SEACOAST PLANTS
OF THE CAROLINAS

A NEW GUIDE FOR

Seacoast

PLANT IDENTIFICATION AND USE

Plants of the

IN THE COASTAL LANDSCAPE

Carolinas

PAUL E. HOSIER

Published by the

UNIVERSITY OF NORTH CAROLINA PRESS, Chapel Hill,

in association with NORTH CAROLINA SEA GRANT

A SOUTHERN GATEWAYS GUIDE

© 2018 North Carolina State University

Unless otherwise credited,
all photos are by Paul E. Hosier.
All rights reserved
Set in Utopia and TheSans types
by Tseng Information Systems, Inc.
Manufactured in the United States of America

The University of North Carolina Press has been a member of the Green Press Initiative since 2003.

Cover photos: Image of ecosystems and plants in Hammocks Beach State Park by Charlie Peek of North Carolina State Parks, courtesy of the North Carolina Department of Natural and Cultural Resources; all rights reserved. Inset photos of *Physalis walteri* fruit, *Amaranthus pumilus* plant, *Erythrina herbacea* fruit, and *Lythrum lineare* flowers by Paul E. Hosier.

Library of Congress Cataloging-in-Publication Data

Names: Hosier, Paul E., author.
Title: Seacoast plants of the Carolinas : a new guide for plant identification and use in the coastal landscape / by Paul E. Hosier.
Other titles: Southern gateways guide. | Sea Grant publication (Raleigh, N.C.) ; UNC-SG-18-01.
Description: [Chapel Hill, North Carolina] : Published by the University of North Carolina Press, Chapel Hill, in association with North Carolina Sea Grant, [2018] | Series: A Southern gateways guide | Series: Sea Grant publication ; UNC-SG-18-01 | Includes bibliographical references and index.
Identifiers: LCCN 2018001033| ISBN 9781469641430 (pbk : alk. paper) | ISBN 9781469641447 (ebook)
Subjects: LCSH: Coastal plants—North Carolina. | Coastal plants—South Carolina. | Coastal plants—North Carolina—Identification. | Coastal plants—South Carolina—Identification. | Landscape gardening—North Carolina. | Landscape gardening—South Carolina.
Classification: LCC QK178 .H67 2018 | DDC 581.9756—dc23 LC record available at https://lccn.loc.gov/2018001033

Southern Gateways Guide™ is a registered trademark of the University of North Carolina Press.

To Elizabeth, Kona, and Greg

CONTENTS

SEACOAST PLANTS

OF THE CAROLINAS

INTRODUCTION

This volume updates and expands upon an earlier book written by Karl Graetz and first published in 1973 by North Carolina Sea Grant. For over four decades, Graetz's book informed residents and visitors to the Carolinas coast about native plants. However, knowledge of coastal processes and the flora and fauna of the region has increased dramatically since 1973. Continued development of coastal resources and new generations of scientists, residents, and visitors have created the need for an update of the original *Seacoast Plants* book.

In this volume, I share information about the unique environments, natural processes, and important plants that surround us when we are at or near the coast. Learning about coastal plants is an intellectual exercise, a way to discover how to use coastal plants wisely in developed spaces, and a prelude to understanding the need to conserve coastal plants, especially those imperiled or found only in certain areas.

This book affords a means of identifying the common plants in the coastal Carolinas. The plant profiles provide physical, chemical, and biological features for each species along with detailed photographs, many displaying seasonal characteristics such as flowers and fruits. The information about each species aids one in understanding and appreciating the ecology of our coastal flora, as well as the wildlife and human uses and values of these distinctive plants.

I describe a range of plants considered one or more of the following: native, exotic, landscape, weedy, or invasive, which are defined in the glossary in Appendix 2. Whether you're planning for your property, making a casual visit, or participating in an extensive field trip, you are likely to encounter these common plants. Understanding the ecological role of our native plants, the usefulness of certain exotic landscape plants, and the effect that invasive and weedy species have on native plants and landscapes leads us to better appreciate, conserve, and preserve native plants in their natural habitats.

I offer practical information that can help you decide which plants to select as part of a pleasing, functional, and low-maintenance landscape plan using native plants. The plant profiles do include some exotic plants, but only those that are especially popular, grow exceptionally well, and have a long history of use in coastal settings with little indication of weediness or invasiveness. Information about introduced plants of special concern—invasive and weedy species—is also included in the plant profiles chapter to alert you about the undesirable growth habits of these problematic species. The descriptions of these species are clearly marked at the beginning of the profile with the cautionary statement, "Not recommended for planting; instead, remove where already growing."

The plant communities described in this book occupy the upland and wetland areas on barrier islands and the adjacent mainland influenced by salt water either through tidal flooding or salt aerosols. Specifically, these communities include dunes ranging from small embryo dunes to mature, well-developed dunes; maritime grasslands; maritime shrub thickets; maritime forests; and freshwater wetlands and saltwater-influenced wetlands, namely brackish marshes, salt marshes, and salt pannes.

The intended audience includes coastal naturalists, ecologists, horticulturalists, landscapers, homeowners, gardeners, students, and visitors to the coast. Individuals with an interest in the nursery trade and representatives of federal, state, local, and nonprofit agencies will find this guide helpful in accomplishing their important work.

Chapter 1 provides the background for understanding the Carolinas coastal environment, including its distinctive and remarkable natural processes and the resulting complex of plant communities. Sandy soils, intense salt aerosols, nearly constant wind, and scarce soil nutrients are examples of what scientists consider distinguishing characteristics of the coastal zone, while the varied plant communities result from the impact of these physical features on the biota.

Chapters 2 through 4 survey the ecology of coastal plants from the wrack line on the beach to the salt marshes that occupy barrier islands, barrier beaches, and nearby mainland estuarine shorelines. These chapters focus on environmental factors to which members of the flora have adapted and the ways in which they have adjusted to surviving in what, for most plants, is a stressful environment.

Chapter 5 identifies plants that are invasive in the coastal Carolinas. Some species are already firmly entrenched with no hope for eradication. Others are nearly under control but require vigilance, lest they expand into natural communities and disrupt the innate balance among species. The ecology of others suggests that they are capable of spreading rapidly if environmental conditions change, possibly in response to climatic change.

Chapter 6 provides practical guidance in selecting native plants to replace current foundation and general property plants. Native plants are adapted to coastal environmental conditions and generally thrive with minimum care. Understanding their ecological requirements allows one to select appropriate native plants. These native species are accustomed to the soils of the Carolinas, resist native pests, and can withstand salt aerosols or saltwater flooding. Exotic species often used as foundation plants are collected from coastal habitats elsewhere in the world and are often well adapted to coastal conditions but sometimes require more care in their new geographic locations. Some introduced species are well-behaved, well-adapted exotic plants, such as Japanese aralia and Chinese podocarpus; these exotic plants can be recommended for landscaping coastal homes and businesses. Planting these species is worth the extra effort in maintenance to enjoy their beauty. Rain gardens are an excellent way to grow native plants that benefit the local environment. Rain gardens are depressions created in the landscape to collect rainwater from impermeable surfaces, such as roads, driveways, and sidewalks. Many native plants are excellent candidates for rain garden plantings.

Chapter 7 considers the effects of frequent coastal storms on vegetation, primarily trees and shrubs in natural and human-centered plant communities. Both research and practical experience show that it is possible to minimize the effects of hurricanes and nor'easters by carefully choosing certain native plants. Pre-storm preparation and post-storm repairs are minimal with the wise selection of native plants for landscaping.

Scientists predict that the rate of change in earth's climate will continue to accelerate in the twenty-first century, with coastlines among the first areas to experience the changes. Chapter 8 explores some of the particular vulnerabilities of the Carolinas coastal region. While the extent cannot be predicted with precision at this time, we can anticipate some climatic changes. It would be prudent to plan for them.

Chapter 9 profiles the plants common to the coast of the Carolinas. This section includes descriptions and other information concerning more than 200 species of common and distinctive coastal plants found in the Carolinas. These profiles include native, exotic, and invasive plants.

The book also includes additional reference materials. Appendix 1 describes 21 natural areas in the coastal Carolinas where you can observe native plants. These areas are reachable by car, foot, or boat. This section notes the specific plant communities that are best expressed at each natural area. Appendix 2 includes a glossary of geological, ecological, and botanical terms. Appendix 3 matches each profiled plant's common name to its respective scientific name. In addition, there is a list of references for further information.

1

ENVIRONMENTAL SETTING FOR THE COASTAL CAROLINAS FLORA

The coast of the Carolinas stretches from the unincorporated community of Carova Beach, N.C., located north of the Outer Banks, to Daufuskie Island, S.C., near the mouth of the Savannah River (fig. 1). Distinctive in many ways, the Carolinas' coastal environment differs from the roller coaster–like piedmont and the imposing Appalachian Mountains. A complex interplay of features gives the coast its identity. There are salty ocean waters and muddy estuaries, nutrient-poor and highly mobile sandy substrates, salt-sheared forests and expansive coastal grasslands, occasional nor'easters and punishing hurricanes. These elements, combined with the dynamic wave and tide actions, merge in time and space to create a unique complex of conditions to which only a limited number of plants and animals have adapted.

The uncommonly attractive yet alien-appearing plant and animal communities created by the intersection of land, sea, and air draw many people to this coastal setting. Millions of people visit this region for action- or leisure-filled vacations each year; hundreds of thousands call the area

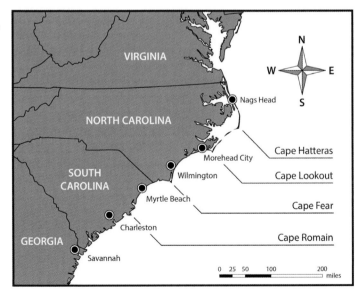

Figure 1. A mix of barrier islands, barrier beaches, capes, mainland beaches, and sea islands comprises more than 500 miles of the ocean shoreline along the Carolinas between Virginia and Georgia. Sounds, bays, and creeks create an immense estuarine shoreline. Illustration by Andrea Dingeldein. Courtesy of North Carolina Sea Grant.

5

home, and tens of thousands find fulfilling work there, ranging from commercial fishing to tourist-oriented service positions. This is all facilitated by—or because of—the existence of coastal communities and their natural surroundings.

UNIQUE COASTAL ENVIRONMENTAL FACTORS

While the Carolinas coast presents a somewhat varying geologic history and pattern of human land use, many environmental factors interact to create the distinctive setting that we sense and recognize as "the coast." These include water (primarily salt water), sand, sun, wind, and storm activity. Here we find unique assemblages of plant and animal communities, including the beaches, dunes, forests, and wetlands. It is in these communities that we discover scores of plants, each exceptionally well adapted to the environment and coexisting with other plants and animals.

The Carolinas coastline varies from the long, narrow barrier islands of the Outer Banks anchored by Cape Hatteras to the high, wide iconic Sea Islands such as Kiawah and Hilton Head islands. Extensive dunes, maritime grasslands, and maritime shrub thickets dominate mile after mile of shoreline along the Outer Banks. In contrast, the topographically diverse and vegetationally complex islands of the southern North Carolina and the South Carolina coasts exhibit a preponderance of salt-aerosol-sheared arborescent vegetation, often with a narrow strip of grassy dunes along the seaward edge (figs. 2 and 3). Brackish marshes and salt marshes sharply define the edges of the upland communities along the estuarine shorelines of the Carolinas. Freshwater swamps, marshes, and ponds are embedded within the dunes and maritime forests.

Compared to the multifaceted and

Figure 2. Beaches, dunes, maritime grasslands, maritime shrub thickets, and occasional freshwater wetlands separate ocean and estuarine environments along the narrow, fragile North Carolina Outer Banks. Courtesy of Outer Banks Visitors Bureau.

Figure 3. Recurved dune ridges create environments for maritime grasslands and maritime shrub thickets (*foreground*) near Captain Sam's Inlet, Kiawah Island, while maritime forests dominate extensive portions of Pleistocene-aged areas of the South Carolina coast. Courtesy of Town of Kiawah Island.

diverse dunes, grasslands, and forests, the marshes appear superficially similar. However, on closer inspection, we see that they range from structurally and vegetationally complex freshwater plant communities found in Currituck Sound to seemingly endless, monotonous expanses of estuarine marshes where but a single plant species dominates thousands of acres of intertidal environments in Port Royal and St. Helena sounds.

GEOLOGY AND GEOMORPHOLOGY

The northernmost barrier islands, including Hatteras and Ocracoke islands in North Carolina, are geologically young, having reached their current dimensions and character less than 5,000 years ago. The South Carolina Sea Islands, best expressed from Bull Island to Hilton Head Island, are composed of both old and new ocean-derived sediments. The central core of these coastal islands is more than 25,000 years old, while a narrow ribbon of sand—usually comprising the ocean shoreline and adjacent dunes—is similar in age to the North Carolina barrier islands.

The region features four major capes: Hatteras, Lookout, and Fear in North Carolina and Romain in South Carolina. Scientists believe that Pleistocene Epoch sediments reworked by ocean waves and tides created these cape features. Cape Hatteras extends well into the Atlantic Ocean, and standing there, one immediately senses that this point of land is a tempting target for Atlantic hurricanes. In contrast to the North Carolina capes, Cape Romain today is composed of several dissembled islands that have evolved into a more or less diffuse cape feature. These complex cape features are typically home to a diverse suite of plants.

OCEAN CURRENTS

Two major ocean currents affect the coastal region of the Carolinas. The Labrador Current flows from its cold-water origin in the Hudson and Davis straits and the Grand Banks of the northwestern Atlantic Ocean south to North Carolina. The warm Gulf Stream flows northward from the coast of Florida, where it arises in the warm waters of the Florida Straits. This surface current generally follows the Carolinas coastline as it moves northward, turning eastward as it passes Cape Hatteras on its path toward the northeastern Atlantic Ocean. Eventually

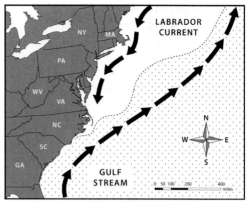

Figure 4. The warm waters of the Gulf Stream flow north, hugging the southeastern U.S. coastline as they approach the Carolinas before moving into the open ocean near Cape Hatteras. The cold waters of the Labrador Current flow south along the New England and mid-Atlantic coast. These major currents influence the distribution of plants and animals along the coastal Carolinas. Illustration by Andrea Dingelein. Courtesy of North Carolina Sea Grant.

the Gulf Stream provides the British Isles with a warmer climate than its far northern latitude deserves. These two currents influence the distribution of plants along the Carolinas coast by bringing species with more northern affinities southward and plants with southern affinities farther north than expected (fig. 4).

Extremes of climate, weather, natural processes, and events such as storms affect the health, survival, and sometimes the distribution of plants and plant communities. The Carolinas coastal environment is agreeable in many ways, but it is not constant. Because individual plants are confined to one site for their entire lifetime, they have evolved wide tolerances for environmental conditions and developed unique adaptations to disruptive events. These conditions include extremes of water availability (flooding and drought), extremes of temperature, wind, and fire. Certainly coastal storms present some of these factors all at once.

Proximity to open water influences the climate along the Carolinas coast; large water bodies tend to moderate the climate by narrowing temperature extremes along the adjacent shores. This region experiences mild winters and hot, humid summers. Temperatures in the coastal Carolinas reach their average maxima of approximately 90°F in July and August and the minima in the mid-30°sF in January and February.

The Outer Banks of North Carolina report generally cooler average high temperatures during July and August (mid-80°s) and warmer average lows in the winter (high 30°s) than the rest of the coast. Because the United States Department of Agriculture (USDA) defines its plant hardiness zones by the average minimum temperature experienced in an area, species adapted to higher minimum temperatures often thrive along a generally cooler coast. Conversely, species adapted to very hot temperatures rarely inhabit coastal plant communities.

Extraordinarily warm or cold temperatures experienced in the coastal Carolinas influence plants, since they have few thermoregulatory mechanisms compared with the animal world. However, plants adapt to at least short periods of heat and cold stress. Excessive heat during the summer leads to water deficits as water moves from roots to leaves and then to the atmosphere. This process desiccates plants and sometimes leads to the death of the plant.

Precipitation is abundant; however, summer droughts lasting for a month are not unusual in the coastal Carolinas. Annual precipitation in the region is evenly distributed throughout the year and averages 50 to 55 inches. The region experiences rainfall maxima in July and August; the least precipitation occurs in November and April. Rains accompanying hurricanes contribute significantly to summer rainfall totals.

The water table is usually close to the surface compared with more inland areas. Many trees and other deeply rooted plants can reach either the water table or the moist zone just above the water table. These deeply rooted plants can survive short periods of drought during the summer, a time when evapotranspiration lowers the water table. Similarly, deep taproots aid dune plants in collecting water during dry periods.

In extended drought conditions, coastal plants react by dropping leaves, which effectively reduces transpiration and therefore water loss. Deep taproots aid dune plants in collecting and storing water during dry periods.

TIDES AND SALT WATER

Tides are diurnal in the coastal Carolinas and increase in range from north to south. The spring tide range at the ocean edge varies from around 3 feet at Duck, N.C., to more than 7 feet at Hilton Head Island, S.C. In the estuaries, spring tides range from less than 1 foot in portions of Pamlico Sound to more than 9 feet in Port Royal Sound.

The presence of salt water is the most influential factor defining the coastal environment. Salt water is ubiquitous in the coastal zone; it is obviously dominant in the ocean and estuaries, but it is also important in the atmosphere in aerosol-sized droplets. In addition, salt water may intrude into the groundwater when coastal aquifers experience excessive freshwater withdrawal. The tidally controlled ebb and flow of estuarine water defines and often delimits the environment in which saltwater-adapted plants live. Adaptation to the presence of salts in their environment is a unique and important attribute of coastal plants (fig. 5).

Figure 5. Huge areas of smooth cordgrass marshes dissected by tidal creeks dominate the coastal areas protected from open ocean waves by barrier islands and sea islands in the Carolinas. Myriad animals ranging from microscopic nematodes to great egrets thrive in these protected creeks and marshes.

Figure 6. Coastal winds transport sand landward from the beach. Only a few plants, such as northern seaside spurge, can grow and reproduce in this environment where rapid burial and sand blast occur continuously.

SOILS

Unconsolidated sands—geologically young with poorly developed soil profiles—comprise the soils of the coastal Carolinas. Much of the coastal plain of the Carolinas is composed of sands successively deposited in thin layers when sea level was considerably higher than it is today. Once the ocean retreated, wave and tidal action separated coarse sands from fine silts and clays. Over time, these processes created today's estuaries, barrier islands, and barrier beaches. Today, winds move sand onshore, where native plants arrest this sand and form dunes. These sandy upland soils are typically coarse, dry, mobile, and nutrient deficient.

Moving water generated by the tides and river currents carries silt and clay into the low-energy estuaries typically found landward of the barrier islands in the coastal Carolinas. In sharp contrast to the dunes, tidal marsh soils are composed of silt and clay particles, and they are poorly aerated, often waterlogged, and frequently flooded with salt water. These markedly different environments support distinctive, easily recognized plant communities.

WIND

Residents and visitors alike usually comment on the omnipresence of wind along the coast. The differential heating and cooling of ocean water and upland environments as well as the low, flat nature of the coastal plain creates conditions that generate and sustain nearly constant winds. The winds are important in shaping coastal environments; for thousands of years, wind and vegetation have interacted to form and reform the hummocky dunes and swales that characterize the Carolinas coast. Over time, winds move prodigious quantities of sand and subject coastal plants to burial of their stems or erosion of sand from around their roots (fig. 6). Winds are responsible for carrying salt aerosols shoreward, where they are deposited on the aerial portions of trees, shrubs, herbs, and grasses.

The coastal Carolinas experience winds from all directions in the course of a year; however, the strongest and most frequent winds blow predominantly from the northeast and southwest quadrants along the Carolinas coast. Variations occur depending on the location, season, and weather patterns.

SALT AEROSOLS

Rooted in place, plants cannot escape salt aerosols carried ashore by onshore winds flowing over breaking waves. Salt aerosols are intense near the beach, and only salt-tolerant plants survive here. Onshore winds deliver salt aerosols in large quantities to the highest dunes closest to the ocean, and aerosols decrease with increasing distance from the beach. In shallow, open estuaries where winds can generate breaking waves, salt aerosols can be carried considerable distances inland by brisk winds. Thus, plants growing near estuaries, sounds, and lagoons must tolerate atmospheric salts as well as elevated soil salinity. Many of the plants described in this guide grow along the estuarine shoreline.

Coastal Carolina native plants vary in response to salt aerosols. Most coastal species exhibit some tolerance. Plants occupying open dunes are well adapted to salt aerosols, while other species occupying, say, the maritime forest floor have no tolerance to elevated salts in the atmosphere—or in the forest soil for that matter. Injury is proportional to the concentration of salt aerosols reaching the plant. Near the ocean, atmospheric salt concentrations are high; at a distance from the ocean, atmospheric salt aerosols are nominal (figs. 7 and 8).

There are telltale symptoms of salt-aerosol damage: reduced stem growth, browning on the tips and margins of leaves, thinning of the leaf crown, premature

Figure 7. Salt aerosols carried by onshore winds dramatically shape shrubs and trees growing near the ocean. Salts, carried in aerosol-sized droplets of seawater, have killed the upper and most seaward needles of this slash pine. The lower and landward portion of the tree is sheltered from salt aerosols by dune grasses and nearby foredunes.

Figure 8. Where trees are far from the ocean, salt aerosols are so diminished that they have little influence on the growth of leaves and branches. This live oak shows only a slight change in shape due to the salt aerosols.

leaf fall, earlier coloration of leaves, and death of twigs on the windward side of a tree or shrub. These symptoms often gradually appear in landscapes as salts build up on plant leaves and twigs or in the surrounding soil. When plants are exposed to chronic salt aerosols, expect to see crown dieback, insect and fungal invasion, and plant mortality. Salt aerosol damage is intensified when the coastal Carolinas experience drought conditions or low humidity for an extended time.

HURRICANES AND NOR'EASTERS

Storms beset the coastal Carolinas throughout the year, but hurricanes usually occur in late summer and early fall. Hurricanes originate in the tropics and reach the coastal Carolinas from the western coast of Africa, where they are usually spawned. These storms track westward, often turning north as they approach the East Coast of the United States. Hurricanes tend to follow the warm Gulf Stream, and records show that storms pass Cape Hatteras more frequently than other parts of the Carolinas. Hurricanes decrease in frequency, but clearly not in intensity, toward southern South Carolina. Less frequently, hurricanes spawned in the Caribbean Sea reach the coastal Carolinas as they track northward.

Hurricanes have severe but relatively short-term impacts on vegetation through various means. For example, the level of salt aerosols accompanying storms is elevated. Also, huge quantities of rain associated with many storms lead to freshwater flooding. In addition, the concomitant surge of ocean water causes major flooding and changes in the position and character of the shoreline. Powerful winds devastate the biota and human developments alike. Overall, however, coastal plants are reasonably well adapted to these insults and recover within several months to a few years after a storm.

This region is also subject to nor'easters, storms with hurricane-like features that do not form in the tropics. These chronic storms tend to hit the Carolinas coast in late fall, winter, and early spring at a rate of about three per month. These low-intensity, but more frequent, nor'easters can, on occasion, inflict severe damage to coastal environments, including flooding and shoreline changes. Plants and plant communities react to nor'easters as they do to hurricanes.

THE CHANGING COAST: THE HUMAN HAND

The environment in the coastal Carolinas has proven to be a challenge for humans hoping to exploit its resources. The area's remoteness led humans to live there transiently and to take the plant and animal resources that it offered without ever attaining dominance over the region. Eventually, we began to use the resources in easily accessible areas, developing commercial centers and recreational areas to support visitors. Ultimately, people became permanent residents of the coastal Carolinas as they sought the unique resources and amenities offered by coastal living.

THE COLONIAL ERA TO THE EARLY TWENTIETH CENTURY

The islands and adjacent mainland areas of the coastal Carolinas were once the domain of fishers, farmers, and with the exception of Wilmington and Charleston, small towns and villages accessible primarily by water. Rivers and the ocean were the highways of the coast before the advent of trains and cars. Inhabitants cut native trees for shipbuilding and shelter. Waterways offered a useful passageway for transit of commercial goods, typically off-loaded from oceangoing vessels and then transported to the inland population. Generally, people who lived there considered these islands and other coastal lowlands quite inhospitable. They were hot, humid, storm ravaged, and besieged by insects; the potential for contracting diseases was high there. As a result, the dunes, maritime forests, and marshes were largely undisturbed, save for some agriculture and grazing on the Outer Banks and larger Sea Islands extending between Bald Head and Hilton Head islands.

Cotton, indigo, sugarcane, and rice were major commodities grown on the southernmost islands in the Carolinas. In removing large swaths of native vegetation to make way for crops, farmers turned Hilton Head and Bald Head islands, for example, into plantations. Extensive agriculture on the Carolinas coast was difficult and short lived. Intense storms and hordes of insects frequently ravaged and destroyed crops. By the early twentieth century, fields had reverted to maritime forests restocked naturally with native trees and shrubs. This change coincided with the decline of the Gullah culture. (The Gullah are West African ethnic groups who were enslaved on island plantations on the Carolinas coast.)

Farmers quickly learned that grazing horses, goats, and sheep on coastal islands provided a significant advantage. Unlike with animal husbandry practiced inland, animals turned out to pasture on the coastal islands required little or no investment in fences. However, livestock preferences for certain species of plants reduced the vegetation cover and altered the landscape. Sand once held firmly in place by plants became mobilized. The legacy of grazing domestic animals in the coastal Carolinas, especially on the Outer Banks of North Carolina, was the creation of thousands of acres of devegetated land covered with extensive mobile dunes. Some scientists speculate that the kind of open, undulating, and bare sand dunes that greeted the Wright brothers at Kitty Hawk was a product of overgrazing by livestock (fig. 9).

It is likely that the introduction of numerous invasive and weed species

Figure 9. Until the middle of the twentieth century, horses, goats, and sheep grazed on coastal Carolina islands. When animals were placed on coastal islands in large numbers, they overgrazed. This posed a constant threat to vegetation cover on dunes and maritime grasslands.

was the by-product of ship-centered commerce. Today, areas around major ports often harbor exotic plants that probably arrived in cargo holds—or even sailors' pants cuffs! Accidental as well as purposeful introductions of nonnative species continue today in the coastal Carolinas.

In the late nineteenth and early twentieth centuries, Currituck Banks and Hilton Head Island became hunting grounds and playgrounds for wealthy northern entrepreneurs. Coastal communities advertised that the "healthy lifestyle" of the coastal Carolinas was due to the clean salt air and unpolluted waters of the region, and they invited those with leisure time to join them at the coast. Heeding the invitation, people congregated at Nags Head, Wrightsville Beach, Myrtle Beach, and Folly Beach to enjoy water sports and the salubrious environment. However, the natural topography and native vegetation were altered only in relatively small spaces where hotels, pavilions, cottages, piers, and boardwalks

Figure 10. This early postcard depicts amenities at Myrtle Beach, S.C., which encouraged people living inland to visit the Carolinas coast. Courtesy of Cecil Brandon/The Brandon Agency.

were built to welcome these first "tourists" (fig. 10).

POST–WORLD WAR II DEVELOPMENT

Following World War II and the prosperous times created by the postwar boom, the modern era of coastal development in the Carolinas began. Charles Fraser created Sea Pines Plantation on Hilton Head Island in the 1950s, and it remains a model community to this day, showing how resort development could be compatible with the conservation and preservation of native plant communities. Myrtle Beach, devastated by Hurricane Hazel in 1954, had a rebirth shortly thereafter, and the golf course era of that region began. In other parts of the coast where privacy was highly regarded, islands such as Figure Eight and Fripp established exclusive gated communities in the coastal Carolinas.

The dense development that we see today along the shoreline of the Carolinas is a relatively new phenomenon. In large measure, extensive and intensive development of first and second homes, as well as myriad recreational outlets, occurred during the latter half of the twentieth century. Development within native plant communities continues unabated as we move into the twenty-first century.

THE COASTAL LANDSCAPING ERA

Development along the Carolinas coast encouraged landscaping for aesthetic as well as safety reasons. With increased interest in landscaping to buffer the harsh coastal environment, homeowners and landscapers tried new plants. Horticulturalists introduced beach vitex to the South Carolina coastal dunes laid waste by the winds and tides of Hurricane Hugo in 1989. Landscapers used thorny elaeagnus to create screening hedgerows and to hold migrating sand dunes in place. Professional landscapers touted Japanese black pine as an excellent landscape tree capable of thriving in harsh coastal conditions. Developers planted thousands of these pines along the coast. Until recently, only a few landscape architects and community planners used native coastal plants extensively in their designs and projects. In hindsight, we realize that many introduced species are or become invasive. Freed from the constraints of their native habitats and pests, these exotics expand into the habitat of native plants and displace them.

Today, with development continuing apace, once-common native plants have disappeared or are declining, while the abundance of many plants adapted to disturbed environments is increasing. For example, seabeach amaranth, a species listed as "threatened" by the U.S. Fish and Wildlife Service, once grew in eight states. Since 1990 that distribution has fallen to only three states. Seabeach knotweed has experienced a similar decline.

Conversely, American beachgrass, once found only in northeastern North Carolina and north to New England, is now common throughout most of the coastal Carolinas. Its wider distribution is due to extensive plantings designed to restore dunes in areas devastated by storms and erosion. This is one of the successful range extensions of plants observed in the coastal Carolinas. There are others. The widespread use of pampas grass as a landscape plant has allowed this plant to become a common inhabitant of nearby natural dunes, maritime grasslands, and even shrub thickets. Common reed and tropical Mexican clover are examples of nonnative plants that thrive in disturbed environments in coastal areas.

Counterbalancing the loss of native plants and their habitats to development started earnestly in the 1950s and continues today with the establishment of public parks, seashores, and other set-asides of land in the coastal Carolinas by federal, state, and local interests. Cape Hatteras and Cape Lookout National Seashores, N.C., and Cape Romain National Wildlife Refuge, S.C., are examples of coastal conservation at the federal level. Hunting Island and Capers Island, S.C., and Bear Island, N.C., resulted from state-sponsored conservation efforts. With most large parcels of land identified and

conserved, efforts to conserve natural coastal communities by conservancies, plant heritage programs, and land trusts have become almost a lot-by-lot effort. For example, the Bald Head Island Conservancy routinely accepts donations of individual lots from landowners.

Recently, the grand designs and intense cultivation of front yards and back yards full of water- and nutrient-requiring exotic plants and picture-perfect lawns have given way to greater interest in low-impact landscaping—the use of native plants, installation of rain gardens, and introduction of drip irrigation. Today, many homeowners have come to appreciate the nearly maintenance-free attributes of native plants. Instead of "keeping up with the Joneses" and landscaping with irrational ostentation, they focus on environmental harmony and naturalness.

The exemplary NC State Extension Master Gardener (SM) program, as well as Clemson Cooperative Extension and N.C. Cooperative Extension, provides coastal homeowners an opportunity to learn and apply horticultural and environmental principles. In the coastal Carolinas, Master Gardener volunteers augment their core training with specialization in shoreline topics of specific interest to coastal homeowners. Encouraging the homeowner to become an "enthusiastic naturalist," the Extension Master Gardener program provides both learning and application goals for homeowners who want to enhance their immediate environment with native plants. A considerable body of research has been amassed concerning the growth, development, and use of coastal plants for revegetation and landscaping. Scientists and engineers studying coastal plants and their environment make this information available to coastal interests through publications and the Internet.

2

ENVIRONMENTS AND FLORA

BEACHES, DUNES, AND MARITIME GRASSLANDS

Along the coast, many of the physical factors affecting plants are clear: salt water, salt aerosols, immature soils with low soil nutrients, storms, occasional fire, and the ebb and flow of tides. These factors can have both short- and long-term effects on plants, and the result is a reasonably consistent and repeatable pattern of plant communities along the Carolinas coast. For ease in identifying the plant communities and their flora, I divided the communities into broad groupings: (1) beaches, dunes, and maritime grasslands; (2) maritime shrub thickets and maritime forests; and (3) palustrine and estuarine wetlands. I subdivided each of these groups into more specific vegetation types based on the dominance of specific plants. These recognizable assemblages occur repeatedly across the coastal Carolinas landscape, a result of the interaction between plants and the unique environments in which they grow (fig. 11).

Covered with extensive plant communities dominated by upland grasses, the beaches, dunes, and maritime grasslands are the signature plant communities in the coastal Carolinas. These principal environmental factors

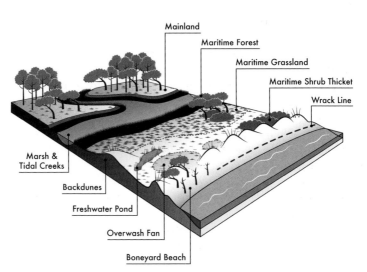

Figure 11. As shown in this idealized cross section of a Carolinas coast and adjacent mainland, distinctly recognizable plant communities develop due to strong environmental influences related to the presence of the ocean and estuaries. Illustration by Andrea Dingeldein. Courtesy of North Carolina Sea Grant.

Mainland
Maritime Forest
Maritime Grassland
Maritime Shrub Thicket
Wrack Line
Marsh & Tidal Creeks
Backdunes
Freshwater Pond
Overwash Fan
Boneyard Beach

delimit, shape, and modify this area: unconsolidated sands moved by coastal winds, intense salt aerosols, and overwash fans created during severe storms. Covering more acreage than the similarly unique, grass-covered Smoky Mountain balds, dunes and grasslands form a nearly continuous strip of vegetation along the Atlantic Ocean shoreline of North Carolina and South Carolina, as well as other coastal states.

BEACHES: HIGHLY MOBILE AND RAPIDLY CHANGING ENVIRONMENTS

Depending on the weather conditions when we visit the coast, waves may be crashing onto the shore or gently swishing up the beach. If we look closely, we can observe small changes along the shoreline occurring over a few minutes or hours. If our visits are separated by days, weeks, or months, the magnitude and extent of changes may elicit gasps of surprise or even horror during subsequent visits. These changes are the result of interactions between unconsolidated sand, ocean waves, and constantly changing tidal and stormwater levels.

During storms, waves move large quantities of sand offshore, hidden from view underwater. Much of that offshore sand is moved back to the beach slowly during quieter wave conditions. Even when wind and water are relatively calm, nearly imperceptible but relentless movement of minute quantities of sand over days or weeks can ultimately result in profound changes in the shoreline shape, position, and character.

FORESHORE AND BACKSHORE ENVIRONMENTS

The beach zone includes the intertidal beach or foreshore, the area between daily low and high tides, and the backshore, the area where beachgoers usually lay their blankets on warm, sunny days. The foreshore is a true marine environment, a highly dynamic zone building and eroding as wave energy changes daily and seasonally. We find no rooted plants here. Waves continuously dissipate their energy on the shore, and this wave action precludes vascular plants from gaining a permanent foothold on the beach. The foreshore is literally the domain of phytoplankton and zooplankton in the water column, as well as mole crabs, coquina clams, and tiny meiofauna buried in the sand.

Rooted vascular plants make their first appearance on the backshore, defined as the region between the average high tide and the base of the dunes. These first plants indicate the landward limit of seasonal erosion of the foreshore during the last year or two. This is where our focus on coastal plants begins. Situated above all but the highest tides, this portion of the beach is dry for much of the growing season. Occasionally, wind-driven seawater or seawater from high spring tides reaches this zone and saturates the sand but does not erode it. Only a scant number of plants survive in the backshore zone, and they are specifically adapted to its occasional seawater flooding, intense salt aerosols, and wind-driven sand grains.

The intertidal beach, backshore, and dune environment changes from season to season. On occasion, these changes occur abruptly. During the long, languid summer, persistent light winds and low-energy waves coincide. Waves gradually move sand landward from offshore bars, and winds blow this sand landward, higher on the beach and into the dunes. Sand accumulates along the beach, trapped there by dune grasses. The beach widens then, and grasses expand upward and outward. Beach weather conditions change dramatically during the winter. Unseen storms blowing far offshore energize waves reaching coastal Carolina beaches. The powerful waves crash onshore, drag sand off the beach, and form long, narrow bars just beyond the breaking waves. Sand that was so painstakingly accumulated during the comparatively quiescent summer disappears from the backshore and sometimes the foredunes, leaving sharp, clifflike scars along the shoreline.

Figure 12. Scattered grasses and herbaceous plants grow along the beach backshore, where competition from other plants is low but environmental conditions are severe. Here seeds germinate and grow on piles of organic debris buried by blowing sand. Once growing, these plants accumulate sand and build small dunes.

WRACK-LINE ECOLOGY

Some of the hardiest shore plants grow near or within an observable zone of plant debris on the upper edge of the backshore. In the fall, winter, and early spring, waves push dead marsh grass stems (primarily smooth cordgrass) and pieces of sargassum, a large, brown seaweed, into a long line of debris high on the beach. Along the shore, flotsam and jetsam—bottles, boards, lightbulbs, twine, and all manner of plastic debris—accumulate along with this organic material. This strip or zone, known as the wrack line or strand line, is more or less continuous along the backshore at the edge of the highest spring tides. This organic material mixes with beach sand and provides an inviting substrate upon which a few plants adapted to an ephemeral life can grow. Wind and water entrain the seeds shed by nearby dune plants, move them around the beach, and ultimately deposit them in this flotsam. During the spring, we find thousands of plants germinating along this visible, bright green wrack line (fig. 12).

Once the organic material accumulated along the wrack line is covered by sand, it acts like a sponge, holding water and releasing nutrients as it decays. On a prograding (seaward-expanding) beach, the wrack line serves as the nucleus for establishing a new dune line. Occasionally, multiple wrack lines form parallel to one another along the beach. This usually indicates a rapidly widening shoreline. Conversely, on an eroding beach, the wrack line may be quite ephemeral, with seedlings, organic material, and sand washed away by waves. Erosion along a shoreline stymies new dune growth. Look for these wrack lines; they can tell you much about the recent history of a beach.

WRACK-LINE FLORA

Plants commonly growing on the wrack line arrive there from the adjacent dunes; however, some species, including a federally "threatened" species called seabeach amaranth, are specifically adapted to living along the wrack line. Sea rocket, northern saltwort, and seabeach knotweed also find this transient environment suitable for growth. All of these species can continuously grow up through accumulating sand and tolerate intense heat and solar radiation. The temporary nature of this zone often requires that these species complete their life cycle within just a few weeks or months.

Seedlings of nearby dune species such as sea oats and sea elder frequently inhabit the wrack line also. These plants can tolerate the highest quantity of salt aerosols and occasional flooding with ocean water. Absent competition or interference from other plants, these species are highly successful in this transient habitat.

DUNES:
UNIQUE COASTAL FEATURES

Landward of the backshore beach, we find foredunes, accumulations of sand stabilized by vegetation. Here, sand from the backshore and foreshore, with help from the wind, moves landward and accumulates around plants. Beginning as small hillocks, dunes grow into hummocky features as individual grasses and herbs capture sand. Dunes in the coastal Carolinas vary in size from embryo dunes, a few feet across and a few inches high, to mammoth dunes covering hundreds of acres and standing more than 50 feet high (fig. 13).

Dunes act as buffers between the ocean and uplands. They are malleable environments, sometimes changing rapidly as constructive or destructive

Figure 13. These are examples of coastal dunes. (a) Embryo dunes develop from a single or small group of seedlings. They may grow rapidly when sand is abundant. (b) Foredunes are the first line of dunes. They coalesce from many individual plants, ultimately forming a nearly straight line of dunes parallel to the beach. (c) Backdunes are located at a distance from the beach. They may have formed originally as foredunes when the shoreline was located at the site where they are found (as shown here). (d) Médanos (Spanish for sandhills) are very large dunes formed when a superabundance of sand is available. Sand builds rapidly into huge piles, and grasses and herbs, buried or undermined, cannot maintain a foothold. Without a cover of vegetation, these dunes migrate in the direction of the dominant wind.

forces dominate the shoreline. During fair weather, light winds carry fine sands landward, dune plants intercept this sand, and dunes build upward and seaward. During the winter and other stormy periods, waves crash onto the beach. Dunes at the edge of the shore are sacrificed as they absorb the energy of the waves. Naturally functioning shorelines allow the alternating processes of dune building and sacrifice to occur unimpeded.

A dune forms as sand collects around a plant in a positive feedback loop; as a plant grows larger, it accumulates sand more effectively and efficiently, and in turn, this sand accretion stimulates the growth and expansion of the plant, resulting in the accumulation of more sand. Embryo dunes represent the earliest stage of dune development. As embryo dunes grow, several often consolidate, forming larger dunes. Large dunes typically coalesce into continuous dune ridges that parallel the shoreline. As time passes, newer dunes form seaward of the older dunes, and the process of dune ridge development is repeated. The parallel dune ridges that you may observe along a shoreline formed in this way. Older dunes become increasingly remote from the foreshore source of sand, and these more remote dunes, called backdunes, stagnate in size. Owing to the relative stability of the backdunes, the density and diversity of plants gradually increases over time.

DUNE ENVIRONMENT

Because foredunes are closest to the beach, they exist in hostile environments where high concentrations of salt aerosols and large quantities of fast-moving sand predominate. Grasses and a few herb species dominate these dunes. Virtually no plant litter accumulates at the ground surface there, and a soil profile is yet to develop. Persistent wind encourages blowouts (explained below), and it subjects plants to the extremes of rapid burial or exposure of their roots. Only plants adapted to these harsh environmental conditions persist season after season. Species that tolerate low soil nutrients and high air and soil temperatures dominate the dunes some distance from the ocean.

WIND AND SAND MOVEMENT

Whether we are at the Carolinas coast, the shore of one of the Great Lakes, or the dunes of White Sands, N.Mex., we will see dunes formed by the interaction of lots of wind and lots of sand. The size and shape, and the amount and direction of dune movement, depend on how, when, and from which direction winds blow.

When prevailing winds blow more or less perpendicular to our coastline, sand moves landward and robust dunes build rapidly, sometimes attaining a height of 6 feet in just a couple of years. The opposite is true when prevailing winds blow parallel to the beach or offshore. In these situations, sand moves predominantly along-shore or offshore, and comparatively small quantities of sand move landward into dunes. Under these conditions, dunes remain modest in size. These dunes may require more than a decade to reach a height of 6 feet.

Wind moves sand by two processes, saltation and surface creep. These processes involve wind lifting or pushing individual sand grains within a narrow zone at or just above the sand surface. Plants growing in the dune-building zone must be able to withstand the effects of saltation and surface creep—essentially, "sandblasting"—in which individual sand grains smash into leaves and stems. Northern seaside spurge and seabeach amaranth have adapted to this hardship by growing close to the ground, effectively reducing the plant surface exposed to blowing sand. Another plant, dune pennywort, has a thick cuticle on the leaf surface that reduces damage caused by moving sand. Some of the dune grasses also possess thick cuticles that not only protect the plants from damage by wind-driven sand grains but also reduce water loss from the leaves.

Plants that continue to grow upward as sand accumulates around them are favored along the coast. Great examples include sea oats, American beachgrass, seaside panicum, saltmeadow cordgrass, and sea elder, which manage to grow upward while being buried by a foot or more of sand in a single year.

SALT AEROSOLS

Salt aerosols are clearly a controlling environmental factor in the coastal area. The presence of aerosols determines the floristic distribution patterns we see on barrier islands, barrier beaches, and the mainland adjacent to estuarine waters. Salt aerosols give the coast the "look and feel" of, well, the coast!

Initially, observers thought that the nearly constant, strong wind typical of coastal areas was the environmental factor that determined plant distribution. For example, scientists believed that desiccating winds were responsible for creating the smooth, sloping surface we see on the trees and shrubs growing close to the ocean. Pioneering research on the North Carolina coast eventually ruled out not only wind per se but soil moisture, soil salinity, air temperature, humidity, or evapotranspiration as the key factor determining coastal plant distribution. Wind remains the vector for delivering the real culprit, salt aerosols, sometimes referred to as "salt spray."

We now know that as waves crest, spill over, and crash onto the shore, they eject tiny aerosol-size droplets of ocean water into the air. Wind lifts these minute droplets, carries them onshore, and deposits them on foliage. On a windy day, you can notice the buildup of these droplets by observing the wetness on plant leaf surfaces facing the ocean. You experience a similar buildup of salt aerosols on your sunglasses when you sit on the beach and face into the wind for an hour or so on a windy day. You will also see a buildup of salt aerosols on your car windshield while it is parked at the beach!

Effects of Salt Aerosols on Plants
The young buds and leaves of plants are the organs most susceptible to the effects of salt aerosols. Necrosis occurs when plants absorb and then translocate salt deposits on leaf, stem, and bud surfaces into actively growing tissues. Unable to detoxify the concentrated salts, cells die and leaf edges and tips turn brown. Gradually, entire leaves and stems succumb to the effects of salt aerosols. Unless dunes or man-made blocking structures shelter trees and shrubs from salt aerosols, they do not persist near the ocean. This is one reason why only grasses and a few specialized herbs dominate coastal dunes nearest the ocean.

Coastal winds deliver salt aerosols after passing over breaking waves and open water. The wind speed and direction influence the intensity of salt aerosols reaching plants. During periods with strong onshore winds, the greatest amount of salt aerosols reaches dune plants. When winds blow parallel to the shore or offshore, salt aerosol intensity is considerably less (fig. 14).

Plant Adaptations to Salt Aerosols
Grasses and herbs survive intense salt aerosols because their growth buds are at or below the surface of the ground and out of the reach of salt aerosols. All

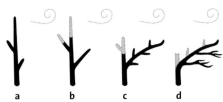

a b c d

Figure 14. Salt aerosols affect the growth of stems and twigs of arborescent vegetation. (a) Normal plant growth without salt-aerosol conditions. (b) Leaves, buds, and twigs with greatest salt accumulation die. (c) Leaves, buds, and twigs continue to grow where salt aerosols are reduced. (d) Over time, differential leaf, bud, and twig growth causes asymmetrical development of trees and shrubs. In this way, trees and shrubs become wedge shaped or appear "sculpted." Modified from Boyce (1954). Illustration by Andrea Dingeldein. Courtesy of North Carolina Sea Grant.

the common dune species—saltmeadow cordgrass, seaside panicum, sea oats, seashore dropseed, and American beachgrass, for example—have growth buds just below the sand surface.

Another way herbs survive salt aerosols is by reducing the amount of salt reaching the broad leaf surfaces. For example, the leaves of dune ground cherry and dune camphorweed have elaborate hairs that intercept salt aerosols, reducing the quantity of salts entering the leaves. Salts accumulate on the hairs and then harmlessly wash off with the next rain. These plants usually exhibit virtually no salt-aerosol damage. Storms, however, deliver salt aerosols to plants growing well beyond the usual range of salt deposition. Hurricane winds carry considerable quantities of salt aerosols, despite some dilution by rainfall, well inland from the ocean or nearby estuaries. Within days of the passage of a hurricane, many dune herbs such as southern horseweed and marsh pink succumb to this exposure to excessive salts. Overall, dunes often look as if winter has arrived in August or September rather than January because of the extensive salt-aerosol damage to plants, which effectively ends their growth season.

Plant Zonation: The Ultimate Outcome of Salt-Aerosol Distribution

In the final analysis, the concentration of salt aerosols controls the distribution of plants across the dunes. Plants best adapted to tolerate salt aerosols grow closest to the ocean. At a distance from the ocean, less-salt-tolerant species predominate. This variation in salt-aerosol deposition and the ability of certain species to tolerate the salts results in the plant zonation we observe from the ocean landward. Sea oats, saltmeadow cordgrass, and other grasses dominate the foredunes because they are less affected by salt spray than other species, such as water oak or loblolly pine.

Variations in zonation occur when large dunes, structures such as buildings or fences, or trees block salt aerosols. For example, common wax myrtle may grow much closer to the ocean than you might expect when large dunes intercept or deflect incoming salt aerosols.

TEMPERATURE

Dunes absorb considerable solar radiation on sunny days, causing the dune surface to heat rapidly. At night, heat flows from the soil to the atmosphere, and soils quickly reach the same temperature as the air. This is especially pronounced within the first 2 to 3 inches of sand, where no organic matter accumulates and dunes retain little water. Scientists have measured temperatures as high as 130°F at the sand surface of dunes, while temperatures just a few inches below were only 80°F. Deeper in the soil, the temperature is moderated by the presence of water and becomes lower and less variable over days and months. The heat load generated by solar radiation can affect the growth and survival of plants.

These high surface temperatures and the relatively constant coastal winds stress any plant without specializations to dissipate heat and reduce water loss. To survive these conditions, coastal plants have developed adaptations such as small leaves, deep or wide-spreading roots, sunken stomata, and light-reflective leaves.

In contrast, dune plants survive cold shock poorly. Plants do best when air and soil temperatures rise or fall slowly. With the onset of cold weather, coastal plants drop their fragile parts. This reduces the water content of the remaining leaves, roots, and stems as they move into dormancy. Sudden frost leads to the formation of ice crystals inside cells, which often break cell walls and release the contents of the cells, resulting in the death of the plants.

We observe adaptations to temperature across the flora of the dunes. Live oak and yaupon are examples of species that have small leaves with thick cuticles. Owing to their small size, the leaves absorb less solar radiation, and the cuticle reflects incoming energy back into the atmosphere. Numerous grasses exhibit sunken stomata on the surfaces of their leaves. Silver-leaf croton, dune camphorweed, and woolly beach heather are examples of common dune plants with specialized light-reflecting hairs on leaves and stems that effectively reduce heat loads.

SOILS AND SOIL WATER

Sandy soils typical of the coastal Carolinas dune environments are geologically young with poorly developed profiles. Unlike mature soils found in the piedmont and mountains, these soils are generally nutrient poor, lacking adequate important nutrient elements such as potassium, phosphorus, magnesium, and some micronutrients. Decaying organic matter and wind-borne, accumulated sand provide some nutrients to growing plants; however, little organic matter accumulates in the young dune soils. Generally, dune soils tend to be highly basic owing to high calcium carbonate concentrations leaching from shell fragments.

Precipitation, predominantly rainfall, is abundant and evenly distributed throughout the year in the coastal Carolinas. Extended droughts occur infrequently. Coarse sands characteristic of dune soils, however, have poor water-holding capacity compared with silt and clay-rich soils. Rainfall percolates into the soil quickly; dune plants with deep roots tap this deeper and more consistent source of water.

Most dune plants have physical or physiological adaptations to survive short drought periods. A number of them store water in their roots, stems, or leaves. The dune prickly-pear stores water in its large, fleshy stems. In fact, dune prickly-pear can serve as an informal measure of the water supply in a dune. Normally, cactus pads appear bright green with a smooth surface. When the pads experience water stress brought on by a drought or extended dry spell, they shrivel and fade to a glaucous, or pale, green.

Adapted to short-term drought, the roots of sea rocket extend surprisingly long distances from the plant, thereby increasing the volume of sand from which the species absorbs water. Sand dayflower utilizes still another strategy. The plant stores water in large, tuberous, finger-shaped roots. Seabeach amaranth demonstrates yet another water storage strategy. It stores water in succulent stems and leaves (fig. 15).

FOREDUNES AND BACKDUNES

Embryo dunes increase in size as they trap sand, and stabilizing grasses grow vigorously in response to continued sand

Figure 15. Growing in sand along the drought-susceptible wrack line, seabeach amaranth has succulent leaves and stems that aid the plant in surviving short periods of drought.

Figure 16. Dune blowouts develop and expand when natural or human disturbance causes part of the vegetation cover to die, exposing dune sand to the chronic coastal winds.

accumulation and nutrient input. When these dunes occur directly landward of the backshore, they are generally referred to as foredunes. In the coastal Carolinas, the iconic sea oats are the most important and dominant plant of the foredune community. When visiting the coast, note the high density of flowering culms visible in a rapidly growing dune system. Compare this view with the density of flowering culms at a distance landward of the young dunes. Here, in the so-called backdunes, the growth and flowering vigor of sea oats diminishes and other plants assume importance. We see several shrub species appear in backdunes, especially in swales where the distance from the source tempers the quantity of salt aerosols. The reduced salt aerosols and lack of sand movement in the backdunes allows many species of plants incapable of surviving in the foredunes to germinate and grow.

BLOWOUTS

Either natural processes or human disturbance can cause the death of plants covering all or some of a dune. Normally, plant cover is sufficient to slow the wind speed near the surface, causing sand to accumulate and the dune to grow larger. When dune plants die or are otherwise removed, a bowl-shaped depression forms as sand that is no longer held in place by plants blows away from the site. This process often results in the formation of barren areas that, once created, continue to expand. The resulting landform is termed a blowout. Blowouts have a tendency to enlarge quickly, and the displaced sand engulfs adjacent vegetation (fig. 16).

Various factors can trigger the formation of a blowout, such as the localized deaths of plants caused by disease or trampling. Wind stops excavating sand at the point where the sand level approaches the top of the water table. At this point, the damp sand cannot be moved by the wind. Buried viable seeds of native plants germinate in the depression, and the increased plant cover further arrests sand movement. At this point, the blowout process ceases.

BIG DUNES: MÉDANOS

Médanos form by either natural processes or human intervention. Both activities result in the removal of the plant cover over a large area, and the sand becomes so mobile that vegetation cannot gain a stabilizing roothold. Jockey's Ridge, N.C., represents one of the few remaining unstabilized médanos along the Carolinas coast. While seeds may occasionally germinate on this large médano, they rarely survive more than a few months—killed by some combination of sand abrasion, burial, and wind erosion. In contrast, the nearby Wright Brothers National Memorial dune represents a médano deliberately stabilized with turf grasses. Contractors planted, irrigated, fertilized, and monitored several species of grasses, primarily Bermudagrass, until a continuous cover was established. Today, the dune is completely stable owing to its dense grass and herb cover and the vigilance of the National Park Service maintenance staff. Blowouts are a constant threat.

Figure 17. Sand live oak, a species capable of withstanding blowing sand and an atmosphere moistened by salt aerosols, thrives on open dunes where few trees or shrubs are capable of growing.

DUNE FLORA

Common foredune grasses include sea oats, seaside panicum, saltmeadow cordgrass, American beachgrass, seashore dropseed, dune sandspur, and purple sandgrass. These dune grasses are tall and flexible. This life form allows grasses to endure strong winds without breaking and to survive rapid burial by wind-driven sand. Herbaceous shrubs exemplified by sea elder and silver-leaf croton grow alongside these grasses in dunes nearest the ocean. Maritime bushy bluestem, coastal little bluestem, and field lovegrass are common floristic elements of backdunes.

Many broad-leaved plants find the backdunes quite hospitable. The predominant species there are dune camphorweed, dune pennywort, seabeach evening primrose, beach evening primrose, dune blue curls, annual sand bean, southern seaside goldenrod, dune ground cherry, northern seaside spurge, and dune finger grass.

Several shrub and tree species thrive in the backdunes. They experience minimal sand movement and reduced salt aerosols there, although specimens frequently show the effects of salt aerosols and sand burial. The most frequently encountered large shrubs and trees are common wax myrtle, northern bayberry, tough bully, toothache tree, and sand live oak (fig. 17).

MARITIME GRASSLAND ENVIRONMENTS

Maritime grasslands develop on the delta-shaped overwash fans and terraces created by moving water that accompanies oceanic overwash. Overwash is important not only in the formation of maritime grassland environments but also in their maintenance. Occasional oceanic overwash rejuvenates the plant community as it buries existing grasses and herbs and creates a nearly barren surface upon which new plants can colonize. The dominant plants that colonize these barren flats are saltmeadow cordgrass and saltmarsh fimbristylis. Here, competition for space is minimal, and these species dominate the area within one or two seasons.

OCEANIC OVERWASH AND MARITIME GRASSLANDS

Oceanic overwash, a process that affects barrier beaches during major hurricanes and nor'easters, occurs when dunes are breached due to increased wave energy and dune erosion during a storm. Storm waves flatten the beach, and within a few minutes to a few hours, the waves erode, then breach, the foredunes. With continued high storm winds, pulses of wave-driven seawater and sand sweep landward across the barrier island. These sand-laden seawater pulses deliver layer upon layer of sand, overspreading and burying existing vegetation, as well as raising the land surface a couple of inches to as much as 3 feet in a single storm. On narrow islands, fans may build across an island from ocean to estuary and even bury saltmarsh vegetation with layers of sand. Over time, grasses grow through the overwash or seed into newly covered areas, thereby revegetating sites where the sand buried existing maritime grasslands and estuarine wetlands (fig. 18).

This process maintains the barrier island's width by transporting sand from the beach and foredune zones landward across the island, elevating and effectively moving the island landward. Fan surfaces typically range from mixtures of coarse, well-drained sand and shell hash close to the beach to fine sand along the landward edge.

Saltmeadow cordgrass is adapted to periodic burial, and it responds to overwash by growing up through the storm-deposited sand. Other plants expand into the grasslands by seeding in from adjacent undisturbed areas. Also,

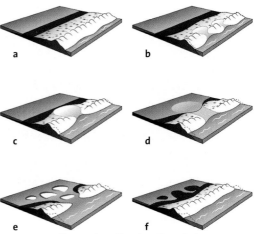

Figure 18. Godfrey and Godfrey (1976) studied the effects of oceanic overwash on low, narrow barrier islands. Continuous, protective foredunes (a) are penetrated by storm-driven ocean water, forming small overwash fans composed of sands moved from the beach to the middle of the island, shown in (b), (c), and (d). New storms then enlarge the overwash fans, pushing sand and seawater farther across the barrier island and burying tidal marsh vegetation. (e) Eventually, overwash fans flatten the island in a way that favors the formation of a tidal inlet. The inlet gradually closes, and new dunes, grasslands, and marshes reestablish in the area. (f) In this process, the entire island (shown in dotted lines) migrates landward. Illustration by Andrea Dingeldein. Courtesy of North Carolina Sea Grant.

species arrive by seed or plant fragment from nearby maritime grasslands and spread quickly, forming dense swards. This environment and its plant community will persist for decades if overwash occurs periodically (fig. 19). If overwash ceases, shrubs and eventually trees begin to take root on these flats. Maritime shrub thicket species will gradually expand in these circumstances, overtopping and shading early grassland-colonizing plants. Given a long period of stability, trees typical of the maritime forest replace most shrubs. Owing to an elevation closer to the water table when compared with nearby dunes,

Figure 19. Graminoids and herbs dominate former overwash fans on Cape Hatteras National Seashore, N.C.

maritime grasslands rarely experience drought.

MARITIME GRASSLANDS AND FIRE

Fires of natural origin are uncommon, but occasional lightning strikes can cause wildfires. Most dune, grassland, and shrub communities easily survive a wildfire. Plants resprout quickly, grow rapidly, and come to dominate because soils are typically enriched with nutrients after a fire. After a fire sweeps through a site, we occasionally find species previously unseen in that area. Species with populations of buried viable seeds in the newly exposed soils thrive briefly in the barren, nutrient-rich soils before the pre-fire vegetation cover is reestablished. For example, hundreds of eastern stargrass plants (*Hypoxis hirsuta*) appeared in a former shrub thicket on Cape Lookout National Seashore within weeks of a wildfire that destroyed the overstory shrubs.

Species capable of surviving sand burial are "pre-adapted" to survive fires. When fire sweeps through dune communities, the aboveground parts of grasses and shrubs burn to the soil level. However, since buds of most grasses grow at or below the surface of the ground, these plants

resume growth from these underground buds. In addition, shrub species such as common wax myrtle and yaupon produce root suckers if their main stems are injured. Oftentimes these species resume growth within a matter of weeks following a light fire.

MARITIME GRASSLANDS FLORA

Probably the best examples of maritime grasslands within the coastal Carolinas occur on Core Banks, N.C. Here, frequent overwash maintains extensive grasslands where the diversity of plants exceeds that of the dune community. Other islands along the North Carolina Outer Banks experience frequent overwash, and this vegetation type generally predominates.

The maritime grasslands bear a physiognomy similar to that of our midwestern short-grass prairies, and they borrow species heavily from adjacent dune and brackish marsh communities. The vegetation cover in maritime grasslands is variable depending upon how long it has been since storm surges affected an area and whether a particular fan or terrace is high and relatively dry or low and moist.

The most consistent and usually dominant species in the maritime grasslands is saltmeadow cordgrass, a species adapted to salt aerosols, saltwater flooding, and storm overwash deposits. The major dune species—American beachgrass, sea oats, seaside panicum, and sea elder—show only a minor presence in the maritime grassland flora. This is the biggest difference in dune and maritime grassland communities.

Associated species in the higher and drier parts of maritime grasslands are switchgrass, poorjoe, coastal little bluestem, bristly foxtail grass, and swallow-wort, while the lower, slightly more moist maritime grasslands tend to feature saltmarsh fimbristylis, saltmarsh wild rye, southern seaside goldenrod, large sea purslane, and marsh pink growing alongside saltmeadow cordgrass.

Common wax myrtle, northern bayberry, loblolly pine, common persimmon, and sea myrtle overspread maritime grasslands as these communities age and overwashes become less frequent. In the coastal Carolinas, maritime grassland communities may grade into dunes, maritime shrub thickets, maritime forests, and salt shrub thickets, as well as brackish and salt marshes.

HUMAN EFFECTS ON THE BEACH, DUNE, AND MARITIME GRASSLANDS FLORA

Human use of coastal environments, especially dunes and grasslands, usually alters plant cover. Dune grasses such as seaside panicum, sea oats, and American beachgrass are easily destroyed by foot and vehicle traffic. Their growth buds and shallowest roots reside just below the surface, and these grasses die quickly when trampling exposes the roots and buds to the air. In contrast, other species thrive nicely in disturbed sites. Ruderal species such as dune wormseed, bitterweed, and narrowleaf plantain thrive in disturbed dune environments. Dune sandspur is an intriguing plant that depends on animals to distribute its seeds. Its presence increases along dune trails frequented by humans or animals. Buildings and constructed dunes provide salt-aerosol reductions. Landward of buildings, sprinkler systems, fertilizer, and landscaping may completely alter the vegetation.

When developers clear natural plant communities, native vegetation is replaced by quickly germinating and fast-growing, ruderal plants. These are usually exotic species that grow best without competition; they assume dominance precisely because the native vegetation is highly disturbed or removed. Thankfully, if left without further disturbance, native species usually replace these pioneering weeds if they can survive competition from invasive species.

Human impact on specific plants in the beach environment ranges from negligible to devastating, although it is generally minor and short lived. Two major impacts, common on a number of North Carolina beaches but less so on South Carolina beaches, are beach nourishment and off-road vehicle use. Beach nourishment widens the foreshore and dunes, creating a wider backshore. It may take a year or more, but seeds of native plants distributed along the shore generally form a new vegetation line on a nourished beach. On developed islands, the maritime grasslands gradually shrink as dune nourishment projects reduce the frequency of oceanic overwash, and development practices promote higher and more continuous dune elevations. In developed areas, parking spaces, streets, buildings, and managed yards replace natural maritime grasslands. Beach nourishment generally buries plants growing on the backshore, but nourished beaches usually have undergone erosion to such an extent that few, if any, plants exist on beaches targeted for nourishment. Anecdotal evidence suggests that when a beach is nourished, seabeach amaranth seeds spread along the beach.

Off-road vehicle use, on the other hand, is detrimental to backshore and dune plants. Many of the plants in this zone are small or juvenile; they are difficult to see and easily destroyed by off-road vehicles. Even heavy foot traffic is detrimental to wrack-line plants. Where foot traffic is concentrated and chronic, such as on popular stretches of beach, wrack-line plants rarely survive a summer season.

Where livestock, primarily horses, still range freely on the dunes, maritime grasslands, and tidal marshes in the

Carolinas, damage is easily observed. This damage is usually devastating where horse populations are unmanaged. Grazing by horses results in less diverse and less complex plant communities compared with undisturbed areas. Grazing animals effectively reduce the overall plant biomass on dunes and eliminate tender flowers and nutritious fruits on coastal plants.

At one time, developers in the Carolinas coastal zone stripped the plant cover and flattened hummocky dunes to create building lots. Today, environmentally conscious developers and potential homeowners more often superintend the coastal development process aided by a healthy dose of coastal management regulations. They have greatly diminished the practice of stripping all dune vegetation on a building lot compared with just four decades ago. We have also gained experience in the increased use of walkways and decks and landscaping with native plants. As a result, it is somewhat less common to see extensive lawns of Bermudagrass, centipede grass, or St. Augustine grass supported by extensive irrigation in the coastal Carolinas. Light pedestrian trampling is sufficient to disturb natural dunes by exposing grass roots and rhizomes to the air, which leads to the death of the grasses. This practice is on the decline with the increased use of dune crossovers, boardwalks, and designated paths. We see similar, but more extensive, damage where off-road vehicles traverse dunes to reach the beach.

We exploit our wild-grown native plants in other ways. For example, sea oats fruiting clusters are large, attractive, and texturally interesting. In years past, collectors stripped thousands of fruiting culms from wild plants to support the floral industry. The industry used thousands of fruiting stems from sea oats annually, often dyed bright colors, in floral arrangements.

Changes in the flora of the maritime grasslands have been minimal except for land development for homes. Because most areas occupied by grasslands are flat and usually treeless, developers find this environment ideal for creating lots and installing necessary utilities. Every coastal development removes some native vegetation in the process. Fortunately, postdevelopment revegetation takes place reasonably quickly.

Another commonly used natural resource is dune hairgrass, which is one of the major natural items used for construction of Low Country coiled baskets. Historically, maritime grasslands have served as the source of this material. Today, this species is in decline, probably as a result of overharvesting. Only with a focused effort to cultivate and market dune hairgrass can we reverse the population decline of this once-abundant plant.

3

**ENVIRONMENTS
AND FLORA
MARITIME SHRUB
THICKETS, MARITIME
FORESTS, AND SALT
SHRUB THICKETS**

The appearance of shrubs and trees in coastal plant communities signals a major change in environmental conditions. With increasing distance from the beach, plants experience less salt aerosols, sandblasting, storm surge, and erosion than plants experience in the beach, dune, and grassland environments. Landward of the beach, high dune ridges build parallel to the shore and act as barriers, further reducing salt-aerosol intensity. Maritime shrub thickets and forests thrive under these conditions (fig. 20). These arborescent communities help stabilize dunes and provide food and habitat for animals. Transformation of an open dune community into one with a continuous arborescent cover typically requires 20 or more years. In the coastal Carolinas, maritime shrub thickets and forests are also present on the mainland fringe where salt aerosols reach the mainland.

GEOGRAPHIC DISTRIBUTION

Maritime shrub thickets and maritime forests are best developed toward the center of barrier islands, the most stable portion of the islands. Maritime forests require several decades or, more likely, several centuries to reach maturity. Given the somewhat different geological histories of islands along the Carolinas coast, the

Figure 20. An important plant community along the coastal Carolinas, the maritime forest covers extensive areas throughout the Sea Island section of South Carolina.

amount and distribution of maritime shrub thickets and maritime forests differ, and coincidentally, this variation roughly breaks down by state. Overwash, dune migration, and inlet formation and migration strongly influence the North Carolina barrier islands. Between the North Carolina–Virginia state line and Sunset Beach, N.C., islands are long and narrow. Stable islands are uncommon, and so are maritime forests. In contrast, the islands south of Myrtle Beach, S.C., many of which have a central core dating from the Pleistocene Epoch, are large, topographically high, and wide. Overwash, dune migration, and small migratory inlets are much less common. Here, maritime forests are extensive and dominate the vegetation cover on many islands, including Bull, Capers (Charleston County), and Hilton Head islands.

The topography within maritime shrub thickets and maritime forests reflects their origin. Profiles vary from "ridge and swale" to hummocky to nearly flat. The ridge-and-swale and hummocky topographies suggest that thickets and forests developed on former dunes. The forests of Nags Head Woods, N.C., and Hunting Island, S.C., are examples of hummocky topography, while Kitty Hawk Woods, N.C., and St. Phillips Island, S.C., are notable examples of forests with a ridge-and-swale profile. Some forested flatlands indicate that thickets and forests developed quite recently on land historically farmed, such as sites on Bald Head Island, N.C., and Hilton Head Island, S.C.

SOILS AND SOIL WATER

Maritime shrub thickets and forests present more mature soil profiles than those found in dunes. The soil profile, however, is much less developed when compared with inner coastal plain and piedmont soils. A horizon of light gray to white, nutrient-poor, and nearly pure quartz sand forms just below a layer of organic matter that includes leaves and twigs, which covers the forest floor. Nutrients leach from this organic layer, move downward as water percolates through the soil, and accumulate deep in the soil, forming a tan to orange, nutrient-rich horizon.

As trees and shrubs shed leaves, branches, and roots, organic matter builds in the soils. The slow decay of thick, tough leaves trickles nutrients into the soil more or less continuously. These changes brought about by the arborescent cover allow other plants with high nutrient and soil water requirements and low salt-aerosol tolerance to survive and reproduce within these environments. Shrub and tree roots are concentrated within the first foot or so of the soil, a favorable location to collect nutrients. A mature soil microfauna composed primarily of mycorrhizae and other soil fungi develops over time. Moist swales and depressions within maritime shrub thickets and forests accumulate considerable organic matter. A fine, sticky, black mud forms as this material breaks down and mixes with sand; some tree species, such as Carolina red maple, thrive in this soil!

SALT AEROSOLS

Salt aerosols influence the character and distribution of maritime shrub thickets and forests, particularly near the ocean. Site factors such as topography, wind, and soil nutrient status modify the salt-aerosol impact. As noted in the discussion of dunes, salt aerosols kill terminal buds and young leaves just as they burst from their buds.

Salt-aerosol damage is often highest in the spring as buds break open and the delicate, thin leaves are exposed to salt injury. A strong onshore wind at this time can cause considerable damage to coastal trees and shrubs within the reach of salt aerosols. Salt enters young leaves through epidermal cracks usually created by leaves

Figure 21. This leaf damage was caused by exposure to airborne salt. Necrosis develops along the leaf margins and tips of leaves exposed to salt aerosols.

Figure 22. Branches and leaves appear as if they have been pruned where maritime shrub thickets and maritime forests grow near the ocean. Leaves, stems, and buds exposed to chronic salt-aerosol deposits die, and this leads to a "windswept" or "sculpted" canopy.

rubbing together. The leaves suffer necrosis and die (fig. 21).

The death of terminal buds stimulates the growth of lateral branches. More leaves and branches survive alee of the source of salt aerosols, and this changes the growth pattern. Differential survival of buds and leaves leads to the development of a "windswept" or "sculpted" growth pattern so often seen in coastal shrubs and trees (fig. 22).

Scientific studies show that the smooth, dense, asymmetrical canopy caused by exposure to salt aerosols reduces the amount of salt reaching plants growing inside the thicket or forest. The tight canopy itself reduces light reaching the interior of the thicket or forest, the temperature within the thicket and forest, and the chance that shrubs and trees would uproot during a storm.

Shrubs and trees with small, unlobed leaves and thick cuticles survive salt aerosols best. The leaves of live oak and sand laurel oak, for example, shed salt aerosols efficiently. Conversely, Carolina red maple and sweet gum are less well adapted to salt aerosols. Their leaves are broad and thin with only a modest cuticle. They grow best as understory trees or distant from the source of salt aerosols.

Because only a relatively small suite of tree and shrub species tolerate salt aerosols, this factor ultimately determines species diversity and composition, as well as the canopy shape and height in shrub and forest communities. Trees and shrubs become progressively larger, and their shape is less "windswept," as the distance from the ocean or estuary (the source of salt aerosols) increases. Once nearly all the salt aerosols drop out of the wind stream, trees grow symmetrically, and the forest and thickets resemble mainland forests in structure and composition.

The canopy is structurally nearly continuous, with the leaf-bearing branches of all the trees concentrated in a thin layer at the top of the forest. Adjacent trees fill in all of the spaces in the canopy. The understory trees are few and scattered, as are the shrubs of the maritime forest.

WATER

Precipitation is the primary source of water for maritime shrub thickets and forests. Precipitation reaching the ground beneath arborescent vegetation infiltrates quickly through the coarse sands. Surficial roots absorb this moisture as it moves into the soil, but deep roots supply most of the water to the trees. The dense canopy intercepts considerable precipitation, especially light rain. Interestingly, a significant proportion of the rainfall evaporates from leaf and stem surfaces almost immediately and never reaches the soil. Coastal fog occurs frequently, and with the dense, tight canopy, the humidity within the forest is higher than in the adjacent dunes. Shrubs or forest trees occupying deep swales typically have roots that access the water table, a reasonably steady water source generated by precipitation. The height of the water table fluctuates over time, depending on the amount of recent rainfall.

Figure 23. Maritime shrub thickets develop in topographically low areas on coastal dunes. Shrubs appear "sculpted" due to the effects of salt aerosols deposited on leaf, stem, and bud surfaces.

FIRE

Fire is an important, but uncommon, factor in the development and maintenance of maritime shrub- and tree-dominated communities in the coastal Carolinas. Lightning ignites most coastal fires. These species survive modest ground wildfires: live oak, loblolly pine, longleaf pine, and slash pine, with their thick bark, as well as cabbage palmetto and saw palmetto, with their thick, persistent leaf bases and fire-resistant trunks. Fire reaching the canopy, however, damages or kills these trees. Despite destruction of the aerial portion of the plant, resprouting occurs in some species, including American holly, red bay, and common wax myrtle. Where ground fires occur frequently, pines gradually assume dominance and the understory thins significantly.

MARITIME SHRUB THICKETS

Maritime shrub thickets originate in many upland settings in the coastal Carolinas. They first appear in patches, often composed of a single shrub landward of the first line of dunes. Maritime shrub thickets also develop in dune swales, on former overwash fans and terraces, and along the seaward edge of maritime forests. Coastal shrubs usually possess multiple stems and achieve a maximum height of around 15 feet. Shrub thickets nearest the ocean exhibit strong salt-aerosol pruning and may be only chest high (fig. 23).

The canopy surface is usually smooth and continuous from the ground to the apex of the thicket. A thin but formidably dense layer of branches and leaves makes this community appear closed and impenetrable. In fact, so smooth is the canopy surface, so gradual is the slope of the canopy, and so densely packed are the leaves and branches that it seems one might easily walk directly to the top of the maritime shrub thicket! (Not so.) However, once you get past the veneer of branches and leaves, the maritime shrub thicket is so open that it's easy to crawl inside the thicket! So little light penetrates the layer of branches and leaves that the ground is usually barren except for maybe a few struggling catbriars or poison ivy. Maritime bushy bluestem and saltmeadow cordgrass typically thrive on the edge of the thicket, where they poke up through the ground-hugging canopy.

While common wax myrtles comprise shrub thickets almost to the exclusion of all other shrubs throughout much of the Carolinas, northern bayberry dominates patchy dune thickets in northern North Carolina. Salt-aerosol-resistant vines straggle across the canopy, most notably dune greenbriar, laurel greenbriar, peppervine, Virginia creeper, poison ivy, and summer grape. Shrubs are the first arborescent vegetation to colonize dune swales and the edges of overwash fans. Within a decade or two, salt-aerosol-resistant trees replace the shrubs.

Thickets generally experience only occasional saltwater flooding, but thickets growing in dune swales may experience periodic freshwater flooding, varying from days to months, especially amid periods of high rainfall or during the winter. Some thickets drain well, while those growing in poorly drained sites remain wet year-round. Thickets grade into a variety of other plant communities, including maritime forests, maritime grasslands, salt shrub thickets, dunes, and interdune ponds.

Most coastal Carolina islands have large acreages of maritime shrub thickets. Bear Island and Sunset Beach, N.C., and Waties Island, S.C., offer excellent examples of extensive, low-growing, nearly impenetrable maritime shrub thickets.

MARITIME FOREST CHARACTERISTICS AND DISTRIBUTION

Scientists classify the maritime forest of the Carolinas coast as a variant of the southeastern evergreen oak/pine forest. This forest type possesses a mixture of broad-leaved evergreen trees, many of which occur in nearby upland forest communities. This type of forest thrives in a warm and humid but temperate and maritime climate.

Maritime forests typically occupy the center or core of barrier islands and some areas of adjacent mainland where elevated salt aerosols skew the mainland forest composition toward a significant presence of salt-tolerant species. Where salt aerosols prune the tree canopy, the forest is only 15 to 30 feet high and surprisingly aerodynamically smooth. Where the maritime forest flourishes directly behind a foredune ridge, intense salt aerosols limit tree growth to a height equal to the top of the foredune. Over time, the maritime forest gradually replaces backdune, maritime grassland, and maritime shrub thicket communities. The terms "coastal hammock" or "maritime hammock" are applied to a maritime forest, especially when it covers dune ridges separated by wetlands—marshes and ponds.

The presence of a mature maritime forest indicates long-term physiographic stability. Along the Outer Banks of North Carolina, maritime forests are uncommon because the region undergoes major physical changes as hurricanes and severe storms strike these islands. Oceanic overwash and inlet formation are major perturbations that affect these islands. Here, maritime forest distribution is discontinuous and patchy. One important forested area on the northern Outer Banks is Nags Head Woods, a globally unique ecosystem. Coastal areas achieve long-term stability along Currituck Banks, Cape Hatteras, and Kitty Hawk Woods, where the island landmasses are wide and topographically high. In North Carolina, wide, high, and stable sites include the aforementioned Nags Head Woods, Buxton Woods, and Bald Head Island Woods. In South Carolina, stable coastal landmasses are common; extensive forests exist on

Figure 24. At a distance from the source of salt aerosols, trees are tall and straight, and the forest exhibits an understory and shrub layer similar to that of a forest inland from the shore.

most of the islands, notably Capers, Hunting, Kiawah, and Hilton Head islands. These forests exist where fronting dunes protect the forests during major storms (fig. 24).

MARITIME FORESTS, THE ENDPOINT OF SUCCESSION

Ecologists consider maritime forest communities the climax, or final and most stable, plant community in the coastal Carolinas. This long-lived community cannot withstand constantly changing environmental conditions. For example, if the protective dunes blow out or the shoreline erodes, increased salt aerosols or infiltration by overwhelming amounts of sand can rapidly destroy a mature forest. It will be many decades before a mature maritime forest can replace itself.

In the center of an island beyond the reach of salt aerosols, maritime forest communities develop that may be nearly indistinguishable from forest assemblages found inland. In these areas, the maritime forest grades into one of several oak/pine associations or a pine/oak/gum association of trees.

BONEYARD BEACHES

There are conditions that dramatically alter the normal position of maritime forests typically well back from the beach. For example, where a section of ocean or estuarine shoreline is adjusting to a new wave climate, wave action can, and often does, erode any grassy dunes separating the maritime forests from the beach. This change exposes the forest to the full effects of salt aerosols, wind, and tidal action. On Hunting, Capers, and Bull islands, S.C., for example, changes in the shape of the islands have resulted in conditions where erosion and saltwater overwashes have destroyed foredunes and left a graveyard of trees and shrubs exposed to ocean waves. The exposed trees die rapidly, leaving roots, trunks, and branches—often in their life positions—littering the surf zone. This feature is called a boneyard beach or sometimes a boneyard forest. The trunks and branches are characteristically twisted and contorted, a reminder of the intense salt-aerosol effects on the overstory trees. Boneyard beaches are simultaneously strikingly beautiful and chillingly eerie as the angular grayish-white trees appear ghostlike along a stretch of sandy shore. The trees symbolize the dynamics of the natural shoreline and the fragility of the plant communities within reach of storm waves and tides (fig. 25).

MARITIME FOREST FLORA

The maritime forest is diverse and variable in respect to species composition. The flora changes with topography, soil moisture, drainage, and salt-aerosol intensity. The dominant tree species in the maritime forests of the coastal Carolinas include live oak, sand laurel oak, cabbage palmetto, slash pine, loblolly pine, southern red oak, southern magnolia, water oak, and pignut hickory. These species resist storms and winds without splitting, breaking, or

Figure 25. A boneyard beach forms where rapid erosion removes the sand from in front of and beneath trees, exposing them to waves and salt water. Tree skeletons remain "frozen" for years in their life position on what is now an ocean beach.

becoming uprooted, and they gradually dominate the maritime forest to the exclusion of less-tolerant species.

Variations in composition of the maritime forest occur in topographically low areas within the forest that may be infrequently wet or seasonally flooded. Black gum, Carolina red maple, sweet gum, bald cypress, water oak, Carolina willow, and loblolly pine characterize plants in these areas (fig. 26).

In high and often drier facets of the maritime forest, loblolly pine, southern red oak, sweet gum, common persimmon, coastal red cedar, black locust, and pignut hickory are important species. In sites nearest the ocean waves, only the hardiest species—live oak, cabbage palmetto, and coastal red cedar—grow well (fig. 27).

Understory trees and shrubs are sparse, which gives the forest an open, parklike feel. The understory trees most frequently encountered are coastal red cedar, American holly, red bay, sassafras, wild olive, flowering dogwood, and coastal American hornbeam. Notable shrubs are common wax myrtle, saw and dwarf palmetto, and yaupon.

Figure 26. Black gums, Carolina red maples, and loblolly pines dominate coastal lowlands that are seasonally or infrequently flooded with fresh water and occasionally with slightly brackish water in Kitty Hawk Woods, N.C. Courtesy of Rachel Veal/North Carolina Coastal Reserve.

Figure 27. This seaward leading edge of a maritime forest in South Carolina is dominated by live oak, coastal red cedar, and cabbage palmetto.

Vines stretch across the smooth forest canopy here—principally maritime catbriar, poison ivy, supplejack, Virginia creeper, peppervine, muscadine, summer grape, Carolina jessamine, and dune and laurel greenbriars. These vines knit the tree crowns into a continuous canopy. Deep in the canopy, light is low, humidity is high, and tree trunks and branches are frequently covered with a variety of crustose, foliose, and fruticose lichens happily sheltered from salt aerosols. The epiphytic Spanish moss hangs in both wisps and long curtains on live oak, Carolina red maple, and other trees.

Ground cover is sparse, yet diverse; the deep shade supports a suite of species adapted to low light. Characteristic plants include ebony spleenwort, partridge berry, finger rot, and common elephant's foot.

Figure 28. This salt shrub thicket developed in a ring surrounding a small patch of maritime forest. Here, sea ox-eye, marsh elder, and yaupon dominate the plant community.

SALT SHRUB THICKET LOCATION AND ENVIRONMENT

The salt shrub thicket is a zone of shrub and herbaceous plants positioned between the upland forest and the brackish or salt marsh on barrier islands. The community lacks a continuous canopy pruned by salt aerosols unless it is adjacent to a large, open-water estuary where winds stir up estuarine whitecaps that put additional salts into the air. Elevations are typically low, and soil moisture is high. Occasional but chronic saltwater flooding excludes species intolerant of elevated soil salinity from this community (fig. 28).

SALT SHRUB THICKET FLORA

The flora consists of a mixture of shrubs, grasses, and broad-leaved herbs. Signature species occurring here include marsh elder, sea myrtle, saltwater false willow, and sea ox-eye. Other species in this community are the ubiquitous saltmeadow cordgrass, switchgrass, yaupon, saltgrass, and, increasingly, common reed. Occasional members of this community are southern seaside goldenrod, common wax myrtle, dune pennywort, eastern bloodleaf, and saltmarsh bulrush.

HUMAN EFFECTS ON THE MARITIME THICKETS AND FORESTS

Loss of forest acreage to development and forest fragmentation pose the greatest threats to maritime forests. These forests are often the first plant communities affected by development because they are high, dry, shaded, and, overall, the safest environment in which to build in the coastal area. Along much of the Carolinas coast, maritime forest environments have undergone at least some development. Constructing homes in the maritime forest invariably breaks the smooth, continuous canopy that deflects salt aerosols, and the loss of this cover allows salts to enter and damage the forest understory.

It is important to avoid breaching this ocean-facing or leading edge of the forest canopy. Understory trees, shrubs, and herbs that are exposed to damaging salt aerosols often die following disruption of the canopy. Houses built in openings cut into the maritime forest can expose the surrounding shrubs and trees to increased salt aerosols. If this occurs, sand fences or similar structures can be installed to block salt aerosols and provide temporary protection to the forest edge while the trees recover. Newly exposed trees and shrubs often continue to die for months, and sometimes years, after construction is finished. This effectively expands the forest openings beyond the first cut of trees.

Similarly, road construction and utilities installation allow salt aerosols to penetrate into the forest. Research indicates that it can take a maritime forest four or more years to reestablish a salt-aerosols-resistant edge, which arrests further loss of forest habitat, after a road is cut through it.

Forest fragmentation effectively increases the edge effect in a forest. While this division increases the edge habitat and supports some interesting species, the total size of contiguous forest plots decreases. This reduces the home territory of some forest animals below a satisfactory size, and they move elsewhere or the population perishes. Development in a maritime forest environment should provide for one or more continuous corridors of natural tree and shrub cover to allow forest-dwelling animals to move from place to place without having to cross open ground. Trails cut through the forest should be few and narrow.

Since we have a better understanding of how development in the maritime forest alters coastal environments, wholesale clearing of building lots is beginning to be replaced by more careful siting of homes and other structures. Today, developers build homes with a clearer understanding of the dynamics of the forest, and they show more consideration for it.

National and state parks, as well as private holdings of various acreages, have preserved and conserved some of the finest examples of the maritime forest

Figure 29. This is evidence of laurel wilt disease. Entire red bay trees die, but surrounding trees and shrubs may be unaffected. Since its introduction in northern Georgia, the disease has spread into Florida, South Carolina, and North Carolina.

in the coastal Carolinas. These include Currituck Banks, Nags Head, Hatteras Island, and Shackleford Banks in North Carolina, where this community type is rare. In addition, Bogue Banks and Bald Head Island, N.C., and North Island, Bull Island, St. Phillip's Island, and Hunting Island, S.C., all preserve exemplary tracts of maritime forest. These efforts help mitigate the losses elsewhere as coastal development proceeds.

Development can pose additional, unexpected hazards, such as the exposure of native plants to pests and diseases not normally found in an undisturbed forest. Laurel wilt disease, for example, is spread by an exotic species that was introduced accidentally. A fungus, *Raffaelea lauricola*, attacks species of the Laurel family, including red bay, causing laurel wilt, which threatens to reduce the presence of red bay in the native flora. The fungus was introduced into coastal red bay populations by the nonnative red bay ambrosia beetle (*Xyleborus glabratus*), which itself was introduced near Savannah, Ga., from Asia in 2003 (fig. 29).

Under natural conditions, the fungus

spreads slowly; however, the ambrosia beetle has increased the rate of the spread of the disease in the coastal Carolinas, Georgia, and Florida. Once the disease affects mature red bay trees, it is nearly always fatal. The disease affects young trees less, and they may not die immediately. The disease can be identified by the presence of entire dead branches on infected trees. The dead, brown leaves remain on the tree for months. The consequences of reduced populations of red bay are unknown, but the loss will likely threaten the survival of the palamedes swallowtail butterfly, which depends on red bay as the primary food plant for its caterpillars. As the internationalization of goods and products continues, diseases similar to laurel wilt will likely continue to appear in coastal vegetation.

4

ENVIRONMENTS
AND FLORA
PALUSTRINE AND
ESTUARINE WETLANDS

Scientists characterize wetlands as environments where terrestrial and aquatic systems intergrade and excess water is the most important environmental factor defining the system. Water determines the nature of the soil that develops and the types of plants that occupy the area. Specialized plants capable of surviving and reproducing while permanently submerged, periodically flooded, or growing in saturated soils are called hydrophytes.

While several kinds of wetlands are present in the coastal Carolinas, we will focus our discussion of the environment and flora on two wetland systems: palustrine and estuarine. Palustrine communities are nontidal wetlands with a mixture of several plant forms: trees, shrubs, grasses, or herbs. The palustrine system includes several freshwater environments, namely ponds, swamps, marshes, and forested wetlands (fig. 30). These communities are periodically covered with water or have a water table close to the surface for at least a portion of the growing season.

Tidal activity influences estuarine communities, with salinities ranging from

Figure 30. On Oak Island, N.C., palustrine wetlands once occupied topographically low sites immediately landward of the foredunes. As development proceeded, these ponds were partially filled. Today, only remnants of these large open-water ponds exist.

seawater strength to nearly fresh water. Emergent vegetation, mostly grasses and rushes, characterizes this system. The estuarine system includes brackish and salt marshes as well as salt pannes.

Wetlands provide valuable functions in a coastal setting. They are buffers against damaging floods and serve as habitat for plants and animals. Natural depressions such as dune swales, marshes, or swamp forests on barrier beaches and barrier islands are important features because they store, filter, and slowly release water.

PALUSTRINE WETLANDS

Most freshwater wetlands we encounter in the coastal Carolinas are relatively small areas when compared with the expansive brackish and salt marshes. Ponds and interdune swales confine and define the freshwater wetlands. Larger freshwater wetlands are typically man-made. For example, ponds on Bull Island, S.C., or Bodie Island and Pea Island, N.C., were constructed to provide resting and feeding sites for wildfowl in the coastal section of the Atlantic Flyway. Natural freshwater wetlands are embedded throughout the upland dunes, maritime grasslands, maritime shrub thickets, and maritime forests. They vary in origin, vegetation, and aspect. Scientists refer to these features by various names, most commonly dune swales, interdune ponds, marshes, swamps, and hollows. Palustrine systems may have some open water. Trees or shrubs may cover all or part of them, or herbaceous plants may dominate. The water regime of deep swales between dunes and dune ridges may be permanent standing water, seasonal or temporary standing water, or damp soils created by a water table that occurs close to the surface. The water table may be several feet below the dune crests but a mere 2 feet or less in the swales,

Figure 31. Densely growing grasses, herbs, and shrubs characterize interdune or swale wetlands. They are easily distinguished from nearby dunes dominated by a sparser cover of primarily dune grasses.

which is a depth well within the root zone of most plants (fig. 31).

These wetland communities undergo succession, the gradual change in the composition of the flora and fauna driven by environmental changes in and around the community. Salt water may occasionally flood these communities when they are subjected to unusually high tides or oceanic overwash. Saltwater flooding kills or damages plants sensitive to elevated soil salts. Dynamic factors influence the floristic composition of palustrine communities; these factors include the amount of salt aerosols received, the hydrologic regime, the presence of an aquaclude, and the amount of organic matter in or on top of the soil.

DUNE SWALES

Dune swales are located in topographical depressions within the dune community. Depending on the landscape, these communities may intergrade imperceptibly with adjacent plant communities over a broad area or have sharp, easily distinguished boundaries. These palustrine communities often have thick, organic-rich, and mucky soils owing to the buildup and partial decay of plant litter.

Dune swales are generally dominated by grasses, rushes, and sedges, including saltmeadow cordgrass, saltmarsh fimbristylis, Olney's threesquare, and narrowleaf white-topped sedge. This is where species such as nodding ladies' tresses, royal fern, and water pimpernel hide amongst the grasses and sedges. Trees and shrubs, along with broad-leaved herbs, are also a part of the swale flora. As succession proceeds, common wax myrtle, red bay, yaupon, and sea myrtle replace these pioneering herbs and grasses. In turn, with the passage of several decades, Carolina red maple, black gum, and bald cypress replace the shrubs.

Depending on the scale of the landscape, swales may range from a fraction of an acre to many acres. Shrubs invade the drier margins first and over time may cover the entire swale. Yaupon, coastal red cedar, and winged sumac also can be found in drier swales, while Carolina willow, common wax myrtle, and sea myrtle are present in moist swales. Dune hairgrass, southern seaside goldenrod, saltmeadow cordgrass, and dune pennywort are typical plants of seasonally wet swales.

INTERDUNE PONDS

Interdune ponds have deeper and more permanent water levels than dune swales. They may have open water or seasonal standing water for a sufficient period to support hydrophytic species. Common duckweed, dotted smartweed, and the exotic and invasive common water hyacinth occupy open water. Water pimpernel, rabbitsfoot grass, lesser quaking grass, Monnier's water-hyssop, St. Augustine grass, marsh fern, eastern

Figure 32. Graminoids dominate the shallow-water edges of freshwater ponds on barrier islands and barrier beaches. Wetlands such as this provide an important source of fresh water as well as nesting and resting places for wildlife.

rose mallow, and common cattail are representative of species that occupy pond edges. Common reed is expanding rapidly in the coastal Carolinas and outcompetes native species in both slightly brackish and freshwater wetlands. Where salt water occasionally intrudes into ponds, giant cordgrass and saw grass are common components of the flora (fig. 32).

South Carolina boasts many wetlands that grade from saltwater- to freshwater-dominated environments. Several South Carolina barrier islands—Bull Island, Capers Island, and Kiawah Island, for example—show historic natural progradation or shoreline accretion, particularly along their northeastern ends. Here, wetland areas nearest the inlet are estuarine with smooth cordgrass, the dominant species. As the swales between successive dune lines narrow and develop farther from salt water, a freshwater flora replaces plants adapted to salt water and brackish water. Swales between dune ridges in Kitty Hawk Woods, N.C., show a similar pattern of plant distribution along the saltwater to freshwater gradient.

IMPORTANCE OF WATER LEVEL TO COASTAL WETLAND PLANTS

Precipitation is the source of fresh water for palustrine wetlands. The water level in ponds is not constant but varies with weather conditions. In periods of high precipitation and low evaporation, wetlands typically maintain high water levels, and hydrophytic plants adjust to these high levels. Hurricanes and nor'easters occasionally dump prodigious quantities of water on the Carolinas coast, raising the water table for weeks or months. These storms can reverse drought conditions in less than 24 hours.

Plants display creative methods for adapting to these conditions. Cattails develop aerenchyma tissue near the base of the plants to ensure that they will receive sufficient oxygen in their roots, even during high-water periods. Virginia buttonweed produces adventitious roots, which absorb oxygen from water when they are nearly submerged due to high water. Carolina red maple, sweet bay, red bay, black gum, and bald cypress all show some measure of buttressing or butt swell when growing at the edge of ponds. This swelling provides extra support for these shallowly rooted trees.

In contrast, during dry years or extended drought, plants frequently adjust their growth based on unfavorable water availability. These responses to drought are species specific, with some wetland trees, shrubs, and herbs shedding leaves as drought advances, thereby reducing water loss. Similarly, plants reduce water loss by closing their stomata when they experience long dry periods. Wetland plants can cope with a varying water supply by either advancing (flushing) or delaying flower and fruit production.

Figure 33. Precipitation is the source of fresh water in ponds, swamps, and marshes on barrier islands such as this pond on Hilton Head Island in South Carolina.

HUMAN EFFECTS ON FRESHWATER WETLANDS

Wetlands seem always to be at the center of human attention. In today's use of this Carolina coastal resource, we are learning to avoid destroying wetland functions while simultaneously accomplishing most of our development goals. We strive to develop our human communities while still preserving wildlife values, protecting natural water storage characteristics, and retaining sediment and nutrients (fig. 33). Freshwater wetlands once met a fate similar to that of coastal salt marshes. Land developers originally altered ponds, swamps, and swales on the Carolina coast by ditching, draining, or filling them. Once scientists understood that these wetlands were not necessarily a nuisance but fulfilled several critical roles in the landscape, agencies adopted new regulations to maintain wetland functions to the greatest extent possible. Developers soon began building near ponds and swales in ways that reduced the disturbance or disruption of their important functions. Today, people can enjoy wetlands using developer-built boardwalks and piers that allow lovers of undisturbed communities to access or traverse them without causing damage.

ESTUARINE WETLANDS

Estuaries are water bodies that are partially open to the ocean. Estuarine wetlands are low-lying, vegetated areas flooded by tidal waters and are considered transitional between uplands and the ocean. The adjacent uplands provide two important functions for the estuary. First, uplands surrounding the estuaries intercept high-energy ocean waves and currents, creating a sheltered environment in which rooted plants can grow. Second, uplands deliver freshwater runoff to the estuary, thereby diluting the salt water. During each tidal cycle, these openings—river mouths and inlets—deliver ocean water to the estuaries and the plant communities they contain, mixing the water in the process. Islands such as Hilton Head, Kiawah, and St. Phillips in South Carolina, as well as Masonboro, Ocracoke, and Core Banks in North Carolina, create and protect hundreds of square miles of wetlands landward of their coastal position (fig. 34). These vary from predominantly shallow, open-water areas like Pamlico and Core sounds to estuaries that are nearly marsh-filled, such as those landward of Edisto Island or those surrounding St. Helena Island. The depth of tidal flooding depends on the geographic and physiographic location of the wetlands. Communities in the open estuaries, Kiawah and Seabrook islands, for example, are covered daily, exhibiting a spring tide range of more than 8 feet of nearly full-strength seawater. In contrast, in northern North Carolina, estuarine plant communities in Currituck Sound experience a tidal range of less than 1 foot with nearly, but not quite, fresh water.

Figure 34. Tidal marsh vegetation nearly fills this estuary landward of the barrier islands in southeastern North Carolina. Estuarine wetlands buffer both the mainland and adjacent islands from destructive waves during storms.

LUNAR AND WIND TIDES

In the estuarine system, plant composition and distribution are affected by daily tide exchanges, precipitation, freshwater runoff, and winds that blow over the estuaries. In the coastal Carolinas, tides are diurnal, with approximately two high tides and two low tides per day. Salinity can vary from greater than ocean water strength (due to evaporation) to nearly fresh water (diluted by runoff). Spring tides cover a larger area of land, leading to occasional saltwater flooding of some portions of the land bordering the estuary. The relative elevation of the marsh substrate, modified by the intensity, duration, and direction of regional winds, affects the flooding frequency.

For example, the combination of an increased volume of fresh water delivered by rivers and winds blowing seawater into the estuary from nearby inlets may increase the depth of the flooding or extend the time of inundation substantially or both. For example, persistent south and southwest winds can cause water to accumulate ("pile up") on the north and northeast shores of Currituck Sound, inundating estuarine plant communities for hours or days. Winds blowing from the opposite direction reduce the geographical extent and time that water covers the plant community in Currituck Sound. The mixing of ocean water and fresh river water delivers water masses with a range of salinities to these wetlands.

The nearly infinite combination of wind speeds and directions interacting with water masses of differing salinity leads to the formation of highly varied estuarine wetlands. These wetlands are regularly to occasionally flooded with water salinities varying from full-strength seawater to nearly fresh water. Often there is no sharp line delineating estuarine plant communities from uplands; they intergrade, with species composition changing depending on the water salinity and the duration of flooding. Depending on topography, the width of the zone dividing the uplands from the estuary varies from a few feet to hundreds of feet.

SALINITY

The salt content of the water flooding the marshes depends on the amount of dilution from fresh water. On a daily basis, seawater bathes estuarine wetlands near inlets, and this action favors plants adapted to daily inundation with full-strength seawater. In contrast, at significant distances from inlets, freshwater rivers and runoff from upland areas dilute the ocean water, favoring plants that survive best in low-salinity environments. A hurricane or major nor'easter disrupts this pattern by temporarily delivering large quantities of rainfall to the estuary. Fresh water pouring into the estuary from the adjacent upland may freshen an estuary for days after the storm.

SALT-TOLERANCE MECHANISMS

Excessive salts in the environment have deadly consequences for many plants.

Large quantities of salts in the soils and soil water upset the internal water balance in plants, causing water to move out of the plants rather than into the plants, which is the normal pattern of water uptake. Once the elevated salts accumulate in plants, they lead to the plant's death.

However, several physiological and physical adaptations have evolved in coastal plants that enable them to survive inundation by salt water. Glassworts, for instance, accumulate salts along with their normal intake of water. These halophytes move the salt to cell vacuoles, where the salts remain isolated from the cell contents during the life of the plant.

Other species internally dilute the salts absorbed by their roots. To compensate, roots absorb additional fresh water, resulting in increased stem and root succulence. Virginia glasswort, for example, appears to detoxify internal salts in this way. Stem segments of this species die once they accumulate a toxic level of salt, ultimately releasing the salts back into the environment.

Smooth cordgrass, saltmeadow cordgrass, and saltgrass possess specialized glands on their leaf surfaces. On hot, dry days, tiny white crystals form on the leaf surfaces of these species. The dry crystals form as water evaporates from a concentrated salt solution exuded from specialized salt-collecting glands on the leaf surfaces (fig. 35). In another example, seabeach orach sheds entire leaves as salt concentrations build within the plant cells. This is an unspecialized, but certainly effective, method of eliminating salt accumulated within the plant.

Research demonstrates that plants related to our coastal halophytes—*Limonium*, *Suaeda*, and *Sporobolus*—use organic compounds synthesized in cells (proline, glycine betaine, and inositol) to counterbalance the intake of

Figure 35. Exuded onto leaf surfaces as a salty brine, large salt crystals form as water evaporates from the exudates. This is a primary mechanism for reducing internal salts in smooth cordgrass (pictured here) and several other halophytes.

environmental salts. They translocate these organic compounds to root cell vacuoles. This action reduces the tendency for water to move from inside the plant to outside the plant in saline environments. Once these compounds build up in root cells, water can move into the roots. Finally, species such as southern seaside goldenrod selectively prevent relatively large ions (Na^+ and Cl^-) from crossing cell membranes into their roots while allowing water molecules to enter.

SOIL OXYGEN STRESS
Aerenchyma tissue forms in plant roots under oxygen stress. Aerenchyma tissue facilitates diffusion from shoots to roots to supply deep roots and rhizomes with oxygen. Black needlerush, smooth cordgrass, saltmeadow cordgrass, giant cordgrass, common and narrow-leaved cattail, and common reed all have air-filled, spongy aerenchyma tissues that aerate their root zones when they grow in waterlogged soils.

ESTUARINE PLANT COMMUNITIES
I have divided the estuarine wetlands communities in the coastal Carolinas into

(a) brackish marshes, (b) salt marshes, and (c) salt pannes (fig. 36). A fourth community, submerged aquatic vegetation, is beyond the scope of this book.

BRACKISH MARSHES: CHARACTERISTICS AND LOCATION
Brackish marshes develop along the upland edge of the estuaries where tidal inundation occurs less than once a day and where the freshwater flow from adjacent uplands dilutes ocean water. In North Carolina, the brackish-marsh plant community is dominated by black needlerush and covers thousands of acres along the shores of the Albemarle and Pamlico sounds. While brackish marshes exist throughout coastal South Carolina, they are less extensive than in North Carolina.

The salinity of brackish marshes ranges from 0.5 ppt (parts per thousand) to about 18 ppt; at its maximum, this level is about half that of ocean-derived water covering salt marshes. At the waterward edge of brackish marshes, saltmarsh plants dominate; at the upper or landward edge, plants called facultative wetland plants flourish. These are plants that can grow in both wet areas and uplands.

Brackish-marsh plant communities regularly grade into salt shrub thickets on the landward side and grade into salt marshes toward open water. Few tidal creeks develop in the brackish marshes owing to the considerably smaller quantity of tidal water moving on and off the marsh. Primary productivity is high but does not equal that of salt marshes. Much of the organic matter remains within the community, since estuarine water only flushes this area intermittently.

Brackish-Marsh Flora
A single plant species, black needlerush, dominates large acreages of brackish

including saltmarsh bulrush, Olney's threesquare, southern seaside goldenrod, saltgrass, perennial saltmarsh aster, and salt-marsh water hemp. Other important plants in the brackish marsh include sea ox-eye, southern saltmarsh fleabane, saltmarsh fimbristylis, narrow-leaved loosestrife, sea lavender, and the seemingly ubiquitous saltmeadow cordgrass. In areas with the lowest salinity soils and where flooding water is the least, the dominant plants are the aggressive, nonnative common reed; eastern rose mallow; giant cordgrass; switchgrass; and common wax myrtle.

SALT MARSHES: CHARACTERISTICS AND LOCATION

Salt marshes are wetland plant communities dominated by emergent vascular plants that are alternately inundated with ocean water and exposed to the air, usually twice a day in the Carolinas. Salt marshes occur on the landward side of barrier islands, in sounds and bays, and at the mouths of coastal rivers such as the Ashepoo, Combahee, Edisto, and Santee in South Carolina and the Pamlico, Albemarle, and Cape Fear in North Carolina. These estuarine embayments in the Carolinas contain some of the largest expanses of salt marshes on the entire Atlantic coast.

Figure 36. Major estuarine plant communities of the coastal Carolinas are (a) brackish marshes, (b) salt marshes, and (c) salt pannes. Plants of brackish marshes typically experience soil water conditions with less-than-full-strength seawater, while salt pannes have soil salt concentrations that exceed that of salt water.

marsh. Few plants co-occur with black needlerush, leading to the formation of extensive monocultures. Depending on elevation, inundation frequency, salinity, and soil conditions, some other common plants of the brackish-water marsh occur,

Saltmarsh Soils
Some salt marshes have poor drainage, leading to waterlogged soils. Under these conditions, plant roots and rhizomes deplete the available oxygen. Plants replenish oxygen to the roots through diffusion from stems and leaves. With low oxygen levels deep in the soil, most estuarine plant roots are concentrated near the surface. Saltmarsh soils are composed of a mixture of fine sands, silts, and clays. In salt marshes, organic matter

decays slowly, and a thick, dense peat accumulates on top of the mineral soil. The breakdown of organic matter in low-oxygen environments results in the formation of sulfides and related compounds indicated by the "rotten eggs" odor that visitors to estuaries commonly experience.

Tidal Creek and Saltmarsh Levee Formation
Flooding and then draining a sheet of ocean water across extensive flats covered with marsh grass plants is hydraulically inefficient. Water does not completely drain from the marsh surface before the next tidal cycle brings fresh floodwaters to the marsh. Ultimately, this natural flooding and draining asymmetry leads to the formation of a network of incised rivulets and creeks. Creeks deliver ocean water on flood tides. On the ebb tide, water leaving the marsh surface carves an extensive and intricate network of channels across the marsh surface. Smooth cordgrass plants growing along creeks slow the movement of flooding and ebbing water to a point that allows fine silt and clay particles to settle on the marsh surface. The greatest deposition of sediment occurs along tidal creeks lined with tall, dense smooth cordgrass culms. Well fortified with nutrients from this sediment, smooth cordgrass grows exceptionally well, and the margins of creek banks increase in elevation. This cycle of sediment capture followed by the increased growth of smooth cordgrass followed by more sediment capture elevates creek margins and results in visibly higher creek margins with visibly taller smooth cordgrass.

Two ecotypes of smooth cordgrass grow in saltmarsh environments. A tall form ranging up to 6 feet tall occupies the distinctive, narrow levee along tidal creeks; the short form grows primarily on muddy flats at a distance from tidal creek margins and adjacent to upland plant communities.

Here, smooth cordgrass may grow only 1 to 3 feet tall.

Water Detention and Quality
Salt marshes buffer water movement during storms and other high-water periods. Salt marshes accumulate, impound, and release water slowly, which decreases the flood potential in estuaries. In addition, marsh grasses absorb the energy of storm waves and currents, thereby serving as the first line of defense against coastal erosion. Together, the saltmarsh flora and fauna maintain water quality. Marsh plants reduce water movement to a level that allows suspended particles of sediment and organic debris to settle from the water column onto the marsh surface. Marsh fauna such as oysters and mussels remove both organic and inorganic compounds from the water column. Scientists estimate that an oyster processes (filters) as much as 50 gallons of water per day.

Saltmarsh Flora
A single plant, smooth cordgrass, almost exclusively dominates the saltmarsh community in the coastal Carolinas. Smooth cordgrass thrives in fine-sediment soils high in salts, low in oxygen, and alternately covered and exposed by estuarine water. Smooth cordgrass initiates saltmarsh growth on newly elevated sandbars and spreads quickly via rhizomes. Over hundreds and hundreds of years, this process created vast acreages of salt marshes in the Carolinas.

Several other salt-tolerant species, called halophytes, compete with smooth cordgrass, most notably saltmeadow cordgrass, black needlerush, saltgrass, and seashore dropseed, especially where tidal waters cover the marsh surface less than twice daily. While grasses dominate the salt marshes, several broad-leaved plants, including sea lavender, sea ox-eye, perennial saltmarsh aster, and saltwort, typically occupy patches of varying sizes in slightly elevated environments. The upland edges of salt marshes display a diversity of salt-tolerant species. Saltmarsh bulrush and southern seaside goldenrod are the dominant plants in these environments. Salt-tolerant shrubs marsh elder and common wax myrtle occur on elevated sites within the marsh.

Rafting of Marsh Grasses

During fall and winter, smooth cordgrass translocates nutrients down to its roots and rhizomes, and the aerial stems die. Wave action breaks these dead stems free, they float to the surface, and currents carry them around the estuary. Large rafts of marsh grass stems, almost exclusively smooth cordgrass, drift out of the estuaries and into the nearshore waters, where they encounter waves and currents that push them onto nearby beaches. Once this organic material reaches the beach backshore, it serves as a water and nutrient source for wrack-line plants that will germinate the following spring.

While some tides and waves carry wrack material to the beaches, winds also drive huge quantities of grass stems back into the salt marshes and irregularly flooded marshes. Here, the leaves and stems are stranded on the marsh surface in immense rafts sometimes a foot thick (fig. 37). The crush of stems smothers the vegetation beneath it, and a "rotten spot" remains when the stems finally disperse or decay in place. These large rafts of partially decomposed stems and leaves contribute to the organic matter buildup in salt marshes. The rotten spots are forensic evidence that patches of organic material once existed in these locations. It may take years, but smooth cordgrass eventually recolonizes rotten spots.

Figure 37. On flood tides during the fall and winter, rafts of dead smooth cordgrass culms accumulate on the marsh surface and may smother living cordgrass. Within a few years, smooth cordgrass grows up through the mats of rafted culms, returning the barren area once again to maximum productivity.

Productivity of Marshes

Salt marshes are one of the earth's most productive plant communities, rivaling tropical rainforest communities. While much of the salt marsh is a monoculture of smooth cordgrass, the diversity of animal species, especially invertebrates, is incredibly high. The marsh grasses provide food and shelter for many animals that inhabit the estuarine environment, such as marine fish fry and aquatic invertebrates. Smooth cordgrass anchors the base of the food web for the entire estuary, primarily in the form of detritus derived from dead stems, leaves, and roots. Herbivores consume tons of organic matter when smooth cordgrass plants are alive, and detritivores process even more organic debris after the plants die.

Twice daily, tides flush the community, carrying as much as 40 percent of the organic matter produced by the marshes into the surrounding estuarine waters. This tidal action also flushes large quantities of nutrients into the estuary and eventually to the ocean.

Communities adjacent to the salt marsh include the brackish marshes, salt shrub thickets, and salt pannes. Mudflats separate salt marshes from estuarine creeks and rivers.

SALT PANNES:
CHARACTERISTICS AND LOCATION
Salt pannes, also known as salt flats, develop on estuarine sites with a nearly impervious subsurface layer of compacted silt, clay, or organic matter. Salt water stands on the surface for extended periods because it percolates so slowly into the ground. Continuous evaporation of standing salt water concentrates salts well above normal seawater strength.

Sparsely vegetated salt pannes are visible along many roadways built to reach coastal islands. Construction of earthen causeways across marshes compacts clay or peat soils, and the washout of fill placed on marshes elevates former marsh environments slightly. Without plant cover, former marshes increase in salinity as flooding and evaporation of salt water alternate over time. Plants with a high tolerance of soil salts survive best in these high-stress environments. After many decades, salt-loving plants reduce soil salt concentrations, improve nutrient availability, and provide shade that paves the way for species less tolerant of elevated salts to colonize these sites.

Salt Panne Flora
Nearly barren, salt pannes support a suite of halophytic plants that grow in concentric zones, notably saltwort, Virginia glasswort, dwarf glasswort, southern sea-blite, sea lavender, seabeach orach, and saltgrass. These species consistently occupy salt pannes throughout the coastal Carolinas, except for saltwort, a species uncommon in North Carolina.

The salt panne community grades into

Figure 38. Brackish marsh and saltmarsh plants grow in zones between the uplands and tidal creeks. In this photograph, bands or "zones" of vegetation are clearly visible between the upland and the estuarine saltmarsh habitat.

brackish and salt marshes and frequently into the salt shrub thicket.

Estuarine Zonation
Competition amongst plants, the amount of soil waterlogging, and salt accumulation in the soils contribute to the formation of distinct vegetation zones in coastal marshes. Smooth cordgrass flourishes in salt marshes because it tolerates the environmental conditions of the marsh and has few competitors in this space. However, smooth cordgrass competes poorly with plants that grow well in the brackish-marsh and salt shrub thicket communities. Likewise, saltmeadow cordgrass cannot grow under saltmarsh environmental conditions, but it outcompetes smooth cordgrass in less salty and less frequently flooded sites. The result of these plant/plant and plant/environment interactions across estuarine environmental conditions leads to aggregations of species along an elevation gradient. We observe these repeatable aggregations of plants as "zonation" within these marsh communities (fig. 38).

PALUSTRINE AND ESTUARINE WETLANDS

49

HUMAN EFFECTS ON COASTAL WETLANDS

Today, we acknowledge that estuarine environments are important coastal features with an incalculable number of organisms dependent on them. Scientists now regard salt marshes and related estuarine areas as critically important coastal resources. It is unlawful to convert these areas to industrial sites or trash dumps or to dredge and fill them for development. In the long view, we have learned to use estuarine environments for a wide variety of purposes—including fishing, shellfishing, boating, hunting, bird-watching, photography, and merely as a quiet refuge from a busy life—without destroying them or eliminating their wetland functions.

Historically, however, we considered estuarine environments unimportant and expendable waste areas. Thousands of acres of brackish marshes and salt marshes in the Carolinas were altered, removed, or smothered in the development process. Coastal interests dredged miles and miles of drainage canals through the marshes under the mistaken assumption that these environments harbored acres of persistently wet areas where mosquitoes bred. This activity led to changes in the amount, frequency, and rate of flooding by salt water and fresh water and altered the functioning of many of our eastern U.S. marshes, including those of the Carolinas. Today, we see the remnants of these narrow drainage channels throughout marshes in the Carolinas. They are particularly prominent in the salt and brackish marshes of Topsail Island, N.C. (fig. 39).

Because salt and brackish marshes exist in such a narrow vertical range associated with the tides, climate change is likely to affect these marshes. The strongest effects

Figure 39. Drainage canals often were cut through brackish marsh environments. Small islands composed of dredged materials subsequently develop salt shrub thicket vegetation. During the 1950s, thousands of miles of canals were dug in a mistaken effort to reduce mosquito populations.

would be expected along the seaward edge and expanding landward into areas once considered high ground. The net effect is likely to be that estuarine vegetation zones would shift landward as sea level rises. The salt marshes of greatest concern are those adjacent to constructed bulkheads. As the seaward edge becomes flooded and no longer supports estuarine plant communities, the bulkhead may not allow them to shift landward. Marshes may drown in place, and the amount and extent of estuarine plant communities may decrease.

Wetlands should be left as natural as possible to avoid changes that alter the natural patterns of water exchange, water circulation, and hydrology. Oftentimes, nearby development tends to reduce water fluctuation in wetlands, and over time, wetlands dry out. Planting nonnative plants in or around wetlands also tends to dry them out and to change their natural capacity to buffer water level changes.

5

INVASIVE PLANTS OF THE COASTAL CAROLINAS

Living on or near the Carolinas coast, one quickly realizes that change is constant and, ultimately, the norm. For example, the shoreline varies seasonally and daily according to the power of the waves and currents; new dunes grow where none existed; large dunes erode, sometimes over just a few days; and newly germinated smooth cordgrass seedlings soon cover barren intertidal sand flats.

A distinctly unwelcome change, however, occurs when we introduce highly aggressive, nonnative plants into an otherwise well-adapted coastal community occupied by native species. Within just a few years, an invasive plant such as the nonnative form of common reed can dominate in a brackish marsh and alter—or even eliminate—a once-thriving community of native plants and animals. Similarly, pampas grass can escape from cultivated landscapes on developed beaches and gradually spread into undisturbed dunes and maritime shrub thickets.

WHAT ARE INVASIVE PLANTS?

Invasive plants (collectively called invasives) are nonindigenous plants. While normally common and naturally well-controlled in their native habitats, invasive plants grow unchecked in their new environments and gradually replace native species. Not all nonnative plants are invasive; some may be quite the opposite. Some nonnative plants may not survive severe drought or a hard winter, or they may not be capable of dispersing seeds beyond the immediate area where they become established. These nonnatives pose little threat to native species.

Plants are considered invasive when, once well established, they are self-sustaining, spread quickly, and often dominate a particular environment. They do this by reducing the availability of resources, including light, water, nutrients, and ultimately, space, for the native flora. To be invasive, a species is one "whose introduction does or is likely to cause economic or environmental harm or harm to human health," according to Executive Order 13112 issued by President Bill Clinton in 1999.

THE COSTS OF INVASIVE PLANTS

Invasive plants are detrimental to virtually all coastal interests. They are costly from both environmental and economic points of view. States in the Southeast have spent thousands of hours and billions of dollars attempting to control invasive plants such as kudzu or the aquatic plant hydrilla. In the future, we will spend similar amounts of time and money trying to control common reed, pampas grass, and many other invasive species with coastal affinities. I discuss some of the most aggressive and thereby probably most costly to control.

One of the factors of most concern is that some nonnative plants offered by nursery and landscaping businesses at first show no invasive tendencies, especially when carefully tended. It seems that aggressive traits emerge when these plants escape cultivation and enter habitats dominated by native plants.

HOW DO INVASIVE PLANTS REACH THE CAROLINAS?

Fundamentally, plants reaching the Carolinas coastlines arrived as a result of the increasing globalization of agriculture, introductions by the nursery trade, or personal travel. Originally introduced as ornamental (landscape) or agricultural plants, some of these species are considered invasive today. We select nonnative ornamentals for our gardens because we enjoy the uniqueness and beauty of their foliage, flowers, or fruits.

Unfortunately, these plants came to the coastal Carolinas without their usual predators or other controlling organisms.

Beach vitex was purposely—and innocently—imported to the United States by landscapers hoping that it would help stabilize our battered dune systems. In contrast, Japanese sedge (*Carex kobomugi*) had an accidental introduction; it was delivered to our shores in ship ballast. This species grows well in dune environments along the mid-Atlantic shoreline as far north as Cape Cod.

Many of our best-known landscape plants are exotics selected by growers for their unique and often useful traits. However, many plants considered weeds have unknowingly accompanied exotic plants introduced for ornamental or agricultural uses in the United States. Chamber bitter (*Phyllanthus urinaria*) is an example of a widely distributed weed species that has spread extensively in the soil of nursery stock.

Most plants introduced to new geographic locations have the potential to upset the natural balance of an ecosystem. Thankfully, few do. Heavenly bamboo (*Nandina* sp.) is a popular coastal landscape plant that produces large numbers of attractive fruits. Unfortunately, offspring from heavenly bamboo can be found considerable distances from their parent plants long after cultivation is abandoned. In contrast, Japanese pittosporum is generally well behaved in a landscaped environment; rarely is it found beyond the parent plant, and rarely does it persist when no longer cultivated. Only occasionally do volunteer seedlings appear in landscaping.

CHARACTERISTICS OF INVASIVE PLANTS

Most plants labeled as invasive (and weeds) share one or more characteristics. Most of them grow quickly, they mature quickly, and they spread quickly. These plants are capable of reproducing by root suckers, runners, stolons, rhizomes, or seeds. Chinese privet is an excellent example of a species with a high reproductive capacity, through both seed production and root suckering. Its spread chokes out the surrounding well-established native plants. This successful invasive plant spreads seeds widely, especially to new areas where the plant is not wanted or into areas where it cannot be contained. These characteristics allow invasive plants to quickly prevail over the local flora. Once growing well, some invasive species are difficult to control, even with a reasonable effort.

The dominance by invasives is a threat to the biodiversity of an area, possibly reaching the point where an invasive plant creates a monoculture in that particular environment. For example, once established, beach vitex can eliminate virtually all other dune plants. The Chinese tallow tree is another example. It spreads rapidly via vegetative means, making it a particularly difficult species to eradicate. Compounding the problem, it produces seeds within three years of germination, a remarkably short period for trees to mature. Invasive species often produce large numbers of seeds and disperse them efficiently and effectively. Pampas grass illustrates this phenomenon; it spreads rapidly as coastal breezes carry its seeds considerable distances.

Invasive species typically leave their normal predators behind in their original geographic range. This allows for rapid expansion, often into disturbed areas where, in the normal course of land development, the norm is to remove all existing plants. Ongoing development in the coastal Carolinas continually disturbs land, thereby providing nonnative plants, including invasives and weeds, with habitats where competition from native plants is minimal.

The tendency for plants to become invasive varies from environment to environment and among hardiness zones. While common water hyacinth is highly invasive in regions where frost is rare or nonexistent, such as in southern Louisiana, the plant cannot currently overwinter in Virginia and presents only a seasonal threat in the coastal Carolinas. However, common water hyacinth may become more aggressive should the coastal Carolinas' climate continue to warm during the twenty-first century.

IMPORTANT INVASIVE AND WEEDY PLANTS

Various federal and state organizations are responsible for designating plants as invasive. Both North Carolina and South Carolina have established committees of experts to designate and track invasive species in an effort to educate the populace concerning these pest plants. The South Carolina Exotic Pest Plant Council's invasive species list includes plants designated by severity of threat, such as "severe threat," "significant threat," and "watch." The North Carolina Invasive Plant Council has identified a large list of invasive plants found throughout the state, including the coastal plain. Both the N.C. and S.C. plant councils are members of the Southeast Exotic Pest Plant Council, an umbrella organization supporting the southeastern states with a forum for exchange of scientific, educational, and technical information. Both North Carolina and South Carolina have also established lists of noxious weeds. The committees meet regularly and revise these lists as necessary. The plants included in this chapter are either threats or on a watch list of plants of concern to interests in the coastal Carolinas. These species are most likely to be encountered on coastal islands or barrier beach properties. Both North Carolina and South Carolina agencies have many more plants on their lists than are noted here. Most are important in other regions in the states; the complete lists can be found on the Internet.

SALTCEDAR
(*TAMARIX RAMOSISSIMA*)

Native to the Mediterranean region and East Asia, saltcedar was first introduced to the United States as an ornamental shrub. Its use was expanded to serve as a streambank stabilizer and windbreak. Landscapers use this species on coastal properties not only for the enjoyment of its light, feathery leaves and its delicate, purple or pink flowers, but also for its high tolerance to salt aerosols and soil salts. Unfortunately, saltcedar's positive landscape traits are overwhelmed by its ability to deplete soil moisture owing to its high rate of transpiration and its tendency to spread beyond its original planting space. Two other species of saltcedar, *T. parviflora* and *T. gallica*, are equally invasive, especially in the dry parts of western North America.

With a similar leaf shape and texture, our native coastal red cedar is a suitable substitute for saltcedar, but coastal red cedar is a larger plant at maturity. In general, it is often difficult to replace one plant with another, and this is certainly true for species considered invasive; substitutes may not have all the same characteristics— such as size, texture, color, foliage, flowers, and fruits. However, replacing invasive species with native plants will always have a positive outcome.

Figure 40. Beach vitex was planted as a ground cover on Topsail Island, N.C. Now considered invasive, it not only filled the intended planting area but also extended onto the adjacent natural dunes. It is a prolific seed producer. Areas infested by the plant should be monitored for years following its removal to prevent regrowth.

BEACH VITEX
(*VITEX ROTUNDIFOLIA*)

Beach vitex has some great assets: highly attractive, pale purple flowers; eye-catching, pale green foliage; and dark, berrylike fruits. Unfortunately, the rampant growth of beach vitex, especially on foredunes, leads to the elimination of virtually all native vegetation. The plant's rapid growth creates a dense monoculture within just a few seasons (fig. 40). Its innate salt tolerance allows this species to grow across the foredunes and into the backshore environment. Here, it is in direct competition with nesting sea turtles, which have great difficulty digging suitable nests on the backshore because the roots and rhizomes of beach vitex grow so shallowly and extensively in this zone. Local governments in coastal North Carolina and South Carolina have enacted ordinances banning the sale and use of beach vitex.

Painting a glyphosate-based herbicide on cut stems of beach vitex will often kill the plant. Contact your local Cooperative Extension agent for specific information on herbicide treatment. The other method of control is to remove offending plants by hand, a difficult and time-consuming job. Regrettably, any stolons and roots not removed will resprout, so periodic maintenance is necessary.

Sea elder, a native species, provides a similar function in coastal dunes. In addition, the native beachgrasses, sea oats, seaside panicum, and saltmeadow cordgrass are excellent substitutes for beach vitex and are more effective for erosion control.

CHINABERRY (*MELIA AZEDARACH*)

Originally introduced to the United States as a shade tree, chinaberry has attractive foliage and deep purple flower clusters that yield yellowish-orange, cherrylike fruits. Often seen near historic dwellings in the coastal Carolinas, chinaberry frequently escapes from these homesteads. It colonizes disturbed habitats, forming thickets owing to its spread by root and stem suckers. Seeds can persist several years, ungerminated, in the soil. Admired for its medicinal properties in its native range, this Asian import can expand into an area rapidly because it is virtually pest free and because it has allelopathic defenses. Plants with allelopathic defenses release chemicals into the environment that eliminate competing species. Removing the tree eliminates the local seed source, and follow-up clearing of seedlings and root suckers eradicates the plant from the area.

Any one of a number of salt-aerosol-resistant tree species, such as southern magnolia, live oak, and sand laurel oak, serve as excellent replacements.

WHITE POPLAR (*POPULUS ALBA*)

The native range of this attractive tree is southern and central Europe and central Asia. Homeowners have frequently used it to add size, color, and texture to landscape plantings. The upper surface of the leaf is green, while the underside is white. In light coastal breezes, the entire tree shimmers. Unfortunately, it has a nasty habit of reproducing by root suckers and often forms dense, spreading, shrublike patches that crowd out native plants. Root suckers swarm around the tree, spreading well beyond the canopy. Where white poplar has been extirpated, sites must be continuously monitored to remove new growth in the form of root suckers. Fortunately, white poplar does not appear to spread beyond the parent plant, so it is only locally invasive. The plant is troublesome in the coastal Carolinas because it can grow in areas with high salinity.

Several native tree species are excellent substitutes for white poplar, including coastal American hornbeam, southern magnolia, American holly, and Carolina laurel cherry.

CHINESE TALLOW (*TRIADICA SEBIFERA*)

This tree is increasingly common in moist soils and wetland habitats in coastal North Carolina and South Carolina. Herbicides are difficult to use in wetland habitats where Chinese tallow thrives, and burning appears to be the only efficient control mechanism where the plant is widespread. The U.S. Fish and Wildlife Service has been only modestly successful at preventing the tree from creating extensive areas of dense monoculture on Bull Island, S.C. Despite major control efforts, Chinese tallow is more common on Bull Island 15 years after Hurricane Hugo than it was before the storm. The plant has two advantages that favor its spread. It becomes reproductive as early as three years old. Also, it is allelopathic, meaning that it releases chemicals into the environment that

Figure 41. Chinese tallow produces prodigious quantities of seeds annually, beginning at an early age. Complete removal of trees is necessary to eliminate the seed source.

eliminate competing species. The plant was once rare in North Carolina, but it appears to be expanding northward along the coast, possibly responding to climate change. Despite its "bad boy" reputation, Chinese tallow is still a component of some home and commercial landscapes (fig. 41).

Chinese tallow was introduced into South Carolina by Benjamin Franklin in 1772, so the story goes. It is highly versatile and grows aggressively in full sunlight or shade, as well as in areas prone to flooding or drought. It shades out and replaces trees that require full sunlight. Unfortunately, if "topped," Chinese tallow can resprout and continue its aggressive growth. Both birds and moving water efficiently spread its white, "popcorn-looking" fruits. It is resistant to attack by pests.

Native species with similar landscape capabilities include sassafras, sweet bay, wild olive, and Carolina red maple.

JAPANESE HONEYSUCKLE (*LONICERA JAPONICA*)

Japanese honeysuckle is a vine with abundant, attractive, and fragrant white flowers; however, left unchecked, Japanese honeysuckle can girdle and overwhelm small trees and shrubs and shade out herbaceous plants. The plant is common along roadsides, forest and field edges, and openings created by disturbances of native vegetation or plant clearing. Remove plants in small infestations by hand-pulling the runners or by spraying with a glyphosate herbicide shortly after the first frost. Both methods involve considerable time and effort, and re-treatment is often necessary, since these treatments rarely remove the entire vine.

Other species of honeysuckle, such as the native coral honeysuckle, behave much better than the Japanese species. Coral honeysuckle does not spread beyond its original planting site, an indication that it does not have invasive tendencies. Appropriate native plant substitutes, in addition to coral honeysuckle, include purple passionflower, trumpet creeper, and Virginia creeper.

THORNY ELAEAGNUS (*ELAEAGNUS PUNGENS*)

Thorny elaeagnus is another plant that was brought to the Carolinas coast originally as an ornamental. This species quickly establishes itself as an unruly mass (or mess!) unless severely pruned annually. If abandoned in a formerly landscaped setting, the plant gradually expands in height and spread. Its dense foliage eliminates virtually any ground cover. Frequently planted in hedgerows, thorny elaeagnus can withstand salt aerosols, which allows it to dominate the landscape in just a few years (fig. 42). Repeated application of herbicides will eventually bring large infestations under control. If herbicides cannot be used, remove plants by digging out the roots. Remove seedlings of this species immediately from all landscape settings. Most of the generic relatives of thorny elaeagnus are equally undesirable. Do not select any species in

Figure 42. If there is no effort to control the size of thorny elaeagnus, this once-innocent hedgerow will engulf a large amount of property. For infestations such as this, eradicating the plant is difficult or, more likely, impossible.

this genus for coastal plantings, especially *E. umbellata* and *E. angustifolia*.

Yaupon, dwarf palmetto, and Spanish dagger are excellent native plant replacements for the invasive thorny elaeagnus. Common wax myrtle can be planted as a windbreak and privacy screen instead of thorny elaeagnus.

COMMON REED
(*PHRAGMITES AUSTRALIS*)

Common reed occurs along the entire East Coast of the United States. The native American form was widespread except in the southeastern United States; however, plant scientists think a much more aggressive European form of common reed was introduced into the United States (probably several times and in several places). This form hybridized with our native form and began expanding aggressively. Its huge size, often up to 12 feet, allows this species to overtop and shade out most native species in wetland habitats. In addition, its abundant windblown seeds travel far and fast!

Plant and animal diversity plummets as common reed expands into a wetland community. It is less desirable both as a food source and as a habitat for native wildlife compared with native plants. The rhizomes and roots of this plant can become so dense that removal requires an axe, or worse yet, a backhoe, to cut them out of the ground. Application of glyphosate herbicides can reduce stem density, but repeated applications are usually required to eliminate the plant. To control an infestation in a limited area, cut stems to ground level and cover them with heavy black plastic for at least one year.

Brackish and tidal marsh species such as giant cordgrass, black needlerush, saltmeadow cordgrass, and sea ox-eye are excellent native species to plant in landscapes once common reed has been removed completely.

PAMPAS GRASS
(*CORTADERIA SELLOANA*)

Pampas grass has a prodigious growth rate, forming tall, graceful plants shaped like pale green, bubbling fountains. Its shape and its large size are what make the plant attractive to landscapers with large spaces to fill. When trimmed annually, the plant remains at landscape scale; when allowed to grow unchecked, these plants become monsters nearly as large as a small car. In the coastal Carolinas, pampas grass becomes a nuisance as seeds drift into dunes and maritime shrub thickets. Their seeds have no special germination requirements, so the plants become part of the coastal landscape at the expense of native plants (fig. 43). Native to the pampas of South America, this species is increasingly invasive as we use it more and more in landscaped settings on the coast.

There are no native bunchgrasses as large as pampas grass, so replacing this species is difficult in large areas in need of landscaping; however, tall switchgrass cultivars such as *Cloud Nine* are good substitutes. Shrubs and small trees such

Figure 43. Similar to other invasive species, pampas grass expands its distribution via seeds spread, in this instance, by the wind. This plant is quite at home as a volunteer amidst an almost impenetrable area of common wax myrtle on Sunset Beach, North Carolina.

as coastal American hornbeam, flowering dogwood, and common persimmon may be the best native substitutes.

SWEET AUTUMN VIRGIN'S BOWER (*CLEMATIS TERNIFLORA*)

Homeowners have planted sweet autumn virgin's bower extensively throughout the coastal Carolinas—no wonder, with its attractive, sweet-smelling flowers that develop in late summer. Following years of use as a landscape plant, sweet autumn virgin's bower is now common along the edges of maritime forests and shrub thickets, roadsides, and gardens. This expansion is the result of self-seeding. Sweet autumn virgin's bower produces prodigious quantities of wind-dispersed seeds. Left unchecked, the plant's rapid growth smothers native trees and shrubs. Digging vines from the soil and applying a glyphosate herbicide are the most effective methods of controlling the plant.

Vines such as coral honeysuckle, peppervine, supplejack, spurred butterfly pea, and Carolina jessamine are excellent native plant substitutes.

ALLIGATORWEED (*ALTERNANTHERA PHILOXEROIDES*)

An accidentally introduced species from South America, alligatorweed has spread throughout many waterways of the United States since the late nineteenth century. It forms extensive mats that can shade submerged aquatic plants and reduce flow in slow-moving, coastal freshwater landscapes. Canoeists report that thick mats of alligatorweed impede their movements in tidal creeks and channels.

Control of alligatorweed is good with the application of a glyphosate or other herbicide labeled for aquatic use and recommended for this species. Alligatorweed can be easily removed from small landscapes such as ponds and slow-moving creeks, but massive infestations are extremely difficult to eliminate. Mechanically removing the plant actually results in fragmentation and spread. While this species has several positive environmental values such as habitat and food resources, its negative characteristics outweigh the positive.

CHINESE PRIVET (*LIGUSTRUM SINENSE*)

Ironically, Chinese privet was deliberately selected to serve as a landscape plant in the United States and elsewhere. Yet this introduction now haunts native plant enthusiasts who monitor noxious plants. This species may displace the native shrub layer and totally prevent regeneration of the native herbaceous flora in some areas. Do not think that Chinese privet can be contained; it spreads rapidly, forming dense, impenetrable thickets. It seeds into adjacent areas and adapts quickly to a wide range of habitats. Chinese privet can reproduce through root and stem suckers as well as seeds. Mechanically removing the plants and then monitoring the site for root suckers can eliminate small areas of infestation. Chemical controls include glyphosate herbicides. Contact your local Cooperative Extension center for recommendations for seasonally effective herbicides, including triclopyr.

Common wax myrtle, beauty berry, winged sumac, and northern bayberry are fine choices for replacing the hedgelike growth of Chinese privet.

RATTLEBOX (*SESBANIA PUNICEA*)

While rattlebox is not among the topmost serious invasive plants in many states, the plant clearly replaces native vegetation, especially in wetlands. Therefore it warrants attention. It is a prolific seed producer, with estimates of seed production ranging up to 1,000 seedpods per plant per year. Seed germination is high, and seeds remain dormant in the soil for several years. Seeds germinate and grow in their own shade, thereby assuring that plants perpetuate themselves and maintain dominance. Scientists have yet to develop a biological control for the plant.

Where rattlebox is well established, remove plants before the annual seed crop is produced, beginning in midsummer, to avoid spreading the species. Cut plants to the ground and treat the stumps with herbicides recommended for wetland areas. Small plants can be pulled by hand. Conduct an annual plant removal for several years to exhaust the population of buried viable seeds in the soil.

Suitable substitutes include eastern coral bean, common elderberry, and red buckeye.

ENGLISH IVY (*HEDERA HELIX*)

English ivy is another example of a good idea gone bad. The species was introduced to the world as a highly suitable evergreen ground cover for landscapes with deep shade. As it turns out, the ability to photosynthesize year-round gives English ivy a distinct advantage over native vegetation. When it grows beyond its intended site, it smothers the ground flora and climbs tree trunks and branches, weakening the trees. The extra weight in the canopy increases the likelihood of limbs or entire trees falling in high winds. Despite its invasive tendencies, it continues to be sold in nurseries. Avoid planting this species, including any cultivars.

Hand-pulling individual vines followed by application of herbicides on cut stems or roots can halt its spread. Since it often enters coastal forests that have been disturbed, limiting forest fragmentation helps reduce invasion by this plant. No biological control agents have been developed to check the spread of this species. In place of English ivy, use peppervine, cross vine, supplejack, Carolina jessamine, or coral honeysuckle.

JAPANESE WISTERIA (*WISTERIA FLORIBUNDA*)

Japanese wisteria is frequently encountered around old homesteads, where it has been abandoned. It is aggressive and hardy, grows rampantly, and forms dense thickets. Once Japanese wisteria begins to spread, the difficulty of containing it increases dramatically. While not as threatening as Japanese honeysuckle or kudzu, it is considered to be invasive in most of the states where it is found. It smothers, strangles (girdles), shades, and overtops nearby trees and shrubs (fig. 44). A heavy infestation can topple trees. This plant can be controlled by cutting vines close to the ground and following up with herbicide applications on cut stumps. In addition, the vine may be hand-pulled, with a follow-up application of herbicides to destroy lingering roots. The most effective herbicides are glyphosate and triclopyr. However, examine the seedpods before applying herbicides or destroying

Figure 44. Japanese wisteria has succeeded in overtopping this loblolly pine. The photograph shows only one of six large pines in the immediate vicinity overtopped and killed by Japanese wisteria.

the plant. The seedpods of our native wisteria, *Wisteria frutescens*, are glabrous, or smooth, not velvety. Destroy only nonnative plants.

Suitable replacements for Japanese wisteria are Carolina jessamine, trumpet creeper, summer grape, and supplejack.

EFFORTS TO ELIMINATE INVASIVE SPECIES

Once an invasive species establishes itself, it becomes a part of our plant communities. It continually interferes with the survival and growth of native plants and animals and forever changes the landscape. Beach vitex is an important exception, and our response after recognizing its threats provides hope that future invasives can

be similarly contained and eventually extirpated.

Coastal managers and landscapers quickly recognized the undesirable traits of beach vitex before it was widely planted to stabilize coastal dunes. With a concerted effort by federal, state, and local environmental agencies and organizations, most of the plants have been located and removed. It took the continuous monitoring of coastal dune systems by interstate agencies, informed landscapers, gardeners, and others to prevent this species from becoming a devastating pest following its introduction into North Carolina and South Carolina.

For many other species, however, the time has long passed for their complete eradication. Chinese privet, common reed, and Chinese tallow are good examples of invasive plants gone wild with little hope for their extirpation. While we can reduce the density or frequency of these species at considerable cost in time, effort, and money, complete eradication seems impossible. These species are likely to be firmly entrenched in coastal plant communities for the near future.

Today, we naively continue planting introduced species that may soon be recognized as invasive. Landscapers and gardeners often rely on and enjoy the landscape value of these species and do not immediately recognize their noxious qualities. It is important to know which species have invasive tendencies and to thus encourage nurseries, landscape businesses, and other sources to abandon growing and using these plants in coastal Carolinas settings. Exemplary offenders in this unwanted category include pampas grass, thorny elaeagnus, and saltcedar, all discussed above.

NEW INVASIVE SUSPECTS EVERY YEAR!

The lists of invasive and weed species for North Carolina and South Carolina continuously change. Committees of experts review new information annually and determine if a particular plant has reached a level of invasiveness that warrants action. For example, if we can extirpate beach vitex, it can be removed from the invasive species list, whereas rugosa rose, Japanese black pine, or other species may become so invasive that they become a pest. With climate change under way, species that seem to be well behaved now may become invasive in the future.

In various environmental situations, plants not currently cataloged as invasive may be labeled as species of concern. While currently not broadly threatening our native flora, these plants may cause disruptions of coastal plant communities on a local basis. These species include white sweet clover, Bermudagrass, centipede grass, common fig, common lantana, common mullein, and northern saltwort.

WHAT YOU CAN DO

Property owners and others interested in maintaining coastal plant communities as natural as possible can help reduce the impact of invasive and weedy species. First, learn to identify invasive species. Recognizing these plants is the initial step toward removing them and protecting natural coastal communities from serious ecological and economic impacts. Report the location of invasive plants to local, state, or federal agencies charged with their control. As noted in the case of beach vitex, early detection followed by continual vigilance creates the opportunity for extirpation of unwanted species.

By using native plants as alternatives to nonnative or exotic species, you can avoid introducing invasive and weedy species into coastal landscapes. Removing invasive species in existing coastal landscapes reduces the possibility of a species "escaping" from cultivation. When pulling an invasive plant from the ground, be sure to remove the entire plant, including its underground roots and rhizomes. In addition, dispose of plant materials in a way that reduces the spread of the plant. The simplest way to do that is to place plant debris in plastic or (preferably) paper bags and store them until the plant material is dry and dead. The bags can then be safely disposed of. Plants may regenerate from roots or stems inadvertently left behind. It is important to monitor the site for several growing seasons. If you use an herbicide, check the label for special conditions pertaining to its use. Using the appropriate chemicals and the recommended seasonal application rates for the target species will reduce the damage that herbicides may cause to surrounding plants and the environment in general. Contact your local Cooperative Extension center for product and application information.

6

LANDSCAPING WITH NATIVE COASTAL PLANTS

Using native plants in landscaping and environmental restoration is a keystone concept in the conservation of natural plant communities. Because they attract wildlife, native plants used in landscaping offer a close-up view of animals (and plants, too) that otherwise would be rarely seen in the areas where we live, work, and play. Native plants provide food and habitat for myriad animals—and habitat for other native plants. For example, sea oat seeds support several bird species during the fall, notably red-winged blackbirds and song sparrows. Likewise, black cherry, Carolina laurel cherry, and sassafras provide food for numerous fruit- and seed-eating birds. Salt-marsh water hemp, an important wetland species, provides nourishing seeds for waterfowl.

The list goes on and on. Live oak trees create the requisite habitat for resurrection ferns and Spanish moss. The dense sand laurel oak canopy of the maritime forest protects flowering dogwoods from intense salt aerosols. Marsh periwinkles graze algae from the culms of smooth cordgrass and then escape the rising tide by scaling the tallest cordgrass culms. Ground-nesting willet collect and assemble the leaves and stems of sea oats into crude but well-camouflaged nest sites. Raccoons and birds relish dune greenbriar and coastal red cedar fruits. Wrens and yellow-rumped warblers feast on common wax myrtle fruits, and colonial waterbirds use this shrub and several others as nest sites. The toothache tree serves as a host plant for the larvae of the giant swallowtail butterfly. White-tailed deer, opossums, and catbirds feed on the foliage and fruits of common persimmon. You get the picture (fig. 45).

Native plants of coastal origin have a natural beauty that equals or exceeds that of many exotic species selected to replace them. Probably the most notable is the passionflower with its stunning

Figure 46. Sea ox-eye adds diversity in shape, texture, and color to a monotonously green salt marsh.

Figure 45. Native plants used as elements of landscaping attract myriad animals, providing diverse types of food and habitat for creatures such as the gulf fritillary butterfly feeding on southern seaside goldenrod nectar.

purple floral displays and novel, egg-sized fruits. In the fall, sea myrtles emerge from obscurity and dominate the landscape, looking much like large cones of cotton candy with their white-plumed seeds ready for dispersal by the wind. The daisylike flowers of sea ox-eye add an ocean of yellow and brown to an otherwise monochromatic green salt marsh (fig. 46).

Species native to our coastal area are attuned to the sunlight, temperatures, precipitation, water regime, atmospheric salts, and soils of the region; they resist native insects and other pests, yet they provide food for native herbivores, including caterpillars. Neither extraordinary irrigation nor fertilization is necessary to keep these plants healthy. Once native plants become established in

the landscape, usually within one or two years, maintenance approaches zero.

In the shade beneath the maritime forest, subordinate native trees such as American witch hazel and coastal American hornbeam thrive and have the added opportunity to grow in a site protected from intense salt aerosols. Conversely, longleaf pine, the coastal oaks, cabbage palmetto, and others prefer the full coastal sun and prosper in open areas.

While native halophytic plants can grow in freshwater conditions, they flourish in sites with elevated soil salts, daily tides, and little competition. Smooth cordgrass, saltgrass, saltmeadow cordgrass, saltwort, and black needlerush grow robustly in soils with elevated salts.

GETTING STARTED

Understanding the ecology of the major native species helps us select suitable species for coastal plantings. Using our knowledge of coastal plants, plant communities, and the factors influencing their development presented in Chapters 2 through 4, we can choose the most appropriate native plants for each zone of the landscape.

Before starting a native plant landscaping project in North Carolina or South Carolina, discuss the plans with personnel in your local coastal management offices and the Cooperative Extension center. Approval is required for projects affecting the beach or foredune area, such as dune bulldozing, constructing sand fencing and dune walkways, or making changes that affect tidal marshes. Your coastal management agency or agencies will have to review these plans. In some communities, adding or removing plants on your property may require review and approval by your homeowners' association.

SELECTING NATIVE SPECIES ADAPTED TO A PARTICULAR SITE

Take the time necessary to assess which plant lifeforms are best suited for the space. One approach is to "read the landscape," looking for clues as to which plants might be suitable. Are any plants already on the site or nearby particularly appealing to you? Maybe you can add more plants of this (or these) species. Are plants modestly or severely pruned by salt aerosols? This effect may guide you to using the appropriate salt-aerosol-resistant species in the landscape plan. Do thickets show signs of growing seaward, or are intense salt aerosols causing them to deteriorate? Ultimately, a variety of plant habits, including large overstory trees, trees of small stature, large and small shrubs, vines, perennial and annual herbs, and grasses, are available to satisfy your site requirements. Descriptions of each species in this book contain information that may guide your plant selection.

FOREDUNES, BACKDUNES, AND MARITIME GRASSLANDS

Before World War II, most development along the shore was focused landward of the dune environments. The rolling topography of dunes made siting structures difficult and costly. Development prospered in relatively flat areas near creeks and channels, which allowed access by boats, the major means of transport along the coast. Later, when bulldozers came into common use, builders typically flattened and denuded the hummocky dunes to allow easy utility installation and home construction. Native vegetation was rarely replaced following development, and if it was, landscapers used materials and techniques designed for inland lots. Surging development during the past 40 years has changed coastal floras and landscapes significantly. The flora one sees today reflects not only the native species but also a range of introduced species and newly created coastal cultivars. In addition to these new plants, native species were introduced into spaces in unusual locations. Today, for example, we see cabbage palmettos planted on the foredunes and beach wormwood planted along the upper edge of tidal marshes.

Developers and homeowners have installed lawns, exotic foundation and yard plants, and trees more at home in inland areas. The hostile environment of the coast takes its toll on lavish landscapes, and unless plants are irrigated and sheltered, over time they succumb to the unusual and severe conditions. Using knowledge gained in coastal urbanization, informed landscapers now discourage use of ill-adapted, nonnative plants and instead consider use of native plants the best approach to landscaping (fig. 47).

Figure 47. Landscaping on properties near the ocean affords homeowners an opportunity to reduce or eliminate "lawnscape" while featuring native plants and time-tested nonnative species.

DUNE MAINTENANCE: THE IMPORTANCE OF FOREDUNES

The foredunes are important as the first, and most important, line of defense during storms. Storms dissipate their energy as the waves they generate crash onto the shore. Energized storm waves pummel the foredunes, eventually leveling some of these dunes. In addition, pulses of seawater wash landward, cutting through low passes in the foredunes. These foredunes are ultimately sacrificed; riptide-like currents move sand from the foredune to the nearshore environments or push sand landward through the foredunes in the form of large overwash fans. Under these circumstances, an oceanfront homeowner wants high, continuous dunes available to be sacrificed when any major storm strikes the beach. Not unexpectedly, storm waves and salt water damage or kill even the hardiest native plants. However, left undisturbed, native plants—especially grasses—will recover or recolonize the dunes.

ERODING, STABLE, OR ACCRETING SHORELINE?

If you live on or near the open ocean shoreline, determine the historical positions as well as the erosion and accretion trends for the shoreline near you, if possible. In the past, has the shoreline been stable? Has it accreted? Or has it eroded? What is the current trend? Understanding the past can often be the key to predicting future changes along the shore. You may gain insights into historic changes in the area by talking with previous owners of your property, longtime owners of nearby properties, or field representatives from the state coastal zone management programs. Local planning offices also typically have a long-term view of changes occurring along the oceanfront, as well as palustrine and estuarine shorelines.

Eroding open ocean shorelines are the greatest concern to homeowners, and unfortunately, these shorelines are the most difficult to stabilize with anything short of shoreline hardening (such as by erecting seawalls, groins, jetties, and similar "hard" structures). The beach and foredune area is a high-energy zone, and plants are no match for waves and moving water. When the long-term erosion rate is greater than about 2 feet per year, it is difficult to use vegetation alone to reduce beach erosion or to restore dunes to their former height and width. Any hardening project, however, should be considered short term and expensive; in addition, these projects always have negative effects on nearby oceanfront properties (fig. 48). North Carolina and South Carolina have regulations that limit erosion-control structures on ocean shorelines.

NATURAL VS. "CONSTRUCTED" DUNES

Planting coastal grasses can effectively augment sand accretion on foredunes, especially where large quantities of sand blow from the intertidal beach and backshore into the dunes. Revegetating the

Figure 48. Chronic erosion-causing, high-energy waves and persistent winds near the beach prevent all but the hardiest coastal plants from thriving (or even surviving) along the immediate shoreline.

Figure 49. Construct wooden crossovers to reduce uncontrolled dune traffic. Crossovers effectively replace unstable footpaths across sensitive dunes. While protecting plants, the boardwalks can also protect feet from dune sandspur and other unpleasant plants.

dunes where they have been disturbed is critical. A dune with a low native species cover often becomes unstable, leading to deflation of the dune. Nonnative species growing on the dunes usually possess a less-extensive root and rhizome system than native grasses have. To reestablish the integrity of dunes, use native grasses to revegetate beach crossovers and other sites

denuded by chronic trampling. Replace uncontrolled footpaths with wooden crossovers (fig. 49). Augmenting any existing plants with highly adapted native grasses is a key rehabilitation measure.

Coastal dune research shows that building foredunes by bulldozing sand from the intertidal zone and piling it up along the shore provides at least emergency protection for structures located landward by mimicking natural dunes simply in terms of sand volume. However, planting dune grasses on constructed dunes after they are built is less effective than planting dune grasses and herbs at the existing grade and allowing the plants to gradually collect sand and build a dune from "scratch." Grasses planted on top of constructed dunes do not develop the extensive root system that would normally draw water from far below the dune surface, especially during extended dry weather. Stressful environmental conditions such as a prolonged summer drought, for example, will probably doom these plants. Unfortunately, there may not be enough time to allow the grasses to build dunes naturally because structures located landward of the developing dunes remain at risk for several years while the natural dune-building process proceeds. The bottom line: aid dunes in developing naturally with plantings and fencing when possible, but having a pile of even poorly vegetated sand on the beachfront is better than no sand at all.

NATIVE FOREDUNE SHRUBS, GRASSES, AND HERBS

Table 1 lists those species most useful in supplementing existing dunes or restoring dunes ravaged by storms in the coastal Carolinas. Consider planting a mixture of at least three of these grasses and herbs to avoid the possibility of losing a single species planting to disease, predation, and other factors. However, if you do plant only one species, American beachgrass would be appropriate from Cape Hatteras north to the Virginia state line. South of Cape Hatteras, sea oats would likely be the most successful. For multiple plantings, mix the key species (either sea oats or American beachgrass) with seaside panicum, saltmeadow cordgrass, seashore dropseed, and sea elder. Seashore dropseed occurs naturally from mid–South Carolina southward, so it is less useful in North Carolina. Bare-root or soil-encapsulated plugs of the native beachgrasses are available from specialized nurseries. Always select plant stock from nurseries that have grown their plants in the climate and soil conditions close to those where they will be planted. Nursery professionals will provide information on planting density, planting season, irrigation requirements, and the fertilization schedule for each species selected (fig. 50).

Figure 50. The science of planting grasses on the ocean shoreline has advanced significantly since the 1930s. Successful projects abound along the Carolinas coast, and unsuccessful plantings have become increasingly rare.

Figure 51. Sand fences are inexpensive and effective in trapping sand in the foredune environment. Fencing installed along shorelines where onshore winds dominate can build large dunes within a few years. Research has yielded efficient sand-trapping designs with minimal disturbance to nesting turtles and other wildlife movements.

SAND FENCES

Sand fences (for transplanted New Englanders, think snow fences) may increase sand accumulation beyond that collected by native plants alone. Rolls of vertical slat-and-wire fences are readily available commercially. These fences slow blowing sand and, in combination with the plants, collect the sand that stimulates the grasses to grow rapidly and expand across the dune. Numerous patterns for installing fencing have been tested, and several work well. Often the successful fence pattern is site specific and geared for local conditions; however, the most successful patterns generally include short fence sections installed perpendicular to the prevailing wind direction. For the greatest sand accumulation and longest-lasting project, place sand fences as far landward as feasible. When sand fences and vegetation successfully trap large quantities of sand, the accumulating sand gradually buries the fences, while the grasses continue to grow upward. A second layer of fencing is easy to install on top of the first fence. The grasses will continue to grow and do not require a second planting (fig. 51).

TABLE 1. Grasses and shrubs suitable for dune restoration and augmentation. The first six species listed are useful in building and stabilizing dunes. The remaining species augment plant diversity on the foredunes.

Common and Scientific Names	Plant Height	Dune Shape
Sea oats *Uniola paniculata*	Leaves grow up to 24 inches. Flowering culms grow to 6 feet and bend gracefully near the top	Steeply sloping to gently sloping; high, hummocky, individual dunes coalesce
American beachgrass *Ammophila breviligulata*	Height 1 to 3 feet, flowering culms to 4 feet	Broad, gently sloping, high, and continuous
Seaside panicum *Panicum amarum*	Reaches 3 to 6 feet tall; flowering culms arch over due to weight of flowers and seeds	Hummocky, steep sides high; individual dunes often remain distinct
Saltmeadow cordgrass *Sporobolus pumilus*	Height ranges up to 4 feet; flowering culms erect	Low, gently rounded, 1 to 3 feet high; lowest of all dunes
Seashore dropseed *Sporobolus virginicus*	Mature plant is 4 to 12 inches tall. Culms have widespread leaves; flowering stalks are erect and narrow	Low, somewhat hummocky; coalesce to form nearly continuous dunes
Sea elder *Iva imbricata*	Up to 3 feet tall, grows upward as sand accumulates	Dunes often distinct, dome shaped; highly efficient sand collection
Sea rocket *Cakile harperi*	Ranges from 6 to 20 inches tall, sometimes with a greater diameter	Forms low mounds as plant traps sand while living and dead
Seabeach amaranth *Amaranthus pumilus*	Ground hugging, 1 to 4 inches, circular footprint	Accumulates 2 to 6 inches of sand
Beach morning glory *Ipomoea imperati*	Grows 1 to 2 inches above the sand; vine grows 10 to 15 feet along the ground; maximum is 25 feet	Trails along the sand surface; little sand accumulation around the plant
Northern seaside spurge *Euphorbia polygonifolia*	Small, circular plant reaching 1 to 2 inches, rarely more	Small sand domes a few inches high
Seabeach knotweed *Polygonum glaucum*	Trailing or upright; height up to 6 inches	Little sand accumulation around the plant

USING NATIVE PLANTS ON BACKDUNES AND MARITIME GRASSLANDS

Plantings in backdune areas are quite successful because these areas are relatively stable and the environment is favorable for growth (for example, there is less sand movement and significantly reduced salt aerosols). The foredune grasses, shrubs, and herbs (Table 1) grow especially well and expand in size because they are stimulated to grow by accumulating sand on the backbeach and foredunes, but do not expect these same species to expand and collect large quantities of sand in the backdunes. You must have a source of sand (such as the beach) adjacent to your plantings for these species to reach their greatest usefulness. Whereas the foredune grasses enjoy more or less constant burial by sand, backdune plants grow best with little or no moving sand.

A plethora of native species grows well

Geographic Range for Dune Restoration	Comments
Throughout the Carolinas	Large, coarse rhizomes with extensive root system. Must be planted deeply. Readily available with local ecotypes; difficult to transplant mature plants
Cape Hatteras northward	Northern dune grass native from New England south to Cape Hatteras. Frequently reroots from plants washed out from dunes. Easy to transplant from mature culms. Rarely flowers south of Cape Hatteras
Throughout the Carolinas	Coarse plant with broad leaves; forms distinctive hummocks composed of several plants
Throughout the Carolinas	Rhizomes near the surface with the potential for culms and roots to develop every few inches. Rhizomes usually dense
Primarily South Carolina and southward	Small grass, but widespread leaves efficiently collect sand; species also grows near salt marshes
Throughout the Carolinas	Broadleaf plant, grows up through sand as it accumulates. Each dune is a single plant, but plants grow large with abundant sand
Throughout the Carolinas	Annual plant; individual plants collect sand when sea rocket grows in the backshore and foredune environment
North Carolina beaches only	Rare, federally protected plant; DO NOT remove from the backshore; annual plant
Primarily South Carolina; outliers grown in North Carolina	Attractive white flowers; interesting leaf shape
Throughout the Carolinas	Annual plant; reseeds into the backbeach easily
Throughout the Carolinas	Uncommon plant; better left alone since it contributes little to sand accumulation on the backshore

in the backdunes and maritime grassland environments (Table 2). Backdune and maritime grassland plant diversity is comparatively large, yielding a variety of plant sizes, forms, textures, and other characteristics. There are few annual plants from which to choose, but perennials typically dominate this environment. Annual sand bean, beach blanket-flower, and dune camphorweed are examples of suitable native annuals (fig. 52). These and other annuals must be planted from seed; however, in subsequent years, some of these species may self-seed.

Many intriguing, attractive, and appealing perennial plants are well adapted to the backdune and maritime grassland environments, including field lovegrass, Spanish dagger, eastern coral bean, and cottonleaf goldenaster. Each adds seasonal color, pleasing leaf shapes and sizes, and a mix of evergreen and deciduous specimens. Table 2 and the plant profiles in Chapter 9 give additional

TABLE 2. Native species suitable for planting in backdune environments

Common and Scientific Names	Habit	Form, Size, and Texture
Beach blanket-flower *Gaillardia pulchella*	Annual herb	Annual, bushy, pale-green, globe-shaped plant covered in flower heads
Dune camphorweed *Heterotheca subaxillaris*	Annual herb	Annual or biennial; erect, bushy, wide spreading, 1 to 3 feet tall; light green leaves
Annual sand bean *Strophostyles helvola*	Annual vine	Profusely branched, trailing and twining green stems; trifoliate leaves
Maritime bushy bluestem *Andropogon tenuispatheus*	Perennial graminoid	Bunchgrass up to 4 feet tall
Field lovegrass *Eragrostis elliotti*	Perennial graminoid	Low-growing grass with bluish-green foliage that gradually turns deep purple or brownish-purple
Dune finger grass *Eustachys petraea*	Perennial graminoid	Stoloniferous bunchgrass; light green to blue-green leaves
Dune hairgrass *Muhlenbergia sericea*	Perennial graminoid	Bunchgrass; 3 to 4 feet tall with inflorescence
Switchgrass *Panicum virgatum*	Perennial graminoid	Loosely arranged bunchgrass, up to 6 feet tall; stems and leaves light to medium green
Coastal little bluestem *Schizachyrium littorale*	Perennial graminoid	Dense bunchgrass, 2 feet tall at the time of flowering
Bristly foxtail grass *Setaria parviflora*	Perennial graminoid	Purplish, lax stems often lie over when not supported; leaf blades up to 12 inches long
Saltmeadow cordgrass *Sporobolus pumilus*	Perennial graminoid	Diffuse, thin-leaved, rhizomatous, up to 4 feet tall
Large-headed rush *Juncus megacephalus*	Perennial graminoid	Plant 1 to 3 feet tall; narrow-bladed leaves, grows from rhizomes
Fire-on-the-mountain *Euphorbia cyathophora*	Perennial herb (annual)	Plant 1 to 3 feet, tall; multistemmed with broad leaves and a small red dot on most leaves
Spotted horsemint *Monarda punctata*	Perennial herb	Plant 1 to 1½ feet tall, bushy, with pubescent leaves
Common frogfruit *Phyla nodiflora*	Perennial herb	Creeping to 6 inches high with purple-tinged stems and leaves
Dune ground cherry *Physalis walteri*	Perennial herb	Arises from rhizomes; 6 to 12 inches tall; pubescent leaves
American germander *Teucrium canadense*	Perennial herb	Plant 2 to 3 feet tall, leafy; arises from rhizomes

Interesting Flowers/Fruits	Sunlight and Soil Moisture	Suitable for Rain Garden?
Prolific flowering, with crimson or rose-purple disk florets and yellow-banded red ray florets; fruiting heads gray	Full sun; well-drained, sandy soils	No
Disk flowers orange; ray flowers yellow; 3/8 to 3/4 inches in diameter	Full sun; dry, sandy soils	No
Pink to pale lavender flowers cluster at the top of 2- to 12-inch racemes; abundant 2- to 4-inch-long, chocolate brown seedpods	Full sun and sandy soils	Yes
Flowers not showy; fruits at dispersal fluffy and white	Full sun; well-drained, sandy soils	Yes
Flowering head may be 2 feet tall, dark purple spikelets	Full sun; dry, sandy soils	Yes
Inflorescence is 2 to 6 racemes at apex of flowering spike	Full sun; dry, sandy soils	Yes
Minute flowers on wispy, purplish-red or pink panicles	Full sun; moist, sandy soils	Yes
Flowering panicle up to nearly 2 feet long; appears reddish-purple	Full sun and partial shade; can survive in poorly drained and nutrient-poor soils (use local genotype adapted to brackish soils)	Yes
One-foot-tall, wispy flowering heads	Full sun, tolerates shade; well-drained, sandy soils	Yes
Bristle-like, pale green, cylindrical flowering head; 1¼ to 2 inches long	Full sun; moist, sandy soils	Yes
Two rows of green spikelets on 1 to 6 thin spikes; spikelets tan at maturity	Full sun, tolerates shade; moist to dry, well-drained soils	Yes
Unassuming flowers in "sunburst" clusters	Full sun to partial shade; moist to wet soils	Yes
Unique flowers deserving close inspection	Full sun, tolerates shade; well-drained, sandy soils	Yes
Bright lavender to pink or white bracts surround whorls of yellow flowers	Full sun and partial shade; well-drained, sandy soils	Yes
Small, globose flower heads with tiny, white corollas	Full sun to partial shade; soils from dry to wet	No
Yellow trumpet-shaped flowers; fruits reminiscent of Japanese lanterns	Full sun; moist to dry, well-drained soils	Yes
White to lavender flowers on spikes	Full sun to partial shade; moist, well-drained soils	Yes

TABLE 2. Continued

Common and Scientific Names	Habit	Form, Size, and Texture
Cottonleaf goldenaster *Chrysopsis gossypina*	Biennial herb (perennial)	One or more stems grow to 1½ to 2½ feet tall in flower, sometimes procumbent
Sand dayflower *Commelina erecta*	Perennial herb	Erect, ascending, or decumbent stems; sparse, clasping, glabrous leaves
Beach evening primrose *Oenothera drummondii*	Perennial herb	Up to 1 foot tall; hairy, grayish-green
Southern dewberry *Rubus trivialis*	Perennial vine	Extends up to 15 feet; bright green, trifoliate leaves; stems with numerous hooked prickles
Swallow-wort *Seutera angustifolia*	Perennial vine	Trailing or climbing on grasses; bright green, glabrous stems with linear, simple leaves
Southern seaside goldenrod *Solidago mexicana*	Perennial herb	Several stout stems grow up to 6 feet tall; dark green, leathery leaves
Spanish dagger *Yucca aloifolia*	Shrub	Cluster of tall, leafy spikes
Silver-leaf croton *Croton punctatus*	Shrub (subshrub)	Plant 1 to 3 feet tall; leaves are silver to grayish green on top and pale green underneath
Eastern coral bean *Erythrina herbacea*	Shrub	Grows to 3 feet high; woody stems from perennial rootstock
Woolly beach heather *Hudsonia tomentosa*	Shrub (subshrub)	Low-growing, bushy plant; dull gray with tiny, appressed leaves
Dune prickly-pear *Opuntia drummondii*	Shrub (subshrub)	Composed of strings of nearly spherical pads with many 1-inch spines
Beargrass *Yucca filamentosa*	Shrub (subshrub)	Basal rosette of spear-shaped leaves with fraying edges
Common wax myrtle *Morella cerifera*	Shrub	Up to 12 feet tall in intense salt-aerosol environments; multistemmed with dense, dark, gray-green evergreen leaves
Northern bayberry *Morella pensylvanica*	Shrub	Up to 8 feet tall; multistemmed with dark green, 1- to 3-inch-long semi-evergreen leaves
Sand live oak *Quercus geminata*	Tree (shrub)	Multistemmed, shrublike dense foliage; usually smooth, salt-aerosol pruned canopy
Common persimmon *Diospyros virginiana*	Tree	Up to 30 feet high with large, simple, deciduous leaves
Cabbage palmetto *Sabal palmetto*	Tree	Evergreen palm up to 30 feet tall; with or without leaf bases on trunk
Toothache tree *Zanthoxylum clava-herculis*	Tree	Squat; often salt-aerosol pruned; pinnately compound, shiny, dark green leaves; deciduous
Spurred butterfly pea *Centrosema virginianum*	Perennial vine	Delicate leaves and stems; trails or twines around vegetation for support

Interesting Flowers/Fruits	Sunlight and Soil Moisture	Suitable for Rain Garden?
Yellow disk and ray flowers, ½ to 1 inch in diameter	Full sun; dry, sandy soils	No
Bright-blue-petaled, three-flowered cyme surrounded by large bract; seeds hidden	Full sun; well-drained, sandy soils	Yes
Numerous large yellow flowers, which last only a day	Full sun; deep, sandy soils	Yes
Flowers 1 inch across with 5 white, wrinkled petals; deep purple fruits	Full sun and sandy soils	No
Greenish-white flowers in axillary clusters; fruit a narrow green follicle	Full sun and sandy soils	No
Large flowering head with dozens of small, yellow flowers	Full sun; moist to dry well-drained soils	Yes
Large, white flowering head; fruits brown capsules with black seeds inside	Full sun; sandy soils	Yes
Small, creamy white flowers; 3-lobed capsule with 3 seeds	Full sun; moist to dry, sandy soils	Yes
Racemes with red, tube-shaped flowers; dark brown fruits split, revealing red seeds	Full sun and partial shade; nutrient-poor, sandy soils	Yes
Abundant, bright yellow flowers; undistinguished brown fruits	Full sun; well-drained sandy soils (North Carolina only)	No
Beautiful, 2½-inch, many-petaled yellow flowers; fruits reddish-purple at maturity	Full sun; dry, sandy soils	Yes
Panicle 3 to 6 feet tall with large, white flowers; fruits are brown, 2 to 3 inches long	Full sun; well-drained, sandy soils	Yes
Dioecious; male and female flowers green and not distinguished; abundant wax-coated, globular, blue-gray, ⅛-inch fruits	Full sun to partial shade; moist to wet soils	Yes
Dioecious; male and female flowers green and not distinguished; abundant wax-coated, globular, gray ¼-inch fruits	Full sun to partial shade; dry, sandy soils (North Carolina only)	Yes
Female flowers are inconspicuous; male flowers are 1- to 2-inch catkins; small acorns	Full sun; well-drained, nutrient-poor, sandy soils	Yes
Dioecious; flowers solitary, sessile, and yellowish-green; fruits are 2-inch, reddish-orange berries	Full sun; moist, well-drained soils; tolerates dry soils	Yes
Arching clusters with hundreds of white to cream-yellow, ¼ inch flowers; fruits black and fleshy	Full sun; moist, sandy soils	Yes
Conspicuous flowering heads; black seeds in clusters	Full sun; deep, sandy soils	No
Bright blue-violet "upside-down" legume flowers; fruit a 5-inch-long pod	Full sun, tolerates some shade; well-drained, sandy soils	Yes

TABLE 2. Continued

Common and Scientific Names	Habit	Form, Size, and Texture
Coastal morning glory *Ipomoea cordatotriloba*	Perennial vine	Trails or twines; abundant, 3-lobed leaves
Dune greenbriar *Smilax auriculata*	Perennial vine	Thick, evergreen leaves; trailing or climbing tendrils
Purple passionflower *Passiflora incarnata*	Perennial vine	Trailing or climbing up to 10 feet; large palmately lobed leaves
Coastal plain bindweed *Calystegia sepium*	Perennial vine	Climbs by twining up to 10 feet on other plants; 2- to 4-inch, arrow-shaped leaves

Figure 52. Among native dune annuals, beach blanket-flower possesses an especially attractive floral display.

information about these and many other species that thrive in dry, sandy soils and experience modest levels of salt aerosols.

CARE OF NATIVE PLANTS: NOT MUCH NEEDED!

By using native plants in backdune and maritime grassland settings, you can take advantage of the low level of care required for native species. For example, you should water new plants only as needed during the first growing season to assure that roots take hold and expand. Thereafter, watering transplants or newly installed plants may actually arrest or even reduce root expansion; this root system is a critical requirement for sustaining coastal plants during drought periods.

The best time for planting varies, but a good generalization is to plant during the dormant season (late fall to early spring, or just as the new year's growth begins). Plants installed during the dry summer months risk desiccation and death.

Note that research studies suggest that heavily fertilized native coastal plants fare poorly. These plants respond with vigorous growth when fertilized, but overly rapid growth results in poorly developed cuticles on leaves and stems. Tattered cuticles create entrances for salt aerosols that eventually kill plants.

Owing to the fact that many coastal plants grow relatively slowly, they require only occasional trimming. Merely remove any dead branches or leaves seasonally. Native plants have adjusted to the presence of most insects and diseases; therefore, death from these agents is low. This low maintenance requirement is one of the dividends for using native plants in coastal landscaping.

Interesting Flowers/Fruits	Sunlight and Soil Moisture	Suitable for Rain Garden?
Pink to purple, 1 to 1½ inches across; deep purple center	Full sun; well-drained, sandy soils	Yes
Small, light green to yellowish-green flowers; prominent, ¼-inch, black or purple berries	Full sun; moist soils	Yes
Purple to white flowers up to 3 inches wide, distinct corona; fruit an egg-sized maypop	Full sun and partial shade; well-drained, sandy soils	Yes
White, funnel-shaped flowers, 2½ to 3 inches; fruits a 2-chambered capsule	Full sun, tolerates shade; moist to dry, well-drained soils	Yes

NATIVE DUNE PLANT SEEDS AND CULTIVARS

Before embarking on a native plant landscaping project, determine which species are available from local and regional plant nurseries, wholesale plant dealers, commercial dealers, garden centers, online nurseries, or other sources. When visiting nurseries, look for cultivars of native coastal plants. Horticulturalists have created some cultivars to enhance certain aspects of the native species, such as pleasing foliage, interesting flowers or fruits, and insect and disease resistance. Current research is under way to determine if cultivars of native plants created by horticulturalists are as useful to wildlife (such as birds and insects) as the native plants. If the purpose of the planting is to restore native plants to a site, using cultivars of native plants may not be appropriate.

Seek out reputable plant sources that can supply native species from the region, rather than digging plants from the wild yourself. Plant poaching—digging, picking, or cutting native plants without permission—is an unacceptable practice. It is acceptable, however, to collect seeds from the wild from native species not available in coastal nurseries. First, secure permission from landowners before collecting any native plant materials, including seeds. Also, collect over a wide area to assure genetic diversity, and take only a small fraction of those available. As a rule of thumb, take less than 10 percent of the seeds from a population at each site. Individual plant descriptions in Chapter 9 give some indication of the availability and processing needs of seeds or plants. If propagation information is available, it is noted for the species.

USING EYE-CATCHING NATIVE PLANTS

To the uninitiated, native plants have the reputation of having small, uninteresting leaves; tiny individual flowers or flower heads; and pedestrian-looking fruits when compared with those of hybrids and other horticultural varieties. Here are a few examples to the contrary: southern seaside goldenrod, spotted horsemint, and beach evening primrose. All of the morning glory species in the genus *Ipomoea* have large and exceptionally beautiful flower clusters, some with long flowering periods. A variety of appealing plant shapes, leaf shapes, textures, and fascinating fruits is expressed in natives, such as dune ground cherry, silver-leaf croton, swallow-wort, and beargrass (fig. 53).

Figure 53. Silver-leaf croton is a compact shrub common on foredunes and backdunes. Its lime green leaves remain attractive well into the fall.

Figure 54. Dozens of insects, especially bees, swarm the dune-dwelling toothache tree when the flowers open.

The backdune and maritime grassland environment is the domain of perennial grasses and herbs; however, a few trees and shrubs are adapted to this environment and would provide plant accents in dune swales or other low-salt-aerosol environments while serving an important wildlife function. Consider planting sand live oak and common persimmon there; southward from Cape Fear, N.C., cabbage palmetto can be used.

DUNE PLANTS WITH HIGH WILDLIFE VALUE

Coastal Carolina dune plants provide subsistence for a wide variety of wildlife. For example, annual sand bean provides abundant seeds for small mammals and ground birds. Southern dewberry provides abundant fruits for birds. Spurred butterfly pea attracts butterflies, as its name implies, while bees and other insects cannot resist the flowers of the toothache tree (fig. 54)!

VINES: ADDING VARIETY TO DUNE PLANTINGS

When we think about vines, tree-climbing monsters like muscadine, Virginia creeper, and poison ivy probably come to mind. While these are welcome in the large trees

Figure 55. Commonly trailing across the maritime grasslands and maritime shrub thickets, the interesting flowers of spurred butterfly pea add splashes of color to coastal plant communities.

of a mature maritime forest, vines like dune greenbriar are much better suited here. It can be trained to grow in dune grasslands in heaps the size of a bushel basket. Swallow-wort, a delicate perennial vine related to milkweeds, twines around saltmeadow cordgrass and other plants. When planted in a maritime grassland environment, coastal morning glory and spurred butterfly pea dot swards with large, bright purple flowers touched with pink (fig. 55).

NATIVE SPECIES SUITABLE FOR MARITIME THICKETS AND FORESTS

The maritime shrub thickets, maritime forests, and salt shrub thickets provide a variety of spaces to enhance with additional native plants. Table 3 lists ground covers, shrubs, understory trees, canopy trees, and vines that are excellent candidates for increasing the diversity of native plants in these arborescent communities.

With many forested sites occupying former hummocky dunes or dune ridges, maritime forest areas usually have deep natural swales that temporarily hold precipitation and provide ideal environments for Carolina red maple, sweet bay, and black gum. Shade-loving plants such as ebony spleenwort and common elephant's foot grow well in forested areas.

You can enhance wildlife values by planting native trees in maritime forest tracts. American holly, flowering dogwood, yaupon, various oak species (*Quercus* sp.), and cherries (*Prunus* sp.) increase the food supply for native animals. These small trees also add color, texture, and diversity to the existing maritime forest.

Mature or overly mature pines are generally vulnerable to storm damage, so avoid placing pines in areas open to the full force of the wind or near structures that could be damaged by falling mature trees. An exception is the longleaf pine. Specimens of this species do not regularly break or uproot owing to their short stature, deep taproot, and strong trunk. Salt aerosols, however, will prune these trees in exposed areas, which is the preferred habitat for this sun-loving species.

Vines are especially common in the coastal Carolinas and represent an unusually large proportion of the total flora, especially in arborescent communities. Many native vines have special attributes, such as attractive flowers or fruits, diverse methods of attaching or twining on supporting trees and shrubs, and wildlife food resources. Vines, including supplejack, summer grape, and Carolina jessamine, are worth planting here. While these vines are large, they rarely overwhelm native trees; however, in fragmented maritime forests, vines growing along the edge may produce sufficient foliage to stress the forest trees. In this situation, active management may be necessary to keep these vines in check.

CREATING, RESTORING, AND ENHANCING PALUSTRINE AND ESTUARINE WETLANDS

Historically, the value of palustrine and estuarine wetlands has not always been fully recognized. Coastal development once focused on converting wetlands to uplands for agriculture, forestry, and urbanization projects. Similarly, dredging and filling were carried on apace to create made-land and to establish deepwater access— for marinas and other water-related activities, for example. Many of these coastal development practices quickly altered, reduced, or eliminated wetland functions and services in the process of expanding human use of the environment. However, we have discovered that these areas were critically important landscapes. Today, we more fully comprehend the role of wetlands and generally agree that it is important to restore and enhance the structure and function of wetlands.

Wetland restoration involves returning a nonfunctioning (former) wetland back into a functioning wetland. In contrast, wetland enhancement focuses on moving one or more functions of a wetland to a higher level. Unfortunately, wetland enhancement may simultaneously lower the level of one or several other wetland functions at the target site. For example, enhancing a fish population by permanently impounding an

TABLE 3. Native plants suitable for planting in maritime shrub thickets and maritime forests

Common and Scientific Names	Habit	Form, Size, and Texture
Ebony spleenwort *Asplenium platyneuron*	Perennial herb	Evergreen; 4 to 15 inches tall; narrow fronds with many pinnae, bright green
Common elephant's foot *Elephantopus tomentosus*	Perennial herb	Basal rosette of leaves; single flower stalk 5 to 15 inches tall from center of rosette
Partridge berry *Mitchella repens*	Perennial herb	Dime-sized evergreen leaves with white veins outlined on the upper surface
Spanish moss *Tillandsia usneoides*	Perennial herb (epiphyte)	Silver-colored strands hang from tree branches
Supplejack *Berchemia scandens*	Perennial vine	Dense tangle of vine stems twining around trees and shrubs; leaves shiny, green
Carolina jessamine *Gelsemium sempervirens*	Perennial vine	Intertwined cluster of reddish-brown stems and shiny, evergreen leaves; grows to 30 feet in trees
Coral honeysuckle *Lonicera sempervirens*	Perennial vine	Woody vine grows 3 to 10 feet; leaves simple, opposite, glaucous green
Muscadine *Muscadinia rotundifolia*	Perennial vine	Grows to 15 to 30 feet high; ovate to round leaves with coarse blunt teeth, green above, glaucous below
Summer grape *Vitis aestivalis*	Perennial vine	Stems with tendrils up to 1 inch in diameter and peeling; 3- to 6-inch, dark green leaves
Beauty berry *Callicarpa americana*	Shrub	Grows to 6 feet tall and 6 feet wide; large, greenish-yellow leaves
American witch hazel *Hamamelis virginiana*	Shrub	Coarse textured; may reach 20 feet high; deciduous, dark green leaves
Yaupon *Ilex vomitoria*	Shrub	Evergreen; grows to 15 to 25 feet; root suckers; dark green, shiny leaves ¾ to 1½ inches long

Interesting Flowers/Fruits	Sunlight and Soil Moisture	Suitable for Rain Garden?	Comments
Brown sori on underside of fertile fronds	Light shade; dry, fertile soils	Yes	Sterile and fertile fronds differ in shape
Small, pink to lavender flowers surrounded by heart-shaped, leafy bracts; fruits inconspicuous	Shade; dry, sandy soils	Yes	Seeds prolifically in suitable habitats; need to thin periodically
Small, paired, white to pinkish-white flowers; bright red, persistent berries	Shade to partial shade; loamy, moist to dry soils	No	Grows via rhizomes; good wildlife food
Flowers and fruits interesting but inconspicuous	Full sun; high humidity	No	Does not harm trees
Small, greenish-white flowers in clusters; blue-black, egg-shaped fruits	Full or partial sun; moist soils	No	Fruits persist into winter
Flowers abundant, bright yellow, 2 inches long, tubular, solitary or clustered; fruits dull, inconspicuous, brown capsule	Full sun and partial shade; moist, sandy soils	Yes	Excellent, fast-growing arbor vine; fragrant flowers; untended, it becomes ratty; cultivars available
Attractive, coral red to orange-red, tubular flowers; fruits red to red-orange berries about ¼ inch in diameter	Full sun; fertile, moist soils	Yes	Not shade tolerant; good wildlife food; cultivars available
Separate male and female plants; inflorescence with inconspicuous flowers; fruit thick-skinned, deep purple or bronze, about ½ inch in diameter	Full sun and partial shade; well-drained, sandy soils	Yes	Fast growing; disease resistant; excellent wildlife food
Flowers greenish-white and inconspicuous; fruits on panicles, 2 to 6 inches long	Full sun or light shade; well-drained, sandy soils	No	Excellent wildlife food; easy to propagate; drought tolerant
Small, pale lavender to pink flowers; fruits form beautiful, deep mauve to magenta rings on stems	Sun or shade; well-drained soils	Yes	Flowers and fruits intensively in full sun; excellent wildlife food; not salt tolerant
Small yellow flowers appear in fall; persistent acornlike fruits	Shaded forest areas; will grow in sun; moist to dry soils	Yes	Leaves turn bright yellow in fall
Flowers small, white clusters on stems; fruits conspicuous red or yellowish-red berries about ¼ inch in diameter; berries on female plant only	Full sun or partial shade; wet to dry soils	Yes	Fruits persistent though the winter; excellent wildlife food; cultivars available

TABLE 3. Continued

Common and Scientific Names	Habit	Form, Size, and Texture
Northern bayberry *Morella pensylvanica*	Shrub	Low-growing, mounded shape; 3 to 4 feet tall; dark green, shiny leaves; deciduous
Dwarf palmetto *Sabal minor*	Shrub	Reaches 6 to 7 feet tall; large, evergreen leaves up to 5 feet in diameter
Saw palmetto *Serenoa repens*	Shrub	Grows 3 to 7 feet tall; mostly horizontal stems; leaves yellowish to bluish-green, hard, stiff, about 3 feet in diameter
Sparkleberry *Vaccinium arboreum*	Shrub	Single, often crooked trunk with rounded crown 8 to 15 feet tall; 1- to 2-inch-long leaves
Tough bully *Sideroxylon tenax*	Tree (shrub)	Grows to 20 to 25 feet tall; 1- to 2½-inch-long evergreen leaves clustered at ends of branches
Carolina red maple *Acer rubrum*	Tree	Grows to 30 feet tall; leaves lobed with red petioles; leaves bright green above, glaucous green below
Coastal American hornbeam *Carpinus caroliniana*	Tree	Reaches 20 to 30 feet with wide crown; 2- to 5-inch-long ovate leaves
Wild olive *Cartrema americanum*	Tree	Grows 10 to 25 feet tall; dark green evergreen leaves; glaucous green leaf underside
Pignut hickory *Carya glabra*	Tree	Grows up to 40 feet tall; deciduous, pinnately compound leaves
Sugarberry *Celtis laevigata*	Tree	Grows to 30 feet; trunk develops distinctive corky warts on bark; leaves light green and simple
Flowering dogwood *Cornus florida*	Tree	Slow growing, reaches height of 30 feet with an equal spread
American holly *Ilex opaca*	Tree	Grows to 15 to 30 feet; bark is light gray with mottled red and white; leaves evergreen and spiny

Interesting Flowers/Fruits	Sunlight and Soil Moisture	Suitable for Rain Garden?	Comments
Flowers inconspicuous; fruits large, gray, and wax-coated	Full sun; dry, sandy soils	Yes	Fruits remain through the winter; stems are weak; good wildlife food; northern North Carolina only
Large clusters of white-petaled flowers on panicles; fruits dark blue to black; persistent	Partial shade; soil moisture range from dry to wet	Yes	Plants occupy a large amount of space; usually available from nurseries
Small, yellowish-white to creamy white flowers on large panicle; fruits black drupes, ¾ inch in diameter	Full sun or light shade; dry, sandy soils	No	Tolerates salinity and drought; becomes ratty looking unless dead leaves removed; South Carolina only
White, bell-shaped flowers on drooping racemes; fruits shiny, black, and persistent into the winter	Prefers partial shade and well-drained soils	Yes	Flaking bark creates a colorful trunk; good wildlife plant
Clusters of small, white flowers in leaf axils; fruits dark brown, fleshy drupes	Full sun or partial shade; poor, dry soils	No	Not commonly available in nurseries; drought and salt tolerant
Separate male and female flowers; bright red clusters appear before leaves; fruits bright red, two-winged samara	Full sun and shade; full range of soils from wet to dry	Yes	Deciduous; grazed by white-tailed deer; cultivars available
Male and female flowers in catkins; leafy bracts surround each fruit	Full or partial sun; fertile soils	Yes	Attractive trunk with longi-tudinal flutes; leaves turn yellow and orange in the fall
Small, creamy white flowers grouped on panicles in leaf axils; fruits persistent, fleshy, dark blue to purplish-black drupes	Full sun or partial shade; moist, well-drained soils	Yes	Highly salt-aerosol and drought tolerant
Male flowers clusters of three catkins; fruits nearly spherical nuts with bright green husks	Full sun, rarely in shade; moist, well-drained, sandy soils	Yes	Leaves turn bright yellow in the fall; drought and salt-aerosol resistant; good wildlife food
Inconspicuous green flowers; fruits purplish-black drupes	Full sun, occasionally shade; fertile, well-drained soil	Yes	Fast growing; drought tolerant
Inconspicuous flowers surrounded by four large, white bracts; fruits persistent clusters of oblong, red drupes	Partial shade, occasionally full sun; moist, well-drained soils	Yes	Leaves turn purplish-red in the fall; good wildlife food; susceptible to the deadly anthracnose fungus
Flowers small clusters, white petaled in axils of the leaves; fruit ¼-inch, red to orange-red drupe in clusters on female plants only	Full sun and shade; well-drained, sandy soils	Yes	Attracts myriad insects during flowering season; salt-aerosol resistant and drought tolerant; plants in full sun flower and fruit heavily

TABLE 3. Continued

Common and Scientific Names	Habit	Form, Size, and Texture
Coastal red cedar *Juniperus virginiana*	Tree	Tall, cylindrical, slow growing; scaly, evergreen leaves; branches droopy
Southern magnolia *Magnolia grandiflora*	Tree	Large, fast growing; large, thick, shiny, evergreen leaves; smooth, gray bark
Sweet bay *Magnolia virginiana*	Tree (shrub)	Grows to 20 to 25 feet high; trunk smooth, gray; leaves leathery, entire, 2½ to 6 inches long, late deciduous
Black gum *Nyssa sylvatica*	Tree	Grows to 30 to 40 feet in coastal areas; dark green, oval to elliptic, and simple leaves
Longleaf pine *Pinus palustris*	Tree	Large, stocky appearance with large spread of branches; needles 10 to 18 inches long
Carolina laurel cherry *Prunus caroliniana*	Tree (shrub)	Fast growing, pyramidal shape; leaves shiny, dark green above, glaucous green below
Black cherry *Prunus serotina*	Tree	Small, but fast growing in the coastal area; dark green, leathery leaves, 2 to 5 inches long
Southern red oak *Quercus falcata*	Tree	Grows to 30 to 40 feet tall; maintains branches near the ground; variably shaped, sharp-pointed leaves, dark green above, glaucous below
Live oak *Quercus virginiana*	Tree	Grows 50 to 70 feet tall; crown spread twice its height; evergreen, shedding last season's dark green leaves as new leaf season begins
Cabbage palmetto *Sabal palmetto*	Tree	Unbranched trunk with or without leaf bases attached; large, fan-shaped leaves clustered at top

Interesting Flowers/Fruits	Sunlight and Soil Moisture	Suitable for Rain Garden?	Comments
Fruits greenish-blue and berrylike	Full sun and occasional light shade; nonacidic, sandy soils	Yes	Resistant to salt aerosols and saltwater flooding; good wildlife food; use only maritime var. *silicicola*
White flowers, 8 to 12 inches across; fruits equally stunning with dozens of bright red seeds	Full sun and shade; moist, well-drained soils	Yes	Cannot withstand extended flooding; highly wind resistant
Fragrant, 3-inch, creamy white flowers with many stamens and pistils; mature fruit splits open, revealing bright red, ¼-inch seeds	Full sun or partial shade; moist or wet soils	Yes	Leaves' upper surface bright green and lower surface whitish-green; good wildlife plant; tree commercially available
Dioecious; flowers inconspicuous; fruits bluish-black, fleshy, oblong drupes	Full sun and partial shade; moist soils; survives occasional flooding	Yes	Good wildlife food; seed production variable from year to year
Male catkins clustered near branch tips; cones 6 to 12 inches long, the largest pinecones in eastern United States	Full sun; well-drained, infertile, sandy soils	Yes	Less susceptible to windthrow during hurricane-force winds than other native pines
Conspicuous creamy white flowers on 2- to 3-inch racemes in leaf axils; ½-inch, fleshy, blue-black drupes	Full sun, occasional shade; well-drained, sandy soils	Yes	A bit messy if wildlife does not have safe access to the fruits; slight tendency to be weedy; cultivars available
Abundant, 1¼- to 4-inch, cylindrical racemes with small, white-petaled flowers; fruit ½-inch, black drupe	Full sun or partial shade; well-drained, sandy soils	Yes	Fruits drop shortly after maturing; salt-aerosol and drought tolerant
Male flowers drooping catkins; female flowers inconspicuous; fruits abundant, orange-brown acorns, ½ to ⅝ inch long	Full sun or light shade; well-drained, sandy soils	Yes	Excellent wildlife food; sustains medium damage in hurricane-force winds
Male flowers clusters of 1- to 3-inch-long catkins; female flowers inconspicuous; acorns about 1 inch long in clusters of 2 to 5	Full sun or shade; well-drained, sandy soils	Yes	Good wildlife food; salt-aerosol and drought tolerant; sustains little long-term damage in hurricane-force winds
Large sprays of white flowers; hundreds of small, fleshy, black fruits	Full sun; well-drained soils	Yes	Tends to be messy, huge flower stalks, large leaves, and thousands of seeds shed annually; highly hurricane resistant

area covered with smooth cordgrass marsh will reduce the input of organic matter into the adjacent estuary. A different wetland function is enhanced by this action. Wetland creation, which is establishing a wetland where none previously existed, is usually more difficult.

Wetland creation, restoration, and enhancement projects can be as simple as inexpensively augmenting existing plants in a small swale. They can also be as grand as taking on massive projects over thousands of acres that demand multiple partners from public, private, and governmental organizations, each with access to considerable scientific expertise and manpower. Creating relatively large wetland areas often requires a precise measurement of elevations and an understanding of soil permeability and hydraulics, as well as the use of a lot of big, expensive equipment—backhoes, graders, front-end loaders, and the like!

In keeping with the theme of this book, I discuss wetland creation, restoration, and enhancement using primarily native plants in situations requiring only modest changes in the landscape. In a later section concerning rain gardens, I consider relatively easy and inexpensive ways to create sites possessing some wetland functions within selected small spaces.

PALUSTRINE WETLAND RESTORATION

Several simple yet effective approaches to restoring and enhancing palustrine (freshwater) wetlands are within the capabilities of homeowners in coastal environments. These approaches are generally low cost and have a reasonably high chance for success. Bear in mind, though, that if only the plant cover has been removed from a wetland in the process of development, doing nothing—except watching—may be the best

approach. Native plant seedbanks are present in wetlands. If you avoid further disturbance of a site, wetland plants will germinate from the seedbank or sprout from rhizomes or roots left in the soil. Also, recolonization will occur naturally in continuously wet areas as plants extend rhizomes, roots, and shoots. As the plants recover and animal food and shelter resources increase (within a season or two), animal species will visit or take up residence. Monitor the site for irruption of invasive species following any disturbance.

If the uppermost layers of soil have been removed, collect seeds of plants from nearby wetlands, especially those noted in Table 4, and scatter the seeds over the entire wetland area, increasing the density of seeds along the moist edges of the site. Work the seeds into the soil with a rake—about ¼ inch deep or just enough to hide the seeds from predators. It may be more expedient to purchase wetland plants listed in Table 4 from plant nurseries or similar sources. Using a dibble, install plugs, rhizome sections, or cuttings in the moist soils on 12- to 18-inch centers. Then monitor the germination and growth of the plants for at least one year. As part of your monitoring program, remove any invasive species that appear; otherwise, they may overtake the native plants. Learn to recognize "volunteer" plants, which germinate from the buried viable seed populations or self-seed from nearby areas. If some of these plants are less desirable, remove them from the wetland as they become identifiable (fig. 56).

Plant shrubs as well as trees such as Carolina red maple, Carolina willow, and bald cypress sourced from nursery stock grown as near to your site as possible. Until demand for these and other native plants increases, locating appropriate nursery stock may be difficult. Avoid siting plants in standing water; most wetland plants

Figure 56. Learn to identify invasive species. This interesting plant grows at the landward edge of a salt marsh (here with no flowers or fruits). Unfortunately, it is an invasive plant, Chinese tallow.

Figure 57. This shoreline is undergoing erosion caused by an open fetch. The shoreline is steepened and denuded of marsh grasses, and upland trees are now imperiled by wave erosion. Courtesy of Spencer Rogers, North Carolina Sea Grant.

germinate and grow best in moist, but not continuously wet, soils, and experienced horticulturalists suggest that container-grown wetland plants may fail to establish in frequently flooded sites. Increase the plant diversity in your wetland by adding a small handful of common duckweed fronds on the open water. Carefully monitor the duckweed reproduction and spread for at least two years. Winter, spring, and fall are the best times for installing wetland plants.

Restoring function to wetland sites that no longer have adequate water flow or retention may require a more serious approach involving design, engineering, and significant earth-moving. Costs add up rapidly in these cases, so if you are not willing to spend significant resources on a restoration project, it may be better to continue to address restoration through plantings only.

ESTUARINE WETLAND RESTORATION: LIVING SHORELINES

Natural, undisturbed estuarine shorelines are generally stable and ecologically fine-tuned to the benefit of existing plants and animals. However, we can create imbalances in the ways plants and animals interact with their new environment if we cover existing vegetation with fill material and "harden" shorelines with concrete, wooden, or rip-rap materials. We might do this, for example, in the course of an urbanization project, such as deepening or altering a channel. These changes could trigger important and undesirable responses. For example, an extensive area of trees or shrubs might fall into the estuary, or scarps or steps composed of exposed peat and sand could form. In addition, clear, progressive, and rapid changes could occur in the position of a shoreline. These changes concomitantly could include losses of vegetation along the estuarine shoreline (fig. 57). Sometimes, affected areas become completely devoid of the plants and animals usually found there. In these situations, coastal scientists support rehabilitation of the damaged shorelines through a technique called living shorelines.

Living shorelines provide a simple,

Common and Scientific Names	Habit	Form, Size, and Texture
Royal Fern *Osmunda spectabilis*	Perennial herb	Large fern with fronds ascending to 4 feet from rhizome; leaves twice pinnately compound
Marsh fern *Thelypteris palustris*	Perennial herb	Forms dense colonies of plants with fronds ranging from 18 to 24 inches tall; bright green; dies back in winter
Giant foxtail grass *Setaria magna*	Annual graminoid	Large, narrow-leaved plant reaching height of 10 feet; leaf blades 2 feet long and 2 inches wide; leaves scruffy
Saw grass *Cladium jamaicense*	Perennial graminoid	Coarse, grasslike plant; growth pattern similar to a bunchgrass; narrow leaves up to 3 feet long
Narrowleaf white-topped sedge *Rhynchospora colorata*	Perennial graminoid	Grasslike plant ranging from 1 to 2 feet tall
Olney's threesquare *Schoenoplectus americanus*	Perennial graminoid	Grows 2 to 4 feet tall; thin, narrow, triangular stems; leaves not evident
Giant cordgrass *Sporobolus cynosuroides*	Perennial graminoid	Plant with inflorescence ranging from 5 to 12 feet tall; dense, creates nearly impenetrable stands
Monnier's water-hyssop *Bacopa monnieri*	Perennial herb	Low growing or ground hugging; grows with taller plants to support vertical growth up to 12 inches
Virginia buttonweed *Diodia virginiana*	Perennial herb	May spread, trail, or ascend up to 18 inches tall
Eastern rose mallow *Hibiscus moscheutos*	Perennial herb	Plant reaches 5 to 6 feet tall; stems die back to the ground in winter
Common duckweed *Lemna perpusilla*	Perennial herb	Yellowish-green to bright green "fronds" float on open-water surface
Water pimpernel *Samolus parviflorus*	Perennial herb (annual)	Plant grows from basal rosette of pale green leaves; plant grows up to 18 inches tall
Nodding ladies' tresses *Spiranthes cernua*	Perennial herb	Grows as single twisted spike up to 20 inches tall
Climbing hempweed *Mikania scandens*	Perennial vine	Plant grows up to 8 feet long and trails over herbs and shrubs; large, arrowhead-shaped leaves
Seashore mallow *Kosteletzkya pentacarpos*	Shrub	Coarse, hairy plant grows 3 to 5 feet high with similar width

Interesting Flowers/Fruits	Comments
Possesses both sterile and fertile fronds. Fertile frond bears sporangia at the plant's apex	Slow growing and long lived; grows well in full sun and full shade
Sterile and fertile fronds appear similar; sori hidden on underside of frond	Prefers full sun; dense colonial growth
Bristly, but unremarkable green flowers on gracefully arching cylindrical spikes	Grows in damp soils or standing water; excellent wildlife food
Mature chestnut brown flowers and fruits droop from tall flowering spikes	Grows in fresh or slightly brackish water; often available at native plant nurseries
Flowering head subtended by several narrow, white-tinged bracts	Grows in damp soils and can tolerate standing water; prefers full sun; attracts many insects
Orange to brown clusters of tiny flowers and fruits appear to emerge laterally on stem	Grows in fresh or slightly brackish water; provides excellent wildlife food and cover
Terminal inflorescence large and attractive; composed of about 20 spikes	Tolerates salinity up to one-third seawater strength; ecologically important marsh plant; excellent wildlife food and shelter
Small white or light blue flowers grow on long peduncles	Grows in damp soils and tolerates some salinity; prefers full sun but can grow in some shade; plants available commercially
Abundant, small, white, sessile flowers; globose, green fruit is undistinguished	Grows in a variety of wet habitats from well drained to standing water; attractive to white-tailed deer, birds, and butterflies; not commercially available
Produces abundant, large, showy, white or pink flowers; fruits are 1- to 2-inch-long capsules	Can grow well in persistently moist soils; grows in full sun and partial shade; collect seeds from wild plants or purchase cultivars
Tiny flowers highly reduced and not visible without a hand lens	Plant reproduces vegetatively and can overwhelm an area of open water in a few seasons; may shade submerged aquatic plants; monitor growth
Flowers are tiny, white-petaled, and widely spaced on terminal racemes	Prefers sunny or lightly shaded areas; collect seeds from wild plants
Small, tightly packed, white flowers line the spike	Not a plant to be taken from the wild; may be available in some native plant nurseries
Flowers clustered in heads; each flower composed of 4 individual florets	Prefers full sun; grows best in salt-free wetlands; salt-aerosol tolerant; propagation through seeds, stem cuttings, and division of rhizomes
Slightly droopy, 1- to 3-inch-wide, light pink to rose pink flowers resembling hollyhocks	Attractive to hummingbirds and butterflies; prefers full sun and moist to wet soils; tolerates some soil salinity

TABLE 4. Continued

Common and Scientific Names	Habit	Form, Size, and Texture
Carolina red maple *Acer rubrum*	Tree	Small tree grows to 30 feet; leaves deciduous
Carolina willow *Salix caroliniana*	Tree (shrub)	Small tree reaching 30 feet tall; long, narrow leaves are green above, glaucous below; crown spreading
Bald cypress *Taxodium distichum*	Tree	One of the largest trees in wetland environments; leaves needlelike and deciduous

low-cost alternative to the installation of constructed solutions commonly in use today. Living shorelines have myriad benefits over these constructed, or "hardened," estuarine shorelines when installed in low to moderately sloped shorelines exhibiting low to moderate wave climates. Living shorelines typically improve water quality, increase biodiversity, reduce wave energy and erosion along the shore, buffer storms, trap sediments, and filter pollutants. More importantly, they create habitats that encourage colonization by many native estuarine plants and animals. This reestablishment of natural shoreline processes and native flora and fauna may increase the overall resiliency of a site faced with the prospect of future sea level change. While the science is far from complete in providing an understanding of the optimum design and installation of living shorelines, our knowledge is growing and is currently sufficient to guide successful installation of site-specific projects in habitat restoration.

Shorelines bordering large, open-water areas are most frequently in need of rehabilitation or restoration. Open-water environments provide an opportunity for fetch to become a major factor affecting the shoreline. Chronic wind-generated waves typically undermine marsh edges, creating abrupt steps from wetland to subtidal environments. Some sites retreat rapidly, and others erode more slowly. Because native grasses, including smooth cordgrass, saltmeadow cordgrass, saltgrass, and others, possess extensive rhizomes, numerous fibrous roots, and flexible stems, they are especially effective in dissipating wave energy and holding sediments in place.

Coastal scientists have proposed a number of designs for living shorelines (fig. 58). Demonstration sites established by local nonprofit organizations and local governments have proven their efficacy, yet each site is unique. Success in one area does not guarantee restoration of ecological services in another. In virtually every example reported, the cost of a living shoreline was lower, and the life of the project was as long or longer than that of projects with hard-structure solutions such as bulkheads. Also, keep in mind that materials and labor costs are incurred even in failed restoration projects.

Interesting Flowers/Fruits	Comments
Separate male and female flowers appear very early in spring before the leaves; fruits a bright red, two-winged samara	Grows well along the margin of wetlands; excellent nesting and roosting site for birds; cultivars available
Dioecious; male and female flowers clustered on catkins; fruit capsules release seeds with white plumelike hairs	Grows well in full sun and partial shade; good food and cover for small animals and birds; readily propagated from both seeds and cuttings
Male flowers are 3- to 5-inch-long catkins; globose cones are ½ to 1½ inches in diameter	Young trees have beautiful shape; interesting "knees"; hurricane wind resistant; chronic saltwater flooding kills the tree

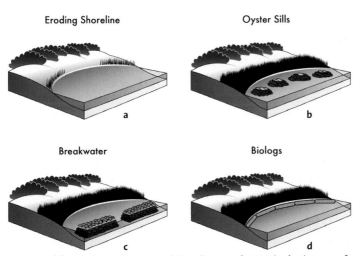

Figure 58. (a) Denuded and steepened shorelines can be repaired using one of several restoration techniques. (b) Oyster-shell-filled bags installed on the water side of the eroded shore absorb wave energy and protect grass plantings from being washed out. (c) At sites of serious and rapid erosion, breakwaters composed of gabions or other hardened materials give long-term protection to planted grasses. (d) Similarly, biologs composed of biodegradable materials that disintegrate in a few seasons give protection to grass plantings long enough for them to develop adequate roots. Illustration by Andrea Dingeldein. Courtesy of North Carolina Sea Grant.

CONSTRUCTION OF LIVING SHORELINES

Are you ready to undertake the establishment of an estuarine living shoreline? In designing and executing a project, you must consider the tidal regime (including the tidal range, wave energy, and salinity), as well as soil characteristics, the structure and composition of nearby shorelines, and the presence of existing or potential vegetation. It would be wise to seek professional help from nearby university personnel, local Extension agents, or coastal management personnel.

Figure 59. For large restoration projects, volunteers plant greenhouse-grown smooth cordgrass seedlings. In the background is an oyster-shell breakwater installed before the planting project began. The breakwater reduces wave energy, and seedlings are less likely to wash away before their roots grow firmly into the sand. Courtesy of North Carolina Coastal Reserve.

Native plants are the centerpiece of living shorelines. Before starting, remove any nonnative plants from the area to be planted. Then select among native estuarine graminoids (Table 5), including smooth cordgrass, saltgrass, seashore dropseed, saltmarsh fimbristylis, and saltmeadow cordgrass. Using a dibble, and at low tide, plant bare-root greenhouse or nursery-grown culms, uniform-aged plugs, or bare-root culms of smooth cordgrass on 6- to 12-inch centers, in staggered rows, 12 to 18 inches apart, in the zone alternately covered and exposed twice daily. Above the intertidal zone, plant a mixture of perennial graminoids at similar depths and spacing. To provide texture and color diversity at higher elevations, sow seeds of a mixture of annual and perennial plants noted in Table 5. Other than the major marsh grasses noted above, few of the other plants listed in Table 5 are commercially available from nurseries or other sources. Therefore, collect a small percentage of the seeds from plants in the adjacent estuarine wetlands and distribute these seeds at the upper fringe of the intertidal zone, gently pressing them into the soil using a rake.

Planting should be accomplished in spring or fall to avoid storms or periods of high wave energy in summer and winter. No watering or fertilization is required in regularly inundated or periodically inundated sites; however, in areas of uplands fringing the estuary, do water native plants weekly until they are firmly rooted (fig. 59).

Establishing a dense and firmly rooted plant cover in the intertidal zone as quickly as possible is important. Early in a project, storms can rip out poorly rooted plants; a dense stand of plants mitigates against this possibility. Should individual plants die or get ripped out of the soil by wave action, replace them as soon as possible. Plan on a loss of 10 to 20 percent of the culms each year during the first few years following installation.

PROJECTS INVOLVING SOIL DISTURBANCE

If you plan to fill, remove, move, or grade soils in wetlands, first consult your state office of coastal management. You may need a permit from either the state or from the U.S. Army Corps of Engineers (Section 404 wetlands) to disturb soils in the wetland environment. Permits for living shoreline projects may take longer to acquire than those for installation of hard structures. Discuss the scope of your project with resource management agencies and determine whether a permit is required, what information is necessary for approval, and how long it will take to obtain a permit.

HYBRID LIVING SHORELINES

Native-plant-based living shorelines can be supplemented or enhanced by minor

Figure 60. Design oyster-shell- or gabion-based breakwaters to fit the size and environmental conditions of the project. Breakwaters may be hundreds of feet long and continuous, such as in the major restoration effort shown here. For projects involving fewer coastal properties, they may be small and discontinuous. Courtesy of North Carolina Coastal Reserve.

hard structures in particular sites. So-called hybrid restoration or stabilization projects include the installation of small breakwaters created by lines of rock- or oyster-shell-filled gabions or by an array of oyster-shell-filled bags. Breakwaters are designed to be completely submerged at high tide. They are permeable yet substantial enough to reduce wave energy and encourage sediment deposition landward of their position. One variation is to use coconut fiber mats to secure native plants in the soil and as an underlayment for gabions and oyster bags. Loose oyster shells or rocks also may be used, depending on specific site conditions. Where slopes to the water are steep, emplacement of one or more rock-edged terraces can break up the steep slope to the water. In some demonstration areas, oyster bags are used as a toe at the base of a project composed of native plants (fig. 60).

OTHER CONSIDERATIONS
Shoreline projects work best when a reasonably large area is rehabilitated. It's helpful to network with neighbors and to request assistance from a homeowners' association, nonprofit, or community organization such as the North Carolina Coastal Federation. These organizations often come with considerable expertise and manpower, allowing a larger project to be undertaken. Also, consider establishing partnerships with a nearby university.

Where marshes have deteriorated owing to foot traffic or other chronic impacts, consider constructing walkways and piers over the affected areas. These are normally expensive, but they allow people to reach the estuarine shoreline without significant degradation of the substrate or loss of the plant cover.

Take note: living shoreline projects are not for the faint of heart. Because the living shoreline ideas are so new and not fully explored, project success is not 100 percent assured. Once you take on a project, monitor the progress of the work, the success of the native plant installations, and the integrity of nonplant components. Correct deviations from the intended outcomes immediately. What do you do if the project fails? With a native-plants-only installation, the project can probably be abandoned with little consequence. If the project includes hard-structure components such as gabions, oyster-shell-filled bags, or other foreign materials, cleanup and removal is necessary. It is important to make provision for the cost and time required to accomplish this possible cleanup in your initial project planning and decisions.

Scientists continue to explore new materials and techniques that could aid in refining the living shorelines concept. The latest information may be obtained through a World Wide Web search on living shorelines. Scientific journals publish timely research reports, and many of these articles, as well as recently published

Common and Scientific Names	Habit	Form, Size, and Texture
Dwarf glasswort *Salicornia bigelovii*	Annual herb	Grows from 2 to 12 inches tall; somewhat bushy with fleshy stems
Southern sea-blite *Suaeda linearis*	Annual herb	Variable, ranging from 4 inches to 2 feet tall; fleshy stems and leaves
Saltgrass *Distichlis spicata*	Perennial graminoid	Ranges from 6 to 18 inches tall; fine stems and leaves
Seashore dropseed *Sporobolus virginicus*	Perennial graminoid	Culms 4 to 12 inches tall; rhizomatous; coarse grass
Smooth cordgrass *Sporobolus alterniflorus*	Perennial graminoid	Plants range from 1 to 7 feet tall, depending upon growing site; wide leaved
Saltmeadow cordgrass *Sporobolus pumilus*	Perennial graminoid	Grows up to 4 feet tall, usually 2 feet; thin leaves and stems; rhizomatous
Saltmarsh wild rye *Elymus virginicus*	Perennial graminoid	Robust; 2½ to 4 feet tall; narrow leaves
Saltmarsh fimbristylis *Fimbristylis castanea*	Perennial graminoid	Resembles a bunchgrass with many thin stems in deliquescent pattern
Black needlerush *Juncus roemerianus*	Perennial graminoid	Coarse, grasslike plant; grows 1 to 6 feet tall; forms dense patches
Saltmarsh bulrush *Bolboschoenus robustus*	Perennial graminoid	Ranging from 2 to 4 feet tall; leaves not evident; grows in loose patches
Sea lavender *Limonium carolinianum*	Perennial herb	Spoon-shaped, dark green, fleshy leaves; flowering head large and open
Virginia glasswort *Salicornia virginica*	Perennial herb (subshrub)	Mat forming with stems 4 to 12 inches high; appears leafless
Perennial saltmarsh aster *Symphyotrichum tenuifolium*	Perennial herb	Slender with narrow leaves; 6 inches to 2 feet tall; scattered in salt marsh
Southern saltmarsh fleabane *Pluchea odorata*	Annual herb (perennial)	Dense, pubescent, broad leaves; 1 to 2 feet tall
Salt-marsh water hemp *Amaranthus cannabinus*	Perennial herb	Stout stems with narrow leaves; height varies from 2 to 8 feet; lanceolate leaves
Eastern bloodleaf *Iresine rhizomatosa*	Perennial herb	Grows 1½ to 3 feet tall
Narrow-leaved loosestrife *Lythrum lineare*	Perennial herb	Plant 1 to 4 feet tall; linear leaves; much branched
Saltmarsh morning glory *Ipomoea sagittata*	Perennial vine	Has large, arrow-shaped leaves
Saltwort *Batis maritima*	Shrub (subshrub)	Fleshy, sessile leaves; prostrate or trailing stems; mat forming; grows up to 2 feet tall
Sea ox-eye *Borrichia frutescens*	Shrub (subshrub)	Rhizomatous; grows 2 to 3 feet tall; usually in patches

Interesting Flowers/Fruits	Comments
No	Turns bright red in fall; grows in saltiest estuarine environments
No	Edible; important wildlife plant
No, small grass inflorescence	Leaves with interesting distichous pattern; tolerates high-salinity soils
No	Equally at home on foredunes and salt marsh (occurs primarily in South Carolina)
No, abundant inflorescences in late summer	Species used most often to revegetate salt marshes; purchase from specialty nurseries
No, modest flowering when growing in estuarine environments	Grows in a zone slightly higher in elevation than smooth cordgrass
Mature flowering head resembles rye grass	Good wildlife food; grows best at upper edge of salt marsh
Flowering and fruiting heads interesting but not colorful	Grows best at upper elevations in salt marshes; important wildlife food
No, flowers/fruits often obscured by dense stems	May provide some erosion protection; important wildlife plant
Persistent clusters of tan or brown spikelets top the stems	Also occurs in freshwater environments; important wildlife plant
Abundant, tiny lavender flowers; bracts paper white, persistent	Cultivars available from specialty nurseries
No	Grows in the saltiest estuarine environments; edible
White ray flowers and yellow disk flowers; attractive but small	Grows mixed with smooth cordgrass
Clusters of bright purplish flowers	Prefers brackish water environments; plant has distinctive odor
No, tiny dioecious flowers; fruits small and green	Excellent wildlife food; grows in brackish and salt marshes
Flowers tiny, green; seeds with tuft of cottony white hairs	Leaves turn reddish-purple in fall
Attractive but small, white flowers; fruits small	May be propagated from seeds or roots
Large, pink, rose, or purple funnel-shaped flowers	Collect seeds from mature plants
Flowers and fruits green, fleshy, undistinguished	Grows best without competing species (South Carolina only)
Bright yellow, daisylike flowers; seed heads brown	Important wildlife plant; propagate from cuttings or seeds

books, can be located with an online search. Illustrations typically accompany these documents and usually provide a clear idea of how to construct and maintain a living shoreline in your area.

NATURAL HOME LANDSCAPING

Horticulturalists and nursery personnel commonly use nonnative species and cultivars for general as well as foundation landscaping in the Carolinas coastal area. Numerous nonnative plants have a long history of use and come in a variety of sizes, shapes, and textures. They are almost universally available at local nurseries. Drawbacks to their use include their susceptibility to various local pests and diseases and the possibility that they become a maintenance nightmare, requiring supplemental water, frequent fertilization, and constant pruning. A serious concern is that some nonnative species such as common lantana already exhibit some invasive tendencies and bear close watching. It is possible that with climate change, accidental crossbreeding, or other events, these plants may become seriously invasive.

A few nonnative species and several native species are highly suitable for foundation landscapes in urbanized coastal environments. Examples of nonnatives include Japanese pittosporum, rosemary, Japanese aralia, bigleaf hydrangea and related cultivars, Japanese shore juniper, oleander, and Indian hawthorn (fig. 61). Each of these species behaves well, has few invasive tendencies, and grows especially well in coastal environments (see individual profiles in Chapter 9). Because these plants are not native, the possibility exists that these, too, may develop invasive tendencies.

Many native species of evergreen shrubs and small trees, including common wax myrtle, cabbage palmetto, dwarf palmetto,

Figure 61. These classic nonnative foundation plants grow well in coastal environments: (a) Indian hawthorn (*Rhaphiolepis indica*) and (b) Japanese pittosporum (*Pittosporum tobira*). Landscapers have observed minimal invasive tendencies in these species if they are maintained and monitored.

yaupon, and coastal red cedar, make fine foundation plants. Deciduous shrubs and trees that are suitable as foundation plants include tough bully, beauty berry, toothache tree, and silver-leaf croton. Since these native species range in height from 1 or 2 feet to 20 or 25 feet, most landscape plans can accommodate at least one of our native trees and shrubs. As with any foundation plant, consider the size of fully grown native plants. Locate these natives so that, at maturity, roots or foliage will not impinge on structures or appear crowded. Tight placement requires additional (and unnecessary) pruning to keep plants away from structures and to prevent damage to nearby foundations. Plantings may look sparse and puny, but you are installing plants for the future; recognize that the plant you install today may be considerably larger in just 5 or 10 years. Bear in mind that fast-growing native shrubs such as common wax myrtle and yaupon must be pruned, but only occasionally; otherwise, they become overgrown, spindly, or dumpy.

When landscaping a coastal home, consider differences in wind direction and aspect. For example, homes constructed near the ocean may block salt aerosols on the leeward side. Japanese aralia may grow well in the microclimate of the sheltered side of a home, but it would almost immediately be killed by salt aerosols if placed on the windward side. This situation can be ameliorated to a certain extent by installing an irrigation system that sprays leaves daily. However, dependence on irrigation creates a maintenance headache and wastes water resources. Also, some municipal or locally sourced well water sprayed on plants may cause leaf damage.

ELIMINATING EXOTIC SPECIES

Once you see the results of planting native species, you may wish to remove the exotic, often weedy species in the area of concern. These interlopers were planted or encouraged in backdune and maritime grassland communities by homeowners in previous generations, and they include thorny elaeagnus (and other elaeagnus species), tropical Mexican clover, common lantana, common mullein, rugosa rose, centipede grass, and Bermudagrass.

Forests are havens for both invasive and weedy plants. Invasive plants sensitive to salt aerosols find refuge in the maritime forests. Chinese tallow is a growing menace in forested areas, especially those with soils that remain moist much of the year. Sweet autumn virgin's bower and Chinese privet are examples of other exotic or weedy species that grow "too well" in the maritime thickets and forests and in small openings. Removing as many of these and other exotic plants as possible from home landscapes enhances the growth of native thicket and forest plants and will prevent seed dispersal to nearby natural areas.

In removing these plants, you should pull up invasive and weedy plants, place them in large bags, allow the plants to dry out, and then dispose of them. Frequently monitor the site for regrowth or the reappearance of root suckers or seedlings. Remove new appearances until you extirpate the species from the area.

RETAINING NATIVE PLANTS IN THEIR HABITATS

As you plan a coastal landscaping project, keep in mind that the native species listed in this chapter's tables were selected for consideration because they have interesting or unusual flowers, fruits, leaves, colors, wildlife use, or other values. Beyond that, each of the *native* species described in the Chapter 9 plant profiles plays a role in the natural plant community (or communities) of the coastal Carolinas to which it belongs. Even if some plants are not especially attractive or we have yet to clearly understand their ecological roles, they still are valuable to the coastal community in which they are found. Leave the existing native plants undisturbed to the extent possible. If in doubt about a plant that is native, let it grow undisturbed, if for no other reason than increasing plant diversity on the site.

RAIN GARDENS

Installing rain gardens is a meaningful way to utilize native plants in coastal communities while also practicing water conservation. Rain gardens, also known as bioretention swales or cells, are shallow,

a

b

Figure 62. Rain gardens can feature (a) a mixture of herbs, grasses, shrubs, and trees or (b) all grasses and herbaceous plants. The size of a rain garden can be scaled up or down depending on the water detention needs of the site, and its shape can be designed to fit the space available. Courtesy of Roger Shew, University of North Carolina Wilmington.

vegetated depressions that collect runoff water from impervious surfaces such as roofs, walkways, driveways, and roads. Essentially, a rain garden is a plant-based water treatment system that mimics an ecosystem. The term "rain garden" first appeared in the landscaping literature beginning in the 1980s, and the use of rain gardens has grown in popularity ever since (fig. 62).

THE ECOLOGICAL ROLE OF RAIN GARDENS

Rain gardens perform important wetland functions in the coastal environment,

and the hummocky backdunes provide a useful model for rain garden design and placement. Natural backdunes possess swales that temporarily collect urban runoff, often called gray water, during a rain and slowly release it into the ground. Urban runoff in any coastal area can become contaminated, necessitating closure of beaches and shellfish beds. Equally important, flooding is reduced in low-lying areas with this water retention. As freshwater runoff is directed into these depressions, it slowly passes through coastal sands and is cooled and filtered of pollutants. The rainwater then slowly infiltrates and recharges groundwater, conserving both water and nutrients. Finally, bioretention or rain garden swales provide habitat for many charismatic bird species, valuable frogs and toads, and myriad insects, including important pollinators.

MANAGING RAINWATER MOVEMENT AND QUALITY

When a particular coastal site is urbanized, the layout and design may call for dunes to be flattened and swales to be infilled, thereby altering the natural infiltration and drainage patterns on barrier beaches and islands. Roofs and pavements also alter natural runoff quantities and patterns. In an effort to move water away from foundations, builders often install underground pipes attached to traditional downspouts. In these situations, piped systems can be extended to rain gardens and environments that simulate predevelopment landscapes in size, shape, and function.

Rain gardens replace the all-too-familiar scene of water rushing along street gutters for hours following a major downpour. Bioretention swales are designed and constructed to hold an inch or more of rainwater as it percolates into the soil. To find the most effective location for a rain garden, note where water from walkways and driveways flows and lingers following a rain. Locate rain gardens strategically in these areas to intercept, collect, and gradually release this water.

RAIN GARDEN DESIGN AND MAINTENANCE

Rain gardens are scalable; their size depends on the quantity of water that a given rain garden must process. Individual property owners can create rain gardens that range from a few square feet to hundreds of square feet. You can make a rain garden a simple do-it-yourself project, join a cooperative neighborhood effort, or support a more complex, professionally designed project. Organizations, institutions, and communities can coordinate planning and undertake large and sometimes interrelated rain gardens. For example, depending on the water management needs of the area, a neighborhood could install several small, individual rain gardens to absorb roof runoff, or it could use a few larger areas such as street medians or unbuildable lots to handle large quantities of runoff.

Establishing undulating topography in a rain garden creates a varied landscape. Place plants with the greatest water requirements in the center of the swale, and plant shrubs or drought-tolerant herbs and grasses on the higher, slightly drier sides of the depression. Plantings may be formal or informal depending on the ambience desired.

Rain garden planning includes core sampling for soil nutrient analysis and measuring the depth to groundwater. The presence of wetland soils or persistent water in the test hole indicates a probable wetland site and an area likely to hold water for longer than 24 hours. Seasonal variation in the groundwater level is common; take a core sample during the winter.

MOSQUITO HEAVEN (HAVEN)?

Scientists have found that rain gardens actually reduce the opportunity for mosquitoes to breed. Mosquitoes require an average of 10 days of standing water for their eggs to hatch and their offspring to grow and emerge as adults. Swales may retain water for a few hours, but certainly no more than 24 hours; hence, a properly constructed rain garden does not provide the water regime required for mosquitoes to breed. In sites where water stands for more than a day or two, you can manage the area as a stormwater wetland. For example, you could plant water-guzzling wetland species there.

MAINTENANCE REQUIREMENTS

Consider rain gardens as an important part of low-impact development. They are visually interesting yet low maintenance, as rain gardens avoid the traditional "lawnscape" and all its maintenance requirements. Following installation, rain gardens require little attention for proper functioning. Initial irrigation does help the plants establish deep and extensive root systems, but it is only important in the first few months following plant installation. Within a single season, native perennials will develop a root system that can withstand considerable drought.

There are just a few annual requirements for maintenance, such as cleaning up dead plant material and placing mulch on the site. The mulch will increase soil moisture, keep weeds at a minimum, lower soil temperature, and improve bioretention by increasing microbial activity. Maintaining a concave profile of the bioretention swale is important. Filling the rain garden to the surrounding ground level defeats the water retention purpose of the swale.

The site may also require periodic weeding to remove unwanted volunteer plants, but no fertilization is necessary. Because water moves directly to the water table, scientists do not recommend using pesticides.

NATIVE SPECIES IN RAIN GARDENS

Native plants thrive in rain gardens; thus projects located in dune swales have dozens of candidate species. See Tables 2 and 3.

Rain gardens in backdune and maritime grassland environments may be open and sunny or shaded. In sunny sites, grasses such as dune hairgrass and coastal little bluestem are excellent choices. As bunchgrasses, they mix well with many herbaceous perennials, including American germander, spotted horsemint, and silver-leaf croton. In shady areas, one or more of the coastal ferns can thrive along with the small shrub beauty berry. Nodding ladies' tresses adds a nice touch of white. Be creative in your selection of native plants to populate a coastal rain garden!

RESOURCES

Availability of native plants is an ongoing issue, but as demand increases, growers are prone to build their native plant stocks. A visit to local and regional nurseries and a search of Internet websites will yield many sources for native coastal plants. Several excellent books, pamphlets, and websites provide detailed information concerning the rain garden concept, including details of style, design, placement, planting, and maintenance.

7

NATIVE VEGETATION AND COASTAL STORMS

The coastal Carolinas are second only to Florida in the number of times they have been pummeled by hurricanes and nor'easters. The temporal patterns of these storms make the Carolinas coast vulnerable to major storms year-round. Both North Carolina and South Carolina often experience hurricanes that either graze or cross the coastline as they spin west and north from the tropics during the late summer and fall (fig. 63). During the winter and spring, powerful extratropical nor'easters track northward, often paralleling the Carolinas coast.

Hurricanes and nor'easters alter coastal landscapes and vegetation patterns in myriad ways. These changes may be immediate, short term, long term, or cumulative. For example, leaves being stripped from trees is an immediate, and sometimes severe, impact of a storm. Flooding in dune swales is often a short-term effect of storms. A cumulative

Figure 63. The track of Hurricane Hugo, a category 4 storm on the Saffir-Simpson Hurricane Wind Scale typical of midsummer to early fall hurricanes in the Southeast. The storm originated near the Cape Verde Islands and moved westward, making landfall near Charleston, S.C., on September 21–22, 1989. Illustration by Andrea Dingeldein based on data from the National Hurricane Center. Courtesy of North Carolina Sea Grant.

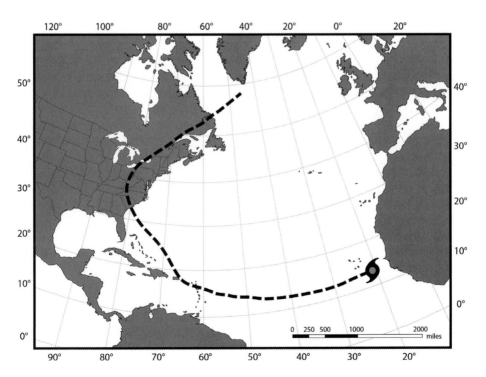

effect occurs when frequent storms successively expand overwash fans until they coalesce and form overwash terraces. Hurricanes and nor'easters influence the geomorphology, hydrology, productivity, nutrient cycling, and community composition of areas in the paths of storms. Individual storm severity varies, owing to differences in the direction and speed of storm approaches and the landfall locations. Storm characteristics and movements affect wind speed, storm surge height, and rainfall accompanying a storm.

Wind, salt aerosols, and saltwater and freshwater flooding during and after severe storms leave visible impacts on native plants and plant communities for years. Often, the extent of coastal vegetation change occurring in a single storm rivals decades of daily changes. These impacts are important but ultimately of less concern when compared with human injury and death, structural damage, and the consequent personal and economic losses.

The species composition and distribution of native coastal vegetation along the Carolinas coast reflects the experience of storms every few years. Plants capable of surviving punishing storms and then recovering rapidly dominate the natural landscapes.

Studying changes caused by storms offers a clear understanding of short- and long-term impacts of these storms on plants, both native and exotic. The aftermath of storms provides us with several opportunities: to measure recovery rates for vegetation; to consider, select, and install new plants; and to minimize future damage in managed landscapes.

PLANT RESILIENCE TO STORMS

As hurricanes reach the Carolinas coast, vegetation receives the brunt of the storm impact. Herbs and grasses are flooded by

Figure 64. This tree damage was sustained during Hurricane Hugo on Bull Island, S.C. The trees are variously uprooted, tilted, stripped of leaves and limbs, and snapped in half by hurricane-force winds.

either fresh water or salt water, or they are smothered by sand washed through the dunes. In some dune zones, sand is washed away, exposing roots and rhizomes of herbs, grasses, and sometimes shrubs. Leaves, branches, and sometimes entire plants are killed either by saltwater or freshwater flooding or by quantities of salt aerosols that exceed the tolerance of the plants. Branches and leaves are often ripped from trees and shrubs. Trees snap, tilt, or uproot (fig. 64).

Despite the magnitude and extent of these storm impacts, coastal environments are resilient to what appear to be, at first glance, devastating changes. Usually, storm effects are barely observable after just a few years. Like plant response to a forest fire, counterintuitively, storm damage is greatest and lasts longer as the interval between major storms *increases*. Trees and shrubs that have not sustained wind damage for decades are the first to be broken or uprooted. Wetlands or uplands not flooded by salt water for many years undergo visible changes in composition as salt-intolerant plants quickly die.

Plant responses to recent storms in the

coastal Carolinas on Brown's Island, N.C., and Bull Island, S.C., illustrate how storms disrupt vegetation on barrier islands. On both islands, major storms killed or damaged much of the maritime forest and maritime shrub thicket vegetation nearest the ocean, creating new, more open habitats. Dog fennel, a notorious weed and a species uncommon on the islands before the storm, subsequently assumed dominance and remained dominant for several years as the overstory thinned. Over time, however, dog fennel was gradually shaded out and replaced as native shrub thickets recovered.

Similarly, loblolly pines were nearly totally removed from the overstory on Bull Island during Hurricane Hugo. Most were snapped in half when they experienced high-speed winds. Today, new young loblolly pines dot the island, but it will take decades before pines again dominate. These situations repeat over and over, from place to place and time to time, ultimately leading to a mosaic of different-aged maritime forests and shrub thickets on the coastal barrier beaches and islands.

Many factors contribute to how (or whether) a given species survives elevated winds, erosion, burial, or freshwater or saltwater flooding. Knowing which species best survive hurricanes or nor'easters along the Carolinas coast helps coastal managers and homeowners install more storm-resistant landscapes. Observations recorded by residents provide valuable information concerning which species survive storms with the least damage in your area. These data are valuable to coastal agencies and community organizations, helping them to select storm-resistant trees and shrubs for future landscaping projects.

PLANT RESPONSES TO FRESHWATER AND SALTWATER FLOODING

Surges in ocean and estuarine water accompany major storms and flood coastal environments, sometimes including entire islands as well as low-lying sections of the mainland. Saltwater or freshwater flooding occurs in areas well above or well landward of regions normally reached by high tides or average water levels in freshwater wetlands. Waves break down dune systems and create large overwash fans landward of the frontal dune. Vegetation is uprooted, buried, or flooded with salt water. Owing to their short lifespan and adaptation to burial by overwash sand, native grasses and forbs recover rapidly—usually within a year or two—following a hurricane or nor'easter. Shrub and tree recovery times are measured in years and decades.

Hurricanes striking the Carolinas coast in the twentieth century produced record rainfalls—usually in less than 24 hours. In 1999, Hurricane Floyd deluged parts of coastal North Carolina with up to 24 inches of rain. Standing water remains for days or even weeks in a flooded region after a major storm. Much of the developed coastline near Corolla, N.C., on the northern Outer Banks, is underlain by a clay layer that slows water percolation into the ground. Plants, especially trees, not adapted to a lengthy period of flooding die at a higher frequency than in other areas.

Freshwater ponds near the ocean shoreline, such as on Oak Island, N.C., experience saltwater intrusion when waves overtop protecting foredunes. High concentrations of salts decrease water uptake by freshwater species, which leads to their death. This intrusion may persist long enough to alter components of the freshwater communities. For example, rabbitsfoot grass, water pimpernel, and eastern rose mallow disappear quickly where chronic intrusions of salt water occur. It may take a decade or more for these species to reappear in the wetland flora.

Flooding due to storm surge or a huge rainfall accompanying a storm is such a massive event that an individual property owner can do little to clean up until the water recedes. Simply removing debris from nearby storm drains may be all that can be done in this instance.

TREE AND SHRUB DAMAGE IN COASTAL STORMS

Owing to their size and longevity, storms affect trees and shrubs to a greater extent than herbaceous species, including grasses and sedges. The trees we observe on barrier islands and beaches have a history of surviving periodic storms; otherwise they would not be part of the landscape we observe. However, some tree species endure storms better than others. Damage to individual trees ravaged by high winds and heavy rainfall ranges from minor branch and leaf loss to death.

Research conducted immediately following storms provides insight into the storm resistance at the species and individual levels. Knowing the factors that allow trees and shrubs to survive storms allows us to select the appropriate trees for landscaping and to site them so that future storms are less devastating. The ability of individual trees to survive hurricanes and major windstorms depends on the species, age, size, structure, health, site characteristics, and storm factors. Post-hurricane observations by coastal scientists show that damage is species specific and that trees and shrubs can be rated on their suitability for planting in hurricane-prone environments (Table 6).

Individual species typically suffer similar types of damage whether storm conditions are fierce or modest. Many trees lose most of their leaves and many of their branches during a storm. This is, in fact, a survival mechanism for some trees. After surviving successive storms over several years, the character of tree crowns changes from dense and crowded to open and loose; therefore, it is best to prune dead branches and to maintain an open structure. This improves wind resistance in all species. Large, mature, and overly mature trees—trees that have deteriorated with age—suffer more damage than younger and smaller trees. Research demonstrates that proactively removing overly mature trees will reduce your storm damage.

At the species level, sweet gum, coastal red cedar, and sand laurel oak typically suffer serious crown damage. In contrast, American holly, live oak, sand live oak, and flowering dogwood experience the least limb injury. The highly flexible cabbage palmetto suffers the least damage of any coastal tree. Among the conifers, longleaf pines survive hurricane winds better than loblolly and slash pines.

Trees and large shrubs with dense crowns are more susceptible to damage compared with open-crowned trees or trees carefully pruned to reduce their fullness. Naturally dense-crowned trees such as live oak, sand laurel oak, and American holly experience significant branch losses, but overall survival is high. With comparatively small crowns, palmettos are rarely uprooted, despite their small, compact root systems. A broken main trunk spells almost certain death for a tree. Post-storm damage surveys find that sand laurel oak, water oak, sweet gum, and coastal red cedar have a higher proportion of trunk breakage when compared with other trees. Massive breakage may shorten the lifespans of these species in the coastal setting.

Conditions before, during, and after

a storm also influence a tree's fate. For example, when soils are saturated with rainwater before a storm reaches the coast or during a hurricane with unusually high rainfall, the incidence of leaning or uprooted trees, regardless of species, is high compared with damage inflicted by "dry" storms delivering less rainfall.

Trees growing closely together often have an advantage, such as interlacing root systems. Trees bound to each other are less likely to be uprooted than single specimens. In addition, solo trees experience the full force of hurricane winds. Trees growing in clumps (not in a line) shield one another, and this arrangement enhances their survival. Clumps composed of a mixture of species endure powerful winds better than clumps of a single species.

Some trees appear fine following a storm, but they later die for no apparent reason—usually during the next growing season. Pines frequently exhibit this pattern of delayed death. Even minor damage to pines opens them to infestations of pine bark beetles, ambrosia beetles, sawyers, and occasionally, blue stain fungus, all of which become fatal when these organisms overwhelm the trees. Frequent inspection of trees following a storm may provide vital information concerning the health of storm-ravaged trees and the likelihood that a particular tree may succumb to the effects of storm damage.

HOW DO SOME TREES AND SHRUBS SURVIVE STORMS?

Physical characteristics of various species—the height, crown shape, and trunk shape—also influence the survival of trees and shrubs. Tall trees, irrespective of species, experience more damage than shorter trees with smaller-diameter trunks. Trees of small stature such as flowering dogwood, common persimmon, American holly,

and live oak fare well in severe storms. In contrast, tall pines with few branches along the trunk are more likely to be damaged. Loblolly pines in particular often snap in two. Young specimens of most species are more flexible and less likely to break during a storm.

Palms, such as cabbage palmetto and South American jelly palm, survive at a higher rate in severe storm conditions compared with broad-leaf trees.

Wood density and elasticity are other important species characteristics affecting the survival of trees in high winds. Having dense wood contributes to the survival of live oak in hurricane-force winds. Likewise, the elastic wood of live oak, slash pine, longleaf pine, southern magnolia, and sand live oak helps these species survive.

Defoliated trees are more likely to survive storms than those with their leaves. High winds rip leaves and small branches from black gums and live oaks early in a storm. These ravaged trees present much less resistance to the wind. Also, once stripped of their leaves, these plants are less likely to be uprooted. Similarly, leaf loss leads to less crown damage. Southern magnolias have large leaves, but they strip easily from the plant, leading to greater survivability when compared with other species (fig. 65).

It is not unusual to see southern magnolias, as well as black gums, toothache trees, and live oaks, regrowing their leaves within a few weeks following a major storm. At the opposite end of the scale, coastal red cedars and loblolly pines resist defoliation and, consequently, experience major wind damage. In addition, the deeply furrowed trunks of many hardwood trees are maladapted for high winds, which quickly dispatch these trees. The deeply furrowed bark gives the wind something to blow against and push the tree over. In contrast, the wind

TABLE 6. Suitability of trees and large shrubs for planting in hurricane-prone environments, based on supporting observations

Common Name	Scientific Name	Hurricane Suitability	Storm-Related Observations
South American jelly palm	*Butia odorata*	High	High wind resistance; shrub-size plant; extensive root system
Coastal American hornbeam	*Carpinus caroliniana*	High	Hard, dense wood; limbs resist breakage; medium-high wind resistance
Flowering dogwood	*Cornus florida*	High	Hard, dense wood; high wind resistance; limbs resist breakage, wind defoliates tree
Common persimmon	*Diospyros virginiana*	High	Hard, dense wood; medium-high wind resistance
American holly	*Ilex opaca*	High	High wind resistance
Yaupon	*Ilex vomitoria*	High	High wind resistance; high flood tolerance
Crape myrtle	*Lagerstroemia indica*	High	High wind resistance, flood tolerant
Southern magnolia	*Magnolia grandiflora*	High	High wind resistance; wind defoliates tree; flood tolerant
Black gum	*Nyssa sylvatica*	High	High flood tolerance; good wind resistance
Sand live oak	*Quercus geminata*	High	Often grows with aerodynamic shape; high wind resistance; deep roots
Live oak	*Quercus virginiana*	High	High wind resistance; wind defoliates tree; deep roots when in well-drained soil; somewhat low profile
Cabbage palmetto	*Sabal palmetto*	High	High flood tolerance; high wind resistance
Tough bully	*Sideroxylon tenax*	High	Hard, dense wood; limbs resist breakage
Bald cypress	*Taxodium distichum*	High	High wind resistance; widespread roots; few branches and leaves; flood tolerant (fresh water only)
Toothache tree	*Zanthoxylum clava-herculis*	High	Often grows with aerodynamic shape; high wind resistance; deep roots
Carolina red maple	*Acer rubrum*	Medium	Flood tolerant; medium-low wind resistance
Wild olive	*Cartrema americanum*	Medium	Limbs resist breakage
Pignut hickory	*Carya glabra*	Medium	Hard, dense wood; medium-high wind resistance
Sugarberry	*Celtis laevigata*	Medium	Medium-low wind resistance

Common name	Scientific name	Rating	Notes
Coastal red cedar	*Juniperus virginiana* var. *silicicola*	Medium	Resists defoliation; low elasticity; flood tolerant
Sweet gum	*Liquidambar styraciflua*	Medium	Medium-high wind resistance; high limb loss
Sweet bay	*Magnolia virginiana*	Medium	Medium-high wind resistance
Northern bayberry	*Morella pensylvanica*	Medium	Often grows with aerodynamic shape; medium-high wind resistance (northern North Carolina only)
Red mulberry	*Morus rubra*	Medium	Medium-low wind resistance
Red bay	*Persea borbonia*	Medium	Medium-low wind resistance
Slash pine	*Pinus elliottii*	Medium	Medium-low wind resistance; tall trunks often snap
Longleaf pine	*Pinus palustris*	Medium	Solid, squat trunk; medium-low wind resistance; deep roots; most wind-resistant conifer
Loblolly pine	*Pinus taeda*	Medium	Medium-low wind resistance; tall trunks often snap
Southern red oak	*Quercus falcata*	Medium	Low wind resistance
Chinaberry	*Melia azedarach*	Low	Brittle wood; **invasive, do not plant; remove existing trees**
Common wax myrtle	*Morella cerifera*	Low	Medium-low wind resistance; resists defoliation
Carolina laurel cherry	*Prunus caroliniana*	Low	Low wind resistance
Black cherry	*Prunus serotina*	Low	Medium-low wind resistance
Sand laurel oak	*Quercus hemisphaerica*	Low	Wind defoliates tree; low wind resistance
Water oak	*Quercus nigra*	Low	Low wind resistance; brittle wood
Black locust	*Robinia pseudoacacia*	Low	Hard, dense wood; brittle wood; high limb loss
Carolina willow	*Salix caroliniana*	Low	Low wind resistance; brittle branches; flood tolerant
Sassafras	*Sassafras albidum*	Low	Root/stem interface weak; small specimens wrenched out of the ground
Chinese tallow	*Triadica sebifera*	Low	Brittle wood; low wind resistance; **invasive, do not plant; remove existing trees**

Figure 65. The nearly complete loss of leaves and branches of southern magnolia early in a storm reduces the tree's wind resistance and contributes to its survival. Almost immediately, new branches and leaves begin to grow on damaged trees.

just "flows" around the magnolia with its smooth bark.

Trees with a single trunk narrowing as it extends upward, such as southern magnolia and American holly, are less susceptible to damage than species with a broad, diffuse crown. Loblolly pine and slash pine are examples of trees that do not taper toward their apex and often sustain considerable wind damage. Trees and shrubs with multiple stems—including northern bayberry, common wax myrtle, and sand live oak—show high survivability.

The depth to which a root system grows and the lateral extent of its root mass are factors related to windthrow in hurricane-force winds. Deeply rooted trees such as live oak and longleaf pine experience

considerably less windthrow than other species. Flowering dogwood, sweet bay, Carolina red maple, and water oak have high windthrow rates because they have relatively shallow, often diffuse, root systems.

Exotic or introduced trees show little difference in the type and amount of wind damage when compared with native species. Species introduced to the Carolinas coast are often native to other coastal environments where windstorms are nearly as frequent as they are in the southeastern United States.

As expected, research reveals that overall damage to trees and shrubs increases with hurricane intensity. Windthrow increases with higher wind speeds. Clearly, tree damage was greater with Hurricane Andrew in Florida with its 145 mph winds than it was with Hurricane Fran in North Carolina, where wind speeds reached 115 mph.

MINIMIZING STORM DAMAGE TO TREES AND SHRUBS

Understanding the type and extent of storm impacts helps coastal managers and homeowners select storm-resistant trees. Storm damage can be minimized in managed landscapes if you opt for trees and shrubs that show the greatest resistance to damage and if you follow a few simple rules for locating and installing them.

Begin by selecting shrubs and trees native to the coastal environment. Table 6 is a starting point for developing a hurricane-resistant tree landscaping plan. This list includes trees and shrubs that will show at least some resistance to wind. Plant a variety of trees and shrubs— different sizes, ages, species, and layers. Birds and insects like diversity, too! A site dominated by only loblolly pines is likely to be devastated by a major storm, whereas an area planted with an array of species will experience less damage.

Plant these trees and shrubs with their mature sizes in mind. Tall trees planted under power lines will have to be removed or severely pruned as they mature. Similarly, trees and shrubs planted under eaves or near decks may cause damage when they outgrow the site. Securely stake all small trees and shrubs with at least three tie-downs until their roots are firmly established, usually one year. Keep landscaping up to date with proper pruning. Remove dead, diseased, and overly mature limbs, as well as stem sprouts, root suckers, or otherwise damaged shrubs and trees, before a storm strikes.

Remove overly mature trees with the lowest suitability rating from your landscape. With low resistance to wind, these are likely to be damaged or to topple during a storm. A homeowner with a beautiful 30-inch loblolly pine located just a few feet from a structure is courting disaster! Replacing the pine with a smaller American holly or flowering dogwood can give one peace of mind.

Avoid planting trees and large shrubs where their root masses may be restricted. For example, planting trees and shrubs too close to a dwelling, a driveway, or a walkway may not allow for full expansion of the roots and may make the plants susceptible to windthrow. Coastal garden clubs, Extension Master Gardener groups, and nurseries with a coastal focus can provide additional information on installing a storm-resistant landscape; consult these resources as necessary. Excellent "how-to" resources populate the Internet.

RECOVERING AFTER A STORM

The big storm is over and it is time to assess and repair damage to trees and

Figure 66. After the storm has passed, cleanup starts! To reduce the potential for insect and disease damage to your remaining vegetation, remove and dispose of all organic debris generated by the storm, including hanging branches. Typically, your community will remove piles of debris you place at the street edge of your property.

shrubs (fig. 66)! It is best to begin cleanup immediately after the storm to prevent downed debris from rotting on the ground. Assess the health of each tree and shrub. Prune dead and damaged branches to allow the tree to resume normal growth; however, do not be surprised if trees and shrubs continue to lose their leaves for several weeks following a storm. Consult a Cooperative Extension agent for pruning guidelines.

Most coastal trees and shrubs are resistant to salt aerosols and soil salts, but after a storm, the leaves and twigs may appear salt burned. Leaves may turn brown within a few days. In the event of salt damage, immediately rinse off the foliage, trim damaged limbs, and water the trees. Fortunately, most trees recover nicely, often regrowing their leaves within a few weeks. Live oak, longleaf pine, coastal red cedar, cabbage palmetto, and black gum revive quickly, whereas Carolina red maple and flowering dogwood may not show signs of recovery until the following spring.

Partially uprooted trees probably have

root damage. For small trees or shrubs that have been uprooted but appear salvageable, immediately cover the roots with burlap or similar breathable fabric to avoid desiccation until they can be righted. Follow up within a few days and right the plants, rebury the roots, fill in the air spaces in the soil, and begin a regimen of weekly watering. Taking these steps quickly will likely save small trees or shrubs. Staking helps stabilize trees and shrubs until the roots are firmly reestablished. Trim away damaged parts of leaning plants, but defer general pruning until spring.

Inspect all trees and shrubs for damage the following spring. Loblolly or longleaf pines may look fine, but they could have been so weakened by the storm that bark beetles and other pests or diseases may have fatally infected the trees. Unhealthy trees and shrubs can spread disease to healthy plants. Trees and shrubs not leafing out the following spring are probably dead. If in doubt, seek the advice of a certified arborist—an invaluable time- and cost-saving experience. Consider the location of a dead tree in relation to structures before removing it. Dead trees or snags add considerable wildlife value if they are not too close to structures or human activity. Finally, make a plan for replacing dead or severely damaged trees and shrubs. Select native plants, keeping in mind the need to establish a diversity of sizes, shapes, textures, and ages that will minimize future damage from hurricanes and nor'easters.

8

CLIMATE CHANGE AND THE FLORA OF THE COASTAL CAROLINAS

Plants and plant communities of the coastal Carolinas are no strangers to change. Sea level clearly is an important factor related to coastal change. Geologic evidence suggests that coastal Carolina shorelines were once positioned more than 50 miles offshore from their current location. The modern Carolina shorelines reached their current location about 5,000 years ago. What is different about today's predicted sea level rise in the context of these past changes? The difference and the center of concern about the Carolinas coastline is the *rate* of change in sea level and, equally important, the *cause* of the change. Tide gauge records in North Carolina indicate that sea level has risen over the last 70 years. This change is a concern for scientists and coastal managers.

Organisms always have thrived in delicate balance with their environments in the relatively narrow zone where the land meets the sea. This coastline has just been in a different position. Plant communities and the species that comprise them have clearly moved in the past. The location, shape, character, and composition of the plant communities have changed and will continue to change. However, past changes along the shore have been measured in century-, millennium-, and epoch-long periods—long enough for plants and animals to adapt to their new surroundings.

Today, many scientists are concerned that the rate of overall climate change on our planet may be accelerating. These changes are signaled by the disruption of local and regional weather, sea level rise, an increase in storm intensity, and changes in other factors. Along the coast of the Carolinas, our local plants face an uncertain future as rapid climate change could shock plants and their environments.

Unlike with past climate changes, the consensus among scientists is that human industry and commerce are contributing to current changes in a major way. We all need to consider our role in this process and how we may affect the plants we enjoy, as so many organisms rely on this coastal environment for their survival.

CLIMATE CHANGE THREATS IN THE CAROLINAS COASTAL ENVIRONMENT

Plants unable to adapt to new environments or to migrate quickly to more favorable environments may perish. Plants are particularly vulnerable to changes in their environment since, unlike many animals, they cannot "pick up and move" to another area. Their movement, expressed as migration, is slow, taking decades, centuries, or even longer. Adapting "in place" to a changing environment is often equally slow. Both migration and adaptation typically lag behind any changes in climate and, in the most recent geological period, behind processes associated with human settlement. Vascular plants may appear to be growing well, but they may be stressed in ways we do not recognize. Climate change and increases in human settlement can fragment plant populations, leaving those populations endangered or even facing extinction.

A number of potential impacts from climate change work together in creating overall threats to thriving plant communities. Shoreline changes (especially erosion), increased storm activity, sea level rise, increased flooding, precipitation changes, and annual average temperature increases are hypothesized to occur in the coastal Carolinas. Confounding these changes is the fact that our understanding of, and predictions about, climate change are continually changing. We add new information and insights to our existing knowledge base continuously. It is within this context that we anticipate that climate change will affect specific environments, natural communities, and native plant populations in the coastal Carolinas in myriad ways.

EFFECTS OF CHANGING TEMPERATURES

According to scientific consensus, the major global response to a buildup of atmospheric carbon dioxide is a warming planet. This is not a recent discovery. We have known this for over a century. The basic theory related to the contribution of carbon dioxide to greenhouse gas warming in the atmosphere goes back to research by Swedish scientist Svante Arrhenius in 1896. The National Climate Assessment of 2014 documented that in the southeastern United States, the average annual temperature has increased by 2°F since 1970. In North Carolina, the mean annual temperature has increased by less than 1°F since 1900, according to a state summary. Long-term climate data show that the Carolinas region has experienced modest warming in winters and summers since the 1980s (fig. 67). Unlike other parts of the country, North Carolina has not experienced an increase in the number of extreme heat days, which are days with a temperature above 95°F. However, in the five-year period of 2010–14, the number of nights with temperatures above 75°F has been greater than in the historical record. Climate experts expect the frequency, duration, and intensity of these events to continue to increase into the twenty-second century.

A shift in the geographic range of key plants in response to temperature changes may already be occurring. Anecdotal evidence includes the fact that 50 years ago, the commonly accepted northern limit

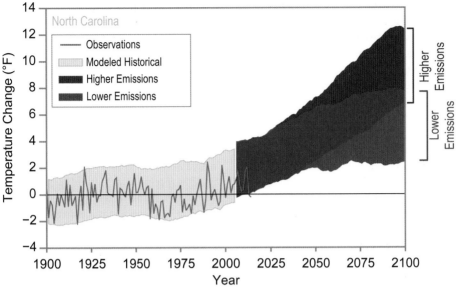

Figure 67. Observed and Projected Temperature Change (North Carolina). Observed and projected changes (compared to the 1901–60 average) in near-surface air temperature for North Carolina. Observed data are for 1900–2014. Projected changes for 2015–2100 are from global climate models for two possible futures: one in which greenhouse gas emissions continue to increase (higher emissions) and another in which greenhouse gas emissions increase at a slower rate (lower emissions). Temperatures in North Carolina (orange line) have risen almost 1°F since the beginning of the twentieth century. Shading indicates the range of annual temperatures from the set of models. Observed temperatures are generally within the envelope of model simulations of the historical period (gray shading). Historically unprecedented warming is projected during the twenty-first century. Less warming is expected under a lower-emissions future (the coldest years being about as warm as the hottest year in the historical record [green shading]), and more warming is expected under a higher-emissions future (the hottest years being about 10°F warmer than the hottest year in the historical record [red shading]). Source: CICS-NC and NOAA NCEI.

of sea oats was located near the mouth of Chesapeake Bay. Today, sea oats have been collected near the Maryland/Virginia state line, 70 miles north. Similarly, the range of American beachgrass has been expanded by extensive plantings much farther south than its natural southern limit, Cape Hatteras. One can predict, however, that this extended range will contract northward as average temperatures climb, droughts become extensive, and heat stress affects the cool-climate-loving beachgrass. This scenario suggests that it may be best to choose more heat-tolerant options for dune reconstruction projects in the Carolinas.

Until recently, Bald Head Island, N.C., was the natural northern limit for cabbage palmetto. Before 1980, cabbage palmetto often failed to survive the occasional cold winters in the Wilmington to Morehead City, N.C., region, even when planted in a landscape setting. With nearly 100 percent mortality every few years, homeowners and landscapers reduced use of the tree in North Carolina. Today, however, we observe landscape cabbage palmettos routinely surviving—and thriving—in the measurably less severe southeastern North Carolina winters. This situation has revived the use of cabbage palmettos in many landscape plans.

As native plants such as cabbage palmetto migrate north, will they displace existing plants? How will these migrations affect the distribution and abundance of other species? Experts need to pay close attention to specific changes in the abundance and distribution of coastal plants for the next several decades, in that current trends are expected to accelerate. As the growing season lengthens in the coastal Carolinas, we particularly need to understand that species considered invasive may spread even more aggressively, replacing native vegetation at a faster rate.

Also, during times of drought and extreme temperatures, the coast may experience an increase in the frequency and intensity of wildfires. While this will minimally affect dunes and maritime grasslands, maritime forests may experience a contraction in distribution and be replaced by plant communities dominated by grasses and herbs better adapted to frequent wildfires.

SEA LEVEL

Sea level rise depends on the rate and amount of global warming and its contribution to the formation of liquid water from melting glaciers and polar ice sheets, coupled with the amount of subsidence, or gradual sinking, of land in a particular area. Where the rate of sea level rise exceeds the rate of sediment deposition, erosion of ocean and estuarine shorelines and wetland drowning are near-certain outcomes. This apparent sea level rise makes the coastal Carolinas especially vulnerable to vegetation change. In northeastern North Carolina, where the land is sinking at the same time sea level is rising, estimates of loss of land, both natural and human built, can be large. In contrast, for stable or rising coastal areas such as the Cape Fear arch near the North

Carolina and South Carolina state line, the coastal zone is less likely to experience comparatively serious erosion or land loss.

Can the extensive tidal marshes covering huge acreages in southeastern South Carolina maintain themselves as sea level rises so rapidly? Possibly not. Will North Carolina's large sounds remain stable in size and depth? Possibly not. Coastal Carolina estuaries may increase in area as well as depth. Generally, tidal marshes receive sufficient sediment from rivers and streams to keep pace with sea level rise, but with an accelerated rise, tipping points may be reached, leading some marshes to drown in place. Where the physiography allows, tidal marshes and tidal freshwater forests can and will retreat landward as the ocean level rises. The currently predicted rates of sea level rise coupled with the likely sediment input into the region may result in loss of land on both ocean and sound sides of islands. This would lead to a reduction in the overall size of these coastal buffers. Protection of coastal uplands from storms may be compromised when buffering vegetation disappears.

If we experience a catastrophically rapid rise in sea level, scientists predict that low-lying barrier islands will fragment. Some islands may disappear entirely. In general, coastal wetland resources are the communities most vulnerable to sea level rise, since they occur in a narrow zone or band at the estuarine edge of islands and uplands. Already today on ocean sides of islands in the region, shoreline erosion predominates over accretion. A specific result of this change is an increasing need for plants, grown on a commercial scale, to address erosion on ocean and estuarine shorelines. We can anticipate that the greenhouse- and field-propagated native coastal plant industry will grow.

STORM ACTIVITY

Climate scientists predict that the intensity of hurricanes and nor'easters will increase with the elevated surface temperatures in the nearshore Atlantic Ocean. Compared with historical records, the number of Atlantic hurricanes reaching categories 4 and 5 on the Saffir-Simpson Hurricane Wind Scale has increased since the 1980s. We do not know if storms like Hurricanes Hugo (1989), Andrew (1992), Fran (1996), and Sandy (2012) will reach the Carolinas coast more frequently. Recent research seems to bolster a developing consensus that although the frequency of hurricanes striking the Southeast has decreased, the intensity of those storms has increased. At the same time, we have no understanding of how climate change will influence storm tracks. Even with no increase in hurricane frequency, coastal storms will likely develop higher wind speeds, deliver more intense rainfalls, and drive higher storm surges ashore. If intense storms take tracks that lead them to landfall along or near our region, shoreline erosion will almost certainly intensify along the Carolinas coast.

More severe coastal storms would have manifold impacts on coastal plants. Oceanic overwash destroys existing plants, but recovery historically has been rapid. Within a decade, the vegetation cover rebuilds. Should storm intensity increase (and therefore overwash intensify) to a point where plants have insufficient time to recover, overall vegetation density may decrease, impairing future recovery. Only anecdotal observations exist for this scenario; longitudinal studies of vegetation will help determine the long-term impacts of increased overwash on barrier island and barrier beach vegetation.

Storm-tolerant arborescent communities (for example, maritime shrub thickets and maritime forests) that normally protect more inland resources are vulnerable to saltwater intrusion during intense storms. As a consequence, maritime forests and freshwater marshes could be expected to decrease in extent throughout the coastal Carolinas.

PRECIPITATION AND FLOODING

Some downscaled climate models project that, on average, coastal areas will experience increased precipitation, but the current models are inconsistent due to the difficulty in simulating land/sea interactions along the immediate coast. Changes in precipitation amounts influence the region's runoff, as well as the frequency and intensity of flooding. Historical hurricane records indicate that the amount of rainfall in the average hurricane is increasing, and rainfalls exceeding 10 inches in a storm are no longer unusual. Precipitation also influences plant composition in wetlands and uplands as new species occupy niches vacated by species unable to tolerate the new precipitation or flooding regimes.

Floods may become deeper and more widespread and may persist for longer periods as sea level rises, as coastal lands sink, or as protective dunes are destroyed by storms (fig. 68). The mantra many suggest is "the exceptionally high tides of today will become the average tides of tomorrow." In flooded areas, oxygen levels in the soil remain lower for longer periods. If this anoxic condition becomes more frequent and severe, it would stress the plants affected. Water quality is, in part, determined by the source and mixing rates of flood waters. Stresses on vegetation may be expressed by changes in species composition in flooded communities.

ESTUARINE SALINITY

The pattern of salinity we observe in coastal waters is a product of complex

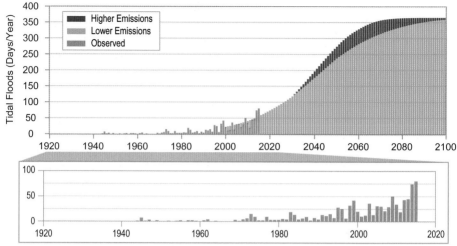

Figure 68. Observed and Projected Annual Number of Tidal Floods for Wilmington, N.C. Number of tidal flood days per year for the observed record (orange bars) and projections for two possible futures: lower emissions (light blue) and higher emissions (dark blue) per calendar year for Wilmington, N.C. Sea level rise has caused an increase in tidal floods associated with nuisance-level impacts. Nuisance floods are events in which water levels exceed the local threshold (set by NOAA's National Weather Service) for minor impacts, such as road closures and overwhelmed storm drains. The greatest number of tidal flood days (all days exceeding the nuisance-level threshold) occurred in 2014 and 2015 at Wilmington. Projected increases are large even under a lower-emissions pathway. Near the end of the century, under both emissions pathways, some models project tidal flooding every day of the year. To see these and other projections under additional emissions pathways, please see the supplemental material on the state summaries website (http://stateclimatesummaries.globalchange.gov). Source: NOAA NOC.

interactions that involve sea level change, local currents, the circulation of water masses, the regional sediment supply, and changes in the elevation of land relative to the water. If changes in any of these factors occur so significantly that vegetation cannot adapt reasonably quickly, an increase in open-water environments is likely (fig. 69). Increased salinity of waters in estuaries typically affects upstream communities as tidal salt marshes replace tidal freshwater marshes. Saltwater intrusion into rivers and groundwater is possible. At the species level, some plants have very narrow habitat requirements in respect to salinity. For example, Monnier's water-hyssop populations will increase or decrease as estuarine salinity changes. Extirpation of the plant from some tidal

marshes is a possibility if soil salinity and inundation change too quickly for the plant to migrate to more suitable habitats.

NONNATIVE AND INVASIVE PLANT RESPONSES TO CLIMATE CHANGE

Warming of the environment allows invasive plants to expand their geographic range and occupy new habitats, ultimately replacing existing plants. We can expect Chinese tallow and saltcedar to continue to invade coastal plant communities, displacing some natives in the process. Under rapidly changing climatic conditions, will other species become invasive or accelerate the disappearance (or arrival) of some species?

Some native species, such as common wax myrtle and sea myrtle, are considered

Figure 69. Low-lying forests such as the one pictured on Bogue Banks, N.C., are increasingly vulnerable to saltwater flooding. Increasingly higher spring tides and storm tides kill or injure trees growing adjacent to brackish and salt marshes.

borderline weedy plants by some botanists. Will their weedy tendencies be dampened or will they become more aggressive when growing in areas experiencing major climatic shifts? Will they become serious pest plants in coastal communities? With the predicted rate of climate change, researchers should identify—and share—answers to these questions.

Shifts in local plant composition will occur as some species retreat to cooler environments. In coastal communities, this change in species composition could lead to niche openings where invasive plants may have an advantage. Clearly, these changes will create new management challenges for coastal landowners, horticulturalists, landscapers, and managers of natural areas.

NATIVE PLANT RESPONSES TO CLIMATE CHANGE

Overall, how will these rapidly changing environmental factors affect native Carolina coastal plants? As best we can tell, there will be impacts, but native plants will fare better than nonnative plants. Thankfully, native plants are well adapted to the environment in which

they are growing. Minor changes in environmental factors typically have little effect on the native flora, and we predict that only modest changes in plant populations would occur, at least in the early stages of accelerated climate change. However, if major changes happen, maritime grasslands may replace dunes, open water may replace tidal marshes, and saltwater communities may replace freshwater communities. While none of these changes in community structure would be catastrophic, these changes may alter the density, abundance, diversity, and interspecific relationships of the plant communities involved.

When plants are under stress, pests are more likely to spike in abundance, taking advantage of the plants' weakened state. Witness the increase in damage by one or more of the common pine bark beetles following major hurricanes. With a rapidly changing climate that stresses plants, communities may experience more frequent or more serious outbreaks of insects and pathogenic organisms.

The salt panne is one of the communities under considerable stress as we experience warmer temperatures and increased evapotranspiration. Any increase in the evaporation of water standing on the salt panne surface could increase soil salinity to the point that populations of Virginia glasswort, dwarf glasswort, southern sea-blite, and similar plants would sustain slower growth and lower productivity overall. Without these plants naturally sequestering environmental salts in salt pannes, plant cover may decrease.

The distribution and abundance of opportunistic plants, better known as weeds, may increase where there are disturbances owing to changes in human land use, land cover changes, and natural variability of weather and climate affecting native plants. Common mullein (a nonnative weed) or dog fennel (a native weed) are two examples included in this volume that may quickly colonize open spaces and available niches where key native species decline.

Currently, cold temperatures in coastal North Carolina winters reduce the growth and spread of the nonnative, common water hyacinth, but it remains an abundant, yet stable, component of the flora. If temperatures rise and the length and depth of the cold season decreases, plants such as common water hyacinth may grow year-round and ultimately express severe invasive tendencies by outcompeting and replacing native plants, as it has done in warmer areas of the Southeast. Similarly, oleander, a nonnative plant used extensively in coastal landscaping throughout the Carolinas, grows best in southern to mid–South Carolina. It suffers periodic dieback when it experiences colder winters in North Carolina. The warming of the climate in the region may lead to a northward extension and success in using this landscape plant along the northern coast of North Carolina and northward.

Increased atmospheric moisture can lead to expansion of suitable habitats by high-profile species, including resurrection fern and Spanish moss. Conversely, over time, an increase in storms may reduce populations of certain coastal trees and shrubs less adapted to high winds or having shallow roots. Southern red oak, sassafras, water oak, black locust, and most of the pine species are examples of trees vulnerable to population reductions with increased storm intensity. Deeply rooted trees, described as windthrow resistant, include live oak, sand live oak, cabbage palmetto, and holly species. They could fill forest niches left by the loss of wind-susceptible trees.

Many coastal species that thrive in warm environments are likely to spread northward as climate change accelerates. Slash pine, Chinese tallow, saltwort, and bay-hops, a species rare in the coastal Carolinas, are just a few examples of natives and nonnatives likely to experience a northward range extension.

Many of the distribution changes cited here may be triggered by simple one-factor changes such as wind, temperature, or salinity, thereby altering the distribution of a particular plant in the coastal Carolinas. When we contemplate more complex and more likely scenarios where multiple factors change rapidly—for example, higher winter air temperatures coupled with more intense and frequent winds and concomitant changes in soil salinity—the response by most native plants may be far too complex to predict with precision.

The good news related to climate change is that native plants are typically more tolerant of saltwater flooding, salt aerosols, high winds, and drought than many nonnative landscape plants. This fortunate circumstance suggests that native plants will survive better than nonnative plants in the face of major changes in the environment predicted by climate change experts. When planning and installing coastal landscapes, go with the species you know will grow best—natives—and avoid using nonnative plants.

9

COASTAL CAROLINA PLANT PROFILES

Each plant profile has accompanying photographs useful in identifying the species and showing the size and shape of the plant as well as its leaves, flowers, and fruits (seeds). I note identifying physical characteristics and seasonal aspects of the plants in both text and photographs. The profiles include information concerning the plant's distribution, natural history, distinctive physical or chemical features, ecology, and use to wildlife and humans. Where appropriate, I note species related or similar to the plant under consideration.

COMMON NAMES

I indicate the most familiar and often-used names. While some plants have a dozen or more local or colloquial names, I cite only the most widely established common names in general use to avoid confusion.

SCIENTIFIC NAMES

I use the traditional binomial nomenclature composed of the genus and species names. Scientists always capitalize the first letter of the genus name, and they write the species name entirely in lowercase letters. The citation, the information following the scientific name, denotes the botanical authority responsible for classifying and naming the species. As taxonomists continue to study species, new information may subsequently lead to a different genus name being assigned to a plant. On occasion, taxonomists change these names as they discover additional information using new molecular phylogenetic techniques. They also gain judgments about species relationships from taxonomists who study plants from a broader geographic perspective.

In instances where taxonomists recently changed a long-standing scientific name, the older name is noted in the text. For one species, the nomenclature has not been officially published to establish a specific epitaph. In this instance, *Trichostema* sp., the specific epitaph [species 1] has been temporarily assigned by taxonomists. I encourage readers to "pencil in" the official species name for this plant once it has been published in the botanical literature. You may wish to do the same for species that taxonomists rename in the future based on new information about species relationships. Nomenclature follows "Flora of the Southern and Mid-Atlantic States," by Alan S. Weakley, made available as a working draft in 2015.

RANGE

The North American geographic range over which the species can be found is noted. Where a plant's range is interesting, such as for a species with a worldwide or Northern Hemisphere distribution, this information is also noted. In this volume, many of the plants are restricted to the coast, such as sea oats or smooth cordgrass; these rarely occur more than a short distance from the ocean or estuary. While other species are present along the coast, they are much more widely distributed, such as common mullein, a plant that occurs throughout the Carolinas from the mountains to the sea. For plants introduced to the Carolinas as landscape plants, I provide the USDA Hardiness Zone information.

HABITAT

Each plant description includes a habitat (or habitats) for each plant. Some plants occur in a wide range of ecological settings, while others occur in only a single community. The description often includes an abundance term, especially for plants considered common or rare. In some circumstances, plants may be locally abundant but rare in the region. Seabeach amaranth, for example, is often locally common, but it occurs on only a

small number of beaches along the entire Atlantic shoreline.

GROWTH HABIT

I note the growth pattern of each species. The designations include ferns, graminoids, herbaceous annuals, herbaceous biennials and perennials, vines, shrubs, and trees. Species may be perennial, biennial, or annual, and I cite this information for each species.

FLOWERING (FL) AND FRUITING (FR) PERIOD

The approximate time during which a species is flowering or fruiting is indicated. For species with distinct flowering and fruit maturation periods, I cite separate times for each. When species occur in both North Carolina and South Carolina, flowering and fruiting generally take place nearer the earliest month cited when the plant occurs in southern South Carolina. Conversely, flowering and fruiting are nearer the latest date cited in northern North Carolina.

WETLAND STATUS

Nearly all species in the region have been assigned a wetland indicator status, found on the 2016 U.S. Army Corps of Engineers' Atlantic and Gulf Coastal Plain Region List of the National Wetlands Plants. This status indicates the likelihood that a particular species occurs in a wetland or in an upland. The list helps scientists address the vegetation factor in determining whether a site is considered a wetland or an upland. The National Technical Committee for Wetland Vegetation established the following wetland categories and definitions:

FAC (Facultative Wetland Plants)— Occur in wetlands and nonwetlands.
FACU (Facultative Upland Plants)—

Usually occur in nonwetlands, but may occur in wetlands.

FACW (Facultative Wetland Plants)—Usually occur in wetlands, but may occur in nonwetlands.

OBL (Obligate Wetland Plants)—Almost always occur in wetlands.

UPL (Upland Plants)—Almost never occur in wetlands.

This book's plant profiles list the designation for plants placed in a wetland status category.

ORIGIN

Origin refers to whether a species is native or a human introduction to the region. I cite the geographic source of the introduction, if known. Some species have become naturalized; they are nonnative species but occupy a distinct niche in the native flora without becoming invasive. As with all nonnative species, there is a possibility that a particular species may develop invasive tendencies, especially with large-scale disturbances such as climate change.

SPECIES DESCRIPTION

Plant features include distinctive characteristics of the roots, stems, leaves, flowers, or fruits (seeds). Use these descriptions in conjunction with the photographs to confirm identification of a particular species. Since the age and growing conditions of a plant can affect the size of an individual specimen, the description includes a size range for many features.

ECOLOGY AND WILDLIFE VALUE

The ecology of a plant refers to the relationship each species has to its environment, including animals. Tolerance to drought and salt aerosols, for example,

are noted. Likewise, I cite important ecological relationships or adaptations developed between a species and its environment; some plants are especially important to wildlife.

HUMAN USES

Human interactions with each species are considered. Some plants have multiple or important uses; others have negative relationships with humans. In cases where I note the use of a plant as a remedy for a disease or condition, understand that these are traditional uses passed on through generations and that they may or may not provide the purported relief or cure. They are part of our cultural heritage.

USEFUL GEOGRAPHIC RANGE

This volume features the coastal plants of North Carolina and South Carolina; however, many of the species range northward into Virginia and the Delmarva Peninsula or southward into Georgia and northern Florida. For example, American beachgrass is the dominant dune species from southern Maine through Virginia, but I present it in this volume because coastal interests have planted it extensively on dunes in North Carolina and South Carolina since the 1970s, and now it is an important component of the flora. Woolly beach heather and northern bayberry are found commonly north of North Carolina; however, specimens of both occur south to the Pea Island National Wildlife Refuge in North Carolina. Thus, I include the species. Saltwort, saw palmetto, and tough bully are common in South Carolina, Georgia, and Florida, yet botanists consider them rare in North Carolina.

The physiographic range includes the plant communities found on barrier islands and beaches on the Carolinas coast as well as freshwater and saltwater marshes near or adjacent to these islands. Where no barrier islands exist, the ocean and adjacent estuaries strongly influence the shore and mainland communities. These species are included because plant distribution reflects the ocean influence sometimes up to a mile inland.

It is difficult to make a book like this comprehensive; an exhaustive treatment of the coastal flora would be a massive tome. The species selected for inclusion are restricted to higher plants: ferns, gymnosperms, and angiosperms; but algae, fungi, mosses, and liverworts lie beyond the scope of this book. I selected species with many different attributes: prominence, rareness, ecological role, historic or economic value, and unusual characteristics or traits.

Ferns

1 EBONY SPLEENWORT

Asplenium platyneuron (Linnaeus) Britton, Sterns & Poggenburg

Family: Aspleniaceae (Spleenwort)
Range: Maine south to Florida and west to Texas and Colorado
Habitat: Maritime forests and maritime shrub thickets; also pine forests and roadsides
Habit: Perennial herb
Flowering/Fruiting Period: FL & FR April–October
Wetland Status: FACU
Origin: Native

a

Ebony spleenwort is one of the most common and easily recognized ferns found in the Carolinas coastal environment. Interestingly, the species is undergoing rapid migration; its distributional limits have moved decidedly northward since it was first described.

Fronds of ebony spleenwort are 4 to 15 inches long and ¾ to 1½ inches wide and arise from short creeping rhizomes that are fed by extensive fibrous roots. Fronds possess 15 to 40 alternately arranged, simple, oblong pinnae (pinna, singular) attached to a lustrous, purplish-brown rachis. Toothed pinnae possess auricles (lobes) that overlap the rachis. Fronds are widest at the middle; the pinnae taper toward the bottom and the top of the frond.

Fertile fronds are erect and exhibit brown, oblong sori (sorus, singular) in pairs on the underside of each pinna. Spores are released from the sori during the summer and early fall. Sterile fronds lack sori and typically grow close to the ground in a spreading pattern radiating from the center of the plant.

Ebony spleenwort prefers moist to slightly dry soils high in calcium, an element often abundant in coastal soils due to the shell content.

Ebony spleenwort has some cover value for wildlife.

b

1. Ebony spleenwort (*Asplenium platyneuron*). (a) Tall, narrow fertile fronds arise from short, creeping rhizomes. (b) Fruiting bodies (sori) are located on the underside of the pinnae of fertile fronds.

Ebony spleenwort grows well in light shade as an ornamental. It has a compact vertical growth pattern and will grow on stone walls as well as tree stumps. Divide it during the winter by separating rhizomes. Ebony spleenwort hybridizes with other species of the genus *Asplenium* when they occur near each other.

---

2 ROYAL FERN

Osmunda spectabilis Willdenow
Family: Osmundaceae (Royal fern)
Other Common Names: American royal fern, flowering fern, bog fern
Range: Eastern North America from Newfoundland to the Mississippi Valley, south to Texas and Florida
Habitat: Edges of freshwater and tidal marshes and swamps; also floodplain woods, streams, bogs, and wet meadows
Habit: Perennial herb
Flowering/Fruiting Period: FL & FR March–June
Wetland Status: OBL
Origin: Native

Royal fern is one of the largest ferns native to North America. Now nearly cosmopolitan, royal fern occurs on all continents except Australia and Antarctica. It is distinctive and imposing when observed in its natural habitat. Look for this plant in freshwater marshes embedded within or at the edge of maritime forests of the coastal Carolinas.

This fern develops from a large, stout rhizome with numerous black, wiry roots that sometimes grow aboveground, especially in continuously wet environments. The fronds are dull green and twice pinnately divided. The fronds may be spreading, ascending, or erect. Fronds grow to about 4 feet high and 12 to 18 inches wide. The stem (called a rachis in ferns) is grooved, shiny, and reddish-brown. Individual leaflets on the fronds,

pinnae, are opposite or nearly so. The pinnae, serrated near the tip, measure 1 to 2 inches long, ¼ to ½ inch wide.

Royal ferns produce two types of fronds, one sterile and the other fertile. The fertile fronds are shorter than the sterile fronds and bear spores in clusters of sporangia at their apices. Sporangia are green during formation and turn brown following release of the spores. The tiny spores are wind dispersed.

Royal fern prefers moist to wet soils and can grow well in full sunlight, partial shade, or full shade. It requires plenty of water and can tolerate occasional flooding.

Little is known concerning the wildlife value of royal fern beyond its serving as an excellent wildlife cover.

You can use spores to propagate royal fern, but the process of producing plants in this way is long and difficult. Instead, propagate the plant easily by dividing the rhizomes and roots in early spring before growth begins. Royal fern is slow growing and long lived. It makes an excellent accent plant and works well with water features. However, it becomes a large plant within a few years!

The fibrous roots, known as osmunda fiber, were once used as an orchid-growing medium, and the plant was so exploited that several states enacted laws to make collection of the plant illegal.

Steam young fiddleheads of royal fern and serve them as a tasty vegetable. People seeking treatment for bruises, burns, sprains, and broken bones report that emollients containing royal fern's rhizomes and roots are effective.

A related fern, cinnamon fern (*Osmundastrum cinnamomeum*), is found in wetland habitats similar to royal fern's habitats in the coastal Carolinas. Fronds of cinnamon fern are dimorphic; each frond is either sterile and photosynthetic or completely fertile.

FERNS

Royal fern is cited as *Osmunda regalis* in legacy literature.

a

b

2. Royal fern (*Osmunda spectabilis*). (a) The spreading, ascending, or erect fronds are dull green and twice pinnately compound. They may grow up to 4 feet high. (b) The shorter fertile fronds bear spores in clusters of sporangia at the apices of the fronds. Initially green, they turn brown at maturity.

3 RESURRECTION FERN

Pleopeltis michauxiana (Weatherby) Hickey & Sprunt

Family: Polypodiaceae (Polypody)

Other Common Names: Gray's polypody, little gray polypody, scaly polypody, miracle fern

Range: Maryland west to Kansas and south to Texas and Florida

Habitat: Maritime forest; also branches of hardwood trees and moss-covered rock surfaces

Habit: Perennial herb (epiphyte)

Flowering/Fruiting Period: FL & FR June–October

Wetland Status: FAC

Origin: Native

As a rule, plants can lose about 10 percent of their internal water before dying from water stress. Humans can lose about 20 percent before succumbing to dehydration. The remarkable resurrection fern gives up 75 percent of its internal water and remains alive and capable of rehydrating and reinitiating growth. This is a *poikilohydrous* strategy (a useful term for *Jeopardy* or conversations at a cocktail party). This ability gives resurrection fern an obvious evolutionary advantage; it can withstand extended droughts, surviving long after neighboring plants are dead. Because of this unusual ecological ability, astronauts have taken resurrection ferns into space on the NASA shuttle to study how the fern behaves as it rehydrates.

As frond blades dry out, they curl, with the underside of the frond facing outward. When rain falls, they rehydrate quickly owing to rapid water absorption by the underside of the blade. As they rehydrate, fronds return to their original shape and a healthy green color within a few hours.

Resurrection fern is an epiphyte that attaches to tree branches in maritime forests, often in association with Spanish moss. The fern is not a parasite; it obtains nutrients from rain and dust and does not harm the tree. The fern's rhizomes are wiry, much branched, and covered with thin, black scales. The rhizome grows in the cracks and furrows of tree bark and gives rise to narrowly triangular, evergreen fronds at short intervals along its length. The smooth-margined fronds are erect, glabrous, leathery, and deeply incised, nearly to the rachis. Usually widest near the middle, frond blades range from 1 to 4 inches long and from 1 to 2 inches wide.

Resurrection fern's spore-producing parts, or sori (sorus, singular), are small, round, dark brown structures on the underside of the fronds. Wind distributes their tiny spores over great distances.

Resurrection fern thrives in full sunlight and partial shade. It is common on large, moss-covered branches of live oak.

The resurrection fern may provide cover for some insects or small animals.

Propagation is by division of rhizomes. Resurrection fern typically grows on high

a

b

c

d

3. Resurrection fern (*Pleopeltis michauxiana*). (a) This plant, possessing many 1- to 4-inch-long fronds, is an epiphyte on trunks and branches of trees in the maritime forest, primarily live oak. (b) When hydrated by rainfall, the fronds are bright green, erect, glabrous, and leathery. (c) When dehydrated following a short drought, the fronds are curled, with the underside of the fronds facing outward. (d) Sori are small, round, dark brown structures near the edges of the underside of the frond.

FERNS

tree branches; simply collect rhizome pieces or entire plants from fallen branches of maritime forest trees.

In a cultivated setting, introduce plant pieces to large limbs of live oaks. Plants can be anchored with chicken wire (poultry netting) until they become established on the bark surface.

Resurrection fern is cited as *Polypodium polypodioides* in legacy literature related to the coastal Carolinas.

---

4 SOUTHERN BRACKEN FERN

Pteridium latiusculum (Desvaux) Hieronymus ex Fries

Family: Dennstaedtiaceae (Bracken)
Other Common Names: Bracken fern, bracken, brake
Range: Throughout North America; also much of the temperate and subtropical regions of the world
Habitat: Maritime forests and maritime grasslands; also dry woods, waste areas, and old fields
Habit: Perennial herb
Flowering/Fruiting Period: FL & FR July–September
Wetland Status: FACU
Origin: Native

With a fossil record beginning around 55 million years ago and a nearly worldwide distribution, bracken fern is considered one of the most successful species on earth. Southern bracken fern has some interesting attributes: rhizomes grow deep in the soil, individual fronds may live up to 3 years, a single frond can produce up to 100,000 spores in a season, and its dominance in some habitats may be due to its allelopathic nature.

Southern bracken ferns produce easily identified, coarse, triangular-shaped, highly dissected fronds on short but fast-growing rhizomes. Highly variable in size in the coastal Carolinas, fronds are typically from 1 to 3 feet high and equally broad. The main stems of fronds may be up to 3/8 inch in diameter at their base. It is unusual to find nectaries in ferns, but southern bracken fern has nectaries at the base of its pinnae that are active during the spring and summer. Ants in particular are attracted to these nectaries, and you may frequently find ants on or around southern bracken fern fronds. The spore-laden sori of southern bracken ferns line the underside edges of the fronds.

Spores are important for colonizing new habitats, but reproduction is primarily vegetative, with new fronds developing from the plant's many rhizomes.

Southern bracken fern grows best in full sun or partial shade. With deep roots, it tolerates drought well and thrives in nutrient-poor, sandy soils. Species commonly found in association with southern bracken ferns are cabbage palmetto, longleaf pine, and live oak.

White-tailed deer avoid the plant; however, a number of herbivorous insects will feed on the plant.

Research studies suggest that southern bracken fern fiddleheads are toxic to livestock and humans, containing thiaminase, an enzyme that causes a reduction of vitamin B_1. Despite this finding, bracken fern fiddleheads are part of the cuisine in many cultures.

Two varieties of the bracken fern are recognized, and both occur in the coastal Carolinas: var. *latiusculum*, the eastern bracken, and the more common var. *pseudocaudatum*, the southern bracken. In legacy literature, this species is cited as *Pteridium aquilinum*.

Generally well behaved in coastal Carolina environments, southern bracken fern is weedy and invasive in some environments, especially in the western United States. While not well suited for coastal native plant gardens, southern bracken fern provides excellent seasonal ground cover for small animals. It is not often available commercially and is difficult to transplant from the wild.

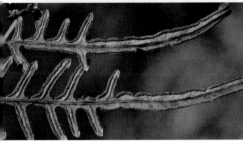

b 4. Southern bracken fern (*Pteridium latiusculum*). (a) Southern bracken fern possesses a coarse, triangular-shaped, and highly dissected frond. Fronds are 1 to 3 feet high and equally broad. (b) Spores are dispersed from brown sori that line the underside edges of fertile fronds.

5 MARSH FERN

Thelypteris palustris Schott
Family: Thelypteridaceae (Marsh fern)
Other Common Names: Meadow fern, eastern marsh fern
Range: Newfoundland west to Saskatchewan, south to Texas and Florida
Habitat: Dune swales, freshwater marshes, swamps, and roadside ditches
Habit: Perennial herb
Flowering/Fruiting Period: FL & FR June–September

Wetland Status: OBL
Origin: Native

Marsh fern forms dense colonies in wet, sunny areas often at the edges of marshes, but it does not grow in clumps like many other ferns, including royal ferns and ebony spleenworts.

The long, shallowly growing, and nearly black rhizomes are about ¹⁄₁₆ to ⅛ inch in diameter and frequently branch. Roots are black and wiry. Fronds of marsh ferns emerge singly along the rhizome, reach an erect height of 18 to 24 inches, and are 4 to 7 inches wide. Fronds are deciduous, dying back as winter approaches.

The species possesses both fertile and sterile fronds; the fertile fronds are slightly smaller than the sterile fronds. Fronds are pinnately compound and taper considerably toward the tip, but just slightly toward the base; fronds are widest just below the middle. Each frond has 14 to 20 pairs of pinnae arranged perpendicular to the central axis, and each pinna is deeply incised near the base but less so near the tips. Frond margins are entire or slightly toothed. Fronds are glabrous on both upper and lower surfaces. The central rachis possesses scattered hairs.

Marsh ferns produce sori on the underside of the fronds, about midway between the midvein and the margin of the pinnae. The edges of fertile fronds roll slightly and partially cover the sori.

Marsh fern prefers full sun but will tolerate light shade. It is most at home in wet soils without surface-standing water. It does not tolerate salt water; thus it occurs only in marshes interior to islands or freshwater tidal marshes.

Like most ferns, it does not serve as a major food source. Where marsh fern occurs, it usually forms a dense, nearly impenetrable cover and can outcompete other plants of similar size and stature. The dense colonial growth pattern creates prime cover for small wildlife in wetland sites.

Marsh ferns transplant easily. You can collect plants from the wild (with landowner permission) in early spring.

The variety *pubescens* is the most common form of marsh fern in the coastal Carolinas.

a b

5. Marsh fern (*Thelypteris palustris*). (a) In sun-filled wetlands, marsh fern grows in dense patches. Pinnately compound fronds emerge singly along a rhizome and grow from 18 to 24 inches high and from 4 to 7 inches wide at maturity. (b) Frond margins are entire or slightly toothed; they are glabrous on upper and lower surfaces, while the central rachis possesses scattered hairs.

Graminoids

6 LESSER QUAKING GRASS

Briza minor Linnaeus
Family: Poaceae (Grass)
Other Common Name: Little quaking grass
Range: Massachusetts south to Florida and
west to New Mexico
Habitat: Wetlands, open woodlands,
roadsides
Habit: Annual graminoid
Flowering/Fruiting Period: FL & FR April–
May
Wetland Status: FAC
Origin: Exotic; native to southern and
western Europe

a

Lesser quaking grass begins its annual
life cycle as a clump of anonymous grass
culms virtually indistinguishable from
nearby grasses. By the time it reaches its
full flowering and fruiting stages, the plant
exhibits its characteristic and unmistakable
heart-shaped clusters of spikelets that
"bobble" or "quake" in the slightest breeze;
hence, its common name.

Culms range from 3½ to 20 inches tall
and possess basal and cauline leaves that
have a characteristic slight twist. Leaf
blades have glabrous surfaces and are 2 to
5 inches long and ⅛ to ⅜ inch wide.

Flowering panicles are 2½ to 8 inches
tall and about 3 inches wide with 15 or
more laterally compressed, triangular
spikelets. Each spikelet is composed of 4 to
7 florets that dangle from thin branches
on open, spherical-shaped panicles. The
spikelets are pale green and white when
florets open. At maturity, the spikelets turn
tan or brown.

Lesser quaking grass grows well in moist
or dry sandy soil where competition from
other plants is low, such as in waste areas
and low-density plant communities. Full
sun endows the plant with its best growth.

The wildlife value of lesser quaking grass
is unknown, but it is likely that ground
birds such as mourning doves eat the tiny
seeds.

b

6. Lesser quaking grass (*Briza minor*). (a) Wind
creates a shimmering movement on a cluster
of lesser quaking grass plants growing in damp
environments. (b) Tiny, delicate spikelets dangle
from springy stalks and "quake" in the slightest
breeze.

7 DUNE SANDSPUR

Cenchrus tribuloides Linnaeus
Family: Poaceae (Grass)
Other Common Names: Sandspur, long-spine sandbur, sand-dune sandbur
Range: Coastal: New York south to Florida and west to Louisiana
Habitat: Dunes and maritime grasslands
Habit: Annual graminoid
Flowering/Fruiting Period: FL June–August; FR July–October
Wetland Status: FACU
Origin: Native

b

Nearly everyone who has stepped off a dune boardwalk or followed a narrow path through the dunes has probably encountered dune sandspur. Usually you feel their spines penetrate your skin before you actually see them. Because dune sandspur easily attaches to animal fur, clothing, and (unfortunately) skin, humans and animals effectively and efficiently disperse its seeds. As a result, dune sandspur is a common—sometimes dominant—plant near paths and other disturbed habitats in the dune environment.

While a few of the shorter culms of dune sandspur are erect and ascending, most culms are long, sprawling, decumbent, and

a

7. Dune sandspur (*Cenchrus tribuloides*). (a) Stems are often long and sprawling. (b) Anthers (tiny orange structures) are exserted in the flower. (c) Fruits become bristly as involucres expand and develop into formidable spines.

c

rooting at the nodes wherever their relaxed habit brings them into contact with moist soil. Culms range from 4 to 28 inches long and possess flat, glabrous leaf blades 1 to 5 inches long and ⅛ to ½ inch wide.

Flowers develop on a dense, spikelike raceme, ¾ to 3 inches long. As fruits mature, the subtending involucre expands to form an irregular ring of sharp bristles. This fruit is the familiar burr of dune sandspur. This species produces the largest burr of all of our native sandspur species, ranging from ¼ to ⅝ inch across.

Research shows that dune sandspur seeds float more than twice as long as those of other sandspur species common in more stable coastal habitats. Experimental removal of dune sandspur spines indicates that the large spines on seeds aid in wind dispersal and protect the seed from predation by crabs and other animals.

Dune sandspur requires full sun and tolerates occasional saltwater flooding. Typically found in dune environments with saltmeadow cordgrass and sea oats, dune sandspur is surprisingly effective in holding sand in place as it roots at the nodes.

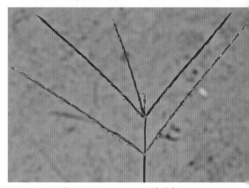

8. Crabgrass (*Digitaria sanguinalis*). (a) A common weed, crabgrass is prostrate and spreading. (b) Flowers are produced on 3 to 9 racemes at the end of an ascending culm.

8 CRABGRASS

Digitaria sanguinalis (Linnaeus) Scopoli
Family: Poaceae (Grass)
Other Common Names: Hairy crabgrass, northern crabgrass, purple crabgrass
Range: Essentially all of North America except the high Arctic
Habitat: Roadsides, fields, lawns, gardens, and waste areas
Habit: Annual graminoid
Flowering/Fruiting Period: FL & FR July–October
Wetland Status: FACU
Origin: Exotic; native to Europe; naturalized over an extensive part of North America

Considered a weedy plant over much of its range, crabgrass is a highly opportunistic plant that typically spreads aggressively in waste areas where competition from other plants is low. Based on gardeners' experience with this plant, one is not surprised to learn that a single plant can produce thousands of seeds per year, and those seeds can remain viable in the soil for many years. Frost usually terminates this annual plant's growth in the fall.

Crabgrass is a coarse, prostrate plant that expands in a wide spreading pattern. When culm nodes touch the soil, they root easily. The additional water and nutrients absorbed by the abundant fibrous roots produced at each node allow this plant to survive in dry and nutrient-poor soils.

Crabgrass leaves are 1 to 8 inches long, ⅛ to ½ inch wide, and densely hairy on both surfaces. Leaves are light green when young and mature to a darker green.

Wind-pollinated flowers are produced on slightly ascending culms. Each inflorescence is composed of 3 to 9 fingerlike racemes that appear whorled at the top of a long stem. Highly variable in size, each raceme ranges in length from ¾ to 5½ inches. Two rows of light green to greenish-brown, one-flowered spikelets are crowded on one side of the raceme. Fruits turn purple at maturity and release ¹⁄₁₆-inch-long shiny, brown seeds.

Crabgrass grows best in moist to dry sandy soils and full sun. It is tolerant of salty soil and salt aerosols; thus, it is a common plant of the Carolinas coastal area.

Songbirds and ground birds eat crabgrass seeds. Small herbivores, including rabbits, occasionally eat the foliage.

A close relative of crabgrass, fonio, produces tiny seeds that are harvested, toasted, and ground into flour.

9 ANNUAL BLUEGRASS
Poa annua Linnaeus
Family: Poaceae (Grass)
Other Common Names: Speargrass, six-weeks grass
Range: Throughout North America
Habitat: Disturbed areas, roadsides, lawns
Habit: Annual graminoid
Flowering/Fruiting Period: FL & FR April–May
Wetland Status: FACU
Origin: Exotic; native to Europe

Because it is a poor competitor with established plants, annual bluegrass is a common colonizer on the edges of paths in dunes, roadsides, and other disturbed sites. It is a cool-weather annual, and by

9. Annual bluegrass (*Poa annua*). (a) Annual bluegrass is an open, loosely tufted plant that grows close to the soil surface. Leaf blades are ½ to 4 inches long and ¹⁄₁₆ to ⅛ inch wide. (b) Producing large numbers of flowering heads, spikelets usually possess 3 or 4 flowers, here with prominent anthers.

GRAMINOIDS

spring, the grass resumes rapid growth and begins flowering within a few weeks. The plant ranges from 1½ to 12 inches tall. It possesses both erect and decumbent bright green stems. It often roots at the nodes. The glabrous, mostly basal leaf blades are ½ to 4 inches long and 1/16 to 1/8 inch wide. Leaf blades are folded lengthwise when young and have a slight wrinkle at the base of each leaf.

Individual plants produce a large number of flowering heads. The inflorescence is pyramidal shaped, varying from ¾ to 4 inches long. Individual spikelets produce 3 to 4 wind-pollinated flowers.

Reproduction is only through seeds. The seeds are brownish-yellow grains shed as soon as they reach maturity. A single plant may produce as many as 300 seeds. Seeds remain viable after passing through the digestive tracts of animals and may live as long as 6 years in the soil seedbank.

Annual bluegrass grows well in moist, nutrient-poor soils but requires full sun for best growth. The plant is moderately tolerant of salt aerosols.

Annual bluegrass serves as an early-season seed source for seed-eating birds. White-tailed deer graze the plant.

c

9. Annual bluegrass (*Poa annua*). (c) Large stigmas capture pollen distributed by the wind.

early summer plants of annual bluegrass have disappeared from the landscape. Annual bluegrass tolerates a wide range of climatic conditions, so one can likely find the plant from the poles to the tropics. Horticulturalists consider it a weed species in the coastal Carolinas.

Annual bluegrass is an open, loosely tufted plant with dense, fibrous roots. It germinates in early fall and overwinters in a vegetative state. With the arrival of

10 RABBITSFOOT GRASS

Polypogon monspeliensis (Linnaeus) Desfontaines

Family: Poaceae (Grass)

Other Common Names: Annual rabbitsfoot grass, annual beardgrass

Range: Throughout North America except for the Ohio River Valley and the Canadian Maritime Provinces

Habitat: Coastal: freshwater and brackish marshes; disturbed areas

Habit: Annual graminoid

Flowering/Fruiting Period: FL May–June; FR June–July

Wetland Status: FACW

Origin: Exotic; native to Europe

a

c

b

10. Rabbitsfoot grass (*Polypogon monspeliensis*).
(a) This plant's height varies from 4 to 30 inches.
Leaf blades are flat, 2 to 8 inches long, and
about ⅓ inch wide. (b) Flowers are produced
on a dense, spikelike panicle 1 to 3 inches long.
(c) Fruiting heads begin to form a more open
panicle with scores of seeds.

Rabbitsfoot grass occurs in moist, sunny
areas near the shoreline of freshwater and
brackish marshes. It derives its name from
its soft, bristly inflorescence reminiscent of
a rabbit's foot.

Rabbitsfoot grass is a tufted grass with
erect or sometimes decumbent culms.
When decumbent, it may root along its
lower nodes. Plant size is highly variable; it
ranges from 4 to 30 inches tall. Leaves are
glabrous or slightly hairy. Leaf blades are
flat and no more than ⅓ inch wide and 2 to
8 inches long.

The species produces wind-pollinated
flowers in dense, spikelike, oblong panicles,
1 to 3 inches long and 1 inch wide. Each
spikelet in the inflorescence has a single
flower. The flowers change from bright
green to grayish-white at maturity.

Like many weedy plants, rabbitsfoot
grass produces large quantities of seeds.
Resembling a grain of wheat, each golden
yellow seed is about 1/16 inch long and
scored with minute horizontal grooves.

Rabbitsfoot grass does not grow well in

GRAMINOIDS

135

competition with other plants, preferring damp, sparsely vegetated sites. It grows best in full sun. Salt-aerosol and saltwater tolerance is modest.

While it is not an important wildlife plant, several species of birds eat the seeds.

Collect seeds at maturity in late spring and sow in the fall to assure that dormancy is broken over the winter.

The species contributes to the spring pollen count and may aggravate asthma and hay fever.

---

11 GIANT FOXTAIL GRASS

Setaria magna Grisebach
Family: Poaceae (Grass)
Other Common Names: Saltmarsh foxtail grass, giant bristlegrass
Range: Coastal: New Jersey to Florida and west to Texas
Habitat: Dune swales, edges of brackish and freshwater marshes, and wet disturbed areas
Habit: Annual graminoid
Flowering/Fruiting Period: FL & FR August–October
Wetland Status: FACW
Origin: Native

Giant foxtail grass is a robust, unmistakable, and beautiful grass when in full flower. Ranging up to 10 feet or taller, its flowering heads stand higher than any other grass with which it is associated, and the graceful, arching inflorescence of long, bristled flowers resembles its namesake, a fox's tail.

Coarse, erect, flat stems may sometimes

11. Giant foxtail grass (*Setaria magna*). (a) This species is an unmistakable member of coastal wetland communities, ranging up to 10 feet tall or more with rough-surfaced leaf blades 20 to 24 inches long and 2 inches wide. (b) The flowering spike is cylindrical and 8 to 18 inches tall with bright green, bristly spikelets. Male and female reproductive parts are visible during flowering time. (c) Spikelet bristles turn brown as they mature.

be 1 inch across, with prop roots growing from nodes close to the ground. Leaf blades are 20 to 24 inches long and 2 inches wide. Both the upper and lower leaf surfaces feel rough to the touch.

The inflorescences are cylindrical spikes at the end of tall culms, ranging from 8 to 18 inches long and ½ to 1 inch wide. The heads are composed of dozens of bright green, bristly spikelets that turn brown as the seeds mature and eventually fall from the inflorescence.

The plant grows best in full sun and requires moist to wet soils. It tolerates standing water for considerable periods. This species is associated with a wide range of wetland plants, including common cattail and saltmeadow cordgrass.

Seeds are an important source of food for game birds, marsh birds, and waterfowl. White-tailed deer and muskrat eat the young shoots of giant foxtail.

Propagate giant foxtail grass by harvesting seeds in the fall and stratifying them at 40°F for 6 weeks. Bury seeds just below the soil surface and maintain moisture until germination is complete.

Use giant foxtail grass in large natural landscape units that are nearly continuously moist, such as pond margins or freshwater to brackish marshes.

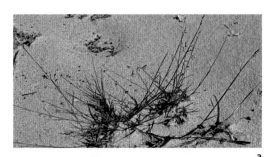

a

b

12. Purple sandgrass (*Triplasis purpurea*). (a) This fine, delicate annual plant with leaves tinged with purple typically remains small and prostrate, but it may grow up to 26 inches high while flowering. (b) Purple-tinged spikelets terminate the widely spreading plant. Prominent purple anthers dangle from tiny flowers.

12 PURPLE SANDGRASS

Triplasis purpurea (Walter) Chapman
Family: Poaceae (Grass)
Range: Coastal: southern Maine south to Florida and west to Texas; also, the Great Lakes states and scattered inland states
Habitat: Dunes, dune swales, sandy waste places, roadsides
Habit: Annual graminoid
Flowering/Fruiting Period: FL & FR August–October
Wetland Status: UPL
Origin: Native

Purple sandgrass is a common plant of dunes in the coastal Carolinas. This annual grass germinates in late spring, and by fall it dominates large areas of open, sparsely vegetated dunes.

This grass possesses culms ascending and spreading from a shallow but extensive root system. When mature, purple sandgrass reaches a height of 12 to 26 inches (rarely larger). The leaves are flat or slightly inrolled and ¹⁄₁₆ to ⅛ inch wide

GRAMINOIDS

137

and 1½ to 3 inches long. Despite thriving on coastal dune sands, purple sandgrass is only moderately tolerant of salt aerosols. Research indicates that intense salt aerosols reduce plant size and reproductive output in purple sandgrass.

The 1- to 2-inch-long, purple-tinged spikelets terminate each widely spreading stem. Purple sandgrass exhibits growth strategies that allow it to flourish in the mobile dune environment. When the plant is buried several inches, its survival is high and growth is stimulated. In addition, seedlings can emerge from seeds buried up to 1½ inches deep.

Birds likely feed on the abundant seeds in the late summer and fall.

Purple sandgrass grows best in open, sandy areas where competition for space and nutrients is not severe. Thus, in a natural garden, the plant should be located away from potentially competing plants. There is no commercial source for this species; collect seeds from mature plants in the fall.

The variety *purpurea* is the common form of purple sandgrass in the coastal Carolinas.

13. American beachgrass (*Ammophila breviligulata*). (a) Culms trap moving sand and build dunes throughout the growing season.

13 AMERICAN BEACHGRASS

Ammophila breviligulata Fernald
Family: Poaceae (Grass)
Other Common Names: Coastal beach-grass, beach grass, American marram
Range: Newfoundland and Labrador, Canada; west through the Great Lakes states; coastal: Maine to South Carolina; also British Columbia, Canada, south to California
Habitat: Wrack lines and dunes
Habit: Perennial graminoid
Flowering/Fruiting Period: FL & FR July–October
Wetland Status: UPL
Origin: Native

American beachgrass is the major native plant colonizing the Atlantic coast from Maine to northern North Carolina and the shorelines of the Great Lakes. It occupies an ecological niche similar to that of sea oats in the coastal Carolinas south of Cape Hatteras. The cool-season grass spreads rapidly, creating high, wide, and stable dunes when and where sand is abundant. American beachgrass plants thrive when buried; rhizomes extend both horizontally and vertically, and culms multiply quickly, a characteristic shared with sea oats. Research demonstrates that American beachgrass survives sand burial up to 14 inches per year. Also, signs of plant vigor, such as the number of culms and the height of the plant, are greatest where sand accumulates rapidly.

One- to 3-foot-tall clumps of narrow leaves arise from rhizomes that can extend up to 10 feet per year under ideal

b 13. American beachgrass (*Ammophila breviligulata*). (b) Large anthers are visible on this flowering spike. (c) The mature fruiting structure contains numerous appressed spikelets.

conditions. Tillering generates many leaves, with each leaf blade ranging from ¼ to ⅜ inch wide and inrolled, especially toward the tip of the leaf. This inrolling reduces the plant's exposure to high heat, intense sunlight, and desiccating winds—all distinctive environmental conditions of coastal environments.

Dense, yellowish, cylindrical flowering spikes, up to 12 inches long, emerge in late summer. These spikes, which often rise a foot or more above the leaves, contain numerous spikelets. Each spikelet possesses one wind-pollinated flower. American beachgrass rarely produces

flowering spikes in southern North Carolina and South Carolina where coastal managers and homeowners have planted the species extensively beyond its natural ecological range. Even within its natural range, seed production is low and unreliable. American beachgrass reproduces primarily through rhizome extension and redistribution of clumps detached from parent plants by erosion.

The extensive root and rhizome system of American beachgrass makes it an excellent plant to stabilize the coastal sands, and when used in mixed plantings of several dune species, it is an excellent plant for stimulating dune growth. In a few years, sea oats naturally replaces American beachgrass as the dominant dune grass in these mixed plantings along the Carolinas coast.

American beachgrass grows best in well-drained, sandy soils and full sun. The plant tolerates salt aerosols and drought well, but summer heat limits its southward range. One of the most studied plants, it is susceptible to damage by off-road vehicles, heavy recreational use, and grazing by horses.

Horticulturalists have developed two major cultivars. *Cape* was cultivated for planting on dunes in the northeastern United States, and *Hatteras* is best adapted for North Carolina and South Carolina dunes. Plant American beachgrass in mid- to late fall in the Carolinas. Plugs are available from nurseries that specialize in growing dune plants.

14 MARITIME BUSHY BLUESTEM

Andropogon tenuispatheus (Nash) Nash
Family: Poaceae (Grass)
Other Common Names: Bushy beargrass, bushy broomgrass, bushy broom-sedge
Range: Southeastern Virginia west to Oklahoma and California, south to Florida and Texas

GRAMINOIDS

139

a

c

b

14. Maritime bushy bluestem (*Andropogon tenuispatheus*). (a) This midsummer-growing plant has narrow, erect culms and fibrous roots. (b) Early fall flowering head nears maturity. (c) Late fall seed heads bear hundreds of seeds poised for wind dispersal.

Habitat: Maritime grasslands, interdune swales, edges of brackish and tidal marshes and maritime shrub thickets; also moist, disturbed areas
Habit: Perennial graminoid
Flowering/Fruiting Period: FL & FR September–November
Wetland Status: FACW
Origin: Native
An inconspicuous grass for much of the year, the bright tan—sometimes nearly orange—leaves and large, fluffy inflorescence make this plant stand out on maritime grasslands and the edges of brackish marsh margins during late fall and early winter. At the time of seed dispersal, the silvery fruiting head expands

dramatically and appears like the bristles of a large artist's paintbrush.

Maritime bushy bluestem is an herbaceous bunchgrass with narrow, erect culms reaching a height of 4 feet. The plant has extensive, fibrous roots capable of supporting the grass during extended drought. Leaves are basal and alternately arranged. Leaf sheaths are flattened and overlapping; leaf blades are 4 to 12 inches long and ⅛ to ¼ inch wide.

Silvery inflorescences are dense, producing purplish-yellow seeds in abundance; a single flowering culm contributes as many as 500 seeds. Attached to each seed is a wispy, ½-inch awn that aids in wind dispersal. Seeds germinate on bare soil, and periodic environmental disturbance maintains the plant in abundance in the coastal Carolinas.

Maritime bushy bluestem grows in full sun and thrives in soils with low nutrients. It dies back completely during the winter, leaving only a stand of dried, reddish-tan culms and empty flower heads.

Birds and small mammals use the plant for cover and nesting and may occasionally eat the seeds.

Propagate maritime bushy bluestem from seeds or by simple plant division. Bag the large seed heads near maturity to collect seeds before they disperse. Seeds also may be commercially available. The plant is useful as a striking coastal ornamental.

15 SALTMARSH BULRUSH

Bolboschoenus robustus (Pursh) Soják
Family: Cyperaceae (Sedge)
Other Common Names: Seacoast bulrush, sturdy bulrush, stout bulrush
Range: Coastal: Nova Scotia, Canada; New Hampshire south to Florida and west to Texas; also California
Habitat: Brackish marshes

Habit: Perennial graminoid
Flowering/Fruiting Period: FL May–June; FR July–September
Wetland Status: OBL
Origin: Native

Scientists have noted a reduction in the geographical distribution and ecological range of saltmarsh bulrush owing to the invasion of common reed in salt marshes along the East Coast of the United States, especially in the New England area. With the recent aggressive expansion of common reed into the Carolinas coastal marshes, this region may see a similar reduction.

This coarse plant with tuberous rhizomes grows to 4 feet tall in brackish and salt marshes. The thick culms are sharply 3-angled in cross section. Leaves arise about halfway up the culms, a characteristic distinguishing this species from other bulrush species. Leaf blades are ¼ to ½ inch wide and up to 30 inches long.

The inflorescence is composed of 3 to 15 cylindrical spikelets. Each orange-brown, ½-inch-long spikelet is either sessile or on a short pedicel, and the entire inflorescence is subtended by 2 or 3 large bracts. Fruits are medium to dark brown, ovoid, glossy achenes covered by a waxy coat. The waxy coating aids the seeds in floating on the water surface.

Plants tolerate periodic flooding up to 3 feet deep. Species often associated with saltmarsh bulrush include smooth cordgrass, giant cordgrass, and narrow-leaved cattail.

Saltmarsh bulrush is an important food for muskrats, ducks, geese, and other waterbirds as well as an important plant for nesting and resting birds. This species should receive major consideration any time you contemplate planting vegetation to enhance waterfowl habitat.

Propagation of saltmarsh bulrush is by

division of the rhizomes and seeds. Seeds germinate readily after falling from the plant. Similarly, rhizomes grow well after division and replanting.

This species is cited as *Scirpus robustus* in legacy literature of the coastal Carolinas.

a

15. Saltmarsh bulrush (*Bolboschoenus robustus*). (a) Mature plants stand 3 to 4 feet tall in brackish and salt marshes. (b) Styles and stigmas are visible on flower heads. (c) At maturity, these ripe spikelets "shatter" and release glossy, dark brown seeds called achenes.

16 SAW GRASS

Cladium jamaicense Crantz
Family: Cyperaceae (Sedge)
Other Common Name: Swamp sawgrass
Range: Virginia south to Florida and west
    to Texas and New Mexico
Habitat: Coastal brackish and freshwater
    marshes; also wet pine forests
Habit: Perennial graminoid
Flowering/Fruiting Period: FL June–August;
    FR August–October
Wetland Status: OBL
Origin: Native

Technically a sedge, saw grass is best
known as the omnipresent and principal
herbaceous plant of the Everglades. It
is the plant Marjory Stoneman Douglas
wrote about so eloquently in her classic
ecology book about the Everglades, *River
of Grass*. In the coastal Carolinas, saw grass

16. Saw grass (*Cladium jamaicense*). (a) Saw
grass forms extensive swaths in brackish
and freshwater marshes. (b) Large flower
inflorescences develop on tall spikes well above
potential flooding water. (c) Each inflorescence is
composed of scores of chestnut brown spikelets.

is an indicator species of brackish water and mucky, organic-rich soil conditions in marshes influenced by the tides.

A coarse plant reaching a height of 6 feet, saw grass typically forms large, dense, monospecific patches in brackish and freshwater marshes. Saw grass secures its place in these marshes through colonization and then extensive growth of stout rhizomes. The culms of saw grass are hollow and 3-angled, characteristics consistent with its plant family, the Sedges. Leaf blades are tough, flat to broadly V-shaped, ½ to ¾ inch wide, and about 3 feet long. Its common name, saw grass, is derived from the fact that the margins and underside midvein of the leaves possess sharp teeth not unlike those of a saw blade. Visible without magnification, these teeth are strong and sharp enough to cut bare skin easily.

The inflorescences of saw grass develop on a tall spike. The entire flowering stem is 1 to 1½ feet long and composed of drooping spikelets in groups of 2 or 3. Spikelets are narrowly ellipsoid and chestnut brown. Fruits are light greenish-brown, glossy achenes, ¹⁄₁₆ inch long, and appear wrinkled toward the base.

Saw grass grows well in full sun and in nutrient-poor, mucky soils high in organic matter. It withstands inundation with fresh or brackish water but is less tolerant of inundation by full-strength seawater. Saw grass cannot survive prolonged drought, and it is sensitive to changes in the hydrologic regime. When the flooding period or the salinity changes, saw grass quickly dies, and other species replace it. For example, if flooding increases, common cattail, pickerelweed (*Pontederia cordata*), and waterlily (*Nymphaea odorata*) increase; if flooding decreases, common wax myrtle, sea myrtle, dune hairgrass, and giant foxtail grass increase.

Saw grass provides food and shelter for raccoons, minks, and otters as well as ducks and other waterbirds.

Propagation is by seeds and plant division. Under natural field conditions, seedling establishment is rare, despite considerable seed production by the species.

Use saw grass in damp natural landscapes and for habitat restoration. It is available from native plant nurseries.

---

17 PAMPAS GRASS

Cortaderia selloana (J. A. & J. H. Schultes)
   Ascherson & Graebner
Family: Poaceae (Grass)
Other Common Names: Silver pampas
   grass, Uruguayan pampas grass
Range: USDA Hardiness Zones 8–10
Habitat: Ornamental
Habit: Perennial graminoid
Flowering/Fruiting Period: FL & FR
   August–October
Wetland Status: FACU
Origin: Exotic; native to Brazil, Chile,
   Uruguay, and Argentina
Not recommended for planting; instead, remove where already growing.

Named for Argentina's signature grassland biome, the pampas, this large tussock grass was introduced into the United States as an ornamental plant. Today, it is a landscape plant found throughout the world. The South Carolina Exotic Pest Plant Council lists pampas grass as a "significant threat" in the coastal plain of South Carolina. In North Carolina, plants have spread into dunes well beyond their original landscape planting sites. Landscapers dislike this plant. It seems to attract vermin such as snakes that scare the life out of you when you are working in or around the plant!

A fast-growing species, pampas grass is recognized by its large size; its tall, "feather duster" flowering heads; and its fountainlike growth habit. Within a few

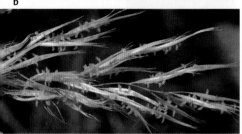

c 17. Pampas grass (*Cortaderia selloana*). (a) Pampas grass's attractive growth appears like a fountain with "feather dusters." (b) Featherlike stigmas are easily seen close-up on female flowers. (c) Anthers are visible on male plant flowers.

plumes persist into the winter, gradually losing their billowy shape and texture as seeds are shed. Pampas grass is a prolific seed producer; botanists have reported that a single plant can produce hundreds of thousands of seeds in its lifetime. Seeds are wind dispersed and can drift for miles on wind currents.

Pampas grass prefers well-drained, fertile soils but will tolerate a range of soil conditions from dry to wet. Growth suffers if the plant is cultivated in environments with frequent periods of standing water. The plant is salt-aerosol and drought tolerant. It prefers full sun, but it will grow under light shade.

Pampas grass has little wildlife value beyond providing cover for small animals.

Interestingly, Hawaiian landscapers first recognized the invasive nature of pampas grass. Only after horticulturalists introduced male plants to the state did the species form viable seeds and begin to invade new habitats.

A similar species (also introduced into the United States) is purple pampas grass (*Cortaderia jubata*), which differs from pampas grass in the height of its flowering culms. In contrast to pampas grass, the gap between the cascade of leaves and the flowering plumes in purple pampas grass is as much as 12 inches.

years after planting, a single plant can reach 12 feet high and 8 feet across. The bluish- or glaucous green leaves are ½ to ¾ inch wide and up to 10 feet long with razor-sharp serrated edges. The leaves fold at the midrib and possess distinctive curly, tapered tips.

Pampas grass is dioecious, with male and female plants needed to produce viable seeds. The flowering heads are about 12 inches long on erect culms that grow just a few inches above the cascade of leaves. Flower heads vary from light tan to silvery-white and pale violet. Like most grasses, its flowers are wind pollinated. The flowering

18 BERMUDAGRASS

Cynodon dactylon (Linnaeus) Persoon
Family: Poaceae (Grass)
Other Common Names: Devilgrass, dog's tooth grass, wire grass
Range: New Hampshire west to Kansas and Washington; south to California, Texas, and Florida
Habitat: Dunes; also waste areas, roadsides, lawns, fields, and pastures
Habit: Perennial graminoid
Flowering/Fruiting Period: FL & FR May–October

GRAMINOIDS

a

b

c

18. Bermudagrass (*Cynodon dactylon*). (a) Light
green to gray-green, narrow leaves characterize
Bermudagrass, an important lawn grass.
Flowering culms have 4 to 7 spikes, each with a
line of tightly appressed spikelets. (b) In sandy
soils, rhizomes grow profusely. (c) Large anthers
and stigmas aid in wind pollination.

Wetland Status: FACU

Origin: Exotic; native area disputed; possibly originated from tropical Africa, the Indo-Malaysian area, and India

Bermudagrass is a highly invasive, highly competitive, fine-leaved, mat-forming grass that tends to thrive in severely disturbed areas and exposed sites. Originally imported as a pasture grass, Bermudagrass became an important grass in the United States in the nineteenth century. The geographic origin of Bermudagrass is obscure because today it is so common in tropical and subtropical regions worldwide.

Bermudagrass is a creeping, warm-season grass that expands through hard, scaly rhizomes and flat stolons. The rhizomes and roots penetrate soil up to 24 inches and help this plant survive severe drought conditions. Stolons rooting at the nodes are responsible for the local spread of the plant. Bermudagrass is normally 2 to 6 inches tall but can reach 16 inches under ideal conditions. The leaves are light green to gray-green, flat, ½ to 6 inches long, and 1/16 to 1/8 inch wide. They are glabrous or sparsely pubescent with rough edges.

Flowering culms are erect with 4 to 7 whorled spikes. Each spike is ¾ to 2½ inches long with 2 rows of tightly appressed spikelets. The wind-pollinated Bermudagrass flowers through the entire length of the growing season. Seeds are tiny, less than 1/16 inch long.

Propagation is by seeds and plant division. Seeds have no dormancy period and germinate immediately after they mature. They are available commercially; however, most landscapers use sod to establish coastal lawns.

Bermudagrass requires full sun; it fails to grow in shaded conditions. The plant thrives when the temperature approaches 100°F, and it can tolerate nutrient-poor soils well. Adapted to coastal environmental conditions, Bermudagrass can survive inundation by fresh and brackish water, and it can grow from rhizomes buried by several inches of sand. While it is salt-aerosol tolerant, Bermudagrass growth slows in continuously elevated soil salinity. Bermudagrass is not cold-hardy, and this limits its distribution. We rarely find it where winter temperatures drop much below 0°F.

The plant provides forage for white-tailed deer, ducks, and geese.

Bermudagrass may displace native species unless its expansion is held in check. Unfortunately, few herbicides control the plant. More than 80 countries have declared it a nuisance weed in cropland.

Bermudagrass is a highly variable and plastic species, and numerous cultivars have been developed for specific purposes, such as lawns, putting greens, and pastures.

19 SALTGRASS

Distichlis spicata (Linnaeus) Greene

Family: Poaceae (Grass)

Other Common Names: Seashore saltgrass, spike grass

Range: Throughout North America except Alaska, West Virginia, Kentucky, Tennessee, Indiana, and Arkansas

Habitat: Coastal: brackish and salt marshes, salt pannes, maritime grasslands, and dredge deposit environments

Habit: Perennial graminoid

Flowering/Fruiting Period: FL & FR June–October

Wetland Status: OBL

Origin: Native

Like smooth cordgrass and black needlerush, saltgrass often forms a near-monoculture in a band or strip along the mean tide level in a marsh. Saltgrass may be mistaken for seashore dropseed in

19. Saltgrass (*Distichlis spicata*). (a) Saltgrass possesses both rhizomes and stolons and grows in dense patches in tidal marshes. Leaves on the culms are narrow and arranged in a distichous (two-ranked) pattern. (b) Stigmas are visible on female flowers. (c) Anthers dangle outside each male flower (*right*).

South Carolina where both species occur. Saltgrass tends to have a finer texture and usually grows taller than seashore dropseed, a species common on foredunes and salt marshes. Because of its value as a forage plant, saltgrass hay was fed to livestock by colonial-era farmers.

Saltgrass is a pale greenish-white, warm-season grass. The plant produces a dense network of rhizomes 4 to 10 inches below the surface; occasionally it produces stolons that extend across the marsh surface. Extensive aerenchyma tissue in its roots and stems allows saltgrass to exchange gases between the atmosphere and the roots under the low-oxygen conditions found in water-saturated soils. Culms are usually erect but occasionally lie over, forming large "cowlicks" in a manner similar to that observed in saltmeadow cordgrass. Culms range from 6 to 18 inches tall; the shortest dominate higher-salinity environments. Leaves are arranged in a distichous pattern (the Greek term *distichos*, meaning "two-ranked," is the derivation of the genus name *Distichlis*). Leaves are about 4 inches long and ¼ inch wide with a pointed tip. The leaves are often inrolled, especially during extended droughts. Saltgrass exudes salts that accumulate in the leaves through specialized two-celled glands found on both the upper and lower leaf surfaces. You can see and feel (and taste!) the salt crystals by running your fingers along the length of a leaf.

Saltgrass is dioecious, with separate male and female plants. The flowering inflorescences are loosely packed panicles, 2 to 2½ inches long, and composed of numerous yellowish-tan, wind-pollinated spikelets; male inflorescences have more spikelets than the female. Each laterally flattened spikelet has from 3 to 10 flowers. Seeds are ¹⁄₁₆-inch, smooth, oval-shaped nutlets. Seeds are usually water dispersed; however, birds and wind also aid seed dispersal.

Saltgrass grows best in ⅓- to ½-strength seawater, but it can survive in soils saturated with more than full-strength seawater. Saltgrass is drought tolerant and grows well in full sun. The tangle of saltgrass rhizomes and roots forms dense, organic mats that resist erosion. Saltgrass grows in association with saltmeadow cordgrass, black needlerush, sea ox-eye, sea lavender, Virginia glasswort, and southern saltmarsh fleabane.

Ducks and geese eat the seeds of saltgrass. Swards provide nesting sites and nesting material for marsh-dwelling animals. Decomposition of saltgrass releases organic matter and nutrients to marsh organisms.

Saltgrass produces many seeds, but the germination rate is low. The simplest propagation is from rhizome sections planted any time of the year. Transplantation success is lower than that of other marsh plants.

20 SALTMARSH WILD RYE

Elymus virginicus Linnaeus
Family: Poaceae (Grass)
Other Common Names: Virginia wild rye, wild rye grass
Range: North America east of the Rocky Mountains, excluding the high Arctic
Habitat: Brackish and salt marshes, maritime forests, dune swales; also streambanks and open woodlands
Habit: Perennial graminoid
Flowering/Fruiting Period: FL & FR June–August
Wetland Status: FAC
Origin: Native

The tall, erect, unbranched saltmarsh wild rye is present in a variety of coastal Carolina habitats, usually growing in clumps from a small root crown with dense, fibrous roots. When it flowers, it reaches a height ranging from 2½ to 4 feet.

Leaves are present along the entire culm of the plant from the ground to the flowering head. They are a bright green to glaucous green but frequently turn brown and die about the time the seeds mature. Leaf blades are ½ inch wide, up to 12 inches long, and typically inrolled, especially if the plant is under drought stress.

Sessile spikelets are densely arranged in pairs on a spike, and these spikes range from 2 to 6 inches tall. Each spikelet has 2 or 3 florets with conspicuous awns up to 1 inch long. The florets are wind pollinated.

a 20. Saltmarsh wild rye (*Elymus virginicus*).
(a) This plant produces fruits that are superficially similar to our food crops wheat and rye. (b) The flowering head is bright green after anthesis. (c) Mature flowering spikes are brown with conspicuous awns up to 1 inch long.

b

c

Saltmarsh wild rye prefers light, sandy soils and is drought tolerant. The plant is most robust in full sun or light shade.

Seeds serve as a good wildfowl food, especially when the plant grows near the water's edge. Numerous herbivorous insects feed on the culms and leaves. White-tailed deer may browse the foliage; the plant is highly nutritive when young, but palatability declines as the plant matures.

Propagation of saltmarsh wild rye is by seeds. Plant seeds of this cool-season grass in the fall.

Seeds are available from specialty nurseries, but these may not necessarily be the coastal variety of this species. Saltmarsh wild rye is particularly effective as a soil stabilizer in environments with moist soils.

Botanists recognize the variety *halophilus* as typically found in brackish marshes, maritime forests, and hammocks in the northeastern United States. Its native range reaches North Carolina but not as far south as South Carolina.

21 FIELD LOVEGRASS

Eragrostis elliottii S. Watson
Family: Poaceae (Grass)
Other Common Name: Elliott's lovegrass
Range: Coastal: North Carolina south to Florida and west to Texas
Habitat: Dunes, dune swales, and maritime grasslands
Habit: Perennial graminoid
Flowering/Fruiting Period: FL & FR August–October
Wetland Status: FACW
Origin: Native

Field lovegrass grows inconspicuously in the secondary dunes and slacks throughout

a

b

21. Field lovegrass (*Eragrostis elliottii*). (a) At maturity, the dark purple flowering panicles exceed the length of the leaves. (b) Individual spikelets are about ¼ inch long and contain 10 to 30 florets.

the spring and early summer. In late summer, however, the plant announces its presence as it produces 1- to 2-foot-tall, diffuse, flowering panicles, each with hundreds of tiny purple spikelets.

Field lovegrass is a fine-textured, warm-season grass that can grow up to 2 feet high and 2 feet wide. It possesses bluish-green foliage with leaf blades ranging from 3 to 12 inches long and ⅛ to ¼ inch wide. As fall approaches, the leaves gradually turn deep purple or brownish-purple.

Each spikelet is about ¼ inch long and contains 10 to 30 florets. As seeds mature, the panicle gradually fades to a light tan. It remains attached to the plant until winter winds break the panicle away from the plant, and it tumbles across the dunes and lodges against other dune plants.

Field lovegrass prefers dry, sandy soils in full sun. It is tolerant of drought conditions and intense salt aerosols.

Field lovegrass makes a good specimen or accent plant. When it is grown in a small cluster, the fall foliage and flowering heads are conspicuous and arresting. Cultivars of field lovegrass are available from commercial growers. *Wind Dancer* and *Tallahassee Sunset* are examples. The plant has no serious insect pests.

Purple lovegrass (*Eragrostis spectabilis*) is a similar species found in the coastal Carolinas. Purple lovegrass possesses short, thick rhizomes.

22 CENTIPEDE GRASS

Eremochloa ophiuroides (Munro) Hackel
Family: Poaceae (Grass)
Range: Coastal: Virginia south to Florida and west to Texas; also Arkansas and Tennessee
Habitat: Dunes, lawns, and roadsides
Habit: Perennial graminoid
Flowering/Fruiting Period: FL & FR August–October
Wetland Status: UPL

GRAMINOIDS

151

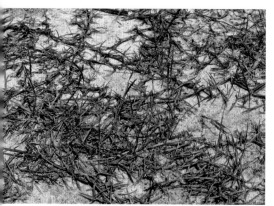

a 22. Centipede grass (*Eremochloa ophiuroides*). (a) Centipede grass usually forms long, crisscrossed runners across sparsely vegetated dunes—often adjacent to existing centipede lawns. (b) Flowering spikes (with dark purple anthers and light purple stigmas) develop on the plant throughout the summer.

Origin: Exotic; native to Southeast Asia (China)

Centipede grass is a slow-growing, coarse-textured, warm-season grass introduced into the southeastern United States in 1916. It is common in many mature dune systems and is probably an escape from cultivated lawns on developed shorelines. The plant spreads over the dunes, forming a loose network of shallowly rooted stolons that root at the nodes.

The alternately arranged leaves are folded in half lengthwise as they begin to grow, but they flatten out as they mature. The glabrous leaves are ½ to 1¼ inches long and ⅛ to ¼ inch wide.

A prolific seed producer, the purplish-brown flowering head of centipede grass is a solitary, terminal raceme about 1¼ to 2½ inches long on a 3- to 5-inch slightly flattened spike. The raceme may be straight or slightly curved. The spikelets are paired and appressed to the flowering stalk. The oval seeds are about 1⁄16 inch long.

Centipede grass is drought tolerant but not as salt tolerant as St. Augustine grass or Bermudagrass. It is adapted to low nutrients and sandy, somewhat acidic soils. It grows best in full sun but will grow in lightly shaded sites. It does not tolerate heavy foot traffic or compaction well. Centipede grass grows more slowly than Bermudagrass. Stolons growing at the ground surface are easier to remove than the deep rhizomes of Bermudagrass.

Propagate centipede grass using seeds, sprigs, plugs, or pieces of sod. Seeds do not require stratification. Available cultivars include *Oklawn*, a drought- and cold-resistant variety, and *Tennessee Hardy*, a cold-tolerant variety. Its northward range expansion is limited by low winter soil temperatures.

Centipede grass is often confused with St. Augustine grass; however, they can be distinguished by the leaf arrangement. St. Augustine grass has opposite leaves at each node.

a 23. Dune finger grass (*Eustachys petraea*). (a) This clumpy grass occurs commonly on mature dunes distant from the oceanfront. (b) Spikelet-lined racemes appear like fingers ascending from a common origin at the top of each flowering stalk. Anthers are visible over much of the flowering stalk; a few nearly transparent styles and stigmas may be visible in the lower left raceme.

23 DUNE FINGER GRASS

Eustachys petraea (Swartz) Desvaux
Family: Poaceae (Grass)
Range: North Carolina south to Florida and west to Texas
Habitat: Dunes, dune swales, and maritime grasslands
Habit: Perennial graminoid
Flowering/Fruiting Period: FL & FR June– October
Wetland Status: FACU
Origin: Native

In coastal dunes, this plant is a common component of the flora, preferring mature dunes located some distance from the ocean. Scientists are studying the ecology of dune finger grass to determine its suitability as a native turf grass as well as to determine its potential use as a cover for highway rights-of-way.

This stoloniferous bunchgrass is characterized by diffuse branching, rooting at the nodes, and flat leaf blades with keeled midribs. The light green to blue-

b

green leaves are glabrous, 4 to 8 inches long, and ⅛ to ¼ inch wide. The basal leaves, arranged in a distichous pattern, often root at the nodes.

The inflorescence possesses from 2 to 6 racemes, each 2 to 3 inches long with a double row of spikelets packed along one side of the raceme. Individual spikelets are ovate, laterally compressed, and about

¹⁄₁₆ inch long. The seed is an ellipsoid, yellowish- to dark brown caryopsis.

Dune finger grass is tolerant of heat, drought, wind, and salt aerosols. Plants commonly associated with this species are dune hairgrass, saltmeadow cordgrass, large-headed rush, common frogfruit, and southern seaside goldenrod.

Seeds may serve as a food source for ground birds, particularly mourning doves.

Propagate dune finger grass by seeds and simple plant division. Seeds germinate best if stratified for at least a month.

In legacy literature concerning coastal plants, this species is cited as *Chloris petraea*.

A closely related species, saltmarsh finger grass (*Eustachys glauca*), is common along the edges of salt marshes of South Carolina and occasionally in North Carolina.

a

24 SALTMARSH FIMBRISTYLIS

Fimbristylis castanea (Michaux) Vahl
Family: Cyperaceae (Sedge)
Other Common Name: Marsh fimbry
Range: New York south to Florida and west to Texas
Habitat: Dune swales, brackish marshes, and salt marshes
Habit: Perennial graminoid
Flowering/Fruiting Period: FL & FR July–September
Wetland Status: OBL
Origin: Native

Often overlooked until its distinctive flowering spike appears during its midsummer reproductive period, saltmarsh fimbristylis is a consistent and important species in brackish-marsh and saltmarsh environments. Except for its dense "bunchgrass" appearance and dark brown leaf bases, the plant is easily mistaken during much of the year for saltmeadow cordgrass, a species that commonly grows in association with it. It is

b

24. Saltmarsh fimbristylis (*Fimbristylis castanea*). (a) Saltmarsh fimbristylis has a dense, clumpy growth form with inflorescences on tall, thick, leafless stems. (b) Several chestnut brown spikelets form the inflorescence. Each flower has 2 nearly transparent, delicate stigmas.

a member of a plant family closely related to the grasses, the Cyperaceae, or Sedges.

Saltmarsh fimbristylis has an extensive, dense network of dark brown, fibrous roots that feed its ascending leathery, needlelike leaves. The leaves rise and then droop away from the center of the plant, forming an interesting fountainlike or deliquescent cascade. The leaves are no more than $\frac{1}{16}$ inch wide with glabrous surfaces that inroll under drought conditions in a manner similar to that of sea oats and American beachgrass. In addition to saltmeadow cordgrass, saltmarsh fimbristylis is often associated with large-headed rush and marsh pink.

Inflorescences develop on thickened, leafless stems. At the top of each flowering stem, each of 3 to 10 short stalks holds from 1 to 4 chestnut brown, elliptical or cylindrical spikelets. The central spikelet is not stalked. Seeds are lustrous, brown achenes with fine vertical lines of pits on the surface visible only with a hand lens. Seeds disperse when the flowering heads mature and shatter, allowing the seeds to fall to the ground.

Seeds are an important waterfowl food, and the plant affords some cover for small animals.

Growing best in saline soils, the plant is suitable only in natural gardens that include brackish-marsh or saltmarsh environments. While saltmarsh fimbristylis does not possess outstanding ornamental value, it should be retained in natural brackish-marsh and saltmarsh environments for the wildlife and cover value of the plant, as well as for its contribution to native marsh diversity.

Carolina fimbry (*Fimbristylis caroliniana*) is a closely related species that occurs in higher, less saline environments of the coastal Carolinas. Carolina fimbry possesses slender rhizomes.

25 LARGE-HEADED RUSH

Juncus megacephalus M. A. Curtis
Family: Juncaceae (Rush)
Other Common Name: Big-head rush
Range: Virginia south to Florida and west to Texas
Habitat: Dune swales, brackish and fresh-water marshes; also roadside ditches
Habit: Perennial graminoid
Flowering/Fruiting Period: FL & FR June–August
Wetland Status: OBL
Origin: Native

Large-headed rush blends with many other grasses, sedges, and rushes in the dune slack and marsh flora until the species begins to reproduce. The plant reveals its identity once the large, distinctive "starburst" flowering heads form at the apex of the culms.

Large-headed rush is a 1- to 3-foot-tall, erect, grasslike plant arising from a $\frac{1}{8}$-inch-diameter rhizome. Several narrow-bladed

a

25. Large-headed rush (*Juncus megacephalus*). (a) Narrow-bladed leaves develop along the length of the culms. Culms are circular in cross section.

b

25. Large-headed rush (*Juncus megacephalus*). (b) The apex of the culm exhibits numerous distinctive starburst-like inflorescences.

leaves grow along the length of the culm. The mature plant possesses roughly 3 to 20 spherical inflorescences, each about ½ inch in diameter, with 40 to 80 flowers originating ostensibly from a single point and creating a starburst effect. Individual flowers have reddish-brown sepals and petals averaging ¼ inch long. The fruit of large-headed rush is a light tan capsule with tiny, yellowish-brown, ovoid seeds.

Large-headed rush prefers sandy soil and full sunlight but can survive in some shade. The plant can grow in brackish or fresh standing water or waterlogged soils, or where the water table is close to the soil surface. Associated species include smooth cordgrass, saltmarsh fimbristylis, and narrowleaf white-topped sedge.

Waterfowl eat the seeds of the large-headed rush. Plants and seeds of this species may be difficult to locate commercially. Take plants from the wild (with owner permission, of course).

26 BLACK NEEDLERUSH

Juncus roemerianus Scheele
Family: Juncaceae (Rush)
Other Common Names: Black rush, needlerush, needlegrass rush
Range: Delaware south to Florida and west to Texas
Habitat: Brackish and salt marshes
Habit: Perennial graminoid
Flowering/Fruiting Period: FL January–May; FR May—November
Wetland Status: OBL
Origin: Native

This coarse, grasslike plant is one of a handful of important and often dominant plant species in the tidal marsh environment of the Carolinas. It spreads slowly, forming monospecific stands within and adjacent to salt marshes. Viewed from a distance, stands of black needlerush appear grayish-green to black throughout the year. The network of shallowly growing rhizomes and deep, fibrous roots decays slowly, gradually forming an organic-rich layer close to the soil surface. This dense, silty, organic layer is highly resistant to erosion and thereby provides significant, long-term erosion protection for needlerush marshes.

Stiff, round leaves arise from hard, dark brown underground rhizomes and taper to a sharp point, giving this plant its common names, needlerush or needlegrass rush. Individual leaves vary from 1 to 6 feet tall and from ⅛ to ¼ inch in diameter at the base. Black needlerush produces new leaves just about year-round. Leaves are shortest and smallest when growing in hypersaline soils. Plants growing in low-salt environments are generally taller and more robust. Black needlerush is commonly associated with smooth cordgrass,

a

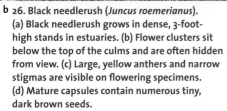

b 26. Black needlerush (*Juncus roemerianus*).
(a) Black needlerush grows in dense, 3-foot-
high stands in estuaries. (b) Flower clusters sit
below the top of the culms and are often hidden
from view. (c) Large, yellow anthers and narrow
stigmas are visible on flowering specimens.
(d) Mature capsules contain numerous tiny,
dark brown seeds.

c

d

saltmeadow cordgrass, saltgrass, and sea
ox-eye.

The bract surrounding the inflorescence
is similar in shape to the stem; therefore,
the terminal flower cluster appears to
emerge laterally on the stem when, in
fact, it is technically terminal on the stem.
Two types of flower clusters, each with
2 to 6 individual flowers, form on black
needlerush—perfect (both male and
female parts) and pistillate (female parts
only). Both kinds of flowers are chestnut to
reddish-brown and about ⅛ inch across.
Pistillate flowers produce more seeds with

a greater viability than the perfect flowers.
Each smooth, brown capsule contains
several shiny, dark brown seeds.

Black needlerush is unpalatable to
many animal species. Herbivores actually
eat only a small proportion of the plant.
Microbes break down this plant after it
dies. This decomposing organic matter
provides food for herbivorous fish and
many other important coastal animals.

Nutria, muskrats, rice rats, and marsh
rabbits live in the black needlerush
environment, and raccoons, cotton mice,
and mink are frequent visitors. More than

60 species of birds reportedly use black needlerush stands at some time during the year, including marsh wrens, rails, and sparrows.

New stands of black needlerush are primarily established by seeds, while existing stands expand through the growth of new culms from current rhizomes. Seeds can remain viable for more than a year and are capable of germinating at any time.

Success in transplanting black needlerush is erratic; it is best to use young, actively growing plants rather than older, established plants when transplanting this species. Horticulturalists have not developed cultivars of black needlerush; however, rhizomes and culms may be available from nurseries specializing in native plants.

27 TWO-FLOWER MELIC GRASS

Melica mutica Walter

Family: Poaceae (Grass)

Other Common Names: Narrow melic grass, two-flower melic, twoflower melic

Range: Maryland west to Iowa and south to Texas and Florida

Habitat: Maritime grasslands, maritime forests, and maritime shrub thickets

Habit: Perennial graminoid

Flowering/Fruiting Period: FL & FR April–May

Wetland Status: UPL

Origin: Native

Lines of light green to nearly white spikelets almost equally spaced along the raceme make two-flower melic grass stand out against a background of grasses and herbs during the spring flowering period for this occasional species.

Two-flower melic grass is a cespitose, rhizomatous plant that can grow to a height of 1½ to 3 feet at maturity. The simple leaves, 4 to 9 inches long, range from ¼ to ½ inch wide. The leaves are alternately arranged and two-ranked.

27. Two-flower melic grass (*Melica mutica*). (a) Cespitose and rhizomatous, this grass grows up to 3 feet tall at maturity and flowers abundantly. (b) Each pendulous spikelet contains 2 flowers, which are scattered along the 3- to 10-inch raceme.

Flowers are produced on 3- to 10-inch panicles, with several spreading branches near the base of the panicle. The upper part of the flowering raceme is often unbranched. Pendulous spikelets are attached by short, thin pedicels. Each spikelet ranges from ¼ to ⅜ inch long and possesses 2 flowers, a characteristic that likely is the source of the name for the plant. Each oblong flower is slightly fleshy. Three anthers complete each flower. Flower color varies from yellow to green to brown.

Two-flower melic grass prefers moist to somewhat dry, calcium-rich sandy soils.

It thrives in full sun but will grow in light shade.

Little is known about the pollination of two-flower melic grass; it is likely wind pollinated. Wildlife use is unknown; ground birds and small mammals may feed on the leaves and seeds.

There appears to be no commercial source for plants. Collect seeds or small plugs of the species from known populations.

a

28 DUNE HAIRGRASS

Muhlenbergia sericea (Michaux)
P. M. Peterson
Family: Poaceae (Grass)
Other Common Names: Sweetgrass, purple muhly grass, long-awn hairgrass, pink muhly grass
Range: Coastal: North Carolina south to Florida and west to Texas
Habitat: Dunes, dune swales, maritime grasslands, brackish and fresh marsh edges
Habit: Perennial graminoid
Flowering/Fruiting Period: FL & FR September—November
Wetland Status: FACW
Origin: Native

b

We know dune hairgrass as "sweetgrass" in the Low Country of South Carolina, where it is collected and dried for use in making baskets. The Gullah/Geechee, descendants of former slaves from West Africa, brought their craft of coiled basketry with them to America. The art of sweetgrass-coiled basketry remains a tradition around Mount Pleasant, S.C., where many individuals accomplished in basket weaving live and pass this skill to younger generations.

28. Dune hairgrass (*Muhlenbergia sericea*). (a) and (b) Dune hairgrass is a bunchgrass with blue-green leaves and unbranched stems. (c) Purplish-red or pink panicles composed of tiny spikelets may grow up to 18 inches high. The inflorescence color fades to tan or fawn in late fall.

GRAMINOIDS

c

Today, concerns center on how best to assure continued availability of this species as development in customary foraging lands of the Low Country continues unabated.

Dune hairgrass is a moderately fast-growing, clump-forming, warm-season plant with an unusual and stunning fall floral display. The stems are unbranched, and the blue-green leaves are upright, stiff, linear, and about 2 feet tall. In full flower, the plant may reach a height of 3 or even 4 feet. Sweetgrass grows best in moist, sandy soils and full sun; it tolerates light shade.

The inflorescence is a mass of wispy, purplish-red or pink panicles up to 18 inches long and 10 inches wide. The much-branched seed heads produce 1/16-inch-long spikelets on thin stalks. After several weeks, the seeds ripen, and the inflorescence gradually fades to a tan or fawn color. You can see outstanding fall floral displays of this plant on the North Carolina Outer Banks. In late fall or winter, the seeds are dispersed by the wind.

Dune hairgrass is tolerant of salt aerosols, drought, heat, humidity, flooding, and nutrient-poor soils; thus it is an excellent landscape plant for beachfront dunes and coastal wetland areas. The plant is available from plant nurseries near Charleston, S.C., and elsewhere. Because it is becoming increasingly uncommon in South Carolina, avoid collecting the plant from the wild.

The plant provides excellent cover for small animals, including mammals and reptiles.

A closely related species, hairgrass (*Muhlenbergia capillaris*), grows in loamy-sand, dry pinelands in the coastal Carolinas.

29 SEASIDE PANICUM

Panicum amarum Elliott
Family: Poaceae (Grass)
Other Common Names: Coastal panic grass, bitter panic grass, bitter seabeach grass
Range: Coastal: Massachusetts south to Florida and west to Texas
Habitat: Dunes, dune swales, and maritime grasslands
Habit: Perennial graminoid
Flowering/Fruiting Period: FL August–September; FR October–November
Wetland Status: FAC
Origin: Native

Along with sea oats, saltmeadow cordgrass, and sea elder, seaside panicum is one of the most important and useful plants in the coastal Carolinas for creating and vegetating coastal dunes and thereby reducing storm impact. Similar to the three other species noted, seaside panicum is an ideal dune plant. Not only is it highly resistant to salt aerosols, moderately drought resistant, and able to tolerate brief tidal inundation that often accompanies storm surges; it is also adapted to the conditions of full sun and low-nutrient soils. In addition, the plant is capable of surviving sand burial and sand abrasion.

Seaside panicum culms arise from short rhizomes. Seaside panicum creates dunes that have a greater stem density and steeper sides than dunes built by sea oats. Growing to a height of 3 to 6 feet, stems are erect to slightly decumbent; leaves are 7 to 14 inches long, 1/4 to 3/4 inch wide, and visibly wider than either American beachgrass or sea oats leaves. The smooth, hairless, alternately arranged leaves have a distinctly bluish-green color that contrasts with the bright green of sea oats leaves. The inflorescence of seaside panicum is a narrow terminal panicle 12 to 15 inches long; it is composed of numerous spikelets and is usually overtopped by

a

b

c

the uppermost leaves. Spikelets contain 2 flowers (florets); the lower floret is male or sterile, and the upper floret possesses both male and female organs.

Seeds provide food for songbirds, and the plant offers modest cover for birds and small mammals.

Seaside panicum produces few viable seeds; propagate by planting sprigs possessing a portion of either rhizome or stem. Sprigging seaside panicum in late winter and early spring assures the greatest success. Sprigs spread rapidly, and the plant begins to trap sand during the first year. For best results in stabilizing dunes, use seaside panicum in mixed plantings with sea oats or American beachgrass.

Seaside panicum is an excellent ornamental species. It grows well as a bunchgrass owing to its short rhizomes. For the Carolinas, the cultivar *Northpa* is appropriate. *Dewey Blue* is another cultivar used primarily as an ornamental. Both are available from commercial sources.

Panicum amarum var. *amarum* is one of two forms of seaside panicum in the coastal Carolinas. Although *Panicum amarulum* is commonly cited in older literature, botanists no longer recognize it as a valid species. Botanists now consider *Panicum amarum* var. *amarulum* a variant of seaside panicum.

29. Seaside panicum (*Panicum amarum*). (a) Found almost exclusively on dunes, this species produces numerous culms (stems) from short rhizomes. Leaves are a distinct bluish-green with leaf blades 7 to 14 inches long and up to ¾ inch wide, visibly wider than either American beachgrass or sea oats leaves. (b) The inflorescence is a terminal panicle 12 to 15 inches long composed of numerous spikelets. (c) Fruits have a reddish-brown tinge at maturity.

30 SWITCHGRASS

Panicum virgatum Linnaeus
Family: Poaceae (Grass)
Other Common Names: Old switch panic grass, tall panic grass
Range: Nova Scotia west to Saskatchewan, Canada; entire United States except the West Coast
Habitat: Coastal: dunes, dune swales, maritime grasslands, edges of brackish marshes; also tall-grass prairies; sandy, open woodlands; and riverbanks
Habit: Perennial graminoid

a
b
c

30. Switchgrass (*Panicum virgatum*). (a) Switchgrass is a light-to-medium green bunchgrass with nearly erect flowering culms (stems) growing up to 6 feet tall. (b) The flowering head is a panicle composed of spikelets, each with 2 flowers. Stigmas and anthers are exserted during flowering. (c) Fruits are typical grass caryopses, light brown and about ¹⁄₁₆ inch long.

Flowering/Fruiting Period: FL & FR June–October

Wetland Status: FAC

Origin: Native

While common in many coastal dune and marsh environments, switchgrass is also a co-dominant plant of the tall-grass prairie along with big bluestem (*Andropogon gerardi*). It is especially well adapted to life on coastal dunes because its long, fibrous roots can obtain water from deep within the sandy soil.

Switchgrass is a fast-growing, warm-season bunchgrass that produces nearly erect flowering culms up to 6 feet tall when planted in ideal conditions. Switchgrass rhizomes are short, and this growth feature creates the bunchgrass variant found in the coastal Carolinas. Culms are light to medium green, round, and glabrous. The

alternately arranged leaves are flat, ½ inch wide, and about 24 inches long. The culms are stiff and strongly ascending in full sun but slightly relaxed when growing in shade.

The open, spreading inflorescence at the top of each culm is 8 to 20 inches long and 4 to 10 inches wide. The flowering head is a panicle composed of small spikelets terminating dozens of slender, reddish-purple branches. Each ¼-inch-long, solitary spikelet is composed of 2 florets, but often only 1 seed is present in each spikelet. Pollination of individual flowers is by wind. The switchgrass seed is an oblong caryopsis about ¹⁄₁₆ inch long. The plant produces large seed crops annually.

Switchgrass prefers full sunlight, but it will grow in partial shade. It is salt-aerosol tolerant and drought tolerant, and it can grow in almost any type of soil, including dry and poorly drained soils. The plant tolerates moderate soil salinity and occasional flooding, but it will die if the water table is persistently high during the growing season. Switchgrass is typically associated with saltmeadow cordgrass, southern seaside goldenrod, and poison ivy.

Switchgrass is a great source of food and shelter for wildlife. A variety of wetland birds and songbirds eat the seeds. White-tailed deer graze the foliage, and the plant provides excellent nesting sites and cover for small mammals.

Propagation is by seeds and rhizomes. Divide roots and rhizomes of large plants or plant seeds in the fall. Alternatively, stratify seeds over the winter and plant them in the spring. Seedlings can withstand gradual burial after emergence, an advantage for surviving and expanding in unstable dune environments.

There are a number of switchgrass cultivars developed for both agricultural and horticultural needs. The ornamental varieties selected for beautiful red, blue, or lavender leaves include *Shenandoah*, *Dallas Blues*, *Heavy Metal*, and *Hänse Herms*.

In addition to choosing switchgrass as an ornamental, use it for restoring devegetated sites and for revegetating dunes. Recent research has suggested that switchgrass has high potential for use as a biofuel. It grows aggressively but is not invasive. Switchgrass self-seeds prolifically and may require management in the landscape.

The switchgrass variety most common in the coastal Carolinas is var. *virgatum*.

---

31 SEASHORE PASPALUM

Paspalum vaginatum Swartz

Family: Poaceae (Grass)

Other Common Names: Seashore crown grass, siltgrass, salt jointgrass, sand knotgrass

Range: Coastal: North Carolina south to Florida and west to Texas

Habitat: Dune swales and brackish marshes

Habit: Perennial graminoid

Flowering/Fruiting Period: FL & FR July-October

Wetland Status: OBL

Origin: Native

Seashore paspalum grows successfully on coastal golf courses and other areas where the soils may have elevated quantities of salts. Horticulturalists use it in naturally saline areas for erosion control, wetland restoration, and site reclamation. In this role, it filters high-nutrient water, stabilizes sediments, provides wildlife habitat, and adds organic matter to the plant community. The plant forms a dense sod and tolerates foot traffic well, so it is an excellent golf course grass. Because of its high tolerance to salts, seashore paspalum thrives under irrigation with brackish water. While irrigation with water at 50 percent of seawater strength depresses growth somewhat, research results show that the plant barely survives when irrigated with full-strength seawater.

Seashore paspalum is a warm-season grass characterized by erect to slightly decumbent culms. In its native habitat, it grows to a height of 20 to 30 inches with individual leaf blades ranging from 1 to 6 inches long and ⅜ inch wide. Leaf blades are flat or folded and taper toward the tip. The leaf surfaces are mostly glabrous with a few scattered long hairs, especially near the base. The plant possesses both stolons and rhizomes. The roots are extensive, and if they penetrate deeply into the soil, the plant is quite drought tolerant.

The flowering head of seashore paspalum is similar to those of other *Paspalum* species with 2 or 3 racemes ranging from ½ to 2½ inches long, which spread at maturity. Spikelets are glabrous

Seashore paspalum grows best in salty areas that experience brackish-water fluctuation just above and below the soil surface. It requires full sun and does not tolerate extended freezing temperatures and deep shade. It is tolerant of salt aerosols and high temperatures. The plant grows well in low-nutrient soils. While not considered invasive in the southeastern United States, it deserves careful monitoring for any undesirable spread beyond the areas in which it is intended to grow.

Geese and rabbits graze seashore paspalum shoots. The plant provides cover for small animals.

Several varieties of this plant are available, primarily for golf course use, in the form of sod. The plant is nutritious and is used as forage for grazing animals. Seashore paspalum is most successful when planted in winter or early spring. Varieties include *Sea Isle 1*, *Salam*, and *Sea Spray*.

A related but nonnative species, bahia grass (*Paspalum notatum*), grows in disturbed soils and established lawns, where it may outcompete other turf grasses.

32 COMMON REED

Phragmites australis (Cavanilles) Trinius Ex Steudel

Family: Poaceae (Grass)

Other Common Name: Phragmites

Range: Throughout North America except Alaska

Habitat: Fresh and brackish marshes; also ditches and disturbed sites

Habit: Perennial graminoid

Flowering/Fruiting Period: FL July–August; FR August–October

Wetland Status: FACW

Origin: Exotic; native to Europe. A native genotype is rare in the Carolinas, occurring primarily from the mid-Atlantic states northward.

a

b

31. Seashore paspalum (*Paspalum vaginatum*). (a) This species possesses erect to slightly decumbent culms (stems) and grows to a height of 20 to 30 inches. One- to 6-inch-long leaves are ⅜ inch wide. (b) Flowering heads exhibit 2 to 3 spreading racemes ranging from ½ to 2½ inches long with numerous small spikelets.

and elliptic to lanceolate in shape, about ⅛ inch long, and ¹⁄₁₆ inch wide. The plant produces dark blue-green spikelets in two rows along the raceme.

The seed produced by seashore paspalum is a yellow caryopsis about ⅛ inch long and slightly flattened.

32. Common reed (*Phragmites australis*). (a) This plant is recognized by its large size and high density of culms; plants grow 6 to 12 feet tall, and stands are nearly impenetrable. (b) Flowers develop in spikelets on 5- to 12-inch-long purplish panicles. (c) As spikelets mature and disperse their seeds, they turn tan, then gray.

Not recommended for planting; instead, remove where already growing.

Until the mid-twentieth century, common reed was a well-behaved member of the North American flora. However, today this common plant behaves as an aggressive weed, especially in disturbed habitats. South Carolina's Exotic Pest Plant Council cites common reed as a "severe threat" on its invasive species list. Scientists believe that new genetic diversity has been introduced to existing populations in North America. This nonnative form behaves poorly, with growth tendencies that are much more invasive than our original native form. These more aggressive populations appear to be moving south and west from New England. Its tendency to outcompete native species and form dense, nearly impenetrable monocultures makes this a highly undesirable invader in southern marshes and other moist or wet habitats.

Common reed, found on every continent except Antarctica, is a colonial grass that spreads primarily through stout rhizomes and occasional stolons. Fibrous roots feed rhizomes that can grow horizontally up to 10 feet per year. Each season, common reed produces many hollow, woody stems ranging from 6 to 12 feet tall. Leaves are lance shaped, 8 to 24 inches long, and ½ to 2½ inches wide. The leaves are glaucous green

GRAMINOIDS

and glabrous. Leaves drop at first frost, but culms remain attached and upright through the winter.

Flowers develop in spikelets on 5- to 12-inch purplish panicles. As the spikelets mature, they turn tan and then gray. Flowers are wind pollinated; seed set is highly variable from year to year.

The plant reproduces by seed, but the primary mode of reproduction is through rhizome and stolon growth. Studies indicate that a single rhizome, stolon, or seed may have started an entire stand of common reed.

Common reed grows best in fresh water, but it can survive in poorly oxygenated brackish water ranging up to two-thirds full-strength seawater, where it easily outcompetes giant cordgrass and wild rice (*Zizania aquatica*).

Common reed has little wildlife value; birds and small mammals prefer other types of plant cover, forage, and seeds.

Common reed has myriad human uses throughout the world, including for herbal medicine, clothing, baskets, mats, jewelry, boats, and roof thatch.

a

b

33. Narrowleaf white-topped sedge (*Rhynchospora colorata*). (a) Four to 6 distinctive green-and-white bracts radiate from the central flowering head. (b) The inflorescence is densely populated with white spikelets.

33 NARROWLEAF WHITE-TOPPED SEDGE

Rhynchospora colorata (Linnaeus) H. Pfeiffer

Family: Cyperaceae (Sedge)
Other Common Names: White-topped sedge, starrush whitetop, star sedge
Range: Virginia south to Florida and west to Texas
Habitat: Dune swales, maritime grasslands, freshwater marshes, and roadside ditches
Habit: Perennial graminoid
Flowering/Fruiting Period: FL & FR May–September
Wetland Status: FACW
Origin: Native

Narrowleaf white-topped sedge is an unusual and distinctive plant, displaying thin, bright white bracts that seem to explode from the center of the flowering heads.

Slender, erect, glabrous culms arising from a thin rhizome characterize narrowleaf white-topped sedge. Plant height ranges from 12 to 25 inches. The erect or spreading culm leaves are typically $\frac{1}{16}$ inch wide.

The inflorescence is terminal, solitary, and densely populated with white spikelets that comprise the reproductive portion of the sedge. Three to 6 narrow, white bracts spread out from the terminal head. Bracts are white at the base and green near each tip. Each bract ranges from 4 to 6 inches long.

Sedges are largely wind pollinated; however, narrowleaf white-topped sedge attracts several species of insects to the inflorescences, and the plant may well be insect pollinated. The laterally compressed spikelets contain many individual florets. Seeds are yellow to brown, lenticular achenes with unique transverse wrinkles.

Propagation of narrowleaf white-topped sedge is primarily by division of the rhizome.

Plants grow best in full sun but tolerate at least some shade. The species is available from native plant nurseries and provides natural plantings with a pleasing color and plant texture for wet locations. Once established, the plant will expand via rhizomes. Florists occasionally use dried stems in flower arrangements.

Sandswamp whitetop (*Rhynchospora latifolia*) can be distinguished from narrowleaf white-topped sedge by the presence of more than 6 white bracts surrounding each flowering head. It may also be found in coastal Carolina plant communities, primarily wet pine savannas.

a

b

34. Coastal little bluestem (*Schizachyrium littorale*). (a) Coastal little bluestem is a densely tufted bunchgrass growing to a height of 2 feet at flowering. (b) Plants turn reddish-brown at maturity. Individual leaves are up to 8 inches long and ¼ inch wide.

34 COASTAL LITTLE BLUESTEM

Schizachyrium littorale (Nash) E. P. Bicknell
Family: Poaceae (Grass)
Other Common Names: Seaside little bluestem, seacoast bluestem, shore bluestem, dune bluestem
Range: Massachusetts south to Florida and west to Texas; occasionally in Great Lakes states
Habitat: Dunes
Habit: Perennial graminoid
Flowering/Fruiting Period: FL & FR August–October
Wetland Status: FAC
Origin: Native

Coastal little bluestem has all of the important environmental tolerances of a coastal foredune plant except one: it does not tolerate rapid burial by sand. Consequently, coastal little bluestem is most common and grows best on sparsely vegetated but stable dunes, those typically located some distance from the shoreline.

Coastal little bluestem is a densely tufted bunchgrass that begins its aerial

GRAMINOIDS

167

c

d

growth late in the spring, reaching a height of about 2 feet in late summer. The coarse, blue-green stems take root at the nodes, and this habit makes the stems appear bent first outward from the center of the plant and then upward. Leaves are smooth and glabrous but may have tufts of hairs where the blades spread from the leaf sheaths. Individual leaf blades are up to 8 inches long and ¼ inch wide.

Flowering heads are about 12 inches long with individual seed clusters about 3 inches long. Short, silvery hairs (awns) develop as the seeds ripen, giving the flowering heads a wispy yet fluffy appearance. The entire plant turns reddish-brown at maturity. The seeds disperse in the fall and early winter. The flowering culms persist on the plant until spring.

Coastal little bluestem tolerates heat, drought, nutrient-poor soils, and salt aerosols. It requires full sunlight and grows best in well-drained environments. Plants often seen growing with coastal little bluestem are sea oats, dune sandspur, woolly beach heather, silver-leaf croton, dune pennywort, and dune camphorweed.

The plant provides excellent cover for ground birds and small mammals that populate the dunes. Along the central North Carolina coast, coastal little bluestem hosts the larvae for the rare crystal skipper butterfly.

Propagation is by seed and plant division, although research indicates that the seed germination rate is poor.

The blue-green leaves of summer, fluffy light tan seed heads of fall, and persistent reddish-brown leaves of winter make this a year-round, attractive specimen for ornamental or native plant garden use. In addition, the plant has no serious insect pests or diseases. The plant is an excellent choice for revegetation or restoration of backdunes.

34. Coastal little bluestem (*Schizachyrium littorale*). (c) Flowering heads are about 12 inches long. Anthers are exserted during the flowering period. (d) Short, silvery hairs develop as the seeds ripen, giving the flowering heads a distinctive fluffy, white-to-silver appearance.

a 35. Olney's threesquare (*Schoenoplectus americanus*). (a) Ranging from 2 to 4 feet tall, Olney's threesquare possesses dark green, triangular stems, with each side of the stem slightly concave. Leaves are short and often not evident. (b) Two to 20 spikelets develop at the top of the stem. Styles and stigmas are prominent in this photograph. The cluster of spikelets appears lateral because the cluster is subtended by an erect bract that gives the impression of being a continuation of the stem.

35 OLNEY'S THREESQUARE

Schoenoplectus americanus (Persoon) Volk
  ex Schinzius & R. Keller
Family: Cyperaceae (Sedge)
Range: Coastal: Nova Scotia and
  Massachusetts south to Florida and
  west to Texas; also western United States
  from California north to Washington
Habitat: Fresh and brackish marshes and
  maritime grasslands
Habit: Perennial graminoid
Flowering/Fruiting Period: FL May–June;
  FR June–September
Wetland Status: OBL
Origin: Native

Olney's threesquare is a locally common plant of fresh, brackish, and tidal marshes in the coastal Carolinas.

Typically ranging from 2 to 4 feet tall,

Olney's threesquare culms arise from stout rhizomes. The culms are dark green and triangular in cross section. Each side of the triangular stem is concave, a distinguishing characteristic of this species of bulrush. Leaves are less than half the length of the total culm and often are not evident. Usually 2 to 20 spikelets develop at the top of the culms, but because the 1- to 2-inch subtending bract is erect and appears as a continuation of the culm, the cluster of terminal spikelets actually appears laterally on the stem.

One-quarter- to ½-inch orange, purple, or brown scales protect the wind-pollinated flowers. The stigmas and anthers are the only flower parts visible during anthesis.

Seeds are dark brown, pointed achenes, each about ⅛ inch long.

GRAMINOIDS

Olney's threesquare prefers full sun but will survive in partial shade. It can tolerate salt aerosols and soil salts. Clearly drought-intolerant, it often grows in standing water. Species consistently associated with Olney's threesquare include narrow-leaved cattail, black needlerush, common reed, giant cordgrass, and saltmeadow cordgrass.

Muskrats and snow geese eat Olney's threesquare rhizomes; ducks and other waterfowl eat the seeds. When growing in dense patches, this species provides great cover for small mammals and birds.

Spring-season division of the rhizomes is the best propagation method for Olney's threesquare. Planting seeds may be more time consuming, but the seeds germinate quickly. Botanists have discovered that Olney's threesquare, growing in ideal habitats, forms short rhizomes. Because of the short rhizomes, the plants grow densely. Plants occupying poorer sites develop long rhizomes, and scientists suggest that long rhizomes allow this species to continuously "explore" the surrounding environment for new and better habitats.

Seeds can be ground into a powder, boiled with water, and eaten as mush. Given the size of the seeds, this seems like a lot of work for a small amount of food!

Olney's threesquare may be available from nurseries that specialize in growing wetland plants.

a

36 BRISTLY FOXTAIL GRASS

Setaria parviflora (Poiret) Kerguélen
Family: Poaceae (Grass)
Other Common Names: Marsh bristlegrass, perennial foxtail grass, knotroot bristlegrass
Range: Massachusetts west to Iowa and south to Texas and Florida
Habitat: Edges of tidal marshes, dune swales; also fields and waste areas
Habit: Perennial graminoid

b

36. Bristly foxtail grass (*Setaria parviflora*). (a) Stems of bristly foxtail grass are weak and decumbent. Whitish-green culms produce hair-covered leaf blades up to 12 inches long and $1/16$ to $1/4$ inch wide. (b) The flowering head is a densely crowded, purplish, cylindrical panicle, $1\frac{1}{4}$ to 2 inches long. Anthers are purple.

c

36. Bristly foxtail grass (*Setaria parviflora*). (c) Ultimately, the whitish seeds drop from the inflorescence, leaving only barren bristles along the raceme.

Flowering/Fruiting Period: FL & FR May–October

Wetland Status: FACW

Origin: Native

Bristly foxtail is aptly named for its distinctive bristle-like, pale green flowering heads that turn yellowish-brown as the seeds mature. The plant is a warm-season grass with weak, decumbent, slender stems. The surrounding grasses, most frequently saltmeadow cordgrass, often provide a scaffold for bristly foxtail, as the plant is prone to lie over on adjacent grassland plants, appearing as if a large animal had rested on it—which it may have!

The short rhizomes of bristly foxtail make the plant culms appear bunched. Culms are usually whitish-green and 10 to 28 inches tall with leaf blades up to 12 inches long and ¹⁄₁₆ to ¼ inch wide. Long hairs cover the upper surface of the leaf blades. In addition, culms may produce adventitious roots at the nodes, especially near the base of the plant.

The flowering head is a densely crowded, purplish, cylindrical panicle 1¼ to 2 inches long and about ³⁄₈ inch wide. Each spikelet sits at the base of 4 to 8 white bristles. Exserted beyond the spikelets, the purple stamens are clearly visible. At maturity, the whitish ellipse-shaped seeds drop from the inflorescence, leaving only bristles on the raceme.

Bristly foxtail thrives in moist, sandy, brackish soils. It can withstand brief flooding by salt water or fresh water. It is often associated with saltmeadow cordgrass and swallow-wort.

Seeds are available to birds and small mammals common in the maritime grasslands.

---

37 SMOOTH CORDGRASS

Sporobolus alterniflorus (Loisel.) P. M. Peterson & Saarela

Family: Poaceae (Grass)

Other Common Names: Saltmarsh cordgrass, marsh grass, Atlantic cordgrass

Range: Coastal: Newfoundland and Quebec, Canada; south to Florida and west to Texas; naturalized in Washington, Oregon, and California

Habitat: Salt marshes

Habit: Perennial graminoid

Flowering/Fruiting Period: FL & FR August-October

Wetland Status: OBL

Origin: Native

Smooth cordgrass is clearly adapted to thriving in habitats subject to the daily ebb and flow of salt water. It is the dominant plant of estuaries along the Atlantic and Gulf coasts of the United States. The plant forms extensive dense, monospecific

GRAMINOIDS

a

c

d

b

37. Smooth cordgrass (*Sporobolus alterniflorus*). (a) Tidal marshes are covered with a monoculture of this species, which arises from dense rhizomes and roots. (b) Female flower parts are seen as nearly transparent stigmas in two ranks on one side of the inflorescence. (c) Male organs are visible as large, white anthers. (d) Seeds are quickly stripped from mature inflorescences by insects.

stands, thereby creating environments unique to the coast, the salt marshes.

Smooth cordgrass culms arise from robust, tough rhizomes stabilized by extensive roots. These culms are composed of erect, coarse stems and leaves with considerable aerenchyma tissue. The stems, up to ½ inch in diameter at their base, range from 1 to 7 feet tall. The average height increases from northern North Carolina to southern South Carolina and by location within the marsh. Along well-drained creek margins and other regularly tidal-flooded habitats, smooth cordgrass is noticeably taller than when it grows in areas away from the edge of tidal creeks or close to the upper limits of tidal influence. The plant expands by producing a profusion of rhizomes. Individual plants spread quickly and easily in the marsh soils, growing up to 2 feet laterally in a single year, forming a compact, interlaced root-and-rhizome system. Leaf blades range from 1 to 2 feet long and ¼ to ⅝ inch wide. The leaf edges roll inward toward the tip of the leaf.

The inflorescence is terminal and compact, varying from 12 to 18 inches long with 10 to 15 spikes. Each spike is composed of 10 to 40 spikelets. Wind-pollinated flowers occur in two rows along the same side of a rachis.

Smooth cordgrass can tolerate anoxic soils and soil salts up to full-strength seawater. When growing in environments with high soil salts, smooth cordgrass excretes salt through special glands embedded in the leaves. In summer, one can see small clumps of salt crystals on the surface of leaves, especially after prolonged dry weather.

Seed production is erratic. The plant produces most seeds in stands along the margins of tidal creeks; little flowering or seed set occurs in stands away from the creek edges. Seeds germinate in spring, and after a summer of growth, smooth cordgrass may produce flowers. Asexual reproduction through growth and extension of rhizomes maintains existing marshes, while seeds often colonize newly created sites near tidal inlets.

While songbirds, marsh birds, and waterfowl relish the seeds, roots are a favorite food of geese. The grass also provides cover and nesting habitat for marsh birds. Commercially important fish and shellfish spend at least a portion of their life cycle in smooth-cordgrass-dominated marshes, which function as nursery beds for many species of marine fishes and invertebrates.

Propagate smooth cordgrass best by division of plants. Stock is available from commercial sources.

Smooth cordgrass has been introduced to the West Coast of the United States, where it has become a seriously invasive plant, altering the natural functioning of native plant and animal communities.

This species is cited as *Spartina alterniflora* in legacy literature for the coastal Carolinas.

38 GIANT CORDGRASS

Sporobolus cynosuroides (Linnaeus) P. M. Peterson & Saarela

Family: Poaceae (Grass)
Other Common Names: Big cordgrass, salt reedgrass
Range: Coastal: Massachusetts south to Florida and west to Texas and Mexico
Habitat: Freshwater and brackish tidal marshes
Habit: Perennial graminoid
Flowering/Fruiting Period: FL June–August; FR August–September
Wetland Status: OBL
Origin: Native

Giant cordgrass grows to a height of 5 to 12 feet, considerably taller and coarser than either of its close relatives, saltmeadow cordgrass or smooth cordgrass. Leaves of the plant are up to 30 inches long and 1 to 1½ inches wide and possess minute serrations that can easily cut the exposed skin of those who venture into a dense stand.

Distinctive, raceme-shaped flower heads ranging from 12 to 18 inches tall and 8 to 10 inches wide top the culms. Each flower head is composed of more than 20 ascending and spreading spikes. Dozens of ¼-inch-long spikelets aligned on one side

GRAMINOIDS

c

38. Giant cordgrass (*Sporobolus cynosuroides*). d
(a) Leaves of this large grass grow up to 30 inches long and 1 to 1½ inches wide. Leaf edges are minutely serrated. (b) Female organs display nearly transparent stigmas in two ranks on the same side of the inflorescence. (c) Male organs are visible as large, white anthers. (d) Flower heads are 12 to 18 inches tall and possess about two dozen spikes.

a

b

of the rachis compose each 1- to 3-inch-long spike.

Typically, giant cordgrass grows in dense, nearly pure stands, forming a thick organic layer of roots and rhizomes. It reproduces from seeds and through new culm production.

Tolerating soil salinity up to about one-third full-strength seawater, giant cordgrass grows in well-drained soils that are occasionally flooded by spring and storm tides. It also grows well in brackish marshes where freshwater runoff from adjacent uplands creates low-salinity soil water. Large, dense patches of the species are common in Currituck Sound, N.C.

Similar to smooth cordgrass, this species contributes large quantities of detritus to the estuarine food web. The plant is an important wildlife food and habitat for small mammals such as muskrat, waterfowl, and songbirds.

The aggressive common reed (*Phragmites australis*) is a plant with similar ecological requirements; it threatens to replace giant cordgrass along the Atlantic coast.

This species is cited as *Spartina cynosuroides* in legacy literature for the coastal Carolinas.

---

39 SALTMEADOW CORDGRASS

Sporobolus pumilus (Roth) P. M. Peterson & Saarela
Family: Poaceae (Grass)
Other Common Names: Marshhay cordgrass, small saltmeadow grass, salt hay
Range: Quebec and the Maritime Provinces, Canada; Maine south to Florida and west to Texas
Habitat: Dunes, dune swales, maritime grasslands, brackish and salt marshes
Habit: Perennial graminoid
Flowering/Fruiting Period: FL June–August; FR August–September
Wetland Status: FACW
Origin: Native

The importance of saltmeadow cordgrass in the coastal area cannot be overestimated. It is one of the most important and valuable plants occurring on the dunes and on the landward edge of tidal marshes along the Atlantic and Gulf coasts of the United States. In addition to its natural occurrence, coastal managers plant saltmeadow cordgrass to stabilize dunes and to restore tidal marshes throughout the coastal Carolinas. In contrast to the steep-sided dunes created by sea oats, saltmeadow cordgrass typically forms broad, low dunes.

This tufted, rhizomatous grass may grow up to 4 feet tall. New culms arise from the base of the previous year's growth and at nodes along the rhizomes that extend

39. Saltmeadow cordgrass (*Sporobolus pumilus*). (a) The long, narrow leaf blades of saltmeadow cordgrass are often inrolled, making them appear tubular. Short rhizomes give the plant a clumped appearance.

considerable distances through moist sand. The long, narrow leaf blades are usually rolled inward, forming a tube that reduces water loss from the leaf surface. The plant is an early colonizer of overwash fans created by hurricanes and other severe coastal storms.

Saltmeadow cordgrass produces a seed head with 1 to 6 spikes ranging from 1 to 3 inches long. Spikelets grow in two rows on one side of the rachis. Propagation through modest seed production and establishment of culms assures the success and rapid expansion of saltmeadow cordgrass.

Saltmeadow cordgrass is tolerant of

GRAMINOIDS

b 39. Saltmeadow cordgrass (*Sporobolus pumilus*). (b) Female organs display nearly transparent stigmas in two ranks on the same side of the inflorescence. (c) Male organs are large anthers. (d) These are mature flowering heads with seeds about ready to disarticulate from the plant.

inundation by fresh water and ocean-strength salt water. It often forms dense, monospecific stands along the upper edge of brackish and tidal salt marshes. Where it grows in large patches, saltmeadow cordgrass characteristically folds over to the ground, forming large features called cowlicks.

Research shows that saltmeadow cordgrass possesses glands on leaf surfaces that excrete salt accumulated by the plants when they grow in high-salinity environments.

Although saltmeadow cordgrass is not very nutritious, coastal farmers once used it as forage for cattle and horses. Geese and other birds feed on the seeds.

Where nearly pure stands of the plant are present along tidal shores, a dense, highly organic soil layer may form beneath saltmeadow cordgrass, a result

of decay-resistant dead roots, rhizomes, stems, and leaves accumulating in the soil. With growth buds located below the ground surface, saltmeadow cordgrass is resistant to fire. In fact, occasional burning enhances its growth.

A species similar to saltmeadow cordgrass, sand cordgrass (*Sporobolus bakeri*), occurs in brackish marshes on southern South Carolina barrier islands.

This species is cited as *Spartina patens* in legacy literature for the coastal Carolinas.

40 SEASHORE DROPSEED

Sporobolus virginicus (Linnaeus) Kunth
Family: Poaceae (Grass)
Other Common Names: Virginia dropseed, coastal dropseed
Range: Southern North Carolina south to Florida and west to Texas

40. Seashore dropseed (*Sporobolus virginicus*). (a) Seashore dropseed stems range from 4 to 12 inches high, and individual leaves are 2 to 4 inches long. (b) Culms terminate with a dense group of single-flowered spikelets arranged along a panicle. (c) These are dense and appressed fruits on the raceme. (d) Seashore dropseed has a distichous pattern of sharply pointed leaves on coarse culms.

Habitat: Dunes, brackish and salt marshes
Habit: Perennial graminoid
Flowering/Fruiting Period: FL & FR
    September–October
Wetland Status: FACW
Origin: Native
Seashore dropseed is an ideal coastal plant, equally at home colonizing windswept

GRAMINOIDS

upper beaches and foredunes as it is thriving in brackish and salt marshes. Seashore dropseed typically develops as a coarse, short plant on the dunes. The plant texture is much finer, and it grows taller in tidal marshes. Seashore dropseed spreads through rhizome growth, often forming dense patches on low, moist dunes and marshes.

The presence of distichous leaves easily identifies seashore dropseed. Without flowering or fruiting material, the plant can be confused with another common species of tidal marshes, saltgrass (*Distichlis spicata*), which also has a distichous leaf arrangement. The flowering heads of the two species are different, and saltgrass does not grow in dunes.

Stems of seashore dropseed range from 4 to 12 inches or more, with leaves 2 to 4 inches long. The edges of the leaves are typically inrolled, especially toward the tip.

Seashore dropseed produces single-flowered spikelets arranged in a dense panicle. The lustrous, reddish grains (seeds) are about ⅟₂₅ inch long.

Seashore dropseed is highly salt tolerant. It thrives in environments with elevated soil salts, such as brackish and salt marshes. Close inspection of seashore dropseed reveals salt crystals on leaf surfaces during periods of hot, dry weather. Specialized glands on the leaf surfaces exude concentrated salts that crystalize as the exudate dries.

Seashore dropseed is an excellent food for geese.

Propagate this species by planting rhizome pieces. It is an excellent plant to use in restoring low, slow-growing dunes. Use this nearly maintenance-free plant as a full-sun turf grass in salty environments. Seashore dropseed is rare in North Carolina but is common in dunes and marshes in South Carolina.

41 ST. AUGUSTINE GRASS

Stenotaphrum secundatum
(Walter) Kuntze

Family: Poaceae (Grass)

Other Common Names: Charleston grass, carpet grass

Range: Virginia south to Florida and west to Texas

Habitat: Dune swales and edges of freshwater and brackish marshes

Habit: Perennial graminoid

Flowering/Fruiting Period: FL & FR July–October

Wetland Status: FAC

Origin: Native

St. Augustine grass is a warm-season grass that is well-behaved, not weedy or aggressive, and has a moderately fast growth rate. Often planted as a turf grass in coastal environments, St. Augustine grass is tolerant of salt aerosols and soil salts. It forms a dense, coarse ground cover and grows especially well in moist, calcareous sandy soils. Its native habitat is coastal wetlands.

St. Augustine grass grows as a much-branched, creeping, stoloniferous plant that forms low, dense mats, with the stolons easily rooting at the nodes. Key identifying characteristics of this species include flattened stems and keeled leaf sheaths. The leaves are dark green and glabrous, with leaf blades 1 to 6 inches long and ⅛ to ½ inch wide.

Terminating each culm is an inflorescence that forms a one-sided spike with an unusually thick central axis 1 to 6 inches long. Individual spikelets are borne on the spike alternately and grow in hollowed-out areas of the spike. The fruit of St. Augustine grass is a dark brown, slightly convex shaped caryopsis.

St. Augustine grass is moderately tolerant of drought, shade, and trampling, but it is not cold tolerant. This trait limits its use to southeastern North Carolina and

a

b

41. St. Augustine grass (*Stenotaphrum secundatum*). (a) St. Augustine grass is a coarse-leaved, much-branched, creeping grass with 1- to 6-inch-long dark green leaf blades. (b) Inflorescences terminate culms, forming one-sided spikes with a 1- to 6-inch-long, thick, central axis.

South Carolina. It grows well in nutrient-poor soils.

St. Augustine grass has modest wildlife value.

Propagation of St. Augustine grass is completely vegetative, with sprigs, plugs, or sod the most common methods of reproducing the plant. Seeds are generally not commercially available.

42 SEA OATS
Uniola paniculata Linnaeus
Family: Poaceae (Grass)
Range: Virginia south to Florida and west to Texas and Mexico; also Bahamas and Cuba
Habitat: Dunes and dune swales
Habit: Perennial graminoid
Flowering/Fruiting Period: FL June–July; FR July–November
Wetland Status: FAC
Origin: Native

Sea oats is a botanical superhero. It can survive rapid sand burial, drought, high winds, salt aerosols, saltwater inundation, high temperatures, and full sun, so it is uniquely adapted to the Carolinas coastal dunes.

Sea oats, a warm-season grass, thrives in a range of shore habitats ranging from the wrack line landward to the seaward edge of shrub thickets and maritime forests. In fact, it rarely occurs inland from the coastal dunes. The plant is the principal dune-building and sand-binding grass of the southeastern United States. It is planted extensively to stabilize sand along shorelines disrupted or eroded by natural or human changes, such as by hurricanes or development.

Sea oats is a coarse rhizomatous plant with an extensive network of near-surface roots complemented by deep, sand-binding roots. Culms arise from the rhizomes that extend laterally and root at nodes when buried by sand. Sea oats tolerates sand burial up to 3 feet per year, with stem growth and tillering stimulated by this burial.

The glaucous green leaves gracefully arch upward from their underground origin, and the tips return to the sandy

GRAMINOIDS

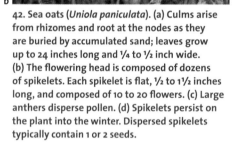

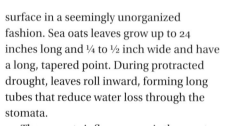

42. Sea oats (*Uniola paniculata*). (a) Culms arise from rhizomes and root at the nodes as they are buried by accumulated sand; leaves grow up to 24 inches long and ¼ to ½ inch wide. (b) The flowering head is composed of dozens of spikelets. Each spikelet is flat, ½ to 1½ inches long, and composed of 10 to 20 flowers. (c) Large anthers disperse pollen. (d) Spikelets persist on the plant into the winter. Dispersed spikelets typically contain 1 or 2 seeds.

surface in a seemingly unorganized fashion. Sea oats leaves grow up to 24 inches long and ¼ to ½ inch wide and have a long, tapered point. During protracted drought, leaves roll inward, forming long tubes that reduce water loss through the stomata.

The sea oats inflorescence is the most familiar and striking feature of the plant. It is composed of dozens of spikelets crowded at the top of 3- to 6-foot culms. The spikelets are flat, ½ to 1½ inches long, ½ inch wide, and composed of 10 to 20

florets. During their maturation, sea oat spikelets turn from blue-green to golden brown. Most flowers do not produce seeds, and research scientists report that spikelets average fewer than 2 seeds each. Spikelets persist on the culms well into the winter. Over time, wind, water currents, and animals disseminate the spikelets.

Birds and small mammals, such as song sparrows, red-winged blackbirds, and mice, consume seeds not quickly buried by blowing sand. Seeds usually remain in the spikelet, as evidenced by the presence of a spikelet almost always entwined by the roots of each germinating seed.

The primary method of reproduction is vegetative growth through rhizome extension and bud formation. Vegetative vigor and flowering of sea oats decrease noticeably in the absence of sand accretion.

The plant grows poorly in habitats with a high water table or continuously saturated soils. Human impacts such as trampling, off-road vehicle use, and urbanization harm the growth and development of sea oats.

It is illegal to collect plants or inflorescences of sea oats in most municipalities in North Carolina and South Carolina without a permit.

Sea oats is available from dune plant growers in the coastal Carolinas. Plugs should be planted in spring or early fall.

Herbs

43 SEABEACH AMARANTH

Amaranthus pumilus Rafinesque

Family: Amaranthaceae (Amaranth)

Other Common Names: Seabeach pigweed, seaside amaranth, dwarf amaranth

Range: New York (Long Island) south to North Carolina

Habitat: Beaches, inlet margins, wrack lines, and dunes

Habit: Annual herb

Flowering/Fruiting Period: FL June–September; FR July–October

Wetland Status: FACW

Origin: Native

Endemic to the Atlantic coast of North America and once found from Massachusetts to South Carolina, seabeach amaranth now only grows on beaches in New York, New Jersey, Maryland, and North Carolina. Beach surveys find that New York and North Carolina have the largest number of seabeach amaranth populations; however, populations have disappeared from the Outer Banks in recent years. The species has been assigned a Global Heritage Status rank of G2 (imperiled) and a National Heritage Status rank of N2 (imperiled). In addition, seabeach amaranth has been designated a "threatened species" by the U.S. Fish and Wildlife Service. North Carolina also lists seabeach amaranth as "threatened." These designations clearly indicate that scientists believe the plant is vulnerable to extinction.

Seabeach amaranth is a low-growing, much-branched plant with pinkish-red, succulent stems that grow close to the ground but do not root at the nodes, a trait common to many other coastal plants. The glabrous stems are prostrate or ascending and often collect sand around them as they grow, thereby creating 10- to 12-inch-diameter "dunes" a few inches above the surrounding ground surface. The wrinkled, fleshy, short-petioled, dark green leaves,

a

b

43. Seabeach amaranth (*Amaranthus pumilus*). (a) Members of the wrack-line flora, mature plants possess pinkish-red, succulent stems. (b) Undistinguished flowers and fruits are clustered in leaf axils.

ranging from ½ to ¾ inch across, crowd together at the tips of branches.

Seabeach amaranth is monoecious, with separate male and female flowers clustered in the axils of the leaves, especially toward the tip of the branches. Unremarkable male and female flowers are intermixed in green flower clusters. Although insects visit the plants, the flowers are not showy and are probably wind pollinated.

The fruit is contained in a ¼-inch-long, water-repellent, air-filled sac, technically a utricle. Seeds are dark reddish-brown and ¹⁄₁₆ to ⅛ inch in diameter. The seed-containing utricle can float on water for a short time. Wind and water disperse seeds in the fall and winter. Seeds germinate beginning the following spring.

Seabeach amaranth is most common just above the spring tide line, a habitat with constant disturbance and low competition from other plants. Common plant associates are sea rocket and northern seaside spurge. The species thrives along the wrack line in quiescent, low-storm years; however, if inundated by salt water during storm surges, seabeach amaranth populations often disappear from that location for that year.

The plant coexists in the same open, sandy habitats where piping plovers and least terns nest.

Many factors have contributed to the decline of seabeach amaranth along the Atlantic coast, such as shoreline development; human trampling; off-road vehicle use; erosion; dune migration; the installation of beach stabilization structures, such as sand fences, jetties, groins, and seawalls; beach scraping; beach raking; and webworm predation.

a

---

44 COMMON RAGWEED

Ambrosia artemisiifolia Linnaeus
Family: Asteraceae (Aster)
Other Common Names: Annual ragweed, Roman wormwood, bitterweed, hay fever weed
Range: Throughout North America
Habitat: Dunes and dune swales; also roadsides, disturbed areas, waste areas, and agricultural fields
Habit: Annual herb
Flowering/Fruiting Period: FL & FR August–November
Wetland Status: FACU
Origin: Native
Common ragweed is a cosmopolitan plant that has a well-deserved poor

b

44. Common ragweed (*Ambrosia artemisiifolia*). (a) Mature, many-branched plants grow in full sun and the dry soil of disturbed areas. (b) Female flowers emerge in leaf axils. Long, thin styles and stigmas are evident in the flowers.

c

44. Common ragweed (*Ambrosia artemisiifolia*). (c) Abundant, pendant male flowers develop on long racemes at the top of the plant.

reputation. Botanists estimate that a single plant can produce a billion pollen grains over a season, and common ragweed pollen grains are allergens in about 10 to 15 percent of the population who show symptoms of what we call "hay fever." Considered a noxious weed and agricultural pest, the plant establishes easily in disturbed areas in the coastal Carolinas, and seeds may remain viable in the soil for 5 or more years. Furthermore, common ragweed appears to release compounds to the soil that are allelopathic; that is, they inhibit growth and development of nearby plants.

Common ragweed is a summer annual growing 4 to 24 inches tall and sometimes larger, depending on the site's environmental conditions and the plant resources available. Following germination, the plant quickly develops a deep taproot and extensive fibrous roots that help it survive drought conditions.

Stems are erect, with many branches above the middle of the plant. Leaves are arranged alternately on the stem. The broadly triangular leaf blades are highly dissected, with entire or slightly toothed margins. The leaf size is highly variable, up to 8 inches long and 4 inches wide. Both upper and lower leaf surfaces are coarsely hairy and glandular.

Common ragweed is monoecious, with separate male and female flowers occurring on a single plant. Male flowers are borne in tall, sometimes lax, 1- to 4-inch racemes at the top of the plant. Inverted, cup-shaped involucres surround tiny flowers, giving them a bell shape. Female flowers form in axils of the upper leaves. The wind-pollinated female flowers are green, and each produces a ⅛-inch, woody, brown achene. The involucres of the female flower form a circle of 4 to 7 hard, spiny projections as the achene ripens. Common ragweed grows best in full sun and is tolerant of dry soil conditions.

The oil-rich seeds of common ragweed are eaten by upland game birds, songbirds, and small mammals.

45 SEABEACH ORACH

Atriplex mucronata Rafinesque
Family: Chenopodiaceae (Goosefoot)
Other Common Names: Spear saltbush, spear saltweed, spreading orach, spearscale
Range: Coastal: New Hampshire to Texas
Habitat: Margins of brackish and tidal marshes, salt flats; also waste areas
Habit: Annual herb
Flowering/Fruiting Period: FL July–October; FR September–November
Wetland Status: FAC
Origin: Exotic; native to Eurasia

An overall powdery gray-green color and red-tinged stems are key identifying characteristics of this distinctive marsh plant.

Seabeach orach is a common erect to prostrate plant that is 1 to 2 feet tall and,

a

b

c

45. Seabeach orach (*Atriplex mucronata*).
(a) Possessing powdery gray-green leaves, seabeach orach is common along the upper edge of tidal marshes where competition from other plants is low. (b) Male flowers are clustered along the terminal raceme at the top of the plant. (c) Female flowers, lacking petals and sepals, cluster in leaf axils, ultimately forming fruits with conspicuous flat wings.

with spreading branches, up to 3 feet in diameter. The stems are smooth and often angular in cross section. The lower leaves are opposite, while the upper leaves are alternately arranged. The 1- to 4-inch-long leaves are entire and become progressively smaller higher on the stem.

Seabeach orach is monoecious, with separate male and female flowers on the same plant. Inconspicuous green, wind-pollinated flowers arise from the leaf axils and the top of the plant in dense clusters on short spikes. The male flower has no petals, and the female flower lacks both petals and sepals. Seabeach orach seeds are solitary and enclosed by 2 fleshy, leaflike bracts. The ⅛-inch brown seeds germinate readily.

Seabeach orach grows well in saline soils under full sunlight. While not invasive, seabeach orach prefers disturbed habitats where competition is low. Seabeach orach is often associated with sea ox-eye, saltmeadow cordgrass, and saltgrass.

We know little about its use as a wildlife food; however, ground-foraging birds eat the seeds of related species.

Propagate seabeach orach from seeds; limited quantities may be available commercially.

Highly tolerant of high soil salts, the plant can add color and texture to an otherwise grass-dominated tidal marsh habitat.

46 SEA ROCKET

Cakile harperi Small
Family: Brassicaceae (Mustard)
Other Common Names: Southeastern sea rocket, American sea rocket
Range: Coastal: North Carolina south to Florida
Habitat: Wrack lines, dunes, and maritime grasslands
Habit: Annual herb
Flowering/Fruiting Period: FL & FR April–June
Wetland Status: FACU
Origin: Native

A member of the nearly ubiquitous Mustard family, sea rocket is a conspicuous plant of the wrack-line and foredune habitat of the Carolinas coast. During any given year, beach scraping, beach grooming, storm overwash, erosion, off-road vehicle use, and development may erase the ephemeral wrack lines occupied by sea rocket; however, extirpation of this resilient plant is not as likely as with seabeach amaranth, a species with an even narrower ecological niche.

Sea rocket is the only large, common herbaceous plant growing near the foredunes. It is 6 to 20 inches tall with bright green, succulent stems and leaves. The smooth, glabrous, entire, or crenate leaves range from 1 to 3 inches long and ½ to 1½ inches wide.

Flowers are arranged in racemes that elongate as the fruits mature. The

46. Sea rocket (*Cakile harperi*). (a) The large, bright green plants are commonplace along the wrack lines and foredunes. (b) Flowers are pale lavender to white with golden anthers.

racemes often reach a length of 8 inches. Pale lavender to white flowers are ¼ inch across and possess 4 sepals and 4 petals. Bees, flies, beetles, moths, and butterflies pollinate the flowers.

Botanically, the fruit of sea rocket is a silique distinguished by the presence of a horizontally transverse joint separating 2 seeds enclosed in a dry, corky, lightweight pod. The shape of the transverse joint is nearly flat; the fruit is 4-angled, and the top and bottom are similar in shape. The

c

46. Sea rocket (*Cakile harperi*). (c) Annual plants die midsummer, leaving 2-seeded fruits on bare tan or gray stems.

¼-inch-long seeds are orange-tan to dark brown, laterally flattened, and ovoid.

The lightweight and buoyant top seed breaks away from the plant and is dispersed by wind or water. The lower portion of the fruit typically remains on the plant and germinates in place if buried by sand accumulating around the dead stem.

Authorities consider sea rocket a "winter annual" in the Carolinas coastal setting: seeds germinate in late summer or early fall and overwinter as small plants. During the following spring and continuing throughout the early summer, the plants flower, set seed, and die. North of the Carolinas, a closely related species, northeastern sea rocket (*Cakile edentula*) reflects the typical annual habit

of spring germination followed by summer flowering.

Sea rocket requires full sun and well-drained sandy soil. It tolerates salt aerosols and low soil nutrients. A poor competitor, it occupies the sparsely vegetated wrack line with plants such as northern saltwort, seabeach amaranth, and northern seaside spurge.

The shape of the transverse joint in the fruit aids in differentiating between the two native coastal Carolina species of sea rocket. In northeastern sea rocket, the lower portion of the silique is deeply notched—clearly V-shaped—and the upper portion is more rounded, almost balloon shaped. The ranges of the species overlap in northern North Carolina.

47 SOUTHERN HORSEWEED

Conyza canadensis (Linnaeus) Cronquist
Family: Asteraceae (Aster)
Other Common Names: Horseweed, Canadian horseweed
Range: Massachusetts west to Indiana and south to Texas and Florida
Habitat: Dunes, dune swales, and maritime grasslands; also old fields, waste areas
Habit: Annual herb
Flowering/Fruiting Period: FL June–October; FR July–November
Wetland Status: FACU
Origin: Native

Common throughout much of North America, southern horseweed (var. *pusilla*) shows how much the environmental conditions present along the coast can affect plant growth and development. Inland, in fertile fields, common horseweed (var. *canadensis*) grows to a height of 4 feet or more and flowers profusely; along the shore of the Carolinas, where southern horseweed is exposed to salt aerosols, desiccating winds, and nutrient-poor soils, it barely reaches 1 foot in height. In fact, it frequently grows less than 6 inches high

HERBS

189

a

b

c

47. Southern horseweed (*Conyza canadensis*).
(a) Horseweed plants are a few inches tall where salt aerosols dominate dune environments.
(b) Tiny flowers are about ¼ inch across.
(c) Fruiting heads appear similar to tiny dandelion heads.

with only modest flowering output. In these environmental extremes, southern horseweed shows adaptability to a wide range of habitats, a trait that characterizes almost all weed species.

A single-stemmed plant, southern horseweed is sparsely hairy, with little branching at the bottom of the plant but extensive branching above. Leaves are slender, coarsely toothed, and hairy. Leaves become progressively smaller toward the stem apex, varying from ¾ to 4 inches long. Southern horseweed may act as a winter annual, with seed germination occurring in late summer or fall. After germination, it grows for a brief time and overwinters in the form of a rosette of basal leaves. The plant bolts the following spring.

Flowers are present on highly branched panicles at the top of the stem. Each individual flower is about ¼ inch across and ¼ inch long. Upon close inspection, flowers look like miniature daisies, possessing 20 to 30 tiny, white ray flowers and 8 to 20 equally petite yellow disk flowers. Flies, bees, wasps, and beetles commonly found on the flowers are probably pollinators. The fruit is an achene with numerous white or tan bristles attached to the seed, which aids in wind dispersal.

Southern horseweed prefers full sun and tolerates drought conditions.

Southern horseweed is reputed to be one of the plants responsible for fall allergies.

In legacy scientific literature, botanists refer to this species as *Erigeron canadensis*.

a

48 POORJOE

Diodella teres (Walter) Small
Family: Rubiaceae (Madder)
Other Common Names: Rough buttonweed, poverty weed
Range: Massachusetts west to Wisconsin, southwest to Texas, and east to Florida; also California, Arizona, and New Mexico
Habitat: Dunes; also agricultural fields, roadsides, and waste places
Habit: Annual herb
Flowering/Fruiting Period: FL June–September; FR August-November
Wetland Status: FACU
Origin: Native

b

Poorjoe is a common field and roadside weed, but it is also a consistent member of the dune and interdune flora of the coastal

c

48. Poorjoe (*Diodella teres*). (a) Poorjoe plants range from a single erect stem to several prostrate or ascending stems. (b) Four-petaled, ¼-inch, pinkish to lavender-white flowers grow from leaf axils. (c) Fruits are top shaped with persistent calyx teeth and spiny seed coats.

Carolinas. Its presence on the dunes indicates that the plant is well adapted to nutrient-poor, sandy soils; high soil and air temperatures; drought; salt aerosols; and full sun.

Arising from a taproot up to 12 inches long at maturity, the plant produces several prostrate to ascending stems that branch beginning close to the ground. Four to 8 inches tall in the dunes, poorjoe grows considerably larger in inland fields and waste areas. Stems are 4-angled, reddish-green, and densely hairy. The leaves are oppositely arranged and linear, ranging from ¾ to 1½ inches long and ⅛ inch wide. They are acute tipped and sessile, with margins that inroll when the plant is water-stressed. Coarse hairs cover the leaves on both surfaces.

The flowers of poorjoe are solitary and sessile in the leaf axils. The corolla is funnel shaped with 4 pinkish to lavender-white petals about ¼ inch long and ¼ inch wide. The stamens and anthers extend beyond the petals.

The fruit is a hard, 2-celled, top-shaped structure with 4 prominent and persistent calyx teeth surrounding the apex. Each cell is about ⅛ inch long and contains 1 light brown, hairy seed. With no specialized mode of dispersal, the mature fruits usually split upon drying, and individual seeds drop to the ground.

The chief mode of propagation for poorjoe is by seeds. Seeds may require a short period of cold stratification, since germination occurs in early spring.

Ground-feeding birds may seek the seeds. Authorities report that whirlabout skippers (*Polites vibex*) swarm poorjoe in search of nectar in the summer.

This species is cited as *Diodia teres* in legacy literature for the coastal Carolinas.

49 DUNE WORMSEED

Dysphania anthelmintica (Linnaeus) Mosyakin & Clemants

Family: Chenopodiaceae (Goosefoot)
Other Common Names: Stinkweed, wormseed, Spanish tea, epazote, Jerusalem tea
Range: Massachusetts south to Florida and west to Kansas and Texas; also California
Habitat: Dunes and dune swales; also roadsides and disturbed areas
Habit: Annual herb
Flowering/Fruiting Period: FL July– September; FR August–October
Wetland Status: FACU
Origin: Exotic; native to Central and South America

The odor of crushed leaves, flowers, or fruits of dune wormseed illustrates why one of the plant's other common names is stinkweed. Dune wormseed is strongly and unpleasantly aromatic; the active terpenes responsible for the aroma are poisonous to livestock, which consistently avoid this plant. The plant is reportedly used as an herb in black bean recipes to "ward off some of the 'negative' side affects [*sic*] of eating beans."

49. Dune wormseed (*Dysphania anthelmintica*). (a) The leaves of dune wormseed are sessile or have short petioles. Numerous flowering heads are produced by a single plant.

49. Dune wormseed (*Dysphania anthelmintica*). (b) Flowers have no petals visible; female styles and stigmas are fully developed; male flowers have prominent anthers, which are about to open in this photograph. **(c)** Each of the abundant fruits contains a reddish-brown to black seed.

c

Growing to a height of 1 to 3 feet, this bright green plant possesses ovate to lanceolate leaves with widely spaced teeth. The leaves are sessile or on short petioles, 1 to 3 inches long, and ⅜ to 1 inch wide.

Arranged in dense terminal and axillary inflorescences, the flowers are interspersed with small elliptical bracts. Petals are absent in the flowers, and 5 green sepals tightly surround the enclosed fruit. Each fruit contains a glossy reddish-brown to black seed.

Dune wormseed prefers sandy soil and full sunlight.

Leaves contain the chemical ascaridole, which is toxic to roundworms, pinworms, and hookworms. Mayans drank epazote tea to ward off worm infestations.

In legacy coastal plant ecology literature, botanists refer to this species as *Chenopodium ambrosioides*.

50 FIREWEED

Erechtites hieraciifolius (Linnaeus)
 Rafinesque. ex A. P. de Candolle
Family: Asteraceae (Aster)
Other Common Names: American
 burnweed, burnweed, pilewort
Range: Nova Scotia, Canada; west to
 Minnesota and South Dakota and south
 to Texas and Florida; also Washington,
 Oregon, and California
Habitat: Dune swales, maritime grasslands,
 and brackish marshes; also woodland
 borders
Habit: Annual herb
Flowering/Fruiting Period: FL July-
 September; FR August-November
Wetland Status: UPL
Origin: Native

Fireweed is a good example of a plant that contributes to ecological diversity without "flair." While this plant is widespread, it presents no showy flowers, no fruits or

a

b

c

50. Fireweed (*Erechtites hieraciifolius*). (a) Each of these widespread, tall, coarse, pale green plants produces hundreds of flowers. (b) Flower heads, composed of disk flowers only, are about ¾ inch long. (c) Seeds possess soft, white bristles that facilitate wind dispersal of the tiny seeds.

seeds upon which wildlife depend, and no direct human benefits; however, it is a frequent pioneer plant that quickly occupies sites after fire or other soil-disturbing events.

Fireweed has a shallow and fibrous root system and fleshy, glabrous, grooved stems often streaked with thin, dark green lines. This coarse, pale green plant varies from 2 to 8 feet tall with ascending branches. Leaves are alternately arranged on the stem and grow up to 8 inches long and 3 inches wide. The margins are serrated, and the upper surfaces have scattered hairs. The lance-shaped leaves attach to short petioles near the base of the plant and are sessile or clasping on the upper portion of the plant.

Upper stems terminate in open panicles with many flower heads composed of disk florets only. The entire flower head is ¾ inch long and ¼ inch across. Linear, glaucous bracts enclose the slightly enlarged heads. The bracts are green or frequently purple tinged. Flowers are greenish-white and barely visible above the bracts. Outer florets on the tightly closed flowers are female, and inner florets are either perfect (possessing both male and female organs) or sterile. Oblong seeds, or achenes, possess tufts of soft, bright white bristles. In fruit, the flowering heads become fluffy masses efficiently distributing the seeds by wind.

While it tolerates some shade, fireweed

prefers full sun and grows best in the moist soils of dune slacks.

Wasps, hornets, bees, and flies visit the flowers. This species constitutes a minor source of food for wildlife.

Use seeds to propagate the species. Seeds that do not germinate shortly after they are shed usually become dormant and may persist for years in the seedbank.

Fireweed may appear as a volunteer plant in native plant gardens.

51 NORTHERN SEASIDE SPURGE

Euphorbia polygonifolia Linnaeus
Family: Euphorbiaceae (Spurge)
Other Common Names: Northern sandmat,
    seaside sandmat, sea milk-purslane,
    dune spurge
Range: Nova Scotia to Ontario and south
    to Florida and west to Mississippi; Great
    Lakes states
Habitat: Wrack lines and dunes
Habit: Annual herb
Flowering/Fruiting Period: FL & FR May–
    October
Wetland Status: FACU
Origin: Native

When stems or leaves of northern seaside spurge are broken, cut, or crushed, milky white sap trickles from the damaged part of the plant, an attribute of many members of the plant family Euphorbiaceae. Familiar members of this family include the South American rubber tree, the holiday-season poinsettia, and the versatile cassava, the source of the dessert ingredient tapioca.

Northern seaside spurge has prostrate stems radiating from a central taproot. At maturity, the plant reaches a dinner-plate size and grows merely 1 or 2 inches above the dune sand surface. Leaves are opposite, or nearly so, entire, elliptic to oblong, ¼ to ⅜ inch long, and ⅛ inch wide. The entire plant is glabrous.

The flowers of northern seaside spurge are arranged in cyathia, flower structures

51. Northern seaside spurge (*Euphorbia polygonifolia*). (a) Stems of this species are prostrate, and the entire plant grows closely appressed to the surface of the ground. (b) Several cyathia and a mature fruit are visible in this view of a stem tip.

particular to plants in the Spurge plant family. The structure, enclosed in leaflike bracts, contains nectar glands, male flowers reduced to stamens only, and female flowers reduced to a single pistil. No petals or sepals are part of the flowers. The cyathia develop at the terminus of each branch.

Mature fruits are composed of a 3-sectioned, 3-seeded capsule. As the capsule matures, the peduncle turns upward, which places the smooth, 1/16-inch, gray seeds above the plant. This may aid in wind dispersal of the seeds.

Northern seaside spurge has little wildlife or landscape use. Ground birds and insects may feed on the seeds.

In the coastal Carolinas, northern seaside spurge is common in sparsely vegetated areas such as the wrack line, inlet shorelines, embryo dunes, and recent overwash fans, where it is typically associated with sea oats, sea rocket, northern saltwort, large sea purslane, and seabeach amaranth.

Northern seaside spurge requires full sun for best growth. It is heat and salt-aerosol tolerant but is not tolerant of high salt concentrations in the soil. The low growth habit of northern seaside spurge appears to reduce the impact of salt aerosols.

The only method of propagating northern seaside spurge is by seeds.

A closely related species, southern seaside spurge (*Euphorbia bombensis*), grows in close proximity to northern seaside spurge. Smaller, darker green leaves and purple stems are key distinguishing characteristics of southern seaside spurge. Southern seaside spurge is locally common in dunes landward of the foredunes.

52 BEACH BLANKET-FLOWER

Gaillardia pulchella Fougeroux
Family: Asteraceae (Aster)
Other Common Names: Fire wheels, Indian blanket, gaillardia
Range: North Carolina south to Florida and west to Texas
Habitat: Dunes; also dry, open waste areas; roadsides
Habit: Annual herb
Flowering/Fruiting Period: FL & FR May–November
Wetland Status: UPL
Origin: Native

A common plant of prairies in the central United States and the state wildflower of Oklahoma, this colorful member of the Aster family is equally at home on Atlantic, Gulf, and Pacific coast dunes. While not considered an aggressive plant, beach blanket-flower spreads easily by seeds.

The bushy beach blanket-flower can grow up to 24 inches high with a similar girth under favorable conditions, but the globe-shaped plant is typically about 10 to 12 inches across. The much-branched plant arises from a shallow taproot. Stems, branches, and leaves are coarsely hairy, and the deeply lobed leaves are mostly basal, alternate, simple, narrow, and clasping. The slightly succulent leaves may be up to 3 inches long and 1¼ inches wide.

Beach blanket-flower has appealing 2- to 3-inch, daisylike flowers with crimson or rose-purple disk florets surrounded by 10 to 20 sterile red or scarlet ray florets, each tinged with a yellow band of varying width at the outer edge of the ray. As the fruits mature, they form small, gray, bristly heads composed of many achenes. Each plant produces enormous quantities of seeds.

Collect the seeds in the fall and plant them the following spring; they germinate readily. A great plant for coastal gardens,

a

b

c

52. Beach blanket-flower (*Gaillardia pulchella*). (a) Many flowers grace the salt-aerosol-resistant and coarsely hairy stems and leaves. (b) Red or scarlet-red ray flowers with yellow-tinged tips surround the rose-purple disk flowers. (c) Fruits are gray with long bristles attached to each achene.

beach blanket-flower is low maintenance and attractive to bees and butterflies. The plant prefers well-drained, sandy soils and is highly drought and salt-aerosol tolerant.

Ground birds and small mammals eat the seeds. This species is a minor proportion of the diet of white-tailed deer.

Several popular cultivars are available commercially, including plants with yellow, orange, red, and multicolored flowers. *Yellow Sun* and *Red Plume* are examples. Beach blanket-flower grows best in full sun and in warm locations, such as near walls and walkways.

The beach blanket-flower variety most common in the coastal Carolinas is *drummondii*.

53 BITTERWEED

Helenium amarum (Rafinesque) H. Rock
Family: Asteraceae (Aster)
Other Common Names: Bitter sneezeweed, narrow-leaved sneezeweed
Range: Massachusetts west to Wisconsin, south to Florida and Texas; also California
Habitat: Fields, roadsides, and waste areas
Habit: Annual herb
Flowering/Fruiting Period: FL & FR June–November
Wetland Status: FACU
Origin: Native

Bitterweed's dense, bright yellow flower heads and linear leaves easily identify this opportunistic weed. It is most common in waste areas and roadsides of the Carolinas coastal area.

Bitterweed grows from 4 to 8 inches tall but can range up to 24 inches in ideal growing conditions. Bitterweed is an erect, compact plant with glabrous stems that are many branched above the middle of the plant. The plant forms a large taproot.

Leaves are numerous, simple, sessile, linear, and alternately arranged on the

a 53. Bitterweed (*Helenium amarum*). (a) Bright yellow flowers with linear leaves help identify this compact plant of disturbed areas. (b) Both disk and ray flowers of bitterweed are yellow. (c) Nutlets are topped with brown, bristle-tipped scales.

stem. Upon close inspection with a hand lens, you can see that the leaves are dotted with small amber-colored glands. The leaves, up to 3 inches long and ¹⁄₁₆ inch wide, are densest near the top of the plant. The lowest leaves usually die before flowering begins. When crushed, the leaves have a disagreeably pungent odor.

Bitterweed flowers prolifically. Flowers are located terminally and in leaf axils. Both disk and ray flowers are yellow and combine to form a flower about ½ to ¾ inch across. The outer edge of each ray flower possesses 3 large, distinctive teeth that are reflexed toward the base of the flower head. The disk flowers have a mounded appearance.

Pollinators include bees and butterflies.

The fruits of bitterweed are brown, pubescent nutlets with bristle-tipped scales on the top of the nutlet. It is best to collect seeds from wild plants in early fall and sow them in early spring. There is no known dormancy requirement for seeds.

Bitterweed requires moist soil and full sun. It grows especially well in sandy soils where competition from other plants is minimal.

The plant is mildly toxic to humans. Livestock eating bitterweed produce bitter-tasting milk.

The variety *amarum* is the most common form of bitterweed in the coastal Carolinas.

54 DUNE CAMPHORWEED

Heterotheca subaxillaris (Lamarck) Britton & Rusby
Family: Asteraceae (Aster)
Other Common Names: Goldenaster, telegraph plant, camphorweed
Range: Coastal: southern Connecticut south to Florida
Habitat: Dunes, dune swales, maritime

a

c

b

54. Dune camphorweed (*Heterotheca subaxillaris*). (a) In dunes and maritime grasslands, individual plants flower profusely and may become several feet across and 3 feet tall. (b) Conspicuous yellow ray flowers surround orange disk flowers. (c) Wind-dispersed achenes detach easily from the mature flower.

grasslands, edges of maritime shrub thickets; also open, sandy disturbed areas; roadsides

Habit: Annual herb (biennial)

Flowering/Fruiting Period: FL & FR July–October

Wetland Status: FACU

Origin: Native

From midsummer through fall, the dunes and other open, sandy environments are ablaze with the bright yellow flowers of dune camphorweed, one of the most abundant and successful plants of the coastal Carolinas. Some ecologists think dune camphorweed is too successful and consider it a noxious weed. During late fall and winter, dunes are dotted with

small rosettes of dune camphorweed, the seedlings of plants that will flourish the following summer.

This erect, bushy, wide-spreading plant ranges from 1 to 3 feet tall and occasionally larger. It possesses a large taproot and extensive roots that supply it with water during extended droughts. Dune camphorweed has alternate, simple leaves that appear light green due to the presence of scattered hairs on both leaf surfaces. The lower leaves are oblong to ovate, up to 4 inches long, ½ to 2 inches wide, irregularly toothed, slightly wrinkled, and long petioled. The smaller upper stem leaves are sessile and clasping. Both leaves and stems release a pungent, camphorlike odor when the foliage is crushed, hence the origin of its common name.

Each somewhat structurally unorganized plant produces scores to hundreds of seeds. An individual flower head is composed of 15 to 30 conspicuous yellow ray flowers, ⅜ to ¾ inch in diameter, and several orange disk flowers, giving the flowering head a pleasing, two-tone, yellow-orange color.

Dune camphorweed is highly attractive to several species of bees and other pollinating insects. It is an important fall nectar source for monarch butterflies and other migratory insects. It is a minor food source for terrestrial birds.

Like the seeds of many members of the Aster family, dune camphorweed seeds (known as achenes) from disk and ray flowers differ in shape and physiology. Disk achenes possess a double pappus; achenes of ray flowers lack a pappus. After being shed in the fall, disk achenes germinate immediately. Ray achenes are dormant when shed, and germination is delayed for a year after dispersal; this occurs because these seeds require a warm period of after-ripening, an environmental condition that does not occur until the following summer. This seed germination strategy assures that this weedy species can survive an environmental disaster such as a serious, yearlong drought.

While not commercially available, seeds can be collected easily on roadsides and in disturbed, sandy areas.

---

55 SOUTHERN SALTMARSH FLEABANE

Pluchea odorata (Linnaeus) Cassini
Family: Asteraceae (Aster)
Other Common Names: Saltmarsh fleabane, marsh fleabane, shrubby camphorweed, stinkweed
Range: Massachusetts south to Florida and west to Texas and California
Habitat: Brackish marshes and edges of salt marshes, fresh marshes, and wet dune swales
Habit: Annual herb (perennial)
Flowering/Fruiting Period: FL & FR August–October
Wetland Status: FACW
Origin: Native

55. Southern saltmarsh fleabane (*Pluchea odorata*). (a) With pubescent stems and leaves, this herbaceous plant grows to a height of 1 to 2 feet, often at the edge of brackish or salt marshes. Alternately arranged leaves are variable in size and shape. (b) Flower clusters are prominent at the apices of the stems. The disk-only flowers range from pink to rose-lavender.

c

55. Southern saltmarsh fleabane (*Pluchea odorata*). (c) Fruits are wind-dispersed achenes, each with a tuft of white hairs.

Southern saltmarsh fleabane is a distinctive broadleaf plant with large, purple flower heads and a characteristic camphorlike odor when the leaves are crushed. The smell is probably the origin of some of its common names, camphorweed and stinkweed. During the fall, when many other brackish-marsh and saltmarsh species have been heavily grazed by feral horses or white-tailed deer, the less palatable southern saltmarsh fleabane stands alone, virtually untouched.

Southern saltmarsh fleabane grows to a height of 1 to 2 feet and possesses pubescent stems and leaves. Leaves are variable, from long and narrow to broad and pointed, and they may be sessile or have short petioles. Leaves possess irregularly toothed margins. Leaves are alternately arranged on the stems and range from 2 to 6 inches long and ⅜ to 1½ inches wide.

Prominent, fragrant flower clusters, 2 to 4 inches across, terminate the ascending stems. The color of individual flower heads ranges from pink to rose-lavender. Possessing only disk flowers in each ¼- to ½-inch flower head, they are usually swarming with pollinating bees, flies, and wasps. The seeds are 1/16-inch-long achenes.

Southern saltmarsh fleabane can tolerate saltwater flooding for a short time. It requires full sun for best growth. Species typically associated with southern saltmarsh fleabane include saltmeadow cordgrass and saltgrass.

The plant persists primarily through seed production. Seeds can be collected from mature wild plants in late fall and used in coastal native plant gardens.

56 TROPICAL MEXICAN CLOVER
Richardia brasiliensis Gomes
Family: Rubiaceae (Madder)
Other Common Names: Brazil pusley, white eye, Mexican clover
Range: Coastal: Virginia south to Florida and west to Texas
Habitat: Fields, lawns, roadsides, and waste areas
Habit: Annual herb (perennial)
Flowering/Fruiting Period: FL & FR May–November
Wetland Status: Not designated
Origin: Exotic; native to South America

Tropical Mexican clover is one of the most common plants occurring along roadsides and lawns in the coastal Carolinas. The plant adapts quickly to periodic mowing, often growing only a few inches tall and spreading laterally up to 12 inches.

When it occurs in backdunes and waste areas, it grows semi-prostrate, highly branched, and from 3 to 12 inches tall. Leaves are simple, oppositely arranged on the stems, 1 to 2 inches long, and ¼ to ¾ inch wide. Hairs are present on the margins and veins of the ovate- or elliptic-shaped leaves. The presence of stipules at

a

b

56. Tropical Mexican clover (*Richardia brasiliensis*). (a) This semi-prostrate to prostrate plant is highly branched with simple, oppositely arranged leaves. (b) Flowers develop in clusters of 20 or more. White petals are joined, forming a funnel-shaped corolla, about ¼ inch long.

the base of the leaves is a distinguishing characteristic of this species.

Flowers develop in terminal, headlike clusters with 20 or more flowers subtended by 2 to 4 leafy, involucral bracts. The flowers are bright white with 6 sepals and 6 petals. The petals are joined, forming a funnel-shaped corolla about ¼ inch long. Stamens extend beyond the petals of the corolla tube. Each fruit splits at maturity to release 3 seeds. Each seed is about ¹⁄₁₆ inch across with abundant long hairs on its surface.

The plant grows best in dry, sandy soil and full sun. It is salt-aerosol tolerant and found growing close to the ocean.

Large and small mammals graze tropical Mexican clover.

Seeds and division of the plant's roots can propagate tropical Mexican clover. Despite its common name, the plant is a member of the Madder family, a group quite distinct from the Clover family, Fabaceae.

Generally considered a weed species in the coastal Carolinas, tropical Mexican clover is not suitable as a component of a coastal native plant garden.

---

57 MARSH PINK

Sabatia stellaris Pursh

Family: Gentianiaceae (Gentian)

Other Common Names: Sea pink, salt marsh pink, annual sea pink

Range: Coastal: Massachusetts south to Florida and west to Louisiana

Habitat: Dune swales, maritime grasslands, and upper edges of brackish and salt marshes

Habit: Annual herb

Flowering/Fruiting Period: FL July–September; FR August–November

Wetland Status: OBL

Origin: Native

While many plants flaunt attractive flowers with a single color, marsh pink displays a striking flower revealing petals with touches of pink, red, yellow, and white that create an interesting and attractive star-shaped center. Occasionally, this species grows in such profusion that the plants turn acres of maritime grasslands into a multicolored display of flowers swaying in the summer breeze.

Marsh pinks are 6 to 20 inches high with slender, erect, loosely branched stems. Leaves, ranging from ½ to 2 inches long, are oppositely arranged, simple, entire, glabrous, and sessile.

Each flower grows on a single pedicel. The 1-inch-wide flowers have 5 short sepals and 5 petals. The stamens and style are yellow. Bumblebees and other small bees such as sweat bees pollinate flowers. Each

a

c

b

57. Marsh pink (*Sabatia stellaris*). (a) Marsh pink ranges from 6 to 20 inches tall with slender, erect, loosely branched stems. Leaves range from ½ to 2 inches long and are simple, entire, glabrous, and sessile. (b) Bright pink flowers are 1 inch wide and have 5 short sepals and 5 petals. Stamens and style are yellow. (c) Fruits are ¼-inch globose capsules that contain more than 100 tiny, brown to black seeds.

fruiting capsule contains about 100 tiny black or brown seeds.

Marsh pink is salt tolerant and commonly associated with brackish environments. It frequently grows amid sea ox-eye, sea lavender, saltmeadow cordgrass, dune finger grass, beach blanket-flower, saltmarsh fimbristylis, and southern seaside goldenrod.

The plant provides nectar for pollinating insects, and various herbivorous insects feed on parts of the plant.

Propagation is only by seeds. Unfortunately, the plant is not commercially available. Collect seeds only where marsh pink is growing in abundance; avoid overcollecting and depleting the annual seed crop. The seeds are tiny, tiny, tiny; just a few seed capsules will generate a lot of seeds!

Marsh pink is either "endangered" or "threatened" in states at the northern limits of its range (Rhode Island, Massachusetts, Connecticut, and New York). This is due, in part, to the expansion of the invasive species common reed into habitats occupied by marsh pink.

Occasionally, we find a similar species, perennial sea pink (*Sabatia dodecandra*), in brackish or freshwater marshes in the coastal Carolinas. Its flowers are twice as large and have 9 to 11 petals.

58 DWARF GLASSWORT

Salicornia bigelovii Torrey
Family: Chenopodiaceae (Goosefoot)
Other Common Names: Pickleweed, dwarf saltwort, woody glasswort
Range: Coastal: Maine to Florida and west to Texas; also California

HERBS

203

a

b

c 58. Dwarf glasswort (*Salicornia bigelovii*).
(a) Dwarf glasswort grows in salt pannes and
salt marshes dominated by smooth cordgrass.
(b) The plant is 2 to 12 inches tall and branched,
with short, jointed, succulent stems that appear
beadlike. Typically, only individual stamens or
styles and stigmas are seen poking out from
nodes near the tip of each stem. (c) The plant
turns bright red in fall.

Habitat: Salt marshes
Habit: Annual herb
Flowering/Fruiting Period: FL August–
September; FR September–October
Wetland Status: OBL
Origin: Native

Dwarf glasswort is a succulent plant
with short, jointed stems that appear to
be composed of strings of "beads." The
opposite leaves are not readily apparent on
the plant; they appear as tiny, fleshy scales.
The plant turns bright red in the fall and
becomes woody as it ages. Botanists named
this unusual-looking marsh plant in honor
of American botanist Jacob Bigelow (1787–
1879). Abundant in the southeastern United
States, dwarf glasswort is designated as a
plant of special concern in Maine and as
a "threatened species" in New Hampshire
and New York.

Dwarf glasswort often forms dense
stands in salt marshes. In this environment,
the plant is erect and typically possesses
primary and secondary branches. Plant
height ranges from 2 to 12 inches.

The flowers of dwarf glasswort develop
on the stem apices. The fertile segments
are larger in diameter than nonfertile parts
of the plant, and these larger segments are
obvious when flowering begins. They occur
on 5 to 25 segments, and each segment
produces 3 small, highly reduced flowers so
sunken into the joints of the stem that only
a single stamen of each flower is visible.
Scale leaves below the flowering spike are
mucronate. The plant is wind pollinated.

Dwarf glasswort's seeds are nutlets.
They are brown or black and barely ¹⁄₁₆ inch
long. Only seeds propagate the plant.
Studies show that germination can occur
in salt-free environments as well as in
soils with up to twice the natural seawater
strength (8 percent salt).

The plant grows best on salt pannes and
in areas of marsh colonized by few other
plants. Dwarf glasswort is consistently

associated with smooth cordgrass, Virginia glasswort, and sea lavender.

Dwarf glasswort is a host plant for the larvae of eastern pigmy blue butterfly (*Brephidium isophthalma*). Decomposition of the plants makes organic matter available to a variety of estuarine organisms.

The plant holds promise as a future fuel; scientists propose using dwarf glasswort seeds as a potential source of biodiesel fuel.

Some people spice up a salad with raw stems. Others enjoy young dwarf glasswort plants, either cooked or pickled. In homeopathy, it is a diuretic and antidote for scurvy.

a

59 NORTHERN SALTWORT

Salsola kali Moench
Family: Chenopodiaceae (Goosefoot)
Other Common Names: Russian thistle, tumbleweed, common saltwort
Range: Essentially throughout North America
Habitat: Wrack lines and dunes
Habit: Annual herb
Flowering/Fruiting Period: FL & FR June–October
Wetland Status: FACU
Origin: Exotic; native to Eurasia

Northern saltwort, a noxious weed and aggressive exotic plant, has spread essentially worldwide in arid and semi-arid environments where competition from native species is minimal. Northern saltwort possesses an extensive root system reported to radiate 3 feet from its base and a physiology that actively takes up nutrients from salt aerosols, allowing it to thrive in the Carolinas' coastal beach and dune habitats.

The bushy northern saltwort has erect branches arising from its base and ranges from 1 to 3 feet tall with an equal girth. Stems of northern saltwort are dark green and are often highlighted with red

b

59. Northern saltwort (*Salsola kali*). (a) Stems of this small shrub, common on the backshore, are dark green tinged with red stripes. Leaves are succulent and spine tipped. (b) Northern saltwort possesses 5 yellow, petal-like anthers.

stripes. The lowest leaves of the plant are succulent, tubular, and ½ to 3 inches long, with a rounded apex. Leaves growing on the upper part of the plant are similar but shorter and spine tipped. Entire plants often turn bright red late in the growing season.

Often overlooked, greenish-white flowers of northern saltwort are solitary in the leaf axils and subtended by 2 succulent bracteoles. The flowers include 5 wing-shaped, papery, persistent, and enlarged sepals, but no petals. Flowering is indeterminate, and the plant continues

HERBS

205

c

59. Northern saltwort (*Salsola kali*). (c) The large, wing-shaped, papery sepals are persistent in the fruits.

60. Southern sea-blite (*Suaeda linearis*). (a) Southern sea-blite varies from 4 to 24 inches tall and is usually much branched. Succulent, linear leaves range from ½ to 1 inch long.

to flower until frost. Seed production is prodigious, with average-sized plants producing thousands of seeds. Seeds remain attached to the plant until they mature; they are scattered by the wind as branches "tumble" along the beach. A tightly coiled embryo is visible through the translucent seed wall. Seeds germinate in March and April as coastal soil temperatures begin to rise.

Little is known of its wildlife value.

60 SOUTHERN SEA-BLITE

Suaeda linearis (Elliott) Moquin
Family: Chenopodiaceae (Goosefoot)
Other Common Names: Sea-blite, narrow leaved seepweed, annual seepweed
Range: Maine south to Florida and west to Texas

Habitat: Beaches, maritime grasslands, and salt pannes
Habit: Annual herb
Flowering/Fruiting Period: FL & FR August–November
Wetland Status: OBL
Origin: Native

Walk across the tidal marsh edge of an overwash fan in the coastal Carolinas, and you are sure to find succulent southern sea-blite plants covering a large area of the fan. After major storms, tidal waters distribute southern sea-blite seeds throughout coastal wet sand environments, and within a year, southern sea-blite dominates the otherwise barren sites. In fact, southern sea-blite is capable of growing in areas where the salt content of the soils is too high for most other species to survive.

The shallowly rooted southern sea-blite possesses glabrous, succulent stems and leaves. Individual plants vary from 4 to 24 inches high and may be profusely branched or nearly unbranched. The alternately arranged, linear leaves range

b 60. Southern sea-blite (*Suaeda linearis*). (b) Pale green flowers form in the axils of leaves near the tips of the upper branches. The flowers have sepals, but no petals. (c) Fruits are tiny; each lobe of the star-shaped fruits contains a single shiny, black seed.

from ½ to 1 inch long. Leaves vary from glaucous green to dark green.

Inconspicuous wind-pollinated flowers are present in leaf axils toward the end of each branch. The slightly zygomorphic flowers have 5 sepals, no petals, 5 stamens, and 2 or 3 stigmas. Rolling the star-shaped fruits between your fingers will tease out the tiny, shiny, black seeds.

Ground birds eat the seeds as they forage on coastal sand flats.

The succulent leaves of southern sea-blite are similar to those of the glasswort (*Salicornia* sp.).

61 DUNE BLUE CURLS

Trichostema [species 1]
Family: Lamiaceae (Mint)
Other Common Name: Carolina blue curls
Range: North Carolina and South Carolina
Habitat: Dunes, dune swales, maritime grasslands, and disturbed areas
Habit: Annual herb
Flowering/Fruiting Period: FL & FR August–November

Wetland Status: Likely UPL
Origin: Native

Dune blue curls derives its name from the 4 beautifully upswept and gracefully arched bluish stamens within its incredibly attractive flower. While not a dominant plant on the dunes, it is common in some localities but easily overlooked when not flowering.

A member of the Mint family, dune blue curls has a square stem that is densely glandular, pubescent, and sticky. Dune blue curls grows from 6 to 18 inches tall but usually remains less than 12 inches tall in dune environments, adapting to an environment with significant salt aerosols. Leaves of dune blue curls are entire, ovate, and arranged oppositely on the stems.

Flowers are solitary or in pairs on much-branched stems that arise from leaf axils. The pale lavender flowers are zygomorphic with 4 fused petals forming the upper lip and a single petal forming the lower lip. The lower lip or tongue is rectangular, slightly inrolled, and covered with large, dark blue splotches. The 4 large stamens and single style occupy the center

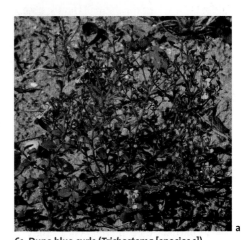

61. Dune blue curls (*Trichostema* [species 1]). (a) This square-stemmed plant is compact, usually remaining less than 12 inches tall, with small, entire, ovate, opposite leaves.

b

c

61. Dune blue curls (*Trichostema* [species 1]).
(b) Strongly zygomorphic flowers are pale
lavender, with 4 fused petals forming an upper
lip and 1 large, dark purplish-blue-splotched petal
forming the lower lip. Four large stamens "curl"
in the center of the flower. (c) Four nutlets are
surrounded by the 5-parted calyx.

provide modest cover for small animals in
the dunes.

The dune blue curls pictured here is
either a separate species or possibly a
variety of common blue curls. Taxonomic
experts have yet to describe and name this
plant. Botanical records indicate that it
may be endemic to the dune communities
of North Carolina and South Carolina.

Because this species appears to have a
restricted range and is yet to be named and
described in the botanical literature, the
U.S. Fish and Wildlife Service designates
this plant a "species of special concern." Do
not remove specimens or seeds from the
dunes.

62 COCKLEBUR

Xanthium strumarium Linnaeus
Family: Asteraceae (Aster)
Other Common Names: Rough cocklebur,
common cocklebur, heartleaf cocklebur
Range: Nova Scotia to British Columbia,
Canada; south to Florida and California
(and worldwide in the temperate zone)
Habitat: Wrack lines and dunes; also waste
places, roadsides, agricultural fields,
and other disturbed environments
Habit: Annual herb
Flowering/Fruiting Period: FL & FR July–
November
Wetland Status: FAC
Origin: Native

Farmers know cocklebur well since it is
an important, often difficult to eradicate
weed in agricultural fields. Many of the
ecological adaptations that make cocklebur
an aggressive weed in cropland allow it to
adapt to frequently disturbed dune areas
on the Carolinas coast.

The bushy, shade-intolerant cocklebur
ranges from 1 to 4 feet tall with alternate,
long-petioled, broadly triangular leaves
that are 1 to 5 inches long with 3 to 5 lobes.
Positively identify this species by the
presence of 3 prominent veins that arise

of the flower. When flowering is complete,
4 nutlets mature within the 5-parted calyx
that remains on the plant.

Dune blue curls grows well in full sun as
well as partial shade. It prefers dry, sandy
soils.

Ground birds and small mammals may
feed on the seeds of this species, and it may

a

c

b

d

62. Cocklebur (*Xanthium strumarium*). (a) This plant's leaves are long-petioled and broadly triangular, ranging from 1 to 5 inches across with 3 to 5 lobes. (b) Separate male flowers grow above the spiny female flowers. (c) Male and female flowers are in close proximity to each other. (d) Fruits are hard, cylindrical burrs with slender, hooked spines.

from the base of the leaf where the blade and petiole meet. Leaf surfaces feel scurfy owing to the presence of numerous stiff, bristly hairs.

Cocklebur possesses separate male and female flowers on each plant. Both cluster in leaf axils, the inconspicuous male flowers higher on the plant than the female flowers. The cocklebur fruit is a ½- to 1-inch-long, hard, cylindrical to ellipsoid burr covered with short, slender, hooked spines and two large, sharp, pointed beaks at one end. The spines resemble the hooked portion of Velcro and help the fruits stick to clothing and fur, an efficient mode of seed dispersal. The burr is initially greenish-yellow, turning brown at maturity.

The burrs can float for at least 30 days, and this trait provides the fruit with an opportunity to be dispersed along beaches as well as to be rolled along the sandy surface by winds. Cocklebur produces 2 different seeds in each fruit. The lower seed germinates in the first year after separating from the plant, while internal physiological conditions delay germination of the upper seed for as long as a year. This strategy assures the persistence of the plant even under unfavorable growth conditions during a particular year.

Cocklebur seeds and cotyledon leaves are poisonous to sheep, cattle, and pigs. A nuisance plant, cocklebur does provide resting and hiding sites for wildlife.

Plant physiologists use cocklebur as a research organism in the study of plant photoperiodism, the roughly 24-hour cycle of biochemical, physiological, or behavioral processes observed in plants.

a

63 ALLIGATORWEED

Alternanthera philoxeroides (Martius) Grisebach
Family: Amaranthaceae (Amaranth)
Other Common Name: Pig weed
Range: Virginia west to Illinois and south to Florida and Texas; also California
Habitat: Shallow water ponds and wet areas; also slow-moving watercourses
Habit: Perennial herb
Flowering/Fruiting Period: FL & FR April–October
Wetland Status: OBL
Origin: Exotic; introduced from Parana River region of South America
Not recommended for planting; instead, remove where already growing.

Alligatorweed, designated an invasive aquatic plant in South Carolina and a noxious weed in other southern states, was accidentally introduced into the United States in the 1890s in Alabama. Since its introduction, the plant has spread throughout the Southeast and into the Midwest and West. This fast-growing

b

63. Alligatorweed (*Alternanthera philoxeroides*). (a) Alligatorweed patches grow partially submerged in open water. Leaves are bright green with a prominent midrib. (b) Individual flowers, possessing bracts and tepals, cluster at the apex of a long peduncle.

plant forms dense mats that displace native aquatic and shoreline plants in the coastal Carolinas. Alligatorweed chokes waterways, creates a habitat for breeding mosquitoes, and blocks drainage wherever it is firmly established.

Alligatorweed typically roots in the substrate, but much of the plant is emergent or floating on the water surface. It forms dense clumps that may be 6 feet or more across. Roots are fibrous and arise at the stem nodes. Alligatorweed stems are fleshy and succulent and may be either creeping or floating. Stems trail horizontally along damp ground; in shallow water, stem tips turn upward. The oppositely arranged leaves sometimes appear whorled. Leaves are elliptical, 2 to 4 inches long, and ¾ inch wide, and they possess neither a petiole nor surface hairs.

The white flower heads of alligatorweed bear a superficial resemblance to those of clover. Heads are about ½ inch in diameter and originate in the upper axils of the plant. Six to 10 individual flowers form the head, and these occur on a peduncle ranging from ½ to 3 inches long. Flowers are composed of papery bracts, ⅛-inch tepals, 5 stamens, and a single pistil.

The fruit contains 1 small seed, but scientists have found that these seeds are usually not viable. Alligatorweed propagation is via vegetative means; fragmentation allows the plant to colonize new locations and habitats.

Alligatorweed grows well on land and in shallow water. It can survive flooding for several days without ill effects. It grows best in open sun and in eutrophic waters. It can tolerate soil salts up to about 10 percent of seawater strength.

Managers of our waterways have attempted to control the plant by releasing 3 predators: a beetle, *Agasicles hygrophila*; a thrip, *Amynothrips andersoni*; and a stem-boring moth, *Arcola malloi*. Their endeavors show some success, especially in the Gulf Coast states. Attempts to remove the plant physically usually result in spreading plant fragments over a larger area.

The plant harbors many species of invertebrates, which provide sustenance for fish, amphibians, and reptiles. In addition, alligatorweed provides some cover for waterfowl.

Although alligatorweed has some redeeming values, remove it from any habitat in which you find it.

64 SALT-MARSH WATER HEMP

Amaranthus cannabinus (Linnaeus) J. D. Sauer
Family: Amaranthaceae (Amaranth)
Other Common Names: Tidal-marsh amaranth, waterhemp ragweed, waterhemp pigweed, water hemp
Range: Coastal: Maine south to Florida and west to Louisiana

64. Salt-marsh water hemp (*Amaranthus cannabinus*). (a) Salt-marsh water hemp grows amongst grasses and other herbaceous plants in wetlands.

b 64. Salt-marsh water hemp (*Amaranthus cannabinus*). (b) Female flowers have no sepals or petals. (c) Male flowers display 3 to 5 stamens.

Habitat: Brackish and salt marshes, tidal riverbanks, and freshwater tidal marshes

Habit: Perennial herb

Flowering/Fruiting Period: FL & FR July–December

Wetland Status: OBL

Origin: Native

Salt-marsh water hemp flowers late in the summer after most marsh grasses have completed their growth for the season. This provides a late-season seed bonanza for wildlife. Salt-marsh water hemp has a broad ecological niche and is capable of growing in marshes of widely varying salinities; thus it is common throughout wetlands of the coastal Carolinas.

Plant height varies from 2 to 8 feet or more. The stems are stout, erect, and smooth. Leaves are narrowly lanceolate, 3 to 6 inches long, about 1½ inches wide, and arranged alternately on the stem. The margins of the leaves are entire, with petioles from 1 to 4 inches long.

Plants are dioecious, and inflorescences are narrow terminal and axillary spikes. Upon inspection with a hand lens, one sees that the female flowers are devoid of sepals and petals, possessing only greenish-yellow pistils with 3 to 5 stigmas. Male flowers have 5 tepals about ⅛ inch long with 3 to 5 stamens.

The fruit is a fleshy utricle with a single shiny, ovoid, black seed. The seed is approximately ⅛ inch in diameter with 3 prominent longitudinal ridges.

Salt-marsh water hemp is commonly associated with smooth cordgrass, saltgrass, and saltmeadow cordgrass.

Despite their value as a wildlife food, salt-marsh water hemp seeds are rarely available commercially. Collect seeds from plants before the waterfowl get them all! This is an important landscape plant for brackish and saltmarsh areas, especially if you are interested in attracting waterfowl.

65 BEACH WORMWOOD

Artemisia stelleriana Besser

Family: Asteraceae (Aster)

Other Common Names: Dusty miller, old-woman, hoary sagebrush; hoary mugwort

Range: Coastal: Newfoundland, Canada, to North Carolina and Great Lakes states; also Washington and Alaska

Habitat: Dunes; also disturbed areas

Habit: Perennial herb

Flowering/Fruiting Period: FL & FR May–September

Wetland Status: FACU

a

b

65. Beach wormwood (*Artemisia stelleriana*). (a) Plants appear gray to white owing to a dense layer of stellate hairs on leaf surfaces. (b) Densely packed yellow flowers develop in terminal clusters.

Origin: Exotic; native to East Asia, Korea, Japan, and Kamchatka Peninsula

Often planted in coastal gardens, beach wormwood is an introduced species that has escaped from cultivation and is now naturalized throughout the dunes of the northeast coast of the United States and Canada. The plant occasionally occurs as far south as northern North Carolina beaches. Despite its northern affinity, beach wormwood thrives as a landscape plant in the coastal Carolinas.

This attractive, bushy, evergreen plant with ascending branches grows up to 2 feet tall. Dense, white, stellate hairs cover the leaves, giving them a soft, woolly feel. The hairs aid in shedding salt aerosols and maintaining a cooler plant during the summer by reflecting light back to the atmosphere. Deeply pinnately lobed leaves are 2 to 4 inches long and 1 inch wide. The upper leaves are sessile; the lower leaves possess petioles.

Golden yellow flowers are densely packed on 3- to 4-inch spikes. Leafy bracts surround each globe-shaped flower. The fruits of beach wormwood are achenes.

Beach wormwood grows best in full sun, but it will tolerate some shade. The plant requires a sandy soil and is tolerant of salt aerosols, heat, and drought.

The plant has little value to our native wildlife, except for pollination.

Propagate this species through seeds and cuttings made in late summer. Seeds require a period of cold stratification to enhance the rate of germination. Plant division is possible because beach wormwood produces robust rhizomes.

66 MONNIER'S WATER-HYSSOP

Bacopa monnieri (Linnaeus) Wettstein

Family: Plantaginaceae (Plantain)

Other Common Names: Water hyssop, herb-of-grace, coastal water-hyssop, moneywort

Range: Primarily coastal: Maryland south to Florida and west to Texas; also Oklahoma, Arizona, and California

Habitat: Edges of brackish and freshwater marshes; also edges of disturbed wetlands, streams, and ponds

Habit: Perennial herb

HERBS

a

b

66. Monnier's water-hyssop (*Bacopa monnieri*). (a) This oft-branched trailing plant forms dense patches that hug the ground. (b) Delicate, white to light blue flowers with 5 fused petals grow on long peduncles.

Flowering/Fruiting Period: FL & FR April–November

Wetland Status: OBL

Origin: Native

Monnier's water-hyssop, a relative of the common snapdragon, exemplifies how a minor component of a plant community can have practical and potentially valuable human uses. Capable of growing completely submerged, Monnier's water-hyssop is one of several favorite plants of freshwater aquarium enthusiasts. In addition, water-hyssop is sold in capsule form as "bacopa," reputed to be a rejuvenating herb for nerve and brain cells, a therapeutic herb for cognitive disorders of aging, and a mild sedative.

Monnier's water-hyssop is most commonly a trailing plant, but it can grow erect when supported by nearby plants. When growing erect, Monnier's water-hyssop rarely reaches 12 inches. Where it trails along moist, sandy ground, the plant roots at the nodes, branches frequently, and forms extensive mats no more than about 3 inches high. The succulent leaves are sessile, entire, obovate, ¼ to ¾ inch long, ⅛ to ¼ inch wide, and oppositely arranged on the stems.

The flowers grow solitary on long peduncles in the axils of the leaves. The flower color varies from white to light blue. Five fused petals form the ⅜-inch-long tubular corolla. Two green bracts surround each flower. The fruit is an ovoid capsule with a pointed tip. Seeds are grayish brown, oblong, and longitudinally ribbed.

Drought intolerant, Monnier's water-hyssop grows best in wet or moist sandy soil, preferably in full sun. It tolerates occasional inundation with brackish or salt water.

Waterfowl may occasionally eat the foliage and seeds.

Propagation is from simple plant division and seeds. Use Monnier's water-hyssop in water gardens and as a ground cover in sunny, moist areas. If it is unavailable in commercial nurseries, obtain specimens from aquarium plant growers.

A related species, blue water-hyssop (*Bacopa caroliniana*), grows in marshes and brackish-water mudflats in the coastal

Carolinas. This species is distinguished by its hairy upper stem and the release of a lemony mint scent when leaves are crushed.

---

67 COTTONLEAF GOLDENASTER

Chrysopsis gossypina (Michaux) Elliott
Family: Asteraceae (Aster)
Other Common Name: Cottony goldenaster
Range: Coastal Virginia south to Florida and west to Alabama
Habitat: Dunes; also sandhills, sandy waste areas, and roadsides
Habit: Biennial herb (perennial)
Flowering/Fruiting Period: FL & FR September–October
Wetland Status: UPL
Origin: Native

It is easy to identify cottonleaf goldenaster with its bright yellow flowers topping a grayish-green plant covered from top to bottom with long, cottony hair.

Cottonleaf goldenaster grows to a length of 1½ to 2½ feet and typically produces a thick taproot with many fibrous roots. Stems are mostly procumbent from the base of the plant; occasionally, stems grow erect. The species may have a single, simple stem or several highly branched stems.

Densely packed, long hairs grow haphazardly over the entire surface of the leaves and stems. The leaves are ¼ to ¾ inch long, cauline, and sessile. Often crowded together, leaf shapes vary from lanceolate to ovate.

Flowering heads of cottonleaf goldenaster grow in loose corymbs. The flowers possess both disk and ray flowers; both are yellow and vary from ½ to 1 inch across.

The seeds of cottonleaf goldenaster are achenes about ¹⁄₁₆ inch long.

Cottonleaf goldenaster grows best in full sun and sandy soils.

The plant is known to be pollinated by goldenaster-specialist bees.

a

b

67. Cottonleaf goldenaster (*Chrysopsis gossypina*). (a) Each cottonleaf goldenaster plant has one to several procumbent stems. Long, densely packed hairs give the stems and leaves a gray-green color. (b) Flower heads, which possess both disk and ray flowers, are ½ to 1 inch across.

Cottonleaf goldenaster is typically not grown commercially, so collect seeds by hand, a few seeds from each plant in the population during the fall. The plant makes an attractive landscape plant where a splash of fall color is desired.

Chrysopsis trichophylla, a closely related species, is found on inland sandhills and dunes of the coastal Carolinas.

a   68. Common yellow thistle (*Cirsium horridulum*). (a) The stem and leaves of this thistle are densely spiny and hairy. (b) The plant produces numerous flowering heads. Each flower is composed of disk flowers only. (c) In a mature flowering head, seeds are dispersed on a plumelike pappus.

68 COMMON YELLOW THISTLE

Cirsium horridulum Michaux

Family: Asteraceae (Aster)

Other Common Name: Bull thistle

Range: Maine south to Florida and west to Texas; primarily coastal states, but also occurs in a few inland states

Habitat: Edges of fresh marshes; also roadsides, fields, and disturbed areas

Habit: Biennial herb (annual)

Flowering/Fruiting Period: FL & FR April–May

Wetland Status: FAC

Origin: Native

Common yellow thistle lives up to its specific epitaph, *horridulum*. It is one of the largest, most extraordinarily spiny plants in the Carolinas coastal area, often reaching 3 feet tall, with individual spines on the leaves ranging from ¼ to 1 inch long.

As a biennial, the plant forms a large, dense basal rosette of spiny leaves and builds a stout taproot and extensive network of thick, lateral roots during the first year. In early spring of the second year of growth, the single stem draws on the stored energy in the taproot and bolts quickly before flowering commences.

In addition to having formidable spines, the stems are densely hairy. The leaves may be glabrous or pubescent with filamentous hairs. Leaves are roughly elliptical and vary from nearly entire to highly dissected. The cauline leaves are sessile and considerably smaller than the basal leaves.

Common yellow thistle produces from

1 to 20 flowering heads, each up to 3 inches across, with up to 50 disk flowers but no ray flowers. Numerous spiny bracts subtend the flowering heads. Flower color varies from light yellow to dark red.

Seeds are smooth nutlets with a plumelike pappus. Under ideal conditions, a common yellow thistle plant produces hundreds of seeds that easily scatter a considerable distance from the parent plant.

The flowers are often teeming with bees and other insect pollinators. The plant is host to the larvae of painted lady and little metalmark butterflies. The dense spines and hairs make this plant less attractive to herbivores.

Taxonomists recognize several varieties of this species throughout the southeastern United States.

69 FINGER ROT

Cnidoscolus stimulosus (Michaux)
  Engelmann & Gray
Family: Euphorbiaceae (Spurge)
Other Common Names: Spurge-nettle, tread-softly, bull-nettle, stinging nettle
Range: Virginia south to Florida and west to Louisiana
Habitat: Maritime forests and maritime shrub thickets; also sandhills and waste areas
Habit: Perennial herb
Flowering/Fruiting Period: FL March–August; FR May–September
Wetland Status: UPL
Origin: Native

Bring together the characteristics of a plant covered with stinging hairs, leaves with 3 to 5 palmately arranged lobes, and

69. Finger rot (*Cnidoscolus stimulosus*). (a) Dark green stems and lobed leaves are covered with stinging hairs. (b) These petal-like flower features are actually sepals. (c) Fruits are covered with stout hairs. Fruits split open, revealing hard-coated, brown seeds.

bright white flowers, and you have the unique coastal plant with the colorful yet menacing common name of finger rot.

Generally low growing but occasionally ranging up to 18 inches, finger rot has alternately arranged, deeply lobed, and coarsely toothed, dark green leaves. Stinging hairs (botanically, trichomes) cover the leaf surfaces. Leaf veins are large and prominent.

The inflorescence is a terminal cyme. The funnel-shaped flowers are monoecious and have 5 bright white sepals that look like petals. The flowers range from ½ to ¾ inch across and have a slight fragrance.

The fruit is a 3-locular capsule, often with a pattern of light and dark green stripes. Hard-coated seeds are brown, about ¼ inch long, and ⅛ inch wide.

Ground birds eat the seeds of finger rot.

While propagated primarily from seed, the plant also spreads by rhizomes.

Finger rot prefers sandy, well-drained soils.

The trichomes on finger rot resemble tiny glass needles. When the trichomes brush across bare skin, they break off and release formic acid. This chemical released on the skin may cause a painful and irritating rash that may last for an hour or longer.

70. Sand dayflower (*Commelina erecta*). (a) Sand dayflower possesses several decumbent, pubescent stems often propped up by nearby vegetation. (b) A bright green bract, resembling a clamshell, surrounds a group of flowers.

70 SAND DAYFLOWER

Commelina erecta Linnaeus
Family: Commelinaceae (Spiderwort)
Other Common Names: Day flower, narrowleaf dayflower, slender dayflower
Range: North Carolina south to Florida and west to Texas and New Mexico
Habitat: Dunes, dune swales, maritime grasslands, edges of maritime shrub thickets; also roadsides, waste areas, and pine and oak forests
Habit: Perennial herb
Flowering/Fruiting Period: FL June–September; FR August–October

Wetland Status: FACU
Origin: Native
Each of sand dayflower's showy blue flowers typically is at its peak for only a few hours. Get to the shore early to see these delicate, ephemeral flowers because the petals wilt quickly, and the plant fades into obscurity until new flowers open the next day.

Several erect or ascending, pubescent stems originate from thick, tuberous roots buried deep in sandy coastal soils. As the stems grow, they often become decumbent, bent to the ground, or propped against nearby herbs and grasses. Alternately arranged, linear to oblanceolate, glabrous leaves clasp the stems. Leaves range from 2 to 4 inches long and ¼ to 1 inch wide.

The inflorescence of sand dayflower is a 3-flowered cyme enclosed in a folded, clamshell-like bract about 1 inch long and ½ inch wide. This distinctive structure protects the delicate flower parts before and after they open. Scentless flowers—each with 2 delicate, bright blue petals and 1 small, white petal—emerge from the bract at the tip of each branch. The 1-inch-wide flowers contain fertile and sterile stamens. Numerous insect species facilitate pollination. Seeds mature in the fruit, a 3-chambered capsule ranging from ⅛ to ¼ inch in diameter.

Sand dayflower prefers well-drained, sandy soils. The deep, fleshy roots aid the plant in surviving extended dry periods. Propagation is by seeds and division of plant roots. Stem cuttings root easily during the growing season. Collect seeds or cuttings from wild plants for use in native gardens.

Research reports indicate that sand dayflower is a preferred food of white-tailed deer. Ground birds such as mourning doves eat the seeds.

Commercial availability is limited.

The variety *angustifolia* is the common form found on barrier islands and barrier beaches in the Carolinas.

71 VIRGINIA BUTTONWEED

Diodia virginiana Linnaeus
Family: Rubiaceae (Madder)
Other Common Name: Large buttonweed
Range: Connecticut south to Florida, west to Texas, and northeast to Missouri and Illinois

Habitat: Dune swales, edges of marshes; also wet meadows, lawns, and roadsides
Habit: Perennial herb
Flowering/Fruiting Period: FL & FR June–November
Wetland Status: FACW
Origin: Native

Virginia buttonweed is one of the plants you are most likely to discover on developed beaches. In the coastal

a

71. Virginia buttonweed (*Diodia virginiana*). (a) Virginia buttonweed plants produce both spreading and ascending branches with opposite leaves.

b

c

71. Virginia buttonweed (*Diodia virginiana*).
(b) Flowers are found in leaf axils and have petals covered with small, white hairs. (c) Fruits are slightly elongated, globular, and pubescent.

and light green below; texturally, they are somewhat leathery with entire margins.

Flowers are sessile and solitary or in pairs in the leaf axils. The bright white corolla is composed of 4 petals united to form a ¼-inch-long corolla tube. The petals are ½ inch wide and covered with small, white hairs. Both stamens and style are prominent. The globular fruit, containing 2 seeds, is ¼ to ⅜ inch long and pubescent.

Virginia buttonweed grows best in open, well-drained, sandy soils in full sun, and it can tolerate flooding conditions for extended periods. There is no need to plant this species in a native coastal plant garden; it will probably appear as a volunteer.

Virginia buttonweed attracts terrestrial birds and butterflies. White-tailed deer occasionally graze it. No detailed studies have assessed the wildlife value of the species.

Poorjoe (*Diodella teres*) is a related species with a similar 4-petaled flower, but it grows in much drier habitats, primarily dunes. Virginia buttonweed may be confused with the exotic tropical Mexican clover (*Richardia brasiliensis*), which also grows well with coastal turf grasses and in waste areas and other disturbed habitats. The flower of tropical Mexican clover has 6 white petals, compared with 4 for Virginia buttonweed.

Carolinas, this small, colorful plant mixes well with turf grasses on properties with maintained lawns. It adapts to close mowing by hugging the ground and producing branches that spread laterally rather than vertically.

In its native habitats, Virginia buttonweed can produce spreading, trailing, or ascending branches up to 18 inches long. Stems are 4-angled and pubescent or glabrous with a reddish tinge. Virginia buttonweed spreads vegetatively as stems root at the nodes. Leaves are opposite and sessile; leaf blades are about 1½ inches long and ½ inch wide. Leaves lower on the stem are elliptic, while those above the middle of the plant are frequently oblong. Leaf surfaces are green above

72 COMMON WATER HYACINTH

Eichhornia crassipes (Martius) Solms-Laubach
Family: Pontederiaceae (Pickerelweed)
Other Common Name: Floating water hyacinth
Range: USDA Hardiness Zones 8–11
Habitat: Freshwater marshes; also bays, lakes, and ponds
Habit: Perennial herb
Flowering/Fruiting Period: FL & FR June–September

a

b

c

72. Common water hyacinth (*Eichhornia crassipes*). (a) Once it gains a foothold in a pond, common water hyacinth can cover the entire water surface and quickly choke out other aquatic plants. (b) A bright yellow dot surrounded by a dark purple ring marks a petal on each flower. (c) Spongy aerenchyma tissue forms a bulbous bladder on each leaf petiole, and these bladders support the plant at or above the water surface.

Wetland Status: OBL

Origin: Exotic; introduced from South America; naturalized worldwide

Common water hyacinth has earned the distinction of being one of the world's most aggressive and invasive aquatic weeds. Because of its rapid growth and floating habit, it excludes other submerged and floating aquatic vegetation, impedes water flow in slow-moving streams, provides excellent mosquito-breeding habitat, and interferes with navigation and recreation in aquatic systems. It cannot get any worse! First introduced into Louisiana in 1885, the species was subsequently released into the St. Johns River in Florida. Over the last century, it has spread throughout the southeastern United States. It is likely to continue spreading northward as climate change occurs along the Atlantic coast.

Common water hyacinth typically grows 6 to 10 inches high. The roots are fibrous and highly branched, appearing almost feathery. They extend out and downward from the plant and are not usually rooted in the substrate.

The leaves are glossy green, leathery, spatula shaped, and up to 8 inches long. Leaf petioles are whorled around a short stem, and they possess a large amount of spongy aerenchyma tissue. The extensive aerenchyma tissue helps keep the plant mostly at or above the water surface.

The inflorescence is a 6-inch raceme with 6 to 7 light blue to lavender flowers. The 6 petals are jointed near the base of the flower, which is 2 to 2½ inches wide. One petal has a distinctive yellow spot surrounded by a dark purple area. This pattern may help pollinating insects orient themselves on the flower.

Fruits develop after the inflorescence

HERBS

221

withers and becomes submerged. The fruit is a 3-celled capsule containing scores of tiny, ribbed seeds. Seeds germinate without a dormancy period and can remain in the aquatic substrate seedbank for 10 to 15 years.

Common water hyacinth reproduces by seeds, fragmentation, and stolon production. New stolons can produce entirely new plants in less than 3 weeks.

The plant requires full sun. An important factor controlling the distribution of common water hyacinth is the fact that it cannot survive air temperatures below 20°F.

As is common with exotic species, there appears to be no significant wildlife value for common water hyacinth. It grows so densely that it does not produce a suitable habitat for small mammals, fishes, or waterfowl.

Scientists have bred 2 predatory weevils and a moth species for release near infected watercourses in an effort to control common water hyacinth. These efforts have shown only moderate success.

73 COMMON ELEPHANT'S FOOT

Elephantopus tomentosus Linnaeus
Family: Asteraceae (Aster)
Other Common Name: Tobaccoweed
Range: Primarily coastal: Maryland south to Florida and west to Texas
Habitat: Maritime shrub thickets and maritime forests
Habit: Perennial herb
Flowering/Fruiting Period: FL & FR July–November
Wetland Status: FAC
Origin: Native

With a vivid imagination, you can see how elephant's foot, a common plant of dry maritime shrub thickets and maritime forests in the coastal Carolinas, received the name by which it is best known. Pressed close to the ground, the large, often

b

73. Common elephant's foot (*Elephantopus tomentosus*). (a) This interesting and attractive plant is characterized by a rosette of large, elliptical leaves closely appressed to the ground and terminal flower clusters arising from a single stem. (b) Only disk flowers compose the flower clusters. The clusters are surrounded by 3 large bracts.

overlapping basal leaves outline an area about the size and shape that an elephant's foot would cover.

Several tomentose, elliptic leaves ranging from 4 to 12 inches long and from 2 to 4 inches wide form a roughly circular basal rosette of leaves. The flat rosette gives rise to a singular peduncle, which bears the flowers. The stem is once or several times divided and ranges from 5 to 15 inches tall. Three leaflike, heart-shaped bracts about ½ inch wide surround each flower cluster. Common elephant's foot possesses only disk flowers surrounded by ⅜-inch-long phyllaries; no ray flowers are present. Two or 3 pale pink to lavender flowers open and close each day, and this pattern continues for several weeks. The fruit associated with each flower is a ribbed nutlet about ⅛ inch long with an attached pappus up to ¼ inch long.

Drought tolerant, common elephant's foot grows best in sandy soils and shade created by overstory trees.

Little information is available concerning wildlife use of this plant; however, it is attractive to butterflies.

Germination requirements for this species are unknown; collect seeds from the plant at the end of the growing season.

A similar species, coastal plain elephant's foot (*Elephantopus nudatus*), occurs in the Carolinas coastal area. Coastal plain elephant's foot exhibits narrower basal leaves (often less than 2 inches wide) and shorter phyllaries surrounding the flowering heads (about ¼ to ⅜ inch) compared with common elephant's foot.

74 DOG FENNEL

Eupatorium capillifolium (Lamarck) Small
Family: Asteraceae (Aster)
Other Common Name: Yankeeweed
Range: New Jersey and Pennsylvania, west to Missouri, south to Florida, and west to Texas

Habitat: Dunes and edges of maritime shrub thickets; also waste areas, roadsides, ditches, pond edges, old fields, and forest margins
Habit: Perennial herb
Flowering/Fruiting Period: FL & FR September–November
Wetland Status: FACU
Origin: Native

a

b

c

74. Dog fennel (*Eupatorium capillifolium*). (a) Large clumps of dog fennel develop from a substantial root base with a deep taproot. The plant may grow to 6 feet tall. (b) Hundreds of tiny, creamy white flowers droop from each stem. (c) Fruits are typical of asters, with dandelion-like, wind-distributed fruits.

This native plant is a common, short-lived perennial ranging in height from 2 to 6 feet. The plant spreads rapidly, and for this reason, botanists generally consider dog fennel a noxious weed, especially in dry, sandy soils. The plant dies back to ground level during the winter and regenerates in spring from overwintering rosettes.

From one to several woody, hairy, reddish stems grow from a substantial root crown possessing a taproot and dense, robust, fibrous roots located just below the soil surface.

Alternate leaves are pinnately or bipinnately dissected into fine divisions about ¹⁄₁₆ inch wide.

A flowering raceme terminates each stem. The ³⁄₈-inch-long flowers are inconspicuous, creamy white, and fragrant. Individual flowers are quite attractive when viewed with a hand lens. One-sixteenth-inch-long seeds are wind dispersed. Seed production is prodigious, and seeds of this species probably comprise a considerable fraction of the seedbank in coastal soils.

Where it is well established, the dense cover of dog fennel effectively blocks other plants from becoming established. Following hurricanes and nor'easters that produce openings in maritime forests and shrub thickets, dog fennel aggressively invades the open space, almost certainly originating from seeds stored in the soil seedbank. Owing to its extensive root system, the plant is drought resistant.

The plant has documented wildlife value; scientists have found that the scarlet-bodied wasp moth feeds on the plant, storing predator-inhibiting toxins in the process. The flowers attract a wide variety of insects, including butterflies and bees.

Dog fennel is aromatic, and the smell of crushed leaves is pungent and unpleasant—probably the source of its colorful common name.

75 FIRE-ON-THE-MOUNTAIN

Euphorbia cyathophora Murray
Family: Euphorbiaceae (Spurge)
Other Common Names: Mexican fireplant, painted leaf, wild poinsettia
Range: Virginia west to Kansas; south to Florida, Texas, and California
Habitat: Dunes; also waste areas and disturbed sites
Habit: Perennial herb (annual)
Flowering/Fruiting Period: FL May–October; FR June–November
Wetland Status: FACU
Origin: Native

Fire-on-the-mountain is instantly recognizable in the field. The bright green stems, deeply scalloped leaves, and red markings immediately remind one of the festive holiday plant poinsettia. Both fire-on-the-mountain and poinsettia are members of the Spurge family and share many of the same characteristics, including milky sap and special flower structures called cyathia (cyathium, singular). Handle this plant with care; when crushed or broken, it exudes milky, white sap that may irritate the skin of sensitive individuals.

Fire-on-the-mountain has erect, glabrous, 1- to 3-foot-tall stems that branch from the base of the plant and become woody as the plant matures. Leaves are highly variable in shape, ranging from round to linear, from ½ to 3 inches long. Lower leaves are usually smooth and entire, while the upper leaves are deeply scalloped with wavy margins. They are oppositely arranged on the stems, often covered with hairs, and clustered toward the ends of the branches. Leaves, especially those surrounding the flowers, have distinctive dark red spots on the upper surface that become more evident as leaves age.

Forming terminal inflorescences, the yellowish-green cyathium consists of a single green ovary, one or more yellow stamens, and a greenish-yellow, cup-

75. Fire-on-the-mountain (*Euphorbia cyathophora*). (a) This slightly woody plant has deeply scalloped, dark green leaves with entire margins. (b) Red leaf spots highlight the cyathia clustered at the apex of each stem.

shaped nectar gland. While no sepals or petals are present, several small bracts splashed with bright red color surround each flower cluster. The brown seeds are nearly spherical, with a roughened surface of small tubercles.

The plant has scant documented wildlife use.

Fire-on-the-mountain grows well under a variety of environmental conditions, including dry, sandy soil and moderate salt aerosols. Survival in these conditions makes it a successful weed along the Carolinas coast.

Propagation of fire-on-the-mountain is by seeds; however, we know little about its seed germination requirements. Placing this species in a native plants garden will give you a summertime opportunity to think of the upcoming holiday season.

---

76 COASTAL BEDSTRAW

Galium bermudense Linnaeus
Family: Rubiaceae (Madder)
Other Common Names: Bedstraw, purple galium
Range: Coastal: New Jersey south to Florida and west to Texas
Habitat: Maritime shrub thickets and maritime forests
Habit: Perennial herb
Flowering/Fruiting Period: FL June–August; FR August–September
Wetland Status: UPL
Origin: Native

Coastal bedstraw is a consistently common component of the coastal flora of the Carolinas. It an evergreen plant with characteristically weak stems. It scrambles over nearby plants, especially grasses that serve as a scaffolding for this sprawling plant. Stiff, bristle-like hairs cover the lower surfaces of the leaves.

Its square stems and whorls of 4 narrow leaves found at each stem node make identification of the plant easy. Stems range from 4 to 12 inches long. The leaves are elliptic, entire, ¼ to ¾ inch long, and about ⅛ inch wide.

Tiny, inconspicuous flowers, usually in pairs, arise in leaf axils near the apex of each branch. The 4 greenish-white petals are difficult to see without a hand lens. The fleshy fruit is a smooth, green, globe-shaped berry about ⅛ inch across. Fruits develop in pairs, and as they mature, the berries turn blue.

HERBS

a

c

76. Coastal bedstraw (*Galium bermudense*).
(a) Whorls of 4 leaves along the stem allow
for quick identification of coastal bedstraw.
(b) Flowers possess 4 tiny, greenish-white petals
and 4 visible stamens. (c) Fruits are paired, blue,
globe shaped, and fleshy.

We know little about the wildlife value
of the plant, but the relatively large fruits
appear to make a tempting meal for ground
birds and other herbivores. The plant is
also valuable to small pollinators.

Coastal bedstraw prefers shady habitats
within or on the edge of shrub thickets and
maritime forests or, occasionally, dunes.

If collected from wild plants, the seeds
should be stratified for 30 days for best
germination results.

This species is cited as *Galium
hispidulum* in legacy literature in the
coastal Carolinas.

77 EASTERN ROSE MALLOW
Hibiscus moscheutos Linnaeus
Family: Malvaceae (Mallow)
Other Common Names: Wild cotton,
swamp rose mallow, marsh hibiscus
Range: Southern Ontario, Canada;

b

a 77. Eastern rose mallow (*Hibiscus moscheutos*).
(a) Eastern rose mallow is a large-leaved,
semiwoody perennial common in or adjacent
to wetlands. (b) Five-petaled white flowers are
tinged in red at their base. Many united stamens
surround the pistil. (c) Several seeds develop in
each of the 5 sections of the fruiting capsule.

Massachusetts west to Wisconsin and
Kansas; south to Florida and Texas
Habitat: Brackish and freshwater marshes;
also roadside ditches
Habit: Perennial herb
Flowering/Fruiting Period: FL June–
September; FR August–October
Wetland Status: OBL
Origin: Native

If you are familiar with cotton, okra, or
hollyhocks, you will instantly see the
familial resemblance of eastern rose
mallow flowers to the flowers of these other
members of the Mallow plant family. The
bold color and large size of the flowers
break the color and pattern monotony of
coastal wetland environments.

Eastern rose mallow, a prolifically
flowering, shrubby perennial, often reaches
a height of 5 or 6 feet. The stems arising
from a sturdy rhizome are round in cross
section, glabrous below, and pubescent
toward the top of the plant. Similar to the
stems of other semiwoody perennials,
the stems of eastern rose mallow die
to the base of the plant in winter; new
growth arises each spring from the root
crown. Alternately arranged leaves are
ovate, longer than broad, and lobed when
growing near the base of the plant but
unlobed on the upper stem. The leaves
are 3 to 8 inches long, 2 to 5 inches wide,
serrated, green and glabrous above, and
white with dense hairs below.

The showy, 5-petaled flowers, borne in

the axils of the upper leaves, are white or pink and up to 6 inches across. The center of the flower varies from pale to deep red. The united stamens surround the pistil, which displays 5 stigmas. The fruit is a 5-section capsule 1 to 2 inches long, with each capsule containing several globose seeds.

Eastern rose mallow is tolerant of slightly saline soils but prefers well-drained, humus-rich soil. The plant grows well in full sun and partial shade.

Propagation is through rhizomes and seeds. Successful germination occurs with direct seeding in moist soil or by sowing seeds in greenhouse flats. Many cultivars of this species exist, and they grow well in coastal environments.

78. Creeping bluet (*Houstonia procumbens*). Ground-hugging creeping bluet grows 1 to 2 inches tall and possesses bright green, simple, and opposite leaves. The plant expands by rooting at the nodes. White flowers arise from leaf axils either singly or in small clusters. Fruits mature underground.

78 CREEPING BLUET

Houstonia procumbens (Walter ex J. F. Gmelin) Standley
Family: Rubiaceae (Madder)
Other Common Names: Roundleaf bluet, fairy footprints, innocence
Range: South Carolina south to Florida and west to eastern Louisiana
Habitat: Dunes and moist, open sandy pinelands
Habit: Perennial herb
Flowering/Fruiting Period: FL & FR October–March
Wetland Status: UPL
Origin: Native

This low-profile plant is rarely seen by the casual observer along the coast because it flowers and fruits over the winter, long past when one expects to find plants in flower. Even when it flowers, creeping bluet is easily overlooked because it is a ground-hugging, mat-forming plant. Its small, white flowers appear to arise directly from the sandy soil.

This plant grows 1 to 2 inches tall and creeps along the ground by rooting at the nodes. Plants possess thin, ovate to elliptical, bright green leaves, a mere ¼ to ⅜ inch wide, slightly longer than wide. The simple leaves are oppositely arranged, rounded at the apex, and evergreen.

Flowers appear in leaf axils either singly or in small clusters on a cyme. The white corolla is ½ inch wide with 4 petals. Besides the bright white flowers, creeping bluet possesses cleistogamous flowers that self-pollinate and produce fruits that remain at or just below the ground surface.

Despite its low stature, creeping bluet has significant connections. It belongs to a well-known genus named after a Scottish botanist, William Houston, who lived from 1695 to 1733. The humble plant also serves a special purpose for the bees, flies, and small butterflies that pollinate its flowers. It is an important food source for these insects, since there are few other plants in flower in late fall and winter. The flowers are within easy reach of crawling insects. After producing flowers, the flower stalk bends into the sand, where the developing fruit matures.

Creeping bluet grows well in dry or moist sandy soil. It prefers full sun but survives in light shade. It is not particularly drought tolerant. It escapes the full impact of salt aerosols owing to its low, creeping growth.

Creeping bluet can be propagated from seeds or cuttings. Collect seedpods when seeds are mature. Stratify the seeds and sow them in the spring. Plants only grow vegetatively during the first year after sowing and flower during the second year.

The tallest of these plants may be confused with tropical Mexican clover; however, the white tropical Mexican clover flowers possess 6 petals.

The species is cited as *Hedyotis procumbens* in legacy literature.

---

79 DUNE PENNYWORT

Hydrocotyle bonariensis Lamarck
Family: Araliaceae (Ginseng)
Other Common Names: Largeleaf pennywort, coastal plain pennywort, dune water pennywort
Range: Coastal: Virginia south to Florida and west to Texas
Habitat: Dunes, dune swales, maritime grasslands, edges of maritime shrub thickets
Habit: Perennial herb
Flowering/Fruiting Period: FL & FR April–November
Wetland Status: FACW
Origin: Native

Dune pennywort is one of the most common yet interesting plants found in dunes and swales of the Carolinas. When you find a patch of dune pennywort growing in loose, dry sand, dig a few inches below the surface and locate the extensive network of thick, white stems (rhizomes). Nearly every node possesses a ring of roots that nourish and water the plant.

Shiny, glabrous leaves and flower heads poke above the ground surface at

a

b

c

79. Dune pennywort (*Hydrocotyle bonariensis*).
(a) Distinctive peltate leaves have scalloped edges and may orient vertically or horizontally, depending on the environmental conditions of its habitat. (b) Flowers and fruits develop on roughly spherical umbels. (c) Fruits contain 2 seeds that split apart and drop to the ground at maturity.

nearly every node, often just a few inches apart. The succulent leaves are peltate with scalloped edges; the pedicels join the leaves at the center. The leaves are variable in size depending on the habitat. In open, grassy dunes, dune pennywort leaves may be about 1 inch in diameter and less than 4 inches tall. Along the edge of shrub thickets and similar deeply shaded habitats, leaves may be up to 4 inches in diameter and more than 10 inches tall. In habitats with full sun, dune pennywort leaves are often oriented perpendicular to the ground, an orientation thought to reduce leaf temperature and the intensity of solar radiation. Dune pennywort is often associated with sea oats, sea elder, saltmeadow cordgrass, dune camphorweed, and seaside panicum.

White to creamy yellow flowers are borne on umbels, an inflorescence typical of the Ginseng family. Flowers are regular with 5 petals. Dune pennywort flowers and fruits continuously from April to November, and it is typical to see both flowers and mature fruits on the same umbel. The dune pennywort fruit is composed of 2 seeds that split apart at maturity. The seeds are 1/8 inch long, yellowish-orange, fleshy, and ribbed.

Dune pennywort thrives in disturbed habitats and areas where competition from other plants is low.

Seeds may be a rich food source for ground birds, such as mourning or ground doves, and small mammals.

Propagation of dune pennywort is by seeds and rhizome extension. Transplant individual stem sections containing at least one node; however, keep in mind that this species is successful at spreading without human intervention! Considered an aggressive pest by many coastal gardeners, the plant is difficult to contain, and many gardeners try to eliminate, not encourage, this plant.

Whorled marsh pennywort (*Hydrocotyle verticillata*), a closely related species, is an obligate wetland plant found primarily in freshwater and brackish wetlands in the coastal Carolinas.

80 EASTERN BLOODLEAF

Iresine rhizomatosa Standley
Family: Amaranthaceae (Amaranth)
Other Common Names: Root-stock bloodleaf, Juda's bush
Range: Pennsylvania west to Kansas and Missouri, south to Texas and Florida
Habitat: Dunes and dune swales, edges of maritime shrub thickets and maritime forests, brackish marshes; also floodplain forests and wet woodlands
Habit: Perennial herb
Flowering/Fruiting Period: FL & FR August–October
Wetland Status: FACW
Origin: Native

It is surprising that eastern bloodleaf, a native higher plant in the United States, was first collected and scientifically described just a century ago. In 1915, botanists discovered eastern bloodleaf plants on Plummers Island, Md., in the Potomac River. While common in other states today, eastern bloodleaf has apparently disappeared from Plummers Island.

Eastern bloodleaf is characterized by an erect, glabrous to sparsely pubescent stem with ascending branches ranging from 1½ to 3 feet tall. The plant arises from a rhizome. The oppositely arranged leaves appear at slightly swollen nodes along the stem. Leaf blades are ovate to elliptic, finely pubescent on both surfaces, and vary from 1½ to 6 inches long and 1 to 3 inches wide. Leaf margins are entire, and the 1-inch-long leaf petioles typically exhibit a reddish tinge.

Difficult to identify in leaf only, eastern bloodleaf is easier to recognize when it is

in full flower or fruit. Eastern bloodleaf is dioecious, with separate male and female flowers occurring on different plants. Panicles of flowers, 3 to 12 inches tall, terminate stems and branches. Smaller panicles arise in leaf axils in the upper half of the plant. Both male and female flowers possess 5 sepals and no petals. The white female flowers are minute, less than 1/16 inch, with a tuft of hairs that persist on the fruit until maturity and aid seed dispersal. The globe-shaped fruit is a thin-walled, indehiscent bladder containing a single lustrous, reddish-brown seed.

The wildlife value of this species is unknown, but it is probably minor.

While hard to find in the commercial marketplace, eastern bloodleaf makes an excellent choice as an ornamental plant in a natural coastal garden due to its fall color and abundant cottony fruits. Collect seeds from wild plants; germination requirements are unknown.

a

b

80. Eastern bloodleaf (*Iresine rhizomatosa*). (a) Fruiting plants are easily identified by the cottonlike, white hairs covering the seeds. (b) Male plants possess minute flowers possessing only greenish-white sepals.

81 BEACH PINWEED

Lechea maritima Leggett ex Britton, Sterns & Poggenburg
Family: Cistaceae (Rockrose)
Other Common Names: Maritime pinweed, hoary pinweed, seaside pinweed
Range: Delaware to North Carolina
Habitat: Dune swales and interdunes
Habit: Perennial herb
Flowering/Fruiting Period: FL June–August; FR July–September
Wetland Status: UPL
Origin: Native

Beach pinweed is common on dunes along the Atlantic coast, reaching its southern limit in northern North Carolina. This curious plant with small, reddish-brown flowers is most likely pollinated by wind, not insects. It has narrow habitat requirements, and continued coastal development reduces the amount of suitable dune habitat. This has led the N.C.

a

b

81. Beach pinweed (*Lechea maritima*). (a) Several stems arise from a taproot that supports beach pinweed. They may be erect or decumbent. (b) Each brown, 3-chambered, spherical capsule contains 4 to 5 seeds.

Plant Conservation Program to list it as imperiled.

Beach pinweed arises from a taproot and reaches a height of 6 to 12 inches with leaves crowded into a dense basal rosette. The alternately arranged, pubescent leaves are elliptic to oblanceolate, range from ½ to 1 inch long, and average ¼ inch wide. An abundance of appressed hairs on the leaf surfaces makes the leaves look grayish-green.

From 1 to 5 shoots arise from the basal rosette, and each produces a panicle with numerous flowers, each about ¹⁄₁₆ inch wide with 3 petals.

The mature fruit is a spherical, 3-chambered capsule that splits open at maturity revealing 4 to 5 seeds. The fruiting stems remain attached and upright during the fall and winter, an aid to seed dispersal by wind and rain.

Plants commonly associated with beach pinweed are American beachgrass, woolly beach heather, seaside panicum, southern seaside goldenrod, purple sandgrass, and northern seaside spurge.

Propagate the plant from seeds collected before they are dispersed in early fall. Seed scarification increases the seed germination rate.

The southern variety recognized as var. *virginica* is represented in North Carolina. A related species, hairy pinweed (*Lechea mucronata*), also occurs on dunes in the coastal Carolinas.

We know little about the wildlife value of beach pinweed; ground birds such as mourning doves may eat the seeds as they forage in the dunes.

82 COMMON DUCKWEED

Lemna perpusilla Torrey
Family: Araceae (Arum)
Other Common Names: Tiny duckweed,
minute duckweed, tropical duckweed
Range: Quebec, Canada; Maine to North

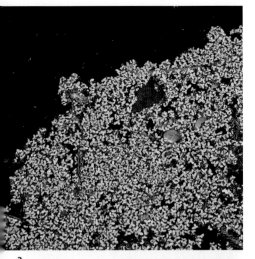

a

b

82. Common duckweed (*Lemna perpusilla*). (a) Fronds—flattened, leaflike stems—float on the surface of freshwater ponds. (b) Sharply pointed, 1-inch-long roots extend vertically downward from the underside of the stem.

Origin: Native

Common duckweed is a small, free-floating, vascular plant of the Arum family whose more familiar representatives include Jack-in-the-pulpit, calla lily, and elephant's ear.

Common duckweed plants consist of a flattened, leaflike stem called a frond. The frond is light green, obovate to elliptic shaped, and up to ⅛ inch across.

We distinguish common duckweed from other duckweed species by the presence of 3 veins impressed on the surface. The frond margins are entire, and the upper surface is convex with several small, round bumps (papilla) visible under magnification. The lower surface of the frond is concave and possesses a single root up to 1 inch long surrounded by a winged sheath where the root joins the frond. Root tips are sharply pointed, another characteristic distinguishing common duckweed from other species. While some species of duckweed have a reddish tinge, common duckweed does not.

Flowers are reduced to a single ovary and a single stamen. The fruit is a thin-walled utricle possessing a single egg-shaped seed covered with longitudinal ridges. The tiny seeds could pass through the eye of a needle.

Vegetative reproduction is more important than seed production in common duckweed. Each frond produces buds from which new fronds develop. Common duckweed grows best in dense clusters of fronds in quiet, wave-free water, such as interdune ponds.

As the name implies, waterfowl consume common duckweed.

Take note, however: common duckweed can be an aggressive invader of ponds and marshes with open water. When duckweed covers the entire surface of a pond or marsh, it blocks sunlight and shades submerged plants. On the other hand,

Dakota and south to Texas and Georgia; also New Mexico and Arizona

Habitat: Interdune ponds and other quiet water environments

Habit: Perennial herb

Flowering/Fruiting Period: FL & FR September–November

Wetland Status: OBL

partial coverage by common duckweed has little effect on pond life. If held in check, common duckweed provides an interesting and colorful plant cover on small ponds in native plant gardens.

Research shows that common duckweed is capable of efficiently removing nutrients from the water, and it has the potential to be used to remediate water polluted with phosphate- and nitrogen-containing compounds.

Common duckweed represents one of several species of duckweed that may occur in various wetland habitats of the coastal Carolinas. A hand lens is necessary to key out the duckweeds.

a

b

83. Sea lavender (*Limonium carolinianum*). (a) Leaves of sea lavender are simple and elliptic or obovate with a strongly developed midvein visible on both sides of the leaf. (b) Large, open panicles composed of buds, flowers, and fruits indicate the presence of sea lavender in grass-dominated marshes.

---

83 SEA LAVENDER

Limonium carolinianum (Walter) Britton
Family: Plumbaginaceae (Leadwort)
Other Common Names: Carolina sea lavender, marsh rosemary, American thrift, seaside thrift
Range: Labrador south to Florida and west to Texas; also Mexico and Bermuda
Habitat: Salt marshes and salt pannes
Habit: Perennial herb
Flowering/Fruiting Period: FL & FR August–October
Wetland Status: OBL
Origin: Native

Collecting and drying sea lavender is a cottage industry in some coastal regions. There is a thriving market for flower heads for use in floral arrangements. When dried, the flower heads (actually the hard, stiff sepals attached to the flowering stems) are quite attractive and add a dollop of straw color to floral arrangements. Since sea lavender reproduces primarily by rhizome extension, it is not surprising that periodic, heavy harvests do not appear to reduce the number of plants in a given site. However, harvesting may reduce sea lavender colonization of new sites.

Sea lavender is a broadleaf marsh plant growing within a "sea" of grasses and grasslike plants in coastal marshes. Leaves are simple and elliptic or obovate, with blades ranging from 2 to 6 inches long and ¼ to 2 inches wide. The petioles equal the length of the leaf blades. Leaves are fleshy with smooth margins. A thin veneer of silt or clay often covers the leaves because suspended particles in the estuarine water column settle out on leaf surfaces. As leaf blades accumulate salts, they gradually shrivel, dry, and drop, especially from

c

d

large, loose panicles reaching 1 to 2 feet high. Flowers are either solitary or in groups of 2 to 3 at nodes on the panicle. A papery, transparent bract and 5 sepals surround each flower. The fruit is a single-seeded utricle.

The species may serve as a food source for waterfowl.

Sea lavender prefers moist soils but can survive under drought conditions for short periods. It requires full sun and grows well in environments frequently flooded with salt water or exposed to salt aerosols. Sea lavender is commonly associated with smooth cordgrass, saltmeadow cordgrass, sea ox-eye, and the glassworts.

Several named cultivars can be obtained through commercial sources.

84 NARROW-LEAVED LOOSESTRIFE

Lythrum lineare Linnaeus
Family: Lythraceae (Loosestrife)
Other Common Name: Narrowleaf
  loosestrife
Range: Coastal: New York south to Florida
  and west to Texas
Habitat: Salt and brackish marshes
Habit: Perennial herb
Flowering/Fruiting Period: FL & FR July–
  October
Wetland Status: OBL
Origin: Native
Narrow-leaved loosestrife is related to the exotic purple loosestrife (*Lythrum salicaria*), a notoriously noxious weed that is highly invasive in wetlands throughout North America, especially the Northeast and the north central United States. Our native narrow-leaved loosestrife shows no such tendency for aggressiveness as seen in its obnoxious cousin.

Mature plant height varies from 1 to 4 feet, depending on environmental conditions. Growing in saline soils tends to reduce the size of the plant. Its pale

83. Sea lavender (*Limonium carolinianum*). (c) Flowers are pale purple to lavender, barely ⅛ inch wide, with 5 petals. (d) Fruits are covered by a persistent, papery calyx.

plants populating highly saline areas. Occasionally, all of the year's leaves are dead by the time flowers appear.

Flowers are tubular shaped and pale purple to lavender. Barely ⅛ inch wide with 5 petals, sea lavender flowers develop on

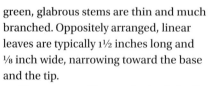

b

84. Narrow-leaved loosestrife (*Lythrum lineare*). (a) Stems of the plant are thin and much branched; flowers are abundant. (b) Six slightly crinkled, white to pale pink petals form small but showy, ¼-inch flowers.

6 petaled, and about ¼ inch across. The ¼-inch-long, narrow, ribbed calyx with sharp apical points forms a distinctive tubular receptacle below the petals. The narrow, fluted capsules hold many tiny, brownish-yellow seeds.

Narrow-leaved loosestrife associates include saltmeadow cordgrass, sea lavender, Virginia glasswort, black needlerush, marsh pink, and sea ox-eye.

We know little about wildlife uses of narrow-leaved loosestrife. It is most likely insect pollinated.

Propagate narrow-leaved loosestrife either by seeds or offshoots from the perennial roots.

green, glabrous stems are thin and much branched. Oppositely arranged, linear leaves are typically 1½ inches long and ⅛ inch wide, narrowing toward the base and the tip.

Flowers are solitary and arise in leaf axils. Each flower is pale pink to white,

85 WHITE SWEET CLOVER

Melilotus albus Medikus

Family: Fabaceae (Legume)

Other Common Names: Sweetclover, white melilot

Range: Throughout North America

Habitat: Dunes and maritime shrub thickets; also roadsides, fields, and waste areas

Habit: Biennial herb

Flowering/Fruiting Period: FL & FR May–September

Wetland Status: FACU

Origin: Exotic; native of Europe and western Asia

About the middle of the eighteenth century, settlers probably introduced this common plant, often considered a weed species, to the United States. A biennial, white sweet clover does not flower during its first year of growth. Initially, the plant directs its energy to the formation of a large, deep taproot. At the beginning of the second year of growth, the plant bolts. After bolting, it flowers profusely, usually reaching a height of 3 to 4 feet and, rarely, up to 8 feet.

At maturity, white sweet clover has

b

a 85. White sweet clover (*Melilotus albus*). (a) White sweet clover reaches a height of 3 to 4 feet and flowers profusely throughout the summer. (b) Each terminal raceme develops 40 to 80 tiny, white, tubular flowers. (c) Fruits turn from green to dark gray or black and contain a single seed with a wrinkled surface.

c

8 to 10 slender, erect, glabrous, light green stems with trifoliate leaves on petioles up to 1 inch long. The grayish-green leaflets are about 1½ inches long, ¼ inch wide, and bluntly toothed near their apices. The middle leaflet has a long petiole, and the adjacent 2 leaflets are sessile. Brushing your hand across the plant releases a sweet fragrance.

Upper stems possess terminal racemes ranging from 2 to 6 inches long, each with 40 to 80 tiny, white flowers. Each flower is tubular at the base, widening out toward the end of the petals. Individual flowers are about ⅓ inch long with a 5-toothed calyx and 5 white petals. Large numbers of bees, wasps, flies, butterflies, and beetles swarm the plant when it is in full flower.

The fruit of white sweet clover is a gray to black oval seedpod about ⅓ inch long containing a single brownish-yellow, wrinkled seed. A prodigious seed producer, a single plant of white sweet clover may form tens of thousands of seeds. Seeds may remain viable for decades in the soil seedbank. One study indicates that some long-lived white sweet clover seeds were 80 years old.

White sweet clover prefers full sun and occurs in a range of soil conditions, from moist to dry. It is quite drought tolerant at maturity. It thrives in fine dune sand and is moderately salt tolerant. Similar to other legumes, white sweet clover fixes nitrogen through a symbiotic relationship with *Rhizobium* bacteria found in its root nodules.

White-tailed deer and rabbits feed on the foliage, and birds and small mammals feed on the seeds. It also serves as a cover plant for small mammals.

The plant was originally introduced as a forage crop for livestock, and ecologists now recognize it as an important nectar plant for bees. However, removing this plant from natural areas is probably a best practice; otherwise, the plants will crowd out more desirable species.

A closely related species, yellow sweet clover (*Melilotus officinalis*), is nearly identical but possesses yellow flowers, is shorter in stature, and is less robust overall. Yellow sweet clover begins to bloom earlier and has a longer blooming season than white sweet clover.

---

86 PARTRIDGE BERRY

Mitchella repens Linnaeus
Family: Rubiaceae (Madder)
Other Common Names: Twinberry, two-eyed berry, squaw berry, deerberry
Range: Newfoundland west to Ontario, Canada; Maine west to Minnesota and south to Florida and Texas
Habitat: Maritime forests; also dry or moist deciduous and coniferous forests
Habit: Perennial herb
Flowering/Fruiting Period: FL April–June; FR June–August
Wetland Status: FACU
Origin: Native

Partridge berry is a common plant found predominantly in forested habitats throughout the eastern half of North America. The genus Mitchella is named after Dr. John Mitchell (1711–68), an American physician and botanist. He is not the same Mitchell (Dr. Elisha) for whom North Carolina's Mt. Mitchell is named.

This small, vinelike, rhizomatous herb typically forms a mat of evergreen leaves beneath the maritime forest canopy. Rooting at the nodes, partridge berry does not climb vegetation and rarely grows more than a few inches high. Individual stems trail along the ground for 12 inches or more. Leaves are oppositely arranged, ovate to nearly round, with prominent white veins on the upper surface. The leaves are dark

a

b

c

green and shiny above and pale yellowish-green below. Partridge berry prefers acidic soils under partial shade.

The fragrant, white to pinkish-white flowers are borne in pairs in the axils of leaves. Thick, white hairs cover the 4 pointed petals comprising each ½ inch-flower. After fertilization, the ovaries of each flower pair fuse, producing a single fruit, a berry. Close inspection of the ½-inch-diameter, bright red fruits reveals scars from the attachment points for 2 flowers on a single berry. Each berry contains 8 seeds, 4 contributed from each flower. The berries remain on the plant and persist throughout the winter.

The plant is tolerant of modest drought conditions and survives in a range of soil-moisture regimes, from moist to dry.

Many species of birds, raccoons, red foxes, mice, and white-tailed deer feed on the berries.

Propagation of partridge berry is by seeds, plant division, and layering. Stratify seeds to increase the rate of germination in the spring. The plant is an excellent but slow-growing ornamental ground cover, an alternative to exotics like vinca and periwinkle.

Native Americans used partridge berry to relieve symptoms of rheumatism and dysentery, as well as to treat kidney disorders and fever.

---

86. Partridge berry (*Mitchella repens*). (a) This plant forms a mat composed of dark green, shiny leaves with prominent white veins on the upper surface. (b) White to pinkish-white, 4-petaled flowers are densely covered with hairs and develop in pairs. (c) Red fruits are ½ inch in diameter and exhibit 2 scars, indicating their origin from 2 individual flowers.

87 SPOTTED HORSEMINT

Monarda punctata Linnaeus
Family: Lamiaceae (Mint)
Other Common Names: Spotted beebalm, eastern horse-mint, American horsemint
Range: Coastal plain: New Jersey south to Florida and west to Texas
Habitat: Dunes; also dry, sandy woods and fields
Habit: Perennial herb

a

b

87. Spotted horsemint (*Monarda punctata*).
(a) The lavender and white bracts surrounding
the flowers of this 12- to 18-inch-high plant are
easily seen from a distance. (b) Flowers are
arranged in tiers in the upper leaf axils and
terminal branches. Purple spots cover the pale
yellow corolla.

Flowering/Fruiting Period: FL July–
September; FR September–October
Wetland Status: FACU
Origin: Native
Spotted horsemint has the signature
Mint family features: aromatic leaves
oppositely arranged on square stems and

zygomorphic flowers. Spotted horsemint
is common on stable interdune areas
along the Carolinas coast, but it seems
somewhat out of place for a broadleaf plant
with prominent and captivating flowers
to be growing in an environment typically
dominated by members of the Grass and
Aster families.

Arising from a sizable taproot, spotted
horsemint grows to a height of 12 to 18
inches. Brownish or reddish, densely
pubescent stems are much branched above
the middle. Leaves are 1 to 3 inches long,
¼ to ½ inch wide, lanceolate to narrowly
oblong, and pubescent. Lower leaves may
be toothed; upper leaves generally have
smooth margins.

Flowers are arranged in tiers of tight
whorls in upper leaf axils and terminating
branches of the plant. An eye-catching
whorl of attractive pink, lavender, or white
bracts similar in shape and size to the
leaves surrounds each flowering head.
The upper lip of the zygomorphic flower
is narrow and arches upward, and the
broader lower lip terminates in 3 lobes;
the central lobe is the largest. Purple
spots cover the pale yellow corolla. The
nectar and pollen attract hummingbirds,
butterflies, honeybees, bumblebees, miner
bees, and plasterer bees. After the flowers
wilt, the showy bracts remain for much of
the summer and fall. Each flower produces
4 nutlets surrounded by a leafy calyx.

Spotted horsemint prefers well-drained,
sandy soils and full sun. The plant tolerates
partial shade, drought, and nutrient-poor
soils. Spotted horsemint is tolerant of salt
aerosols.

Propagate the plant by seeds, plant
division, and stem cuttings. Cuttings and
plant division are most successful if taken
during the summer. Collect and stratify
seeds before planting in the spring. Seeds
of spotted horsemint are available from
commercial nurseries. This species would

be an excellent choice for a native plant garden. No significant insect pests or diseases affect spotted horsemint.

Spotted horsemint possesses the essential oil thymol, an antiseptic found in some mouthwashes. Native Americans drank tea made from the leaves to treat flu, colds, and fever.

Several varieties of spotted horsemint are recognized; the variety common to the coastal Carolinas is var. *punctata*.

a

88 BEACH EVENING PRIMROSE

Oenothera drummondii Hooker
Family: Onagraceae (Evening primrose)
Other Common Name: Drummond's evening primrose
Range: Southern North Carolina south to Florida and west to Louisiana and Texas
Habitat: Dunes and maritime grasslands
Habit: Perennial herb
Flowering/Fruiting Period: FL & FR April–November
Wetland Status: UPL
Origin: Native

Rare in North Carolina but common in South Carolina, this low-growing dune plant adds a touch of bright yellow to the summer dunes and maritime grasslands. But to enjoy these flowers you need to attune yourself to the plant's daily cycle. Similar to most evening primroses, its flowers open in late afternoon or evening and close by late morning. Look for the subtle petal color change from pale yellow to orange and the wilting of the petals. This

b

88. Beach evening primrose (*Oenothera drummondii*). (a) Beach evening primrose's large, yellow flowers typically open in the late afternoon. (b) Flowers are 2 to 3 inches across with 4 petals, a long floral tube, and prominent stamens and a pistil extending beyond the floral tube. (c) The 1- to 2-inch, dry, hairy fruits peel open as they mature, releasing seeds from each of 4 chambers.

c

is a signal to potential pollinators that the flower nectar reward is exhausted.

A deep taproot supports an erect or sprawling, slightly woody plant arising from a rosette of basal leaves. The densely pubescent stems range from 8 to 20 inches long and possess glandular, pubescent, grayish-green leaves. The simple basal leaves are elliptic, shallowly lobed, and 2 to 5 inches long by ½ to ¾ inch wide. Stem leaves are considerably smaller, sessile, entire or shallowly toothed, and alternately arranged. Leaves tend to cluster at the ends of branches. The ground cover created by this plant reduces sand movement and helps stabilize dunes.

The inflorescence is an open spike developing in the leaf axils with only 1 flower open per stem at a time. Long, narrow, upturned floral tubes support 2- to 3-inch, 4-petaled, yellow flowers. The dry, hairy fruit resembles a tiny banana as it "peels" open at maturity. It is 1 to 2 inches long with 2 rows of seeds in each of 4 chambers. Seeds are ¹⁄₁₆ inch, brown, ellipsoid, and pitted on their surfaces.

Beach evening primrose grows best in full sun and on the leeward side of dunes and other areas where it is sheltered from the direct effects of salt aerosols. The plant tolerates summer heat and occasional sandblasting.

Beach evening primrose serves as a nectar source for pollinating moths.

Propagate the plant easily from seeds; also, cuttings can be successfully rooted. The floral display of our native beach evening primrose rivals that of any ornamental dune plant bred for large, colorful flowers.

The subspecies *drummondii* is the common form of beach evening primrose in the coastal Carolinas.

89 SEABEACH EVENING PRIMROSE

Oenothera humifusa Nuttall
Family: Onagraceae (Evening primrose)
Other Common Name: Spreading evening primrose
Range: Coastal: New Jersey south to Florida and west to Louisiana
Habitat: Dunes and maritime grasslands
Habit: Perennial herb
Flowering/Fruiting Period: FL & FR May–September
Wetland Status: UPL
Origin: Native

Faithful to its name, the pale yellow, almost butter-colored flowers of seabeach evening primrose are open from early evening until early morning each day during summer and early fall. Only when the weather is cloudy and cool do the flowers open at midday. Throughout the coastal Carolinas, the plant prefers mature dunes and sparsely vegetated maritime grasslands, where it can grow with little competition from other plants.

Seabeach evening primrose is an erect to procumbent, woody, much-branched plant ranging in height from 4 to 20 inches. Typically, one finds it growing nearly prostrate against the sand. Dense hairs on the stem and leaves give the plant a distinctive grayish-green color. Ground-hugging rosettes of leaves are common on the dunes during the coastal Carolinas winter. Rosette leaves are spatula shaped, toothed, 2 to 3½ inches long, and about ½ inch wide. Stem leaves are slightly smaller and oblong to elliptic.

Flowers are ¾ inch wide and develop on lateral branches throughout the summer. Flowers are composed of a ½- to 1-inch floral tube capped by 4 broadly ovate, yellow petals. Each day, a single flower opens on each spike. As the fruit ripens, it changes from a densely pubescent, gray-green, cylindrical structure to a light brown,

a

b

c

89. Seabeach evening primrose (*Oenothera humifusa*). (a) Seabeach evening primrose is much smaller than its close relative, beach evening primrose. Four to 20 inches high, it prefers open, sparsely vegetated dunes. (b) Flowers are ½ to 1 inch wide with a long floral tube. (c) Fruiting capsules are ½ to 1½ inches long and ⅛ inch in diameter with 4 longitudinal chambers.

dehiscent capsule. The 4-angled capsule is ½ to 1½ inches long and ⅛ inch in diameter. Capsules look like tiny bananas and split longitudinally along 4 sutures to release numerous light brown seeds.

Common associated plants include northern seaside spurge, southern seaside goldenrod, seaside panicum, dune sandspur, sea oats, and purple sandgrass.

The wildlife value of seabeach evening primrose is modest. Ground birds occasionally eat the seeds.

Seeds may be available from some nurseries, garden stores, or plant dealers.

90 MORNING HONEYSUCKLE

Oenothera simulans (Small) W. L. Wagner
  & Hoch
Family: Onagraceae (Evening primrose)
Other Common Names: Southeastern
  gaura, southern beeblossom
Range: North Carolina to Florida and west
  to Texas
Habitat: Dunes; also forest edges and
  roadsides
Habit: Perennial herb (annual)
Flowering/Fruiting Period: FL & FR May–
  September
Wetland Status: UPL
Origin: Native

Morning honeysuckle is a native plant easily overlooked in the dunes and along forest margins. While the plant can grow quite tall, the flower clusters often appear thin, pale, and delicate, blending into a background typically composed of robust grasses and broadleaf trees and shrubs.

The plant possesses a basal rosette of elliptical leaves and narrow stem leaves that are borne singly and alternately on a stem that may reach a height of 5 or 6 feet. Stem leaves are sharply toothed, vary from 1½ to 3 inches long, and range from ovate to narrowly lanceolate. The leaves become progressively smaller toward the top of the plant.

90. Morning honeysuckle (*Oenothera simulans*). (a) Several flowering racemes cluster at the top of the plant. (b) Reddish-pink sepals surround delicate, pink petals. Stamens and style are prominent. (c) Three- or 4-angled, football-shaped fruits mature upward from the base of the flowering raceme.

Flowers appear in clusters of racemes at the ends of the branches. The calyx is cylindrical with 3 to 4 lobes. The ¼-inch-wide petals are white or pink depending on the time since opening. Flowers first open in the afternoon and are white; they turn pale pink before closing the following morning. The 4 petals appear to cluster on one side of the flower, giving the flower a bilaterally symmetrical look. Each flower possesses 8 stamens and a long style with a 4-lobed stigma.

Morning honeysuckle produces 3- or 4-angled, football-shaped fruits that drop from the plant shortly after reaching maturity.

Morning honeysuckle grows best in sunny sites with moist, well-drained, sandy soils. It makes an interesting, but not showy, background plant in a native plant garden. Collect seeds from wild plants.

The species appears to be of modest interest to wildlife except for pollinators and seed-eating insects.

This species is cited as *Gaura angustifolia* in legacy literature for the coastal Carolinas.

---

91 DOTTED SMARTWEED

Persicaria punctata (Elliott) Small
Family: Polygonaceae (Smartweed)
Range: Nova Scotia west to British Columbia, Canada; the United States excepting the cold desert states of Utah and Nevada
Habitat: Freshwater wetlands and other marshes; also pond edges and floodplain forests
Habit: Perennial herb (annual)
Flowering/Fruiting Period: FL & FR July–November
Wetland Status: OBL
Origin: Native
Numerous species of the genus *Persicaria*

occur in the Carolinas, but dotted smartweed is one of the most common in coastal wetland environments. It is related to two familiar plants in our everyday life: buckwheat and rhubarb.

a

b

c

91. Dotted smartweed (*Persicaria punctata*). (a) One to 2 feet tall, dotted smartweed plants grow exclusively in wetlands. Long, smooth leaves are ¼ to ½ inch wide and taper at both ends. (b) Greenish-white flowers are sparsely distributed on long racemes. (c) Using a hand lens, you can see tiny, dark glands on the calyx.

The 1- to 2-foot-tall, dotted smartweed may grow erect or decumbent. Reddish-green, branched stems with swollen joints characterize the plant. Surrounding each joint is a thin, often translucent sheath called an ocrea. The ocrea is a key identifying characteristic of the Polygonaceae (Buckwheat family).

Leaves are simple, smooth, petiolate, and glabrous. They are up to 8 inches long and ¼ to ½ inch wide, and they taper at both ends. Leaves contain a compound that is acrid or bitter when placed on the tongue and lips, thus giving rise to its common name, smartweed.

The flowers are sparsely distributed along the erect, 2- to 6-inch-long racemes. The flowers are greenish-white, and the sepals are dotted with tiny, dark glands. The botanical term associated with plant parts dotted with small glands is "punctate," hence the origin of dotted smartweed's specific epitaph.

The seeds are brownish-black, 3-sided, shiny nutlets.

Dotted smartweed grows in full sun and partial shade. The plant prefers moist to wet conditions and can survive in standing water for several weeks. Dotted smartweed occasionally occurs in brackish water.

Bees, wasps, and flies are common visitors to the flowers. Dotted smartweed seeds serve as excellent food for waterfowl, marsh birds, shorebirds, songbirds, and small mammals.

Propagation of dotted smartweed is by seeds and, to a lesser extent, rhizomes. Seeds are available commercially. Plant them in wetland areas to attract wildlife.

92 COMMON FROGFRUIT

Phyla nodiflora (Linnaeus) Greene
Family: Verbenaceae (Verbena)
Other Common Names: Creeping frogfruit, turkey tangle frogfruit, capeweed
Range: New Jersey west to Missouri and

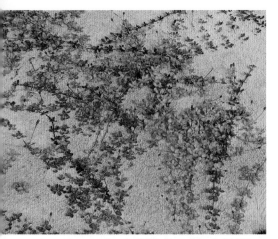

a 92. Common frogfruit (*Phyla nodiflora*). (a) This prostrate plant spreads by stolons that root at the nodes. (b) Leaves are coarsely serrate from the midpoint to the tip. They range from ½ to 1½ inches long and are about ½ inch wide. Globe-shaped flower clusters arise in leaf axils. (c) Flower heads sit atop 1- to 4-inch peduncles; each produces dozens of pink to lavender, slightly zygomorphic flowers.

Oregon and south to Florida; also California, Mexico, and the Caribbean

Habitat: Dunes, dune swales, dune ponds, brackish marshes, ditches, and disturbed areas

Habit: Perennial herb

Flowering/Fruiting Period: FL & FR May–November

Wetland Status: FAC

Origin: Native

Common frogfruit is a minor but appealing ground cover common throughout the coastal Carolinas.

Common frogfruit is a fast-growing, prostrate, sometimes weedy plant that grows just 2 to 6 inches above the ground surface. It spreads via stolons that root at stem nodes and tightly anchor the plant in sandy soils. The obovate to oblanceolate leaves of common frogfruit are arranged alternately along the angled stems. The leaves are coarsely serrate from the midpoint to the tip—there are typically

5 teeth on each leaf side—and they range in size from ½ to 1½ inches long and about ½ inch wide.

The closely packed, globelike clusters of flowers are ¼ to ½ inch long and ¼ inch in diameter. They sit atop 1- to 4-inch peduncles that arise from the leaf axils. Each ¹⁄₁₆-inch, slightly zygomorphic flower has a corolla composed of 4 fused petals ranging across the color spectrum from white to lavender and pink. Common frogfruit flowers continuously from spring until fall. The fruit is a capsule containing 2 seeds.

Common frogfruit survives in a wide variety of environmental conditions, from drought-prone, nutrient-poor dune sand to standing brackish water. The plant is common in infrequently flooded dune swales and exhibits slight leaf succulence when growing in saline soils. Like many other sun-loving species, common frogfruit flowers freely in full sun but infrequently when growing in shade. The plant is evergreen in mild winters, especially in the southern portion of its range.

White-tailed deer graze common frogfruit. Frogfruit is the host for the phaon crescent butterfly caterpillar; therefore, avoid removing this plant from coastal environments where it is found.

Propagate common frogfruit from seeds and by dividing the plant.

Common frogfruit tolerates trampling and provides color, interest, and texture when grown on or along paths in a native plant garden.

A related species, marsh frogfruit (*Phyla lanceolata*), occurs in brackish wetlands of the coastal Carolinas. Marsh frogfruit has larger leaves with 7 to 11 teeth on each leaf side.

a

b

c

93 DUNE GROUND CHERRY
Physalis walteri Nuttall
Family: Solanaceae (Nightshade)
Other Common Name: Walter's ground cherry
Range: Coastal: Virginia south to Florida and west to Louisiana
Habitat: Dunes, swales, edges of maritime forests; also pine forests
Habit: Perennial herb
Flowering/Fruiting Period: FL & FR May–September
Wetland Status: UPL
Origin: Native

Dune ground cherry is closely related to the highly prized tomatillo *Physalis ixocarpa*, a common ingredient in traditional Mexican cuisine and a distant relative of the familiar tomato. You can easily recognize this plant

93. Dune ground cherry (*Physalis walteri*).
(a) Stellate hairs cover stems and leaves, giving this plant a gray-green color and a velvety feel. Flowers are solitary, pale yellow, and trumpet shaped with 5 united petals and a large calyx.
(b) Fruits are loosely covered by a thin, dry calyx.
(c) The fruit is a yellow to orange, smooth-skinned berry.

when it is reproductive by the 5-lobed, papery calyx covering the ripening fruit, a structure reminiscent of Japanese lanterns.

Dune ground cherry is 6 to 12 inches tall and occasionally larger. Under ideal conditions, it is found in small colonies facilitated by the growth of extensive rhizomes about 1/16 inch in diameter. Stellate hairs cover the gray-green stems and leaves, making them feel velvety soft. Lance- to oval-shaped leaves are entire

HERBS

247

and about 1 to 2½ inches long and ½ to 1½ inches wide.

Solitary flowers arising from leaf axils are bell shaped, with 5 united petals and a large calyx. The pale yellow corolla with a grayish center is ½ to ¾ inch long and about as broad.

The fruit of dune ground cherry, a yellow to orange berry, is similar to a small tomato. It is approximately ½ inch in diameter and loosely covered by a thin, dry calyx, ¾ to 1½ inches long by ¾ inch across.

Dune ground cherry requires full sun and prefers moist to dry, well-drained sandy soils. Long-term flooding by salt water or brackish water will kill the plant. Drought and salt-aerosol tolerances in this species are high.

As the fruits dry and break open, dozens of small, disk-shaped seeds become available for ground-feeding birds.

Propagation is by seeds and root division. Although somewhat mealy, the fruits can be dried and eaten like figs or apricots. This plant is a wonderful native plant for use in natural or wildflower gardens and in habitat restoration projects.

a

b

c

94 MARITIME POKEWEED

Phytolacca rigida Small

Family: Phytolaccaceae (Pokeweed)

Other Common Names: American pokeweed, pigeonberry, pokeberry, Virginia poke

Range: Virginia south to Florida and west to Texas

Habitat: Dunes, dune swales, edges of maritime forests and maritime shrub thickets; also disturbed areas

Habit: Perennial herb

Flowering/Fruiting Period: FL & FR May–November

Wetland Status: FACU

Origin: Native

94. Maritime pokeweed (*Phytolacca rigida*). (a) Mature plants may be up to 6 feet tall with green to purplish-red stems and large, bright green, entire leaves. (b) Numerous white to greenish-white flowers are loosely spaced on short pedicels in axillary racemes. (c) Mature fruits are slightly compressed, dark blue spheres containing several seeds.

Maritime pokeweed is a coarse weed that is in a "gray area" of acceptability as an ornamental native plant. Because of the danger of poisoning, avoid planting this species in areas where children are likely to play and be attracted to the berries. Otherwise, maritime pokeweed is a gorgeous plant with red, green, and deep purple colors that also provides important wildlife food.

The combination of a stout, reddish stem; entire, smooth, alternate leaves; and dark blue berries distinguishes maritime pokeweed from similar species. Annually, new stems arise from a thick, long, branching taproot that may grow to a diameter of several inches. The mature plant stands up to 6 feet tall and 3 to 5 feet wide. Maritime pokeweed stems, which change from green to purplish-red as the fall approaches, are glabrous and much branched above the middle of the plant. Leaves are ovate to oblanceolate and tapered at both ends. They range from 3 to 8 inches long and from 1½ to 3 inches wide. The leaves have an unpleasant odor when bruised. Maritime pokeweed grows best in full sun but can grow in partial shade.

Clusters of small, white to greenish-white flowers form in erect axillary racemes. A dozen or more flowers on short pedicels are spaced along the 2½- to 3½-inch-long raceme. Flowers are about ¼ inch across, with 5 delicate, white sepals surrounding a bright green ovary. (The flower has no petals.) In full flower, the racemes are always abuzz with pollinating bees and flies. The large juicy, shiny berries are slightly compressed spheres, each containing about 10 flattened, oval, black seeds.

Maritime pokeweed propagation is by seeds and division of the taproot.

The plant has considerable ecological value. Berries are important to robins, towhees, mockingbirds, mourning doves, catbirds, and bluebirds. Gray foxes, raccoons, and opossums also eat the berries. All of these animals are responsible for distributing the seeds, often at a considerable distance from the parent plant.

Its widely distributed, close relative, *Phytolacca americana*, tends to be aggressive. It differs by having longer, arching, or drooping racemes.

Native Americans used this plant for relieving skin maladies and as an emetic, a spring tonic, a purgative, and an expectorant. The juice of the fruits makes a red dye and ink. Maritime pokeweed is reputed to have delicious-tasting leaves when "properly cooked" (southern style: with bacon drippings and salt)!

---

95 NARROWLEAF PLANTAIN

Plantago lanceolata Linnaeus
Family: Plantaginaceae (Plantain)
Other Common Names: English plantain, ribwort, lanceleaf plantain
Range: Throughout North America
Habitat: Roadsides, fields, lawns, disturbed areas
Habit: Perennial herb
Flowering/Fruiting Period: FL & FR April—November
Wetland Status: FACU
Origin: Exotic; native to Eurasia

Narrowleaf plantain, a common weed of disturbed areas, is considered a noxious weed over much of North America. Early European settlers probably brought it with them in their "medicine cabinet" and thereby introduced it into North America. As a medicinal plant, it is used to alleviate respiratory disorders, whooping cough, and bronchial asthma. The entire plant is used in preparing a tea, poultice, syrup, or infusion. Some research reports note that "whole plant extracts" have antibacterial properties.

Narrowleaf plantain possesses a shallow taproot and numerous coarse, fibrous roots. The plant develops a rosette of basal leaves and then produces a tall, thin flowering stalk. Leaves are linear and taper at each end. They are dark green, glabrous or sparsely hairy, about 6 inches long, and ½ inch wide. The margins are entire and have 3 to 5 prominent, parallel veins that run the length of the leaf, reflecting one of its common names, ribwort.

HERBS

a

b

95. Narrowleaf plantain (*Plantago lanceolata*). (a) This plant produces a basal rosette of narrow leaves that taper at each end. They have 3 to 5 prominent veins that run the length of the 6-inch-long, ½-inch-wide leaves. **(b)** Peduncles are 6 to 18 inches long and possess inflorescences from ½ to 2 inches long. Greenish-white flowers open from the base toward the apex. White stamens and clear styles and stigmas (*top*) are prominent.

Flowering stalks are leafless and range from 6 to 18 inches tall. A short, densely packed column of flowers (a spike) tops each stalk. This inflorescence varies from ½ to 2 inches long, and individual flowers open from the base to the tip of the inflorescence. Over a period of a week or more, the short, blunt inflorescence elongates, and flowers open sequentially upward. The wind-pollinated flowers have 4 small, greenish-white sepals and 4 whitish petals. At anthesis, the distinctive white stamens of individual flowers extend well beyond the petals.

The fruit is an ovoid capsule about ⅛ inch long. Upon splitting open, it releases 2 dark brown, shiny seeds, each deeply grooved along one side. Seeds

become mucilaginous when wet, which aids their dispersal. Seeds are the only mode of reproduction in narrowleaf plantain. A single plant can produce up to 1,000 seeds, making it an excellent weed species!

Narrowleaf plantain prefers full sun and sandy soils. It is tolerant of salt aerosols and soil salts. It grows in a range of soil moistures, from moist to dry. The presence of mycorrhizae associated with the roots of narrowleaf plantain may help the plant grow in nutrient-poor soils.

Seeds may provide nutrition for songbirds and ground birds. Plantain species serve as larval hosts for the buckeye butterfly, tiger moths, and giant leopard moth.

b

96. Seabeach knotweed (*Polygonum glaucum*). (a) Stems of this species may grow prostrate or upright. The fleshy leaves are entire, bluish-green to glaucous green, and ¾ to 1½ inches long. (b) Flowers develop in leaf axils and have 5 thin, whitish sepals and no petals. The sepals persist beyond the maturation of the reddish-brown to black, 3-sided achenes.

96 SEABEACH KNOTWEED

Polygonum glaucum Nuttall
Family: Polygonaceae (Smartweed)
Other Common Names: Seaside knotweed, glaucous knotweed
Range: Coastal: Massachusetts to Florida
Habitat: Wrack lines and dunes
Habit: Perennial herb
Flowering/Fruiting Period: FL & FR May–November
Wetland Status: FACU
Origin: Native

Of the 12 states in which seabeach knotweed is found, 7 list it as rare, of special concern, or endangered, and the other states will probably soon file their own designation of concern. Seabeach knotweed is a pioneer plant of the shoreline, occurring in a narrow habitat between the high spring tide lines and the developing dunes—more or less the wrack-line region, where the plant has few competitors. Unfortunately for this species, its habitat is coincident with the area of many human impacts: sunbathing, beach sweeping, off-road vehicle use, dune stabilization, beach nourishment, and development. Where shoreline and dune stabilization efforts have reduced the incidence of naturally occurring overwashes, both the number of sites and the total number of seabeach knotweed plants have clearly decreased.

Seabeach knotweed is rarely more than 6 inches high, with multiple branched, prostrate, or ascending stems arising from the base of the plant. The ¾- to 1½-inch-long and ⅜-inch-wide fleshy leaves of seabeach knotweed are bluish-green to glaucous green and elliptical with entire margins. Leaves typically curl under along their edges.

Flowers develop in the axils of the leaves in 1 to 3 flowered clusters, with each flower from ¹⁄₁₆ to ⅛ inch in diameter. The flowers display 5 thin, whitish sepals, but no petals. Seabeach knotweed is probably self-pollinated owing to the large distances between plants; however, occasional insect visits may result in some cross-pollination. The sepals persist past the flowering period and extend beyond the tip of the mature fruit, an achene. The tiny, reddish-brown to black achenes have 3 shiny, smooth facets.

Several species of birds feed on the seeds and probably distribute seeds from beach to beach.

Because this is an imperiled plant in the coastal Carolinas, leave this species in its natural beach environment.

97 JUNIPERLEAF

Polypremum procumbens Linnaeus
Family: Tetrachondraceae (Tetrachondra)
Other Common Names: Rustweed, wireweed, polypremum
Range: New York west to Missouri and south to Florida and Texas
Habitat: Dunes; also fields and disturbed areas
Habit: Perennial herb
Flowering/Fruiting Period: FL May–September; FR August–October
Wetland Status: FACU
Origin: Native

Juniperleaf is an occasional member of the flora of the dunes in the Carolinas. Juniperleaf is a small, low-growing, glabrous plant that reaches the size of a dinner plate. Several stems extend from the center of the plant like the spokes of a wheel. The stems are up to 5 inches long and branch frequently.

Leaves are abundant, simple, linear (¼ to 1 inch long), and narrow toward the tip and base. The leaves are nearly sessile, possess entire margins, and are glabrous on both the upper and lower surfaces.

a

b

97. Juniperleaf (*Polypremum procumbens*).
(a) Juniperleaf is a low-growing plant, with oft-branched stems radiating from a central taproot. Stems and leaves become reddish-brown or reddish-orange as they mature. Leaves are nearly sessile, simple, linear, glabrous, and narrow toward the tip and base. (b) Flowers are solitary, sessile, and tiny. Four white petals surround a tuft of hairs in the center of the flower.

Stems and leaves may become reddish-brown or reddish-orange at maturity.

Juniperleaf flowers are solitary, axillary, sessile, and tiny—about ³⁄₁₆ inch across. Each flower is white with 4 lobed petals. The center of the flower is hairy, usually hiding 4 stamens.

The fruit is a spherical, 2-chambered capsule about ¹⁄₁₆ inch across, with sharply pointed, persistent sepals surrounding the fruit.

The seeds are likely a food source for ground birds foraging in the dunes.

The shape, texture, and seasonal colors of juniperleaf make this plant an attractive addition to a coastal native plant garden. Collect seeds from wild plants.

98 ROSEMARY

Rosmarinus officinalis Linnaeus
Family: Lamiaceae (Mint)
Other Common Names: Pilgrim's plant, Mary's mantle, compass weed
Range: USDA Hardiness Zones (6) 7–8 (9)
Habitat: Dunes and cultivated areas
Habit: Perennial herb (shrub)
Flowering/Fruiting Period: FL & FR October–April
Wetland Status: Not designated
Origin: Exotic; native to the region surrounding the Mediterranean Sea

Found from coastal sand dunes to 3,000-foot mountains in countries surrounding the Mediterranean Sea, rosemary has a broad ecological range. It also has a long history of human use, primarily in the areas of pharmacology and culinary arts. Rosemary has beneficial uses ranging from a topical antiseptic to a spice in meat and vegetable dishes. For coastal Carolinas, the bonus is that it thrives in environments with warm temperatures, well-drained sandy soil, and salt aerosols. In other words, rosemary is a great coastal plant.

Rosemary is an evergreen, woody shrub with square stems, needle-shaped leaves, and bark that is gray and scaly. Under ideal growth conditions, rosemary can reach a height of 6 feet with a spread of 3 to 5 feet. The 1-inch-long leaves grow in clusters of 2 to 3. The leaves are dark green above and pale green and pubescent below. A light brush by your hand across the leaves releases a warm and inviting fragrance.

The flowers are typical of the Mint family, with bilateral symmetry created by a 2-lobed upper lip and a 3-lobed lower lip. Flowers range from pale to deep lavender

a

b

98. Rosemary (*Rosmarinus officinalis*). (a) A low-growing evergreen shrub, rosemary possesses square stems and dark green, needle-shaped leaves growing in clusters of 2 or 3. (b) Half-inch flowers are bilaterally symmetrical with a 2-lobed upper lip, a 3-lobed lower lip, and prominent arching stamens. Flowers vary from pale to deep lavender.

and are about ½ inch long. Seeds are small and yellowish-brown.

Rosemary is most easily propagated by cuttings or layering. You can divide roots in the spring. Seed germination is variable, and this propagation method is not the best for reproducing the plant.

Rosemary prefers full sun, and it grows especially well in nutrient-poor, dry, sandy soil. The plant tolerates high soil temperatures.

The flowers attract butterflies and bees; some people consider the honey produced from its flowers among the best. The shrub may provide some cover for small mammals and ground birds.

Rosemary heightens the aroma of sachets, potpourris, soap, lotions, perfumes, and shampoos. Rubbing rosemary leaves on exposed skin serves as an insect repellent.

Rosemary is a staple in any herb garden, and numerous cultivars have been developed.

99 VIRGINIA GLASSWORT

Salicornia virginica Linnaeus
Family: Chenopodiaceae (Goosefoot)
Other Common Names: Woody glasswort, saltwort, samphire, pickleweed
Range: Coastal: Newfoundland, Canada; south to Florida and west to Texas
Habitat: Salt marshes and salt pannes
Habit: Perennial herb (subshrub)
Flowering/Fruiting Period: FL & FR August–October
Wetland Status: OBL
Origin: Native

Two distinct species of glasswort are common in the coastal Carolinas. One is an annual, dwarf glasswort (*Salicornia bigelovii*), which turns bright reddish-purple during the fall. The other is a perennial species that typically remains green throughout the fall, Virginia glasswort.

99. Virginia glasswort (*Salicornia virginica*). (a) Virginia glasswort grows in dense mats in the tidal marsh and salt pannes. Stems are bright green and succulent. Flowers develop in nodes near the top of stems. Flowers are highly reduced and inconspicuous; sometimes merely a single stamen (b) or style and stigma (c) is visible.

Virginia glasswort is the most common and widespread glasswort species, ranging from 4 to 12 inches tall and often growing in crowded mats of mostly unbranched stems. Arising from a dense network of rhizomes and roots, the bright green, succulent stems may be erect, spreading, or decumbent. Arranged oppositely, the leaves of Virginia glasswort are reduced in size to small appressed, fleshy, scalelike appendages. As Virginia glasswort absorbs salts and accumulates them throughout the plant, stem tissues die, release the salts back to the environment, and thereby allow the plant to continue growing in salty environments. This loss of salts can be seen as summer and fall progress. Section by section, stems of Virginia glasswort lose their succulence and turn gray or brown until virtually all of the stem sections appear dead.

Flowering heads, similar in shape and size to the lower stem segments, develop as spikes near the top of individual stems. Scale leaves below the flowering spike are obtuse. Three flowers develop in each fertile node. Each of the highly reduced and inconspicuous flowers possesses 1 or 2 stamens and a single pistil. Seeds of Virginia glasswort are ovoid, brown or gray, and about 1/16 inch in diameter.

Virginia glasswort is common on salt flats or pannes, environments within salt marshes that drain poorly. Here, evaporation of seawater increases soil salinity above natural seawater strength. The plant does not tolerate competition from other plants and grows best in moist, sandy soils and full sun.

Propagation of Virginia glasswort is by seeds and plant division. Seeds can germinate immediately after they are shed in the fall, or they may remain dormant until spring. Seedlings are distinctive; they look superficially like the seedlings of many cacti.

Species often associated with Virginia glasswort are dwarf glasswort, smooth cordgrass, and sea lavender.

The wildlife value of Virginia glasswort has not been well documented.

The stems are edible; include them in a fresh salad for a different texture and for saltiness.

100 WATER PIMPERNEL

Samolus parviflorus Rafinesque
Family: Primulaceae (Primrose)
Other Common Names: Seaside brookweed, water brookweed, smallflower water pimpernel
Range: Throughout North America except for the Rocky Mountain states
Habitat: Freshwater and brackish marshes;

a

100. Water pimpernel (*Samolus parviflorus*).
(a) Water pimpernel is typically found in wetland habitats. Its basal leaves are pale green and rounded with entire margins. Upper leaves are sessile.

b

c

d

100. Water pimpernel (*Samolus parviflorus*). (b) Tiny flowers with long peduncles are widely spaced on terminal racemes. (c) Flowers have 5 white petals and 5 bright yellow anthers visible in the center. (d) Fruits are light brown capsules with 5 sharp calyx teeth. Note the seeds inside the capsule.

also swamps, edges of streams, and ditches

Habit: Perennial herb (annual)

Flowering/Fruiting Period: FL & FR April–October

Wetland Status: OBL

Origin: Native

In environments throughout the coastal Carolinas where you are likely to get your feet wet and muddy, you are apt to encounter water pimpernel. This plant is most at home in sunny, wetland habitats.

Water pimpernel ranges from 6 to 18 inches tall with dense, shallow, fibrous roots. Plants arise from ground-level rosettes of leaves. These basal leaves are pale green and obovate with entire margins. The basal leaves range from 1 to 3 inches long and 1 inch wide and often persist through the winter. Lower leaves possess petioles; upper leaves are sessile. Leaves are rounded at the tips and gradually narrow at the bases. Alternately arranged stem leaves decrease in size from the base to the top of the plant. The entire plant is glabrous.

Tiny flowers are widely spaced on terminal racemes. Each flower is white, cup shaped, and barely ⅛ inch across. Flowers have 5 petals, 5 bright yellow anthers, and a single stigma; each flower terminates a long, thin peduncle. Water pimpernel blooms profusely throughout the summer. The fruit is a nearly globose, brown capsule with 5 sharp calyx teeth. The fruit contains numerous reddish-brown seeds.

The wildlife value of this plant is unknown, but seeds may be part of the diet of waterfowl.

Propagation is from seeds collected from wild plants. In a native garden, water pimpernel would grow best in a wetland environment that receives spray from a water feature. Plants can grow in both light shade and full sun.

a

b

101 LARGE SEA PURSLANE

Sesuvium portulacastrum (Linnaeus) Linnaeus

Family: Aizoaceae (Fig Marigold)

Other Common Name: Shoreline sea purslane

Range: Southeastern North Carolina south to Florida and west to Texas

Habitat: Wrack lines, dunes, maritime grassland, edges of tidal marshes; also waste places

Habit: Perennial herb

Flowering/Fruiting Period: FL & FR May–December

Wetland Status: FACW

Origin: Native

Large sea purslane adds red, green, and pink to the summer and fall palette of the extensive grass-dominated flats near inlet margins and on overwash fans in the coastal Carolinas. Large sea purslane, with individual plants growing to a diameter of

c

101. Large sea purslane (*Sesuvium portulacastrum*). (a) Large sea purslane grows only a few inches above the sand surface. It possesses reddish-green, succulent stems and prefers areas with little competition from other plants. (b) Leaves are simple, entire, and oblanceolate, ranging from ¾ to 2 inches long and ⅛ to ⅜ inch wide. (c) Flowers are ½ to ¾ inch across, bright pink, and star shaped with numerous stamens and 5 sepals that are green on the outside and pink on the inside. The flowers have no petals.

HERBS

257

3 feet, effectively traps blowing sand, which often results in a modest increase in the elevation of sites where it grows.

Large sea purslane is a low-growing plant usually only 1 to 2 inches above the ground surface. Noticeably succulent stems are reddish-green, glabrous, and highly branched; they root at the leaf nodes. Leaves are opposite, simple, entire, and oblanceolate shaped, ranging from ¾ to 2 inches long and ⅛ to ⅜ inch wide.

Bright pink flowers are ½ to ¾ inch across and appear on ¼- to ¾-inch pedicels. These showy flowers possess 5 sepals, green on the outside and pink on the inside, with 20 or more stamens. Each flower only opens for a short time, but an entire plant displays numerous flowers each day for weeks. The fruit of large sea purslane is a cone-shaped capsule up to ⅜ inch long. The plant has no special seed dispersal mechanism; the 30 or more shiny, black seeds in each capsule merely fall to the ground near the parent plant. Wind or water may move seeds elsewhere along the shore.

Large sea purslane is drought resistant and tolerates high soil salt concentrations, full sun, and low-nutrient sandy soils. Well adapted to the coastal environment, large sea purslane grows best where competition from other plants is low. If used in a coastal native plant garden, give it plenty of space to grow without competition.

Propagation is exclusively from seeds; severed stem sections perish quickly.

Large sea purslane is a minor component of the diet of small mammals.

Small sea purslane (*Sesuvium maritimum*) is a closely related species that also occurs in the coastal Carolinas in similar habitats. While similar to large sea purslane, the flowers and fruits of small sea purslane are sessile. Flowers have only 5 stamens.

102 SOUTHERN SEASIDE GOLDENROD

Solidago mexicana Linnaeus
Family: Asteraceae (Aster)
Range: Coastal: Massachusetts south to Florida and west to Texas
Habitat: Dunes, dune swales, maritime grasslands, edges of maritime shrub thickets, edges of brackish and salt marshes
Habit: Perennial herb
Flowering/Fruiting Period: FL & FR August–November
Wetland Status: FACW
Origin: Native

With one of the largest flowering heads of the goldenrod species, the hardy southern seaside goldenrod brings bright yellow to a variety of habitats from dunes to salt marshes.

Ranging to a height of 6 feet, southern seaside goldenrod is an erect or slightly arching plant with a basal rosette composed of large, evergreen leaves. A mature plant will often have several stout stems arising from rhizomes. Stem leaves are alternately arranged, becoming progressively smaller toward the flower head. The oblanceolate basal leaves vary from 2 to 8 inches long, while the upper-stem leaves are about 1 inch long. The leaves, either sessile or clasping the stem, are dark green, glabrous, entire, and somewhat succulent. Succulence is pronounced in leaves exposed to concentrated salt aerosols or soil salts.

The flowering head is large, showy, and secund. A dense pyramidal or club-shaped cluster of bright yellow flowers comprises the inflorescence. Each individual flower of the inflorescence is about ¼ inch across and includes 7 to 10 ray florets and 10 to 16 disk florets. The flowers attract bees, butterflies, and beetles. One can scarcely take a photograph of southern seaside goldenrod without including an insect or

a

b

102. Southern seaside goldenrod (*Solidago mexicana*). (a) Erect or slightly arching, southern seaside goldenrod has oblanceolate basal leaves ranging from 2 to 8 inches long, while the upper-stem leaves are about 1 inch long. (b) Bright yellow flowers about ¼ inch across include disk and ray florets.

two foraging in the flowers. The fruit is an achene topped with long, white hairs that aid in wind dispersal of the seeds.

Southern seaside goldenrod requires full sun and moist soils, but the plant is quite drought resistant. It prefers sandy soils and can withstand occasional inundation with brackish or salt water. Storms occurring during the growing season appear to have little impact on the plant, and it continues to flower even after sustaining wind damage and saltwater flooding. Common associated plants include saltmeadow cordgrass and sea oats.

Butterflies and moths swarm over the flowers when pollen is available. Several species of birds, including goldfinches, eat the seeds.

Propagate southern seaside goldenrod

from seed and by plant division. Seeds may be collected from wild plants, air dried, and sowed immediately. Plant division is most successful in the spring when rhizomes begin to extend from the plant. Southern seaside goldenrod is available from commercial nurseries.

Southern seaside goldenrod and other goldenrods have often been considered the cause of hay fever, but this is rarely the case. Common ragweed deserves the credit as the real culprit.

103 NODDING LADIES' TRESSES

Spiranthes cernua (Linnaeus) L. C. Richard
Family: Orchidaceae (Orchid)
Other Common Names: Fragrant ladies' tresses, white nodding ladies' tresses
Range: Canadian Maritime Provinces west to Minnesota and Nebraska and south to Georgia and Texas
Habitat: Dune swales and maritime grasslands; also swamps, marshes, and bogs
Habit: Perennial herb
Flowering/Fruiting Period: FL & FR July–November
Wetland Status: FACW
Origin: Native

During late summer and early fall, the flowers of nodding ladies' tresses provide a sliver of bright white and green within the season-ending brown background of the grasses and herbs in dune swales.

Nodding ladies' tresses sends up a single flowering stem from a tuberous root deep in the soil. The stem has from 3 to 6 leaves that are small and scalelike.

A spirally twisted spike of delicate, white flowers tops the upper third of the glabrous stem that ranges from 10 to 20 inches high. Tightly packed along the stem are 15 to 30 sessile flowers. Each flower and subtending bract is finely pubescent with nearly transparent hairs, a key identifying characteristic of this species. The 3 upper

HERBS

a

b

103. Nodding ladies' tresses (*Spiranthes cernua*).
(a) A dense flower spike terminates nodding
ladies' tresses stems. Three to 6 small, scalelike
leaves are spaced along the stem. (b) The 10-
to 20-inch flower spike is spirally twisted with
delicate, white flowers, each subtended by a
bract covered with thin, nearly transparent hairs.

petals form a tubular-shaped hood, with
each petal tip slightly upturned. The flower
has a faintly toothed and wrinkled lower
petal about ¼ to ⅜ inch long.

A similar species also found in the
coastal area, especially along roadsides, is
spring ladies' tresses (*Spiranthes vernalis*).
It flowers early in the summer and displays
its white flowers in a similarly stacked,
spiral arrangement. It features abundant,
short, simple hairs on the upper portion of
the stem.

Both nodding ladies' tresses and
spring ladies' tresses grow in moist swales
dominated by grasses and forbs. They
are early colonizers of this environment
and disappear when shrubs invade dune
swales.

We know little of the wildlife value of
nodding ladies' tresses. There is likely an
insect/plant interaction in the pollination
process.

The plant may be available from
specialized native plant nurseries. Avoid

collecting the plant or its seeds from the wild.

104 PERENNIAL SALTMARSH ASTER

Symphyotrichum tenuifolium (Linnaeus) G. L. Nesom

Family: Asteraceae (Aster)

Other Common Names: Salt marsh aster, saline aster

Range: Massachusetts south to Florida and west to Texas

Habitat: Brackish and salt marshes

Habit: Perennial herb

Flowering/Fruiting Period: FL & FR July–November

Wetland Status: OBL

Origin: Native

In late summer, perennial saltmarsh asters dot brackish and tidal marshes with miniature yellow-and-white, daisylike flowers.

Generally found above the mean high-tide level, this plant spreads by slender rhizomes possessing many fibrous roots. Perennial saltmarsh aster has glabrous stems and erect to spreading branches that vary from 6 to 24 inches tall. Leaves are widely spaced and scattered along the stem. They are linear to elliptic, fleshy, entire, and alternately arranged on the stem. The leaves, 1 to 6 inches long and ⅛ inch wide, are shed continuously as the plant grows during the summer and fall.

a

b

104. Perennial saltmarsh aster (*Symphyotrichum tenuifolium*). (a) Stems of perennial saltmarsh aster are glabrous and erect or spreading. Linear to elliptic leaves are succulent and widely spaced along the stem of plants, which vary from 6 to 24 inches tall. (b) Numerous phyllaries subtend the flowering head.

c

d

104. Perennial saltmarsh aster (*Symphyotrichum tenuifolium*). (c) Flowers are composed of both disk and ray flowers. Ray flowers are pale lavender to white, while disk flowers are yellow to purplish-yellow. (d) Fruiting heads are globose and reminiscent of the familiar dandelion fruiting heads.

Each plant displays several flowers composed of both ray and disk flowers on the tips of branches; the flowers range from ½ to ¾ inch across. Ray flowers have pale lavender to white petals; in contrast, the disk flowers vary from yellow to purplish-yellow. Bracts that subtend the flower heads are white with a green midrib. The fruit is a ribbed nutlet that is ⅛ to ¼ inch long and shaped like a grain of rice. The seed has a distinct ¼-inch pappus. Perennial saltmarsh aster is salt tolerant and able to survive in saltmarsh environments.

This plant is adapted to salt marshes and is less suitable as a native garden specimen.

An annual species related to perennial saltmarsh aster is the eastern annual saltmarsh aster (*Symphyotrichum subulatum*), which occurs in similar habitats in the Carolinas. In contrast to the perennial saltmarsh aster, the eastern annual saltmarsh aster has no rhizomes and grows from a taproot. Its flowers are smaller, up to ½ inch across. The plants are otherwise similar. In legacy coastal literature, botanists cite these two aster species as *Aster tenuifolius* (perennial) and *Aster subulatus* (annual).

105 AMERICAN GERMANDER

Teucrium canadense Linnaeus

Family: Lamiaceae (Mint)

Other Common Names: Canada germander, common germander

Range: Coastal: Nova Scotia, Canada; south to Florida and west to Texas

Habitat: Dunes and maritime forest edges; also waste areas and moist roadside ditches

Habit: Perennial herb

Flowering/Fruiting Period: FL & FR June–August

Wetland Status: FACW

Origin: Native

a

b

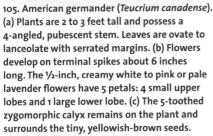

105. American germander (*Teucrium canadense*).
(a) Plants are 2 to 3 feet tall and possess a
4-angled, pubescent stem. Leaves are ovate to
lanceolate with serrated margins. (b) Flowers
develop on terminal spikes about 6 inches
long. The ½-inch, creamy white to pink or pale
lavender flowers have 5 petals: 4 small upper
lobes and 1 large lower lobe. (c) The 5-toothed
zygomorphic calyx remains on the plant and
surrounds the tiny, yellowish-brown seeds.

The genus name for American germander,
an aromatic member of the Mint family,
comes from "Teucer," a Greek hero of
the Trojan War. Despite its native status,
American germander spreads easily and
quickly through the growth of slender
rhizomes, and some states consider it a
highly aggressive species.

Typically ranging from 2 to 3 feet
tall, American germander possesses a
distinctive 4-angled, pubescent stem and
has ovate to lanceolate, opposite leaves
with serrated margins. The sharply pointed
leaves grow on short petioles and are 2 to
5 inches long and 1 to 2 inches wide.

c

Flowers develop on terminal spikes that average about 6 inches long. The pubescent calyx is 5-toothed. The ½-inch flowers are zygomorphic with 4 small upper lobes and 1 large lower lobe (petal), varying from creamy white to pink or pale lavender. Each flower possesses 4 stamens of two different lengths. Bees and butterflies pollinate the flowers.

The ellipsoid seeds, about ¹⁄₁₆ inch long, are yellowish-brown. Each flower produces 4 seeds. To propagate American germander, sow seeds in the spring or make cuttings in July to August.

American germander prefers full or partial sun and requires moist but well-drained soils. It is not particularly drought or salt-aerosol tolerant.

Brewed leaves of the plant act as a diuretic. This brew can also be used externally as a gargle and an antiseptic.

Several varieties of American germander are recognized. The most common variety found in the coastal Carolinas is var. *canadense*.

---

106 SPANISH MOSS

Tillandsia usneoides (Linnaeus) Linnaeus
Family: Bromeliaceae (Pineapple)
Other Common Names: Florida moss, grandfather's whiskers
Range: Virginia south to Florida and west across the Gulf of Mexico coast
Habitat: Maritime forests and coastal bottomland forests
Habit: Perennial herb (epiphyte)
Flowering/Fruiting Period: FL & FR April–June
Wetland Status: FAC
Origin: Native

b

106. Spanish moss (*Tillandsia usneoides*). (a) Spanish moss is characterized by dense, silver-gray threads hanging from the branches of live oak and other species. (b) Tiny flowers, subtended by two bracts, are solitary and pendant. Each possesses 3 yellow-green petals.

Neither from Spain nor botanically classified as a moss, Spanish moss is actually in the same family as the pineapple. It is commonly associated with grand plantations and coastal swamps of the southeastern Atlantic and Gulf seacoasts. Only locally persistent beyond the coastline or open water, Spanish moss grows best in locales with a mild climate and high humidity.

Spanish moss may grow to lengths of 10 to 20 feet under the ideal condition of

c

d

strong morning sun; however, the living portion of an individual plant is often only about 20 inches long. When viewed under a microscope, the stems and leaves appear to be covered with silver-colored peltate scales that lend an overall gray-green color to the plant. The scales are responsible for reducing moisture loss and increasing nutrient capture in the plant's leaves and stems. Traces of particulate and dissolved nutrients reach Spanish moss via rainfall and dry deposition.

In the early summer, solitary, pendant, yellow-green flowers subtended by 2 bracts appear on the stems. The 1-inch-long, 3-parted capsules about the diameter of a pencil lead contain from 2 to 20 feathery seeds. Seedpods open in the summer.

The plant thrives on large branches of trees such as oaks and cypress; it is less common on pines. Spanish moss is not a parasite, and it does not harm the host trees upon which it grows.

Birds and wind are responsible for spreading Spanish moss from tree to tree, and birds often use plant pieces in constructing their nests.

Propagate Spanish moss from seeds or by simple division of the plant.

Because of its natural resilience to crushing and its resistance to insect attack, Spanish moss was once used extensively as mattress filler, in overstuffed furniture, and as filling for car seats. Today, the uses of Spanish moss are limited to mulch for potted plants and source material for various arts and crafts.

106. Spanish moss (*Tillandsia usneoides*). (c) Fruiting capsules are 1 inch long and about the diameter of a pencil lead. (d) Capsules dry and split, releasing 2 to 20 seeds with long, white, wispy hairs.

107 NARROW-LEAVED CATTAIL

Typha angustifolia Linnaeus
Family: Typhaceae (Cattail)
Other Common Name: Cattail
Range: Nova Scotia west to North Dakota and south to South Carolina; also Louisiana and Texas
Habitat: Brackish and salt marshes,

HERBS

265

a

b

107. Narrow-leaved cattail (*Typha angustifolia*).
(a) Narrow-leaved cattail ranges from 4 to
10 feet tall with narrow, bright green leaves
extending well above the top of the flowering
spike. (b) Male flowers (*top*) and female flowers
(*bottom*) are clustered at the top of the flowering
spike. Male and female flowering sections are
separated by ½ to 2 inches.

freshwater marshes; also swamps and roadside ditches

Flowering/Fruiting Period: FL May–July; FR June–November

Habit: Perennial herb

Wetland Status: OBL

Origin: Exotic; native to Europe

Narrow-leaved cattail is one of the most versatile plants known. Virtually every part of the plant is either edible (including the pollen, which can be used to enrich flour) or useful for other purposes, such as bedding, tinder, thatching, matting, stuffing, and compost and in making baskets, shoes, paper, rope, and boats. Some scientists believe that narrow-leaved cattail, which is native to Europe, was introduced into New England around 1820. It subsequently migrated westward and southward.

Narrow-leaved cattail is a rhizomatous

aquatic or semi-aquatic plant varying from 4 to 10 feet tall with bright green leaves extending well above the top of the flowering spike. The rhizome is up to 2 feet long and approximately 1 inch in diameter. Leaves are erect and linear and ¼ to ½ inch wide, a characteristic that distinguishes it from common cattail, a species with wider leaves.

Flowering stems are 3 to 6 feet tall and topped with a characteristic 4- to 8-inch, dense, cylindrical flowering head containing thousands of seeds. Both staminate and pistillate flowers are present on the same stem, separated by ½ to 2 inches. Seeds of narrow-leaved cattail are nutlets surrounded by brown, downy hairs about ¹⁄₁₆ inch long.

Stands of narrow-leaved cattail provide shelter and nesting material for rails, coots, bitterns, red-winged blackbirds, and marsh wrens; white-tailed deer may use the stands for cover, while geese and muskrats eat the roots and rhizomes.

Narrow-leaved cattail propagates vegetatively and from seeds. Seeds germinate immediately after they mature. Narrow-leaved cattail is invasive in disturbed habitats, expands quickly, and outcompetes native species. Gain control of the plant by reducing nutrient input and by maintaining high salinity in the environment. Narrow-leaved cattail will replace smooth cordgrass if tidal flow is restricted, such as when salt marshes are diked.

This species prefers deeper water than common cattail, up to 3 feet deep, and will tolerate higher salinities. The soils in large stands are typically high in organic matter generated by the plant leaves, stems, and rhizomes.

Because this plant has a tendency to become invasive, use it only with considerable caution and vigilance in a coastal native plant garden setting.

108. Common cattail (*Typha latifolia*). (a) Leaves a are linear (3 to 8 feet long), ³⁄₈ to 1 inch wide, flat on both sides, and pale green or gray-green.

108 COMMON CATTAIL

Typha latifolia Linnaeus
Family: Typhaceae (Cattail)
Other Common Names: Cattail, broadleaf cattail, broad-leaved cattail
Range: North America (introduced worldwide)
Habitat: Freshwater marshes, swamps, and roadside ditches
Habit: Perennial herb
Flowering/Fruiting Period: FL May–July; FR June–November
Wetland Status: OBL
Origin: Native

Common cattail is one of the most widespread plants distributed, from the coldest high Arctic communities to tropical climates virtually throughout the world. Whether you dipped the dry "corn-dog-shaped" flower heads in kerosene and lit them for "torches" or tore the flower heads apart out of curiosity, inadvertently covering yourself with great wads of soft fluff, you likely experienced cattails sometime during your childhood.

Leaves of common cattail are linear, flat on both sides, and pale green or gray-

The staminate section is not persistent after flowering, usually breaking off about ¼ inch above the pistillate section.

Despite the fact that it can withstand some soil salinity, common cattail occurs most frequently in shallow coastal freshwater environments.

Common cattail may provide shelter and nesting material for several species of birds and small mammals.

Common cattail may hybridize with narrow-leaved cattail when they grow in proximity. The offspring of this mating are a hybrid, *Typha* x *glauca*, a highly aggressive cattail that can outcompete most aquatic plants, including its parents.

Propagation of common cattail in existing stands is through rhizome extension. Advances into new environments typically occur through seeds dispersed by wind, water, or animals.

Wetland restoration projects may include common cattail. Cultivars of the species are available commercially. As with its sister species, narrow-leaved cattail, vigilance is important to ensure that this species does not take over the environment in which it is placed.

b 108. Common cattail (*Typha latifolia*). (b) Male flowers (*top*) and female flowers (*bottom*) grow at the top of the flowering spike with less than ½ inch between them (oftentimes touching). (c) Male flowers gradually fall or drift away from the fruit.

green. The leaves, arising from a stout rhizome with fibrous roots, vary from 3 to 8 feet long and range from ⅜ to 1 inch wide—shorter and wider than those of the narrow-leaved cattail.

Flowers are yellow-green to green at the start of the flowering season, turning dark brown as they mature. The wind-pollinated flowers develop on separate parts of the same stem, which grows to about the same height as the leaves. A key differentiating characteristic between common and narrow-leaved cattails is the relationship between the two types of flowers that characterize the species, pistillate and staminate flowers. The distance between staminate and pistillate flowers is less than ½ inch in common cattail and usually more than ½ inch on narrow-leaved cattails.

109 COMMON MULLEIN

Verbascum thapsus Linnaeus

Family: Scrophulariaceae (Figwort)

Other Common Names: Woolly mullein, velvet dock, flannel plant

Range: North American continent and elsewhere

Habitat: Waste places, disturbed sites, roadsides

Habit: Biennial herb

Flowering/Fruiting Period: FL June– September; FR July–October

Wetland Status: FACU

Origin: Exotic; native to Europe and Asia; introduced throughout much of the temperate world

Introduced to North America from Europe

109. Common mullein (*Verbascum thapsus*).
(a) The identifying characteristic of this 3- to
7-foot-tall plant is the gray-green leaves densely
covered with star-shaped hairs, making the
leaves soft to the touch. (b) Plants produce one or
more racemes up to 24 inches long with densely
packed, ½- to 1-inch, slightly zygomorphic
flowers. (c) Fruiting capsules are about ¼ inch in
diameter and split open as they dry.

in the 1700s, common mullein spread across the United States and Canada over the next 100 years. Crushed seeds were used as a fish poison, while various parts of the plant were processed into emollients, ointments, and poultices and used to treat asthma, skin diseases, diarrhea, and headaches.

In the first year of growth, the plant forms a ground-hugging rosette of gray-green, soft, pubescent leaves with a thick taproot surrounded by fibrous roots. The rosette leaves are large, ranging from 5 to 20 inches long and 1 to 5 inches wide. As a biennial, the plant grows vegetatively during its first year and remains green over the winter. In the second year, a thick, flowering stem emerges and bolts to a height of 3 to 7 feet. Alternately arranged stem leaves decrease in size toward the top of the plant.

Numerous tightly packed and slightly zygomorphic yellow flowers surround the upper third of the stem, each having 5 petals and 5 sepals. This distinctive rod-shaped flowering head may be up to 24 inches long. Each flower opens for a single day, and flowering progresses up the stem for as long as 2 months. The fruit is a nearly spherical capsule about ¼ inch in diameter. As the fruit dries, it splits open, releasing myriad brown, pitted seeds.

A single large plant can produce more than 100,000 seeds in a year, and the seeds can remain viable for years. This makes the plant difficult to eradicate; however, the plant does not spread aggressively, and botanists do not currently consider it invasive.

The plant prefers sandy soils. Common mullein is a pioneer species in disturbed habitats and frequents human-influenced environments, such as picnic areas or trails through dunes and overwashes. The species disappears from an area as the amount of bare soil decreases.

The plant has little wildlife value beyond bee and butterfly pollination. White-tailed deer will graze on the plant if their preferred foods are not available.

Grow the sun-loving common mullein in a native plant garden; it is a strikingly attractive addition in drier sites. Seeds germinate best on bare soil in the spring.

Vines

110 SUPPLEJACK

Berchemia scandens (Hill) K. Koch
Family: Rhamnaceae (Buckthorn)
Other Common Names: Rattan vine,
    American rattan, Alabama supplejack
Range: Maryland west to Illinois;
    Oklahoma south to Texas and Florida
Habitat: Maritime shrub thickets and
    maritime forests; also swamp and
    bottomland forests
Habit: Perennial vine
Flowering/Fruiting Period: FL April–May;
    FR August–October
Wetland Status: FAC
Origin: Native

Supplejack is one of a seemingly large
number of vine species in the coastal
shrub thickets and maritime forests of the
coastal Carolinas. The plant is a climbing,
deciduous vine that often forms a dense
tangle over and within shrubs and trees,
such as common wax myrtle and live oak.

With stems growing up to 1 inch in
diameter, supplejack has bark that is
smooth and grayish-green with white
streaks. This vine grows to over 30 feet
by twisting around trees and shrubs, in
contrast to vines such as poison ivy that
cling to trunks and branches with many
adventitious roots. Leaves of supplejack
are shiny green, slightly serrate, elliptical,
and alternately arranged on the stems. The
leaves are 1 to 2 inches long and ½ to 1 inch
wide, with wavy edges and conspicuous
pinnate venation.

The flowers have 5 greenish-white petals
about 1⁄16 inch across. They are arranged
in terminal panicles on short, lateral
branches. The fruit of supplejack is a blue-
black, egg-shaped drupe up to 3⁄8 inch long.
The fruits often persist far into the winter.

Supplejack prefers continuously moist
soils typical of coastal shrub thickets and
maritime forests. It grows well in both
partial and full sun.

Birds and small mammals feast on the

110. Supplejack (*Berchemia scandens*).
(a) Alternately arranged, shiny, wavy-edged
leaves characterize this woody vine. (b) Terminal
clusters of flowers typically develop high in the
maritime forest canopy. (c) Fruits mature from
green to red to bluish-black late in the growing
season.

fruits, and white-tailed deer occasionally browse the plant. Reports indicate that the fruits are poisonous to humans.

Owing to its smooth stems of nearly uniform diameter interrupted only by thin branches, supplejack is useful in making wickerware items, hence the common name rattan vine.

---

111 COASTAL PLAIN BINDWEED

Calystegia sepium (Linnaeus) R. Brown
Family: Convolvulaceae (Morning glory)
Other Common Names: Wild morning glory, hedge bindweed, hedge false bindweed
Range: Virginia south to Florida and west to New Mexico; also California and Nevada
Habitat: Edges of maritime forests and maritime shrub thickets; also roadsides and disturbed areas
Habit: Perennial vine
Flowering/Fruiting Period: FL & FR June–September
Wetland Status: FAC
Origin: Native

Represented by several varieties, coastal plain bindweed is a common and widespread plant. We know it by more than 20 common names! It is usually found climbing on other herbs and shrubs; the freely branching stem may trail or climb up to 10 feet. It spreads far from its rhizomatous base by twining around other plants and objects.

Leaves are alternately arranged on the stem and triangular or arrow shaped. They range from 2 to 4 inches long and 2 to 3 inches across. The leaves are glabrous and entire.

The solitary, funnel-shaped flowers are 2½ to 3 inches wide and grow on 2- to 6-inch-long, angular pedicels in the axils of the leaves. The flowers are composed of 5 fused, white or occasionally pink petals. In bud, 2 green, leafy bracts cover the

a

b

111. Coastal plain bindweed (*Calystegia sepium*). (a) Arrow-shaped leaves surround the nearly 3-inch flowers composed of 5 fused white petals. (b) Each 2-chambered fruiting capsule contains 2 to 4 large seeds.

sepals and petals. In some varieties, the white flowers possess pale pink stripes radiating from the center.

Characteristically, the 5 stamens fuse together and surround a single pistil with 2 stigmas. Like many members of the Morning glory family, coastal plain bindweed flowers open in the morning and close in the afternoon or evening on fair

273

days. Curiously, in this species, we observe that flowers are twisted in the bud stage. When flowering is complete, the flowers re-twist as they close.

The fruit is a 2-chambered capsule containing 2 to 4 dark brown seeds that are about ¼ inch long.

Coastal plain bindweed prefers moist, sandy soils that are poor in nutrients. It grows best in full sun, but it will survive in partial shade.

Many bee species pollinate the scentless flowers, seeking nectar in return. A few species of birds eat the seeds.

The species has a tendency to become weedy and aggressive. It is difficult to eradicate because of its deep roots. Under ideal growing conditions, it can smother the nearby plants on which it grows.

The subspecies *limnophila* is the most common subspecies of bindweed in the coastal Carolinas.

a

b

112 TRUMPET CREEPER

Campsis radicans (Linnaeus) Seemmann ex Bureau

Family: Bignoniaceae (Bignonia)
Other Common Names: Trumpet flower, cow-itch, trumpet vine, cow vine
Range: Massachusetts west to Iowa and south to Texas and Florida; naturalized north and west of these boundaries
Habitat: Edges of maritime forests; also dry woods, thickets, bottomland forests, waste areas, disturbed areas, roadsides, and fencerows
Habit: Perennial vine
Flowering/Fruiting Period: FL June–July; FR September–October
Wetland Status: FAC
Origin: Native

Coastal native plant gardeners have a love/hate relationship with trumpet creeper. On one hand, the leaves, flowers, and fruits of trumpet creeper are quite handsome in large garden settings, and the

c

112. Trumpet creeper (*Campsis radicans*). (a) Coarsely toothed, dark green, shiny leaves are pinnately compound and oppositely arranged. (b) Slightly asymmetrical flowers cluster at the ends of new branches. (c) The fruit, a curved woody pod, contains dozens of wind-dispersed seeds.

plant is attractive to wildlife. Conversely, trumpet creeper is a fast-growing, high-climbing, and tightly clinging vine that many charitably describe as "weedy" and "invasive." However, with constant attention and care, you can hold the weedy tendencies of this woody vine in check and enjoy the more delightful features of the plant.

A deciduous vine, trumpet creeper grows nearly straight up vertical objects without twining. Great numbers of adventitious aerial rootlets arise all along the stem and aid the plant in clinging to posts, walls, and trees, allowing the vine to grow to heights of 30 feet or more. The distinctive shredding bark on the stems is light tan when young and pale brown when mature. Leaves are oppositely arranged, 6 to 12 inches long, and pinnately compound with up to 11 leaflets. Each leaflet is about 2 inches long and 1 inch wide; they are shiny and dark green above, a lighter green on the lower surface.

Strikingly showy flowers are borne in clusters of 4 to 12 individuals at the ends of new branches. The flowers are tubular, slightly asymmetrical, and about 3 inches long, with orange to red corollas.

The fruit is a smooth, slightly curved, cylindrical woody pod, 4 to 7 inches long and nearly 1 inch wide. Two ridges run lengthwise, and the pod tapers at both ends. Each pod contains dozens of flat, transparent-winged seeds that are wind dispersed. Trumpet creeper prefers full sun and well-drained soils. It is drought and heat tolerant.

Cuttings and root suckers easily propagate trumpet creeper. Collect and stratify seeds in the fall before planting in the spring.

Possessing large nectar glands, trumpet creeper is especially attractive to hummingbirds, butterflies, and long-tongued bees. The plant also attracts ants,

and rarely is there a time when you cannot find them on the flowers and other parts of the plant.

Trumpet creeper is a good screen or cover plant for fences, trellises, and arbors, but because it produces suckers at the ends of the aerial roots, it can damage wood if allowed to grow unchecked. In fact, planting it near structures is not recommended. Trumpet creeper has few insect or disease pests.

A closely related plant, cross vine (*Bignonia capreolata*), occurs in similar habitats of the coastal Carolinas. Its flowers range from orange to reddish-orange. Monitor the growth of this vine; it has a tendency to proliferate through root suckers.

---

113 SPURRED BUTTERFLY PEA

Centrosema virginianum (Linnaeus) Bentham
Family: Fabaceae (Legume)
Other Common Name: Butterfly pea
Range: New Jersey west to Illinois and Missouri, south to Texas and Florida
Habitat: Dunes, maritime grasslands, edges of maritime shrub thickets and maritime forests
Habit: Perennial vine
Flowering/Fruiting Period: FL June–August; FR July–October
Wetland Status: UPL
Origin: Native

Flowers of members of the Legume family typically have a standard, or single large petal, that appears at the top of the flower with 4 other petals (called keels) that appear below the standard. In the spurred butterfly pea flower, the positions of the standard and keel petals are reversed; the flowers of spurred butterfly pea develop with the standard emerging at the bottom of the flower.

Spurred butterfly pea is a low-climbing or trailing vine that twines around natural

a 113. Spurred butterfly pea (*Centrosema virginianum*). (a) The large purple- to nearly white-colored petal, called the standard, aids in identifying this attractive flower. (b) The fruit is a long, narrow pod containing 13 to 16 dark brown or black seeds.

b

or fabricated supports on slender stems. Without support, it will sprawl across the ground. In the coastal Carolinas, spurred butterfly pea drapes across the various grasses in dune swales and the maritime grassland community. Leaves are trifoliate, entire, deciduous, and alternately arranged on the stem. Individual leaflets are linear to ovate with an acute tip, and they range from ¾ to 2¾ inches long and ½ to 1 inch wide. Leaves may be glabrous or minutely pubescent on both upper and lower surfaces.

The inflorescence is a short, axillary raceme with 1 to 4 bee-pollinated flowers. The calyx surrounds the petals and possesses 5 deeply lobed segments. Predominantly blue-violet, the corolla varies from purple to nearly white. The standard is about 1 inch long and 1¼ inches wide. The fruit is a flattened pod (legume) 2½ to 5½ inches long and ¼ inch wide containing a dozen or more dark brown or black seeds. Similar to the pods of other legume species, the halves of the spurred butterfly pea pod twist upon drying and explosively throw the seeds in all directions.

Spurred butterfly pea has nitrogen-fixing bacteria in root nodules that allow it to grow well in nitrogen-poor, sandy soils. It grows best in full sun, but it will tolerate some shade. It is not tolerant of waterlogged soils or soils containing salts; however, it is drought resistant and salt-aerosol tolerant.

Ground birds and small mammals eat the seeds.

Grow spurred butterfly pea from seeds; bag fruits at maturity to prevent the seeds from being scattered by its volatile and efficient dispersal mechanism. With its large and attractive flowers, spurred butterfly pea makes an outstanding and showy plant for native plant gardens.

Look for a similar, related species, butterfly pea (*Clitoria mariana*), in similar habitats.

a

114 SWEET AUTUMN VIRGIN'S BOWER

Clematis terniflora A. P. de Candolle
Family: Ranunculaceae (Buttercup)
Other Common Names: Leatherleaf clematis, sweet autumn clematis, yam-leaved clematis, Japanese virgin's bower
Range: USDA Hardiness Zones (4) 5–9
Habitat: Ornamental
Habit: Perennial vine
Flowering/Fruiting Period: FL & FR July–October
Wetland Status: FACU
Origin: Exotic; native to Japan, China, Korea, and Taiwan
Not recommended for planting; instead, remove where already growing.

Sweet autumn virgin's bower possesses elements of both beauty and beast. It has a stunningly beautiful and pleasantly fragrant floral display in late summer and early fall. On the other hand, sweet autumn virgin's bower is a tough, weedy, aggressive species with a rampant, sprawling growth habit. Left unchecked, the plant can engulf and overwhelm even shrubs and trees. Recognizing this tendency, the South

b

114. Sweet autumn virgin's bower (*Clematis terniflora*). (a) At peak flowering, vines are virtually covered with flowers bearing white sepals and no petals. (b) Fruits are brown, with each achene possessing a long, curly plume that aids in wind dispersal.

VINES

277

Carolina Exotic Pest Plant Council has listed sweet autumn virgin's bower on its invasive species "Watch List."

Unlike other species of vines with tendrils or adventitious roots, sweet autumn virgin's bower possesses neither. It climbs up to 30 feet by twisting its stems and leaves around arbors, trellises, tree and shrub branches, or other supports. If no supports are available, the thin stems of sweet autumn virgin's bower form an unruly mound of foliage at ground level.

Young stems are green and glabrous; older stems are brown. Leaves are pinnately compound with 5 leaflets, 2 to 3 inches long and ½ to 1 inch wide. The leaflets are ovate, cordate, and entire. The upper sides of the leaves are dark green, and the lower sides are light green.

The plant flowers prolifically; at the peak of flowering, the entire plant appears white. Borne on branching panicles in the axils of the upper leaves, the 1-inch-wide, nectar-bearing flowers have 4 petal-like sepals (no petals), many long stamens, and 5 to 6 pistils. Bees, wasps, and flies pollinate the flowers. The fruit is a cluster of achenes with long, spreading, curly plumes (actually styles) covered with long, silver to grayish-white hairs that aid in wind dispersal of the achenes.

Sweet autumn virgin's bower stems, leaves, and flowers prefer full sun. The plant is a prolific seed producer. Without a dormancy requirement, seeds germinate readily. This semiwoody vine is deciduous over much of the Carolinas, dying back to the ground after the first frost.

The foliage of sweet autumn virgin's bower contains toxins, and the plant is unpalatable to white-tailed deer and small mammals.

Marsh clematis (*Clematis crispa*), a native species of clematis, is an excellent substitute for sweet autumn virgin's bower in a coastal Carolina native plant garden.

115 CAROLINA JESSAMINE

Gelsemium sempervirens (Linnaeus) St. Hilaire

Family: Gelsemiaceae (Jessamine)
Other Common Names: Yellow jessamine, evening trumpetflower, Carolina jasmine
Range: Virginia south to Florida and west to Texas
Habitat: Maritime shrub thickets, maritime forests, and dunes; also fencerows, thickets, and swamp forests
Habit: Perennial vine
Flowering/Fruiting Period: FL March–April; FR September–November
Wetland Status: FAC
Origin: Native

Spring in the coastal Carolinas arrives not strictly by the calendar but by the appearance of the beautiful and fragrant Carolina jessamine. Its characteristic torch-shaped flower buds and bright yellow, funnel-shaped flowers appear suddenly along the edges of shrub thickets and maritime forests and occasionally in the dunes. Forever popular, Carolina jessamine was enthusiastically awarded the status of state flower by the South Carolina legislature in 1924.

Carolina jessamine is a bushy vine that grows to a height of about 30 feet. Its reddish-brown stems twine up any support, such as a tree or fence post. Without support, it forms a large mound of intertwined stems and leaves or sends long branches all over the ground. The oblong or lanceolate leaves, 2 to 3 inches long and ½ inch wide, are shiny and evergreen. The leaves are somewhat leathery and oppositely arranged on the stems. They exhibit sharply pointed tips and smooth margins.

Five fused petals form the 2-inch-long, tube-shaped flowers, which occur either solitary or in clusters of 2 or 3 in the leaf axils of the vine. Flowering is especially prolific in full sun, where bumblebees,

a 115. Carolina jessamine (*Gelsemium sempervirens*). (a) Dense, twining stems grow across the tops of large shrubs and small trees, producing a brilliant floral display. (b) Fused golden yellow petals form distinctive tubular flowers. (c) The laterally compressed capsules contain winged seeds.

honeybees, and other insects pollinate the 1-inch broad flowers. The sweet fragrance of Carolina jessamine is similar to the flower fragrance of the Old World jasmine (*Jasminum* sp.). The fruit of Carolina jessamine is a brown capsule, laterally compressed, ½ to ¾ inch long, and about ½ inch wide. The capsule contains numerous brown, winged seeds.

Carolina jessamine is fast growing and drought tolerant but prefers moist, sandy soils. It grows well in both full sun, where it is dense and compact, and partial shade, where it grows in a loose, relaxed pattern. The plant is moderately tolerant of salt aerosols.

Carolina jessamine is low maintenance, generally disease and insect free, and an excellent choice for covering trellises and arbors in the coastal Carolinas. Propagate Carolina jessamine from seeds, layering, and simple cuttings made in the spring. Seeds and plants are available from commercial growers throughout the Carolinas. Cultivars include *Pride of Augusta*, *Major Wheeler*, *Leo*, and *Margarita*. All parts of the plant are poisonous to humans.

A related species, Rankin's yellow jessamine (*Gelsemium rankinii*), occurs in the Low Country swamps of the Carolinas and farther south. While similar

VINES

279

in appearance, it lacks the fragrance of Carolina jessamine.

116 ENGLISH IVY

Hedera helix Linnaeus
Family: Araliaceae (Ginseng)
Other Common Name: Common ivy
Range: USDA Hardiness Zones 4–9; New York and Massachusetts south to Florida and west to Texas and Missouri
Habitat: Old homesites, forest margins, and disturbed areas
Habit: Perennial vine
Flowering/Fruiting Period: FL & FR June–July
Wetland Status: FACU
Origin: Exotic; native to Eurasia
Not recommended for planting; instead, remove where already growing.

When Rome ruled the world, English ivy wreaths adorned the heads of the winners of poetry and other cerebral contests. It seems that English ivy was a symbol of intellectual achievement. Dionysus, the Greek god of wine, is typically depicted wearing a crown of ivy on his head. Europeans used an alepole, consisting of a branch covered with ivy leaves, to indicate sites where wine or ale was sold. To other folks, English ivy was considered an excellent landscape plant owing to its evergreen foliage, its ability to thrive in shade, and its suitability as a ground cover. With this pedigree, English ivy was introduced as an ornamental throughout much of the world. Brought to the United States in the early 1700s, this import is now considered a nasty invasive plant, amply demonstrating its ability to displace our native plants wherever it grows. Given time, it can completely cover mature trees. Today, due to its popularity, nearly 400 cultivars are known for English ivy.

English ivy is a vine capable either of growing to heights of 80 feet in trees or of forming a 6- to 9-inch-high ground cover.

116. English ivy (*Hedera helix*). (a) English ivy possesses deep green, 3-lobed leaves called juvenile leaves. (b) Adventitious roots develop on stout vines when English ivy climbs trees.

The vine does not have an extensive root system, and its roots penetrate just 3 to 6 inches belowground. Its bark is light brown and scaly. Leaves are alternately arranged on the stem, dark green to blue-green, waxy, and leathery. They are 2 to 4 inches long and highly variable in shape, with unlobed, 3-lobed, and 5-lobed leaves represented on a single vine. White lines outline major veins.

English Ivy grows in two distinct forms: a juvenile stage (vegetative phase) and an adult stage (reproductive phase). In the juvenile stage, which is the most common

c

d

116. English ivy (*Hedera helix*). (c) Greenish-white flowers cluster in umbels on adult plants; compare the shape of adult leaves to the shape of juvenile leaves. (d) Mature fruits turn bluish-black. Fruits contain 5 seeds, each with a hard seed coat.

black drupes about ¼ inch in diameter. The outer layer is fleshy, and each fruit contains 5 hard seeds. Seeds germinate quickly with a high percentage of success.

English ivy typically invades deciduous forest communities, but it is present along the edges and disturbed areas within maritime forests and other mature forests in the coastal area. English ivy is intolerant of salinity. It grows best in loamy soil and in partial to full shade, but it will tolerate full sun and some drought.

White-tailed deer graze English ivy. Starlings, cedar waxwings, robins, mockingbirds, and house sparrows feed on the seeds and aid in their dispersal. The dense, evergreen foliage is important for winter shelter and food for animals owing to the abundance of insects hiding and resting among the leaves and stems.

Early herbalists believed English ivy fruits could counteract the unwanted side effects of alcohol consumption. But the fruits are mildly toxic to humans, causing gastrointestinal upset. So, eating the fruits may replace one undesirable side effect with another!

phase, the plant forms an extensive ground cover as stems root at the nodes. The leaves are thickened, and most are distinctly lobed. It does not produce flowers. In the adult stage, stems grow vertically, producing few adventitious roots. Elliptic or ovate leaves predominate, and flowers are abundant.

The greenish-white flowers of English ivy develop on spherical umbels, each possessing 8 to 20 flowers. Umbels cluster at the tip of the stems in groups of 3. Wasps, moths, flies, hoverflies, and bumblebees pollinate the flowers. Fruits are bluish-

117 COASTAL MORNING GLORY

Ipomoea cordatotriloba Dennstedt
Family: Convolvulaceae (Morning glory)
Other Common Names: Purple bindweed, cotton morning glory, tie-vine, sharp-pod morning glory
Range: Coastal: North Carolina to Florida and west to Texas
Habitat: Dunes, roadsides, and disturbed areas
Habit: Perennial vine
Flowering/Fruiting Period: FL & FR August–October
Wetland Status: FACU
Origin: Native

While coastal morning glory plants can add a nice touch of late-summer color to a native plant garden or natural area, their

VINES

a 117. Coastal morning glory (*Ipomoea cordatotriloba*). (a) Coastal morning glory has heart-shaped leaves and pink to purple flowers; it often aggressively grows over other plants. (b) Flowers open to 1 to 1½ inches across with a deep purple throat. (c) The hairy, brown capsule contains 4 seeds.

growth should be carefully monitored. Under ideal growing conditions, this species tends to be aggressive and can quickly overtake nearby plants. Growing from a large root crown, individual stems of coastal morning glory can grow to 15 feet long, twining or trailing across grasses, herbs, and low shrubs.

Coastal morning glory leaves are heart shaped and 3-lobed with pointed tips and entire margins. The leaves are alternately arranged on the stem and may grow to 3 inches long and 2 inches wide.

Coastal morning glory produces a cluster of up to 5 flowers on each peduncle. The color of the funnel-shaped corolla ranges from pink to purple with a deep purple center. Flowers are 1 to 1½ inches across with stamens shorter than the floral tube. The sepals are hairy, short, and leathery with a sharp tip.

The fruit is a nearly spherical, hairy capsule up to ⅜ inch across, containing 2 chambers, each with 2 seeds. Propagate coastal morning glory using seeds.

Coastal morning glory prefers to grow in full sun and sandy soils.

Several species of insects pollinate the flowers, including bumblebees and the hawk moth. White-tailed deer graze the plant; terrestrial birds consume minor amounts of the seeds.

Exhibiting several forms across its range, the variety *cordatotriloba* is common in the coastal Carolinas.

118 BAY-HOPS

Ipomoea pes-caprae (Linnaeus) R. Brown
Family: Convolvulaceae (Morning glory)
Other Common Names: Railroad vine,
  goat's foot, beach morning glory
Range: South Carolina to Florida and west
  to Texas
Habitat: Wrack lines and foredunes
Habit: Perennial vine
Flowering/Fruiting Period: FL & FR: May–
  September
Wetland Status: FAC
Origin: Native

Bay-hops is a familiar sight on tropical shores around the world. It is found on five continents (although not Europe). Scientific research suggests that the populations along the shorelines are genetically similar, pointing to the probability that long-distance dispersal maintains similar populations on distant beaches. Supporting this argument is the fact that seeds of bay-hops can float in seawater for more than 90 days.

118. Bay-hops (*Ipomoea pes-caprae*). The fleshy, alternate leaves with entire margins are 2½ to 4 inches long, notched at the apex, and slightly folded. The 2½- to 3-inch, funnel-shaped flowers develop singly or in clusters at plant axils.

The occasional and short-term presence of bay-hops on North Carolina and South Carolina beaches suggests that the Gulf Stream current transported the seeds from tropical population centers. The current likely entrains and distributes the bay-hops seeds northward to the Carolinas coast. Truly a tropical plant unable to tolerate prolonged frost, bay-hops does not survive most coastal South Carolina winters.

Bay-hops is found only on the wrack line and foredunes, creeping rarely more than 2 to 6 inches above the ground. The plant possesses a large, thick taproot and adventitious roots that arise at nodes along the vine where it touches the beach sand. The glabrous stems grow 10 to 20 feet or more, radiating in all directions from the main roots. When injured, stems exude a milky sap.

Leaves are fleshy, alternate, leathery, and slightly elliptical. They have entire margins and range from 2½ to 4 inches long. Leaves are notched at the apex and slightly folded at the midvein.

Showy, funnel-shaped flowers are erect, axillary, and 2½ to 3 inches in diameter. They vary from pink to lavender to purple with a darker purple center. Each flower opens in the morning and closes in the afternoon. Individual fruits produce 4 black or dark brown seeds. Covered with hairs, the seeds are ¼ to ⅜ inch in diameter.

Large nectaries at the base of each flower attract many pollinating insects, including bees, flies, beetles, wasps, moths, butterflies, and ants.

Bay-hops reproduces by seeds and stem cuttings. Seeds must be abraded before they will germinate.

The bay-hops variety present along the coast of the Carolinas is var. *emarginata*.

119 BEACH MORNING GLORY

Ipomoea imperati (Vahl) Grisebach

Family: Convolvulaceae (Morning glory)

Other Common Name: Fiddleleaf morning glory

Range: Southern North Carolina south to Florida and west to Texas

Habitat: Wrack lines and dunes

Habit: Perennial vine

Flowering/Fruiting Period: FL & FR August–November

Wetland Status: FACU

Origin: Native

119. Beach morning glory (*Ipomoea imperati*). (a) Long stolons run along the surface or are just barely covered by sand. Entire to deeply lobed leaves emerge at nodes on the stolons. (b) Insect-pollinated, white flowers rise a few inches above the sand surface in the foredune habitat.

Beach morning glory is an example of a plant distributed by the ocean and limited by temperature. It occurs throughout tropical and subtropical climates on six continents. The frequency, duration, and severity of freezing temperatures limit its distribution. Although the plant may briefly persist farther north, botanists consider southern North Carolina dunes its northern natural limit.

Beach morning glory is a prostrate, herbaceous vine with slightly succulent stolons (stems) and leaves. Annually, the plant initiates growth from a perennial taproot that may extend from 15 to more than 60 inches into the soil. The reddish-brown, nearly unbranched stems grow 25 feet long under optimum conditions, often developing adventitious roots at the nodes. The glabrous stems exude thick, white latex when severed. Leaves are simple, leathery, and alternately arranged on the stolon. Leaves may be oblong to ovate with entire margins ranging from ½ to 4 inches long and from ½ to 2 inches wide. Leaves frequently exhibit 3 to 7 deep lobes extending nearly to the midrib.

Solitary, bright white flowers develop in leaf axils. The 1-inch pedicels hold the flowers erect. The trumpet- or funnel-shaped flowers are 2 to 3 inches wide and 1¼ inches long, with a corolla composed of 5 fused petals. Flowers generally open only during part of a single day. The fruit of beach morning glory is a nearly spherical, glabrous capsule divided into 4 chambers. Each chamber contains from 1 to 4 light brown seeds covered with short hairs.

Beach morning glory is a pioneer plant in the coastal strand. It is common in areas of unstable sands, such as the wrack line, where competition from other species is low, and on sparsely vegetated dunes close to the ocean. Plants frequently associated with beach morning glory include sea rocket, northern seaside spurge, northern saltwort, sea oats, and seaside panicum.

Beach morning glory is tolerant of

salt aerosols, sand blast, and high air and soil temperatures. It grows well in nutrient-poor, sandy soils. The plant traps moving sand and tolerates moderate burial, thus promoting dune formation and stabilization. Beach morning glory's narrow habitat in the coastal environment makes it susceptible to destruction by off-road vehicle use, trampling, and storms.

Butterflies are major pollinators. Small mammals and ground birds feed on the seeds of beach morning glory.

Most wrack-line and foredune plants grow best in an environment characterized by dry sand that blows into the places where the plants grow and the sand gradually accumulates around them. This would be the preferred habitat of beach morning glory in a coastal native plant garden.

Botanists refer to beach morning glory as *Ipomoea stolonifera* in legacy coastal literature.

a

b

120 SALTMARSH MORNING GLORY

Ipomoea sagittata Poiret
Family: Convolvulaceae (Morning glory)
Other Common Name: Glades morning glory
Range: North Carolina south to Florida and west to Texas
Habitat: Edges of fresh, brackish, and salt marshes; dune swales; and maritime grasslands
Habit: Perennial vine
Flowering/Fruiting Period: FL & FR July–September
Wetland Status: FACW
Origin: Native

From early summer to early fall, the large flowers of saltmarsh morning glory punctuate the edges of grass-dominated coastal environments of the Carolinas with bright, delicate circles of pink or purple.

This fast-growing vine secures itself by

c

120. Saltmarsh morning glory (*Ipomoea sagittata*). (a) Large, funnel-shaped flowers range up to 3 inches across and 3 inches deep. Leaves are arrow shaped and alternately arranged on stems. (b) and (c) The fruit is a large capsule containing several seeds. Each seed is covered with short, thick, brown hairs.

twining on nearby shrubs as it optimizes its position to receive full sunlight; where unsupported by other plants, it grows back over itself, creating a dense, tangled pile of stems, leaves, and flowers. At maturity,

VINES

saltmarsh morning glory may reach a height of 6 to 8 feet via thin, smooth, green stems. Leaves are distinctly arrow shaped, 1½ to 3½ inches long, ½ inch wide, and alternately arranged on the stems. Saltmarsh morning glory is deciduous, dying back to the ground at the end of the growing season.

Its funnel-shaped flowers are 2 to 3 inches across and 2 to 3 inches long. Corollas may be pink, rose, or purple and either solitary or arranged in groups of 2 or 3. Unlike other species in the Morning glory family on the Carolinas coast, the stamens and pistil are included in the corolla and not exserted beyond the flared portion of the corolla tube. On sunny, warm days, flowers wilt quickly, rarely lasting more than a few hours in the morning. The fruit is a capsule, ⅜ to ½ inch in diameter, that contains numerous seeds covered in short, thick, brown hairs.

Saltmarsh morning glory requires full sun for best growth. The plant is tolerant of brackish water in the soil and moderate amounts of salt aerosols.

Saltmarsh morning glory serves as a nectar source for pollinating insects and provides cover for small mammals and insects.

Collect seeds from mature wild plants. Stratify seeds over the winter to increase the germination percentage.

---

121 JAPANESE HONEYSUCKLE

Lonicera japonica Thunberg

Family: Caprifoliaceae (Honeysuckle)

Other Common Name: Chinese honeysuckle

Range: Ontario, Canada; Maine to Nebraska and California; south to Arizona, Texas, and Florida

Habitat: Maritime shrub thickets and maritime forests; also edges of woodlands, roadsides, disturbed areas, and fencerows

Habit: Perennial vine

Flowering/Fruiting Period: FL & FR April–November

Wetland Status: FACU

Origin: Exotic; native to East Asia, including Japan and Korea

Not recommended for planting; instead, remove where already growing.

With the best intentions, Japanese honeysuckle was introduced into the United States as an ornamental plant in the early 1800s. It is now one of the most common vines in the Carolinas. Nearly all of the states in the Northeast, mid-Atlantic, and Southeast consider it a noxious weed (or worse!). North Carolina lists this invasive plant as a "moderate threat," and South Carolina lists it as a "severe threat." Japanese honeysuckle has all the characteristics of a noxious weed. When left unchecked, it outcompetes and eliminates native flora due to its rapid growth, strongly competitive roots and rhizomes, wide seed dispersal, adaptation to a variety of habitats, long growing season, and few natural enemies.

Japanese honeysuckle is a twining vine that grows to 30 feet into shrubs and trees. Larger stems are woody, with tan to reddish bark shredding in long strips. Leaves are dark green, opposite, evergreen, and elliptic or oval. They vary from 2 to 3 inches long and from 1 to 1½ inches wide. Young leaves and stems are pubescent. Leaves are entire except for those appearing on vigorous spring growth, where the leaves are frequently deeply lobed. In addition to climbing, Japanese honeysuckle also spreads across the ground and displaces native plants.

Fragrant flowers bloom throughout the growing season. A day after opening, the bright white flowers fade to a light orange or creamy white. Borne in leaf axils near the branch tips, the tube-shaped flowers are about 1½ inches long with 2 widely

a

b

c

121. Japanese honeysuckle (*Lonicera japonica*). (a) Japanese honeysuckle is typically found growing over, around, and on other plants in both sunny and shaded environments. (b) Newly opened flowers are bright white, while day-old flowers turn a distinctive creamy white to light orange. (c) Fruits are paired, blue-black drupes about ¼ inch in diameter.

spreading lips. The upper lip is composed of 4 petals united at the base, and the lower lip is a single petal. Japanese honeysuckle produces paired, globose, blue-black, fleshy drupes about ¼ inch in diameter. Each fruit contains 2 to 3 dark brown, oblong seeds.

Japanese honeysuckle tolerates drought and thrives in full and partial sun as well as forest shade.

White-tailed deer, rabbits, and birds eat the fruits of Japanese honeysuckle, and all these animals distribute the seeds widely. The plant provides modest cover for terrestrial birds and small mammals.

Japanese honeysuckle spreads rapidly through vegetative growth and seeds. It produces long, aboveground runners that firmly attach to the soil by adventitious roots. Scientists report that such runners may grow up to 25 feet per year. Rhizomes also spread the plant locally, especially in sandy coastal soils. The plant is difficult to eradicate completely; it simply resprouts when cut back to ground level.

122 CORAL HONEYSUCKLE
Lonicera sempervirens Linnaeus
Family: Caprifoliaceae (Honeysuckle)
Other Common Name: Trumpet honeysuckle
Range: Southern Quebec and Ontario, Canada; Maine west to Iowa and south to Florida and Texas
Habitat: Margins of maritime forests and maritime shrub thickets
Habit: Perennial vine
Flowering/Fruiting Period: FL March–July; FR July–September
Wetland Status: FACU
Origin: Native

Coral honeysuckle brings together bright green and red in an attractive and useful plant. The red flowers are especially attractive to butterflies and birds. The leaves are evergreen in the southern part of its range and late deciduous in northerly populations. Unlike its weedy relative Japanese honeysuckle, coral honeysuckle is not an aggressive or noxious plant.

Coral honeysuckle is a fast-growing, drought-resistant, twining or trailing, woody vine typically growing 3 to 10 feet

VINES

b

c

a 122. Coral honeysuckle (*Lonicera sempervirens*). (a) This climbing vine is easily recognized in flower or fruit, producing bright red splotches of color as it grows on and around plants or other supports. (b) The coral red to orange-red, tube-shaped flowers are clustered at the ends of branches. (c) Fruits are ¼-inch red berries.

high. Possessing sessile or short petioles, the leaves of coral honeysuckle are opposite, simple, and evenly spaced along the stems. Young stems are light green, smooth, and glabrous; old stems tend to be light orange-brown or light yellowish-green.

Sessile bracts surround the whorled flower cluster at the end of new or one-year-old twigs. The hummingbird- and insect-pollinated flowers are tube shaped, coral red to orange-red, and 1 to 1½ inches long by ½ inch wide. The flower tube may be lined with yellow. Fruits are red to red-orange berries, about ¼ inch in diameter. In contrast to Japanese honeysuckle, the flowers of coral honeysuckle are not fragrant, but the sprays of red flowers are striking.

Coral honeysuckle grows best in full sunlight. It is not shade tolerant, producing few flowers and fruits in the shade.

The fruits serve as a food for various songbirds, including robins, catbirds, cedar waxwings, and cardinals. Coral

honeysuckle hosts larvae of the hummingbird clearwing moth.

Propagate coral honeysuckle through seeds, layering, and cuttings. Local nurseries may have several cultivars.

123 CLIMBING HEMPWEED

Mikania scandens (Linnaeus) Willdenow
Family: Asteraceae (Aster)
Other Common Name: Climbing hempvine
Range: Ontario, Canada; Maine to Illinois and south to Texas and Florida
Habitat: Dune swales, edges of freshwater wetlands, maritime shrub thickets; also swamps and marshes

a 123. Climbing hempweed (*Mikania scandens*).
(a) Key identifying characteristics of this vine
are simple, opposite, triangular leaves on
long petioles with 3 distinctive veins. (b) Each
flowering head is composed of 4 disk florets.
(c) Wind-dispersed fruits are small, dark achenes
with pinkish-white bristles.

Habit: Perennial vine
Flowering/Fruiting Period: FL & FR July–
 October
Wetland Status: FACW
Origin: Native

During mid- to late summer, climbing
hempweed is easily identified by its
arrowhead-shaped leaves and large, flat-
topped clusters of white to purplish-
white flower heads twining and sprawling
across shrubs, grasses, and herbs in dune
swales and other moist, open coastal
environments.

This aggressive vine is characterized
by sparsely pubescent, highly branched,

4-angled stems that grow to 8 feet long
during the summer and fall and then die
back to the ground each winter. The leaves
of climbing hempweed are opposite,
simple, and triangular, with long petioles
and 3 distinctive veins on each leaf. The
leaves are mostly glabrous, 1 to 5 inches
long, and ¾ to 2½ inches wide, with wavy,
blunt-toothed edges.

Clusters of flower heads arise in the leaf
axils. Each ¼-inch flower head is composed
of 4 disk florets. The fruits of climbing
hempweed are small, dark brown, 5-angled
achenes with pinkish-white bristles. Resin
glands, visible under a hand lens, cover

VINES

289

the achene surface. Wind is the primary dispersal agent for the seeds.

Climbing hempweed prefers moist, well-drained soils and full sun. It survives well in nutrient-poor sands. While it does not tolerate long-term saltwater inundation, the plant has a high tolerance to salt aerosols.

Propagate this species by seeds, stem cuttings, and division of the plant rhizomes. Each node of the vine can produce roots.

When the plant is in full flower, bumblebees, honeybees, wasps, butterflies, and flies swarm the flower heads seeking nectar and pollen.

Climbing hempweed is an interesting native ornamental suitable for a native plant garden. It may be difficult to find this plant in commercial nurseries; collect seeds or plants sparingly from wild stock. Take care, though, if you place climbing hempweed in a native plant garden because it may overwhelm nearby plants.

A related species, heartleaf climbing hempweed (*Mikania cordifolia*), occupies similar habitats in southeastern South Carolina.

124 MUSCADINE

Muscadinia rotundifolia (Michaux) Small
Family: Vitaceae (Grape)
Other Common Name: Scuppernong
Range: Delaware and Maryland west to Oklahoma and Texas, and south and east to Florida
Habitat: Dunes, maritime shrub thickets, and maritime forests; also dry forests, swamps, and roadsides
Habit: Perennial vine
Flowering/Fruiting Period: FL May–June; FR August–October
Wetland Status: FAC
Origin: Native
Muscadine can be differentiated from the other species of grapes in the

a

b

c

124. Muscadine (*Muscadinia rotundifolia*). (a) Leaves are green and glabrous above and glaucous green below. Leaves are 2 to 4 inches wide with large, coarse, blunt teeth. (b) Male flowers and female flowers grow on separate plants. Male flowers (*shown here*) exhibit a starburst pattern of stamens. (c) Fruits are ¼ to ¾ inch in diameter, thick-skinned, and mature from green to deep purple.

coastal Carolinas by this combination of characteristics: smooth bark (not peeling in strips), large stem lenticels, brown pith continuous through stem nodes, and unbranched tendrils.

Vines grow to a height between 15 to 30 feet, with alternately arranged leaves that are green and glabrous above and glaucous green below. The ovate to roundish leaves are 2 to 4 inches wide with coarse, blunt teeth.

Muscadine is dioecious, with separate male and female flowers occurring on different plants. The inflorescence is a compound panicle arising in the leaf axils with 5-petaled, nearly inconspicuous flowers. The flowers are wind and insect pollinated. The thick-skinned, deep-purple- or bronze-colored berry is borne singly or in small clusters. Each fruit is ¼ to ¾ inch in diameter and contains 5 seeds.

Muscadine tolerates salt aerosols well, rarely showing the characteristic necrosis from salt-aerosol deposition on the leaves. Muscadine grows well in full sun as well as in partial shade. It grows best in slightly acidic soils but languishes in wet soils.

A wide variety of birds and small mammals, including raccoons, opossums, cardinals, robins, cedar waxwings, and mourning doves, relies heavily on muscadine fruits for food during the summer and early fall. White-tailed deer also feed on the fruits.

To propagate muscadine, layer canes (stems) during the summer and plant seeds in the fall. A useful, attractive, and fast-growing ornamental plant, muscadine is disease resistant. Its fruits produce a musky, sweet wine and a flavorful jelly—both products of commerce in the Carolinas.

Numerous cultivars, such as *Carlos*, *Noble*, and *Scuppernong*, are available commercially.

The variety *rotundifolia* is recognized as the plant common to the coastal Carolinas.

125. Peppervine (*Nekemias arborea*). (a) Coarsely serrate, bi- and tri-pinnately compound leaves grow best in full sunlight.

125 PEPPERVINE

Nekemias arborea (Linnaeus) J. Wen & Boggan
Family: Vitaceae (Grape)
Other Common Name: Buckvine
Range: Maryland and Virginia west to Illinois and Missouri, south to Florida; also Texas, New Mexico, and Mexico
Habitat: Edges of brackish and freshwater marshes, maritime shrub thickets, maritime forests, and waste places
Habit: Perennial vine
Flowering/Fruiting Period: FL & FR May–October
Wetland Status: FAC
Origin: Native

Peppervine is a fast-growing, drought-tolerant, deciduous, woody vine. You can confirm its aggressive nature by observing this plant covering fences, walls, and other structures along the coast. In fact, the specific epitaph *arborea* refers to its climbing habit.

The leaves are dark green above and light green below, arranged alternately with tendrils along their stems. Young growing stems and leaves are often reddish-green to purplish-green, especially when growing in full sun. Peppervine leaves are bi- and

b

c

125. Peppervine (*Nekemias arborea*). (b) Flower clusters are borne on stems opposite the leaves. (c) Mature, pea-sized fruits are fleshy and contain 2 to 5 seeds.

tri-pinnately compound, thus appearing highly dissected. Each leaflet is coarsely serrate.

The ¼-inch, greenish-white to white flowers possess 5 petals and are borne in clusters on the stem opposite the leaves. Technically drupes, the green, inedible, pea-sized, smooth-skinned fruits of peppervine turn red and then blue-black as they mature throughout the summer. Each fruit contains 2 to 5 seeds.

Birds and raccoons eat peppervine fruits; sometimes white-tailed deer browse the leaves.

Peppervine grows in the shade of both overstory trees and shrubs; the vine often grows atop the trees when the forest or shrub canopy is less than 30 feet tall. Peppervine leaves add yellow or red accents to coastal vegetation in the fall.

The plant has been reported to cause skin rashes and allergic reactions with some individuals. Peppervine is rarely cultivated because of its aggressive and weedy nature, but if you do introduce it into natural gardens, you can easily propagate it by seeds or cuttings.

In legacy literature, authors cite this species as *Ampelopsis arborea*.

126 VIRGINIA CREEPER

Parthenocissus quinquefolia (Linnaeus) Planchon

Family: Vitaceae (Grape)

Other Common Names: Woodbine, American ivy, five-leaved ivy

Range: Throughout North America east of the Rocky Mountains

Habitat: Maritime forests and maritime shrub thickets; also fencerows, upland forests, and streambanks

Habit: Perennial vine

Flowering/Fruiting Period: FL May–July; FR July–August

Wetland Status: FACU

Origin: Native

A common member of numerous plant communities throughout North America, including maritime forests and maritime shrub thickets, Virginia creeper is both an important resource for wildlife and a native ornamental plant. The plant provides cover and food for many species of birds and mammals and displays handsome summer and fall foliage colors. Unfortunately, this harmless and attractive plant is easily confused with poison ivy, which has 3 shiny leaflets; Virginia creeper has 5 leaflets. The mature fruits of poison ivy are similar in size to Virginia creeper's but are always

a 126. Virginia creeper (*Parthenocissus quinquefolia*). (a) Virginia creeper is a deciduous, woody, high-climbing vine with many fine, adventitious aerial roots. Characteristic 5-leaflet, palmately compound leaves differentiate this species from poison ivy, which possesses 3 leaflets. (b) Flowers are borne on long-stemmed clusters 4 to 6 inches wide in leaf axils. (c) Fruits are bluish-black drupes containing 2 or 3 shiny, brown seeds.

b

c

grayish-white, while Virginia creeper's are bluish-black.

Virginia creeper is a woody, deciduous, high-climbing vine with gray-brown stems that produce many fine, adventitious aerial roots. This fast-growing plant will climb to 60 feet or more on natural or fabricated structures, such as barns, trees, and poles. The plant attaches to objects by branched tendrils that produce cuplike adhesive pads when in contact with a solid surface. In the absence of structures, Virginia creeper will form a pile of foliage up to a foot high and several feet in diameter.

Young stems are reddish-green and glabrous, turning brown and woody as they mature. The leaves are dull green, alternately arranged on stems and palmately compound with 5 ovate or elliptic leaflets. The coarsely toothed leaflets range from 2 to 6 inches long and from 1 to 3 inches wide. In the fall, the leaves of Virginia creeper usually turn an intense red.

Inconspicuous 5-petaled, green flowers are borne in complex, long-stemmed clusters about 4 to 6 inches wide that form in leaf axils, especially near the tips of stems. Fruits are bluish-black, ¼-inch drupes; each contains 2 to 3 shiny, brown seeds. Pedicels turn from green to red as the fruits mature.

Virginia creeper prefers moist and well-drained soils but can survive in dry soils. It grows well in full sun and nutrient-poor, sandy soils. Moderate amounts of salt aerosols have little effect on the growth of Virginia creeper.

VINES

293

Bees and other insects are attracted to the pollen and nectar produced by the plant. Songbirds, mice, squirrels, rabbits, and white-tailed deer eat the fruits and are responsible for dispersal of Virginia creeper seeds.

Propagation is by seeds, layering (it roots at stem nodes), and stem cuttings. Stratify seeds to increase the germination rate when sowing seeds in the spring.

Virginia creeper can be unruly. Prune this vine to keep it under control, and avoid planting it where the adhesive disks on the tendrils could damage surfaces. The vine sends up many sprouts from horizontal, aboveground stems, and it may self-seed into areas adjacent to where it is growing. It is an excellent native plant for covering trellises and arbors as well as for erosion control projects; however, if you allow Virginia creeper to grow up a tree or a shrub unchecked, it can eventually shade out the plant and kill it.

Virginia creeper cultivars such as the small-leaved *Engelmannii* are better behaved than native wild plants.

Virginia creeper berries are toxic to humans, and the sap many cause skin irritation in susceptible individuals.

127. Purple passionflower (*Passiflora incarnata*). (a) The complex flower is axillary, short peduncled, solitary, and about 3 inches across. Between the sepals and petals and the reproductive organs is an unmistakable corona of fine, crumpled, purple-and-white-striped filaments.

---

127 PURPLE PASSIONFLOWER

Passiflora incarnata Linnaeus
Family: Passifloraceae (Passionflower)
Other Common Names: Maypops, purple passion vine
Range: New York west to Iowa and Kansas, south to Florida and Texas
Habitat: Maritime shrub thickets; also disturbed areas, open fields, edges of woods, and roadsides
Habit: Perennial vine
Flowering/Fruiting Period: FL May–August FR; July–October
Wetland Status: UPL
Origin: Native

The name passionflower was given to this plant because early Spanish explorers assigned Christian symbols to the plant's petals, stamens, stigmas, and corona. Collectively, these parts were said to represent the story of the crucifixion or passion of Christ. Its beautiful and unique flowers aside, purple passionflower is a potentially invasive species in the coastal Carolinas. It grows profusely and spreads quickly by root suckers.

Exhibiting considerable variation in morphology and ecology, the stems may be smooth or slightly pubescent and creeping or climbing. Abundant tendrils arise in leaf axils. Where shrubs or other support structures are available, the plant can grow to a height of 10 feet, with tendrils holding the plant tightly to the objects it has climbed. Stems branch frequently from leaf axils, forming a dense network of stems, leaves, flowers, and fruits. The leaves of purple passionflower are palmately veined

the sepals and petals and reproductive organs is a corona featuring dozens of crimped, purple-and-white-striped filaments. Pollinated by bumblebees, the flower possesses large stamens and a distinctive 3-lobed stigma. The fruit of purple passionflower is called a maypop and expands to about the size and shape of a small chicken egg, about 1½ to 3 inches long. At maturity, the maypop surface is yellow-green and smooth. Each maypop contains many brown seeds, ¼ inch in diameter and surrounded by juicy, edible pulp.

The vine grows best in full sun, but it will tolerate partial shade. It prefers moist, well-drained, sandy soils. It is tolerant of both drought and salt aerosols.

Passionflower is a minor food source for terrestrial birds and the host plant for both Gulf and variegated fritillary larvae.

Propagation is by seed or cuttings; however, seed germination is slow and unreliable.

Grow purple passionflower on fences, arbors, trellises, and walls or even over the top of shrubs and small trees. However, because purple passionflower is potentially invasive, be careful to keep it under cultivation; do not allow it to grow beyond tended areas. The plant is available from commercial sources.

Purple passionflower is a traditional herbal medicine reputed to reduce anxiety, insomnia, and liver problems. Native Americans grew vines for the fruits, which they ate raw or boiled to make syrup.

A similar species, eastern yellow passionflower (*Passiflora lutea*), occurs in coastal Carolina. The flowers of eastern yellow passionflower are considerably smaller than purple passionflower's and produce small, black, berrylike fruits. It prefers moist woods and thickets.

b

127. Purple passionflower (*Passiflora incarnata*). (b) Fruits, called maypops, are green and about the size and shape of a small chicken egg.

and alternately arranged on the stems. They typically have 3 or 5 lobes and are 6 to 8 inches long and 5 to 6 inches wide. Dark green above and light green below, leaves have nectar glands at the intersection of the leaf blades and petioles. The vine builds a large root over time, and the plant dies back to ground level following the first fall frosts along the coast.

The complex flower is axillary, short stalked, and solitary. Each purple to white flower is about 3 inches across, with 5 green sepals and 5 purple petals. Between

128 SOUTHERN DEWBERRY

Rubus trivialis Michaux

Family: Rosaceae (Rose)

Other Common Name: Coastal plain dewberry

Range: Pennsylvania west to Kansas and south to Texas and Florida

Habitat: Dunes and dune swales; also roadsides and fields

Habit: Perennial vine

Flowering/Fruiting Period: FL March–April; FR April–May

Wetland Status: FACU

Origin: Native

128. Southern dewberry (*Rubus trivialis*). (a) Flowers are solitary or grow in groups of 2 or 3. They are about 1 inch across with 5 crinkly, white petals. (b) Mature fruits are deep purple, about 1 inch long, and ½ to ¾ inch wide.

One of the first flowering plants to brighten the winter-worn dunes is the southern dewberry, a hairy, woody vine with a deep taproot. The plant is not a climber and tends to crisscross through the dune grasses via low and often arching stems. The stems extend up to 15 feet from the base of the plant. They are green when young and turn reddish-brown as they age. Both old and young stems have scores of hooked prickles along their length.

The compound leaves are trifoliate but occasionally may have 5 leaflets. Individual leaflets are up to 3 inches long and 1 inch wide, lanceolate, and serrate or sometimes doubly serrate. The terminal leaflet is on a short petiole; the lateral leaflets are sessile. Alternately arranged on the stems, each glabrous leaf has stipules at the base of the petiole. The upper leaf surface is bright green, and the lower surface is pale green.

Southern dewberry flowers are solitary or grow in groups of 2 to 3. The flower is about 1 inch across with 5 white (or, rarely, slightly pink) wrinkled petals. The flowers typically open during the day and close at night or during inclement weather. Each flower possesses numerous stamens.

The fruit is a compound drupe up to 1 inch long and ½ to ¾ inch wide. As they mature, the drupes change from green to red and finally deep purple.

Southern dewberry prefers sandy dune soils. The species grows well both in full sun and in the shadow of dune shrubs.

A good wildlife plant, its fruits are food for songbirds, ground birds, raccoons, and mice. Rabbits and white-tailed deer graze the leaves and stems. Since it is a valuable native food and cover resource for many animals, consider planting southern dewberry in any native plant garden.

Southern dewberry reproduces primarily by seeds, which birds and small mammals efficiently disperse. Occasionally the stems will root at the nodes and spread vegetatively.

The edible fruits are juicy and sweet when ripe, and they make delicious pies and jams. Several varieties of dewberry are available commercially.

129 SWALLOW-WORT

Seutera angustifolia (Persoon) Fishbein & W. D. Stevens

Family: Apocynaceae (Dogbane)
Other Common Name: Climbing milkweed
Range: Coastal: North Carolina south to Florida and west to Texas
Habitat: Dune swales, maritime grasslands, shrub thickets, and brackish marshes
Habit: Perennial vine
Flowering/Fruiting Period: FL June–July; FR July–October
Wetland Status: FACW
Origin: Native

You can recognize swallow-wort in the field by its haphazard, clambering growth pattern on shrubs and grasses and by its droopy leaves and fruits. A trailing or climbing vine, it appears to weave together common wax myrtles, sea myrtles, saltmeadow cordgrass, or other coastal plants with its slender, bright green, glabrous stems. Twining over many different plants of dune swales and brackish marshes, it even loops back and twines on itself. Identification is certain when white, milky sap exudes from broken or cut leaves and stems.

Leaves of swallow-wort are linear, simple, and pointed at the tip. Ranging from 1½ to 3 inches long and about ¼ inch wide, the leaves are oppositely arranged on the stem. The leaves exhibit entire margins and have sparse hairs on the surface. The stems, growing up to 4 feet long, die back to the ground each winter.

Greenish-white flowers develop in axillary clusters. The nearly spherical clusters have several ¼-inch flowers, each possessing 5 sepals and 5 petals tinged with a bit of rose or pink. Fruits are narrow, green follicles measuring 1½ to 2½ inches long and ¼ inch wide. When mature, dozens of seeds with long, silky, white hairs are efficiently dispersed from the follicles by the wind.

a

129. Swallow-wort (*Seutera angustifolia*). (a) A trailing or climbing vine, the plant bleeds white sap when stems or leaves are broken or cut. Leaves are linear, 1½ to 3 inches long, and ¼ inch wide.

VINES

129. Swallow-wort (*Seutera angustifolia*). (b) Flowers are greenish-white and develop in spherical clusters in leaf axils. (c) Fruits are narrow, green follicles. Silky, white, plumed seeds are dispersed by the wind in typical milkweed fashion.

Propagate swallow-wort by seeds collected from wild stock, since the plant is unavailable from commercial nurseries.

Swallow-wort affords some cover for small animals in dense maritime grasslands. The plant is a nectar source for pollinators.

In legacy literature, authors cite this species as *Cynanchum angustifolium*.

130 DUNE GREENBRIAR

Smilax auriculata Walter
Family: Liliaceae (Lily)
Other Common Names: Earleaf greenbriar, eared greenbriar
Range: Coastal: North Carolina south to Florida and west to Louisiana
Habitat: Dunes, maritime grasslands, edges of maritime forests, and maritime shrub thickets
Habit: Perennial vine
Flowering/Fruiting Period: FL May–July; FR October–November
Wetland Status: FACU
Origin: Native

Dune greenbriar is an important coastal dune stabilizer. It is commonly found growing across the canopy of dune shrubs, such as common wax myrtle. If no shrubs are available for climbing, the vine forms a low mound (usually composed of just a single plant) that resembles a low-growing shrub.

The rhizomes of this species are large and grow in dense clusters like potatoes. The branches of this vine often form a zigzag shape and possess numerous prickles toward the base of the stems. In contrast, the growing tips of the stems have only a few prickles. Dune greenbriar possesses tendrils that originate in the leaf axils.

The ovate to nearly elliptical leaves are alternately arranged on the stems and often stand erect. The distal ends of the leaves are rounded, with small, abruptly pointed tips. Glabrous and green on top and bottom surfaces, the 2- to 4½-inch-long leaves exhibit outer edges that are smooth. An identifying characteristic for this species is the presence of 3 major veins raised above the surface on the underside of the leaves.

Dioecious flowers are produced in umbels that arise from leaf axils. Each umbel possesses from 5 to 25 flowers. The male flower is slightly larger than the

a

b

c

d

130. Dune greenbriar (*Smilax auriculata*).
(a) The most common coastal catbriar, this species possesses stems prickly at the base. Ovate to elliptical leaves terminate in small, abruptly pointed tips. Best seen from the underside, 3 major veins run the length of the leaves. Separate light green male (b) and female (c) flowers arise in umbels formed in leaf axils. (d) One-quarter-inch fruits are produced on peduncles that are longer than the petiole of the subtending leaf.

female, about ¼ inch across. Both male and female flowers range from light green to yellowish-green. The flowers appear to have 6 petals, but flowers are actually composed of 3 sepals and 3 petals that are nearly identical.

Fruits are berries produced on peduncles that are longer than the petiole of the subtending leaf, a key identifying characteristic. The berries are purple or black and about ¼ inch in diameter. While the fruits of maritime catbriar (*Smilax bona-nox*) are single seeded, fruits of dune greenbriar each contain 2 to 3 seeds.

Dune greenbriar requires moist soil, and while tolerating some shade, it grows best in full sun.

Numerous species of birds and small mammals that inhabit the dunes and maritime shrub thickets consume the berries.

Seeds germinate well but require at least a month of cold stratification. Divide rhizomes in the spring. Root cuttings in the summer.

Native Americans produced flour from

VINES

299

dried and ground rhizomes. They also made a tea from the leaves and stems; the tea was used to treat rheumatism and stomach problems.

131 MARITIME CATBRIAR

Smilax bona-nox Linnaeus
Family: Liliaceae (Lily)
Other Common Names: Greenbriar, catbriar, fringed greenbriar
Range: Virginia west to Kansas and south to Florida and Texas
Habitat: Dunes, maritime shrub thickets, and maritime forests
Habit: Perennial vine
Flowering/Fruiting Period: FL April–May; FR September–November
Wetland Status: FAC
Origin: Native

Maritime catbriar is a woody vine capable of growing up to 20 feet into a forest canopy. More typically, though, the plant forms a dense, dome-shaped, tangled patch on the ground, occasionally reaching a diameter of 10 feet, or it climbs over dune shrubs.

A highly variable species, maritime catbriar has bright green, woody, glabrous stems that arise from a tuberous rhizome. The stems may or may not exhibit small, stout prickles. Stems have ovate to ovate-lanceolate leaves with prominent, lateral

131. Maritime catbriar (*Smilax bona-nox*).
(a) Leathery, evergreen leaves of catbriar are 1½ to 3 inches long with bristly margins and prominent lateral lobes. (b) Pale green flowers are either male or female and have 6 nearly identical sepals and petals (tepals). (c) Mature fruits are black berries containing a single seed.

lobes. The leathery, evergreen leaves are often mottled, 1½ to 3 inches long, and 1½ inches wide, with bristly margins. Tendrils are present at the base of the leaves.

Maritime catbriar has separate male and female plants. Pale green flowers, clustered in umbels of 10 to 15 each, develop in leaf axils. The 3 sepals and 3 petals are similar in shape and size and form a 6-parted perianth. Black berries, appearing in late summer, are about ¼ inch in diameter and contain a single brown seed.

Seeds are common in the diet of a variety of small mammals and birds. Undigested seeds may compose the majority of the feces of raccoons during the fall.

Propagate this plant by sowing seeds in sandy soil; cuttings have also been successfully grown.

You can eat young shoots raw or cooked. The root, stem prickles, and leaves are reputed to have medicinal properties and have been used to treat dropsy, rheumatism, and stomach ailments.

The variety *littoralis* is the most common form of this species of catbriar in the coastal Carolinas.

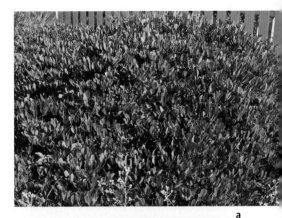
a

b

132 LAUREL GREENBRIAR

Smilax laurifolia Linnaeus
Family: Liliaceae (Lily)
Other Common Names: Bamboo vine, laurel leaf greenbriar, laurel briar
Range: New Jersey south to Florida and west to Texas, including the lower Mississippi Valley
Habitat: Wet maritime forests; also swamp forests and pocosins
Habit: Perennial vine
Flowering/Fruiting Period: FL July–August; FR September–October (2nd year)
Wetland Status: FACW
Origin: Native

Laurel greenbriar is one of several species of the genus *Smilax* that are high-climbing,

c

132. Laurel greenbriar (*Smilax laurifolia*). (a) Oblong to elliptical, evergreen leaves exhibit a prominent midvein, smooth margins, and short petioles. (b) Male flowers are borne in axillary clusters. Individual, yellow-green flowers have 6 tepals. (c) Fruits are about ¼ inch in diameter, fleshy, black, and clustered in groups of 5 to 25.

VINES

thorny vines that grow from large tuberous rhizomes. In the maritime forest, species such as laurel greenbriar are often so abundant that they seem to knit the tree canopy together.

Botanists report that stems of laurel greenbriar grow up to 2 inches a day in ideal conditions as they form dense thickets. The stems are round, green, and tough; they range from sparsely to densely prickly. Tendrils assist the plant in reaching the canopy.

Laurel greenbriar leaves are evergreen and leathery with smooth margins. Leaves have short petioles and oblong to elliptical blades; they are 2 to 6 inches long and ½ to 3 inches wide. A key characteristic is that the leaf midvein is more prominent than the 2 lateral veins.

The dioecious flowers are borne in axillary clusters. The sepals and petals are similar and together form small, yellow-green, fragrant flowers.

The abundant shiny, black, fleshy berries of laurel greenbriar occur in clusters ranging from 5 to 25. The fruits, about ¼ inch in diameter, require 2 years to mature. In the first year, the fruits remain green.

Laurel greenbriar grows best in mucky, peaty soils low in oxygen and frequently saturated or flooded. Maximum growth occurs in full sunlight. Species frequently occurring near this plant include Carolina red maple and red bay.

Several species of songbirds and waterfowl eat and disperse the berries. White-tailed deer browse the plant, especially the young, nonwoody stems.

Propagate laurel greenbriar either by seeds or by rhizomes.

The leaves and stems make a refreshing tea.

133 ANNUAL SAND BEAN

Strophostyles helvola (Linnaeus) Elliott
Family: Fabaceae (Legume)
Other Common Names: Trailing wild bean, beach bean, annual woolly-bean
Range: Quebec, Canada; west to Minnesota and South Dakota; south to Florida and Texas
Habitat: Dunes, dune swales, maritime grasslands, and sandy, open waste areas
Habit: Annual vine
Flowering/Fruiting Period: FL June–September; FR August–October

133. Annual sand bean (*Strophostyles helvola*). (a) Annual sand bean trails and twines around grasses and herbs in the dunes. Dark green, sparsely hairy leaves are trifoliate. (b) Bilaterally symmetrical, pink to pale lavender flowers are clustered at the top of racemes. Fruits are 2 to 4 inches long and chocolate brown with brown seeds at maturity.

Wetland Status: FAC

Origin: Native

Squeeze one of the mature, 2- to 4-inch-long, chocolate brown seedpods (resembling a garden bean) of annual sand bean and the seedpod will suddenly split open, forcefully ejecting its 4 to 8 woolly seeds. This interesting feature of the plant assures the effective and efficient dispersal of seeds at a considerable distance from the parent plant.

American beachgrass, sea oats, saltmeadow cordgrass, and seaside panicum often serve as support for this lush, trailing and twining dune plant with thin, green stems and profuse branching. Leaves are compound and grow on opposite sides of the stem. Sparse hairs cover the trifoliate leaves.

Pink to pale lavender flowers cluster at the top of racemes arising from leaf axils along the stem. The racemes range from 2 to 12 inches tall, often protruding well above the trailing stem and leaves. The characteristic bean flower is from ¼ to ½ inch long, with lower petals modified into an elongate, hornlike structure. As the growing season progresses, both flowers and seedpods are present on the rapidly spreading vine. Mycorrhizae and nitrogen-fixing bacteria associated with the roots of annual sand bean aid in absorption of water and nitrogen nutrition.

Several species of bees, wasps, ants, flies, and beetles visit the flowers, while birds and small mammals eat the seeds.

Archeological research into pre-Columbian coastal human habitations shows that the annual sand bean was likely used for food and as a remedy for several diseases. One of the nearest relatives of annual sand bean is the invaluable seed crop soybeans.

Annual sand bean has limited landscape value but provides food for wildlife in a coastal native plant garden.

134. Poison ivy (*Toxicodendron radicans*). (a) Each of the 3 leaflets is glabrous, shiny, 1 to 4½ inches long, and 2 to 2½ inches wide. Margins may be entire or coarsely toothed.

134 POISON IVY

Toxicodendron radicans (Linnaeus) Kuntze

Family: Anacardiaceae (Cashew)

Other Common Name: Eastern poison ivy

Range: Nova Scotia, Canada; west to Minnesota and South Dakota; south to Texas and Florida

Habitat: Maritime forests, maritime shrub thickets, dunes and dune swales, brackish marshes; also roadsides, waste areas

Habit: Perennial vine

Flowering/Fruiting Period: FL April–May; FR August–October

Wetland Status: FAC

Origin: Native

People often find poison ivy difficult to identify in the field—and with good reason. Depending on the habitat in which it is found, poison ivy can appear as a 50-foot-long, high-climbing vine; a 3-foot, bushy shrub; or a ground-hugging herbaceous plant growing no more than 6 inches tall. Add to this its relatively inconspicuous flowers and highly variable leaflet shape, and you have several opportunities to misidentify the plant. Assure positive identification, however, by observing the presence of trifoliate leaves alternately

VINES

303

b

c

134. Poison ivy (*Toxicodendron radicans*).
(b) Yellowish-green flowers are clustered in
leaf axils. Each ⅛-inch-broad flower possesses
5 triangular petals. (c) Fruits are hard, greenish-
white drupes about ¼ inch in diameter; they
persist on the plant until dispersed or eaten
(birds love them!).

arranged on stems with no thorns. *Leaves of three, let it be!*

Woody poison ivy stems reach the forest canopy when many small, adventitious roots attach to tree trunks, allowing stems to elongate skyward. Plants trailing along the ground develop roots where stems touch the ground. New shoots sprout from existing roots and rhizomes.

Twigs are slender, reddish-brown, and densely covered with adventitious roots. Each glabrous leaflet of poison ivy is 1 to 4½ inches long and 2 to 2½ inches wide, turning bright red or yellow in the fall. On some plants, the leaflets have a few large teeth; on others, leaf edges are entire.

Yellowish-green flowers cluster in leaf axils. Each flower has 5 triangular petals about ⅛ inch across. Fruits are hard, round, greenish-white drupes, each containing a single seed.

Poison ivy can grow in full shade and full sun and in moist to dry, sandy soil.

The somewhat waxy, ¼-inch drupes persist through the winter, serving as food for woodpeckers, thrushes, sapsuckers, flickers, and other species. Seeds distributed by wildlife are the primary source of new plants.

Toxicodendron is of Greek origin and translated as "poison tree." Aptly named, the plant produces urushiol, a skin irritant. Present in all parts of the plant, urushiol causes severe itching, reddish inflammation, and blistering. Severe cases may require hydrocortisone or steroids to relieve the itching. Burning poison ivy releases the same compound into the air, causing similar responses within our lungs. The oil takes years to break down, so dead plants are toxic, too. Research indicates that about 85 percent of humans are susceptible to the effects of urushiol. Some individuals who are allergic to poison ivy may also be allergic to mangos, since mango skins have a chemical compound similar to urushiol.

Several forms of poison ivy are recognized; the eastern poison ivy variety *radicans* is the most common form in the coastal Carolinas. Legacy scientific literature cites poison ivy as *Rhus radicans*.

135 SUMMER GRAPE

Vitis aestivalis Michaux

Family: Vitaceae (Grape)

Other Common Names: Pigeon grape, silverleaf grape, blueleaf grape

Range: Southern Ontario, Canada; Maine west to Minnesota and Nebraska; south to Texas and Florida

Habitat: Maritime forests and maritime shrub thickets; also woodlands

Habit: Perennial vine

Flowering/Fruiting Period: FL May–June; FR September–October

Wetland Status: FACU

Origin: Native

Several commercially grown cultivars of the native summer grape produce a delightful, dry red wine. In addition, the ¼- to ½-inch, blue-black fruits make a flavorful jelly. After a small fire or a hurricane has opened the canopy of the maritime forest or shrub thicket, large quantities of summer grape seeds germinate and quickly recolonize the disturbed habitat. Along the North Carolina and South Carolina coast, summer grape grows best in well-drained, sandy soils. It is drought tolerant and prefers full sun or semishade.

b

c

a 135. Summer grape (*Vitis aestivalis*). (a) Coarsely toothed leaves are 3 to 6 inches across and may have no lobes or 3 to 5 deep lobes. (b) Greenish-white flowers are produced on 2- to 6-inch-long panicles. (c) Fruits are blue-black and about ¼ to ½ inch in diameter.

VINES

305

Leaves of summer grape are arranged alternately on stems nearly round in cross section. On mature stems that may be as large as 1 inch in diameter, the bark is reddish-brown and frequently peels in narrow strips. Young stems are tomentose but become glabrous with age. Coarsely toothed and slightly elliptical, the leaves may have no lobes or may have 3 to 5 deep lobes. They vary from 3 to 6 inches across, and they are pale green to glaucous beneath.

Summer grape produces small, greenish-white, insect-pollinated flowers in panicles from 2 to 6 inches long. The flowers open at the same time as leaf buds break in the spring. The branched tendrils of summer grape allow this fast-growing vine to reach the top of the forest canopy in one season. A key identifying characteristic of this species is that a flower inflorescence or tendril is absent from opposite every third leaf along the stem.

Summer grape seeds not consumed by birds or other wildlife accumulate in the soil seed bank. Birds and small mammals feed on mature fruits, with summer grape accounting for up to 25 percent of their diet. Birds find the bark strips useful in lining their nests.

Seeds, layering, and cuttings made from the current year's wood are ways to propagate summer grape.

The variety *aestivalis* is the common form of summer grape found in the coastal Carolinas.

136 JAPANESE WISTERIA

Wisteria floribunda (Willdenow) A. P. de Candolle
Family: Fabaceae (Legume)
Range: Maine to Florida and west to Texas and Illinois; USDA Hardiness Zones 5–9
Habitat: Old homesites, forest margins, and disturbed areas

Habit: Perennial vine
Flowering/Fruiting Period: FL April–June; FR June–October
Wetland Status: Not designated
Origin: Exotic; native to Japan
Not recommended for planting; instead, remove where already growing.

Japanese wisteria was introduced into the United States in about 1830 as an ornamental plant. The plant is still popular in the nursery trade despite its invasive tendencies. The deep green foliage and large clusters of attractive flowers make this plant particularly pleasing when grown as a covering for gazebos and similar landscape structures in the southeastern United States. Unfortunately, the invasive tendencies of Japanese wisteria exceed the plant's ornamental value.

Japanese wisteria is a deciduous, woody, twining vine. It reaches a height of 50 feet but is reported to grow up to 70 feet long as it trails along the ground. An identifying characteristic is the vine's habit of twining upward in a dextrorotatory (clockwise) direction. Hairy when young, the light gray to nearly white stems become smooth with age. Some older specimens are reported to reach 50 years of age with stems up to 12 inches in diameter. Such old, heavy vines, combined with tightly constricting stems, can bring down mature trees.

Leaves of Japanese wisteria are dark green, pinnately compound, and alternately arranged on the stem. The leaves range from 4 to 16 inches long with 13 to 19 leaflets. Leaflets have long, smooth edges; tapered tips; and wavy margins.

Flowers appear at the same time that leaves expand. The abundant, showy, and fragrant flowers form on long, pendulous racemes measuring 9 to 20 inches long with more than 100 flowers on each raceme. Flower color ranges from white to lavender to pink, and flowers are insect pollinated.

a 136. Japanese wisteria (*Wisteria floribunda*). (a) Dozens of 9- to 20-inch-long flowering racemes hang from a single vine. (b) Up to 100 insect-pollinated, lavender flowers open sequentially from the base to the tip of each cluster. (c) Densely pubescent flattened pods gently outline individual seeds.

b

c

The pealike flowers open sequentially from the base to the tip of the cluster. From 1 to 8 seeds are contained in brown, velvety, flattened pods varying from 4 to 7 inches long. Pods often persist on the vine into the winter, when the ½-inch-diameter, flattened seeds are released.

Japanese wisteria prefers open sun but will grow and reproduce in partial shade. It grows best in loamy, well-drained soils. Nitrogen-fixing bacteria are symbiotic in the roots of Japanese wisteria, which allows the plant to obtain additional nitrogen in nutrient-poor soils.

Bobwhite quail eat minor quantities of the seeds.

Japanese wisteria reproduces through sprouts from roots, stolons, and— more rarely and less reliably—seeds. Ungerminated seeds in the soil are relatively short lived.

The leaves, flowers, fruits, and seeds are reported to be poisonous, causing nausea and vomiting, among other symptoms.

Chinese wisteria (*Wisteria sinensis*) is closely related to Japanese wisteria. It is also invasive. Chinese wisteria possesses compound leaves with 7 to 13 leaflets and flower clusters with fewer than 100 flowers that open more or less simultaneously. Individual specimens may not be clearly identifiable as either Chinese or Japanese wisteria because the two species hybridize easily. Hybrids often exhibit a mix of physical characteristics that are either intermediate between the two species or similar to one or the other species of wisteria.

Shrubs

137 SALTWATER FALSE WILLOW

Baccharis angustifolia Michaux
Family: Asteraceae (Aster)
Other Common Names: Narrowleaf
  baccharis, false willow
Range: Coastal: North Carolina south to
  Florida and west to Louisiana
Habitat: Brackish marshes, maritime shrub
  thickets, and dune swales
Habit: Shrub
Flowering/Fruiting Period: FL & FR
  September–November
Wetland Status: FACW
Origin: Native

Saltwater false willow grows in low, moist,
shrub-dominated thickets and wet dune
swales along the Carolinas and the south

Atlantic and Gulf of Mexico coasts. It is
smaller in stature and has smaller white-
plumed seeds than its sister species, sea
myrtle.

This multistemmed and much-
branched shrub ranges from 3 to 6 feet tall
and is 3 feet across. The simple, alternately
arranged, slightly fleshy leaves feature resin
glands on the upper and lower surfaces.
Leaf blades are ¾ to 2¼ inches long and
⅛ to ¼ inch wide.

Saltwater false willow is dioecious,
with separate male and female flowers
occurring on different plants. Flower heads
cluster in groups of 3 to 4 near branch
tips, and each head is composed of 15 to
20 white disk florets; saltwater false willow
possesses no ray flowers.

Wind-dispersed fruits are brown

137. Saltwater false willow (*Baccharis angustifolia*).
(a) Mature plants range from 3 to 6 feet high
with simple, narrow, slightly fleshy leaves.
(b) Flowers on male plants are massed at the tips
of branches. (c) Female plants possess showy
disk flowers in the fall. (d) Plumed seeds are wind
dispersed.

achenes with slender, white bristles up to ½ inch long attached to the top of each achene. In the fall, a mass of plumed seeds forms an attractive blanket of white fluff across the top of the plant.

Saltwater false willow is tolerant of salt aerosols and salt water, and it prefers moist soil in full sun. The plant often grows with sea myrtle, but the narrow, fleshy leaves of saltwater false willow distinguish it from sea myrtle's much larger and wider, gray-green leaves.

When occurring in dense patches, the plant provides cover for a variety of small mammals and birds. The flowers of saltwater false willow attract a variety of insects, especially butterflies.

Propagate saltwater false willow through seeds and cuttings. This species, with its moderate growth rate, is a good substitute for nonnative ornamental shrubs. Specimens are available from commercial sources.

Baccharis glomeruliflora is a related species that grows in similar environments in southern North Carolina (although rarely) and in South Carolina. The dense flowering heads of this species arise in the leaf axils, rather than at the branch tips.

138 SEA MYRTLE

Baccharis halimifolia Linnaeus
Family: Asteraceae (Aster)
Other Common Names: Eastern baccharis, silverling, groundsel tree, high-tide bush, mullet bush
Range: Massachusetts south to Florida and west to Texas; also Arkansas and Oklahoma
Habitat: Edges of brackish marshes, maritime shrub thickets, maritime grasslands, dune swales; also disturbed sites, ditches, roadsides
Habit: Shrub
Flowering/Fruiting Period: FL & FR September–November

Wetland Status: FAC
Origin: Native

During mid- to late fall, masses of white-plumed seeds cover the tops of sea myrtle, the largest species of the Aster family in the Carolinas. Once flowering and fruiting begins, sea myrtle transforms from an anonymous background plant to the focal point of the shrub communities in which it grows.

Sea myrtle arises from either a single stem or multiple stems, with deep furrows and reddish-brown bark. Its wood is weak

138. Sea myrtle (*Baccharis halimifolia*). (a) Sea myrtle is an inconspicuous coastal shrub until midfall. (b) A spectacular display occurs in late fall as the plant flowers.

c

d

138. Sea myrtle (*Baccharis halimifolia*).
(c) Yellowish-white flowers develop on male plants at the ends of branches. (d) Flowers on female plants are responsible for the exploding white color of the fall plant.

green into the spring before giving way to the new season's growth.

Sea myrtle is dioecious, with separate male and female plants. White to greenish flowers develop in small, dense clusters surrounded by involucral bracts. Bees and butterflies swarm plants in early fall and pollinate the flowers.

On mature achenes, the silvery-white, ½-inch-long bristles are responsible for the distinctive white, cottony masses of seeds characteristic of this species. The bristles on each achene aid in seed dispersal.

Other than during pollination, sea myrtle is not an especially important wildlife plant; birds may nest in the shrub, and white-tailed deer graze the plant.

Sea myrtle is tolerant of salt aerosols, soil salts, and saturated soil. It thrives in moist, nutrient-poor soil with full sun, but it will survive in light shade. Horticulturalists report no major disease or insect problems for sea myrtle. Common associates are common wax myrtle, sea ox-eye, and marsh elder, a plant with which it is often confused. Marsh elder is distinctive in having opposite leaves with fine, regular teeth.

Propagation is primarily by seeds, which are commercially available, and by cuttings taken in the summer.

This coastal species' range is rapidly expanding inland. It appears well adapted to roadside wetland environments (ditches) that are especially prevalent along interstate highways. These environments provide sea myrtle with extensive new, exploitable habitats. In fact, its ability to invade open or disturbed wetlands or natural areas has caused land managers to initiate sea myrtle control programs.

and frequently shed, as evidenced by the many dead twigs and branches on the ground surrounding the plant.

Alternately arranged and coarsely toothed, the elliptical, gray-green leaves are 2 to 4 inches long and ¼ to ½ inch wide. Leaf surfaces often have small resin glands. The leaves closest to the apex of the plant are the smallest and have no teeth. This rapidly growing shrub is late deciduous, with leaves overwintering and remaining

139 SALTWORT

Batis maritima Linnaeus

Family: Bataceae (Batis)

Other Common Names: Turtleweed, seaside saltwort, beachwort, pickleweed

Range: South Carolina south to Florida and west to Texas

Habitat: Brackish and salt marshes, salt pannes

Habit: Shrub (subshrub)

Flowering/Fruiting Period: FL June–July; FR October

Wetland Status: OBL

Origin: Native

If you are slogging your way along the edge of a tidal marsh or observing a marsh from a boardwalk at Hunting Island, Hilton Head, or a nearby island in South Carolina

c

a

b

d

139. Saltwort (*Batis maritima*). (a) and (b) Woody, succulent saltwort grows in salty, waterlogged soils called pannes. (c) Stamens appear on flowering specimens. (d) Mature fruits are approximately the size of large pearls.

or farther south, you are likely to encounter this odd-looking, small, succulent shrub, saltwort.

Saltwort has substantial, woody stems, either prostrate or trailing along the ground. It usually grows to a height of 2 feet, rarely taller. New stems arise at nodes where weak stems bend and touch the soil surface. New adventitious roots form and solidly anchor the yellowish-green stems to the marsh surface. As it spreads, the plant forms a mat, patch, or loose cluster of stems often interspersed among culms of the dominant marsh species, smooth cordgrass. Saltwort leaves are oppositely arranged, fleshy, and sessile, with a gently curved shape like miniature bananas. The smooth, pale green leaves are up to 1¼ inches long and possess a strong odor when crushed.

Saltwort is dioecious, with separate male and female plants. The flowering branches are usually erect; both male and female flowers form in cone-shaped axillary inflorescences. Each female flower produces 2 to 8 small fruits that usually drop near the parent plant but subsequently may be transported considerable distances by water.

Saltwort requires full sun or light shade. It survives saltwater flooding and long periods in waterlogged soils. It survives these conditions by absorbing excess salts through the roots, accumulating these salts in leaf cell vacuoles, and then dropping the salt-laden leaves as they die. Saltwort is not competitive with other plants, so it grows best in frequently disturbed areas or in sites with few other plants, such as salt pannes. In addition to smooth cordgrass, sea ox-eye and Virginia glasswort commonly grow with saltwort.

Propagate saltwort through seeds, cuttings, layering, and simple plant division. Commercial growers typically start new plants from cuttings. This

interesting succulent plant is a good conversation starter in a coastal native plant garden. It is little affected by diseases, insects, or grazing.

Saltwort is reported to be an herbal medicine used to alleviate rheumatism and gout, as well as a skin treatment for conditions such as psoriasis.

---

140 SEA OX-EYE

Borrichia frutescens (Linnaeus) A. P. de Candolle

Family: Asteraceae (Aster)

Other Common Names: Sea ox-eye daisy, bushy seaside tansy, seaside ox-eye, sea daisy

Range: Virginia south to Florida and west to Texas; also Mexico

Habitat: Brackish and salt marshes

Habit: Shrub (subshrub)

Flowering/Fruiting Period: FL & FR May–September

Wetland Status: OBL

Origin: Native

This colonial shrub is rarely taller than 2 to 3 feet, typically growing in nearly pure stands along the upper edge of brackish

140. Sea ox-eye (*Borrichia frutescens*). (a) The fleshy-leaved plant grows in large patches in brackish and salt marshes.

b

c

140. Sea ox-eye (*Borrichia frutescens*). (b) Daisylike flowers terminate woody branches. (c) Spine-tipped bracts on fruiting heads protect seeds as they mature.

below the soil surface in the plant's wetland habitat. Thick, fleshy, oppositely arranged leaves are pubescent on both upper and lower surfaces. These simple, silvery to gray-green, obovate leaves are evergreen, 1 to 3 inches long, and ⅜ to 1¼ inches wide. The leaves are slightly aromatic when crushed.

Bold, yellow, daisylike flowers borne on short peduncles terminate the shrub's short branches. Fifteen to 30 bright yellow ray flowers surround a center of 20 to 75 brownish-yellow disk flowers, and these combine to create a 1-inch-wide flower head. Overlapping, spine-tipped bracts subtend the flower heads. As seeds are set, each flower head turns brown and gradually breaks apart, releasing dozens of 4-sided achenes.

Sea ox-eye grows best in wet soils, and it tolerates saturated soils and frequent inundation by salt water. This sun-loving plant is salt-aerosol tolerant. Common plants associated with sea ox-eye are smooth cordgrass, black needlerush, saltmeadow cordgrass, and marsh elder.

The plant serves as cover and food source for small mammals and birds; the flowers attract several species of butterflies.

Propagated by seeds and stem cuttings, sea ox-eye is widely cultivated. Generally pest free, sea ox-eye may still endure attacks by a gall-forming fly, *Asphondylia borrichiae*, and by *Paracantha forficula*, a fly whose larvae feed on the achenes.

and tidal marshes. The erect, sparsely branched stems of sea ox-eye form large, dense patches at a surprisingly uniform height in each patch.

The woody stems of sea ox-eye are round in cross section and arise from myriad short rhizomes that extend well

141 BEAUTY BERRY

Callicarpa americana Linnaeus
Family: Lamiaceae (Mint)
Other Common Names: American beauty-berry, French mulberry, American mulberry
Range: Maryland south to Florida and west to Texas; also Mexico and the West Indies

SHRUBS

315

Habitat: Maritime shrub thickets and maritime forests; also disturbed sites

Habit: Shrub

Flowering/Fruiting Period: FL June–July; FR August–October

Wetland Status: FACU

Origin: Native

Beauty berry is a striking and unmistakable plant when seen in full fruit in the early fall along the edge of maritime shrub thickets or in a maritime forest. Typically, the fruit-laden stems bend away from the center of the plant in a beautiful, deliquescent pattern.

Beauty berry grows to 6 feet tall and 6 feet wide, occasionally larger. The large, simple, opposite leaves are ovate to rhombic and greenish-yellow with coarsely serrated edges. They vary from 4 to 6 inches long and 2 to 3 inches wide.

The ⅛-inch-long flowers are pale lavender to pinkish with united petals that create a narrow tube. The flowers develop on new wood and cluster in the axils of the leaves. When the mauve to magenta, 4-seeded fruits are mature, they form dense, bracelet-like rings around the woody stems.

While beauty berry grows well in shaded sites, its fruits reach the deepest, most intense color when grown in sunny habitats. Well-drained, sandy coastal soils are most suitable for the plant's growth. Beauty berry is moderately drought resistant but not salt tolerant.

Raccoons, opossums, gray foxes, and several species of birds feed on the fruits, while white-tailed deer browse the leaves.

The fleshy fruits often persist on the stems well into the winter, long after the leaves have turned yellow and dropped from the plant. In cultivation, beauty berry can be heavily pruned to the ground in late fall or winter. The plant is generally disease free. Propagate beauty berry from seeds, cuttings, and layering.

a

b

141. Beauty berry (*Callicarpa americana*). (a) Delicate, pale lavender to pinkish flower petals are united above the middle. The stamens are prominent. (b) Fleshy, purple fruits encircle the stems at each pair of leaf axils. The ovate leaves are greenish-yellow and simple with coarsely serrated margins.

Beauty berry fruits are edible; they are customarily used to make jelly. The plant is reputed to have numerous traditional medicinal uses; tea made from the roots was used in treating dysentery, upset stomach, and colic. A natural compound extracted from beauty berry called callicarpenal has shown significant repellent properties against mosquitoes, ticks, and fire ants. Callicarpenal may prove to be useful as a natural deterrent to biting pests.

---

142 SILVER-LEAF CROTON

Croton punctatus Jacquin
Family: Euphorbiaceae (Spurge)
Other Common Names: Beach croton, beach tea, gulf croton
Range: North Carolina south to Florida and west to Texas; also Mexico, Caribbean Islands

Habitat: Wrack lines, dunes, dune swales, and maritime grasslands
Habit: Shrub (subshrub)
Flowering/Fruiting Period: FL & FR May–November
Wetland Status: UPL
Origin: Native

Silver-leaf croton, a common plant found only in coastal environments in the Carolinas, is a highly attractive member of one of the largest genera of flowering plants that includes trees, shrubs, herbs, and vines. Generally considered a rhizomatous perennial plant, it survives only one year in North Carolina, the northern limit of this species. This limit is

142. Silver-leaf croton (*Croton punctatus*). (a) The distinctive grayish-green color and stellate hairs covering the stems help identify this common species. Female (b) and male (c) flowers occur on the same plant. (d) Fruits are 3-lobed and 3-seeded, ¼ to ½ inch across.

likely a result of the severity, duration, and frequency of freezing temperatures.

Ranging from 1 to 3 feet high, the erect stems are yellowish-orange to tan and exude a yellowish-orange sap when cut. Simple, slightly succulent leaves are borne in an alternate arrangement on numerous branches covered with stellate hairs. The upper side of the leaf is silver to grayish-green and efficiently reflects sunlight. The underside is pale green. Leaves are ovate to lanceolate with entire margins. They are ¾ to 2 inches long and ⅜ to 1½ inches wide.

Silver-leaf croton is monoecious, with separate creamy white male and female flowers occurring on compact terminal racemes. The insect-pollinated flowers are small with 5 triangular sepals and no petals. The minutely pubescent fruit is a 3-lobed, 3-seeded capsule about ¼ to ½ inch across. Individual seeds are light brown with purple flecks. Silver-leaf croton produces large quantities of seeds; these are forcibly ejected from the capsules in warm, dry weather. Fruits and seeds are buoyant in seawater, likely an aid in dispersal, although birds, small mammals, and reptiles often disseminate the seeds.

Silver-leaf croton occurs most commonly in sparsely vegetated dunes and maritime grasslands. More landward, silver-leaf croton is outcompeted or shaded by other plants. It can tolerate burial by sand up to about 8 inches per year, forming adventitious roots along the stem as sand accumulates around the plant. Silver-leaf croton is quite resistant to salt aerosols; salt injury to leaves is rarely apparent. A plant useful for stabilizing dunes, it prefers moist to dry, sandy soils and tolerates low soil-nutrient levels and high soil temperatures. Silver-leaf croton is intolerant of flooding by either salt water or fresh water. It often, but temporarily, disappears from the beach and dune environment after a major hurricane. This plant is commonly

associated with seaside panicum, sea oats, dune pennywort, and dune camphorweed.

The wildlife value of silver-leaf croton is unknown. Plants may serve as cover for ground birds and small mammals on sparsely vegetated dunes.

Propagate the plant by seeds. Germination rates are high if seeds are scarified and planted in the fall or early spring.

143 THORNY ELAEAGNUS

Elaeagnus pungens Thunberg
Family: Elaeagnaceae (Oleaster)
Other Common Names: Silverthorn, thorny olive, spotted elaeagnus, autumn silverberry
Range: USDA Hardiness Zones 7–10
Habitat: Ornamental
Habit: Shrub
Flowering/Fruiting Period: FL October–November; FR February–April
Wetland Status: Not designated
Origin: Exotic; native to East Asia and Japan
Not recommended for planting; instead, remove where already growing.

Left without horticultural care such as trimming and pruning, thorny elaeagnus will form large, dense, cascading mounds

143. Thorny elaeagnus (*Elaeagnus pungens*). (a) The unruly tangle of high-arching stems suggests rapid growth for this weedy plant.

a

b

c

143. Thorny elaeagnus (*Elaeagnus pungens*). (b) Small, white, gardenia-scented flowers develop in clusters along the stems during late fall. (c) Mature, bright orange, juicy fruits attract birds.

or hedges of high-arching stems and root suckers. Rapid growth allows this naturally aggressive plant in the coastal Carolinas to outcompete nearby plants for water, space, and sunlight. Thorny elaeagnus is included in the "severe threat" category on the South Carolina Exotic Pest Plant Council list and is on invasive species lists for nearby states.

Thorny elaeagnus is a multistemmed

shrub with scaly, reddish-brown bark and twigs. Thin offshoots of the main branches have the look and feel of thorns but are actually short branches. Plants can grow from 10 to 20 feet tall with a spread of 10 to 15 feet. Leaves are thick, alternate, evergreen, and 2 to 4 inches long with wavy edges. Unique brown scales dot the upper side of the bright, glossy green leaves. In contrast, silvery scales cover the underside of the leaves.

The small, ivory white or cream-colored pendant flowers open in late fall. The flowers have a sweet fragrance similar to the familiar scent of gardenia. Withered flowers remain attached to the distal end of the growing fruits for several weeks. By spring, the large, brown, scale-covered fruits turn bright reddish-orange. The single-seeded, juicy, ½- to 1-inch fruits are attractive to birds.

Thorny elaeagnus grows in both sun and shade; it tolerates salts in the soil, salt aerosols, and drought conditions. With roots capable of fixing nitrogen, the plant grows well in soils low in nutrients.

Small mammals and birds eat the fleshy fruits. Butterflies feed on the nectar of flowers during migration, and the tangle of dense stems provides birds and small mammals with an excellent environment for nesting, resting, and hiding.

144 EASTERN CORAL BEAN

Erythrina herbacea Linnaeus
Family: Fabaceae (Legume)
Other Common Names: Red cardinal, Cherokee bean, coral bean lily, cardinal spear
Range: Central North Carolina south to Florida and west to Texas; also Mexico
Habitat: Dunes, maritime forests, and waste areas; also open, sandy woods
Habit: Shrub
Flowering/Fruiting Period: FL May–July; FR July–September

SHRUBS

a

b

c

144. Eastern coral bean (*Erythrina herbacea*).
(a) Numerous flowering stems develop from
a woody rootstock. (b) Red flowers open
progressively from the base of the raceme toward
the apex. (c) Individual, bright red seeds remain
attached to the fruit for some time after the pod
splits open.

Wetland Status: UPL
Origin: Native

Eastern coral bean is a small, moderately
fast-growing, handsome, and showy
shrub topped with distinctive scarlet-red-
flowered racemes. Identify this plant once
and you will not confuse it with any other
coastal plant.

Growing to a height of 3 feet, this
semiherbaceous shrub produces annual
stems from a woody, perennial, tuberous
root. In the coastal Carolinas, expect
the stems of the plant to die back to the
ground each winter following freezing
temperatures. Short, slightly curved spines
arm the stems of eastern coral bean.
The deciduous, alternately arranged,
compound leaves are composed of
3 distinct leaflets with bulging centers and
pointed tips. The entire leaf is 6 to 8 inches
long, with individual leaflets 3 to 5 inches
long by 3½ to 4 inches wide. Leaves are
light to medium green with prickles on the

midribs and undersides of leaflets. Leaves
are reputed to track the sun position
throughout the day.

The flowering racemes of eastern coral
bean develop at the top of each stem. The
2-inch-long, tube-shaped flowers have
5 petals, with the upper petal wrapped
around the lower 4 petals. Since dozens
of flowers populate each inflorescence,
a single plant can flower for several
weeks. The distinctive fruit is a hard, dark
brown pod ranging from 3 to 6 inches
long, splitting open at maturity to reveal
5 to 10 bright red seeds that are ¼ inch
in diameter. The fruit often persists on
the plant into the winter. The seeds are
reported to be toxic to humans.

Eastern coral bean thrives in full sun and partial shade. It is drought tolerant and grows well in nutrient-poor, sandy soils owing, in part, to the presence of nitrogen-fixing bacteria in root nodules. Moderate levels of soil salts do not reduce the growth of the plant.

Eastern coral bean attracts hummingbirds, butterflies, and other pollinating insects. Propagation is primarily by seeds and stem cuttings. Scarify seeds for faster germination. Commercially available, eastern coral bean is a low-maintenance plant without serious pests. With attractive leaves, flowers, and fruits, it makes an outstanding accent or specimen plant and serves as a native substitute for exotics such as common lantana.

a

145 JAPANESE ARALIA

Fatsia japonica (Thunberg) Decaisne & Planchon
Family: Araliaceae (Ginseng)
Other Common Names: Japanese fatsia, paperplant, Japanese rice tree
Range: USDA Hardiness Zones 8–10
Habitat: Ornamental
Habit: Shrub
Flowering/Fruiting Period: FL September–November; FR October–December
Wetland Status: Not designated
Origin: Exotic; native to Korea, Japan, and Ryukyu Islands

b

The tropical-looking Japanese aralia tolerates the effects of light salt aerosols and grows well in seacoast areas protected from desiccating winds. It makes an excellent foundation planting for structures located landward of the primary dunes.

Deeply palmately lobed, the nearly orbicular leaves are leathery, dark green above, and pale green below; they range from 8 to 16 inches across. The stem is coarse, thick, and occasionally branched. Japanese aralia may grow to a height of 15 feet, but the plant typically does not

c

145. Japanese aralia (*Fatsia japonica*). (a) Shiny, dark green, leathery leaves are salt-aerosol resistant. (b) Spherical flowering heads are composed of dozens of cream to white flowers. (c) Blue-black berries persist through the winter.

SHRUBS

321

grow taller than 8 feet with a diameter of 8 feet.

Each spherical flowering head is 1 to 2 inches in diameter with cream to white flower clusters; fruits are individual blue-black berries, ¼ inch in diameter, and persistent on the plant throughout the winter.

The plant tolerates a variety of soil types, including deep, well-drained sands characteristic of the coastal area. The coarse-textured Japanese aralia grows well in nearly full sun and deep shade; however, too much sun may burn the leaves.

Japanese aralia appears to be pest free; however, attacks by scale and mealy bugs have been reported. A hard frost will kill the leaves and stems, but if protected with mulch, the roots will survive. Prune Japanese aralia to the ground in spring to rejuvenate the plant. Prune suckers at any time to maintain plant shape and to increase leaf growth at the bottom of the plant.

Cuttings made in early summer root easily. Germination is high with seeds sown in spring or fall. All parts of the plant are considered poisonous.

The Japanese traditionally plant Japanese aralia on the north side of homes to ward off evil spirits.

---

146 COMMON FIG

Ficus carica Linnaeus
Family: Moraceae (Mulberry)
Other Common Names: Edible fig, garden fig
Range: USDA Hardiness Zones 8–10
Habitat: Ornamental, fruit tree
Habit: Shrub
Flowering/Fruiting Period: FL May–August; FR August–October
Wetland Status: UPL
Origin: Exotic; native to Asia Minor and carried to the Mediterranean by humans; now distributed worldwide

The common fig, one of the first plants purposefully cultivated by humans, was introduced into North America in Virginia in 1769. Since its introduction, it has spread throughout the southeastern United States. A major item of Asian and Mediterranean food commerce for centuries, the fig is related to another staple food plant, the Pacific Island breadfruit (*Artocarpus altilis*).

In the coastal Carolinas, common fig grows as a large, mound-shaped plant reaching a height of 10 to 15 feet and a diameter of 50 feet. It possesses multiple, wide-spreading stems. Branches and leaves grow from the ground to the apex; the dense canopy shades out all plants growing beneath it in just a few years. The wood is weak, and branches suffer extensive damage by hurricane winds, but it recovers rapidly. Shallow, extensive roots grow well beyond the outer edge of the plant.

The bark is smooth and silvery-gray. Common fig leaves are bright green, thick, simple, and deeply lobed with 2 to 5 lobes. The leaves can grow up to 12 inches across; they are irregularly toothed on the margins, palmately veined, hairy, rough on the upper surface, and velvety soft on the lower surface.

The flower head is unusual. Scores of flowers are packed inside a pear-shaped structure called a syconium. In the syconium, inward-pointing flowers line the inside. In the common fig, all of the flowers are female and no pollination is necessary; they are self-pollinating. Other fig species require pollination by a minute wasp, and the insect's only access to the flowers is through a tiny opening at the top of the syconium.

Figs bear 2 fruit crops each year; the first spring crop, called the *breba* crop, is produced on last year's wood. A second crop, called the *main* crop, follows on the new wood of the current year. The first crop is usually composed of small, unpalatable

Propagate the common fig by cuttings. Prepare cuttings from 2-year-old branches in the winter and plant immediately.

Eat figs fresh or dried. Fruits have been used in making pies, cakes, jams, preserves, and ice cream for generations. The filling in the popular Fig Newtons cookie is fig paste.

Horticulturalists recognize numerous cultivars—some reports indicate that there are more than 700! Examples of popular varieties include *Black Mission*, *Celeste*, *Magnolia*, and *Brown Turkey*.

---

147 AMERICAN WITCH HAZEL

Hamamelis virginiana Linnaeus
Family: Hamamelidaceae (Witch hazel)
Other Common Names: Witch hazel, northern witch hazel
Range: Nova Scotia west to Ontario, Canada; south to Florida and Texas
Habitat: Maritime forests; also moist to dry forests
Habit: Shrub
Flowering/Fruiting Period: FL October–December; FR September–November (2nd year)
Wetland Status: FACU
Origin: Native

Witch hazel, a steam distillate of the bark of the American witch hazel plant dissolved in alcohol, is still found on drugstore shelves today. Before the advent of modern aftershave lotions, I remember my father using witch hazel as a refreshing postshave styptic. A small witch hazel industry still exists today in Connecticut, where manufacturers harvest twigs annually and distill flavonoids, tannins, and volatile oils from the plant.

American witch hazel is a coarse shrub with one or more stems. The shrub is deciduous with crooked, spreading branches that form an angular, asymmetrical open crown. The slow-growing shrub eventually reaches a height

a

b

146. Common fig (*Ficus carica*). (a) The mound-shaped plant forms a dense, impenetrable canopy. (b) Leaves are dark green, thick, and possess 2 to 5 deep lobes. The syconium fruit has tiny, inward-pointing flowers.

fruits, while the second crop is edible. The fruits may be yellowish-green, bronze, or purple at maturity. Ranging from 1 to 4 inches in diameter, the fruits possess a tough outer skin that cracks and exposes the inner rind. Inside, a white rind encircles a mass of seeds; each seed is surrounded by a jellylike pulp.

Common fig produces the best fruit when growing in full sun. The plant is drought and salt-aerosol tolerant and grows well in nutrient-poor soils.

Figs constitute a minor part of the diets of local birds and small mammals. Because of the potential size of a mature tree, plant common fig only in a large space. On grassy dunes in the coastal Carolinas, they serve as excellent sand stabilizers.

a

c

b

147. American witch hazel (*Hamamelis virginiana*). (a) The large, alternately arranged leaves are typical of those on many understory trees. The leaves have short petioles and wavy margins. (b) Long, narrow, wrinkled yellow petals dominate flowers with 4 stamens and 2 styles. (c) On reaching maturity, the hard, woody, acorn-shaped capsules forcefully eject seeds.

of 20 feet, sometimes taller. A taproot anchors the shrub. Nearly as wide as it is tall, the shrub possesses smooth, thin, light brown or grayish bark, becoming scaly at maturity.

The leaves are dark green above and pale green below. The upper surface of the leaf is typically smooth, while the underside is hairy along the veins. The leaves turn bright yellow in the fall.

Curiously, the shrub flowers in mid- to late fall after the leaves have been shed. Flowers have yellow petals that appear wrinkled, as if they had been folded haphazardly in the flower bud. The flower is composed of 4 small sepals and 4 bright yellow petals. The petals are about ½ to ¾ inch long and ¹⁄₁₆ inch wide. Four stamens and 2 styles are visible in each flower. The flowers produce nectar and are

successful in attracting several species of flies that aid in pollination.

Fruits are brown, woody, acorn-shaped, pubescent capsules about ⅝ inch long. The seed coat is extremely hard. When the capsules open the following summer, the shiny, black, ½-inch seeds are violently ejected several feet from the capsule.

Typically found in moist to dry woods, American witch hazel is present but uncommon in the coastal maritime forests. It tolerates full sun as well as shade. American witch hazel is not drought tolerant, and its salt tolerance is low; it relies on overstory trees to limit its exposure to salt aerosols.

Reproduction is primarily by seeds, and American witch hazel seeds may take 12 months or more to germinate. Scarification may enhance the success and speed of germination. American witch hazel also reproduces by suckers.

American witch hazel can be planted in a maritime forest or a natural area; be mindful, though, to avoid full exposure to salt aerosols.

White-tailed deer eat the fruits, twigs, and leaves; small mammals and birds feed on the fruits.

American witch hazel is a traditional herb of Native Americans. In addition to being used as an astringent and styptic, its bark was also used to treat cuts and bruises. Taken internally, it is reputed to treat internal bleeding, coughs, and colds.

Cultivars of American witch hazel with large flowers are available commercially. Pests and diseases are not generally a problem with this species.

The variety *virginiana* is the form common in the coastal Carolinas.

a

b

148. Woolly beach heather (*Hudsonia tomentosa*). (a) A low-growing, shrubby dune plant, woolly beach heather has tiny, overlapping, grayish-green leaves. (b) Bright yellow flower clusters grow at the tips of new branches.

148 WOOLLY BEACH HEATHER

Hudsonia tomentosa Nuttall

Family: Cistaceae (Rockrose)

Other Common Names: Woolly hudsonia, beach heather, sand-heather, sand golden-heather

Range: Eastern Canadian provinces, Maine south to North Carolina, west to the Great Lakes states

Habitat: Dunes

Habit: Shrub (subshrub)

Flowering/Fruiting Period: FL May–June; FR June–September

Wetland Status: UPL

Origin: Native

Woolly beach heather, a plant more common north of the Carolinas, is present along the North Carolina coast as far south as Nags Head, the natural southern limit for this species. When in full bloom in the spring, woolly beach heather flowers brighten an otherwise gray and dull dune community.

Woolly beach heather is a low shrub rarely growing taller than 1 foot above the open dune sands, its primary habitat. The plant forms dense, bushy patches as individual plants expand and cover large patches of older, stabilized dunes. Leaves are grayish-green with dense, whitish hairs that cover the scalelike leaves. These small, simple, alternately arranged leaves overlap in a way reminiscent of the leaves of coastal red cedar. Older stems become gray to reddish-brown.

The bright yellow, ¼-inch, five-petaled flowers cluster near the tips of the branches. The fruit of woolly beach heather is a smooth, round capsule containing 1 to several seeds.

SHRUBS

325

Woolly beach heather is a good dune stabilizer in the northeastern United States, but it is susceptible to damage and uprooting by trampling. Off-road vehicle use and continued development in dune environments threaten the plant's continued existence in North Carolina. The distribution of this plant may contract northward as climate changes occur.

Because woolly beach heather is rare in North Carolina, native populations should be admired but not disturbed.

We know little of the use of woolly beach heather by wildlife. Where it grows in large, dense patches, small mammals likely use the plants for hiding, resting, and nesting. Flowers are insect pollinated.

Woolly beach heather may be available from specialized coastal native plant nurseries. It makes a colorful, low-maintenance landscape plant that is moderately salt tolerant but not, unfortunately, particularly heat tolerant.

a

b

149 BIGLEAF HYDRANGEA

Hydrangea macrophylla (Thunberg) Seringe

Family: Hydrangeaceae (Hydrangea)
Other Common Names: French hydrangea, mophead hydrangea, garden hydrangea
Range: USDA Hardiness Zones 6–9
Habitat: Ornamental
Habit: Shrub
Flowering/Fruiting Period: FL & FR June–August
Wetland Status: Not designated
Origin: Exotic; native to Japan, China, and Korea

149. Bigleaf hydrangea (*Hydrangea macrophylla*). (a) A prolific summer bloomer, bigleaf hydrangea possesses flowering heads that range from deep blue to bright pink. (b) Each individual mophead hydrangea flower has 4 large sepals and no petals.

Soil pH controls flower color in bigleaf hydrangea. Where soils are relatively acid and high in aluminum, bigleaf hydrangea produces deep blue flowers; where soils are neutral or basic, flowers are bright pink. Coastal landscape gardeners can change the flower color expressed by a particular plant. When aluminum sulfate ($AlSO_4$) is added to the soil in late fall or early spring, the pH is decreased (making the soil more acid), and the blue flower color is expressed. Conversely, when calcium carbonate ($CaCO_3$) is added to the soil, the pH is increased (making the soil more basic), and bright pink flowers are produced. Yes, flowers are purple when you add both $CaCO_3$ and $AlSO_4$ to the soil!

Flowering throughout the summer, the bushy bigleaf hydrangea grows from

3 to 6 feet high and 3 to 6 feet across. This coarse, fast-growing plant possesses stout, erect, and unbranched stems. The leaves are deciduous, opposite, simple, obovate to elliptic, 4 to 8 inches long, and 3 to 6 inches wide. The serrated leaves are bright green above and paler green below with scattered hairs.

Two flower forms occur on varieties of bigleaf hydrangea. *Lacecaps* have flower heads that are flat on top with large, sterile flowers surrounding numerous inner, small, fertile flowers. *Mopheads* bear many large, fertile flowers borne in rounded corymbs that form nearly spherical flower heads up to 8 inches across. Bee-pollinated, individual flowers have showy sepals but no petals. The fruit of bigleaf hydrangea is a capsule.

The species is tolerant of salt aerosols and coastal winds, but tolerance of soil salts is low. It prefers sites with morning sun and afternoon shade. Soils must be moist and well drained.

Since bigleaf hydrangea is an introduced plant, native wildlife makes little use of it. But it can provide cover for small animals and ground birds.

Propagate bigleaf hydrangea by cuttings in the summer, a time when they root easily. Bigleaf hydrangea makes a good summer flowering foundation or accent plant in the coastal Carolinas. Mopheads make a great addition to either fresh or dried flower arrangements. The species has no serious insect pests or diseases. Some of the many cultivars are *Nikko Blue*, *Quadricolor*, *Forever Pink*, *Blue Prince*, and *All Summer Beauty*. Bigleaf hydrangea is well behaved and not invasive.

150 YAUPON

Ilex vomitoria Aiton
Family: Aquifoliaceae (Holly)
Other Common Names: Yaupon holly, evergreen holly, Christmas berry

Range: Virginia south to Florida and west to Texas
Habitat: Dune swales, maritime shrub thickets, maritime forests, brackish and tidal marsh shorelines; also pine flatwoods and forested wetlands
Habit: Shrub
Flowering/Fruiting Period: FL March–May; FR October–November
Wetland Status: FAC
Origin: Native

Yaupon is a coastal plant noted for its uses in holiday decorations and as a source of the "black drink" that Native Americans made from its leaves and stems. The highly concentrated drink was reportedly used

150. Yaupon (*Ilex vomitoria*). (a) Yaupon is a small tree reaching a maximum height of 25 feet.

b

c

150. Yaupon (*Ilex vomitoria*). (b) Flowers are white with 4 petals. Male (*shown here*) and female flowers occur on separate plants. (c) Each of the bright red or yellowish-red berries contains 4 seeds. Finely crenate margins characterize the small, elliptical leaves. (d) The bark is smooth, thin, and light gray.

d

as a medicine to induce vomiting and as a laxative. When diluted, Native Americans and European settlers consumed the brew as a caffeine-containing social drink.

Yaupon is a large shrub or small tree reaching a height of 15 to 25 feet and a spread of 15 feet. It often grows from root sprouts, creating dense, almost impenetrable stands that provide exceptional cover and nesting sites for birds. The trunk is rarely more than 6 inches in diameter—more typically 1 to 3 inches—with smooth, thin, light gray bark. Yaupon possesses small, leathery, elliptical leaves that are ¾ to 1½ inches long and ¼ to ½ inch wide. The leaf margins are crenate and shiny. The leaves are alternately arranged on the stem, and

they are gray-green above and glaucous green below.

Yaupon is dioecious, with male and female flowers occurring on separate plants. The ¼-inch, 4-petaled, and 4-sepaled flowers emerge from the axils of leaves and from nodes between the leaves, either singly or in groups of 2 or 3.

The nearly spherical fruit is a bright, translucent, red or yellowish-red drupe approximately ¼ inch in diameter.

The 4-seeded fruit remains on the plant throughout the winter or until birds strip the berries, whichever comes first! Raccoons and squirrels, as well as mockingbirds, bluebirds, robins, cedar waxwings, and mourning doves, relish yaupon's fruit and are primarily responsible for dispersing the seeds. Yaupon is a favorite browse for white-tailed deer.

Yaupon thrives in a range of soil types, from dry to wet. It can withstand desiccating wind, high temperatures, full sunlight, and high concentrations of salt aerosols. Yaupon often exhibits a "sheared" profile, a response to salt aerosols being deposited on the plant.

Propagate yaupon from seeds and from cuttings of mature wood. It is cultivated as an ornamental; representative cultivars are *Jewel*, *Nana*, and *Pride of Houston*.

a

b

151. Marsh elder (*Iva frutescens*). (a) This bushy shrub grows 3 to 8 feet tall and almost exclusively along the upland-estuarine boundary. (b) Leaves are dull green and slightly succulent with toothed margins 1¼ to 4 inches long.

151 MARSH ELDER

Iva frutescens Linnaeus
Family: Asteraceae (Aster)
Other Common Names: Southern maritime marsh elder, high tide bush, saltmarsh elder
Range: Coastal: New Jersey south to Florida and west to Texas
Habitat: Upland edges of brackish and salt marshes
Habit: Shrub
Flowering/Fruiting Period: FL August; FR September–November
Wetland Status: FACW
Origin: Native

Marsh elder is a common but often overlooked shrub species found almost exclusively along the landward limit of tidal marshes and slightly elevated sites within these marshes. Marsh elder and other shrub-sized plants form a plant community—the salt shrub thicket—that outlines the transition or ecotone from marsh to upland along estuarine shorelines in the Carolinas. Some of the other shrubs are common wax myrtle, coastal red cedar, sea ox-eye, and sea myrtle. The most robust marsh elder plants grow at elevations in the marsh that are flooded less than 10 percent of the growing season.

c

151. Marsh elder (*Iva frutescens*). (c) Flowering heads are pendant and composed of disk flowers only. Small, leafy bracts surround each flowering head.

Marsh elder ranges from 3 to 8 feet tall with a spread of 4 to 6 feet. It is multistemmed and much branched. The grayish-green, woody stems are brittle and sometimes appear warty. Scientists report that marsh elder stems have a rapid turnover; most stems live less than 6 years before being replaced by new stems. Marsh elder leaves are dull green, with toothed margins and 3 prominent veins running the length of each leaf. The leaves are pubescent on both surfaces, 1¼ to 4 inches long, and ⅛ to ¾ inch wide. The late-deciduous, slightly succulent leaves are simple, opposite, and lanceolate shaped. Upper leaves sometimes appear alternately arranged on the stem.

The inconspicuous flowering heads are pendant on terminal racemes that vary from 1 to 4 inches long. The individual greenish-white flower heads are composed of disk florets only; several small, leafy, imbricate bracts subtend each head. Individual florets are male or female.

Fruits are blackish-brown achenes covered with pale resin dots.

Marsh elder prefers full sun and exhibits a high degree of salt tolerance; however, high salt aerosols associated with major storms kill back the leaves and stems. Marsh elder exhibits excellent growth in areas with a high water table and occasional flooding. It is moderately drought tolerant.

Marsh elder serves as a nesting and resting site for various birds, including red-winged blackbirds, painted buntings, and marsh wrens.

Propagate marsh elder through seeds. Cuttings and plants are available commercially.

Marsh elder and sea elder are closely related, but they occupy distinctly different coastal habitats and are easily distinguished from each other. Sea elder possesses thick, succulent leaves with entire margins and is common on wrack lines and dunes.

Without flowers, marsh elder is easily confused with sea myrtle. Marsh elder has oppositely arranged leaves with prominent teeth along the entire edge. Sea myrtle leaves are toothed only above the middle and are arranged alternately along the stem.

The variety *frutescens* is the primary form of marsh elder present along the coast of the Carolinas.

152 SEA ELDER

Iva imbricata Walter

Family: Asteraceae (Aster)

Other Common Names: Beach-elder, dune marsh-elder

Range: Coastal: Virginia south to Florida and west to Texas

Habitat: Wrack lines, dunes, and maritime grasslands

a

b

c

152. Sea elder (*Iva imbricata*). (a) This semiwoody plant intercepts blowing sand and grows in height and girth as sand accumulates around it. (b) Individual flower heads contain numerous flowers surrounded by large, green bracts. (c) When mature, fruits are released and scattered along the shore by wind and water.

Habit: Shrub
Flowering/Fruiting Period: FL & FR
August–November
Wetland Status: FACW
Origin: Native

Sea elder joins sea oats, seaside panicum, and saltmeadow cordgrass as one of the four most important dune-colonizing plants in the Carolinas. Sea elder is a pioneer plant of the wrack line and dunes, capable of withstanding desiccating winds, strong sunlight, high temperatures, sand burial, scarce soil nutrients, and intense salt aerosols so characteristic of the environment directly adjacent to the beach. Expanding upward and outward as sand accumulates around it, sea elder becomes the nucleus of low, rounded dunes.

This semiwoody, much-branched plant grows to a height of about 3 feet. Sand accumulation stimulates sea elder to form new stems and roots at stem nodes buried by the sand. The leaves of sea elder are alternately arranged, elliptical, shallowly toothed, 1 to 2 inches long, and ¼ to ½ inch wide. The leaves are glabrous, fleshy, and sessile, and they possess a thick cuticle, a feature that is most likely responsible for sea elder being one of the most salt-aerosol-resistant coastal plants.

Its numerous flower heads develop in terminal racemes ranging from 2 to 12 inches long. Individual flower heads are from ⅛ to ⅜ inch in diameter; the fruit is a yellow-brown achene typical of the Aster family. Sea elder produces large quantities of seeds that germinate soon after dispersal by wind and water. Studies show that seeds can germinate when covered by up to 1½ inches of sand. Seedlings are abundant on the dunes over the winter and into spring, but few survive to maturity.

Interestingly, sea elder grows most profusely when continually buried by sand. The plant tends to become leggy when little sand accumulates around it; thus, it is not a particularly attractive landscape plant.

A prolific seed producer, sea elder releases seeds in late summer. The seeds may serve as food for small mammals and ground birds.

Propagation of sea elder is by seeds and cuttings. Collect and prepare cuttings during the fall. Plants are also available from commercial dune plant growers.

153 JAPANESE SHORE JUNIPER

Juniperus conferta Parlatore

Family: Cupressaceae (Cypress)
Range: USDA Hardiness Zones (5) 6–9
Habitat: Ornamental
Habit: Shrub (subshrub)
Flowering/Fruiting Period: FL April–May; FR September–October
Wetland Status: Not designated
Origin: Exotic; native to the coasts of Hokkaido, Japan, and Sakhalin Island, Russia

Japanese shore juniper is an example of an introduced species that has remained well behaved. The plant shows no tendency to become invasive or weedy, and it stabilizes coastal sands well and grows relatively fast. These are characteristics that make it a good plant for foundation, mass, and slope plantings for residential and commercial structures built in the coastal dune environment of the Carolinas.

Japanese shore juniper is an evergreen shrub with reddish-brown stems that rarely grows higher than 12 inches or wider than 5 to 10 feet. The stems and branches grow parallel to the ground, occasionally rooting where a stem touches the sand. The waxy-coated leaves are aromatic, bluish-green, and needlelike, about ½ inch long with a stiff, pointed tip.

Japanese shore juniper is dioecious; yellowish-brown, ¼-inch, round male cones are produced on plants separate from the ¼- to ½-inch, dark blue female cones. The 3-seeded cones, produced on 2-year-old branches, are covered with a whitish bloom.

Japanese shore juniper requires full sun and well-drained, sandy soils. It tolerates heat, salt aerosols, nutrient-poor soils, and drought.

The species is not a major source of food or shelter for birds or small mammals.

Propagate Japanese shore juniper from

a

b

c

153. Japanese shore juniper (*Juniperus conferta*). (a) Shore juniper spreads slowly and remains close to the ground, usually less than 12 inches above the soil surface. (b) Female cones containing 3 seeds are found on 2-year-old branches. (c) Male cones are about ¼ inch in diameter and occur on separate plants.

cuttings taken in the dormant season. It is a low-maintenance plant and easy to transplant. If you are growing from seeds, stratify the seeds over the winter. Expect them to germinate slowly. With adequate water and fertilizer, the plant does form a dense cover. However, be aware that the plant is prone to fungal diseases, mites, and scale. These problems may shorten the useful lifespan in the landscape.

Many cultivars of Japanese shore juniper are available commercially, including *Blue Pacific, Silver Mist, Emerald Sea*, and *Blue Lagoon*.

---

154 SEASHORE MALLOW

Kosteletzkya pentacarpos (Linnaeus) Ledebour

Family: Malvaceae (Mallow)

Other Common Names: Virginia saltmarsh mallow, saltmarsh mallow, seaside mallow, pink mallow

Range: New York south to Florida and west to Texas

Habitat: Freshwater and brackish marshes, edges of wet maritime shrub thickets; also swamps

Habit: Shrub

Flowering/Fruiting Period: FL & FR June–October

Wetland Status: OBL

Origin: Native

Seashore mallow is a distinctive wetland plant of the Carolinas coast that possesses large, attractive flowers. This plant is easy to spot amid the less colorful grasses and sedges that dominate our swamps and marshes. Seashore mallow is a relative of marsh mallow (*Althaea officinalis*), a plant used as a medicinal herb and a food delicacy since Roman times. Other close relatives include rose mallow, which is another Carolinas marsh plant, as well as the agricultural crops of cotton and okra.

The seashore mallow plant is coarse

SHRUBS

a

c

154. Seashore mallow (*Kosteletzkya pentacarpos*). (a) Seashore mallow grows to a height of 3 to 5 feet and possesses triangular to ovate, gray-green leaves. (b) Solitary flowers with 5 light pink to rose pink petals have a distinctive yellow column of united stamens at the center. (c) The fruit is a 5-seeded, brown capsule covered with short, white bristles.

b

and hairy, with many branches and stems that develop from a crown of roots. Under ideal conditions, seashore mallow may grow to a height of 6 feet, but it normally ranges from 3 to 5 feet tall with a spread of 3 to 4 feet. Leaves are alternately arranged on the stem. They are triangular to ovate, with distinctive triangular lobes at the base and large, irregular teeth along the margin. Considerably variable in shape and size, the leaves range from 3 to 7 inches long and 1½ to 3½ inches wide. Dense, coarse stellate hairs give the leaves a gray-green color.

The solitary flowers develop on long pedicels originating in the axils of the leaves. Flowers are slightly droopy and

1 to 3 inches across, with 5 light pink to rose pink petals and a distinctive central column of bright yellow, united stamens. Flowers are either insect- or self-pollinated, and each lasts a single day. The fruit is a 5-seeded, brown capsule covered with stiff, white bristles, approximately ½ inch across. Seeds are dark brown with a smooth surface.

Seashore mallow prefers full sun and moist soils. It will tolerate some shade, but it is not drought tolerant. Seashore mallow grows best in standing fresh water or in salt water that is up to about one-third of full strength. Modest quantities of salt aerosols have little effect on the plants; however, plants do not grow where they are exposed to persistent salt-laden winds.

The flower nectar of seashore mallow

attracts butterflies and hummingbirds, which aid in pollination.

Wild-collected seeds germinate readily. Propagate the plant from cuttings taken any time before flowering begins. Attractive and easy to grow, seashore mallow is available commercially.

In the coastal Carolinas, this species is referred to as *Kosteletzkya virginica* in legacy plant literature.

---

155 COMMON LANTANA

Lantana strigocamara R. W. Sanders
Family: Verbenaceae (Verbena)
Other Common Names: Largeleaf lantana, shrub verbena, hedgeflower
Range: Coastal: southeastern North Carolina south to Florida and west to Texas
Habitat: Roadsides, waste areas, pastures
Habit: Shrub (subshrub)
Flowering/Fruiting Period: FL & FR May–December
Wetland Status: FACU

Origin: Exotic; native to Central America, South America, and the Caribbean

A native of the American tropics, common lantana is an invasive plant and a noxious weed over much of the tropical world and adjacent regions that rarely experience killing frosts. In a frost-free environment, common lantana spreads rapidly and forms low, dense thickets. Left unmanaged, common lantana becomes firmly established, spreads rapidly by vegetative means, and gradually reduces species diversity in the area. Currently, the

b

c

a 155. Common lantana (*Lantana strigocamara*). (a) Multiple woody stems with ovate, wrinkled leaves characterize this commonly cultivated species. (b) Dome-shaped flowering heads produce numerous tubular flowers in leaf axils. (c) The ¼-inch fruits are 2-seeded drupes that turn black at maturity.

entire Carolinas coast has sufficient days with temperatures below freezing to ensure that plants are killed back each year. How climate change will affect common lantana during this century is a concern; invasive tendencies may appear.

Multiple, woody stems often armed with prickles distinguish the vegetative part of common lantana. Its identifying characteristics include oppositely arranged, ovate leaves that have a wrinkled texture; they are 3 to 5 inches long and 1 to 2 inches wide. The leaves are pubescent and toothed and emit a strong, unpleasant odor when crushed.

Common lantana produces flowers in profusion throughout the summer and fall. Several species of butterflies and nectar-feeding insects pollinate the flowers. Densely packed tubular flowers comprise the dome-shaped umbels that develop in the leaf axils. Flowers are commonly yellow, but cultivars may have white, orange, red, pink, or purple flowers. More than one color is sometimes present in a single flower head, and to complicate the situation, individual flowers change color slightly as they age.

The fruit of common lantana is a fleshy, 2-seeded drupe about ¼ inch in diameter that turns black at maturity.

Common lantana grows well in poor soils, tolerates salt aerosols well, and survives extended drought. It requires full sun for best growth and thrives in warm environments.

Birds are the major disseminators of common lantana's abundant seeds.

Plants may be propagated through stem cuttings taken in midsummer. However, it is best to purchase one of the numerous, well-behaved cultivars, including dwarf, trailing, upright, and weeping growth forms. Seeds and foliage are toxic to livestock and pets. Common lantana normally grows 1 to 3 feet above the ground, but it can extend vinelike up to 6 to 8 feet when provided with lattice or other growth supports.

---

156 CHINESE PRIVET

Ligustrum sinense Loureiro
Family: Oleaceae (Olive)
Other Common Names: Chinese ligustrum, common Chinese privet
Range: New England to Florida and west to Kansas, Oklahoma, and Texas
Habitat: Shrub thickets, maritime forests, and disturbed sites
Habit: Shrub (tree)
Flowering/Fruiting Period: FL April–June; FR August–September
Wetland Status: FAC
Origin: Exotic; native to China and Southeast Asia
Not recommended for planting; instead, remove where already growing.

Endowed with attractive and abundant white flowers and distinctive fruits, Chinese privet was introduced into the United States in the mid-1800s. Since its introduction, it has escaped cultivation and become naturalized throughout its range, especially in the Southeast, where it benefits from fire, flooding, timber cutting, cultivation, and other habitat disturbances. It is so widespread, abundant, and noxious that it is included on all state lists of invasive species where it is found.

Chinese privet ranges from a shrub to a small tree, often growing to a height of 12 feet; it can even grow to 30 feet, though rarely. Many stems typically arise from the extensive and shallow root system. Bark is smooth, gray, and dotted with lenticels. Branches are densely pubescent and characteristically project outward from the stems at nearly right angles. Similarly, leaves extend outward from the twigs at right angles. The plant is evergreen to semideciduous with short-petioled leaves that are bright green above and

a

b

c

156. Chinese privet (*Ligustrum sinense*).
(a) A multistemmed, evergreen to semideciduous shrub, Chinese privet possesses simple, opposite leaves. Flowers are abundant. (b) White flowers grow on cone-shaped panicles. Each flower possesses 4 petals. Two stamens are exserted beyond the corolla. (c) One-quarter-inch, fleshy berries turn blue-black at maturity.

glaucous green below. Leaves are simple and opposite and grow to a length of ¾ to 1½ inches and a width of ½ to 1 inch. The midvein on the underside of the leaf bears abundant fine hairs.

Flowers develop on cone-shaped panicles at the tips of branches. Short-pediceled, yellowish-white flowers display 4 petals and 2 exserted stamens. The ¼-inch-long ellipsoid fruit is a fleshy berry, blue-black to black, containing a single hard seed. Seeds are produced in profusion and persist on the plant until they are eaten or fall off the following spring.

Bobwhite quail and other birds consume the fruits. White-tailed deer forage the plant, especially when their preferred food is scarce. The dense tangle of stems and leaves provides some low-quality cover for a few animal species.

The plant grows exceptionally well in a variety of habitats, particularly disturbed areas. It can grow in both moist and dry environments.

Chinese privet propagates through root and stem suckers and seeds. Reproductive

SHRUBS

337

capacity is high, which makes it difficult to eradicate. The Pollen Library lists this species as a "severe allergen." Do not facilitate the spread of Chinese privet by planting it anywhere for any reason!

A related species, the evergreen Japanese privet (*Ligustrum japonicum*), is naturalized in similar environments throughout the coastal Carolinas. This invasive plant is also unwelcome along our coast.

157 COMMON WAX MYRTLE
Morella cerifera (Linnaeus) Small
Family: Myricaceae (Bayberry)
Other Common Names: Southern bayberry, southern wax myrtle
Range: Southern New Jersey south to Florida and west to Texas
Habitat: Dunes and dune swales, maritime forests, maritime shrub thickets; edges of freshwater marshes, brackish marshes, and salt marshes
Habit: Shrub
Flowering/Fruiting Period: FL March–April; FR August–October
Wetland Status: FAC
Origin: Native

A common shrub of the Carolinas, common wax myrtle shows up in most coastal habitats, from the landward edge of the primary dunes to the upper edge of tidal marshes. Its abundance along the Horry County shore led to the naming of Myrtle Beach, S.C., after this plant.

This evergreen shrub with dense, attractive foliage grows up to 25 feet high but more commonly reaches a height of only 10 to 12 feet, especially under the influence of salt aerosols. The trunk and branches of the fast-growing common wax myrtle are weak and tend to break easily. Hurricanes usually damage both leaves and branches, but the plants respond by sprouting and releafing within weeks after a storm. Common wax myrtle may

157. Common wax myrtle (*Morella cerifera*). (a) This seemingly ubiquitous evergreen shrub has dark, gray-green leaves and grows to a height of 10 to 12 feet. (b) Female flower clusters develop in the axils of the leaves.

c

e

d 157. Common wax myrtle (*Morella cerifera*).
(c) Male flowers grow similarly and are composed
of stamens only. (d) Fruits are blue-gray, wax-
coated berries about ⅛ inch in diameter. (e) The
bark is thin, gray to grayish-brown, and smooth.

develop a single trunk, but numerous suckers frequently form on young, vigorously growing plants, creating a dense, multistemmed shrub.

Leaves are simple, entire, dark gray-green on the upper surface, and glaucous green on the lower surface. Leaves cluster near the ends of branches in an alternate pattern and persist on the plant for up to 2 years. The leathery, waxy leaves are 1 to 3 inches long, ¾ inch wide, and aromatic when crushed. Resin glands cover both upper and lower leaf surfaces.

Common wax myrtle is dioecious, and male and female plants produce flower clusters in the axils of terminal branches. Male flowers are yellowish-green catkins up to 1 inch long; female catkins are much shorter and grow inconspicuously along the stem. Fruits are wax-coated, globular, blue-gray berries, densely packed along the stems and about ⅛ inch in diameter.

Despite its tolerance to ocean-derived salts, the frequently observed wedge-shaped canopy of common wax myrtle growing near the beach is a result of pruning by salt aerosols. Common wax myrtle is often the first woody plant to invade backdunes and swales. It is moderately tolerant of drought and salts in the soil. Its ability to fix nitrogen in the roots allows the plant to thrive in nutrient-poor, sandy soils.

Seeds serve as a food source for tree swallows, Carolina wrens, sparrows, and migratory warblers. Colonial waterbirds may use common wax myrtle thickets located in remote and inaccessible areas as rookeries.

Propagate common wax myrtle by seed and cuttings. Seeds require stratification over the winter before they will germinate. This species is available commercially.

Where common wax myrtle and northern bayberry overlap in distribution, the two species can be confused. Common wax myrtle has resin glands on both surfaces of the leaf, while northern bayberry's resin glands are only on the underside of its leaves. Also, the waxy fruit of northern bayberry is about twice the diameter of common wax myrtle's fruit, about ¼ inch in diameter. Leaves of northern bayberry are deciduous; common wax myrtle leaves are evergreen.

In the legacy plant literature, botanists refer to common wax myrtle as *Myrica cerifera*.

158. Northern bayberry (*Morella pensylvanica*). **a** (a) This shrub species is low growing, usually less than 8 feet tall, and has multiple stems.

158 NORTHERN BAYBERRY

Morella pensylvanica (Mirbel) Kartesz
Family: Myricaceae (Bayberry)
Other Common Names: Bayberry, candleberry, waxberry, tallow bayberry
Range: Coastal: Canadian Maritime Provinces to northeast North Carolina; also Great Lakes states
Habitat: Dunes, dune swales, maritime grasslands, and edges of maritime forests
Habit: Shrub
Flowering/Fruiting Period: FL March–April; FR August–October
Wetland Status: FAC
Origin: Native

"Bayberry" and "candles" are terms inextricably linked by history and lore. The first colonists strained floating wax from great quantities of boiled berries gathered from this abundant shrub they found growing on New England dunes. Its pale green, fragrant wax is prized for making excellent, hard, slow-burning candles. Soap and sealing wax were also made from the waxy seed coat of northern bayberry.

Northern bayberry is a low-growing, upright shrub occasionally 8 feet tall but usually only 3 to 4 feet tall. The shrub's bark is gray-brown, thin, and smooth. The plant typically exhibits multiple twisted stems growing in a clonal growth habit. The stems are weak and easily broken by storm winds.

The leaves of northern bayberry are dark green and shiny above, pale green and pubescent below. They are alternately arranged on the stem, deciduous, simple, and leathery. Leaves are also ovate, 1 to 3 inches long, ¾ inch wide, and entire but occasionally toothed near the tip of the leaf. Yellow resin glands are present primarily on the lower leaf surface, an identifying characteristic that separates northern bayberry from common wax myrtle. Common wax myrtle has resin glands on both sides of the leaf. When you crush a plant part, you can smell the "bayberry" aroma.

Northern bayberry is dioecious, with separate male and female plants. One-half-inch-long, inconspicuous catkins develop in early spring before the leaves appear; they are composed of many flowers without either sepals or petals. The northern bayberry fruit is a silver or grayish-purple drupe, ¼ inch in diameter or about twice the size of the drupe produced by its southern relative, common wax myrtle. Abundant fruits develop on second-year wood and often remain on the plant well into winter.

Northern bayberry is drought tolerant and has considerable tolerance of soil salts

b

e

c

d

158. Northern bayberry (*Morella pensylvanica*).
(b) Northern bayberry possesses alternately arranged, ovate, dark green leaves. Female flowers (c) and male flowers (d) are borne on separate plants and appear before the shrub leafs out. (e) Fruits are ¼ inch in diameter and have a thick, silver or grayish-purple waxy coating.

as well as salt aerosols. An excellent coastal dune stabilizer, it grows best on sparsely vegetated, nutrient-poor dunes in full sun, where it can spread easily with minimal competition from other plants. It grows well in environments with accumulating sand. Common associates often found growing with northern bayberry are American beachgrass, yaupon, poison ivy, and—where their ranges overlap—common wax myrtle.

The ripe fruits of the plant attract a variety of birds and small mammals.

Chickadees, tree swallows, catbirds, and bluebirds eat the fruits, while northern bayberry thickets provide ideal nest sites.

The plant grows best when allowed to spread naturally by root suckers. Sow seeds in the spring after stratification and prepare cuttings from young twigs during the summer. Cultivars of the species are available from native plant nurseries, but the plant is suitable for growing only in the most northern coastal counties in North Carolina. Its natural range is as far south as Pea Island National Wildlife Refuge in Rodanthe.

In legacy literature, authors cite this species as *Myrica pensylvanica*.

159 OLEANDER

Nerium oleander Linnaeus
Family: Apocynaceae (Dogbane)
Other Common Name: Common oleander
Range: USDA Hardiness Zones (8) 9–11
Habitat: Ornamental
Habit: Shrub

b

c

a 159. Oleander (*Nerium oleander*). (a) An excellent landscape plant for the coastal area, oleander's cultivars vary in flower color; pink and white are the most common. (b) Abundant, fragrant flowers composed of 5 fused petals are up to 2 inches across and grow clustered at stem tips. (c) Fruits are brown pods, 4 to 7 inches long. They split lengthwise to release white-plumed seeds.

Flowering/Fruiting Period: FL June–August; FR July–October

Wetland Status: Not designated

Origin: Exotic; native to the Mediterranean region and Eurasia

The bright green foliage and large, long-lasting flowers of oleander welcome and brighten the spirits of many visitors to the southern North Carolina and South Carolina coasts. Oleander is an example of the successful introduction of an exotic plant to a new environment. It shows no growth or reproductive characteristics that would lead it to be classified as an invasive plant.

Oleander is a fast-growing shrub normally pruned to maintain a height and girth of 10 feet; however, it can grow to 20 feet tall if untended. Stems are canelike, green, and smooth when young, graying as the plant ages. Leaves are bright green above, glaucous green below, glossy, somewhat leathery, and linear or lanceolate shaped; they range from 4 to 10 inches long and from 2 to 4 inches wide. Leaves are evergreen and opposite or whorled on the stem. Along the North Carolina coast, winter temperatures below 20°F damage foliage; stem damage occurs below 15°F. Otherwise, oleander tolerates drought, high heat, high soil salts, high winds, high salt aerosols, and nutrient-poor soils well. Oleander prefers full sun, but it will grow in shade.

The large, abundant, and fragrant flowers cluster at the end of the stems.

Five fused petals form a floral tube up to 2 inches wide and 1½ inches long. Flower color varies depending on the cultivar: white, pink, red, salmon, or yellow. The 4- to 7-inch-long green pods ripen to a medium brown, then split to release dozens of white-plumed seeds.

The plant is attractive to bees and may serve as a bird habitat.

This ornamental is easy to grow in most coastal settings as a single stem or multistemmed plant; it works well as a hedge or a specimen plant. To propagate oleander, divide large plants or take stem cuttings in the summer. Seed germination is least desirable because seeds may not breed true if the parent plant is the result of a genetic cross. *Calypso, Hawaii, Petit Salmon*, and *Sister Agnes* are among the multitude of introduced varieties.

Warning: All parts of the plant are poisonous to humans—even the smoke from a burning plant. Oleander contains several cardio-active glycosides, including oleandrin, which is similar in action to the active compound found in the foxglove plant, digitalis. Ingesting oleander may cause nausea, vomiting, cramps, cardiac arrest, and possibly death.

a

---

160 DUNE PRICKLY-PEAR

Opuntia drummondii Graham
Family: Cactaceae (Cactus)
Other Common Names: Sandbur pricklypear, cockspur pricklypear
Range: Coastal: North Carolina south to northern Florida and west to Texas
Habitat: Dunes and maritime grasslands
Habit: Shrub (subshrub)
Flowering/Fruiting Period: FL April–June; FR August–October
Wetland Status: UPL
Origin: Native

Dune prickly-pear has evolved an interesting mechanism for spreading to new locations. When bumped by passing

b

160. Dune prickly-pear (*Opuntia drummondii*). (a) The plant is mat-forming with cylindrical or elliptical pads tinged with purple. The pads disarticulate from the plant easily. (b) Bright yellow flowers with numerous stamens are about 2½ inches across and usually form near the apex of the distal pads. Fruits are ¾ to 1 inch long and purplish-red at maturity.

humans or large animals such as white-tailed deer or raccoons, its large spines are driven into fur, skin, shoe leather, pant legs, or socks. When discovered, dislodged, and tossed aside, dune prickly-pear has been efficiently "dispersed" from the parent plant!

Dune prickly-pear is a trailing or mat-forming plant with green stems (called pads) tinged with purplish or reddish highlights, especially when the plant grows in full sun. The pads are elliptical or cylindrical, slightly flattened, and typically 1 to 2 inches long and ½ to 1 inch wide. One or 2 stout, 1-inch, strongly barbed spines (modified leaves) arise from each areole, principally those areoles located near the apex of each pad. In addition to aiding dispersal, the large spines reduce herbivory on the pads. Numerous pale yellow or brown glochids located in each areole add additional armor to the plant.

The yellow flowers have numerous petals and many yellow stamens; they are about 2½ inches across and open only for one day. The flowers often form near the apex of the outermost pads. Fruits gradually change from green to purplish-red at maturity. They are roughly cylindrical, ¾ to 1 inch long, and ½ inch in diameter. The fruits are glabrous and fleshy with no spines; however, they do possess glochids (tiny bristly hairs) in the areoles. Seeds are tan, disk shaped, and ¼ inch in diameter.

Dune prickly-pear prefers dry, sandy soils with no major competition from other species. It is consistently found in association with sea oats and dune camphorweed.

White-tailed deer may graze this cactus early in the spring. Several ground species, including doves, thrashers, woodpeckers, squirrels, and rabbits, eat the seeds.

Propagation is by seeds and detached pads placed on moist sand until

adventitious roots form. Seed germination is apparently low.

Dune prickly-pear can be used as an ornamental in natural gardens.

---

161 EASTERN PRICKLY-PEAR
Opuntia humifusa (Rafinesque) Rafinesque
Family: Cactaceae (Cactus)
Other Common Names: Creeping prickly pear, smooth prickly pear, devil's tongue
Range: Massachusetts west to Minnesota and south to New Mexico, Texas, and Florida
Habitat: Dunes and maritime grasslands; also dry, open, sandy pine woodlands
Habit: Shrub (subshrub)
Flowering/Fruiting Period: FL May–July; FR August–October
Wetland Status: UPL
Origin: Native

The eastern prickly-pear is the only species of cactus common throughout the eastern half of the United States. It has one of the largest, simplest, yet most spectacular flowers in the coastal Carolinas flora.

Eastern prickly-pear forms dense, spreading, evergreen clumps of segmented stems or "pads." Pads grow to about 6 to 10 inches high and up to 3 feet in diameter. The plant develops an extensive, shallow root system composed of fibrous roots. Succulent stems are bright green to yellowish-green, oblong, flattened, 2 to 6 inches long, 2 to 3 inches wide, and ⅜ inch thick.

Usually, eastern prickly-pear is spineless; however, some plants produce long, sharp spines, especially near the apex of the pads. When present, spines are brown or gray and about 1 inch long. Widely spaced areoles with tufts of tiny, reddish-brown barbed bristles called glochids cover the pads. These bristles are much more bothersome to people and animals than the big spines. When the

a   b

161. Eastern prickly-pear (*Opuntia humifusa*). (a) Pads are oval, bright green to yellowish-green, and 2 to 6 inches long. They may or may not have spines. Flowers are bright yellow and 3 to 4 inches across, with 8 to 12 shiny petals and numerous stamens. (b) Fruits are ovoid, 1 to 2 inches long, and turn red at maturity.

areoles are touched, these fine glochids work their way into the skin and are quite painful. Occasionally, you may find small, green, cone-shaped structures near the areoles. These are highly reduced leaves and may grow for some time before they drop from the plant in early summer.

The flowers of eastern prickly-pear are bright yellow and 3 to 4 inches broad, with 8 to 12 shiny petals and numerous yellow stamens. They often occur roughly in a row along the upper edge of the topmost pads. Large plants may have dozens of flower buds, but only 1 or 2 flowers open at a time on each pad, and each lasts just 1 day. The flowers are insect pollinated, and you will observe numerous bees and other insects foraging around open flowers. The fruits (called tunas) are ovoid, reddish-green, about 1 to 2 inches long, and ½ inch across. The pulp of the tuna is red, sweet, and

edible. Remove the tiny glochids before eating!

Small mammals, including mice and rabbits, eat the tan, disk-shaped seeds.

Propagation can be accomplished by breaking pads off a parent plant and burying the pads about ½ inch deep in moist soil until adventitious roots are formed. Stem segments do not disarticulate as easily as in the dune prickly-pear; they must be carefully broken or cut off the plant. Collect seeds from wild plants, being sure to avoid the glochids. Stratify the seeds to assure successful germination.

Eastern prickly-pear prefers full sun and thrives in nutrient-poor, sandy soils. The plant tolerates drought conditions but tends to lose water and shrivel when dried. When suitable growing conditions return, pads rehydrate, becoming smooth and firm.

SHRUBS

345

Eastern prickly-pear is an excellent choice for a coastal native plant garden. Strategically placed, it can create a barrier to foot traffic for people or animals.

Another species of prickly-pear cactus, *Opuntia stricta*, occurs in coastal environments in the Carolinas (although less commonly in North Carolina). It is represented by two varieties: *dillenii* and *stricta*. This species is considerably larger than either dune prickly-pear or eastern prickly-pear and possesses large, ovate to obovate, strongly flattened pads. Its mature fruits are typically dark red to purple.

162. American mistletoe (*Phoradendron leucarpum*). (a) American mistletoe haustoria bore into the wood of host trees, and the plant eventually develops a spherical shape.

162 AMERICAN MISTLETOE

Phoradendron leucarpum (Rafinesque) Reveal & M. C. Johnston
Family: Santalaceae (Sandalwood)
Other Common Names: Mistletoe, Christmas mistletoe, oak mistletoe
Range: New York west to Ohio and Missouri, south to Texas and Florida
Habitat: Maritime forests and forested swamps
Habit: Shrub (subshrub)
Flowering/Fruiting Period: FL October–November; FR November–January
Wetland Status: Not designated
Origin: Native

For much of the year, American mistletoe grows virtually unseen on tree branches high in the forest canopy. When host trees shed their leaves in late fall and winter, this hemiparasitic plant is revealed for all to see. The slow-growing American mistletoe does not permanently damage the host tree, and scientists consider it a natural component of a healthy forest. American mistletoe is most common in habitats where atmospheric moisture is high, such as maritime forests and forested swamps.

American mistletoe has modified roots called haustoria that bore into the wood of host trees, such as oaks, pecans, gums, elms, and maples. The haustoria extract water, nutrients, and some sugars from the host plant's water- and food-conducting tissues. The branches of host trees swell where the haustoria infect this water- and food-transporting tissue, creating a "bump" on the infected branch. Mature plants grow up to 3 feet across and appear as roughly spherical balls composed of multibranched stems. Stems are brittle, green, and photosynthetic. Leaves are dark green, thick, fleshy, and leathery, ranging from ½ to 3 inches long and ⅜ to 1 inch wide. The simple, elliptical leaves with entire margins are oppositely arranged on the stems.

American mistletoe is dioecious; male and female flowers occur on separate plants. The flowers are small, only about ⅛ inch across, and possess 3 green sepals and no petals. Flowers of both sexes develop on spikes that are ½ to 1½ inches long. The fruit is a globose, translucent, white berry containing a single seed. The ⅛- to ¼-inch diameter fruits often persist on the plant into the spring.

The seeds are poisonous to humans; however, birds such as cedar waxwings,

c

d

162. American mistletoe (*Phoradendron leucarpum*). (b) The male flowers develop on a spike. (c) Female flowers also develop on a spike and possess 3 sepals but no petals. (d) Fruits are ⅛- to ¼-inch, semitransparent, globose berries that can persist until spring.

bluebirds, and robins relish the seeds and are responsible for spreading the plant from tree to tree. Seeds pass through birds undigested and may be deposited on limbs in their droppings. Seeds also spread when birds wipe their beaks on tree limbs to rid themselves of the sticky substance contained in the fruits.

Scientists report that the caterpillar of the great purple hairstreak (*Atlides halesus*) feeds on American mistletoe. The butterfly lays its eggs on mistletoe. After hatching, the caterpillars feast on the plant. Mistletoe is also an important nectar and pollen source for native bees.

Propagate the plant by pressing ripe

berries against a tree branch, taking advantage of the sticky substance that surrounds each seed. It may take 12 to 18 months for the seed to germinate and send haustoria into the branch.

Exchanging a kiss under mistletoe is variously interpreted as a prediction of marriage, happiness, or long life. This tradition has reached us through Greek, Celtic, and Norse customs.

The subspecies *leucarpum* is the most common form of American mistletoe in the coastal Carolinas.

163 JAPANESE PITTOSPORUM

Pittosporum tobira (Thunberg) W. T. Aiton
Family: Pittosporaceae (Pittosporum)
Other Common Names: Japanese
    mockorange, tobira, Australian laurel
Range: USDA Hardiness Zones 8–10
Habitat: Ornamental
Habit: Shrub
Flowering/Fruiting Period: FL April–May;
    FR September–November
Wetland Status: Not designated
Origin: Exotic; native to Korea, Japan,
    Taiwan, and China

Virtually unaffected by salt aerosols, drought, and heat, Japanese pittosporum is one of the best plants that can be selected to address many seacoast landscaping situations. As an added bonus, this nonnative plant requires little fertilization. Seedlings do, however, appear in landscaping, suggesting invasive tendencies. Time will tell!

The intensely bright green and dense foliage is composed of shiny, dark, simple, leathery leaves, 1 to 4 inches long and up to 1 inch wide. The edge of each leaf characteristically curls under. When not trimmed, Japanese pittosporum exhibits a mounded shape and grows to about 12 feet with a spread of 4 to 8 feet.

In late spring, Japanese pittosporum displays highly fragrant, white to creamy

163. Japanese pittosporum (*Pittosporum tobira*). (a) Foliage of this landscape shrub is bright green, shiny, and leathery. Leaves are 1 to 4 inches long and 1 inch wide. (b) Five-petaled flowers are fragrant, white to creamy white, and grow in clusters. (c) Fruits are green, woody capsules.

white flowers in 2- to 3-inch clusters that contrast sharply and dramatically with the dark green foliage. Each flower is about ½ inch in diameter and has 5 sepals and 5 petals. The fruit of Japanese pittosporum is a woody capsule containing seeds covered with a resinous substance.

This moderately fast-growing plant is equally at home in sun or partial shade. Japanese pittosporum performs well in well-drained, sandy environments but languishes in poorly drained soils, especially when water saturates the soil for extended periods.

Japanese pittosporum provides cover for small mammals and birds. Despite producing large numbers of fruits and seeds, the plant has little native wildlife food value.

As a landscape plant, Japanese pittosporum serves well as a foundation plant, a ground cover, a hedge, or—with the lower branches pruned—a multistemmed small tree. Propagate Japanese pittosporum from cuttings of mature stems if they have been treated by a root-promoting compound. *Variegata* and *Compacta* are popular cultivars.

a

164 INDIAN HAWTHORN

Rhaphiolepis indica (Linnaeus) Lindley
Family: Rosaceae (Rose)
Other Common Name: Rhaphiolepis
Range: USDA Hardiness Zones 8–11
Habitat: Ornamental
Habit: Shrub
Flowering/Fruiting Period: FL April–May;
    FR September–October
Wetland Status: Not designated
Origin: Exotic; native to Japan and Korea

Indian hawthorn and its larger, more sprawling relative—yedda hawthorn (*Rhaphiolepis umbellata*), also sometimes referred to as Indian hawthorn—are clearly two of the best and most popular nonnative evergreen shrubs available for landscaping in the coastal Carolinas.

Indian hawthorn reaches an average height of 4 feet and has a similar breadth. The plant requires little maintenance and is quite colorful in a foundation or garden

b

c

164. Indian hawthorn (*Rhaphiolepis indica*). (a) This species may reach 4 feet in height with a similar spread. The thick, leathery, simple, ovate, and serrated leaves tend to cluster at the tips of the branches. (b) White flowers are about ½ inch across and grow in 4- to 5-inch clusters. (c) Purplish-black fruits are spherical and about ½ inch in diameter. They often persist on the plant through the winter.

SHRUBS

setting. Leaves tend to cluster at the tips of the branches of this relatively slow-growing shrub. The thick, leathery leaves are bright green above and glaucous green below. Alternately arranged on the stems, the leaves are simple, ovate, serrated, 1 to 1½ inches long, and ¾ to 1¼ inches wide.

Individual fragrant, white flowers are about ½ inch in diameter and grow in large 4- to 5-inch clusters. Numerous species of insects visit the flowers in the spring. Purplish-black fruits are slightly less than ½ inch in diameter and contain 1 to 2 seeds. They mature early in the fall but often persist on the plant through the winter.

Indian hawthorn is well adapted to the coastal environment. It is salt-aerosol and drought tolerant and grows best in full sun and sandy soils. Capable of surviving in light shade, it prefers moist, well-drained soils.

Propagate Indian hawthorn using seeds and cuttings. Seeds germinate easily, and cuttings made during the summer usually grow roots successfully.

The seeds are a winter source of food for mockingbirds, towhees, sparrows, and cardinals. White-tailed deer will browse the plant, but only when preferred plants are in short supply.

Numerous cultivars are available, including *Majestic Beauty*, a large shrub; the compact, pink *Indian Princess*; and the pink, cold-tolerant *Eleanor Taber*. Look for cultivars that are less susceptible to leaf spot disease caused by *Entomosporium*, a fungus. Yedda hawthorn (*Rhaphiolepis umbellata*) is a similar but larger plant, often reaching 6 to 8 feet tall with a similar spread. Indian hawthorn is a good substitute for Japanese azalea in the coastal Carolinas.

165 WINGED SUMAC

Rhus copallinum Linnaeus
Family: Anacardiaceae (Cashew)
Other Common Names: Flameleaf sumac, dwarf sumac, shining sumac
Range: Maine south to Florida and west to Texas
Habitat: Maritime shrub thickets; also open fields, roadsides, and waste areas
Habit: Shrub
Flowering/Fruiting Period: FL July–September; FR August–October
Wetland Status: UPL
Origin: Native

Winged sumac deserves a better reputation than it has as a native plant and potential ornamental plant. Despite an aggressive tendency through root suckering, it has attractive flowering heads; eye-catching, bright red fruits; striking red fall leaf color; rapid growth in both single and multistemmed forms; and outstanding value to wildlife.

Winged sumac is a deciduous shrub that may grow to 10 feet tall (but usually half that height), with drooping branches. Once established, winged sumac expands through root sprouts and forms a dense stand that attracts wildlife seeking thick plant cover. Tan pubescence covers the thin bark of the stems and twigs. Leaves are 12 to 18 inches long and pinnately compound, usually with 11 leaflets. Its central rachis is winged, a key identifying characteristic of the species. Leaflets have mostly smooth margins; they are dark green above and glaucous green below, 1 to 4 inches long, and ½ to 1½ inches wide.

Winged sumac is dioecious, with male and female flowers on different plants; rarely do both sexes occur on the same plant. Flowers develop on dense and compact, pyramidal-shaped panicles that are 4 to 8 inches high and nearly as wide. Bees, wasps, and flies are attracted to the greenish-yellow flowers and are

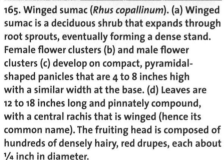

165. Winged sumac (*Rhus copallinum*). (a) Winged sumac is a deciduous shrub that expands through root sprouts, eventually forming a dense stand. Female flower clusters **(b)** and male flower clusters **(c)** develop on compact, pyramidal-shaped panicles that are 4 to 8 inches high with a similar width at the base. **(d)** Leaves are 12 to 18 inches long and pinnately compound, with a central rachis that is winged (hence its common name). The fruiting head is composed of hundreds of densely hairy, red drupes, each about ¼ inch in diameter.

responsible for pollination. The fruiting head is composed of hundreds of densely hairy, red drupes. Each drupe is about ¼ inch in diameter and contains 1 seed. The drupes turn a tawny, port brown color and then black in late fall. The fruits may persist on the plant through the winter.

In addition to providing cover, winged sumac also supplies winter food that wildlife eat after their preferred food is exhausted. Research indicates that more than 100 species of birds eat the fruits. Rabbits eat the bark and leaves; white-tailed deer eat fruits, stems, and leaves.

Winged sumac prefers well-drained, somewhat dry sandy soils and full sun. It can survive considerable drought and persists in nutrient-poor soils.

Propagation is through seeds and division of roots. Seed germination is enhanced by passage through the gut of birds or small mammals.

Winged sumac has good potential as an ornamental shrub or small tree in native garden settings. With conscientious pruning, this weedy plant tames easily! Cultivars are available commercially, and new, less aggressive cultivars are under development. The species is relatively free of pests and diseases.

The variety *copallinum* is the common form of winged sumac in the coastal Carolinas.

---

166 RUGOSA ROSE

Rosa rugosa Thunberg
Family: Rosaceae (Rose)
Other Common Names: Japanese rose, wrinkled rose, beach rose, saltspray rose
Range: USDA Hardiness Zones 2–7 (8)
Habitat: Dunes and disturbed sites
Habit: Shrub
Flowering/Fruiting Period: FL & FR June–August
Wetland Status: FACU
Origin: Exotic; native to China, Korea, and Japan

Coastal New Englanders consider rugosa rose a noxious and invasive plant. Introduced about 150 years ago, rugosa rose has expanded throughout much of the eastern half of the United States. To its credit, the plant is attractive. It possesses beautiful, dark green foliage; large magenta flowers; and cherry-tomato-sized fruits. However, the plant tends to displace native species on coastal dunes and is a major problem on New England dunes.

Rugosa rose is an erect, many-branched, somewhat coarse, fast-growing shrub that forms dense and sometimes sprawling clumps on dune systems. It produces root suckers easily and quickly and can reach heights of 4 to 5 feet. Scores of fine, gray thorns, some reaching ½ inch long, cover the stems.

The deciduous leaves are pinnately compound with 5 to 9 leaflets, and the leaves are alternately arranged on the plant stems. Leaves are fleshy and distinctively

166. Rugosa rose (*Rosa rugosa*). (a) Rugosa rose is a many-branched, dense shrub with fine, gray thorns covering the stems. Leaves are pinnately compound with 5 to 9 leaflets. (b) The magenta flowers are 2 to 3 inches across and possess numerous yellow stamens. (c) At maturity, fruits are bright red, about an inch in diameter, and possess narrowly triangular calyx lobes.

crinkled. The leaflets are elliptic or obovate, 1 to 2½ inches long, and have serrated edges. The upper leaf surfaces are glabrous, and the lower surfaces are pubescent.

The flowers develop singly or in clusters on short pedicels. Flowers are 2 to 3 inches across and possess numerous stamens. Rugosa rose blooms continuously throughout the summer. The flowers offer a slight fragrance.

The bright red fruits, called hips, are about 1 inch in diameter and contain dozens of seeds. Long, narrowly triangular calyx lobes remain on the fruit after the flower has faded.

Rugosa rose is capable of withstanding high concentrations of salt aerosols, allowing it to survive seaward of many other coastal plants. Although it will tolerate some shade, the plant prefers sandy soils with good drainage and full sun.

The plant serves as good cover for small mammals and birds. Rugosa rose attracts bees, while white-tailed deer and rabbits tend to avoid it due to its spiny stems.

Rugosa rose is useful for pedestrian control in dune areas, and coastal managers recognize it as a species of some value in dune stabilization. But it must be constantly monitored for aggressive tendencies bordering on invasive!

Propagate the plant through seeds, plant division, and cuttings. It transplants easily but requires a large space at maturity. Seeds have a dormancy requirement that can be satisfied by sowing seeds in the fall for spring germination. It works well as a single specimen plant or a hedgerow.

Leaves have been used as a mild laxative. Rose oil derived from the plant has uses as an antiseptic and a perfume.

167. Dwarf palmetto (*Sabal minor*). (a) Dwarf   a
palmetto grows no more than 6 to 7 feet tall.
It has blue-green, fan-shaped evergreen leaves.

167 DWARF PALMETTO

Sabal minor (Jacquin) Persoon
Family: Arecaceae (Palm)
Other Common Names: Dwarf palm, bush palmetto, scrub palmetto
Range: Coastal plain: North Carolina south to Florida and west to Texas
Habitat: Maritime forests; also bottomland and swamp forests
Habit: Shrub
Flowering/Fruiting Period: FL May–July; FR September–November
Wetland Status: FACW
Origin: Native

Dwarf palmetto, a close relative of cabbage palmetto, is the hardiest native palm growing along the East Coast of the United States. Common as far north as northern North Carolina, this species of fan palm is at home in both maritime forests and a number of low-lying plant communities in the southeast Atlantic and Gulf coastal plain.

Four to 10 blue-green, fan-shaped evergreen leaves ranging from 1 to 5 feet in diameter arise from an underground stem. The low-growing plant rarely reaches more than 6 to 7 feet high. The short, 1- to 2-inch midrib clearly differentiates dwarf palmetto from young cabbage palmettos that have much longer, more prominent midribs. The smooth petiole, about 24 inches

SHRUBS

b 167. Dwarf palmetto (*Sabal minor*). (b) Dozens of small, white flowers line erect panicles. (c) Flowers are ⅛ to ¼ inch across with 3 white petals. Stamens are prominent. (d) The drupes are ¼ to ½ inch in diameter and contain a single seed. Fruits mature to dark blue to black. (e) A key identifying element is the presence of a short midrib (1 to 2 inches) that is easy to observe on the bottom (back) side of the leaf.

long, distinguishes dwarf palmetto from a related species—saw palmetto (*Serenoa repens*)—which has rows of sharp, spiny teeth along the length of its petiole.

Standing above the tallest leaves, the flowers of dwarf palmetto cluster on large, erect panicles. Each of the dozens of ⅛- to ¼-inch-diameter flowers displays 3 white petals. The fruits are dark blue to black drupes that are ½ inch in diameter and contain a single seed. The increasing weight of the fruits as they mature often causes the entire inflorescence to gracefully arch over and touch the ground. The seeds often persist on the plant into the winter.

Dwarf palmetto grows best in partial shade. The plant is tolerant of salt aerosols and short-term drought, and it can survive short freezes down to about –10°F. Mature plants survive these conditions better than

seedlings and young plants. Associated species include black gum and Carolina red maple.

Birds and small mammals, such as mockingbirds, robins, raccoons, and squirrels, feed on ripe fruits.

Propagation of this species is through seeds sown immediately after they mature. Collect seeds from the wild in early fall. Plants from seeds grow slowly, forming sizable taproots before many leaves develop. Dwarf palmetto makes an interesting addition to a native plant garden. Make room for them, though; they occupy a large space at maturity! Nursery-grown stock is increasingly available.

168 COMMON ELDERBERRY

Sambucus canadensis Linnaeus
Family: Adoxaceae (Moschatel)
Other Common Names: American black

elderberry, American elder, sweet elder, black-berried elder

Range: North America east of the Rocky Mountains

Habitat: Edges of maritime shrub thickets and maritime forests; also fields and roadsides

Habit: Shrub

Flowering/Fruiting Period: FL April–July; FR July–August

Wetland Status: FACW

Origin: Native

Common elderberry is a versatile and practical plant with a rich history of human use. You can eat the berries dried, raw, or cooked, and most people associate the plant with wine, jam, syrup, or pie. These uses represent just a few of the products derived from the plant. Hollowed-out common elderberry stems make crude whistles, and the fruits are useful as a dye in basketry. An interesting but nonintuitive use is to dip flower clusters in batter and deep-fry them. I know they do this in Maine! Common elderberry is also an important food and medicinal plant for Native Americans. Bark, flowers, and fruits all have medicinal properties. **Caution:** The leaves and unripe fruits exhibit some toxicity.

Common elderberry is a dense, multistemmed shrub that grows to a height of 4 to 12 feet. The bark is thin and grayish brown. Corky lenticels cover the stems, which tend to bend outward from the center of the plant in a gentle arc. A rapidly growing plant, common elderberry has stems that are somewhat weak and brittle and often arise as suckers from the roots. Most of the aboveground plant dies back in winter.

Leaves are pinnately compound, bright green above, and pale green below. Leaflets are ovate to oblong, deciduous, and oppositely arranged on the stems. The leaves range from 6 to 14 inches long.

a

b

c

168. Common elderberry (*Sambucus canadensis*). (a) A dense, multistemmed shrub, common elderberry has leaves that are thin, pinnately compound, bright green above, and pale green below. (b) The inflorescence is a flat-topped cyme with dozens of white to cream-colored, ¼-inch, 5-petaled flowers. (c) Fruits are ¼ inch in diameter, fleshy, and dark purple, containing 3 to 5 seeds.

They have 5 to 9 serrated leaflets, each 2 to 4 inches long and 1 to 2 inches wide.

The inflorescence is a flat-topped cyme ranging from 2 to 8 inches across. Each cyme has dozens of white to cream-colored flowers with a delectable fragrance. Flowers are about ¼ inch across with 5 corolla lobes. The flowers attract a variety of bees, flies, and beetles that serve as pollinators.

Fruits are drupes about ¼ inch in diameter and turn from green and red early in the season to dark purple at maturity. Each contains 3 to 5 small seeds. Common elderberry usually produces a large seed crop each year. A hard seed coat helps the seeds remain viable for a dozen or more years in the soil.

Common elderberry prefers moist, seasonally wet to well-drained sites in full sun, but it will tolerate light shade. It is moderately drought tolerant.

Common elderberry is an outstanding wildlife plant. Birds and small mammals are efficient seed dispersers. White-tailed deer graze on common elderberry twigs, foliage, and fruits; rabbits graze on stems and bark. The fruits and seeds provide food for a score of songbirds and ground birds, and the plant also supplies cover and nesting sites for several species of birds and small mammals.

Sow seeds in the fall for spring germination or stratify them in the fall and plant in the spring. Prepare cuttings in winter or early spring; however, the success rate for cuttings is low.

The species is generally well behaved but appears unkempt without a touch of pruning. Common elderberry tends to self-seed into the environment.

Common elderberry is available from commercial sources. Cultivars such as *Aurea* (red berries), *Maxima* (large flower clusters), and *York* (large fruits) provide a great visual display from late spring through summer.

169 SAW PALMETTO

Serenoa repens (Bartram) Small
Family: Arecaceae (Palm)
Other Common Name: American dwarf palm tree
Range: Central South Carolina south to Florida and west to Louisiana
Habitat: Dunes and maritime forests; also pine flatwoods
Habit: Shrub
Flowering/Fruiting Period: FL May–July; FR October–November
Wetland Status: FACU
Origin: Native

A relative of the cabbage palmetto and one of the most distinctive palms in the United States, saw palmetto thrives naturally as far north as the southernmost coastal counties of South Carolina. Individual plants may spread over an area 20 feet in diameter.

Saw palmetto usually grows to a height of 3 to 7 feet but may occasionally reach a treelike height of 10 feet under ideal growing conditions. Composed of much-branched, horizontal stems, this shrub creeps along the ground and forms a dense, sometimes almost impenetrable, uninviting tangle of vegetation, including current-year leaves and an accumulation of hard, stiff, decay-resistant foliage from previous years.

The nearly circular leaves are yellowish- to bluish-green, alternately arranged on the stem, and 2 to 3 feet in diameter. Each tough, hard leaf is palmately compound and fan shaped. The plant adds 3 to 7 leaves each year at each node. Leaf petioles may be up to 3 feet long and have strongly serrated edges, a feature that distinguishes saw palmetto from a young cabbage palmetto or the dwarf palmetto. Another important distinguishing feature of this species is the small triangular hastula found on both sides of the leaf.

Flowers of saw palmetto are fragrant, yellowish-white or creamy white, and

a

b

c

d

169. Saw palmetto (*Serenoa repens*). (a) Saw palmetto produces a dense tangle of leaves and stems up to 20 feet in diameter and 3 to 7 feet tall. It may create a near monoculture in some environments. (b) Petioles of the fan-shaped leaves may be 3 feet long and possess serrated edges. The small triangular hastula (brown tissue) is a distinguishing characteristic feature of this species. (c) Hundreds of white flowers are produced by each plant. (d) Ovate fruits are about ¾ inch long and black at maturity.

develop on a large panicle up to 3 feet long. The flowers are ⅛ to ¼ inch in diameter and have 3 sepals and 3 petals. Flowers are abundant in some years and virtually nonexistent in other years. Bees that pollinate these flowers exclusively make a distinctive, high-quality honey. Fruits of saw palmetto are black, ovate drupes approximately ¾ inch in diameter.

Saw palmetto grows well in full sun and tolerates partial shade. The plant can endure high soil salinity, drought, and nutrient-poor, sandy soils.

Birds, white-tailed deer, opossums, raccoons, and foxes eat the seeds of saw palmetto.

Seeds may not germinate for up to 6 months after they are shed, and young plants grow slowly. Saw palmetto is almost impossible to transplant successfully. Saw palmetto frequently grows in environments prone to recurrent fires. Its trunk is highly resistant to fire, and following a light fire, the plant resprouts quickly.

The seeds are a source of an herbal medicine reputed to reduce swelling of the prostate gland and to treat baldness. Cultivars such as *Silver saw palmetto* are available commercially.

---

170 RATTLEBOX

Sesbania punicea (Cavanilles) Bentham
Family: Fabaceae (Legume)
Other Common Names: Spanish gold, scarlet wisteria, false poinciana, purple sesbane
Range: USDA Hardiness Zones 6–9; Virginia south to Florida and west to Texas; also California
Habitat: Edges of coastal wetlands, marshes, ponds, and watercourses
Habit: Shrub
Flowering/Fruiting Period: FL June– October; FR August–November
Wetland Status: FAC
Origin: Exotic; native to Argentina, Brazil, Paraguay, and Uruguay
Not recommended for planting; instead, remove where already growing.

Homeowners and landscapers recognized rattlebox as a classy ornamental shrub, with its attractive, bright flower clusters; distinctive and persistent fruits; and unusual, dark green leaves. Well, forget it! Rattlebox defies control and consistently and aggressively escapes from cultivation, to the considerable detriment of nearby native plants.

Rattlebox leaves are pinnately

a 170. Rattlebox (*Sesbania punicea*). (a) A cluster of rattlebox plants is growing in a disturbed area, a common habitat for this species. (b) Bright reddish-orange, beanlike flowers develop in pendulous clusters. (c) Four to 10 seeds "rattle" in dried pods. This feature gives the plant its common name.

compound, deciduous, alternately arranged on the stems, and range from 5 to 7 inches long. The shrub routinely reaches a height of 8 feet and occasionally higher. It usually forms dense, nearly impenetrable thickets. Bark is gray to reddish-brown and covered with conspicuous horizontal lenticels. Rattlebox leaves have 6 to 20 pairs of 1-inch, elliptical, smooth-margined leaflets. The leaflets are dark green above and pale green below.

Flower clusters are pendulous and up to 10 inches long. The individual beanlike flowers are ½ to 1 inch across and bright reddish-orange to reddish-purple. Fruits are dark brown, conspicuously 4-winged pods borne on a ½-inch peduncle; they are 3 to 4 inches long and pointed at the end. Pods persist into the winter and contain 4 to 10 seeds that are released when the dried pod breaks apart. Loosely held seeds "rattle" in the pod when shaken by the wind.

Ecologically, rattlebox prefers full sun and moist to wet locations. Its densest growth occurs along the edge of freshwater ponds, marshes, and watercourses.

Rattlebox has little food value for wildlife. All parts of the plant, especially the seeds, are poisonous to birds and mammals, including livestock. The active compounds are saponin glycosides, which cause nausea, vomiting, abdominal pain, diarrhea, and on rare occasions, death.

The plant is root hardy and can survive hard freezes but not sustained freezing temperatures. This probably limits its distribution in North America.

In legacy literature, rattlebox is referred to as *Daubentonia punicea*.

171 SALTCEDAR

Tamarix ramosissima Ledebour
Family: Tamaricaceae (Tamarisk)
Other Common Names: Tamarisk, tamarix
Range: Coastal: Virginia south to Georgia

Habitat: Dunes, edges of brackish and salt marshes; also waste areas
Habit: Shrub (tree)
Flowering/Fruiting Period: FL April–May; FR June–July
Wetland Status: FACW
Origin: Exotic; native to southern Europe, northern Africa, and eastern Asia
Not recommended for planting; instead, remove where already growing.

Fast-growing saltcedar was enthusiastically introduced into the United States as an ornamental in the

a

171. Saltcedar (*Tamarix ramosissima*). (a) Saltcedar grows to a height of 15 to 25 feet with a spread of about 10 feet. Branches are characteristically slender and drooping with bluish, gray-green, scalelike leaves.

b

171. Saltcedar (*Tamarix ramosissima*). (b) Two-inch-long racemes of pink flowers are produced near the ends of branches.

early 1820s and sometime later was used as a windbreak tree and soil stabilizer along streambanks. Saltcedar and its close relatives quickly became established beyond cultivation, and they have become a significantly noxious and invasive species throughout the arid Southwest and in southern coastal environments. Saltcedar represents only one of several species of *Tamarix* introduced into the coastal Carolinas.

Saltcedar is relatively short lived, growing to a height of 15 to 25 feet with a spread of 10 feet or more. The abundant, highly branched, slender, drooping stems possess bluish, gray-green, scalelike deciduous leaves. From a distance, the plant resembles our native coastal red cedar. Saltcedar leaves possess salt glands; when growing in saline environments, these glands exude salts.

Flowering begins within 1 or 2 years after germinating. In the spring, saltcedar produces abundant, 2-inch-long racemes of pink flowers at the ends of branches. Wind and water distribute the tiny,

reddish-brown seeds shed from the plant continuously throughout the summer.

Propagation is by seed and vegetative regrowth. Seeds have no dormancy period. A single plant reportedly can produce thousands of seeds per year.

The plant prefers well-drained, sandy soils and full sun. It grows well in saline soils and can tolerate some drought. It survives in a variety of habitats.

Once established, the deep taproot of this phreatophyte allows the plant to persist through significant droughts, and it easily outcompetes native plants for water, sunlight, and nutrients. It is highly salt resistant and grows well in moist, saline coastal environments.

The plant is of little use to wildlife; animals neither eat the seeds nor browse the plant.

We find saltcedar infrequently in coastal North Carolina and South Carolina, but without continuous monitoring and control, the plant could quickly overrun additional sites, since it is especially invasive in disturbed habitats. Mechanical control by cutting the tree followed by removal of the stump appears effective; however, take care to avoid shredding branches and limbs, since this practice can lead to its reestablishment from stem fragments. Avoid planting this and any other saltcedar species or varieties!

172 SPARKLEBERRY

Vaccinium arboreum Marshall
Family: Ericaceae (Blueberry)
Other Common Names: Farkleberry, huckleberry
Range: Virginia west to Indiana and Kansas, south to Texas and Florida
Habitat: Maritime forest; also open woods
Habit: Shrub
Flowering/Fruiting Period: FL April–June; FR September–October

a

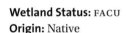

b

c

172. Sparkleberry (*Vaccinium arboreum*).
(a) Leaves are ovate to elliptical, dark green,
1 to 2 inches long, and ½ to 1½ inches wide.
(b) The bell-shaped, white flowers are nearly
¼ inch broad. They are produced on a panicle
with a small, green bract at the base of each
petiole. (c) Mottled bark is smooth and
exfoliates in strips.

Wetland Status: FACU
Origin: Native

Every coastal home needs a sparkleberry!
The single-trunked shrub is manageable
in size; has abundant, attractive flowers;
produces persistent fruits eaten by wildlife;
and serves as a home to butterfly larvae.
To top it all off, sparkleberry is drought
tolerant! What more could you ask for in
a native plant destined to be a landscape
plant?

The much-branched, often-leaning,
nearly evergreen shrub grows from 8 to
15 feet tall and produces an appealing,
rounded crown. Some old specimens may
reach tree size at 25 or 30 feet tall. The
smooth, thin, colorful, crooked trunk has
flaking bark that reveals grays, browns, and
oranges as it shreds.

The ovate to elliptical, leathery leaves
are alternately arranged, 1 to 2 inches
long, and ½ to 1½ inches wide. The upper
surfaces of the leaves are dark green and
shiny, while the lower surfaces are pale
green. Occasionally, the leaves are minutely
serrate. Leaves turn reddish in the fall.

Sparkleberry produces clusters of white,
bell-shaped flowers on drooping racemes
or panicles. These flowers develop on
2-year-old branches. Each flower is globe
shaped with 5 lobes on the fused petals.
The dainty flowers grow up to ½ inch long
and ¼ to ⅜ inch across. Flower production
varies somewhat from year to year. Dry,
hard, BB-sized berries mature in late
summer and often persist into the winter.
The shiny, black fruits contain about 10
kidney-shaped seeds.

Sparkleberry flowers are pollinated by bees seeking the nectar and pollen. Birds and mammals eat the berries. Robins, bluebirds, catbirds, and bluejays enjoy the fruits and aid in seed dispersal. White-tailed deer occasionally browse the plant, and foxes, opossums, and raccoons relish the berries. The plant is attractive to butterflies and is larval host of Henry's elfin (*Callophrys henrici*) and striped hairstreak (*Satyrium liparops*).

Sparkleberry prefers partial shade but will grow fine in full sun. It prefers dry, sandy soils. It grows in the maritime forest with trees such as live oak, slash pine, and loblolly pine.

Propagate sparkleberry through seeds and cuttings from young wood. Plants are also commercially available; that's a good thing, since sparkleberry does not transplant well. Native Americans apparently used a root extract of the plant as a treatment for diarrhea.

173 BEACH VITEX

Vitex rotundifolia Linnaeus f.
Family: Lamiaceae (Mint)
Other Common Names: Chaste tree, round-leaf chaste tree, roundleaf vitex
Range: Cape Lookout, N.C., to Charleston, S.C.; Florida, Alabama
Habitat: Dunes, dune swales, and maritime grasslands
Habit: Shrub
Flowering/Fruiting Period: FL May–September; FR June–December
Wetland Status: Not designated
Origin: Exotic; native to the Pacific Rim (Korea and Japan to Malaysia, Indonesia, and Australia)
Not recommended for planting; instead, remove where already growing.

Beach vitex was imported to serve as an attractive ornamental that could also function as a shoreline stabilizer. But its introduction almost turned into an

173. Beach vitex (*Vitex rotundifolia*). (a) Beach vitex is a prostrate, rambling, woody-stemmed shrub. Leaves are oval shaped, about 2 inches by 1½ inches, and bluish-green on the upper surfaces. (b) Zygomorphic flowers are blue to purple, an inch long, and clustered in the leaf axils. (c) Fruits are spherical, ¼ inch in diameter, and purple or black when ripe.

ecological disaster; horticulturalists refer to the plant as "kudzu of the beach." Less than 20 years after its introduction, this species has proven to be aggressive. Within 1 or 2 growing seasons it can easily outcompete all plants, including sea oats, American beachgrass, and seaside panicum, creating a monoculture on the dunes it inhabits.

Beach vitex is a prostrate, rambling shrub with woody stems ranging from 1 to 4 feet high. Individual plants can grow in patches up to 12 feet in diameter. Stems root at the nodes, and individual runners are reported to be up to 60 feet long.

The deciduous leaves are oval shaped, approximately 2 inches by 1½ inches, and green to bluish-green on top and glaucous green on the underside. Leaves have a strong scent when crushed.

Attractive zygomorphic flowers are borne on short inflorescences arising in the axils of the leaves closest to the terminal end of the upright stems. The fragrant, bluish to purple flowers are 1 inch across. Fruits are round, ¼ inch in diameter, and purple or black when ripe. Beach vitex produces prodigious quantities of seeds. Waves and currents distribute the buoyant seeds to nearby beach environments. Wind and water also easily transport fragments of beach vitex to adjacent beaches, where they quickly establish new colonies.

Beach vitex exhibits high salt and drought tolerance; the plant requires full sun and prefers well-drained, sandy soils.

Coastal managers report that an extensive covering of beach vitex compromises or reduces suitable sea turtle nesting habitat. The threat of this plant to native vegetation on coastal dunes has been reduced by the aggressive action of the Carolinas Beach Vitex Task Force, and the plant has been nearly extirpated locally.

174 SPANISH DAGGER

Yucca aloifolia Linnaeus
Family: Agavaceae (Agave)
Other Common Names: Spanish bayonet, palm lily
Range: North Carolina south to Florida and west to Louisiana
Habitat: Dunes, dune swales, maritime grasslands, and edges of maritime shrub thickets
Habit: Shrub
Flowering/Fruiting Period: FL June–July; FR October–December
Wetland Status: UPL
Origin: Native

174. Spanish dagger (*Yucca aloifolia*). (a) Spanish dagger forms colonies of 3- to 4-foot-high plants. Stems are surrounded by 1- to 2-foot-long leaves, each tapering to a stout, sharp point. (b) Flowers are globose and pendant with creamy white, nearly identical sepals and petals. (c) Fruits are brown and leathery, about 3 inches long.

Spanish dagger stands as a tall sentinel plant overseeing the grasses and forbs of coastal Carolina dunes and swales. The softly rounded, showy, 3- to 4-foot spike of fragrant, creamy white flowers splashed with red or purple contrasts dramatically with the manifold sharp, pointed, swordlike leaves that make up the body of the plant. Often, Spanish dagger forms colonies of plants—tall and short, branched and unbranched.

The shrub begins growth as a ground-level rosette of leaves; over time, the plant extends skyward a few inches each year, creating a thick, fleshy trunk. Numerous leaves surround each branch; the leaves are 1 to 2 feet long and 2 inches wide, tapering to a stout, sharp point. The leaf margins are serrated like a fine saw; you can check this characteristic by carefully running your hand along the edges of the leaves.

Large, cone-shaped panicles hold dozens of individual flowers. The flowers sport 3 petals and 3 sepals that are virtually identical in size and shape. The flowers are globose, pendant, and 2 to 3 inches long by 1 inch wide. The brown, leathery fruits are about 3 inches long. Seeds are ovate, shiny, black, thin, and about ¼ inch in diameter. The seeds are stacked within the fruit like rolls of coins.

Spanish dagger is tolerant of salt aerosols and drought, and it grows best in full sun and nutrient-poor, sandy soils. Propagate Spanish dagger from seeds. In addition, stem cuttings and offsets (small suckers) from the parent plant are easy to collect and have a high success rate.

Seeds are often missing from mature seedpods, suggesting that insects probably feed on the seeds as they mature. Spanish dagger provides modest cover for small mammals and reptiles.

The plant is an excellent accent plant in coastal Carolina landscapes. Since the leaves are stiff and pointed, the plant is useful in establishing natural protective borders or barriers.

Mound-lily yucca (*Yucca gloriosa*) is similar to Spanish dagger and found in similar habitats. Mound-lily yucca is distinguished from Spanish dagger by the presence of more flexible, swordlike leaves with smooth edges and unbranched stems.

175 BEARGRASS

Yucca filamentosa Linnaeus
Family: Agavaceae (Agave)
Other Common Names: Adam's needle yucca, curly leaf yucca, silkgrass, spoonleaf yucca
Range: New Jersey south to Florida and west to Louisiana and Texas (naturalized range is more extensive)
Habitat: Dunes and maritime grasslands; also vacant lots and waste ground
Habit: Shrub (subshrub)
Flowering/Fruiting Period: FL May–June; FR September–October
Wetland Status: UPL
Origin: Native

175. Beargrass (*Yucca filamentosa*). (a) Beargrass is 3 feet tall with gracefully drooping flowers.

b

d

c

175. Beargrass (*Yucca filamentosa*). (b) The center of the plant shows characteristic "filaments" produced as the leaf margins shred. (c) Flowers include 6 white tepals. (d) Three-sectioned pods hold stacks of jet black, coin-shaped seeds.

One of the alternate common names of beargrass, Adam's needle yucca, alludes to the plant's distinctive characteristics: long, thin, spine-tipped leaves with curly, fibrous strands fraying along leaf margins. It reminds one of needles and thread. Beargrass is one of three yucca species found along the Carolinas coast; however, it is the only one that forms a rosette of lanceolate leaves at or near ground level. It also stands out by rarely growing more than 1 foot above the soil surface—except when it is in flower.

SHRUBS

The medium green, leathery leaves are slightly inrolled and flexible, yet they exhibit stiff, stout spines at each leaf tip. Young plants may have leaves that are 4 to 6 inches long, while mature plants have leaves up to 20 to 30 inches long and 2 to 4 inches wide. While locally common on coastal dunes, the deep taproot of beargrass does little to bind dune sands.

During May and June, a 3- to 6-foot-tall panicle of bell-shaped flowers adorns the plant for several weeks. The creamy white to greenish-white flowers are composed of sepals and petals of similar shape and size, 1 to 2 inches long and 1 inch wide. Two to 3-inch-long green fruits turn brown before releasing dozens of dull, black, pancake-shaped seeds "stacked" inside the 3 compartments of each fruit.

Propagate beargrass from seeds, root segments, and division of large plants. Scientists report that the plant is especially tolerant of urban environments and the accompanying high heat, drought, trampling, and sun exposure. Beargrass is tolerant of salt aerosols and has few insect pests.

The yucca moth (*Tegeticula* sp.) has a mutualistic relationship with beargrass. First, the moth pollinates beargrass, and then the seeds provide a food source for yucca moth larvae. The yucca moth lays her eggs inside the ovary of the flower before pollinating the stigma, assuring that sufficient seeds will develop to nourish the offspring.

Trees

176 CAROLINA RED MAPLE

Acer rubrum Linnaeus

Family: Sapindaceae (Soapberry)

Other Common Names: Swamp maple, soft maple, scarlet maple, water maple

Range: Eastern North America from Newfoundland to Manitoba, Canada; south and west to Florida and Texas

Habitat: Edges of tidal and nontidal freshwater swamps and marshes, maritime forests; also bottomland, upland, and riverine forests

Habit: Tree

Flowering/Fruiting Period: FL January–March; FR February–June

Wetland Status: FAC

Origin: Native

One of the first indications that springtime is not far away is the sight of the bright red flowers of Carolina red maple. Flowering time for Carolina red maple in the coastal Carolinas is long before the first leaves appear on it or any other deciduous species.

The Carolina red maple is a medium-sized tree of great ecological and geographic range, including coastal environments. It is common throughout the eastern United States, from sea level to an elevation of 3,000 feet, from swamps to rocky uplands, and in open sun and deep shade. In the coastal Carolinas, Carolina red maple regularly occurs in wet habitats, where it is tolerant of occasional flooding and waterlogged soils. Although the tree can grow to 60 feet high with an equal spread, Carolina red maples growing in maritime forests typically remain small trees, reaching about 30 feet.

The bark of young trees is smooth and light gray; older trunks are furrowed and dark gray, almost black. The leaves possess 3 shallow lobes, bright green upper surfaces, and gray-green undersides. Leaves are up to 4 inches long and 5 inches wide with red petioles. Buds and young twigs are reddish.

176. Carolina red maple (*Acer rubrum*). (a) Bright red petioles bear 3-lobed leaves. (b) Female flowers are identified by the presence of 2 large stigmas. (c) Each male flower in a cluster possesses numerous stamens.

Clustered on young twigs, separate male and female flowers may occur on the same tree or on separate trees. Wind and insects pollinate the flowers.

The fruit is a ½- to 1-inch, bright red, 2-winged samara. The samaras are wind dispersed in early summer. Seeds are often produced in great quantities and germinate immediately after they are shed.

Carolina red maple takes advantage of openings in coastal forests disturbed by hurricanes or nor'easters. Look for seedlings to appear in these openings within a year or two of a storm.

White-tailed deer graze the foliage; the tree provides nest cavities and roosting sites for birds. It also serves as an early-season nectar source for native bees.

Carolina red maple leaves turn a vivid and attractive red or red-orange in the fall. *Autumn Flame* and *Red Sunset* are two examples of the many cultivars developed for the horticulture market.

The variety *trilobum* is the most common form of Carolina red maple in the coastal Carolinas.

177 RED BUCKEYE

Aesculus pavia Linnaeus
Family: Sapindaceae (Soapberry)
Other Common Names: Scarlet buckeye, firecracker plant
Range: Virginia west to Illinois and southwest to Texas and east to Florida
Habitat: Maritime forests and swamp forests
Habit: Tree (shrub)
Flowering/Fruiting Period: FL April–May; FR July–August
Wetland Status: FACU
Origin: Native

Reportedly pollinated by ruby-throated hummingbirds, red buckeye is one of the first red flowers to appear in spring, and it possibly sustains hummingbirds until additional nectar-bearing plants appear.

176. Carolina red maple (*Acer rubrum*). (d) Paired, red, winged samaras comprise the fruit. (e) Dark, pronounced fissures split the light gray bark as the tree matures.

a

c

b

d

177. Red buckeye (*Aesculus pavia*). (a) Terminal flower clusters develop in spring after the leaves expand. (b) Flowers are tubular and zygomorphic. (c) Style and stamens extend beyond the petals. (d) Each large fruit contains 1 to 3 chestnut-sized seeds.

Red buckeye is a shrub or small tree with a single or multiple grayish-brown stems ranging from 4 to 15 feet tall, occasionally reaching 20 feet, and spreading 6 to 10 feet across. It has a coarse texture and an open branching pattern. Red buckeye produces branches along the trunk beginning close to the ground, and these persist throughout the plant's relatively short lifespan.

Leaves are palmately compound with 5 (and occasionally 7) sessile, oblong or lanceolate leaflets. Leaflets are present on 4- to 6-inch petioles and are typically 5 to 10 inches across. Leaves are dark green, oppositely arranged, shiny, serrated, and slightly pubescent below. Red buckeye drops its leaves in late summer with only a slight yellowish-brown color change.

Flowering begins in early spring, just after the leaves expand. The showy, tubular flowers are bright red or orange-red and form a cone-shaped terminal raceme. Flowers are zygomorphic, with the style and stamens exserted just beyond the petals. Individual flowers are 1 to 1½ inches long.

The fruit is a nearly smooth, light tan, thin-walled globular capsule that is 1 to 1½ inches in diameter. Each capsule contains from 1 to 3 seeds similar in shape and color to a chestnut. In the fall, the capsule splits open, releasing the large seeds. The seeds can germinate immediately after falling to the ground.

Red buckeye typically grows near forested streams but also occurs within and at the edge of maritime forests in the coastal Carolinas.

The seeds are poisonous and not eaten by wildlife.

Red buckeye grows best and produces more flowers and fruits in full sun; however, it tolerates some shade and brief flooding. While preferring moist, well-drained, sandy soils, red buckeye is modestly drought tolerant. It is moderately salt-aerosol tolerant.

The fast-growing tree is available commercially. Several cultivars have been developed, including *Humilis*, a low-growing variety with small flowers, and *Atrosanguinea*, a variety with deep red flowers. Red buckeye grows easily in a natural garden and flowers when only 2 to 3 years old.

The variety *pavia* is the common form of red buckeye in the coastal region from southern North Carolina to Florida and west to Texas.

---

178 SOUTH AMERICAN JELLY PALM

Butia odorata (Barbosa Rodrigues) Noblick
Family: Arecaceae (Palm)
Other Common Names: Pindo palm, Brazilian butia
Range: USDA Hardiness Zones 8–11
Habitat: Ornamental
Habit: Tree
Flowering/Fruiting Period: FL May–June; FR July–August
Wetland Status: Not designated

Origin: Exotic; native to Argentina, Uruguay, and southern Brazil

The most cold-hardy of all palms planted along the southeastern United States coast, South American jelly palm is easily recognized as a short, stocky cousin of the tall, graceful cabbage palmetto. The South American jelly palm is originally from the grasslands and savannas of South America and only reaches a height of 15 feet, even after decades of growth. South American jelly palm is a magnificently sculpted plant with a dome-shaped canopy of bluish-green to silvery fronds that curve up and out in a graceful deliquescent pattern.

a

b

178. South American jelly palm (*Butia odorata*). (a) This cold-hardy, nonnative plant grows up to 15 feet high in coastal settings. (b) Separate male and female flowering stalks produce spectacular displays, with hundreds of individual white flowers.

c

d

178. South American jelly palm (*Butia odorata*).
(c) Male flowers are bright and showy. (d) The
soft, fleshy fruits are bright orange when mature.

The trunk of mature specimens is up to 18 inches in diameter at the ground level. Typically, the trunk appears cone shaped, narrowing toward the top of the plant. South American jelly palm has persistent leaf bases attached to its trunk throughout its life. Its leaves are pinnately compound and 4 to 8 feet long, with 80 to 150 leaflets. The leaves are coarse, with long spines in a line along the leaf petioles.

The species is monoecious, with separate male and female flowers on a single plant. The magnificent flowering stalk may have 50 to 100 branches, each lined with small, white flowers. Each flower has 3 sepals and 3 petals. Male flowers have 6 stamens. The flowers are about ¼ inch across and develop in a spectacular and unusual woody spathe that often persists after flowering and fruiting are complete. The South American jelly palm fruit is 1 to 1½ inches in diameter, bright orange or orange-yellow, and contains 1 large seed. Produced in huge quantities, the fruits are often seen scattered around the base of the plant after they mature and dehisce in midsummer.

South American jelly palm is drought resistant and tolerant of salt aerosols. The plant grows well in the full sun of coastal dunes, but it will survive in light shade. Well-drained, sandy soils are the most suitable for the plant. South American jelly palm survives hurricane-force winds well; the flexible leaves and short trunk resist breakage.

The fruits are attractive to squirrels and other small mammals.

The edible fruits look and taste like apricots; however, the juicy pulp tends to be stringy and fibrous. The fruits do make good jams and jellies. Propagate South American jelly palm by planting seeds, but understand that they take months to germinate.

South American jelly palm is available in most local nurseries. It is a favorite of coastal landscapers, given its lack of diseases and other pests, the ease in growing the plant, and its availability. Its graceful shape also makes it a great specimen tree. The species shows no tendency to be aggressive or invasive. The major drawback to the plant is that it creates significant litter of leaves and fruits throughout the year.

179 COASTAL AMERICAN HORNBEAM

Carpinus caroliniana Walter
Family: Betulaceae (Birch)
Other Common Names: Ironwood, musclewood, muscle beech, blue beech
Range: Maine south to Florida and west to Texas and Illinois
Habitat: Maritime forests; also bottomland hardwood and streambank forests
Habit: Tree
Flowering/Fruiting Period: FL March–April; FR August–October

179. Coastal American hornbeam (*Carpinus caroliniana*). (a) Coastal American hornbeam leaves are alternately arranged on the stem and have doubly serrate margins. (b) Male flowers develop on 1- to 2½-inch catkins. A female flower cluster is visible at the top right. (c) The pendant fruit has leafy bracts surrounding each seed. (d) The bark is smooth with prominent longitudinal ridges. It is typically encrusted with lichens.

Wetland Status: FAC
Origin: Native

Whether possessing a single or a multistemmed trunk, coastal American hornbeam is easy to identify any time of the year. This small, deciduous, understory tree of the coastal Carolinas maritime forest has a gray or blue-gray trunk that is smooth with prominent longitudinal ridges or flutes resembling rippled arm or leg muscles.

Coastal American hornbeam grows to a height of 20 to 30 feet and possesses a wide, flat-topped crown. The 2- to 5-inch-long ovate leaves have doubly serrated margins and are arranged alternately along the stems. The leaves are glabrous on the upper side and pubescent on the underside. They turn yellow and orange in the fall.

Coastal American hornbeam is monoecious, with separate male and female flowers on the same plant. Male catkins are yellowish-green and 1 to 2½ inches long, while female catkins are similar in color but only ½ to 1 inch long. Both flowers and new leaves of the season appear at about the same time in the spring. Fruits are ribbed nutlets about ¼ inch long. A narrow, 3-winged, leaflike bract surrounds each fruit. Bracts are initially green but gradually turn brown as the seeds mature. Several fruits together create a distinctive pendulous cluster, 1 to 4 inches long.

Rabbits and white-tailed deer feed on the leaves and twigs. Birds feed on the nutlets and are responsible for their dissemination. Fruit production is uneven, with large crops occurring every 3 to 5 years.

Seeds and cuttings propagate coastal American hornbeam. Seeds require stratification prior to germination, and cuttings are rather hard to root. Transplantation is difficult and usually unsuccessful because coastal American hornbeam produces a deep taproot. Specialized nurseries often carry specimens of this species. Horticultural specialists report few insect or disease problems.

The slow-growing coastal American hornbeam prefers deep, fertile soils and full or partial sun. It is not drought tolerant and grows best in sandy soils with abundant moisture and good drainage. It is not especially tolerant of salt aerosols or soil salts and typically remains an understory tree throughout its lifetime in the maritime forest. Coastal American hornbeam is frequently associated with American holly, live oak, southern magnolia, and Carolina laurel cherry.

The small, twisted stems have little commercial value. However, craftsmen have used the wood to make tool handles, mallet heads, and similar items requiring heavy, hard, close-grained wood.

Botanists recognize two varieties of American hornbeam; the variety *caroliniana* is native to the coastal Carolinas.

---

180 WILD OLIVE

Cartrema americanum (Linnaeus) Nesom
Family: Oleaceae (Olive)
Other Common Names: American olive, devilwood, American devilwood
Range: Virginia south to Florida and west to Louisiana
Habitat: Maritime forests; also dry woods, along streams
Habit: Tree
Flowering/Fruiting Period: FL March–May; FR August—October
Wetland Status: FAC
Origin: Native

Wild olive is a plant often overlooked as a potential ornamental tree. It has notable positive attributes: dark green, evergreen leaves; unusual and fragrant flowers; and long-lasting fruits attractive to wildlife.

a

c

b

180. Wild olive (*Cartrema americanum*).
(a) A small tree, wild olive has simple, entire, leathery leaves sub-oppositely arranged on the branches. (b) Small, 4-petaled, white flowers are found on panicles in the axils of the leaves. (c) Fruits are dark blue or purplish-black, single-seeded drupes about ½ inch in diameter. (d) The bark is thin, smooth, and gray.

d

A member of the Olive family, wild olive is closely related to the olives of commerce and the exotic tea olives *Osmanthus fragrans* and *Osmanthus heterophyllus*.

Wild olive grows 10 to 25 feet high and occasionally larger, with an 8- to 15-foot spread. Slightly drooping branches characterize this slow-growing tree. The bark of wild olive is gray and smooth. Leaves are simple, entire, leathery, and sub-oppositely arranged along the branches. The undersides of the elliptic-shaped leaves are glaucous green. Leaves are 2 to 6 inches long and 1 to 1¾ inches wide, tapering at both ends.

Flowers are borne on short panicles

TREES

375

in the axils of leaves. The flowers form in late fall and slowly enlarge until they open in the spring. The 4-petaled flowers are creamy white, fragrant, and about ³⁄₁₆ inch wide. Fruits are 1-seeded, fleshy drupes that gradually turn dark blue or purplish-black in late fall. Resembling small olives, the ½-inch fruits typically remain on the tree until the following spring.

Birds and squirrels feed on the fruits; in fact, you may see a flock of robins or cedar waxwings attack a tree and strip the entire annual fruit crop within minutes.

Wild olive grows well in both partial shade and full sun. It is salt-aerosol and drought tolerant. It prefers moist but well-drained, sandy soils. Wild olive usually remains an understory tree of the maritime forest, where it is often associated with live oak and loblolly pine.

Propagate wild olive from seeds, volunteer seedlings, and cuttings. However, seed germination is erratic, and cuttings are difficult to root; so transplant volunteer seedlings for best results.

Wild olive is becoming increasingly available commercially from native plant growers and online nurseries, but it is rarely found in retail garden centers. Horticulturalists prefer it as a substitute for nonnative *Ligustrum* species. The wood is typical of olives; it is tough and difficult to split or work and has little commercial value. Just for fun, try breaking a small branch off this tree. It is virtually impossible! Wild olive's use today is limited to woodworking and small hand items.

Authors cite this species as *Osmanthus americanus* in legacy literature in the coastal Carolinas.

a

b

181. Pignut hickory (*Carya glabra*). (a) Five leaflets are typical for the pinnately compound leaves of pignut hickory. (b) Drooping triplets of catkins bear the male flowers.

181 PIGNUT HICKORY

Carya glabra (P. Miller) Sweet
Family: Juglandaceae (Walnut)
Other Common Name: Smoothbark hickory

Range: Ontario, Canada; New Hampshire west to Illinois and south to Louisiana and Florida
Habitat: Maritime forests; also upland forests
Habit: Tree
Flowering/Fruiting Period: FL March–April; FR October
Wetland Status: FACU
Origin: Native

c

d

181. Pignut hickory (*Carya glabra*). (c) Mature fruits turn dark brown or black and split along sutures. (d) The bark of young trees is smooth and gray; as trees mature, the bark transitions to dark gray and develops ridges.

Pignut hickory is a common, but not abundant, species in the coastal Carolinas that is closely related to several economically important tree species, including pecan, butternut, and black walnut. Unlike the fruits of its relatives, the meat of coastal pignut hickory tastes quite bitter and unappealing.

While usually only reaching a height of about 40 feet in maritime forests, pignut hickory can grow to 100 feet tall with a crown reaching 20 to 25 feet across under ideal conditions some distance from the coast. This deciduous-leaved tree has smooth, gray, mottled bark when young. As trees mature, the bark becomes ridged and scaly, but never shaggy. The leaves of pignut hickory are 8 to 12 inches long, pinnately compound with 5 (and occasionally 3 or 7) leaflets, and are alternately arranged on the branches. Each 3- to 6-inch-long ovate or elliptic leaflet is sharply serrated, dark green, and glabrous on the upper surface and glaucous green beneath. Often the terminal leaflet is the largest. Leaves turn bright yellow in the fall.

Pignut hickory is monoecious, with both male and female flowers present on the same tree. Typically, pignut hickory trees do not bear flowers and fruits until they reach at least 20 years of age. Male flowers are produced on distinctive drooping catkins clustered in 3s in the leaf axils of branches formed in the previous season. The wind-pollinated female flowers occur in clusters on ¼-inch-long spikes at the ends of twigs. The fruit contains a single nearly spherical nut surrounded by a thin, bright green husk. The husk turns dark brown or black at maturity and splits into several sections as it releases the nut. The nut is ¾ to 1¼ inches in diameter, light brown, and thick-shelled.

Pignut hickory grows best in full sun but can tolerate some shade. It grows well in nitrogen-poor soils. It is highly drought and somewhat salt-aerosol resistant, but its growth suffers in soils containing salts.

The nuts and bark are excellent food

for squirrels, raccoons, rabbits, and foxes. Researchers on coastal islands in the southeastern United States found that white-tailed deer and feral pigs tend to graze tender seedlings and are responsible for reducing the number of pignut hickory seedlings in maritime forests.

Propagation is by seeds that require stratification over the winter before germination takes place. Pignut hickory develops a large taproot that is hard to remove from the soil intact, making transplantation difficult.

The moderately fast-growing pignut hickory has a number of attributes that make it an excellent choice for a shade or specimen tree, including a lack of serious insect and disease pests and excellent resistance to limb breakage in high winds. When choosing a site for this species, avoid planting it in high-traffic areas, due to the large amount of debris created by the fruit drop.

The wood of pignut hickory is hard and strong, and it was once used for handles of tools, including rakes and axes. In the past, brooms were also made from narrow splits of the wood. Today, the wood of this and other hickory species is used for fuel and for smoking meats and fish.

182 SUGARBERRY

Celtis laevigata Willdenow
Family: Cannabaceae (Hops)
Other Common Names: Southern hackberry, sugar hackberry, hackberry
Range: Maryland west to Wyoming and Washington, south to California, Texas, and Florida
Habitat: Maritime forests, edges of freshwater and salt marshes; also bottomland hardwood forests
Habit: Tree
Flowering/Fruiting Period: FL April–May; FR August–October
Wetland Status: FACW

Origin: Native

Sugarberry is an uncommon tree with a narrow ecological range in the coastal environments of the Carolinas. It is closely related to elms and possesses a broad crown of spreading, slightly drooping branches. Owing to its high tolerance for salt aerosols and salts in the soil, sugarberry is a minor but consistent component of the canopy in maritime forests. The leaves with the highest exposure to salt aerosols often appear brown, curled, and burned.

a

b

182. Sugarberry (*Celtis laevigata*). (a) The characteristic broad crown is evident in this open-grown sugarberry. (b) Leaves are light green and alternately arranged. Fruits become reddish-brown as they mature.

c

d

182. Sugarberry (*Celtis laevigata*). (c) Male flowers are clustered on twigs as leaves emerge in the spring. (d) Corky protuberances develop on the bark of mature trees.

Sugarberry is a fast-growing tree reaching a maximum height of about 30 feet, but often it has a much smaller stature in the maritime forest. The bark is light gray and smooth when young. As it ages, the trunk develops large, corky warts, a key characteristic in identifying the tree. The leaves are light green, simple, and slightly serrate. They are arranged alternately on the stems. The leaves are lanceolate, 2 to 5 inches long, and 1½ inches wide, tapering to a narrow point at the apex. The leaves turn bright yellow in fall.

Sugarberry is monoecious. Inconspicuous green male flowers occur in clusters on the twigs. Solitary greenish-white female flowers, ⅛ inch across, develop on ½-inch-long pedicels. Both flower types appear just before—or concurrent with—spring leaf development. Fruits are spherical drupes, ¼ to ⅜ inch in diameter, and contain a single round seed. As they mature, the sweet, fleshy, thick-skinned fruits change from orange to reddish-brown and finally to purplish-black. They frequently persist into the winter.

Sugarberry is shade and wind tolerant but grows best in the full sun as part of the maritime forest canopy. Despite having shallow roots, sugarberry is quite drought tolerant and grows well in nutrient-poor, sandy soils. It is common in both wet and dry habitats, including the edges of salt marshes and freshwater wetlands. Typical plants associated with sugarberry include live oak, red mulberry, southern red oak, water oak, and Carolina red maple.

Small mammals, birds, and water disperse the seeds. White-tailed deer browse sugarberry after their preferred food is exhausted. Sugarberry is the caterpillar food plant for several butterflies, including hackberry emperor, question mark, mourning cloak, and American snout.

Make cuttings in the fall to propagate the plant. Seeds require stratification to enhance germination. The plant is not prone to insect attack or disease and is available from specialized nurseries. A few cultivars, including *All Seasons* and

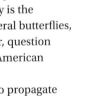

Magnifica, are available. There is little commercial use for the sugarberry wood; it is occasionally used for fence posts, furniture, plywood, and veneer.

183 FLOWERING DOGWOOD

Cornus florida Linnaeus
Family: Cornaceae (Dogwood)
Other Common Names: Dogwood, eastern flowering dogwood
Range: Maine to Michigan to Kansas, south to Texas and Florida
Habitat: Maritime forests; also upland forests
Habit: Tree
Flowering/Fruiting Period: FL March–May; FR September–October
Wetland Status: FACU
Origin: Native

The state tree of North Carolina, Virginia, and Missouri, flowering dogwood is one of the most recognizable native plants in the coastal Carolinas and throughout its range. It has magnificent white "flowers" in the spring, bright red berries in the summer, and spectacularly colorful foliage in the fall. No wonder this compact and graceful native plant is so popular. Flowering dogwood is common in maritime forests in the Carolinas—Nags Head Woods, Bald Head Island, Hunting Island, and many others.

A small, slow-growing tree, it often reaches a height of 30 feet with a similar spread. Flowering dogwood possesses single or multiple trunks with nearly horizontal branches and a rounded crown. It remains an understory tree in the maritime forest, shielded from salt aerosols by an overstory of live oak, loblolly pine, and others. The mature bark is broken into small, dark gray to black squares resembling the blocky markings on an alligator's back. Flowering dogwood leaves are oppositely arranged on branches, ovate to oval shaped, 3 to 6 inches long,

183. Flowering dogwood (*Cornus florida*). (a) Flowering structures open before the leaves reach full size. (b) Four white bracts surround the flower cluster in the center.

and 1½ to 3 inches wide. The leaves turn a beautiful red or purple in fall.

Flower buds are large and distinctive; they open before the leaf buds break. The inflorescence is composed of about 20 small, yellowish-green flowers. Four white bracts, each 1 to 2 inches across, surround the inflorescence and give the entire floral structure a 4-inch spread. Thus, the "showy" parts of the flowers are not the petals, but the petal-like bracts. The fruits are composed of an upright cluster of 2 to 6 oblong, bright red drupes, each about ½ inch long. Persisting into the winter, each fruit contains 1 or 2 elliptical seeds covered by a mealy pulp.

c

d

183. Flowering dogwood (*Cornus florida*).
(c) Fruits are oblong, bright red, fleshy drupes.
Sometimes they persist into the winter. (d) The
bark is characterized as "resembling the marking
pattern on the back of an alligator."

Flowering dogwood grows best in
moist, well-drained soils in partial shade;
however, the plant can tolerate full sun.
Excessive heat and salt in the soil or
atmosphere stress the plant; its shallow

roots prevent it from being drought
tolerant.

A number of birds and mammals,
including cedar waxwings, cardinals,
flickers, mockingbirds, robins, squirrels,
and white-tailed deer, eat the fruits.

Unfortunately, the species has been
ravaged by dogwood anthracnose (*Discula
destructiva*), a fungus that first seriously
infected flowering dogwoods in the 1970s
and has spread throughout the range of the
species.

Propagate flowering dogwood from
cuttings of young branches taken in spring,
cuttings from older wood planted during
the summer, and seeds. Dozens of cultivars
have been developed, including *Cherokee
Chief, Cloud Nine, First Lady, Pink Sachet*,
and *Royal Red*. The newest cultivars resist
canker and anthracnose.

Because of its small stature, flowering
dogwood has little commercial value.
The wood is used for specialty items such
as tool handles that require wood that is
strong, hard, and shock resistant.

184 COMMON PERSIMMON

Diospyros virginiana Linnaeus
Family: Ebenaceae (Ebony)
Other Common Names: American
    persimmon, eastern persimmon,
    possumwood
Range: Massachusetts west to Nebraska
    and south to Texas and Florida; also
    Utah and California
Habitat: Dunes, dune swales, edges of
    maritime shrub thickets, and maritime
    forests; also sandy woodlands, river
    bottoms, and abandoned fields
Habit: Tree
Flowering/Fruiting Period: FL May–June;
    FR September–October
Wetland Status: FAC
Origin: Native
Common persimmon is a member of the
Ebony wood family. Its wood is strong,

TREES

a

c

d

b

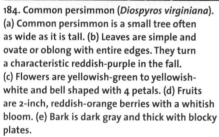

184. Common persimmon (*Diospyros virginiana*).
(a) Common persimmon is a small tree often
as wide as it is tall. (b) Leaves are simple and
ovate or oblong with entire edges. They turn
a characteristic reddish-purple in the fall.
(c) Flowers are yellowish-green to yellowish-
white and bell shaped with 4 petals. (d) Fruits
are 2-inch, reddish-orange berries with a whitish
bloom. (e) Bark is dark gray and thick with blocky
plates.

hard, smooth, and even-textured. These
traits were important when common
persimmon wood was used for textile
shuttles, golf club driver heads, and pool
cues. Today, synthetic materials have
replaced common persimmon wood
for these items. Even use of common
persimmon fruits in making cakes, cookies,
and puddings is, for the most part, just a
memory.

A small, slow-growing tree, common
persimmon ranges from 15 to 60 feet tall

e

and 20 feet across, but it rarely exceeds 30 feet in the coastal Carolinas. The bark is dark gray, thick, and blocky like a checkerboard. Leaves are simple, ovate or oblong with entire edges, and alternately arranged on the branches. The upper surfaces of the leaves are green, and the lower surfaces are light green. The leaves turn reddish-purple in fall. The somewhat leathery leaves range from 4 to 6 inches long and from 1½ to 3 inches wide.

Common persimmon is dioecious, with male and female flowers on separate trees. Female flowers are solitary, sessile, and yellowish-green to yellowish-white. The flowers look much like lily-of-the-valley flowers and appear after the tree is in full leaf. The bell-shaped flowers have 4 petals and are about 1 inch across and ¾ inch long. Male flowers occur in clusters of 2 to 3 and are similar in shape and color to female flowers but smaller, about ½ inch long. The 2-inch fruits develop as hard, greenish-yellow berries and mature after the first frost to soft, reddish-orange berries with a distinctive white surface bloom. Studies show that common persimmon produces good fruit crops about every 2 years.

Common persimmon tolerates hot, dry, and nutrient poor-soils; however, it grows best in moist, well-drained soils in full sun. The plant is salt-aerosol tolerant and has a moderate tolerance to soil salts.

White-tailed deer feed on the leaves and twigs of common persimmon, and birds such as cedar waxwings and catbirds eat and disseminate the fruits. Small mammals, including opossums, squirrels, rabbits, and foxes also enjoy the fruits.

Propagation is by cuttings and seeds. Germination will be highest when seeds are stratified over the winter and planted in the spring. Transplantation of common persimmon is difficult owing to its large, deep taproot. Common persimmons are messy trees because they drop copious quantities of leaves, twigs, and fruits throughout the year. They are commercially available, and some cultivars have great fruit quality. Japanese persimmon (*Diospyros kaki*) is similar to common persimmon and grows well in coastal environments.

Eat persimmons when they are just about to fall off the tree, but test them with a tiny bite first. They are delicious when ripe but bitter, bitter, bitter when not yet ripe! The traditional method of harvesting persimmons involves spreading an old sheet under the tree to make collection of the fruit easier.

185 AMERICAN HOLLY

Ilex opaca Aiton
Family: Aquifoliaceae (Holly)
Other Common Names: Christmas holly, dune holly, hummock holly
Range: Massachusetts and New York west to Illinois and Missouri, south to Texas and Florida
Habitat: Maritime forests; also moist, upland deciduous forests
Habit: Tree
Flowering/Fruiting Period: FL April–June; FR September–October
Wetland Status: FAC
Origin: Native

American holly is one of the most easily recognized and popular trees in the coastal maritime forests of the Carolinas. Because it retains its attractive, scalloped, evergreen leaves and red berries into the winter, American holly has become an iconic holiday decoration. Today, much to the benefit of the species but not to the environment, indestructible plastic or silk American holly look-alikes have largely replaced live plants as seasonal decorations.

Along the coast, American holly grows to a height of 15 to 30 feet, occasionally 50 feet. Where salt aerosols are a significant

a

c

b

185. American holly (*Ilex opaca*). (a) Shiny,
evergreen leaves are thick and leathery with
spine-tipped margins. (b) Creamy white male and
female flowers (occurring on separate trees) are
similar, but only female trees produce bright red
fruits (c) on the current year's growth. (d) Bark
of mature trees is mottled with brightly colored
lichens.

d

environmental factor, the tree loses its pyramidal form and may develop a contorted shape. The tree has thin, light gray bark mottled with lichens of several colors. American holly leaves are alternately arranged, elliptical, 2 to 4 inches long, and 1 to 2 inches wide. The thick, shiny, leathery leaves possess spine-tipped margins. Individual leaves live more than 1 year. About one-third of the leaves are shed each year.

American holly is dioecious, with separate male and female trees. In both sexes, the white flowers with 4 petals and 4 sepals arise from the leaf axils and nodes along the twigs of the current year's growth. Bees, ants, wasps, and night-flying insects pollinate sweet-smelling flowers. The fruit is a dull red to orange-red drupe ¼ to ½ inch in diameter. Each drupe typically contains 4 seeds. Plants in full sun produce the most fruits. Heavy spring rains or late frosts can diminish seed production.

American holly is resistant to salt aerosols. Shade and drought tolerant, it thrives in well-drained, slightly acidic soils.

Mourning doves, cedar waxwings, goldfinches, and several other species of songbirds eat American holly fruits. White-tailed deer and squirrels also consume the fruit.

Propagate American holly from cuttings of current-year wood and from seeds. The cultivars *Carolina #2*, *Miss Helen*, and *Steward's Silver Crown* are examples of ornamental varieties (usually female) available from commercial growers.

The wood is nearly pure white and is used for wood turning and specialty cabinetwork.

---

186 COASTAL RED CEDAR

Juniperus virginiana Linnaeus
Family: Cupressaceae (Cypress)
Other Common Names: Southern red cedar, American juniper

Range: Southern Quebec and Ontario, Canada; Maine, west to North Dakota and south to Florida and Texas
Habitat: Dunes, maritime forests, margins of brackish and salt marshes; also old fields
Habit: Tree
Flowering/Fruiting Period: FL January–March; FR September–November
Wetland Status: FACU
Origin: Native

a

b

186. Coastal red cedar (*Juniperus virginiana*). (a) Coastal red cedar is one of the first arborescent trees or shrubs to appear on grass-dominated dunes. (b) Yellowish-brown male cones develop on branch tips.

TREES

385

c

d

186. Coastal red cedar (*Juniperus virginiana*).
(c) Smooth female cones mature to a deep bluish-green. They also develop near branch tips. (d) The bark is reddish-brown and shaggy.

and berries that are slightly smaller than eastern red cedar's (var. *virginiana*). It also has a significantly higher salt tolerance than eastern red cedar.

Coastal red cedar is a relatively slow-growing evergreen tree that grows up to 60 feet tall with an 8- to 20-foot spread. Drought tolerant and shade intolerant, coastal red cedar may grow to an age of 250 to 300 years.

Large coastal red cedar trees possess reddish-brown, shaggy bark. The trunk is typically straight, but under the influence of salt aerosols it may be contorted; the entire tree may be stunted, and the foliage may appear sheared. Typically, leaves are short scales, closely appressed, and overlapping on the stem. Leaves vary in color from yellowish-green to bluish-green. Flowers are either male or female and occur on separate trees.

Male flowers appear yellow, and female flowers are green. Both develop at the tips of small branches. Botanically, coastal red cedar fruits are cones, but they look like berries. Each smooth, greenish-blue to "frosted blue" berry contains 1 or 2 seeds.

Coastal red cedar is tolerant of salt aerosols and occasional flooding by brackish water that often accompanies hurricanes or nor'easters. The tree frequently grows on shell middens in the coastal area where soil acidity is moderated.

Birds and small mammals, including cedar waxwings, bobwhites, rabbits, foxes, raccoons, and opossums, feed on the berries. White-tailed deer may browse coastal red cedar but only if their preferred foliage is not available.

Coastal red cedar is the alternate host of the cedar-apple rust (a fungus).

The wood is used for fence posts, lumber, paneling, chests, and linen closets. At one time coastal red cedar was used in manufacturing pencils. Its fruits serve

In the coastal Carolinas, the variety *silicicola* is distinctive from the predominant red cedar variety found throughout the eastern United States. This variety possesses drooping branch tips

as a flavoring in soup. The essential oils extracted from the tree were once used in soaps and insecticides and as moth repellents. Leaves, crushed and spread around, function as an insect repellent.

Propagate coastal red cedar from seeds; however, nursery specimens are readily available.

187 CRAPE MYRTLE OR "CREPE MYRTLE"

Lagerstroemia indica Linnaeus
Family: Lythraceae (Loosestrife)
Range: USDA Hardiness Zones (6) 7–9
Habitat: Ornamental
Habit: Tree (shrub)

Flowering/Fruiting Period: FL & FR June–September
Wetland Status: Not designated
Origin: Exotic; native to China and Korea; cultivated throughout the world

Introduced into the United States in the mid-1700s, crape myrtle is one of the most common and easily recognized cultivated trees in the coastal Carolinas—and throughout the South for that matter. This

187. Crape myrtle or crepe myrtle (*Lagerstroemia indica*). (a) Crape myrtle may be cultivated as a single stem, a much-branched shrub, or a small tree. (b) Flower petals are crinkled, giving the flower an overall crepe-paper-like appearance. (c) Persistent fruiting capsules have 6 chambers, each with numerous seeds.

1- to 2-inch flowers. The large petals appear crinkled like crepe paper. Bright yellow stamens contrast sharply with the colorful petals. The plant is available commercially with flowers in a variety of colors and shades, including white, pink, red, purple, and lavender.

The fruits are brown to dark brown, globose capsules with 6 chambers. Each chamber contains several disk-shaped seeds. The fruits tend to persist through the winter.

The plant has modest wildlife value; songbirds and other birds may occasionally nest in the branches, and various insects provide pollination services.

Propagate crape myrtle from either seeds or cuttings. Seeds can be collected in the fall; they germinate immediately with no pretreatment. Plants root easily from summer, fall, or winter wood. It has few insect pests or diseases; however, powdery mildew can become serious under humid conditions. Disease-resistant varieties are now available from nurseries. The tree is quite resistant to damage by high winds.

Crape myrtle prefers moist, well-drained soil in full sunlight. While it cannot tolerate soil salts, it does tolerate salt aerosols well. It is somewhat drought tolerant.

The plant easily produces stem suckers from the base and tends to seed into nearby areas; however, it does not show the undesirable growth characteristics of an invasive plant. Nevertheless, its growth bears careful monitoring.

Most plants available from nurseries today are hybrids of *Lagerstroemia indica* and *L. fauriei* or *L. speciosa*. Nurseries continue to develop new hybrids that extend the range of the plant beyond its current distribution. Examples of cultivars include *Biloxi*, a mildew-resistant, pink-flowered variety; *Centennial Spirit*, with dark red flowers; *Natchez*, a white-flowered

d

187. Crape myrtle or crepe myrtle (*Lagerstroemia indica*). (d) As the plant grows, the smooth, gray bark flakes off, revealing a caramel color when first exposed.

rapidly growing plant ranges in size from a small shrub just a few feet tall to a tree that grows up to 30 feet tall. It is prized for its graceful and symmetrical, vaselike shape; beautiful green leaves; prolific and long-lasting summer flowering; and striking mottled bark that is tan, brown, orange, and gray.

Crape myrtle can be cultivated with single or multiple trunks. The fluted stems and branches exfoliate annually, revealing a bright, clean, smooth surface. Foliage and flowers grow on the upper half of the plant. The simple, dark green leaves range from 1 to 3 inches long. They are alternate to nearly opposite, entire, glossy, and glabrous.

Long blooming, the tree flowers continuously throughout the summer. Flowers occur as large, pyramidal or cone-shaped terminal panicles that range from 5 to 12 inches long and possess hundreds of

variety; *Tonto*, a small to medium-sized tree with raspberry red flowers; and many, many others.

Use crape myrtle as a specimen tree in a small garden. Clusters of different sizes, shapes, and colors create a spectacular display when placed in a larger area.

188 SWEET GUM

Liquidambar styraciflua Linnaeus
Family: Altingiaceae (Sweet gum)
Other Common Names: American sweet gum, red gum, sap gum, starleaf gum
Range: Connecticut southwest to Missouri and Oklahoma, south to Texas and Florida
Habitat: Maritime forests; also bottomland forests, streambanks, old fields, and disturbed areas
Habit: Tree
Flowering/Fruiting Period: FL March–April; FR August–October
Wetland Status: FAC
Origin: Native

The fruits of sweet gum, known colloquially as "gum balls," are a familiar sight in myriad places, from bottomland forests to driveways throughout the eastern United States. They make walking difficult and cleanup a chore wherever they are a part of the human landscape, yet the spiny spheres remain a fascinating curiosity for young and old.

Sweet gum, an occasional member of the maritime forest in the coastal Carolinas, is a large, rapidly growing, deciduous tree capable of attaining a height of 100 feet and a crown diameter of 40 feet under ideal conditions. In coastal environments, the tree rarely reaches 40 feet in height. It is pyramidal in shape with a deep taproot and many widely spreading, shallow lateral roots. A unique, interesting, and highly variable trait of sweet gum is its development of corky, winglike growths on young twigs.

a

b

c

188. Sweet gum (*Liquidambar styraciflua*). (a) Leaves are easily recognized as they resemble a 5-pointed star. (b) Separate male flowers (upper) and female flowers (lower) often appear close together on the same stem. (c) Characteristic "gum-ball" fruits are spiny spheres about 1 to 1½ inches in diameter.

TREES

389

d

188. Sweet gum (*Liquidambar styraciflua*). (d) Deep, longitudinal furrows characterize the medium gray bark of a mature tree.

The leaves are easy to recognize; they are roughly star shaped and palmately lobed and veined, ranging from 4 to 7 inches across. The slightly aromatic leaves are alternately arranged, simple, shiny dark green above, and pale green below. In the fall, the leaves turn a mix of bright yellow, orange, red, and purple.

Sweet gum is monoecious, with separate male and female flowers occurring on the same tree. Female flowers are yellowish-green, arising in leaf axils on a slender pedicel. The globose head, ¼ inch across, is composed of numerous ovaries. The male flowers appear in a dense, pyramidal, cone-shaped raceme about 2 to 3 inches long. Both flowers appear at the same time—just as the leaves begin to unfold. The fruit is the familiar spiny, pendant sphere about 1 to 1½ inches in diameter. Green in the summer, the fruits mature to dark brown in the fall when the beaked capsules open and seeds drop to the ground while the gum balls are still attached to the tree. The seeds are brown and asymmetrically winged. Sweet gum usually produces a bumper crop of seeds every 2 or 3 years.

Sweet gum is shade intolerant, preferring open sun. It grows best in soils with medium or high moisture and can tolerate short-term flooding. The tree survives with moderate salt aerosols, but with brittle wood and branches that break easily in windy conditions.

At least a dozen species of birds and small mammals eat sweet gum seeds. White-tailed deer occasionally browse the foliage.

Propagation is through seeds, cuttings of young stems, and root sprouts. The seed germination rate increases following stratification over the winter.

With moderately fast growth and tolerance to a variety of environmental conditions, sweet gum makes a good shade or specimen tree in the coastal Carolinas. It has few insect pests or diseases.

Sweet gum sap has a rich history of medicinal uses, including as a cure for dysentery, diarrhea, and skin problems.

One of the more commercially important hardwood trees in the Southeast, sweet gum is used for lumber, veneer, plywood, pulpwood, and millwork.

189 SOUTHERN MAGNOLIA

Magnolia grandiflora Linnaeus
Family: Magnoliaceae (Magnolia)
Other Common Names: Bull-bay, large-flower magnolia, evergreen magnolia
Range: Coastal plain: North Carolina to

189. Southern magnolia (*Magnolia grandiflora*). (a) This broad-leaved evergreen tree can attain a height of 90 feet and a trunk diameter of 3 feet. (b) Flowers are 8 to 12 inches across with creamy white petals and dozens of stamens surrounding a dome-shaped column of pistils. (c) Bright red seeds are expressed from the fruit as it dries. Look for seeds dangling from thin, white threads.

central Florida and west to east Texas; also Tennessee and Arkansas

Habitat: Maritime forests; also swamp margins and moist forests

Habit: Tree

Flowering/Fruiting Period: FL May–June; FR September–October

Wetland Status: FAC

Origin: Native

The huge, glossy leaves and massive, fragrant, white flowers of southern magnolia are instantly recognizable by all who encounter this tree. The state flower of Mississippi and Louisiana, this large, pyramid-shaped tree has become emblematic of southern living.

The broad-leaved evergreen tree grows to 60 to 90 feet high with a trunk diameter of 2 to 3 feet under ideal conditions, but it rarely reaches this height and trunk girth in salt-aerosol-influenced maritime forests along the Carolinas coast. The broadly elliptic leaves are dark green above and densely pubescent below with dark brown hairs. The thick, alternately arranged leaves with entire margins vary from 4 to 12 inches

more than 20 years as an understory tree before reaching the canopy. It prefers moist, well-drained bottomland soils but cannot tolerate extended flooding. In the maritime forest, southern magnolia is often associated with cabbage palmetto, live oak, coastal red cedar, and sweet gum.

Birds and small mammals eat the seeds.

Propagation is by seeds planted shortly after they mature; otherwise, they must undergo stratification. Take cuttings during the summer. Southern magnolia has more than 100 cultivars, including the popular *Little Gem, Samuel Sommer,* and *Majestic Beauty.*

Southern magnolia is resistant to storm impacts. Its extensive root structure supports the large tree and helps reduce the possibility of uprooting during storms. In severe hurricanes, leaves and branches are stripped from the trees; however, recovery is rapid, as trees produce new branches and leaves within a few weeks.

At one time uncommon in northern North Carolina forests, southern magnolia is now widespread, owing to birds distributing seeds from plants established in ornamental landscapes.

189. Southern magnolia (*Magnolia grandiflora*).
(d) The light gray bark is thin and smooth.

long and from 1½ to 6 inches wide. The leaves of southern magnolia are legendary in their resistance to decay.

The showy, bowl-shaped flowers are 8 to 12 inches across with 6 creamy white petals and dozens of matchstick-sized stamens surrounding a dome-shaped column of pistils. The abundant fruits are grayish- or greenish-brown, 3 to 5 inches long, and 2 to 3 inches wide. Bright red seeds, ¼ to ½ inch across, have a soft, fleshy outer coat (called an aril) and a single hard seed. As the fruit dries and contracts, seeds erupt and dangle from the fruit by thin, white threads.

Southern magnolia grows well in both full sun and shade. It can survive

190 SWEET BAY

Magnolia virginiana Linnaeus
Family: Magnoliaceae (Magnolia)
Other Common Names: Sweetbay magnolia, swamp magnolia, white bay
Range: Coastal: Massachusetts south to Florida and west to Texas
Habitat: Maritime forests; also bay forests, evergreen shrub bogs, pocosins, and pine and hardwood forests
Habit: Tree (shrub)
Flowering/Fruiting Period: FL April–June; FR June–October
Wetland Status: FACW
Origin: Native

Sweet bay is a member of a large group of plants common on the coastal plain of the

a

b

c

d

190. Sweet bay (*Magnolia virginiana*). (a) Sweet bay is a small tree or shrub with simple, elliptical, evergreen leaves. (b) Flowers are about 3 inches wide and possess 10 to 15 creamy white petals and sepals. (c) Mature fruits split open, revealing numerous ¼-inch, bright red seeds. (d) The bark is thin, smooth, and light gray. It is often mottled.

Carolinas called "bays." This taxonomically diverse group of bays is superficially similar. They are broad-leaf evergreen trees and shrubs possessing simple, elliptical leaves with entire margins and aromatic foliage. Sweet bay occurs occasionally in the wettest parts of maritime forests and the edges of swamps on the coastal islands. A tree of the southeastern United States, it is "endangered" or "threatened" at the northern edge of its range in Massachusetts, New York, and Pennsylvania.

A rapidly growing, small to medium, multistemmed tree, sweet bay attains a height of 20 to 25 feet in salt-aerosol-influenced locations, but it may grow to a tall and columnar 60 feet under ideal conditions. The trunk is gray, smooth, and thin. The leathery leaves are alternately arranged, simple, and entire. They are elliptical to oblong, 2½ to 6 inches long, and 1 to 3 inches across. Whitish-green beneath, the upper surface of the leaves is dark green and shiny. Last year's leaves gradually drop during the winter and early spring and lie on the ground by the time the new leaves of the season begin to appear. When crushed or bruised, the leaves release a pleasant aroma.

Sweet bay welcomes spring with large, lemon-scented, creamy white, insect-pollinated flowers formed at the end of branches. They are about 3 inches across and possess 10 to 15 petals and sepals. A flower opens and closes each day for up to 3 days, revealing 50 to 90 yellow stamens and 20 to 30 pistils. As the 1- to 2-inch fruit matures, it changes from green to reddish-brown. In the fall, the fruit dries, splits, and exposes the hard-covered, bright red, ¼-inch seeds. Wind, water, and animals help disperse the seeds.

Sweet bay grows in full sun or partial shade, but the environment must be moist or wet. It can survive occasional, but not extended, flooding. Tolerance to salt aerosols and soil salinity is low; one typically finds the plant a considerable distance from the ocean and estuarine shores. Other species often associated with sweet bay in the coastal Carolinas include black gum, Carolina red maple, water oak, sand laurel oak, American holly, and southern magnolia.

Birds, squirrels, and other small mammals feed on the seeds of sweet bay, and white-tailed deer browse the leaves and twigs.

Propagate sweet bay from seeds and cuttings; seeds require stratification before planting in the spring. Use sweet bay as an ornamental in moist or wet areas. It can be trained as a multistemmed shrub or a single-trunk tree. Plants are commercially available. Few insect pests or diseases affect sweet bay.

Its wood has little commercial value; larger trees are used for pulpwood, veneer, and box lumber.

Sweet bay may be confused with red bay, which occupies similar habitats. The whitish underside of sweet bay leaves contrasts with the pale green underside of red bay. Red bay has inconspicuous yellow-green flowers and dark blue to purple fruits. Crushed red bay leaves are spice scented; sweet bay leaves have a citruslike fragrance.

The distribution of the two varieties of sweet bay, *virginiana* (southern sweet bay) and *australis* (northern sweet bay), overlaps in the coastal Carolinas. Both the leaf midveins and last year's stem are pubescent in northern sweet bay, while southern sweet bay possesses scattered hairs on the midvein and glabrous second-year stems.

---

191 CHINABERRY

Melia azedarach Linnaeus
Family: Meliaceae (Mahogany)
Other Common Names: Chinaberry tree, Carolina mahogany, umbrella tree, Indian lilac
Range: USDA Hardiness Zones 7–11
Habitat: Ornamental; an escape on roadsides and waste areas
Habit: Tree
Flowering/Fruiting Period: FL March–May; FR June–September
Wetland Status: UPL
Origin: Exotic; native to Southeast Asia and northern Australia
Not recommended for planting; instead, remove where already growing.

a

c

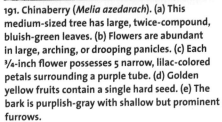

b

d

e

191. Chinaberry (*Melia azedarach*). (a) This medium-sized tree has large, twice-compound, bluish-green leaves. **(b)** Flowers are abundant in large, arching, or drooping panicles. **(c)** Each ¾-inch flower possesses 5 narrow, lilac-colored petals surrounding a purple tube. **(d)** Golden yellow fruits contain a single hard seed. **(e)** The bark is purplish-gray with shallow but prominent furrows.

Introduced into South Carolina in the late 1700s, this member of the Mahogany family was once a popular ornamental tree. Today, its shortcomings are better known, and its use as an ornamental has declined precipitously. Despite having attractive flowers and fruits, the rapidly growing chinaberry has escaped from cultivation and invaded native plant communities, and it is listed as a "severe threat" by the South Carolina Exotic Pest Plant Council. The state of Florida has banned use of the tree.

Chinaberry can grow to 50 feet, but 30-foot specimens are more common. The bark is rough and purplish-gray. Leaves are alternately arranged on the branches, twice compound and large, ranging from 8 to 24 inches wide. The dark, bluish-green leaflets are 1 to 2 inches long and serrated. They turn brownish-yellow in the fall.

Beautiful, showy, fragrant, lilac-colored flowers mass in arching or drooping panicles, attracting bees and butterflies. Each flower is about ¾ inch across and has 5 narrow petals surrounding a purple tube. Mature fruits are round, yellow to rusty-yellow, marble-sized drupes resembling cherries. Each slightly wrinkled, sticky fruit contains a single hard seed and persists on the tree into the next spring. Seeds can remain dormant in the soil for at least 2 years, making the tree difficult to eradicate.

Chinaberry exhibits a tolerance to drought and salt aerosols. It grows well in both sun and shade.

Birds may occasionally eat the fruits, but overall the tree has little wildlife value.

Chinaberry has the important characteristics of a successful weed: it is highly adaptable to a variety of environmental conditions, pest free, and allelopathic to surrounding plants, and it thrives in open, disturbed habitats. Its wood is weak; the branches are easily broken.

Owing to chinaberry's invasive tendencies, it is best not to plant the tree under any circumstances.

The fruits are poisonous to humans and other mammals, but not to birds. Chinaberry is reputed to have a peptide in its leaf tissue that is effective against the herpes simplex virus. Chinaberry seeds were once used as beads for rosaries.

---

192 RED MULBERRY

Morus rubra Linnaeus
Family: Moraceae (Mulberry)
Range: Massachusetts west to South Dakota and south to Texas and Florida
Habitat: Maritime forests; also bottomland hardwood forests
Habit: Tree
Flowering/Fruiting Period: FL April–May; FR May–June
Wetland Status: FACU
Origin: Native

Red mulberry, our only native mulberry, is related to white mulberry (*Morus alba*), a tree introduced into the United States during our colonial period in a failed attempt to start a silkworm industry. Much better behaved than its weedy and decrepit relative, red mulberry has redeeming values for wildlife and human use. It is an infrequent component of maritime forests, although it is occasionally locally abundant.

Rarely growing more than 30 to 40 feet tall, the tree exhibits a broadly rounded crown with gray-brown, furrowed bark. Leaves are 3 to 7 inches long and 3 to 5 inches wide. Leaves of mature trees are typically unlobed, but leaves of young trees often have 2 or 3 lobes. The upper surface of the finely serrated leaf is green and rough to the touch. The lower side is pale green and covered with soft hairs. Milky white sap oozes from the petiole when a leaf is removed from the plant.

Red mulberry is dioecious, with male and female flowers appearing on separate trees. However, flowers may occasionally occur together on the same tree, but on separate branches. Both male and female flowers are yellow- or reddish-green and open as the leaves expand. Male flowers occur on drooping catkins 1 to 2 inches

a

c

d

b

e

192. Red mulberry (*Morus rubra*). (a) This small, highly branched tree is rarely more than 30 to 40 feet tall with a broadly rounded crown. (b) Red mulberry possesses finely serrated, ovate leaves whose upper surfaces are rough to the touch. (c) Drooping catkins of male flowers are 1 to 2 inches long. (d) Fruits range from ¾ to 1¼ inches long, changing from green to deep purple as they mature. (e) The bark is grayish-brown and furrowed.

long. Female catkins are cylindrical and about 1 inch long. Composed of several small drupes clustered together, red mulberry fruits look like large, elongated blackberries. Ranging from ¾ to 1¼ inches long, the fruits change from green to red and then to deep purple as they ripen. The ripe fruit is edible and sweet; however, *unripe* fruits are apparently toxic and can cause an upset stomach as the major symptom. Each drupe of the aggregate fruit contains a single yellowish, oval, slightly flattened seed.

Red mulberry grows best in full sun and in well-drained, sandy soils with high organic matter. It will tolerate partial shade.

Songbirds flock to red mulberry trees when fruits ripen. Squirrels, raccoons, opossums, and foxes also eat the fruits.

Propagate the tree from seeds stratified

for at least 90 days. Several red mulberry cultivars are available from native plant nurseries. The tree makes a poor ornamental; it is relatively short lived and quite messy. The fruits will stain walkways and driveways, and the plant is susceptible to breakage in high winds.

The fruits are used in making jams, pies, and wine. Native Americans made tea of red mulberry leaves for treatment of dysentery and as a laxative.

Red mulberry is imperiled in other parts of its range, including Vermont, Connecticut, Massachusetts, and Michigan.

---

193 BLACK GUM

Nyssa sylvatica Marshall

Family: Nyssaceae (Tupelo)

Other Common Names: Tupelo gum, tupelo, sour gum

Range: Maine west to Wisconsin and Kansas and south to Texas and Florida

Habitat: Maritime forests; also low, moist woods, swamps, and streambanks

Habit: Tree

Flowering/Fruiting Period: FL April–June; FR August–October

Wetland Status: FAC

Origin: Native

Botanists look upon black gum with great admiration and interest. The tree is reputed to be the longest-living hardwood species in the forests of the eastern United States, capable of reaching 650 years of age. Black gum is at home in both upland and lowland environments. It is a slow-growing, shade-tolerant tree found in many different forest types, yet virtually nowhere is it the dominant tree in the forest communities in which it is present.

Black gums of maritime forests are always considerably shorter than the 60- to 80-foot height that trees growing inland can attain. Black gum is cone shaped when young, maturing to a tree with a wide, flat-topped crown and dense foliage. The bark

193. Black gum (*Nyssa sylvatica*). (a) In the coastal environment, black gum is a medium-sized tree with dense, glossy, oval to elliptic leaves that are 2 to 5 inches long and 1½ to 3 inches wide. (b) Male flowers are clustered and display many stamens. Flowers are often swarmed by bees and other insects.

of black gum is grayish-brown with deep, irregular ridges broken into rectangular blocks. Leaves are glossy green, oval to elliptic, and simple. The somewhat leathery leaves are alternately arranged on stems

c

d

e

193. Black gum (*Nyssa sylvatica*). (c) Female flowers are greenish-white and arise in small clusters at the ends of long peduncles. They occur on trees separate from male trees. (d) Fruits are single-seeded, oblong drupes that turn bluish-black at maturity. (e) The bark is grayish-brown with irregular fissures breaking the bark into rectangular blocks.

and 2 to 5 inches long and 1½ to 3 inches wide. Leaf margins are wavy but not toothed. New leaves are typically reddish-purple and turn dark green as they age. In the fall, leaves turn a strikingly beautiful, deep, burgundy red.

Black gum is dioecious, with male and female flowers on separate trees. Flowers are greenish-white, arising in axillary clusters of 3 or more flowers at the end of each peduncle. Male clusters are many flowered. The flowers are bee pollinated and appear concomitant with or just after the leaves emerge. Fruits of black gum are bluish-black, fleshy, oblong drupes

about ½ inch long. Fruits usually fall to the ground shortly after ripening; occasionally they persist until late fall. Each fruit contains a single large, ribbed seed. Fruit and seed production is highly variable from year to year.

Black gum grows best in sandy soils and full sun or partial shade. It is moderately salt-aerosol and soil salt tolerant. It can withstand brief spring flooding as well as considerable drought. Black gum is commonly associated with Carolina laurel cherry, flowering dogwood, yaupon, red bay, and several species of oaks.

Black gum provides cover and food

for a variety of forest animals. Robins, woodpeckers, mockingbirds, and brown thrashers, just to name a few, eat the fruits. Like many fruit-bearing trees, a black gum can be stripped clean by a flock of hungry birds in a matter of minutes. White-tailed deer seek out the twigs, foliage, and young sprouts. Large trees provide nest cavities for a variety of birds and mammals.

Seeds are the primary propagation method. Stratify the seeds for successful germination. The tree is difficult to transplant owing to its large, deep taproot. Cuttings are not usually successful.

Black gum is highly desirable as a shade or specimen tree in the coastal Carolinas. Although the fruits are a nuisance when falling on driveways and walkways, the tree has few insect or disease problems and has attractive foliage color in the fall.

Two other species of gum—water tupelo (*Nyssa aquatica*) and swamp tupelo (*Nyssa biflora*)—may occur in coastal forested wetland environments.

---

194 RED BAY

Persea borbonia (Linnaeus) Sprengel
Family: Lauraceae (Laurel)
Other Common Names: Silkbay, shorebay
Range: Coastal: central North Carolina
south to Florida and west to Texas
Habitat: Dunes and maritime forests
Habit: Tree
Flowering/Fruiting Period: FL May–June;
FR September–October
Wetland Status: FACW
Origin: Native

Red bay trees are dying of laurel wilt disease at an alarming rate in the southeastern United States. This is owing to the introduction of a lethal fungus, *Raffaelea lauricola*, and the simultaneous arrival of the red bay ambrosia beetle (*Xyleborus glabratus*) from Asia, which is responsible for spreading the fungus. First found in Savannah, Ga., in 2002, red

bay ambrosia beetle apparently harbors the lethal fungus and inoculates red bay trees with it. The disease has spread south throughout much of Georgia and northern Florida and northward into South Carolina and North Carolina. Today, many red bay trees on Hunting Island, S.C., for example, have succumbed to the disease. Research suggests that other members of the Laurel family, including sassafras (*Sassafras albidum*), are also susceptible to the disease, which puts their continued existence along the Carolinas coast in jeopardy.

Red bay is an evergreen that grows to a height of 20 to 25 feet in the coastal Carolinas, but it can reach 50 feet with a crown spread equal to its height in ideal conditions. Like many bays, its wood is weak and susceptible to breaking in strong winds. The bark is distinctively reddish-brown. A reddish-brown pubescence covers young branches. The branches become glabrous with age, a characteristic that distinguishes red bay from a close relative, swamp bay (*Persea palustris*), a species also found in the maritime forests of the coastal Carolinas. (The young twigs and leaf undersides of swamp bay are densely pubescent with cinnamon brown hairs.) Red bay's leaves are shiny, leathery, simple, entire, and alternately arranged on the branches. They are oblong, tapered at the apex and base, and range from 2 to 6 inches long and from 1 to 2 inches wide. They give off a spicy aroma when crushed. The leaf undersides are pale green with a few light brown hairs principally along the veins.

The plants are virtually 100 percent infected with insect galls that form along leaf margins. These galls are caused by the red bay psyllid (*Trioza magnoliae*), an insect related to leafhoppers, aphids, and shield bugs. While aesthetically unappealing, the galls cause little long-term damage but are so consistent and

194. Red bay (*Persea borbonia*). (a) This plant is a small tree with shiny, leathery, simple, and entire leaves alternately arranged on the branches. **(b)** Fruits are ½ inch in diameter and change from green to dark blue or black as they mature. **(c)** The red bay psyllid (*Trioza magnoliae*) is responsible for disfiguring, but not killing, the leaves. **(d)** The bark is distinctively reddish-brown with shallow furrows.

distinctive that they instantly confirm the identity of red bay.

Red bay grows in full sun or partial shade. It is tolerant of nutrient-poor soils, soil salts, drought, salt aerosols, heat, and short-term soil saturation. Red bay is often associated with Carolina red maple, sweet gum, black gum, cabbage palmetto, loblolly pine, and coastal red cedar. Its natural northern limit is Ocracoke Island, N.C.

The flowers of red bay develop in small axillary clusters and open after the leaves emerge in the spring. The wind- and insect-pollinated flowers are about ¼ inch long, yellowish-green, and inconspicuous. The ½-inch-diameter, dark blue to black fruits ripen in the fall.

Red bay is an important wildlife plant. Many species, including bluebirds, robins, and squirrels, eat the seeds. White-tailed deer browse the foliage and consume seeds. Red bay is also the larval food plant for the Palamedes swallowtail butterfly (*Papilio palamedes*).

Since so many red bay plants are succumbing to laurel wilt disease, avoid planting red bay trees in a coastal setting unless they are purchased from a reputable nursery and certified as disease resistant.

Red bay and sweet bay are often confused in the field. Sweet bay has large, showy, white flowers; bright red seeds; and whitish undersides on the leaves.

Two important plants of human commerce and enjoyment are related to red bay. Red bay is in the same genus as a popular food—avocado (*Persea americana*), a native of Mexico and Central America. Also, the bay leaf spice (*Laurus nobilis*), which is native to the Mediterranean Sea area, is in the same plant family as red bay.

195. Slash pine (*Pinus elliottii*). (a) Slash pine is a medium-sized tree in the South Carolina coastal area. (b) Needle leaves are 7 to 12 inches long and are found in dark green to bluish-green clusters of 2 (occasionally 3). Numerous male cones are produced at stem tips and release pollen early in the year—typically January and February.

195 SLASH PINE

Pinus elliottii Engelmann

Family: Pinaceae (Pine)

Other Common Names: Yellow slash pine, south Florida slash pine, Honduras pine

Range: South Carolina south to Florida and west to Texas

Habitat: Maritime forests; also pine flatwoods and floodplain forests

Habit: Tree

Flowering/Fruiting Period: FL January–February; FR October–November (2nd year)

Wetland Status: FACW

Origin: Native

Slash pine is one of the most economically important coniferous trees in the southeastern United States. Native from Charleston, S.C., southward, slash pine has wood that is hard, strong, and durable, second only to longleaf pine's. Today, forest managers plant this species extensively in various reforestation projects and timber plantations, including a few sites in North Carolina, well beyond its native range.

Under ideal conditions, this rapidly growing evergreen tree can reach more than 100 feet tall with a trunk diameter of 2 to 4 feet. The tree has many lateral roots near the surface and a deep taproot. The bark of slash pine is reddish-brown with thin, scaly plates that slough off as the tree grows. On the South Carolina Sea

c

d

195. Slash pine (*Pinus elliottii*). (c) Female cones are glossy and brown, varying from 3 to 6 inches long. (d) The bark is reddish-brown with thin, scaly plates that slough off as the tree grows.

loblolly and longleaf pines, which have 3 needles per cluster. The dark green to bluish-green clusters of slash pine needles are alternately arranged on the branches. Its needles typically persist on the tree for 2 full seasons.

Slash pine is monoecious, with both male and female flowers present on the same tree. Male cones shed pollen in January and February, while female cones require 2 seasons to develop. The glossy, brown, varnished-looking cones mature in September of the following year, and the seeds fall in October. The prickly cones are 3 to 6 inches long, intermediate in size between loblolly's and longleaf pine's cones. Slash pine's cones also grow on short stalks, unlike those of loblolly and longleaf pines. Slash pine produces good seed crops about every 3 years.

Slash pine is shade intolerant, preferring open areas with little competition from other tree species. It is more tolerant of wet soils than most pines. Slash pine has a high tolerance to salt aerosols, but its growth slows in soils with measurable salinity. It grows well in nutrient-poor soils and is moderately drought tolerant. Slash pine is commonly associated with live oak, cabbage palmetto, saw palmetto, loblolly pine, and coastal red cedar.

Birds eat the seeds of slash pine; small mammals, including gray and fox squirrels and white-tailed deer, browse the seedlings. When grown in managed stands, slash pine provides an excellent habitat for small mammals and birds.

Propagation of slash pine is by seeds. Germination usually occurs within weeks of seed fall, and seedlings grow slowly during their first year.

Slash pine is an excellent tree for a natural garden space. Due to its shallow lateral root system, be sure to locate the tree away from walkways and driveways.

Islands, slash pine is a medium-sized tree reaching a height of 50 feet. Slash pine has 2 or 3 7- to 12-inch needles in each cluster. This feature easily distinguishes it from the other major coastal pine species,

TREES

196 LONGLEAF PINE

Pinus palustris P. Miller

Family: Pinaceae (Pine)

Other Common Names: Southern yellow pine, southern pine, Georgia pine

Range: Coastal Plain: Virginia south to Florida and west to Texas

Habitat: Maritime forests; also pine savannas and pine/oak woodlands on sandhills

Habit: Tree

Flowering/Fruiting Period: FL March–April; FR September–October (2nd year)

Wetland Status: FACU

Origin: Native

Longleaf pine, the largest of the southern pines, once covered large areas of the coastal plain of the Carolinas and provided important naval stores such as turpentine, pitch, and tar for a growing nation. The nickname "tarheel" is associated with those who burned the heartwood to collect pitch needed to produce the naval stores. It is an occasional component of maritime forests in the Carolinas.

Under ideal conditions, longleaf pine is a beautiful, stocky, open-crowned tree that can attain heights of 100 feet or more with a 30- to 40-foot canopy spread. However, under the influence of salt aerosols near the coast, the tree rarely reaches 50 feet, a height similar to that of the surrounding trees. The bark of longleaf pine is light brown with coarse, rectangular plates that continuously flake off the trunk. Needles are typically grouped in 3s per fascicle, occasionally in 2s. Needles are 8 to 18 inches long, slightly drooping, bright green, and tufted at branch tips. New buds are silvery-white.

Male cones shed large quantities of pollen from numerous dense, cylindrical clusters near branch tips. Purplish, sessile female cones, 1 to 3 inches long, grow on upturned branch tips. Mature longleaf pine cones are the largest in the eastern

196. Longleaf pine (*Pinus palustris*). (a) The largest of the native pines, this tree usually grows less than 50 feet tall in salt-aerosol-influenced areas; needles are 8 to 18 inches long, drooping, and tufted at the ends of the branches. (b) The numerous male cones are cylindrical and concentrated at the tips of the branches.

c

d

196. Longleaf pine (*Pinus palustris*). (c) Female cones may be 6 to 12 inches long at maturity. (d) The light brown bark sheds large plates.

building a large, deep taproot and an extensive root system; during this time the plant shows little height growth. This is termed the "grass stage" in the tree's life history. Once the roots are fully developed, the tree grows rapidly, as much as 15 feet over 3 or 4 years. Longleaf pine is a component of fire-dependent plant communities and has become rarer owing to human development and fire suppression. Where the tree dominates, the canopy is high and open, allowing a diverse herbaceous plant layer to establish.

Longleaf pine is the preferred nesting tree of the imperiled red-cockaded woodpecker (*Picoides borealis*). Common associates include southern red oak, flowering dogwood, black gum, sweet gum, and common persimmon.

Squirrels and other small mammals feed on the seeds.

Intolerant of shade, longleaf pine grows best in full sun. The tree is drought and salt-aerosol tolerant and thrives in well-drained, nutrient-poor, sandy soils. Like most pines, longleaf pine is susceptible to breakage in storms, but other pine species are more vulnerable to breakage.

Propagation is by seeds; seedlings taken from the wild do not transplant well due to their large taproots. Seeds germinate within a few weeks after they fall from the tree. Six weeks of stratification will improve the germination rate. Seeds are commercially available for this outstanding ornamental tree.

North Carolinians claim the longleaf pine as their state tree.

United States at 6 to 12 inches long. Cones fertilized in the spring develop and mature over 2 seasons, releasing their seeds to the wind in the fall of the second year. Seed production is variable with an exceptionally good crop every few years.

Following germination, a seedling of longleaf pine spends 5 or more years

197 LOBLOLLY PINE

Pinus taeda Linnaeus
Family: Pinaceae (Pine)
Other Common Names: North Carolina pine, old-field pine, bull pine
Range: New Jersey south to Florida and west to Texas

TREES

Habitat: Maritime forests; also swamp forests and open fields

Habit: Tree

Flowering/Fruiting Period: FL March–April; FR October–November (2nd year)

Wetland Status: FAC

Origin: Native

A nearly uniform stand of 80-year-old loblolly pines dominated Bull Island, S.C., before Hurricane Hugo struck in 1989. The hurricane-force winds that pounded the island snapped most of the large loblolly pines in half, and they subsequently died. Since then, however, loblolly pine has made a rapid and widespread recovery, and growth models predict loblolly pine will again dominate the uplands on Bull Island.

Loblolly pine is a rapidly growing tree that frequently can reach a height of 100 feet or more in the southeastern United States. Depending on the amount of salt aerosols reaching its needles and growing tips, loblolly pine may vary from a straight tree 50 feet tall to a short, gnarly shrub less than 30 feet tall. In either set of conditions, loblolly pine produces a deep taproot. The bark of loblolly pine is reddish- to purplish-brown and scaly when young; the bark of older trees is thick and furrowed with flat, scaly plates. The needles of loblolly pine are 6 to 8 inches long; there are 3 needles per fascicle (occasionally 2), with fascicles arranged alternately along the branches. Individual needles live 2 to 3 years, and a third of the needles drop throughout the winter each year. Common tree and shrub associates of loblolly pine are cabbage palmetto, live oak, common wax myrtle, coastal red cedar, red bay, and American holly.

Loblolly pine is monoecious, with separate male and female flowers occurring on the same tree. During early spring, reddish-yellow male cones cluster at branch tips. These cones, about 1 inch

197. Loblolly pine (*Pinus taeda*). (a) The level of salt aerosols in the air determines whether loblolly pines will be tall and straight or short and gnarly. (b) Approximately 1-inch-long male cones are clustered near the growing tips of branches.

long and ¼ inch in diameter, drop from the tree after distributing prodigious quantities of pollen. Female reproductive structures are small yellowish to purple cones about ½ inch long. The mature fruits of loblolly pine are 3- to 6-inch, reddish-brown cones

c

d

197. Loblolly pine (*Pinus taeda*). (c) Mature cones are 3 to 6 inches long and are armed with short, sharp, stout spines. Requiring 2 years to mature, both young, 1-year old cones and mature cones can be found on a single branch, as seen here. (d) The bark of mature trees is thick, brown, and furrowed with flat, scaly plates.

armed with short, sharp, stout spines. The cones require 2 years to mature. Cones dropping to the ground in early fall were fertilized during the spring of the previous year. Seeds are produced in large quantities nearly every year; they are reddish-brown and ¼ inch long with a thin, membranous, ¾-inch wing.

Loblolly pine grows best in full sunlight. Once established, it is drought tolerant and moderately tolerant of salt aerosols.

Loblolly pine propagation is by seed, and germination is usually high. Trees over about 4 feet tall are difficult to transplant and will not survive if the long taproot is severed.

Gray squirrels favor (and savor) loblolly pine seeds.

Loblolly pine is the most commercially important tree species in the southeastern United States. Trees growing close to the coast are rarely harvested due to their size and often gnarly shape; however, loblolly pine is extensively and intensively cultivated for lumber and pulp inland, away from the coastline.

Pine bark beetles and other pests attack loblolly pines after major hurricanes weaken the trees. Avoid planting loblolly pines close to human habitations because their spreading roots growing near the ground surface can lift sidewalks, driveways, and even structures.

198 JAPANESE BLACK PINE

Pinus thunbergii Parlatore
Family: Pinaceae (Pine)
Other Common Name: Black pine
Range: USDA Hardiness Zones (5) 6–8
Habitat: Ornamental
Habit: Tree
Flowering/Fruiting Period: FL March–April; FR October–November
Wetland Status: Not designated
Origin: Exotic; native to Japan, South Korea, and China

Brought to the United States in the late nineteenth century and once commonly planted along coastal areas, Japanese black pine has fallen out of favor as a landscape plant because it is potentially invasive. Volunteer seedlings have begun to appear

TREES

407

a

c

d

b

198. Japanese black pine (*Pinus thunbergii*). (a) This small tree grows in an irregular shape often influenced by salt aerosols; needles grow in fascicles of 2. (b) Female cones of the current year are reddish-brown and about ½ inch across. (c) Numerous ½-inch-long male cones cluster at the growing tips of branches. (d) Mature cones are oval, 2 to 3½ inches long, and 1½ to 2 inches wide with prickles.

in areas where Japanese black pine has been planted. Recently it has developed considerable susceptibility to insects and diseases, especially along mid-Atlantic states shorelines.

In coastal settings, this irregularly shaped conifer grows to 25 to 30 feet tall and 20 to 30 feet wide; inland, it can grow considerably larger. A moderate growth rate translates to a height growth of 12 to 18 inches per year for Japanese black pine. The tree does not have a single point of growth like most conifers; thus it often appears as a multistemmed tree or shrub with a contorted trunk. The dark green, rigid needles are 2½ to 5 inches long and grow in fascicles of 2. They persist on the tree for 2 or 3 years. The distinctive silvery-white buds are ½ to ¾ inch long and are a distinguishing characteristic of this tree in the winter.

Japanese black pine produces cones within 4 or 5 years of planting. Cones are oval, 2 to 3½ inches long, and 1½ to 2 inches wide. Cones usually have tiny prickles on each scale.

Japanese black pine requires both full sun and well-drained soils for optimum growth. Compared to native pines, Japanese black pine is more tolerant of drought, salt aerosols, and heat. Despite the suitability of Japanese black pine, consider using native pines in any landscaping project in the coastal Carolinas.

Like many exotic plants, Japanese black pine has little wildlife value.

It is reported that Japanese black pine is susceptible to attacks by turpentine beetles (*Dendroctonus terebrans*), bluestain fungus (*Leptographium* sp.), and pinewood nematodes (*Bursaphelenchus xylophilus*); these attacks especially occur when the tree is stressed by unusually long, cold winters or extended drought.

The scientific name for Japanese black pine used in legacy publications is *Pinus thunbergiana*.

---

199 CHINESE PODOCARPUS

Podocarpus macrophyllus (Thunberg) D. Don

Family: Podocarpaceae (Podocarp)
Other Common Names: Podocarpus, Japanese yew, plum pine, yew podocarpus

Range: USDA Hardiness Zones 8–10
Habitat: Ornamental
Habit: Tree (shrub)
Flowering/Fruiting Period: FL April–May; FR October
Wetland Status: Not designated
Origin: Exotic; native to Japan and southern China

Chinese podocarpus is a member of the Podocarp family, a close relative of the pines, spruces, and cedars. It has a slow to moderate growth rate but can attain the size of a tall shrub or small tree (20 to 30 feet) if not frequently pruned.

The bark is light brown, aging to light gray. Leaves are alternately arranged on the stems but are so close together that they appear to be whorled. Leaves are evergreen, linear, pointed, simple, entire, and fragrant when crushed. They are thick, leathery, and bright green above and

a

199. Chinese podocarpus (*Podocarpus macrophyllus*). (a) A tall shrub or small tree, Chinese podocarpus reaches a height of 20 to 30 feet if left unpruned.

TREES

409

199. Chinese podocarpus (*Podocarpus macrophyllus*). (b) Leaves are linear, pointed, simple, entire, and alternately arranged on the stems. (c) Male plants produce many white to cream-colored, catkinlike cones about 1 inch long. (d) Mature female cones are bluish-green and solitary. They develop into 1-inch-long, blue or purple berrylike features.

glaucous green below. The leaves are ½ to 3 inches long and typically less than ⅜ inch wide.

Chinese podocarpus is dioecious, with male plants producing white to cream-colored, catkinlike cones about 1 inch long in leaf axils. Female plants produce solitary bluish-green, wind-pollinated cones that develop into fruits with a berrylike appearance. Over 2 years, the 1-inch-long ovoid fruits ripen from green to red or purple.

Chinese podocarpus grows in shade or sun; however, it does not grow well in wet soils, preferring fertile, well-drained soils. It is highly tolerant of drought, salt aerosols, and soil salts.

Birds eat the fruits and are responsible for dispersal of the seeds. White-tailed deer find the fruits unpalatable.

The fruits are safe to eat; adventurous people can eat them directly from the tree or bake them into pies and cakes.

Propagation is by hardwood cuttings, which root easily. Horticulturalists rarely use seeds as a source for Chinese podocarpus stock because the seeds do not germinate readily.

Prune Chinese podocarpus in a variety of shapes, including hedges, specimen trees, and foundation shrubs. The foliage lasts a long time when used in cut-flower arrangements. It is virtually pest- and disease-free and a great choice for coastal gardens. In North Carolina, Chinese podocarpus is nearly at its northern range limit. Several cultivars are commercially available.

200 WHITE POPLAR

Populus alba Linnaeus
Family: Salicaceae (Willow)
Other Common Names: Silver-leaved poplar, silver poplar
Range: USDA Hardiness Zones (3) 4–9
Habitat: Ornamental

Habit: Tree

Flowering/Fruiting Period: FL March–April; FR May

Wetland Status: Not designated

Origin: Exotic; native to southern and central Europe and central Asia

Not recommended for planting; instead, remove where already growing.

Introduced into North America in the mid-1700s, white poplar is now considered a noxious weed in several states and is banned from sale in some states. The South Carolina Exotic Pest Plant Council lists it as a significant threat. Time has revealed many faults with the tree, including brittle wood that breaks easily during storms, roots thirsty for sewer and water lines, roots lifting sidewalks and driveways, susceptibility to diseases and insect pests, and the characteristics of an all-around messy tree with a rain of debris—twigs, catkins, and leaves—throughout the year.

White poplar is a fast-growing, short-lived, medium-sized tree growing 50 to 80 feet tall with a 40-foot spread. The bark is smooth and greenish- to grayish-white with large lenticels when young. The bark is black and fissured when old, especially at the base. The light-colored trunk contrasting with green and white leaves does make white poplar an interesting ornamental tree. The leaves are 2½ to 5 inches long, coarsely toothed, and alternately arranged on the branches; they resemble five-lobed maple leaves. The upper sides of the leaves are shiny and dark green, while a thick layer of silvery-white hairs covers the undersides. Leaves turn bright yellow in the fall.

White poplar is dioecious, with male and female flowers on separate trees. Flowers appear before the new leaves. The male flowers are gray catkins up to 3 inches long, and the grayish-green female flowers are smaller, about 2 inches long. Female catkins lengthen to about 3 inches after pollination

a

b

200. White poplar (*Populus alba*). (a) White poplar is an oft-planted tree because it tolerates salt aerosols well and grows quickly. (b) Leaves are coarsely toothed, shiny and dark green on top, and covered with silvery-white hairs on the underside.

takes place. Seed capsules mature in late spring, and each capsule contains several light brown seeds with cottony hairs that aid in dispersal by the wind.

The tree prefers full sun and moist soil, but it is quite drought tolerant. The tree

c

d

200. White poplar (*Populus alba*). (c) Female flowers are produced along 2-inch, grayish-green catkins in the spring. (d) The bark is smooth and greenish- to grayish-white with large lenticels when young; it becomes black and fissured when mature.

exhibits a high tolerance to salt aerosols and soil salts.

White poplar also spreads by suckers owing to the development of adventitious buds on its shallow roots exposed at the soil surface, thereby forming dense thickets.

201 CAROLINA LAUREL CHERRY

Prunus caroliniana (P. Miller) Aiton

Family: Rosaceae (Rose)

Other Common Names: Laurel cherry, American cherry laurel

Range: Coastal: central North Carolina south to Florida and west to Texas; also California

Habitat: Maritime forests; also low woods, old fields, roadsides, and fencerows

Habit: Tree (shrub)

Flowering/Fruiting Period: FL March–April; FR September–October

Wetland Status: FACU

Origin: Native

Carolina laurel cherry once grew only in maritime settings in a geographically narrow strip along the Atlantic coast, but today it is naturalized and planted inland in the piedmont province. It is an attractive evergreen tree with high wildlife value. As an ornamental tree, it requires little maintenance. While remaining shrub-sized along the Carolinas coast, this tree may grow to 40 feet high with a 10-inch-diameter trunk in ideal inland habitats.

Carolina laurel cherry is a fast-growing tree or tall shrub with a pyramid-shaped canopy; smooth, gray bark with prominent lenticels; and a shallow root system. Its common names reflect the fact that the branches smell like cherries when bruised or broken. Leaves are alternately arranged on the branches and are shiny, dark green above and dull, glaucous green below. The leaves are 2 to 3 inches long and an inch wide; they are simple with entire margins or a few small teeth near the apex.

a

c

d

b

201. Carolina laurel cherry (*Prunus caroliniana*).
(a) Carolina laurel cherry is a small tree or large
shrub in maritime forests. (b) Leaves are shiny
and dark green above, a dull and glaucous green
below. Simple leaves are 2 to 3 inches long and
1 inch wide with entire margins. (c) Flowers
are creamy white and develop on 2- to 3-inch
racemes that arise in the leaf axils of last year's
wood. (d) Slightly elongated, ½-inch, blue-black,
thick-skinned fruits may persist on the plant
through the winter.

The creamy white flowers develop on
2- to 3-inch racemes that arise from the
leaf axils of last year's wood. The ¼-inch-
wide flowers are 5-petaled and fragrant,
and they attract many pollinating bees.
The green, fleshy fruits are ½ inch long
and ⅜ inch in diameter, maturing to blue-
black, thick-skinned drupes that may
persist on the plant through the winter.

Birds are primarily responsible for
disseminating the seeds; however, squirrels
and other small mammals also eat the
fruits and aid in dispersal.

Carolina laurel cherry prefers full
sunlight but will tolerate some shade. It
is both drought and salt-aerosol tolerant.
Flowering and fruiting are greatest when
the plant grows in full sunlight.

Propagate this species from seeds, root

e

201. Carolina laurel cherry (*Prunus caroliniana*). (e) The bark is thin, smooth, and gray with prominent lenticels.

202 BLACK CHERRY

Prunus serotina Ehrhart

Family: Rosaceae (Rose)

Other Common Names: Black chokecherry, wild black cherry, wild cherry

Range: Nova Scotia, New Brunswick, Quebec, and Ontario, Canada; Maine west to North Dakota and south to Texas and Florida; also Arizona and New Mexico

Habitat: Maritime forests; also hardwood forests, old fields, and fencerows

Habit: Tree

Flowering/Fruiting Period: FL April–May; FR July–August

Wetland Status: FACU

Origin: Native

While black cherry was once one of the largest and most commercially valuable trees of the deciduous forests of the eastern United States, it often achieves only sapling or small-tree size with no commercial value in the maritime forests of the coastal Carolinas. Growing under the influence of salt aerosols, it typically develops a short, gnarly trunk.

The bark is thin and gray with conspicuous lenticels that are especially prominent when the tree is young. As the tree ages, the bark becomes dark gray, fissured, and scaly.

Leaves of black cherry are simple, ovate-oblong to lanceolate, 2 to 5 inches long, and 1 to 2 inches wide. They are dark green, glabrous, and leathery, releasing a fruity aroma when crushed. Leaf margins are finely toothed, and the leaves have brown hairs along the midrib on the underside of the leaves.

First flowering when the tree is about 10 years old, the inflorescences are slightly drooping, cylindrical racemes, 1¼ to 4 inches long, each with numerous fragrant flowers. Individual flowers are about ¼ inch across with 5 bright white petals, a single pistil, and many stamens.

suckers, or cuttings. Seeds sown in the fall germinate the following spring. Collect seedlings of Carolina laurel cherry from where the plant has seeded in naturally and subsequently germinated.

The plant should be considered more often for planting in natural gardens. While it does tend to be weedy, pruning reduces this tendency. A handsome and hardy tree, Carolina laurel cherry transplants easily and serves well as a hedge or specimen plant. It has few insect pests or diseases. Cultivars such as *Bright 'n' Tight* and *Compacta* are available from commercial growers.

a

b

c

202. Black cherry (*Prunus serotina*). (a) Leaves of this species are simple, ovate-oblong to lanceolate, dark green, glabrous, and slightly leathery. Leaf margins are finely toothed.
(b) Flower inflorescences are cylindrical racemes. Flowers are about ¼ inch across with 5 white petals, a single pistil, and many stamens.
(c) Mature fruits are ½ inch in diameter, thin-skinned, and black at maturity. (d) Bark is dark gray, fissured, and scaly in mature specimens.

d

The flowers open after the leaves have expanded and bees and flies accomplish pollination.

The fruit is a thin-skinned, nearly spherical, 1-seeded drupe about ½ inch in diameter. The drupe matures first to red and then to black. Fruits fall soon after ripening. Like many other trees, black cherry has an abundant crop of seeds every 3 to 4 years. Seed dormancy varies amongst the seeds, with an entire crop germinating over a period of 3 years. Where black cherry grows in a maritime forest, there is always a large black cherry seedbank in the soil, an important source of new, fast-growing trees following a hurricane.

Black cherry is shade intolerant, usually occurring as an early successional species. In addition to preferring full sun or partial shade, the species is tolerant of salt aerosols, soil salts, and drought. It grows best in well-drained soils; it fares poorly in wet sites. Common black cherry associates include sassafras, live oak, and American holly.

White-tailed deer browse seedlings and saplings; fruits are an important source of food for robins, mockingbirds, bluebirds, catbirds, blue jays, cardinals, cedar waxwings, grackles, and sparrows. Seeds are part of the diet of red foxes, raccoons, opossums, squirrels, and rabbits. Seeds commonly pass through birds and small mammals undigested, a process that aids in dispersal of the seeds. Black cherry is the food host for many butterflies and moths, including the red-spotted purple and eastern tiger swallowtail.

Propagation of black cherry is by cuttings and seeds. Stratify seeds for successful germination. Alternatively, transplant the volunteer seedlings that germinate near existing trees. Cultivars of black cherry are available from commercial sources.

Black cherry is not a particularly good plant near patios and driveways. The annual fruit drop is unsightly and stains concrete surfaces. Because the major roots are shallow, the tree is susceptible to windthrow during storms.

The variety *serotina* is the common form of black cherry found in the coastal Carolinas.

203 SOUTHERN RED OAK

Quercus falcata Michaux
Family: Fagaceae (Beech)
Other Common Names: Spanish oak, red oak
Range: New Jersey west to Missouri and south to Oklahoma, Texas, and Florida

Habitat: Maritime forests; also upland forests
Habit: Tree
Flowering/Fruiting Period: FL April–May; FR September–October (2nd year)
Wetland Status: FACU
Origin: Native

Southern red oak is a common, easily recognized tree in the maritime forest along the Carolinas coast. Capable of growing to 90 feet tall under the best environmental conditions, the tree rarely exceeds 30 or 40 feet in areas influenced by salt aerosols. Not a self-pruning tree species, mature specimens often have branches and leaves that nearly touch the ground. Long, droopy leaves are a simple but distinctive characteristic used to identify this tree in the field.

Young trees have smooth, light gray bark; the bark of mature trees is dark gray with deep, narrow ridges and furrows. Leaves are variable in shape, simple, bristle tipped, and alternately arranged on the stems. They range from 5 to 9 inches long and 4 to 6 inches wide. Some leaves have 3 lobes, while others, especially those on the upper branches, have 5 or 7 lobes. Each leaf lobe has 1 to 3 bristles and deep sinuses. They are shiny green above and glaucous green below, with reddish-brown hairs along the major veins. The leaf blades are U-shaped at the base and noticeably lopsided on either side of the petiole. The terminal lobe is much longer than the other lobes. Leaves are late deciduous, gradually falling from the tree over the winter and before new leaves expand in the spring.

The tree is monoecious, with male flowers developing on 3- to 5-inch-long, drooping, yellowish-green catkins that mature at the same time the leaves appear. The wind-pollinated female flowers are borne on short spikes, each with 2 flowers. The fruit is an orange-brown acorn ½ to ⅝ inch long. Reddish-brown hairy scales

a

b

203. Southern red oak (*Quercus falcata*).
(a) Leaves are variable in shape with 5 to 7 deep lobes (occasionally only 3). The leaves are bristle tipped and range from 5 to 9 inches long and 4 to 6 inches wide. (b) At maturity, acorns are orange-brown with a similarly colored cap covering less than one-third of the nut. (c) The bark is dark gray with deep, narrow ridges and furrows.

c

cover the cap, which extends over less than one-third of the nut. The acorns, either solitary or paired, mature in the fall of the second year after pollination. Acorn production begins when the tree reaches about 25 years old.

Southern red oak prefers full sun or light shade and well-drained, sandy soils. Trees are highly drought tolerant at maturity and tolerate moderate salt aerosols.

Propagation is by seeds (acorns) only; planting seeds in the fall assures the best germination.

Acorns are a significant wildlife food for white-tailed deer and squirrels. Small mammals are important agents for dispersing the seeds. Oak trees, including southern red oak, are hosts for larvae of hairstreak butterflies and many moths.

While intolerant of root disturbance, southern red oak is a long-lived and fast-growing shade tree. The long taproot of southern red oak diminishes transplant success. Best used as a specimen tree in native garden settings, southern red oak has branches that are resistant to breakage and can withstand hurricane-force winds.

Southern red oak wood is hard, making it useful for lumber, furniture, flooring, and firewood. The bark is used as an antiseptic, astringent, and tonic.

TREES

417

204 SAND LIVE OAK

Quercus geminata Small
Family: Fagaceae (Beech)
Range: Coastal: North Carolina south to
Florida and west to Louisiana
Habitat: Dunes; also dry coastal plain
woods and sandhills
Habit: Tree (shrub)
Flowering/Fruiting Period: FL March–April;
FR September–November
Wetland Status: UPL
Origin: Native

Most common along the coast from
Cape Lookout, N.C., and southward,
fast-growing sand live oak possesses
leaves that superficially resemble those
of live oak (*Quercus virginiana*). But sand
live oak usually forms low, rounded,
multistemmed, nearly impenetrable
thickets typically no more than 10 to 15 feet
tall. Growing close to the shoreline, the
canopy often exhibits a smooth, sheared,
aerodynamic shape common to trees and
shrubs affected by intense salt aerosols.

The bark of sand live oak is gray, dark
gray, or nearly black and furrowed. The
alternately arranged, lanceolate- to elliptic-
shaped leaves are leathery with entire
margins. The upper leaf surface is dark
green and glossy. The lower leaf surface
is whitish or glaucous green and densely
covered with stellate hairs. Leaf size is from
1½ to 2½ inches long and ½ to 1 inch wide.
The leaves of sand live oak are strongly
inrolled toward the underside of the leaf,
and the midvein and secondary veins are
outlined on the upper surface. In contrast,
live oak leaf edges are flat to slightly
inrolled, and the veins are not evident
when viewed from the upper surface.
The leaves of sand live oak remain on the
branches over the winter, with old leaves
gradually dropping a few days before new
leaves expand.

Sand live oak is monoecious, with

204. Sand live oak (*Quercus geminata*). (a) Sand
live oak forms low, salt-aerosol-pruned, nearly
impenetrable thickets, as well as open, parklike
stands. (b) Thick, shiny leaves are strongly
inrolled toward the underside of the leaf. The
midvein and secondary veins are outlined on
the upper surface of the leaf. (c) Young female
flowers cluster at the end of thick peduncles
arising in the leaf axils.

d

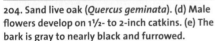

204. Sand live oak (*Quercus geminata*). (d) Male
flowers develop on 1½- to 2-inch catkins. (e) The
bark is gray to nearly black and furrowed.

e

male flowers present on catkins about 1 to
2 inches long. Several inconspicuous, pale
green female flowers cluster on ½-inch
peduncles arising in the axils of leaves. The
acorns mature in a single season.

Sand live oak grows best in full sunlight
in deep, nutrient-poor, sandy soils. Once
established, they are drought and salt-
aerosol tolerant.

Acorns are an excellent wildlife food,
especially for white-tailed deer and small
mammals.

Seeds propagate this species. Plant
seeds (acorns) in the fall; germination
occurs the following spring.

The wood of sand live oak is not

as dense or strong as that of live oak.
Scientific research indicates that up to
80 percent of sand live oak's total biomass
is underground.

Sand live oak makes an attractive
specimen or accent tree in a coastal natural
plant garden. It is suitable for planting
in confined spaces where live oak would
become too large and overwhelm the site.

205 SAND LAUREL OAK

Quercus hemisphaerica Bartram ex
    Willdenow
Family: Fagaceae (Beech)
Other Common Names: Darlington oak,
    coast laurel oak, upland laurel oak

TREES

a

b

c

205. Sand laurel oak (*Quercus hemisphaerica*). (a) A fast-growing semi-evergreen, sand laurel oak reaches a height of about 25 feet in the maritime forest. (b) Leaves are glabrous, simple, thick, entire, and about 1 to 3½ inches long and ¾ to 1¼ inches wide. (c) Yellowish-green male flowers populate drooping, 1½- to 3-inch catkins.

Range: Coastal: Virginia south to Florida and west to Texas

Habitat: Maritime forests; also coastal sandhills

Habit: Tree

Flowering/Fruiting Period: FL March–April; FR September–November (2nd year)

Wetland Status: FACU

Origin: Native

A common tree of the coastal Carolinas, this medium-sized tree is fast growing and semi-evergreen (late deciduous). It has smooth, brown or gray bark when young and dark, ridged bark when it is older. Although capable of reaching a height of 60 feet under ideal soil and atmospheric conditions, it can only reach about 25 feet or less in the maritime forest.

Leaves are simple, entire, leathery, and alternately arranged on the branches. Leaves from the previous year turn brown and are shed in early spring just as the new leaves begin to expand. They are glabrous and shiny above and light green and glabrous below. Each leaf is 1 to 3½ inches long and ¾ to 1¼ inches wide. Leaves on stem sprouts and young trees are often lobed and toothed. The leaves are widest just above the middle and often possess a short bristle tip.

Sand laurel oak is monoecious, with male flowers present on yellowish-green, drooping catkins that range from 1½ to 3 inches long. Female flowers develop on short, thick spikes in the leaf axils. The tree often flowers a week or two before the old leaves drop from the branches. Acorns are nearly sessile on the twigs and measure

d

e

205. Sand laurel oak (*Quercus hemisphaerica*).
(d) The nearly sessile acorns have a shallow cap covering about one-quarter of the fruit. (e) The bark is gray and ridged.

⅜ to ⅝ inch in diameter with faint stripes running lengthwise. The cup is shallow, covering only about one-quarter of the fruit. The acorns require 2 years to mature; annual seed crops are quite large.

Squirrels, raccoons, white-tailed deer, and many bird species eat the acorns.

Sand laurel oak grows well in full sun and prefers well-drained, nutrient-poor, sandy soils. The tree is fairly drought tolerant. Associated species in the coastal Carolinas include live oak, loblolly pine, coastal red cedar, red bay, wild olive, and American holly.

Sand laurel oak is prone to breakage during storms, rotting, and early death, often living only 25 to 50 years. This makes it less suitable for a cultivated landscape. Sand laurel oak hybridizes freely with other oak species.

Laurel oak (*Quercus laurifolia*) is similar in appearance to sand laurel oak. It is found in wet swales in swamps and maritime forests. Laurel oak has stellate hairs in vein axils, and the leaves have rounded tips without bristles.

---

206 WATER OAK

Quercus nigra Linnaeus
Family: Fagaceae (Beech)
Other Common Names: Possum oak,
    spotted oak, paddle oak
Range: New Jersey southwest to Oklahoma
    and south to Florida and Texas
Habitat: Maritime forests; also bottomland
    forests
Habit: Tree
Flowering/Fruiting Period: FL April;
    FR September–November (2nd year)
Wetland Status: FAC
Origin: Native

Despite its name, water oak is not particularly adapted to wet locations and clearly cannot tolerate constantly saturated soils. Water oak is a fast-growing tree with shallow, spreading roots that make it easy to transplant when young. The tree grows well in full sun or partial shade and prefers well-drained but moist, sandy soils.

In the coastal Carolinas, water oak can attain a height of 40 to 50 feet and a similar canopy width. Under ideal conditions in more inland environments, water oak may reach 60 to 80 feet tall with a trunk

TREES

206. Water oak (*Quercus nigra*). (a) Leaves are simple, entire, and range from 2 to 5 inches long and ½ to 2 inches wide. They are widest above the middle. (b) Male flowers line 2- to 3-inch reddish catkins. In this photograph, male flowers are about to release pollen. (c) Tiny female flowers develop on short spikes. (d) Acorns are ½ inch long, dark brown, and solitary or in pairs. (e) The bark is dark gray to black and furrowed.

diameter of 2 to 3 feet. The bark is dark gray and smooth when young; mature trees have black, furrowed bark. Water oak leaves are variable in shape but are usually spoon shaped and widest just above the middle. Leaves are simple and entire with 2 to 4 lobes. They are alternately arranged on branches and range from 2 to 5 inches long and ½ to 2 inches wide. The upper sides of the leaves are dark bluish-black, and the undersides are pale green.

The tree is monoecious, with both male and female wind-pollinated flowers present on the same tree. Flowering commences just as new leaves emerge or shortly before. Male flowers are packed along 2- to 3-inch, reddish catkins, and female flowers appear on short, hairy spikes with prominent red stigmas. Acorns mature in the second year after fertilization; acorns falling this year were pollinated last year. Acorns are ½ inch long, dark brown, and solitary or in pairs. The acorn crop of water oak varies from year to year, but acorns are generally abundant. Gravity, animals, and water disseminate the acorns.

White-tailed deer and squirrels eat water oak acorns; deer browse the buds and young twigs.

Trees typically associated with water oak are sand laurel oak, black gum, flowering dogwood, southern magnolia, coastal American hornbeam, and sugarberry.

Water oak tolerates drought and salt aerosols well; however, it is intolerant of soil salts.

Stratify the acorns over the winter before planting in the spring.

Like many oak species, water oak hybridizes with several closely related oaks, including southern red oak.

While widely planted as a shade tree, water oak does have drawbacks for use in landscaping. The tree is short lived, usually surviving about 30 to 50 years. The wood is weak, and the tree is subject to hurricane damage. During the fall, tannins leaching from acorns may stain walkways and driveways.

Not a commercially important tree, water oak has poor-quality wood commonly used for veneers, boxes, pulpwood, and rough-cut lumber.

---

207 LIVE OAK

Quercus virginiana P. Miller
Family: Fagaceae (Beech)
Other Common Names: Southern live oak, Virginia live oak, coastal live oak
Range: Virginia south to Florida and west to Texas
Habitat: Maritime forests and maritime shrub thickets, edges of coastal marshes, and dunes
Habit: Tree
Flowering/Fruiting Period: FL March–April; FR September–November
Wetland Status: FACU
Origin: Native

In addition to serving as home to Spanish moss, resurrection fern, and occasionally American mistletoe, live oak is one of the best-known plants in the southern United States; in fact, it has become an icon of southern coastal living. Its instantly recognized profile graces many coastal business logos ranging from landscapers' and law firms' to restaurants' and banks'.

When growing in ideal conditions, live oak produces a short, thick trunk often between 2 and 4 feet in diameter and reaches a height of 50 to 70 feet with a crown spread sometimes twice its height. Live oak is evergreen or semideciduous; it always appears green, shedding last year's leaves within a few weeks of developing new leaves in the spring. Large branches close to the ground grow nearly horizontally, sometimes dipping toward the ground before ascending to the edge of the crown. Live oak leaves are alternately arranged, elliptical, and leathery with

a

c

b

d

207. Live oak (*Quercus virginiana*). (a) Live oak produces a short trunk, and the tree spreads laterally, sometimes to twice its height. (b) Leaves are elliptical and leathery with entire edges that are slightly rolled under. The upper surface is shiny. (c) Male flowers are borne on catkins, 1 to 3 inches long. (d) Acorns are chestnut brown, about 1 inch long, and ½ to ⅝ inch wide, with the cap covering one-third to one-half of the acorn. (e) The bark is dark gray and furrowed.

e

entire edges that are slightly rolled under, a key to identification of this species. The dark green leaves range from 1½ to 3½ inches long, ½ to 1½ inches wide, and occasionally possess bristle-tipped teeth, especially at the apex. The upper surface is shiny, and the lower surface is light green with some pubescence.

Live oak is monoecious, with male flowers borne on catkins 1 to 3 inches long and wind-pollinated female flowers borne on spikes arising in the axils of leaves. Acorns are chestnut brown, about 1 inch long, and ½ to ⅝ inch wide with the cap covering one-third to one-half of the acorn. They occur singly or in clusters of 2 to 5. In contrast to the acorns of sand laurel oak and water oak, live oak acorns mature in 1 year and geminate shortly after falling from the tree.

Acorns serve as a food source for birds, squirrels, and white-tailed deer.

Live oak is the climax tree of the maritime forest in the Carolinas due to its adaptation to salt aerosols, soil salinity, and wind. Live oak tolerates salt aerosols well, but it takes on a characteristic wedge-shaped profile where and when salt-laden winds kill the buds and leaves on the windward side of the tree. Live oak grows well in full sun or shade, and it tolerates moderate drought, occasional flooding with salt water, and nutrient-poor soils as long as the soil remains unsaturated.

During severe hurricanes, the tree's broad, squat profile reduces the possibility that it will topple. Hurricane-force winds strip the leaves and small branches from live oak; however, the tree sprouts new branches and leaves within a few weeks.

Live oaks are fast-growing trees, especially when they are young. They often live 200 to 300 years or longer. Propagate live oak from seed, or plant sapling live oaks that are available commercially. Trees larger than saplings do not transplant well. With adequate space, live oaks develop into spectacular ornamental and shade trees.

---

208 BLACK LOCUST

Robinia pseudoacacia Linnaeus
Family: Fabaceae (Legume)
Other Common Names: False acacia, yellow locust, common locust
Range: North America, except Alaska; north and central Canadian provinces
Habitat: Coastal: roadsides and waste areas
Habit: Tree

Flowering/Fruiting Period: FL April–June; FR July–November
Wetland Status: UPL
Origin: Native to the Appalachian Mountains; now spread throughout the United States and Canada

The original range of the fast-growing black locust centered in the Appalachian Mountains from Pennsylvania to Alabama. Today, the tree has been introduced into new areas, and it now grows well beyond its geographic origins. In many of parts of the United States, it is a noxious weed or an aggressive plant that can and will crowd out native vegetation. In parts of Europe, black locust is a seriously invasive tree.

Black locust may grow to 50 feet tall, rarely taller, with a spread of 20 to 30 feet. The canopy is open, allowing sunlight to reach the ground. The roots are shallow and extensive. The bark of black locust is light gray to dark gray and deeply furrowed in a diamond-shaped pattern, a form replicated by expanded metal mesh (the material used to make porch furniture).

Alternately arranged leaves are pinnately compound and range from 8 to 13 inches long. The node where each leaf originates on young branches has 2 stout, sharp thorns sometimes up to ¾ inch long. Each leaf has 7 to 19 light bluish-green leaflets. Leaflets are oval or elliptical and about 1 inch long. Margins of the thin leaflets are entire. Leaflets are slightly hairy above and glabrous below. Leaves consistently turn yellow in late summer and usually drop before fall begins.

Flowers are creamy white, showy, and fragrant. They are produced in the axils of leaves and develop after the tree leafs out. Flowers arise on a cone-shaped, drooping raceme, a shape similar to a cluster of grapes. The entire inflorescence ranges from 4 to 8 inches long. Individual flowers are about 1 inch across with the

a

c

b

208. Black locust (*Robinia pseudoacacia*).
(a) Growing less than 50 feet tall with an open
canopy, this species possesses alternately
arranged, pinnately compound, bluish-green
leaves. (b) Creamy white flowers arise on cone-
shaped, drooping racemes about 6 inches long.
(c) Fruits are flat, brown, and about 2 to 4 inches
long. They persist on the tree into the winter.
(d) The bark is light gray to dark gray and deeply
furrowed.

d

characteristic pealike flower of the Legume family. The flowers are always abuzz with bees and produce excellent honey.

The fruit is a flat, brown or black pod 2 to 4 inches long and 1 inch wide, containing 4 to 8 reddish-brown seeds. Seedpods often persist on the tree into the winter. The tree produces a good seed crop every second or third year. Seeds can remain dormant in the soil for several years and germinate after soil disturbance.

Black locust is of limited use as a wildlife plant, but it does provide cover for animals and food for pollinating insects, especially bees. Also, it serves as the host tree for skipper butterfly caterpillars, especially the silver-spotted skipper.

Seldom grown from seed, black locust is easily propagated by softwood, hardwood, and root cuttings.

Black locust prefers full sun, but it will survive in partial shade. The plant grows well in sandy soils. It survives slightly elevated salinity in the soil and tolerates drought. Black locust grows well in poor soils, probably because the nitrogen-fixing bacteria associated with its roots can convert atmospheric nitrogen into nitrates important for plant nutrition.

The tree does have detracting features. It is prone to produce root suckers, and it spreads beyond where one would wish it to grow. It is susceptible to insect damage from the locust leaf miner and the black locust borer. Black locust branches are brittle and break easily during storms. The tree also tends to be messy; it continuously drops branches, leaves, seeds, and seedpods. Roots can lift walkways and driveways when located too close to these structures. It's a tree that probably should not be planted or otherwise encouraged!

209 CABBAGE PALMETTO

Sabal palmetto (Walter) Loddiges ex J. A. & J. H. Schultes

Family: Arecaceae (Palm)

Other Common Names: Cabbage palm, Carolina palmetto, common palmetto, palmetto palm

Range: Southern North Carolina south to Florida and west to Louisiana; the Bahamas and Cuba

Habitat: Dunes and maritime forests

Habit: Tree

Flowering/Fruiting Period: FL June–July; FR October–November

Wetland Status: FAC

Origin: Native

Cabbage palmetto is an important symbol for the states of South Carolina and Florida. It serves as the official tree in both states and is depicted on each state's great seal, state flag, and commemorative quarter-

a

209. Cabbage palmetto (*Sabal palmetto*). (a) Cabbage palmetto is a medium-sized, unbranched evergreen plant.

TREES

209. Cabbage palmetto (*Sabal palmetto*).
(b) Flowers are borne on high, arching clusters
ranging from 5 to 8 feet long. (c) White to cream-
yellow flowers are ¼ inch across. (d) Fruits
at maturity are black, fleshy, ¼ to ½ inch in
diameter, and contain a single seed. The leaf
bases of some individuals remain attached (e),
while the leaf bases of other trees slough off,
leaving the trunk smooth (f).

dollar. In North Carolina and South Carolina, it generally grows within about 10 miles of the coast. Makers of South Carolina Low Country sweetgrass baskets use strips of cabbage palmetto to bind bundles of coiled-grass leaves.

This medium-sized, unbranched, evergreen palm possesses a short, bulbous underground stem with many, many fibrous roots extending downward and laterally into the soil. Young cabbage palmettos typically require several years to develop an aboveground trunk; however, under poor growing conditions, it may take as long as 20 years to develop a trunk. At maturity, the tree measures from 12 to 24 inches in diameter and more than 30 feet tall. On some trees, the leaf bases remain attached to the trunk from the base to the crown, while in other specimens the leaf bases slough off, leaving a smooth trunk. Cabbage palmetto possesses a compact, spherical crown of fan-shaped leaves with a strong midrib down the center of the leaf. Leaves are alternate, dark green, and up to 5 or 6 feet long and 7 to 8 feet wide. They rustle loudly when moved by the wind.

Cabbage palmetto flowers are borne on high, arching clusters 5 to 8 feet long. The fragrant, bee-pollinated, white to cream-yellow flowers are ¼ inch across and ⅛ inch long. Black, fleshy fruits, each ¼ to ½ inch in diameter, contain a single brown seed. The seeds remain on the tree until wind, rain, or birds remove them. Cabbage palmettos produce prodigious quantities of seeds each year.

Birds and small mammals consume most of the seeds and play an important role in dispersing them. Seeds are buoyant and, unlike the parent plant, tolerate lengthy inundation with salt water. Thus, the seeds may be water distributed also. The plant provides some cover for small mammals and birds.

Cabbage palmetto grows well in calcium-rich, sandy soils, especially along the edge of brackish and freshwater marshes. Cabbage palmetto is clearly the most hurricane-resistant tree along the southeastern coast of the United States. Trees may bend nearly to the ground when hurricane winds reach 100 mph, but the stems return upright as wind speed decreases. With a deeply buried bud in the crown of the tree and a thick trunk, cabbage palmetto survives ground fires, often without damage.

Human uses of cabbage palmetto have included food (bread), wharf pilings, and pipes. Historically, cabbage palmetto logs were used in coastal fortifications such as Fort Moultrie, S.C., because they were able to absorb the impact of cannonballs.

Propagate cabbage palmetto from seeds.

The centrally located terminal bud tastes much like its namesake, cabbage, when eaten raw or cooked. Unfortunately, cabbage palmetto contains only 1 bud; once the "cabbage" is removed or dies, the tree dies.

Cabbage palmetto is an excellent ornamental tree; it is shade tolerant and has few damaging insect pests or diseases. It fits nicely into a coastal native plant garden.

210 CAROLINA WILLOW

Salix caroliniana Michaux
Family: Salicaceae (Willow)
Other Common Name: Coastal plain willow
Range: New Jersey and Pennsylvania west to Kansas and south to Texas and Florida
Habitat: Dune swales, ponds, and edges of freshwater marshes; also riverbanks and sandbars
Habit: Tree (shrub)
Flowering/Fruiting Period: FL & FR February–May
Wetland Status: OBL
Origin: Native

210. Carolina willow (*Salix caroliniana*). (a) This species is occasionally found in moist swales surrounded by dunes. This specimen is being buried by a migrating dune. Female catkins (b) and male catkins (c) occur on separate trees. (d) Mature seed capsules split, releasing white-plumed seeds.

A predicable indicator that spring has finally arrived is the presence of abundant, fluffy seeds of Carolina willow swirling in the wind and floating on the surface of open water near the plant. Carolina willow is often found leaning over the edge of open water in dune swales and freshwater marshes; its spreading crown, arching branches, and long, narrow leaves are key indicators that the small tree or shrub is Carolina willow.

This fast-growing tree has a short trunk with grayish-brown, furrowed bark. It reaches a height of 15 to 30 feet in coastal Carolinas environments. The leaves of Carolina willow are deciduous. They are glaucous green and sparsely pubescent on the underside. They are alternately arranged on the stems, up to 7 inches long, and 1 inch wide with finely toothed margins. Yellow glands residing at the tips of the teeth help confirm the identity of this species.

Similar to several other tree species of the Carolinas coast, Carolina willow is dioecious, with separate male and female trees that bear flowers before or simultaneously with the emergence of the leaves. Female flowers cluster on 3- to 4-inch, greenish-white, drooping catkins. Male flowers similarly cluster on erect catkins. After releasing their pollen, male catkins dry and drop from the plant. Mature female inflorescences form long clusters of capsules; each capsule is about ¼ inch long and contains several seeds. White, plumelike hairs on the seeds aid dispersal.

Carolina willow grows well in full sun and partial shade. The tree requires wet soils but tolerates nutrient-poor soils. While it has some resistance to salt aerosols, the roots cannot tolerate flooding by brackish or salt water. Associated species include cabbage palmetto and peppervine.

Carolina willow provides cover for small animals and birds and forage for herbivorous insects.

Propagation is by seeds and cuttings, which root readily.

Ornamentally, Carolina willow can serve as an accent or specimen tree near ponds or other wetlands. The plant is available commercially. Be careful not to mistakenly purchase the nonnative weeping willow (*Salix babylonica*) instead of Carolina willow.

Carolina willow can be confused with another native willow, black willow (*Salix nigra*). Black willow has pale green lower-leaf surfaces (not glaucous) with red glands on the marginal teeth, distinguishing it from Carolina willow's yellow glands.

---

211 SASSAFRAS

Sassafras albidum (Nuttall) Nees
Family: Lauraceae (Laurel)
Other Common Names: Common sassafras, white sassafras, red sassafras, silky sassafras
Range: Maine southwest to Iowa and south to Texas and east to Florida
Habitat: Maritime forests; also hardwood forests, fields, and disturbed areas
Habit: Tree
Flowering/Fruiting Period: FL March–April; FR June–July

Wetland Status: FACU
Origin: Native

As a youngster, you knew this tree as the "mitten tree," indicating the shape of its leaves. Possessing left-, right-, double-, and no-thumbed leaves, this tree can reach 80 feet in height in mature inland forests, but normally it does not exceed 25 feet in the Carolinas maritime forests.

The tree is slender and pyramidal with shallow lateral roots and nearly horizontal branches. The bark grows reddish-brown and smooth when the tree is young; with age, the bark becomes gray to brown and furrowed. When damaged, the tree usually develops new stems from root suckers. The easily recognizable leaves are generally elliptical shaped, 2 to 6 inches long, and 2 to 4 inches wide. They are simple, alternately arranged on the stems, and somewhat fragrant when crushed. The fall brings a display of yellow-orange or red leaves.

One of the earliest spring-flowering trees, sassafras is dioecious, producing small, fragrant, greenish-yellow male or female flowers that appear near the ends of the uppermost branches before the leaves expand. Individual flowers are ¼ inch across and pollinated by insects,

211. Sassafras (*Sassafras albidum*). (a) Leaves may have 0, 1, or 2 deep sinuses, mimicking the "mitten" shape with which they are often associated.

b

d

c

211. Sassafras (*Sassafras albidum*). Female flowers
(b) possess clearly evident pistils, while male
flowers (c) display large stamens with bright
yellow anthers. (d) Fruits are fleshy, ovoid drupes
about ¼ to ½ inch in diameter, which turn dark
blue at maturity. (e) Bark is slightly reddish-
brown and fairly smooth.

e

especially bees. Fruits are fleshy, shiny, dark blue, ovoid drupes about ¼ to ½ inch in diameter with a single seed in each fruit.

Sassafras prefers moist, well-drained sandy soils and full sun. The tree is fairly drought tolerant. Species often associated with sassafras include flowering dogwood, sweet gum, coastal red cedar, and coastal American hornbeam.

Small mammals and birds such as mockingbirds, sapsuckers, and kingbirds eat the fruits as quickly as they mature. White-tailed deer browse leaves and the young growth in spring and twigs during the winter.

A prolific seed producer, sassafras can be propagated from seeds. Stratify seeds for 4 months prior to planting, or sow them in the fall, allowing them to overwinter before germinating in the spring. Sassafras also can be propagated from root cuttings. A large tree is difficult to transplant due to its large taproot.

Sassafras is an excellent choice for planting in a coastal native plant garden. It works well as a specimen tree or in a mass planting with single or multiple stems.

Filè powder is made from the ground leaves of sassafras. It is used today as a condiment and soup thickener in Cajun cuisine. Oil of sassafras was once extracted from the root bark and used as a flavoring in root beer. This practice is now unpopular due to the large concentration of the compound safrole, deemed carcinogenic, found in the oil. Sassafras has had a long and colorful history of herbal use to ameliorate myriad ailments.

---

212 TOUGH BULLY

Sideroxylon tenax Linnaeus
Family: Sapotaceae (Sapodilla)
Other Common Names: Tough buckthorn, tough bumelia, silver buckthorn
Range: Southern North Carolina south to Florida

Habitat: Maritime shrub thickets and maritime forests
Habit: Tree (shrub)
Flowering/Fruiting Period: FL May–June; FR September–October
Wetland Status: UPL
Origin: Native

Tough bully derives its common name from its tough branches that are virtually impossible to twist, snap, or break off; you must absolutely cut twigs with a sharp knife! The 1-inch-long, short stems that

a

b

212. Tough bully (*Sideroxylon tenax*). (a) Often clustered near the ends of branches, the leaves are elliptical to oval shaped, widest above the middle, and range from 1 to 2½ inches long and ¼ to ¾ inch wide. The underside of the leaf is densely covered with silky hairs. (b) Flowers develop in clusters in leaf axils. Petals are greenish-white.

TREES

433

c

d

212. Tough bully (*Sideroxylon tenax*). (c) Dark brown to black fruits range from ³/₈ to ½ inch in diameter. (d) Stout spines arise near the nodes on twigs. (e) Bark is reddish-brown to gray with flat, scaly ridges.

e

appear and act as spines on branches give added support to the name "tough bully." This shrub or small tree is rare along the North Carolina coast but is common in thickets and forests in South Carolina and southward.

This large shrub or small tree grows to 20 to 25 feet under ideal conditions and may have a trunk up to 4 inches in diameter. The bark is reddish-brown to gray and furrowed, with flat, scaly ridges. Young stems and twigs are pubescent with cinnamon-colored hairs. The dark green, deciduous, but sometimes evergreen leaves are alternate, elliptical to oval shaped, and widest above the middle. The leaves

are often clustered at branch ends, have entire margins, and taper to a point at their base. They range from 1 to 2½ inches long and ¼ to ¾ inch wide. In addition, white to chocolate-colored silky hairs cover the undersides of the leaves.

Tough bully blooms profusely, with clusters of flowers arising in the axils of the leaves. The flowers are bell shaped with 5 greenish-white petals. The fruit is a ³/₈- to ½-inch, dark brown to black, fleshy drupe containing a single seed.

The plant prefers dry, sandy soils and full sun but can survive in partial shade. Tough bully is tolerant of low-nutrient soils, drought, and salt aerosols.

Tough bully is insect pollinated; seeds form a minor part of the diet of several coastal bird species.

Seeds, stem cuttings, and air layering propagate the plant. It is not commonly available in nurseries.

A similar species, buckthorn bully (*Sideroxylon lycioides*), is also found in the maritime shrub thickets and maritime forests of the coastal Carolinas. Buckthorn bully has young twigs that are initially pubescent but become glabrous with age. It possesses larger leaves (3 to 4½ inches) with only scattered hairs on the lower surface.

In legacy literature, authors refer to tough bully as *Bumelia tenax*.

---

213 BALD CYPRESS

Taxodium distichum (Linnaeus)
    L. C. Richard
Family: Cupressaceae (Cypress)
Other Common Names: Cypress, southern cypress, swamp cypress
Range: Coastal: Delaware south to Florida and west to Texas
Habitat: Estuarine shorelines (low salinity) and black-water swamps
Habit: Tree
Flowering/Fruiting Period: FL March–April; FR October
Wetland Status: OBL
Origin: Native

The "bald" in bald cypress is probably derived from the observation that it is one of the few deciduous conifer trees. Bald cypress is a long-lived tree that grows from 50 to 100 feet tall. Height growth ceases when it reaches about 200 years old and a broad, flat, irregular crown gradually replaces the pyramidal crown shape of its youth. In virgin forests, specimens of bald cypress reach 80 to 100 inches in diameter, with some particularly large individuals reaching 140 inches. Bases of the large trees have wide, spreading buttresses.

213. Bald cypress (*Taxodium distichum*). (a) Bald cypress trees reach 50 to 100 feet high with a trunk diameter of 80 to 100 inches. (b) Leaves are light green, ½ to ¾ inch long, and flat. (c) Female cones form at the tips of branches.

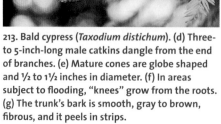

d

f

e

g

213. Bald cypress (*Taxodium distichum*). (d) Three-
to 5-inch-long male catkins dangle from the end
of branches. (e) Mature cones are globe shaped
and ½ to 1½ inches in diameter. (f) In areas
subject to flooding, "knees" grow from the roots.
(g) The trunk's bark is smooth, gray to brown,
fibrous, and it peels in strips.

Branches spread horizontally up to 50 feet in mammoth trees. Much of the biomass of bald cypress is located in the trunk and roots; few leaves support even the largest trees. Spanish moss typically drapes the limbs of bald cypress.

The trunk possesses a smooth, gray to brown, fibrous bark, usually peeling away in strips. Bald cypress possesses a large taproot and numerous lateral roots. These lateral roots give rise to the well-known "knees" of bald cypress. Although the knees were once thought to aid in aeration of the roots, scientists have yet to reach consensus concerning the function of these knees.

The leaves are light green, ½ to ¾ inch long, flat, and alternately arranged on the branches. In the fall, the leaves turn orange to cinnamon brown.

Bald cypress is monoecious; separate male and female flowers develop on the same plant. Purple male catkins, 3 to 5 inches long, develop in clusters of 2 or more. In contrast, female cones are small and occur in clusters of 2 or 3. Mature cones are globe shaped and ½ to 1½ inches in diameter, with 9 to 15 scales that break apart at maturity and release small, triangular seeds. Good seed years occur every 3 to 5 years. Water is the most important dispersal mechanism for the seeds.

Seeds can remain viable in flooded soil conditions for extended periods without the embryos being killed. For germination, seeds require moist but not flooded conditions. Bald cypress also reproduces by root or stump sprouts.

Field observations indicate that turkeys, evening grosbeaks, squirrels, and wood ducks eat bald cypress seeds. Bald eagles and ospreys frequently use the flat-topped trees as nest sites.

Bald cypress grows best in acidic, wet clayey or sandy soils. It prefers full sun but will tolerate some shade. Trees survive frequent, prolonged flooding by fresh water; flooding by more than one-third full-strength salt water kills these trees.

Associated species include Carolina red maple, sugarberry, sweet gum, sweet bay, cabbage palmetto, and black gum.

The wood of bald cypress is highly resistant to decay and therefore finds great use in boat construction, flooring, cabinetry, shingles, and siding.

Bald cypress is a highly appropriate plant for a native plant garden. It makes a beautiful specimen tree, and once established under cultivation, the tree does not require wet soil; it can grow in dry, upland soils. Look for cultivars developed by the nursery industry. Bald cypress has few insect and disease pests. The tree is hurricane resistant and difficult to topple.

Pond cypress (*Taxodium ascendens*) may occasionally occur in the Carolinas coastal area. Unlike bald cypress leaves, the needlelike leaves of pond cypress are mostly appressed to the twigs and branches.

---

214 CHINESE TALLOW

Triadica sebifera (Linnaeus) Small
Family: Euphorbiaceae (Spurge)
Other Common Names: Popcorn tree, chicken tree, white wax berry
Range: Southern North Carolina south to Florida and west to Texas
Habitat: Edges of brackish marshes, disturbed areas, wetlands
Habit: Tree
Flowering/Fruiting Period: FL May–June; FR August—November
Wetland Status: FAC
Origin: Exotic; native to China and Japan
Not recommended for planting; instead, remove where already growing.

Introduced into the United States in the eighteenth century, Chinese tallow was widely planted as an ornamental before it revealed its undesirable qualities.

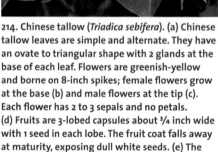

214. Chinese tallow (*Triadica sebifera*). (a) Chinese tallow leaves are simple and alternate. They have an ovate to triangular shape with 2 glands at the base of each leaf. Flowers are greenish-yellow and borne on 8-inch spikes; female flowers grow at the base (b) and male flowers at the tip (c). Each flower has 2 to 3 sepals and no petals. (d) Fruits are 3-lobed capsules about ¾ inch wide with 1 seed in each lobe. The fruit coat falls away at maturity, exposing dull white seeds. (e) The gray bark is furrowed, revealing a light brown color beneath.

Following its introduction, it escaped cultivation and invaded numerous habitats, including wetlands and bottomland hardwood forests, rapidly replacing native vegetation. It quickly spread to fields and disturbed areas due to its prodigious seed production. As a result of this tendency, Florida, Alabama, Mississippi, and Texas label Chinese tallow as a noxious weed. It is rapidly replacing native vegetation in Florida wetlands. It is designated a "severe threat" on the invasive species list by the South Carolina Exotic Pest Plant Council. The U.S. Fish and Wildlife Service is finding it difficult to eradicate the species on Bull Island, S.C. Land managers throughout the Carolinas work to eliminate it wherever and whenever it occurs.

This quickly maturing tree grows up to 20 to 25 feet tall in the coastal Carolinas. Under ideal growing conditions, Chinese tallow may form dense thickets. It begins to flower after just 2 or 3 years of growth. Chinese tallow produces a deep taproot that allows it to survive extended droughts. In addition, it has extensive lateral roots that grow close to the surface. Leaves are simple, alternately arranged on the stems, and ovate to triangular on 1- to 2-inch petioles. Leaves range from 1½ to 3½ inches long and 1½ to 4 inches wide, with 2 glands located at the leaf base.

Chinese tallow is monoecious, with greenish-yellow flowers borne on 8-inch spikes. Typically, female flowers occur on the lower part (base) of the spike, and male flowers are on the upper part (tip) of the spike. Each flower has 2 to 3 sepals and no petals. Honeybees pollinate the flowers. Fruits are 3-lobed capsules about ¾ inch wide with 1 seed in each lobe. The covering of the fruit turns black at maturity and falls away to expose dull white seeds, hence the name popcorn tree. The seeds persist for a few weeks, then drop to the ground. Trees may produce as many as 100,000 fruits in a single season. Water and birds, including robins, flickers, cardinals, and red-winged blackbirds, distribute seeds.

The tree appears to be of little value to native animals as a food source; birds and insects have been observed eating various plant parts, but the nutritional value is undetermined.

Chinese tallow grows in full sunlight and partial shade. Seedlings are shade tolerant and grow rapidly under a variety of environmental conditions. It can tolerate soil salinity and considerable salt aerosols. In the southeastern United States, hard frosts limit its distribution. Because of Chinese tallow's phenomenal seed production, high seed germination rate, and wide tolerances to environmental conditions, horticulturalists do not recommend this species as a landscape plant in the coastal Carolinas. In fact, if seedlings appear on your property, get rid of them! Once they are established, they are difficult to eliminate.

In Asia, the tree is a source of vegetable tallow, oil, and food. The oil can be refined into machine oil, lamp oil, and varnishes. A soft wood, Chinese tallow is used for carving. Similar to other members of the Spurge family, Chinese tallow may be toxic to animals and humans. Eating the fruits causes nausea and vomiting, and the white, milky sap causes skin irritation.

215 TOOTHACHE TREE

Zanthoxylum clava-herculis Linnaeus
Family: Rutaceae (Citrus)
Other Common Names: Hercules' club, southern prickly ash, tingle-tongue
Range: Virginia south to Florida and west to Oklahoma and Texas
Habitat: Dunes, maritime shrub thickets, and maritime forests
Habit: Tree
Flowering/Fruiting Period: FL April–May; FR July–September
Wetland Status: FAC
Origin: Native
The identification of this short, stocky tree, less than 20 feet high, is confirmed by the presence of large, corky, thorn-tipped protuberances on the trunk and sharp spines on both twigs and the rachis of its compound leaves. The common toothache

a

d

b

c

e

215. Toothache tree (*Zanthoxylum clava-herculis*).
(a) This tree is common on the grassy coastal
dunes; it is often salt-aerosol pruned. (b) Flower
clusters are positioned at branch apices.
(c) Green fruits form dense clusters at apices.
(d) Dark, shiny seeds are released from fruits at
maturity. (e) A mature trunk has numerous corky
protuberances, each armed with a single stout
prickle.

tree is in leaf from March through midfall. Related to grapefruit, lemon, lime, and orange trees, the toothache tree has leaves with a citruslike odor when crushed.

Toothache tree leaves are pinnately compound and composed of 7 to 17 leaflets. The leathery leaves are dark green on their upper surface and glaucous green below. The bark is light gray, thin, and often mottled.

Toothache tree flowers, typically abuzz with bees and other insect pollinators, appear on wood produced the previous year. The light green flowers possess 4 to 6 sepals and an equal number of petals. The plant is dioecious, with male and female flowers occurring on separate trees. The shiny, black, ⅛-inch-diameter seeds are encased in a dark brown husk that splits open at maturity, releasing the seeds in the fall.

Toothache tree prefers full sun and tolerates drought well. In its preferred dune habitat, the tree often displays a salt-aerosol-pruned shape—often a low, wide dome. When stripped of leaves by a late summer or early fall storm, toothache tree may immediately releaf and even flower out of season.

Propagation of the toothache tree is only from seeds. Seeds germinate if planted immediately upon ripening; otherwise, they require 3 months of cold stratification.

Scientists report that toothache tree is a host plant for giant swallowtail butterfly larvae (*Papilio cresphontes*) and leaf beetle (*Derospidea brevicollis*).

Toothache tree is a well-known herbal medicine source. The seeds and bark, both rich in aromatic oils, are used as a diuretic and antirheumatic. The astringent taste experienced in chewing bark or leaves has been used to soothe toothache pain. You can experience the unique taste of the toothache tree by stripping a small piece of bark or a leaf and chewing it.

APPENDIX 1 ACCESSIBLE NATURAL AREAS FOR VIEWING COASTAL PLANTS AND PLANT COMMUNITIES

The citizens of North Carolina and South Carolina point with pride to myriad accessible, natural maritime communities managed for future generations. These sites vary from an acre or two representing a single plant community to tens of thousands of acres composed of dozens of complex, interdependent communities. These properties have been set aside by an array of coastal interests, including individuals, nonprofit organizations, and communities, as well as municipal, county, state, and federal governments. This brief list contains some of the most undisturbed, unique, and extensive plant (and animal) communities accessible to the public. These sites can be reached easily by car or ferry (usually for a fee). Some parks and preserves are publicly supported by entrance (user) fees. You can observe and study these relatively undisturbed coastal environments; in addition, at some you may be allowed to walk on the beaches, camp, boat, hike, swim, fish, and enjoy other activities. Many areas have educational centers, interpreted nature trails, and outdoor programs. None feature minigolf courses, waterslides, or boutique shopping! This list of natural areas is necessarily limited by space; as you explore the Carolinas coast, you will discover dozens of other unique and interesting natural areas.

1. CURRITUCK NATIONAL WILDLIFE REFUGE, NORTH CAROLINA

This site is composed of nearly 10,000 acres of dunes, maritime shrub thickets, maritime forest, and fresh and brackish marshes. It occupies a large part of the northern Outer Banks beginning less than a mile north of the town of Corolla. While some areas are closed owing to their fragile nature, much of the reserve and refuge properties can be reached on foot or by four-wheel-drive vehicle. Beach, dune, maritime shrub thicket, and maritime forest vegetation are relatively undisturbed within the refuge. There are no on-site visitor amenities—including roads and trails—so plan accordingly. The National

Wildlife Refuge visitor center in Manteo shares information with visitors and offers exhibits that introduce the mission and features of the refuge.

2. CURRITUCK BANKS NATIONAL ESTUARINE RESEARCH RESERVE, NORTH CAROLINA

Located in an area of Currituck Banks occupied by tidal inlets 200 years ago, the Currituck Banks National Estuarine Research Reserve covers nearly 1,000 acres of natural maritime habitat. The reserve is within an extensive, undeveloped part of the northern Outer Banks. Two nature trails—one a boardwalk trail—meander through extensive dunes, maritime shrub thickets, maritime forest, freshwater marshes, and salt marshes. The beach is accessible by four-wheel-drive vehicle at the northern terminus of N.C. Highway 12. The warm Gulf Stream and the cold Labrador currents mix near Currituck Banks, and this happenstance creates conditions where northern and southern floras intermingle. On the reserve, you can see a unique, low-salinity estuary and the famous Corolla wild horses, as well as catch a view of how the Outer Banks looked before development overtook many areas. The reserve encourages fishing, hunting, birding, hiking, and photography. The N.C. Coastal Reserve's sites also include Kitty Hawk Woods and Buxton Woods. Trail information is available at the N.C. Coastal Reserve's offices in Kitty Hawk or online.

3. PINE ISLAND AUDUBON CENTER, NORTH CAROLINA

Pine Island includes 2,600 acres between Corolla and Nags Head that stretch from the barrier island across Currituck Sound to the mainland. The area includes outstanding examples of dunes, maritime (wet) grasslands, maritime shrub thickets, maritime forest, freshwater ponds, and expansive marshes in Currituck Sound. A well-maintained, 2.5-mile nature trail accessed from N.C. Highway 12 meanders through the major plant communities on the property. Kayak tours and educational programs, as well as access to other areas within the site, are available by prior arrangement. Plan your visit knowing that Pine Island has no general visitor facilities.

4. NAGS HEAD WOODS NATURE PRESERVE, NORTH CAROLINA

This 1,100-acre Nature Conservancy–managed preserve boasts over 5 miles of hiking trails ranging from easy to strenuous. The trails wind through one of the finest remaining maritime forests covering steep dune ridges and deep swales with interdune ponds and marshes. The maritime forest here shows the structure and composition of a plant community protected from salt aerosols by surrounding dunes. You can also access excellent examples of brackish marsh on Roanoke Sound from the preserve. Visitor facilities are available at the Information Center.

5. JOCKEYS RIDGE STATE PARK, NORTH CAROLINA

Visitors climb an extensive "live" unvegetated sand dune, or médano, that rises 80 feet to gain a commanding view of the Outer Banks. When you have scaled it, you will have reached the top of the tallest natural sand dune along the East Coast of the United States. The area surrounding the dunes is replete with examples of freshwater and brackish marshes, all accessible using a mile-long, self-guided nature trail. Mature shrub thickets abound on the site, and since some are in the path of the migrating dune, you can observe the shrubs being buried by a wall of sand. Kite flying, picnicking, and hiking are encouraged. Hang gliding is allowed if you're certified. The park is handicapped accessible, although assistance must be scheduled in advance. A plant checklist is available at the visitor center and museum.

6. CAPE HATTERAS NATIONAL SEASHORE AND VICINITY, NORTH CAROLINA

Cape Hatteras National Seashore stretches 70 miles along the Outer Banks from Bodie Island to Ocracoke Island. The park abounds with unrivaled examples of dunes, shrub thickets, maritime grasslands, maritime forests, and freshwater and saltwater marshes.

The seashore and recreation area has several small parking lots with short dune crossings you can use to reach the beach or to enjoy informative interpretative trails. A half-mile hiking trail passes through representative plant communities at Bodie Island Lighthouse and ends at an elevated platform. Near the Cape Hatteras Lighthouse, the Buxton Woods trail traverses maritime forest growing on high dunes. Ocracoke Island is dominated by a combination of natural and man-made dunes. Some of the constructed dunes date from the 1930s. Extensive maritime shrub thickets and maritime forest have matured during the past 75 years on Ocracoke Island. These features can be observed from roadside turnouts. The self-guided, half-mile-long Hammock Hills Nature Trail transects plant communities typically found on Ocracoke Island. The National Park Service maintains four campgrounds on the seashore; each has minimal camping amenities.

Under separate jurisdiction, Pea Island National Wildlife Refuge manages several man-made impoundments. The impoundments and surrounding vegetation harbor a variety of wetland plants. These sites are important to wildlife and seasonally attract huge numbers of waterfowl. Refuge information and parking are available at the National Wildlife Refuge visitor center on N.C. Highway 12 near Rodanthe.

The state-owned, 1,000-acre Buxton Woods Coastal Reserve near Cape Hatteras is one of the largest remaining tracts of maritime forest on the North Carolina coast. Trails meander across stabilized dune ridges with maritime forest, shrub thickets, and freshwater-wetland-filled depressions between dune ridges. An extensive hiking trail system has been constructed throughout the forest, and this system links to adjacent National Seashore trails. For more information, consult local maps for directions to the maritime forests, visit the N.C. Coastal Reserve offices in Kitty Hawk, or go online.

Managed by the N.C. Coastal Land Trust, Springers Point Preserve encompasses approximately 120 acres of maritime forest, maritime grasslands, and tidal marsh easily accessible from Ocracoke Village.

7. CAPE LOOKOUT NATIONAL SEASHORE AND VICINITY, NORTH CAROLINA

Extensive dunes, maritime grasslands, shrub thickets, and tidal marshes cover Core Banks, one of three major islands comprising Cape Lookout National Seashore. Private ferries depart from Beaufort, Harkers Island, Davis, Atlantic, and Ocracoke Island, bound for various landings on Shackleford, Core, and Portsmouth islands, including the Cape Lookout Lighthouse area. There are no designated hiking trails on the islands. Visitors are welcome to hike throughout the park. Beach walking, swimming, fishing, primitive camping, and boating are encouraged at Cape Lookout National Seashore. There are few services in the Cape Lookout area or Shackleford Banks. North and South Core Banks have a limited number of rustic cabins for rent. Visitors so inclined may walk or use an off-road vehicle to reach specific plant communities and other sites on Core and Portsmouth islands. Just south of the abandoned village of Portsmouth, there is a unique, expansive, nearly barren sand flat often flooded by salt water. The maritime forest, maritime shrub thickets, dunes, and dune swales on Shackleford Banks should not be missed. Portsmouth Island and Core and Shackleford banks can also be reached by personal boat.

Expansive, irregularly flooded brackish and freshwater marshes cover nearly 5,000 acres between the town of Beaufort and Cedar Island. The marshes are part of the Cedar Island National Wildlife Refuge. These important marshes are difficult to observe closely without a boat, but you can view them as you drive or bicycle to the state-run Cedar Island–Ocracoke ferry terminal.

8. THEODORE ROOSEVELT STATE NATURAL AREA, NORTH CAROLINA

This 300-acre natural area is located roughly in the center of Bogue Banks. It features an attractive and interesting hiking trail that is about 1 mile, with a shorter loop. It is an easy, albeit insect-infested, walk. The trail immerses you in a complex maritime forest and beautiful salt marsh adjacent to Bogue Sound. The start of the trail is accessed from the west end of the parking lot adjacent to the N.C. Aquarium at Pine Knoll Shores. Visitor amenities are available at the aquarium for a fee. The aquarium, which includes several coastal-themed exhibits, is a rewarding stop.

9. BEAR ISLAND, NORTH CAROLINA

Bear Island is one of three components of Hammocks Beach State Park. Bear Island is accessible by ferry for a fee from the park's headquarters near Swansboro. The ferry approaches the island through a broad expanse of saltmarsh vegetation highly dissected by tidal creeks and mudflats. Extensive undisturbed dunes and maritime shrub thickets occupy the bulk of the island. Many exceptional plant communities are accessible by walking the wide, flat beach. For example, you can observe a wall of sand burying a small pocket of maritime forest on the northeastern end of the island. Bear Island has no designated hiking trails. Swimming is permitted; bathhouse facilities are seasonally available. Primitive camping is permitted.

10. BALD HEAD WOODS COASTAL RESERVE, NORTH CAROLINA

Bald Head Island can be reached by a regularly scheduled private ferry from the town of Southport for a fee. Once on Bald Head Island, you can reach the coastal reserve by foot, bicycle, or golf cart. No cars are allowed on the island. The coastal reserve occupies approximately 200 acres that include 2 miles of self-guided hiking trails and many unusually large specimens of live oak. The outstanding maritime forest is protected from ocean winds and waves by a large seaward dune ridge. Within the forest are several impressive freshwater dune ponds. This forest is the natural northern limit of cabbage palmetto. A portion of the hiking trail is handicapped accessible.

11. MASONBORO ISLAND, NORTH CAROLINA

Masonboro Island, a component of the National Estuarine Research Reserve program, is an undeveloped island accessible only by boat. There are public and private boat ramps there, and a ferry services the island and surrounding coastal environments for a fee. The narrow, low-lying, 8-mile-long island is an excellent example of a barrier island exhibiting little natural dune recovery following major storms. Good examples of maritime grasslands on overwash terraces abound on the island. No visitor amenities are available. Primitive camping is allowed.

12. BIRD ISLAND COASTAL RESERVE, NORTH CAROLINA

Bird Island was once the last barrier island in North Carolina, distinct and separate from Sunset Beach. But with the closure of Mad Inlet, this 1,000-acre reserve became continuous with Sunset Beach and easily accessible on foot from there. Part of the N.C. Coastal Reserve, the island is composed of a noteworthy mix of young, undeveloped, and undisturbed natural dune, maritime grassland, maritime shrub thicket, and tidal marsh plant communities. The reserve currently has no visitor amenities. Parking on Sunset Beach near Bird Island is limited.

13. MYRTLE BEACH STATE PARK, SOUTH CAROLINA

Myrtle Beach State Park is a popular, family-friendly, natural area in the most intensely developed part of Myrtle Beach. Accessible by car, the park boasts several easy walking trails and boardwalks to the beachfront. Maritime forests and freshwater ponds are represented in this landscape. Activities such as beach walking, fishing, camping, bicycling, and picnicking are supported by considerable infrastructure, including cabins for rent. The park is heavily used throughout much of the year, especially on weekends.

14. HUNTINGTON BEACH STATE PARK, SOUTH CAROLINA

The park is an oasis of natural environments along South Carolina's Grand Strand. Huntington Beach State Park features a boardwalk and nature trails that traverse 3 miles of natural ocean shoreline and dunes, extensive freshwater wetlands, and fine examples of maritime forest and tidal marsh communities. There are conveniently located campsites, picnic areas, and an educational center with coastal-themed exhibits. The park is also a well-regarded birding spot.

15. CAPE ROMAIN NATIONAL WILDLIFE REFUGE, SOUTH CAROLINA

More than 60,000 acres of barrier beaches, maritime forest, tidal marshes, and freshwater and brackish impoundments constitute the Cape Romain National Wildlife Refuge. Outstanding examples of all these habitats occur throughout the refuge. Bull and Cape islands have excellent examples of maritime forests. A regularly scheduled ferry delivers visitors to Bull Island for a fee. Other upland and wetland sites can be reached by personal watercraft.

16. CAPERS ISLAND, SOUTH CAROLINA

Capers Island is an undeveloped, state-owned island just south of Cape Romain National Wildlife Refuge. The island possesses excellent examples of dunes, maritime shrub thickets, maritime forests, and salt marshes. It can be accessed only by boat or by a ferry for a fee. A maritime forest tree skeleton "boneyard" covers much of the Capers Island beachfront. Capers Island is a wonderful location for beach walking, nature appreciation, photography, and solitude. In the 1960s, the island owners at the time constructed brackish marsh impoundments to attract waterfowl. A mix of freshwater- and saltwater-tolerant flora and fauna occupies these interesting environments today.

17. FORT MOULTRIE (FORT SUMTER NATIONAL MONUMENT) AND SULLIVAN'S ISLAND, SOUTH CAROLINA

Various permutations of maritime shrub thickets cover much of the undeveloped part of this site, but probably none of the fort's original vegetation remains. The maritime shrub thickets between the fort and the beach illustrate the impact that invasive plants can have on a community. Chinese privet, Japanese honeysuckle, chinaberry, Chinese tallow, and other invasives are replacing the native species. The visitor center displays information about how palmetto logs were used in constructing the earliest fort on this site.

18. FOLLY BEACH COUNTY PARK, SOUTH CAROLINA

Folly Beach County Park, located at the western end of Folly Beach, covers 100 acres with coastal dunes, maritime grasslands, and small patches of maritime shrub thickets that clearly struggle to survive under the impact of oceanic overwash and an environment of high salt aerosols. Extensive tidal marshes occur along the estuarine shore of Folly River. The compact nature of the park allows you to observe the major plant communities in less than an hour's walk. Parking is available for a fee. Birding, biking, picnicking, and fishing are encouraged. Showers, dressing rooms, and restrooms are available.

19. EDISTO BEACH STATE PARK, SOUTH CAROLINA

Edisto Beach State Park provides access to prime tidal marsh areas, a somewhat patchy maritime forest community, and an extensive area of beach dunes–maritime grasslands that extends ¾ of a mile northeast of the campground. The park boasts an interpretative center with interactive displays, and it frequently hosts programs centered on coastal education and research in partnership with the ACE Basin National Estuarine Research Reserve Program. Edisto Beach State Park offers amenities associated with beach walking, hiking, swimming, boating, fishing, camping, and picnicking.

20. HUNTING ISLAND STATE PARK, SOUTH CAROLINA

The vegetation of Hunting Island State Park has experienced relatively little disturbance at this much-visited site in coastal South Carolina. The eastern end of the island has naturally eroded for decades, which created a sweeping boneyard beach. The extensive maritime forest provides outstanding examples of the variation in a maritime forest in the Carolinas. A fabulous boardwalk and trail complex crosses tidal marshes and a maritime forest on the landward side of the island.

21. HILTON HEAD ISLAND AND VICINITY, SOUTH CAROLINA

Hilton Head Island boasts hundreds of acres of undisturbed coastal plant communities. Environmentally sensitive signs indicate numerous access points where the public can enjoy outstanding examples of beach and dune plant communities. Other public access points open exquisite maritime forests, freshwater wetlands, and tidal marshes for observation and enjoyment by the public. Maps of these areas are available at the Hilton Head Island Welcome Center and online.

The Sea Pines Forest Preserve, a 600-acre property on Hilton Head Island, has been carefully protected from development. The preserve encompasses a complex of maritime forests, wetlands, and land once farmed for rice, indigo, and cotton. Well-marked 1- and 2-mile-long trails traverse these diverse plant communities.

accretion: the increase in size or buildup of a beach, shoreline, dune, marsh, or other feature by the gradual addition of layers of matter; the opposite of erosion

achene: a dry, indehiscent fruit that contains a single seed

acute: tapering to a narrow point

adventitious: a plant organ (roots, stems, or leaves) arising from an unusual position

aerenchyma: plant tissue containing large air spaces; often found in aquatic plants. The tissue creates buoyancy and allows circulation of gases

aggregate fruit: a fruit formed from several separate flowers, such as mulberry

allelopathy, allelopathic: a chemical inhibition of one plant by another plant that releases germination, growth, or reproduction inhibitors into the environment

annual: a plant that germinates, grows, flowers, fruits, and dies within one year (or season)

anoxic: an environment lacking oxygen; a reducing environment

anther: the part of a stamen bearing pollen

anthesis: the time when a flower opens and is available for pollination

appressed: growing close to the stem; the opposite of spreading

aquaclude: an impermeable layer or stratum that acts as a barrier and prevents water from flowing freely

arborescent: pertaining to trees and large shrubs; not herbaceous

areole: a small pit containing a tuft of tiny spines or bristles; a common feature of cacti species

aril: a fleshy seed coat; especially prominent on seeds of magnolia

asexual reproduction: reproduction without the union of gametes; includes root and stem suckers, cuttings, and plugs

awn: a bristle-like appendage; often a key identifying characteristic on grass flowers

axial: pertaining to branches arising from buds in leaf axils

axil: the angle between a leaf and the stem to which it is attached; buds develop in leaf axils

axillary: a plant part, such as a bud, when it is located near the axil

barrier beach: a mainland beach or spit formed by the transport of sand by wind, waves, and tides; it protects either upland or estuarine environments

barrier island: an elongated island that protects estuarine environments landward of its location

basal: located at or near the base of a plant stem; typically refers to a cluster of leaves

berry: a multiseeded fruit derived from one pistil; indehiscent and often fleshy

biennial: a plant that completes its life cycle in two years; it germinates and grows during one year (season) and grows, flowers, fruits, and dies during the second year (season)

bilateral symmetry: symmetry in which a plant body or organ can be divided by one plane into mirror-image halves

biomass: organic material derived from living plants that can be converted to energy by biological or chemical means

bipinnate: twice pinnate

bloom: a white (usually powdery) coating on leaves or fruits

blowout: a depression in the dunes or grasslands created by wind after vegetation is disturbed

bolt: when plants grow rapidly from a short, leafy state to a tall, flowering state

bract: a small, leaflike organ usually associated with an inflorescence or single flower

bracteole: a small bract

bristle: a short, stiff plant hair

bulbous: swollen or bulb shaped

bunchgrass: a grass species that grows in a clump as opposed to a mat or sod

burr: a rough, prickly case surrounding a plant seed

calyx: the outer set of perianth segments covering a flower; they are usually green and smaller than the flower petals

capsule: a dry fruit that splits open upon ripening, creating segments; the split may occur along the circumference, at the top of the capsule, or longitudinally

caryopsis: a one-seeded grass fruit; similar to an achene

catkin: a flexible, pendulous inflorescence with scaly bracts surrounding unisexual flowers; usually occurs on oaks and willows

cauline: pertaining to the stem of a plant

cespitose: a growth pattern that is densely clumped or tufted; often seen in graminoids

clasping: a leaf without a stem; usually, the leaf blade partially surrounds the stem

cleistogamous: having flowers that do not open and are self-pollinated

climax (community): a self-perpetuating community where species composition remains stable over time; the endpoint of succession

compound: a leaf composed of two to several leaflets; leaflets are arranged pinnately or palmately

cone: a unisexual reproductive structure of a conifer; the structure may possess woody, leathery, or fleshy scales; each scale bears pollen sacs or one or more seeds

cordate: heart shaped; usually pertains to the base of a leaf

corolla: collectively, the inner, delicate petals of a flower, which are usually a color other than green

corymb: a flat-topped inflorescence; the outer flowers open first

crenate: a rounded, wavy, or scalloped margin of a plant organ, such as a leaf

crown: the aboveground parts of a plant, including stems, leaves, and flowers; usually associated with trees

culm: the aerial stem of a grass or sedge

cultivar: a variety of a wild plant that has been selected and maintained through cultivation

cuticle: a thin, waxy layer on a leaf that prevents water loss and blocks other substances from entering

cutting: technique for vegetatively propagating a plant from a piece of stem or root

cyathium (pl. cyanthia): an inflorescence that includes nectaries, bracts, and several highly reduced flowers; peculiar to plants in the Euphorbiaceae (Spurge) family

cyme: a flat-topped inflorescence; the inner flowers open first

deciduous: a plant with foliage shed annually at the end of the growing season; in late-deciduous plants, shedding is delayed to as late as the beginning of the next growing season

decumbent: reclining or lying flat along the ground with an ascending tip or extremity

deflation: erosion of sand from a surface by action of the wind

dehiscent: splitting open naturally at maturity along lines of weakness or where parts join; usually applied to seedpods

deliquescent: a branching pattern in which branches radiate from the central axis of a plant that does not possess a single stem

detritivore: an organism that feeds on, and derives energy from, detritus, the partially decomposed remains of plants and animals

dioecious: a species in which male and female flowers occur on separate plants; compare with monoecious

disk flowers: small, tubular flowers in the central disk of flowers in the Aster family

dissected: deeply divided into numerous segments; typically associated with the characterization of a leaf

distal: refers to a plant part or organ farthest from the base

distichous: alternate arrangement of plant organs in two vertical rows on opposite sides of an axis

drupe: a fleshy indehiscent fruit possessing a single seed surrounded by a hard covering; cherry and olive fruits are examples

ecotone: the transition between two distinct plant communities; the transition may be abrupt or gradual and is usually recognized by a change in the dominant plant species

edge effect: a change in plant and animal community structure at the boundary of two types of habitat such as grasslands and forest. Small community patches have large edge effects

ellipsoid: a shape created by elongating a sphere; football shaped

elliptical: a plant part or organ having the shape of an ellipse

endemic: refers to a native species found exclusively in a particular area and nowhere else; endemics typically are found only in small geographic areas

entire: having a smooth, continuous margin without indentations or teeth, such as a leaf

estuary, estuarine: an area where fresh water and ocean water mix

evapotranspiration: the combined loss of water via evaporation from the soil and transpiration from plants in a given area

evergreen: a plant with foliage that persists and remains green throughout the year

exotic: not native to the area in which it is found; introduced from a different place, such as another continent

exserted: protruding beyond an enclosing structure; stamens or stigmas may extend beyond the corolla

fascicle: a bundle or cluster of stems, leaves, or flowers; many pines have fascicles of leaves

fibrous: a root system consisting of thin, branching roots from the base of the plant

fiddlehead: the furled or unexpanded frond of a fern; it is shaped like the end of a violin

floral tube: a structure created by united, elongated petals; stamens and pistils often emerge from this tube; common floral structure in the Convolvulaceae (Morning glory) family

floret: a small flower; usually refers to flowers of the Grass, Sedge, and Aster families; grass and sedge florets lack sepals and petals; asters may possess ray or disk florets or both

follicle: a dehiscent seedpod that splits along only one side; swallow-wort, a member of the Apocynaceae (Dogbane) family, produces this type of seedpod

frond: leaf or leaflike part of a fern or a palm

gabion: a hard engineering structure; a cage or box filled with rocks or soil and used to reduce the impact of waves along an estuarine shoreline

genus (pl. genera): a taxonomic group containing one or more species with a fundamentally similar structure

glabrous: a plant surface, such as a leaf or stem, that is hairless

glandular: a plant surface possessing glands, which are minute, oil-secreting structures

glaucous: a grayish-green or whitish-green plant surface; also, a smooth plant surface covered with a whitish bloom that rubs off easily

globose: a structure with a globular or roughly spherical shape

glochid: one of a number of tiny, usually barbed, bristles found in the areole of many cacti

graminoid: an herbaceous plant with grasslike morphology. Graminoid plants have long culms and leaf blades. Refers to grasses, sedges, rushes, arrow-grasses, and quillworts

gray water: wastewater generated by humans that has not been contaminated by fecal matter; relatively clean water

halophyte: a plant capable of growing and reproducing in a saline environment

hastula: a triangular flange of tough material on the upper side of the petiole where it joins the frond blade of some palm fronds; the point where the petiole and frond join

haustorium (pl. haustoria): a projection from the root of a parasitic plant, such as mistletoe, that enables the parasite to penetrate the host plant tissues and derive nutrition

head: a short, compact inflorescence at the top of a stem usually associated with members of the Aster family

hemiparasite: a plant that obtains food from both photosynthesis and parasitism of another plant

herbaceous: a plant with leaves and stems that die back to the ground at the end of the growing season; not woody

herbivory: the consumption of vegetation by animals; herbivory usually does not result in the death of the plant

hydrologic cycle: the sequence of events involved in moving water coming from water vapor through precipitation, surface water, and groundwater and back into the atmosphere via evaporation and transpiration

hydrophyte: a plant adapted to growing in water

hypersaline: a condition in which the water in the environment is saltier than normal seawater; usually achieved by the evaporation of seawater

imbricate: arrangement of leaves and other plant parts in a closely packed, overlapping pattern

incised: deeply, sharply, and sometimes irregularly cut, such as the edge of a leaf

indehiscent: not splitting open naturally at maturity; usually applied to seedpods

indeterminate: a plant inflorescence in which the lower flowers bloom first. This allows indefinite elongation of the flowering stem

indigenous (nonindigenous): native to a particular area (nonnative to a particular area)

inflorescence: the flowering head of a plant, including associated stems, bracts, and flowers; also refers to the arrangement of flowers on a stem

inlet: a waterway between barrier islands or barrier beaches connecting the ocean and a lagoon, bay, sound, or tidal creek

inrolled: rolled inward; often refers to leaves

invasive plant: an aggressive, nonnative species that can outcompete native plants in undisturbed natural areas and alter the natural balance of the plant community

involucre: one or more bracts arising from beneath a flower cluster and surrounding it

joint: a point of articulation on a stem; often bears a leaf

keel: the two lower or front fused petals of a flower in the Fabaceae (Bean) family, which form a boatlike structure surrounding the stamens and pistil; also, any ridged structure on a plant

lanceolate: description of any plant structure, usually a leaf, that is longer than it is wide, is broad at the base, and has a long, pointed apex

lateral: any plant organ (flower, bud, or stem) borne at the side

layering: a method of plant propagation in which an intact stem or branch is placed in contact with the soil, encouraging it to form new roots

leaflet: one of the individual segments of a compound leaf

legume: the fruit of a member of the Fabaceae (Bean) family that splits into two halves; the seeds are attached to one edge of the fruit

lenticel: a small, lens-shaped pore on young woody stems that allows gas exchange between the atmosphere and internal plant tissues

linear: a long, narrow plant structure; grass leaves are typically linear

made-land: formerly a wetland, an area of land that has been man-made through the use of fill material during a reclamation project

margin: the edge of a leaf blade; types of leaf margins include lobed, toothed, and entire

médano (Spanish for dune): a large, unvegetated, or nearly unvegetated dune

meiofauna: collectively, the group of tiny benthic organisms living among the grains of sand and shell in the intertidal beach zone

mesic: a habitat characterized as being moist, but not wet

midrib: the central or middle rib of a leaf or leaflet

midvein: the main vascular supply to a leaf or leaflet

monoecious: a plant species that possesses both male and female unisexual flowers on the same plant; compare with dioecious

mottled: possessing different shades or colors; spotted

mucilaginous: a moist, viscous plant secretion; slimy

mucronate: a leaf with a short projection at the tip

mycorrhiza (pl. mycorrhizae): a fungus that grows in association with plant roots in a symbiotic relationship

native: a plant that originated in the area in which it grows

nectar gland: a fluid-secreting organ in a flower, leaf, or stem; usually sweet

needle: the narrow, stiff leaf of members of the Pinaceae (Pine) family

node: the position on a plant stem where branches or leaves originate

nodule: a small, knoblike growth on the roots of members of the Fabaceae (Bean) family that contains nitrogen-fixing bacteria

nutlet: a small nut; a single-seeded section of the fruit of members of the Lamiaceae (Mint) family

oblanceolate: lance shaped, but broadest above the middle and tapering toward the base; often refers to a leaf

oblong: elongated with approximately parallel sides

obovate: roughly egg shaped, but widest above the middle and narrowing toward the base

obovoid: three-dimensional, egg-shaped structure with its narrow end at the base

ocrea: a sheath formed from fused stipules around the node of a stem; a key characteristic of some members of the Polygonaceae (Smartweed) family

orbicular: circular; often refers to a leaf that is nearly circular and flat

ovary: a part of the female reproductive organ of a flower; the part of the pistil that contains the ovule or ovules

ovate: egg-shaped in outline; broadest just below the middle

overwash; oceanic overwash: a process in which a storm surge pushes water and sand across a barrier island or barrier beach and deposits it at a distance from the beach

pad: the flattened stem of a member of the Cactaceae (Cactus) family; a round, floating leaf of an aquatic plant such as a water lily

palmate: possessing three or more lobes, veins, or other plant parts radiating fanlike from a central point; digitate, like a hand

palustrine: wetlands lacking flowing water and dominated by trees, shrubs, and herbs; also, wetlands in tidal areas with a salinity of less than five parts per thousand

panicle: an inflorescence in which the branches are racemes; a common form of inflorescence in the Poaceae (Grass) family

panne: a slightly depressed coastal wetland, with or without standing water; typically in a salt marsh

pantropical: distributed throughout the tropical regions of the world

pappus: a tuft of fine hairs, bristles, or scales attached to the seed coat of many members of the Asteraceae (Aster) family; the pappus aids in wind dispersal

pedicle: a stalk bearing a single flower or fruit in an inflorescence

peduncle: a stalk bearing an entire flower cluster, or a single flower (fruit) when that flower is solitary on the plant

peltate: a leaf whose petiole is attached near the center of the lower surface rather than the margin; umbrella shaped; small scales on a plant organ, such as a leaf, may have similarly constructed hairs

pendant: hanging on a stalk with the apex pointed vertically downward; typically a flower or fruit

perennial: a plant with a life cycle longer than two years

perfect (flower): having functional stamens and pistils

perianth: collectively, the outer covering of a flower; composed of sepals or petals or both

petal: one unit of the outer covering of a flower; a division of a corolla; usually brightly colored and showy

petiole: the stalk that attaches a leaf to the stem

phreatophyte: a plant with deep roots that collect water from at or near the water table; the plant is usually drought tolerant

phyllary (pl. phyllaries): one of several modified leaves (bracts) that surround the involucre in flowers of members in the Asteraceae (Aster) family

pinna (pl. pinnae): a primary division of a pinnate leaf; a single leaflet of a compound leaf; in ferns, a division attached to the main stem (rachis)

pinnate: featherlike; leaflets or other divisions arranged on either side of a common stalk

pinnately compound: pinnately arranged leaflets or other divisions that are divided again; twice-divided pinnate arrangement of leaflets or other divisions

pistil: the female, seed-bearing part of a flower composed of (when complete) ovary, style, and stigma

pistillate (flowers): having one or more functional pistils but no functional stamens

Pleistocene Epoch: the geological time period between 1.8 million and 17,700 years ago

pocosin: a forested wetland plant community with water-saturated, sandy soil; other names include bay, bay head, evergreen shrub bog, and forested bog

pod: a dry, dehiscent, several-seeded fruit; fruits of species in the Fabaceae (Bean) family are referred to as pods

prickles: a small, often hard, spinelike extension of the epidermis of a plant stem; many rose species have prickles

primary productivity: the rate at which photosynthesis occurs; usually measured in a particular area

procumbent: the condition of a plant stem that

lies flat against the ground but does not root at the nodes

prostrate: growing flat along the ground; plant stems often grow in this manner

pubescent: covered with short, soft hairs; downy

punctate: a plant surface (for example, a leaf, petal, or sepal) that is dotted with glands

raceme: a type of inflorescence with stalked flowers arranged singly along an unbranched axis

rachis: the main stem of an inflorescence; the stalk of a pinnately compound leaf

ray flower: flowers lining the outside edge of the disk in members of the Aster family; usually the ray flowers have one large petal; the outer flowers of a daisy

receptacle: the thickened part of a stem on which the flower parts are borne—parts such as the pistil, stamens, and petals

resin gland: a tiny, yellow- or amber-colored protuberance on the surface of a plant structure such as a leaf

rhizome: a horizontal underground stem capable of sending out shoots and roots; possesses nodes, buds, and occasionally, scalelike leaves

rootlet: a small or fine branch of a root; an adventitious aerial root

rosette: a circular arrangement of leaves around a stem; an arrangement near the base of a plant is called a basal rosette

runner: slender stem growing horizontally along the ground; may give rise to roots or stems at the distal end or at a node

samara: a dry, dehiscent, single-seeded fruit bearing a wing; Carolina red maple fruits are an example

secund: arranged on only one side; for example, flowers arranged on one side of an inflorescence

seedbank: seeds naturally deposited and residing in the soil ungerminated for more than one season

semideciduous: leaves persistent on a plant past the usual fall season but dropping before leaves emerge the following spring

sepal: one of the separate, usually green, parts forming the calyx that surrounds a flower

serrate: having a saw-toothed edge with teeth pointing forward; usually refers to the margin of a leaf

sessile: not possessing a stalk; attached directly to the stem

shell midden: a mound or deposit containing shells; indicates the site of a human habitation

silique: an elongated fruit with two valves; usually refers to the fruit of the Brassicaceae (Mustard) family

simple: a leaf not divided into leaflets; not compound; an inflorescence that is unbranched

sorus (pl. sori): a spore-bearing cluster of sporangia on the underside of a fern frond

spathe: a modified bract that surrounds the flowers of members of the Arecaceae (Palm) family and the Araceae (Arum) family; it may be herbaceous and colored or dry, hard, and woody

species: a category of taxonomic classification that ranks below a genus; a group of plants that produce similar offspring

spike: an elongated, unbranched inflorescence with sessile flowers arranged singly

spikelet: a small or secondary spike; the floral unit of a Poaceae grass composed of flowers and their surrounding bracts

spine: a hard, pointed structure on a plant stem

sporangium (pl. sporangia): in ferns, a structure in which spores are produced

spore: a reproductive body resistant to desiccation and heat; often refers to ferns

spring tide: tide that coincides with a new and full moon where the highest high tide (and lowest low tide) is recorded

stamen: the pollen-producing organ of a flower; composed of an anther and a filament

staminate (flowers): having one or more functional stamens but no functional pistils

standard: the single, expanded, erect, large petal surrounded by lateral and keel petals; characteristic of some members of the Fabaceae (Bean) family

stellate: star shaped

stemflow: redirection of water down plant branches and stems; usually refers to water reaching the ground after flowing down a tree trunk

stigma: the apex of a pistil that is receptive to pollen

stipule: a small appendage at the base of a petiole; usually in pairs

stolon: a horizontal stem that produces adventitious roots and buds at the nodes; runners

stomate (pl. stomata): a small pore on a leaf surface or stem surrounded by guard cells; site of gas exchange in a leaf

stratification: the process of pretreating seeds of some plant species with a period of cold that simulates winter conditions; stratification usually improves the germination rate

style: in a flower, the slender part of a pistil located between the stigma and the ovary

sub-opposite: nearly opposite; refers to the position of leaves on a stem

subtend: the condition of occupying a position below and adjacent; usually refers to one plant part located relative to another plant part

succulent: stems or leaves that store water

sucker (root): a shoot produced from the roots or base of a woody plant that can give rise to a new plant

swale: a shallow depression in the ground that is often moist and may be the product of a blowout

syconium: the fruit of a fig; a large, fleshy, hollowed-out receptacle that contains a mass of tiny seeds

symbiosis: a close association between two or more individuals of different species that may or may not benefit each member

taproot: the long, large, straight, tapering main root of a plant that grows straight downward; lateral roots branch from the taproot

tendril: a leaf or stem modified into a threadlike structure that twines around an object, allowing a plant to climb

tepal: a segment of plant parts surrounding the outside of a flower that has no differentiation between petals and sepals

terminal: positioned at the distal end of a stem or branch

throughfall: the portion of precipitation reaching the ground after passing through the forest canopy

tiller (tillering): a shoot that sprouts from the base of a grass plant; the process of sprouting new shoots

tomentose: covered with dense, soft, sometimes matted hairs or filaments

trichome: a hairlike or bristle-like outgrowth from the epidermis of a plant; often glandular

trifoliate: having three leaves, leaflets, or leaflike parts

tubercle: a small, rounded nodule or protuberance on a surface of a plant part. Some plants have many tiny tubercles on the seed coat

tuberous (tuber): having the qualities of an enlarged, fleshy, underground stem that bears buds from which new plants arise

tuna: the edible fruit of a cactus

umbel: an inflorescence in which the flower stalks originate from a common point and are nearly equal in length; the top of the inflorescence is flat or slightly curved

utricle: a small, bladderlike, one-seeded indehiscent fruit; common fruit type in the Amaranthaceae (Amaranth) family

variety: a subdivision of a species below the subspecies level; divergence from the species or subspecies is minor, but the variety breeds true to these differences

venation: the pattern or arrangement of the venous system on a leaf blade

wavy: undulating, with alternating concave and convex curves

weed: a plant growing where it is not wanted, often competing with landscape and other plants; weeds tend to grow aggressively and reproduce prolifically

wetland: "Those areas that are inundated or saturated by surface or ground water at a frequency and duration sufficient to support, and that under normal circumstances do support, a prevalence of vegetation typically adapted for life in saturated soil conditions. Wetlands generally include swamps, marshes, bogs, and similar areas." (Source: U.S. Army Corps of Engineers)

whorl (whorled): arrangement of three or more plant organs, such as leaves, radiating from a single node

windthrow: trees (and large shrubs) uprooted or broken by high winds

winged: possessing a dry, membranous, winglike appendage

winter annual: an annual plant that germinates in the fall or winter, lives through the winter, and typically blooms in the spring

woody: composed of wood—a dead, hard, xylem tissue; woody stems do not die back to the ground at the end of the growing season

wrack line: the line or zone of debris left high on the backshore after storms or high tides; it includes organic matter and flotsam and jetsam such as plastics

xerophyte: a plant adapted for growth in an environment with limited water; a plant that exhibits adaptations for water storage or water conservation

zygomorphic: having only one plane of symmetry; bilaterally symmetrical

APPENDIX 3
COMMON NAME TO SCIENTIFIC NAME SYNONYMY

COMMON NAME	SCIENTIFIC NAME	PROFILE NUMBER
alligatorweed	*Alternanthera philoxeroides*	63
American beachgrass	*Ammophila breviligulata*	13
American germander	*Teucrium canadense*	105
American holly	*Ilex opaca*	185
American mistletoe	*Phoradendron leucarpum*	162
American witch hazel	*Hamamelis virginiana*	147
annual bluegrass	*Poa annua*	9
annual sand bean	*Strophostyles helvola*	133
bald cypress	*Taxodium distichum*	213
bay-hops	*Ipomoea pes-caprae*	118
beach blanket-flower	*Gaillardia pulchella*	52
beach evening primrose	*Oenothera drummondii*	88
beach morning glory	*Ipomoea imperati*	119
beach pinweed	*Lechea maritima*	81
beach vitex	*Vitex rotundifolia*	173
beach wormwood	*Artemisia stelleriana*	65
beargrass	*Yucca filamentosa*	175
beauty berry	*Callicarpa americana*	141
Bermudagrass	*Cynodon dactylon*	18
bigleaf hydrangea	*Hydrangea macrophylla*	149
bitterweed	*Helenium amarum*	53
black cherry	*Prunus serotina*	202
black gum	*Nyssa sylvatica*	193
black locust	*Robinia pseudoacacia*	208
black needlerush	*Juncus roemerianus*	26
bristly foxtail grass	*Setaria parviflora*	36
cabbage palmetto	*Sabal palmetto*	209
Carolina jessamine	*Gelsemium sempervirens*	115
Carolina laurel cherry	*Prunus caroliniana*	201
Carolina red maple	*Acer rubrum*	176
Carolina willow	*Salix caroliniana*	210
centipede grass	*Eremochloa ophiuroides*	22
chinaberry	*Melia azedarach*	191
Chinese podocarpus	*Podocarpus macrophyllus*	199
Chinese privet	*Ligustrum sinense*	156
Chinese tallow	*Triadica sebifera*	214
climbing hempweed	*Mikania scandens*	123
coastal American hornbeam	*Carpinus caroliniana*	179
coastal bedstraw	*Galium bermudense*	76
coastal little bluestem	*Schizachyrium littorale*	34
coastal morning glory	*Ipomoea cordatotriloba*	117
coastal plain bindweed	*Calystegia sepium*	111
coastal red cedar	*Juniperus virginiana*	186
cocklebur	*Xanthium strumarium*	62

COMMON NAME	SCIENTIFIC NAME	PROFILE NUMBER
common cattail	*Typha latifolia*	108
common duckweed	*Lemna perpusilla*	82
common elderberry	*Sambucus canadensis*	168
common elephant's foot	*Elephantopus tomentosus*	73
common fig	*Ficus carica*	146
common frogfruit	*Phyla nodiflora*	92
common lantana	*Lantana strigocamara*	155
common mullein	*Verbascum thapsus*	109
common persimmon	*Diospyros virginiana*	184
common ragweed	*Ambrosia artemisiifolia*	44
common reed	*Phragmites australis*	32
common water hyacinth	*Eichhornia crassipes*	72
common wax myrtle	*Morella cerifera*	157
common yellow thistle	*Cirsium horridulum*	68
coral honeysuckle	*Lonicera sempervirens*	122
cottonleaf goldenaster	*Chrysopsis gossypina*	67
crabgrass	*Digitaria sanguinalis*	8
crape myrtle / crepe myrtle	*Lagerstroemia indica*	187
creeping bluet	*Houstonia procumbens*	78
dog fennel	*Eupatorium capillifolium*	74
dotted smartweed	*Persicaria punctata*	91
dune blue curls	*Trichostema* [species 1]	61
dune camphorweed	*Heterotheca subaxillaris*	54
dune finger grass	*Eustachys petraea*	23
dune greenbriar	*Smilax auriculata*	130
dune ground cherry	*Physalis walteri*	93
dune hairgrass	*Muhlenbergia sericea*	28
dune pennywort	*Hydrocotyle bonariensis*	79
dune prickly-pear	*Opuntia drummondii*	160
dune sandspur	*Cenchrus tribuloides*	7
dune wormseed	*Dysphania anthelmintica*	49
dwarf glasswort	*Salicornia bigelovii*	58
dwarf palmetto	*Sabal minor*	167
eastern bloodleaf	*Iresine rhizomatosa*	80
eastern coral bean	*Erythrina herbacea*	144
eastern prickly-pear	*Opuntia humifusa*	161
eastern rose mallow	*Hibiscus moscheutos*	77
ebony spleenwort	*Asplenium platyneuron*	1
English ivy	*Hedera helix*	116
field lovegrass	*Eragrostis elliottii*	21
finger rot	*Cnidoscolus stimulosus*	69
fire-on-the-mountain	*Euphorbia cyathophora*	75
fireweed	*Erechtites hieraciifolius*	50
flowering dogwood	*Cornus florida*	183
giant cordgrass	*Sporobolus cynosuroides*	38
giant foxtail grass	*Setaria magna*	11
Indian hawthorn	*Rhaphiolepis indica*	164
Japanese aralia	*Fatsia japonica*	145
Japanese black pine	*Pinus thunbergii*	198

COMMON NAME	SCIENTIFIC NAME	PROFILE NUMBER
Japanese honeysuckle	*Lonicera japonica*	121
Japanese pittosporum	*Pittosporum tobira*	163
Japanese shore juniper	*Juniperus conferta*	153
Japanese wisteria	*Wisteria floribunda*	136
juniperleaf	*Polypremum procumbens*	97
large-headed rush	*Juncus megacephalus*	25
large sea purslane	*Sesuvium portulacastrum*	101
laurel greenbriar	*Smilax laurifolia*	132
lesser quaking grass	*Briza minor*	6
live oak	*Quercus virginiana*	207
loblolly pine	*Pinus taeda*	197
longleaf pine	*Pinus palustris*	196
maritime bushy bluestem	*Andropogon tenuispatheus*	14
maritime catbriar	*Smilax bona-nox*	131
maritime pokeweed	*Phytolacca rigida*	94
marsh elder	*Iva frutescens*	151
marsh fern	*Thelypteris palustris*	5
marsh pink	*Sabatia stellaris*	57
Monnier's water-hyssop	*Bacopa monnieri*	66
morning honeysuckle	*Oenothera simulans*	90
muscadine	*Muscadinia rotundifolia*	124
narrowleaf plantain	*Plantago lanceolata*	95
narrowleaf white-topped sedge	*Rhynchospora colorata*	33
narrow-leaved cattail	*Typha angustifolia*	107
narrow-leaved loosestrife	*Lythrum lineare*	84
nodding ladies' tresses	*Spiranthes cernua*	103
northern bayberry	*Morella pensylvanica*	158
northern saltwort	*Salsola kali*	59
northern seaside spurge	*Euphorbia polygonifolia*	51
oleander	*Nerium oleander*	159
Olney's threesquare	*Schoenoplectus americanus*	35
pampas grass	*Cortaderia selloana*	17
partridge berry	*Mitchella repens*	86
peppervine	*Nekemias arborea*	125
perennial saltmarsh aster	*Symphyotrichum tenuifolium*	104
pignut hickory	*Carya glabra*	181
poison ivy	*Toxicodendron radicans*	134
poorjoe	*Diodella teres*	48
purple passionflower	*Passiflora incarnata*	127
purple sandgrass	*Triplasis purpurea*	12
rabbitsfoot grass	*Polypogon monspeliensis*	10
rattlebox	*Sesbania punicea*	170
red bay	*Persea borbonia*	194
red buckeye	*Aesculus pavia*	177
red mulberry	*Morus rubra*	192
resurrection fern	*Pleopeltis michauxiana*	3
rosemary	*Rosmarinus officinalis*	98
royal fern	*Osmunda spectabilis*	2
rugosa rose	*Rosa rugosa*	166

COMMON NAME	SCIENTIFIC NAME	PROFILE NUMBER
saltcedar	*Tamarix ramosissima*	171
saltgrass	*Distichlis spicata*	19
saltmarsh bulrush	*Bolboschoenus robustus*	15
saltmarsh fimbristylis	*Fimbristylis castanea*	24
saltmarsh morning glory	*Ipomoea sagittata*	120
salt-marsh water hemp	*Amaranthus cannabinus*	64
saltmarsh wild rye	*Elymus virginicus*	20
saltmeadow cordgrass	*Sporobolus pumilus*	39
saltwater false willow	*Baccharis angustifolia*	137
saltwort	*Batis maritima*	139
sand dayflower	*Commelina erecta*	70
sand laurel oak	*Quercus hemisphaerica*	205
sand live oak	*Quercus geminata*	204
sassafras	*Sassafras albidum*	211
saw grass	*Cladium jamaicense*	16
saw palmetto	*Serenoa repens*	169
seabeach amaranth	*Amaranthus pumilus*	43
seabeach evening primrose	*Oenothera humifusa*	89
seabeach knotweed	*Polygonum glaucum*	96
seabeach orach	*Atriplex mucronata*	45
sea elder	*Iva imbricata*	152
sea lavender	*Limonium carolinianum*	83
sea myrtle	*Baccharis halimifolia*	138
sea oats	*Uniola paniculata*	42
sea ox-eye	*Borrichia frutescens*	140
sea rocket	*Cakile harperi*	46
seashore dropseed	*Sporobolus virginicus*	40
seashore mallow	*Kosteletzkya pentacarpos*	154
seashore paspalum	*Paspalum vaginatum*	31
seaside panicum	*Panicum amarum*	29
silver-leaf croton	*Croton punctatus*	142
slash pine	*Pinus elliottii*	195
smooth cordgrass	*Sporobolus alterniflorus*	37
South American jelly palm	*Butia odorata*	178
southern bracken fern	*Pteridium latiusculum*	4
southern dewberry	*Rubus trivialis*	128
southern horseweed	*Conyza canadensis*	47
southern magnolia	*Magnolia grandiflora*	189
southern red oak	*Quercus falcata*	203
southern saltmarsh fleabane	*Pluchea odorata*	55
southern sea-blite	*Suaeda linearis*	60
southern seaside goldenrod	*Solidago mexicana*	102
Spanish dagger	*Yucca aloifolia*	174
Spanish moss	*Tillandsia usneoides*	106
sparkleberry	*Vaccinium arboreum*	172
spotted horsemint	*Monarda punctata*	87
spurred butterfly pea	*Centrosema virginianum*	113
St. Augustine grass	*Stenotaphrum secundatum*	41
sugarberry	*Celtis laevigata*	182

COMMON NAME	SCIENTIFIC NAME	PROFILE NUMBER
summer grape	*Vitis aestivalis*	135
supplejack	*Berchemia scandens*	110
swallow-wort	*Seutera angustifolia*	129
sweet autumn virgin's bower	*Clematis terniflora*	114
sweet bay	*Magnolia virginiana*	190
sweet gum	*Liquidambar styraciflua*	188
switchgrass	*Panicum virgatum*	30
thorny elaeagnus	*Elaeagnus pungens*	143
toothache tree	*Zanthoxylum clava-herculis*	215
tough bully	*Sideroxylon tenax*	212
tropical Mexican clover	*Richardia brasiliensis*	56
trumpet creeper	*Campsis radicans*	112
two-flower melic grass	*Melica mutica*	27
Virginia buttonweed	*Diodia virginiana*	71
Virginia creeper	*Parthenocissus quinquefolia*	126
Virginia glasswort	*Salicornia virginica*	99
water oak	*Quercus nigra*	206
water pimpernel	*Samolus parviflorus*	100
white poplar	*Populus alba*	200
white sweet clover	*Melilotus albus*	85
wild olive	*Cartrema americanum*	180
winged sumac	*Rhus copallinum*	165
woolly beach heather	*Hudsonia tomentosa*	148
yaupon	*Ilex vomitoria*	150

ACKNOWLEDGMENTS

A book such as *Seacoast Plants of the Carolinas* is never the product of one or even a small number of individuals. This book represents the observations of eyewitnesses to the natural world—scientists, natural historians, and casual spectators whose research and understanding of coastal ecosystems form our accumulated knowledge. It is the sum of the experiences, reflections, and actions of many individuals who have aided me in the compilation and presentation of information related to coastal plant ecology.

The University of North Carolina Wilmington afforded me the time, opportunity, and resources to pursue this endeavor. I am indebted to Drs. Martin Posey, Chris Finelli, and Heather Koopman, chairs of the Biology and Marine Biology Department, for their support. Personnel from William Madison Randall Library and technical support from the Information Technology Systems Division provided critical and timely intervention.

My experiences in the classroom and especially on myriad coastal-themed field trips with undergraduate and graduate students shaped the content and style of this volume. Students love to be able to identify native plants and to understand the role of each in the coastal environment. Similarly, members of various nonprofit organizations with coastal interests helped me to see the need to organize basic information on how native plants can be used in our daily living. Their joy in understanding the natural world demonstrated this truth as I made presentations and led field trips. To all these individuals, I am grateful for their suggestions and direction.

Over the years, North Carolina Sea Grant extension specialists, especially Dr. Lundie Spence and Spencer Rogers, have cited the value of Karl Graetz's original *Seacoast Plants of the Carolinas*. Upon their suggestions— echoed by David Perry during his tenure as UNC Press editorial director and by many partners all along the Carolinas coast—Katie Mosher, Sea Grant's communications director, pushed for an update of this original work. Her efforts included assembling a team to address this need, providing a focal point for input, serving as chief advocate for the project, infusing others with enthusiasm for the new book, and continuously serving as a resource, critic, and inspiration to this author. In their roles as North Carolina Sea Grant's executive director, Drs. Susan White and Michael Voiland enthusiastically supported the overall effort, from the manuscript development through book production.

Katharine Braly Elks completed the initial compilation of the books, documents, reports, and other information that formed the basis of the plant profiles. Cary Paynter, Lara Berkley, and Dr. Eric Bolen provided critical reviews of early drafts, sharing suggestions and corrections that enhanced the manuscript.

My gratitude also goes to Drs. Darin Pennys, Jessica Whitehead, Alan Weakley, and the late Dick Dillaman. I give further thanks to Spencer Rogers, Gloria Putnam, and Tracy Skrabal. Each of these individuals had a hand in shaping the manuscript, from identifying and locating plants and other resource materials to reviewing draft documents and constantly encouraging completion of the overall tasks. Their ideas are woven into and clearly evident throughout the manuscript. Two anonymous readers also provided immensely helpful suggestions and encouragement to pursue publication.

Debbi Sykes Braswell, with a turn of phrase, change in punctuation, or selection of a more appropriate word, made readability of the manuscript soar and brought my pedantic language to life. Pam Smith set the content and tone of the plant profiles section with her editorial remarks. Andrea Dingeldein turned written words, verbal comments, and scribbled diagrams into works of art in preparing the illustrations.

Any errors of omission or commission are my responsibility.

In the preparation of this manuscript,

I could not have had a better editorial team than UNC Press Editorial Director Mark Simpson-Vos, Associate Editor Jessica Newman, and their colleagues. Mark and his team provided guidance, assistance, and timely feedback concerning the manuscript, as well as editorial guidance on other elements.

To my spouse, Elizabeth, I offer my most warm and affectionate thank you. You have endured long lectures and presentations on coastal ecology, endless field trips in fair and foul weather, innumerable photo sessions with native plants, and my occasional moodiness and habitual distraction while the book matured in my mind and on paper. Yet, in return, you have provided decades of continuous, enthusiastic, and unwavering support and encouragement.

My royalties from the sale of this book will be donated to the Paul E. Hosier Undergraduate Research and Creativity Fellowship in the Center for Support of Undergraduate Research and Fellowships (CSURF) at UNC Wilmington.

Paul E. Hosier
Wilmington, North Carolina

BOOKS

Alexander, J., and J. Lazell. 2000. *Ribbon of Sand: The Convergence of the Ocean and the Outer Banks*. Chapel Hill: University of North Carolina Press. 256 pp.

Barry, J. M. 1980. *Natural Vegetation of South Carolina*. Columbia: University of South Carolina Press. 214 pp.

Batson, W. T. 1984. *Landscape Plants for the Southeast*. Columbia: University of South Carolina Press. 427 pp.

————. 1987. *Wild Flowers in the Carolinas*. Columbia: University of South Carolina Press. 153 pp.

Bell, C. R., and B. J. Taylor. 1982. *Florida Wild Flowers and Roadside Plants*. Chapel Hill: University of North Carolina Press. 308 pp.

Brown, C. L., and L. K. Kirkman. 1990. *Trees of Georgia and Adjacent States*. Portland, Ore.: Timber Press. 372 pp.

Brown, C. A., and G. N. Montz. 1986. *Bald Cypress: The Tree Unique, the Wood Eternal*. Baton Rouge, La.: Claitor's Publishing Division. 139 pp.

Cox, D. D. 2003. *A Naturalist's Guide to Seashore Plants: An Ecology for Eastern North America*. Syracuse, N.Y.: Syracuse University Press. 156 pp.

Daiber, F. C. 1986. *Conservation of Tidal Marshes*. New York: Van Nostrand Reinhold. 341 pp.

Dirr, M. A. 2009. *Manual of Woody Landscape Plants: Their Identification, Ornamental Characteristics, Culture, Propagation, and Uses*. 6th ed. Champaign, Ill.: Stipes Publishing. 1187 pp.

Douglas, M. S. 1947. *The Everglades: River of Grass*. New York: Rinehart and Co. 406 pp.

Duke, J. A. 1997. *The Green Pharmacy*. New York: St. Martin's Press. 507 pp.

Dunbar, L. 1989. *Ferns of the Coastal Plain: Their Lore, Legends, and Uses*. Columbia: University of South Carolina Press. 128 pp.

Duncan, W. H, and M. B. Duncan. 1987. *Seaside Plants of the Gulf and Atlantic Coasts*. Washington, D.C.: Smithsonian Institution Press. 409 pp.

————. 1988. *Trees of the Southeastern United States*. Athens: University of Georgia Press. 336 pp.

————. 1999. *Wildflowers of the Eastern United States*. Athens: University of Georgia Press. 416 pp.

Eleuterius, L. N. 1990. *Tidal Marsh Plants*. Gretna, La.: Pelican Publishing. 168 pp.

Foote, L. E., and S. B. Jones Jr. 1989. *Native Shrubs and Woody Vines of the Southeast: Landscaping Uses and Identification*. Portland, Ore.: Timber Press. 255 pp.

Frankenberg, Dirk. 1995. *The Nature of the Outer Banks: Environmental Processes, Field Sites, and Development Issues, Corolla to Ocracoke*. Chapel Hill: University of North Carolina Press. 157 pp.

————. 1997. *The Nature of North Carolina's Southern Coast: Barrier Islands, Coastal Waters, and Wetlands*. Chapel Hill: University of North Carolina Press. 250 pp.

Gledhill, D. 2008. *The Names of Plants*. 4th ed. Cambridge: Cambridge University Press. 436 pp.

Godfrey, R. K. 1988. *Trees, Shrubs, and Woody Vines of Northern Florida and Adjacent Georgia and Alabama*. Athens: University of Georgia Press. 734 pp.

Godfrey, R. K., and J. W. Wooten. 1979. *Aquatic and Wetland Plants of the Southeastern United States: Dicotyledons*. Athens: University of Georgia Press. 944 pp.

————. 1979. *Aquatic and Wetland Plants of the Southeastern United States: Monocotyledons*. Athens: University of Georgia Press. 712 pp.

Graetz, K. E. 1973. *Seacoast Plants of the Carolinas for Conservation and Beautification*. UNC Sea Grant Publication UNC-SG-73-06. 206 pp.

Gruenberg, B. U. 2014. *The Wild Horse Dilemma: Conflicts and Controversies of the Atlantic Coast Herds*. Strasburg, Pa.: Quagga Press. 597 pp.

Gupton, O. W., and F. C. Swope. 1982. *Wildflowers of Tidewater Virginia*. Charlottesville: University of Virginia Press. 208 pp.

Hackney C. T., S. M. Adams, and W. H. Martin, eds. 1992. *Biodiversity of the Southeastern United States: Aquatic Communities.* New York: John Wiley and Sons. 779 pp.

Halfacre, G. R., and A. Shawcroft. 1989. *Landscape Plants of the Southeast.* Raleigh, N.C.: Sparks Press. 325 pp.

Justice, W. S., C. R. Bell, and A. H. Lindsey. 2005. *Wild Flowers of North Carolina.* 2nd ed. Chapel Hill: University of North Carolina Press. 325 pp.

Kaplan, E. H. 1988. *A Field Guide to Southeastern and Caribbean Seashores: Cape Hatteras to the Gulf Coast, Florida, and the Caribbean.* Boston: Houghton Mifflin. 425 pp.

Kartesz, J. T. 1994. *A Synonymized Checklist of the Vascular Flora of the United States, Canada, and Greenland.* 2nd ed. 2 vols. Portland, Ore.: Timber Press. 622 pp. 816 pp.

Kraus, E. J. W. 1988. *A Guide to Ocean Dune Plants Common to North Carolina.* Chapel Hill: University of North Carolina Press. 72 pp.

Krings, A. 2010. *Manual of the Vascular Flora of Nags Head Woods, Outer Banks, North Carolina.* Memoirs of the New York Botanical Garden 103. New York: New York Botanical Garden Press. 308 pp.

Leatherman, S. P. 1988. *Barrier Island Handbook.* 3rd ed. Coastal Publication Series. College Park: University of Maryland Press. 92 pp.

Manning, P. 1995. *Palmetto Journal: Walks in the Natural Areas of South Carolina.* Winston-Salem, N.C.: John F. Blair. 238 pp.

Martin, L. C., and M. Magellan. 1989. *Southern Wildflowers.* Atlanta: Longstreet Press. 272 pp.

Martinez, M. L., and N. P. Psuty, eds. 2004. *Coastal Dunes: Ecology and Conservation.* Springer Ecological Studies. Berlin: Springer-Verlag. 386 pp.

Miller, J. H., and K. V. Miller. 2005. *Forest Plants of the Southeast and Their Wildlife Uses.* Athens: University of Georgia Press. 454 pp.

Mitsch, W. J., and J. G. Gosselink. 2000. *Wetlands.* 3rd ed. New York: John Wiley and Sons. 920 pp.

Nourse, H., and C. Nourse. 2000. *Wildflowers of Georgia.* Athens: University of Georgia Press. 120 pp.

Pilkey, O. H., Jr., W. J. Neal, O. H. Pilkey Sr., and S. R. Riggs. 1978. *From Currituck to Calabash: Living with North Carolina's Barrier Islands.* 2nd ed. Durham, N.C.: Duke University Press. 244 pp.

Porcher, R. D. 1995. *Wildflowers of the Carolina Lowcountry and Lower Pee Dee.* Columbia: University of South Carolina Press. 302 pp.

Porcher, R. D., and D. A. Raynor. 2001. *A Guide to the Wildflowers of South Carolina.* Columbia: University of South Carolina Press. 551 pp.

Radford, A. E., H. E. Ahles, and C. R. Bell. 1968. *Manual of the Vascular Flora of the Carolinas.* Chapel Hill: University of North Carolina Press. 1,183 pp.

Reimold, R. J., and W. H. Queen, eds. 1974. *Ecology of Halophytes.* New York: Academic Press. 605 pp.

Silberhorn, G. M. 1999. *Common Plants of the Mid-Atlantic Coast: A Field Guide.* Rev. ed. Baltimore: Johns Hopkins University Press. 294 pp.

Sillman, T. R., E. D. Grosholz, and M. D. Bertness, eds. 2009. *Human Impacts on Salt Marshes: A Global Perspective.* Berkeley: University of California Press. 413 pp.

Stuckey, I. H., and L. L. Gould. 2000. *Coastal Plants from Cape Cod to Cape Canaveral.* Chapel Hill: University of North Carolina Press. 305 pp.

Sullivan, B. J. 2003. *Garden Perennials for the Coastal South.* Chapel Hill: University of North Carolina Press. 268 pp.

Taylor, W. K. 1992. *The Guide to Florida Wildflowers.* Dallas: Taylor Publishing Co. 320 pp.

Tiner, R. W. 1993. *Coastal Wetland Plants of the Southeastern United States.* Amherst: University of Massachusetts Press. 328 pp.

Webster, W. D., J. F. Parnell, and W. C. Biggs Jr. 1985. *Mammals of the Carolinas, Virginia, and Maryland.* Chapel Hill: University of North Carolina Press. 255 pp.

Wells, B. W. 1932. *The Natural Gardens of North Carolina.* Chapel Hill: University of North Carolina Press. 458 pp.

Woelfle-Erskine, C., and A. Uncapher. 2012. *Creating Rain Gardens: Capturing the Rain for Your Own Water-Efficient Garden.* Portland, Ore.: Timber Press. 203 pp.

Wood, V. S. 1981. *Live Oaking: Southern Timber for Tall Ships*. Boston: Northeastern University Press. 206 pp.

SCIENTIFIC JOURNAL ARTICLES

Adams, D. S. 1963. "Factors Influencing Vascular Plant Zonation in North Carolina Salt Marshes." *Ecology* 44:445–56.

Arrhenius, S. 1896. "On the Influence of Carbonic Acid in the Air upon the Temperature of the Ground." *Philosophical Magazine and Journal of Science*, ser. 5, 41:237–76.

Art, H. W., F. H. Bormann, G. K. Voigt, and G. M. Woodwell. 1974. "Barrier Island Forest Ecosystem: Role of Meteorological Nutrient Inputs." *Science* 184: 60–62.

Boyce, S. G. 1954. "The Salt Spray Community." *Ecological Monographs* 24:29–67.

Burk, C. J. 1962. "The North Carolina Outer Banks: A Floristic Interpretation." *Journal of the Elisha Mitchell Scientific Society* 78:21–28.

Colosi, J. C., and J. F. McCormick. 1978. "Population Structure of *Iva imbricata* in Five Coastal Dune Habitats." *Bulletin of the Torrey Botanical Club* 105:175–86.

Conner, W. H, W. D. Mixon II, and G. W. Wood. 2005. "Maritime Forest Habitat Dynamics on Bulls Island, Cape Romain National Refuge, SC, Following Hurricane Hugo." *Forest Ecology and Management* 212:127–34.

Cooper, A. W., and E. D. Waits. 1973. "Vegetation Types in an Irregularly Flooded Salt Marsh on the North Carolina Outer Banks." *Journal of the Elisha Mitchell Scientific Society* 89:78–91.

Craig R. M. 1977. "Herbaceous Plants for Coastal Dune Areas." *Proceedings of the Florida State Horticultural Society* 90:108–10.

Dolan, R., H. Lins, and B. Hayden. 1988. "Mid-Atlantic Storms." *Journal of Coastal Research* 4:417–33.

Duryea, M. L., E. Kampf, and R. C. Littell. 2007. "Hurricanes and the Urban Forest: I. Effects on Southeastern United States Coastal Plain Tree Species." *Arboriculture and Urban Forestry* 33:83–97.

Eaton, T. E. 1979. "Natural and Artificially Altered Patterns of Salt Spray across a Forested Barrier Island." *Atmospheric Environment* 13: 705–9.

Ezer, T., and L. P. Atkinson. 2014. "Accelerated Flooding along the U.S. East Coast: On the Impact of Sea-Level Rise, Tides, Storms, the Gulf Stream, and the North Atlantic Oscillations." *Earth's Future* 2:362–82 (DOI: 10.1002/2014EF000252).

Hayden, B. P., M. C. F. V. Santos, G. Shao, and R. C. Kochel. 1995. "Geomorphological Controls on Coastal Vegetation at the Virginia Coast Reserve." *Geomorphology* 13:283–300.

Hill, S. R., and C. N. Horn. 1997. "Additions to the Flora of South Carolina." *Castanea* 62: 194–208.

Kirwan, M. L., G. R. Guntenspergen, A. d'Alpaos, J. T. Morris, S. M. Mudd, and S. Temmerman. 2010. "Limits on the Adaptability of Coastal Marshes to Rising Sea Level." *Geophysical Research Letters* 37 L23401. 5 pp. (DOI: 10.1029/2010GL045489).

Kopp, R. E., C. C. Hay, C. M. Little, and J. X. Mitrovica. 2015. "Geographic Variability of Sea-Level Change." *Current Climate Change Reports* 1:192–204.

Kopp, R. E., G. P. Horton, A. C. Kemp, and C. Tebaldi. 2015. "Past and Future Sea-Level Rise along the Coast of North Carolina, USA." *Climatic Change* 132:693–707.

Krings, A. 2002. "The Nags Head Woods Collections of the National Park Service Cape Hatteras National Seashore Herbarium (CAHA)." *Journal of the North Carolina Academy of Science* 118:145–55.

Lentz E. E., E. R. Thieler, N. G. Plant, S. R. Stippa, R. M. Horton, and D. B. Gesch. 2016. "Evaluation of Dynamic Coastal Response to Sea-Level Rise Modifies Inundation Likelihood." *Nature Climate Change* 6:696–700 (DOI: 10.1038./NCLIMATE2957).

Lonard, R. I., F. W Judd, et al. 1999 to date. "The Biological Flora of Coastal Dunes and Wetlands." *Journal of Coastal Research*. Series of journal articles with comprehensive reference lists for each species.

Masterson, J. P., M. N. Fienen, E. R. Thieler, D. B Gesch, B. T. Gutierrez, and N. G. Plant. 2014. "Effects of Sea-Level Rise on Barrier Island Groundwater System Dynamics— Ecohydrological Implications." *Ecohydrology* 7:1064–71.

Michener, W. K., E. R. Blood, K. L. Bildstein, M. M. Brinson, and L. R. Gardner. 1997.

"Climate Change, Hurricanes and Tropical Storms, and Rising Sea Level in Coastal Wetlands." *Ecological Applications* 7:770–801.

Miryeganeh, M., K. Takayama, Y. Tateishi, and T. Kajita. 2014. "Long-Distance Dispersal by Sea-Drifted Seeds Has Maintained the Global Distribution of *Ipomoea pes-caprae* subsp. *brasiliensis* (Convolvulaceae)." *PLOS ONE* 9(4). 10 pp. http://www.plosone.org.

Oosting, H. J. 1954. "Ecological Processes and Vegetation of the Maritime Strand in the Southeastern United States." *Botanical Review* 20:226–62.

Oosting, H. J., and W. D. Billings. 1942. "Factors Affecting Vegetation Zonation on Coastal Dunes." *Ecology* 23:131–42.

Rayner, D. A., and W. T. Batson. 1976. "Maritime Closed Dune Vegetation in South Carolina." *Castanea* 41:58–76.

Rozema, J., P. Bijwaard, G. Prast, and R. Brockman. 1985. "Ecophysiological Adaptations of Coastal Halophytes from Foredunes and Salt Marshes." *Vegetatio* 62: 499–521.

Russell, A. B. 1995. "Coastal Plants from A to Z." *American Nurseryman* 182.

Stalter, R. 1984. "The Flora of Bull Island, Charleston County, South Carolina." *Bartonia* 50:27–30.

Sweet, W. V., and J. Park. 2014. "From the Extreme and the Mean: Acceleration and Tipping Point of Coastal Inundation from Sea Level Rise." *Earth's Future* 2:579–600 (DOI:10.1002/2014EF000272).

Van der Valk, A. 1974. "Mineral Cycling in Coastal Foredune Plant Communities in Cape Hatteras National Seashore." *Ecology* 55: 1351–58.

———. 1975. "The Floristic Composition and Structure of Foredune Plant Communities on Cape Hatteras National Seashore." *Chesapeake Science* 16:115–26.

Wagner, R. H. 1964. "The Ecology of *Uniola paniculata* L. in the Dune-Strand Habitat of North Carolina." *Ecological Monographs* 34: 79–96.

Weakley, A. S. 2005. "Why Are Plant Names Changing So Much?" *Native Plants Journal* 6:52–58.

Zimmerman, J. K., E. M. Everham III, R. B.

Waide, D. J. Lodge, C. M. Taylor, and N. V. I. Brokaw. 1994. "Responses of Tree Species to Hurricane Winds in Subtropical Wet Forests in Puerto Rico: Implications for Tropical Tree Life Histories." *Journal of Ecology* 82:911–22.

OTHER DOCUMENTS

Au, Shu-Fun. 1974. *Vegetation and Ecological Processes on Shackleford Banks, North Carolina*. National Park Service Scientific Monograph Series, No. 6. Washington, D.C.: U.S. Government Printing Office. 86 pp.

Beal, E. O. 1977. "A Manual of Marsh and Aquatic Vascular Plants of North Carolina with Habitat Data." North Carolina Agricultural Experiment Station, North Carolina State University, Raleigh. 298 pp.

Bellis, V. J. 1995. *Ecology of Maritime Forests of the Southern Atlantic Coast: A Community Profile*. Biological Report 30. Washington, D.C.: National Biological Service, U.S. Department of the Interior. 95 pp.

Carlton, J. M. 1977. *A Survey of Selected Vegetation Communities of Florida*. St. Petersburg: Florida Department of Natural Resources Marine Research Laboratory Publication, Number 30. 40 pp.

Carter, L. M., J. W. Jones, L. Berry, V. Burkett, J. F. Murley, J. Obeysekera, P. J. Schramm, and D. Wear. 2014. "Ch. 17: Southeast and the Caribbean. Climate Change Impacts in the United States: The Third National Climate Assessment." In J. M. Melillo, T. C. Richmond, and G. W. Yohe, eds., *U.S. Global Change Research Program*, 396–417 (DOI:10.7930/J0NP22CB). Online at http://nca2014.global change.gov/report/regions/southeast. First published May 2014; PDF revised October 2014.

Clark, R. K., A. Krings, J. M. Stucky, and H. J. Kleiss. 2016. *Guide to the Vascular Flora of Kitty Hawk Woods (Dare County, North Carolina, U.S.A.)*. Botanical Miscellany Series 45. Ft. Worth: Botanical Research Institute of Texas Press. 208 pp.

Cowardin, L. M., V. Carter, F. C. Golet, and E. T. LaRoe. 1979. *Classification of Wetland and Deepwater Habitats of the United States*. Washington, D.C.: U.S. Department of the Interior, U.S. Fish and Wildlife Service. 131 pp.

Craig, R. M. 1991. "Plants for Coastal Dunes of the Gulf and South Atlantic Coast and Puerto Rico." U.S. Department of Agriculture, Soil Conservation Service, *Agriculture Information Bulletin* 460. 41 pp.

Frankson, R., K. Kunkel, L. Stevens, D. Easterling, W. Sweet, A. Wootten, and R. Boyles. 2017. North Carolina State Climate Summary. *NOAA Technical Report NESDIS 149-NC*, 3 pp. Online at https://statesummaries.ncics.org/nc.

Godfrey, P. J., and M. M. Godfrey. 1976. *Barrier Island Ecology of Cape Lookout National Seashore and Vicinity, North Carolina.* National Park Service Scientific Monograph Series, No. 9. Washington, D.C.: U.S. Government Printing Office.

Kay, S. H. 2001. *Invasive Aquatic and Wetland Plants: A Field Guide.* Edited by B. Doll. Raleigh: North Carolina Sea Grant. 43 pp.

Kraus, E. J. W. 1981. *A Guide to Salt Marsh Plants Common to North Carolina.* UNC Sea Grant Publication. UNC-SG-81-04.

Lichvar, R. W., N. C. Melvin, M. L. Butterwick, and W. N. Kirchner. 2012. "National Wetland Plant List Indicator Rating Definitions. ERDC/CRREL TR-12–1." U.S. Army Engineer Research and Development Center, Cold Regions Research and Engineering Laboratory, Hanover, N.H. 7 pp.

Lopazanski, M. J., J. P. Evans, and R. E. Shaw. 1988. *An Assessment of Maritime Forest Resources on the North Carolina Coast.* Raleigh: North Carolina Department of Natural Resources and Community Development. 108 pp.

Matthews, T., F. Stapor Jr., C. Richter, J. Miglarese, M. McKenzie, and L. Barclay. 1980. *Ecological Characterization of the Sea Island Coastal Region of South Carolina and Georgia.* Vol. 1, *Physical Features of the Characterization Area.* Washington, D.C.: Office of Biological Services, U.S. Fish and Wildlife Service. 212 pp. Online at https://www.nwrc.usgs.gov/wdb/pub/others/FWS _79-40.pdf.

Rogers, S., and D. Nash. 2003. *The Dune Book.* Raleigh: North Carolina Sea Grant. 28 pp.

Runkle, J., K. Kunkel, L. Stevens, R. Frankson, B. Stewart, and W. Sweet. 2017. South Carolina State Climate Summary. *NOAA Technical Report NESDIS 149-SC.* 4 pp. Online at https://statesummaries.ncics.org/sc.

Shafale, M. P. 2012. *Guide to the Natural Communities of North Carolina. Fourth Approximation.* Raleigh: North Carolina Department of Environment and Natural Resources. North Carolina Natural Heritage Program. 208 pp.

Shafale, M. P., and A. S. Weakley. 1990. *Classification of the Natural Communities of North Carolina. Third Approximation.* Raleigh: North Carolina Department of Environment, Health, and Natural Resources, Division of Parks and Recreation, Natural Heritage Program. 321 pp.

Teal, J. M. 1986. *The Ecology of Regularly Flooded Salt Marshes in New England: A Community Profile.* Washington, D.C.: U.S. Fish and Wildlife Services Biological Report 85 (7.4). 61 pp.

Weakley, A. S. 2015. "Flora of the Southern and Mid-Atlantic States." Working Draft of 21 May 2015. University of North Carolina Herbarium, Chapel Hill. 1,320 pp.

Whitaker, J. D., J. W. McCord, P. P. Maier, A. L. Segars, M. L. Rekow, N. Shea, J. Ayers, and R. Browder. 2004. *An Ecological Characterization of Coastal Hammock Islands in South Carolina.* South Carolina Department of Natural Resources, Final Report to Ocean and Coastal Resource Management, Department of Health and Environmental Control. Project Number 475774. 115 pp.

Wiegert, R. G., and B. J. Freeman. 1990. *Tidal Salt Marshes of the Southeast Atlantic Coast: A Community Profile.* Biological Report 85 (7.29). Washington, D.C.: U.S. Fish and Wildlife Service. 70 pp. Online at https:// www.nwrc.usgs.gov/techrpt/85-7-29.pdf.

ANNOTATED INTERNET RESOURCES

Appleton, B., V. Greene, A. Smith, S. French, B. Kane, L. Fox, A. Downing, and T. Gilland. "Trees and Shrubs that Tolerate Saline Soils and Salt Spray Drift." Virginia Cooperative Extension, Virginia Tech, Virginia State University. Publication 430-031. 9 pp. https:// pubs.ext.vt.edu/430/430-031/430-031_pdf .pdf. Accessed 26 August 2017. Website discusses issues with plants associated with elevated soil salts and aerosol salts typical of coastal environments, and it provides a list of plants with some resistance to these salts.

The Center for Invasive Species and Ecosystem Health. "Invasive Species 101: An Introduction to Invasive Species." https://www.invasive.org/101/. Accessed 26 August 2017. Website addresses the question, Why should I care about invasive species?

Clemson Cooperative Extension. "A Guide to Rain Gardens in South Carolina." https://www.clemson.edu/extension/raingarden/clemson_rain_garden_manual_2016.pdf. Accessed 26 August 2017. Website covers siting, sizing, shaping, and planting rain gardens.

Duryea, M. L., and E. Kampf. "Wind and Trees: Lessons Learned from Hurricanes." Document FOR118, revised. Institute of Food and Agricultural Sciences (IFAS), University of Florida, Gainesville. 16 pp. http://edis.ifas.ufl.edu/pdffiles/FR/FR17300.pdf. Accessed 26 August 2017. This document reviews storm damage to trees, lists recommended trees, and provides numerous suggestions for planting trees to survive hurricanes.

Florida Living Shorelines. "Types of Living Shorelines." http://floridalivingshorelines.com/types-of-living-shorelines/. Accessed 26 August 2017. Site describes various types of shoreline protection.

———. "What Is a Living Shoreline?" floridalivingshorelines.com/what-is-a-livingshoreline/. Accessed 26 August 2017. Although focused on Florida coastal environments, the information is applicable to the coastal Carolinas. Includes discussion of why this approach is beneficial.

Gilman, E. F., M. L. Duryea, E. Kampf, T. J. Partin, A. Delgado, and C. J. Lehtola. "Assessing Damage and Restoring Trees after a Hurricane: Urban Forest Hurricane Recovery Program." http://www.miamidade.gov/environment/library/reports/trees-damage-assess.pdf. Accessed 26 August 2017. Website provides important safety information, damage assessment advice, and tips for restoration pruning of trees affected by hurricanes.

Glen, Charlotte. "Plants for Rain Gardens. Recommended for Southeastern North Carolina." www.ces.ncsu.edu/wp-content/uploads/2013/04/Coastal-Plains-Plants.doc. Accessed 26 August 2017. The author provides a list of suitable plants for coastal plantings based on size, salinity tolerance, and life span.

Living Shorelines Academy. https://www.livingshorelinesacademy.org. Accessed 26 August 2017. Document explores what living shorelines are, how to design and build them, and why they are important to coastal environments. Information is presented in "course" format.

Massachusetts Office of Coastal Zone Management. "Landscaping to Protect Your Coastal Property from Storm Damage and Flooding." StormSmart Coasts Fact Sheet 6. http://www.mass.gov/eea/docs/czm/stormsmart/ssc/ssc6-landscaping.pdf. Accessed 26 August 2017. Although the information is specific to Massachusetts, it is general enough to apply, in some instances, to the coastal Carolinas.

National Oceanic and Atmospheric Administration (NOAA). "Habitat Conservation: Living Shorelines." http://www.habitat.noaa.gov/restoration/techniques/livingshorelines.html. Accessed 26 August 2017. Website provides information on planning and implementing a living shoreline.

National Oceanic and Atmospheric Administration, the U.S. Environmental Protection Agency, the U.S. Army Corps of Engineers, the U.S. Fish and Wildlife Service, and the Natural Resources Conservation Service (an interagency group). "An Introduction and User's Guide to Wetland Restoration, Creation, and Enhancement." http://www.habitat.noaa.gov/pdf/pub_wetlands_restore_guide.pdf. Accessed 26 August 2017. Document includes information on project planning, implementation, and monitoring.

Native and Naturalized Plants of the Carolinas and Georgia. http://www.namethatplant.net/index.shtml. Accessed 26 August 2017. Website is a compilation of information including native plant websites in the Southeast. Includes information on coastal plants and plant communities.

Nelson, J. B. "The Natural Communities of South Carolina: Initial Classification and Description." 1986. S.C. Wildlife and Marine Resources Department. http://m.namethat plant.net/PDFs/JBNDoc.pdf. Accessed 26 August 2017. Document characterizes each of the plant communities recognized in South Carolina. Several coastal communities are included in the listing.

North American Pollinator Protection Campaign. http://pollinator.org/nappc/. Accessed 26 August 2017. Describes classes of pollinators and some of the major plants to which they are attracted. Provides bloom periods for native plants and their pollinators.

North Carolina Coastal Federation. "Living Shorelines." https://www.nccoast.org/protect -the-coast/restore/living-shorelines/. Accessed 26 August 2017. The website introduces living shorelines as a coastal protection measure, including descriptions and photos of successful Coastal Federation restoration projects.

N.C. Cooperative Extension Service. "Salt Tolerant Plants Recommended for Pender County Landscapes." Urban Horticulture Leaflet 14. https://pender.ces.ncsu.edu/files /library/71/Salt%20Tolerant%20Plants.pdf. Accessed 26 August 2017. Document provides lists of trees, shrubs, vines, and other plants suitable for planting in shoreline areas.

N.C. Invasive Plant Council. http://www.nc-ipc .weebly.com. Accessed 26 August 2017. Website includes an introduction to invasives, as well as information on outreach and education, management and control, laws and policies, and a listing of invasive plants in North Carolina.

Rain Garden Network. "How to Build a Rain Garden: Ten Steps." http://www.raingarden network.com/how-to-build-a-rain-garden -in-10-steps/. Accessed 26 April 2015. Basic steps for building your own rain garden.

———. "What Is a Rain Garden?" http://www .raingardennetwork.com. Accessed 26 August 2017. Website gives background information about the benefits that rain gardens bring to homeowners. It also gives information on design, construction, and maintenance of rain gardens.

Smith, Cherri. "Invasive Exotic Plants of North Carolina." 2008. North Carolina Department of Transportation, Raleigh, N.C. 185 pp. https://www.se-eppc.org/northcarolina /NCDOT_Invasive_Exotic_Plants.pdf. Accessed 26 August 2017. Website includes a comprehensive list, description, identification guide, and methods of control for over 70 species of exotic plants.

South Atlantic Living Shorelines Summit. Summary Report. http://southatlantic alliance.org/south-atlantic-living-shorelines -summit/. Accessed 26 August 2017. Website includes information on management, research, regulation, and implementation of living shorelines in the South Atlantic region.

South Carolina Department of Natural Resources. "Characterization of the Ashepoo-Combahee-Edisto (ACE) Basin, South Carolina." http://www.dnr.sc.gov/marine /mrri/acechar/resourcemanagement /taskforce.html. Accessed 26 August 2017. Describes management strategies for resource protection in the Ashepoo-Combahee-Edisto Task Force Basin.

South Carolina Exotic Pest Plant Council (SC-EPPC). https://www.se-eppc.org /southcarolina. Accessed 26 August 2017. Website provides state and national information concerning invasive plant pest species in South Carolina.

Southeast Exotic Pest Plant Council. https:// www.se-eppc.org. Accessed 26 August 2017. Website focuses on invasive plant news nationally and from the Southeast.

Urban Forest Hurricane Recovery Program. "Trees and Hurricanes." http://hort.ifas .ufl.edu/treesandhurricanes/. Accessed 26 August 2017. This comprehensive website gives coastal homeowners important and useful information about establishing and maintaining a wind-resistant tree environment. While Florida-based, the information also applies to coastal Carolinas urban trees and shrubs.

U.S. Department of Agriculture. Agricultural Research Service. "USDA Plant Hardiness

Zone Map." http://planthardiness.ars.usda .gov/PHZMWeb/. Accessed 26 August 2017. Website provides a dynamic and interactive map of U.S. plant hardiness zones.

U.S. Department of Agriculture. National Invasive Species Information Center (NISIC). "Gateway to Invasive Species Information." https://www.invasivespeciesinfo.gov/. Accessed 26 August 2017. The site displays images of invasive species and provides basic information about how to eliminate or control them.

U.S. Department of Agriculture. Natural Resources Conservation Service (NRCS). "USDA Plants Database." https://plants.usda .gov/. Accessed 26 August 2017. Information concerns native and exotic plants found in the United States. Includes fact sheets on many plants.

U.S. Environmental Protection Agency (EPA). "Coastal Wetlands." https://www.epa.gov /wetlands/coastal-wetlands. Accessed 26 August 2017. Website defines coastal wetlands, explains why they are important, tells why we are losing them, and provides suggestions for preserving wetlands.

U.S. Fish and Wildlife Service. "Native Plants for Wildlife Habitat and Conservation Landscaping: Chesapeake Bay Watershed." https://www.nps.gov/plants/pubs/chesa peake/toc.htm. Accessed 26 August 2017. Although specific to the Chesapeake Bay, this website has useful elements for the Carolinas, such as, Why use natives? The website provides lists of plants suitable for coastal dunes and saltwater and brackish water marshes.

Virginia Department of Environmental Quality. "What Makes Eastern Shore Native Plants So Special?" http://deq.state.va.us/Programs /CoastalZoneManagement/CZMIssues Initiatives/NativePlants/PlantESNatives /Benefits.aspx. Accessed 26 August 2017. Site provides information concerning the importance of coastal native plants for water quality, economics, wildlife, and aesthetics.

Whitaker, J. D., J. W. McCord, B. Pulley, and E. Mullins. "Best Management Practices for Wildlife in Maritime Forest Developments." 2009. South Carolina Department of Natural Resources. 76 pp. www.dnr.sc.gov/marine /pub/BMPSforCoastWeb.pdf. Accessed 26 August 2017. Website covers birds, amphibians, reptiles, and mammals.

Williams, M. J. "Native Plants for Coastal Dune Restoration: What, When, and How for Florida." U.S. Department of Agriculture, Natural Resources Conservation Service. https://www.nrcs.usda.gov/Internet/FSE _PLANTMATERIALS/publications/flpmspu 7474.pdf. Accessed 26 August 2017. Information on general coastal ecology, sand fencing, dune vegetation maintenance, and consideration of specific trees, shrubs, and herbs for planting on coastal dunes. Much is applicable to the Carolinas.

Bold page numbers indicate extended topical information. *Italicized page numbers indicate information presented pictorially or graphically.*

PAUL E. HOSIER

is a coastal plant ecologist with a Ph.D. from Duke University. He served as professor of biology at the University of North Carolina Wilmington for forty-one years and is currently professor emeritus at the institution. Throughout his university career, he taught undergraduate and graduate courses in general ecology, barrier island ecology, and coastal management. He has conducted coastal research along the North Carolina, South Carolina, and Georgia coasts, including a study of the effects of hurricanes on the vegetation of Cape Lookout National Seashore. He studied the effects of off-road vehicles on the vegetation and coastal processes at Cape Hatteras National Seashore, a project supported by the North Carolina Sea Grant Program. Sea Grant supported his research on vegetation patterns and succession in oceanic overwash environments along North Carolina's barrier islands. Hosier also studied dune and marsh vegetation on Kiawah Island prior to development of the island. He has served as a member of the board of directors of the Friends of Plant Conservation and currently serves on the board of directors of North Carolina's Coastal Land Trust. Hosier is a coauthor of the book *Living with the Georgia Shore* (Duke University Press, 1992).

NORTH CAROLINA SEA GRANT

Through integrated, unbiased research and outreach efforts, North Carolina Sea Grant enhances sustainable use and conservation of ocean, coastal, and watershed resources to benefit communities, economies, and ecosystems. The Sea Grant team provides key leadership to address urgent and long-term needs via sound science, educational excellence, and extensive and effective collaborations. An interinstitutional program of the University of North Carolina system through a partnership with the National Oceanic and Atmospheric Administration, North Carolina Sea Grant has its headquarters at North Carolina State University in Raleigh. Coastal offices are in Wanchese, Morehead City, and Wilmington. Learn more at ncseagrant.org.

Other **Southern Gateways Guides** you might enjoy

Living at the Water's Edge
A Heritage Guide to the Outer Banks Byway

BARBARA GARRITY-BLAKE AND KAREN WILLIS AMSPACHER

A unique guide to the byway's people and places

Lessons from the Sand
Family-Friendly Science Activities You Can Do on a Carolina Beach

CHARLES O. PILKEY AND ORRIN H. PILKEY

Fun ways to learn about the beach and its surrounding environment

Life along the Inner Coast
A Naturalist's Guide to the Sounds, Inlets, Rivers, and Intracoastal Waterway from Norfolk to Key West

ROBERT L. LIPPSON AND ALICE JANE LIPPSON
ILLUSTRATIONS BY ALICE JANE LIPPSON

More than 800 species from fresh, brackish, and salty waters

Available at bookstores, by phone at **1-800-848-6224**, or on the web at **www.uncpress.org**